THE ENCYCLOPEDIA OF
UNSOLVED CRIMES

THE ENCYCLOPEDIA OF
UNSOLVED CRIMES

Second Edition

Michael Newton

Checkmark Books®
An imprint of Infobase Publishing

The Encyclopedia of Unsolved Crimes, Second Edition

Checkmark Books
An imprint of Infobase Publishing
132 West 31st Street
New York NY 10001

Library of Congress Cataloging-in-Publication Data

Newton, Michael, 1951–
The encyclopedia of unsolved crimes / Michael Newton.
p. cm.
Includes bibliographical references and index.
ISBN-13: 978-0-8160-7818-9 (hardcover : alk. paper)
ISBN-10: 0-8160-7818-1 (hardcover : alk. paper)
ISBN-13: 978-0-8160-7819-6 (pbk. : alk. paper)
ISBN-10: 0-8160-7819-X (pbk : alk. paper)
1. Crime—Encyclopedias. 2. Homicide—Encyclopedias. I. Title.

HV6251.N48 2010
364.103—dc22

2008045073

Checkmark Books are available at special discounts when purchased in bulk quantities for businesses, associations, institutions, or sales promotions. Please call our Special Sales Department in New York at (212) 967-8800 or (800) 322-8755.

You can find Facts On File on the World Wide Web at http://www.factsonfile.com

Text design by Erika K. Arroyo
Cover design by Keith Trego

Printed in the United States of America

MP MSRF 10 9 8 7 6 5 4 3

This book is printed on acid-free paper and contains 30 percent postconsumer recycled content.

For Margaret

_____

Contents

Introduction   ix

Entries A–Z   1

Bibliography   421

Index   429

Introduction

It is not true, as pop star Bonnie Tyler suggests in her hit song "Driving Me Wild," that everyone loves a mystery. While fictional enigmas exert an enduring appeal, from the Sherlock Holmes adventures penned by Sir Arthur Conan Doyle to the best-selling novels of Patricia Cornwell, real-life mysteries are something else entirely.

Police officers and prosecutors hate mysteries, preferring their criminal cases tied up into neat, easily explained packages. Defense attorneys generally share that sentiment—unless a phantom suspect helps win an acquittal in court. Friends and family of crime victims or missing persons crave nothing more than an absence of doubt. Archaeologists, psychologists, medical researchers, "intelligence" agents—all these and more devote their lives to the proposition that no riddle should remain unsolved.

And yet . . .

These plentiful exceptions notwithstanding, there *is* something in an unsolved mystery that appeals to many of us. Some go so far as to publicly hope that this or that classic case will never be solved, comparing mysterious cases to gaily wrapped presents forever unopened, never losing their appeal for armchair detectives. When the package is opened, its contents revealed, no amount of excitement or pleasure can ward off the inevitable letdown. We want to see the gift, possess it but . . . perhaps *not yet*.

In the real world, as it happens, unsolved mysteries are distressingly common. The solution rate for U.S. murders has declined from 90-odd percent in the late 1950s to an average 70 percent (and less, in some regions) a half century later. Lesser crimes are even more likely to go unsolved. Fewer than half of all rapes are reported to authorities, much less "cleared" by arrest and conviction. Thousands of thefts go unsolved every year; the number unreported (or unnoticed, for that matter) is unknown. Authorities cannot agree on the number of children who vanish yearly in America, much less on what has become of them. As for missing adults, barring obvious signs of foul play, no agency even attempts to keep track of the lost.

In the face of those odds, a curious researcher may be startled to learn how many cases *do* get solved (albeit slowly in some cases, taking years or even decades). During preparation of this volume, late-breaking investigations forced deletion of various tantalizing cases, including (but not limited to) the following:

- A stalker of prostitutes in Vancouver, British Columbia, theoretically linked to the disappearance of 67 victims since the 1970s;
- Wichita's "BTK Strangler," linked to six slayings in 1974–77, then proved guilty of 10 when a suspect confessed in 2005;
- Seattle's "Green River Killer," blamed for the deaths of 49 women between 1982 and 1984;
- The stabbing deaths of at least eight gay men, murdered around Chesapeake, Virginia, between 1987 and 1995;
- A series of hit-and-run murders that claimed two female joggers and a male bicyclist during 1991, in Porterville, California;
- New York's "Last Call Killer," linked to the slayings of five men, lured from gay bars and dismembered before their remains were scattered along New Jersey highways in 1991–92;
- The mysterious deaths of 48 patients at Truman Memorial Veterans Hospital in Columbia, Missouri, between January and August 1992;
- The grisly deaths of three Minneapolis prostitutes in 1996, stabbed and beaten before they were doused with gasoline and set afire in Theodore Wirth Park;

- The kidnap-murders of three adolescent girls at Spotsylvania, Virginia, in 1996–97;
- The 2000 murder of Jill Behrman in Bloomington, Indiana, apparently solved with the conviction of defendant John Myers in 2006 (though some critics maintain that Myers is innocent).

Homicide investigators frequently remind us that the first 24 to 48 hours are critical to solving a crime, but these cases and others like them, cracked long after the fact, serve as a daily reminder that justice is often delayed. "Cold" cases *can* be solved by discovery of new evidence, by confession—and, increasingly, by the scientific miracle of DNA profiling.

That said, what constitutes an unsolved case? Typically, the term applies to a crime in which no suspects are identified, but that need not be the case. Some crimes are "cleared" by arrest and conviction of an innocent suspect, whether by chance or through a deliberate frame-up, thus leaving the real offender at large. Others, some notorious, remain technically unsolved after a known offender was acquitted by a biased or dim-witted jury. In some cases, authorities have branded a suspect as guilty on the flimsiest of evidence and without benefit of trial. Other crimes are "solved" by confessions that, upon closer examination, seem to be the product of police coercion or disordered minds. For purposes of this volume, we shall consider unsolved cases to include:

- Crimes in which no suspect is identified;
- Cases in which the offender is known to police or the public but cannot be charged for lack of concrete evidence;
- Miscarriages of justice, including cases wherein innocent suspects are convicted (or otherwise officially blamed), and those in which guilty parties are wrongfully acquitted.

Cases in the text are alphabetically arranged, most often by the victim's name, although some headers refer to an event (e.g., St. Valentine's Day Massacre) or to the popular nickname of an unidentified offender (e.g., "Jack the Ripper"). Cases with multiple victims are identified either by the geographical location (e.g., Atlanta child murders) or by some recognized media label (e.g., "Golden Years murders"). Blind entries link individual victims to entries profiling a serial murder or similar crimes (e.g., Eddowes, Catherine: See "Jack the Ripper"). References within the text to subjects possessing their own discrete entries appear in LARGE AND SMALL CAPITAL LETTERS.

This second edition of the *Encyclopedia of Unsolved Crimes* includes 93 completely new entries, plus various additions to the original bibliography. Many others have been updated with new information received since 2002, and several entries from the first edition were deleted, based on solution of the crimes in question by arrest and conviction of the perpetrators. In cases where suspects or "persons of interest" have been named by police, but no trial has been held, the cases remain officially unsolved.

As in the previous edition, certain cases listed by authorities as solved or "cleared" also appear within these pages, where substantial evidence casts doubt on the official verdicts. In those cases, whether simple error or deliberate frame-ups are indicated, both sides of the ongoing debate are presented, leaving readers to serve as the ultimate jury. Exposure of government misconduct over the past quarter century, combined with scientific exoneration of 328 wrongfully convicted defendants since 1989, clearly demonstrates that official declarations of guilt sometimes deserve close and critical scrutiny.

Special thanks are owed to David Frasier, friend, author, and reference librarian extraordinaire at Indiana University in Bloomington; to William A. Kingman, for sharing his insight on the case of the New Orleans Axeman; and to Heather Locken. Every effort has been made to ensure accuracy in the text that follows. Anyone with further knowledge of the cases covered—or of unsolved crimes in general—is invited to contact the author, in care of Facts On File.

Entries A–Z

ABDULLAH, Ahmet gangland murder victim (1991)

An adopted son of the Arif family, a group of Middle Eastern racketeers and armed robbers residing in London's Stockwell district, Ahmet Abdullah was identified by Scotland Yard as a narcotics dealer, nicknamed "Turkish Abbi." On March 11, 1991, Abdullah was ambushed by rival mobsters at a betting shop on Bagshot Street, Walworth. Witnesses reported that he begged for his life, then briefly used another of the shop's patrons as a human shield before fleeing into the street, where Abdullah was shot in the back and fatally wounded.

Suspects Patrick and Tony Brindle were charged with the murder, held over for trial at the Old Bailey court in early 1992. Frightened witnesses to the shooting testified behind screens to conceal their faces, identified only by numbers in court. Patrick Brindle declined to testify, but brother Tony produced evidence that he had been drinking and playing cards in a London pub, The Bell, when Abdullah was shot. The defendants' mother described her sons as softhearted young men who wept when their parakeet died, and who made a habit of helping elderly women cross the street. Jurors acquitted the brothers on May 16, 1992, whereupon police pronounced the case closed.

ABEL, Robert William   See "I-45 Murders"

ADAMS, Mrs. Wesley   See San Diego murders (1931–36)

ADKINS, Francis Roy murder victim (1990)

A suspected London mobster, Francis Adkins was identified as the boss of a narcotics smuggling ring in January 1990, in sworn testimony offered to a Chelmsford court. That testimony was presented by Charles Wilson, a convicted participant in England's "Great Train Robbery" of 1978, who was himself murdered a short time later (allegedly on orders from Adkins). Police initially suspected that Adkins might have been killed in reprisal for Wilson's slaying, but detectives later determined Wilson's death to be an unrelated incident.

On the night he was killed, September 28, 1990, Adkins met with two Colombians in the Nightwatch bar of the American Hotel in Amsterdam, Netherlands. Subsequent testimony indicated that Adkins was involved in smuggling stolen emeralds through Holland and that he had completed several runs without difficulty prior to the night of September 28. On the latest run, however, one of the packets containing hot gems had been stolen, a circumstance that did not prevent the Colombian suppliers from demanding full payment on schedule.

Accomplice Sam O'Neil, earlier acquitted on charges of smuggling £10 million worth of cocaine into England (while three Colombian codefendants received 18-year prison terms), saw Adkins in the Nightwatch bar on September 28, but later told police that Adkins made a furtive gesture to keep O'Neil moving. As he left the hotel, O'Neil heard a flurry of gunshots but claimed not to know Adkins had been killed until he

1

read a newspaper account of the murder next morning. The gunmen were never identified, and the case remains open today, with no realistic hope of solution.

ADKINS, Joseph assassination victim (1869)

A Republican member of Georgia's state senate during the troubled years of Reconstruction (1865–77), Joseph Adkins was elected to his seat from Warren County. White Democrats in the region (then known as Conservatives) reviled Adkins for his "radical" politics—i.e., support for black civil rights and allegiance to the Union victors in the recent War Between the States—and denounced him as a "scalawag" (a native Southerner disloyal to the late Confederacy). Adkins further outraged white opinion in April 1868, when he posted a statutory bond for Sheriff John Norris, another Republican hated by Conservatives and the night-riding Ku Klux Klan.

Warren County was among the state's most violent districts in those days, and Adkins led a delegation to Washington, D.C., in the spring of 1869, seeking a restoration of military rule in Georgia until the vigilante outrages could be suppressed. Sheriff Norris warned Adkins not to return, but Adkins ignored the many threats against his life. On May 10, 1869, a gang of racist thugs was waiting for him when Adkins disembarked from a train at Dearing, Georgia. The gunmen "confiscated" his horse and buggy, leaving Adkins with a walk of several miles to reach his home. Along the way he was ambushed and mortally wounded by gunfire. His wife and daughter found him lying in the road. Adkins lived long enough to name at least one of the shooters, who had failed to don their usual Klan disguises.

While Adkins's family refused to publicly identify the shooters, they informed military authorities that one triggerman had been Ellis Adams, a member of the gang that harassed Adkins at the Dearing railroad depot. Adams bore a special grudge against Adkins, since Adkins had reported him for stabbing a black man and other racist crimes. Adams was also a prime suspect in the murders of victim PERRY JEFFERS and his family near the Dearing station.

Warren County Democrats initially tried to blame the murder on blacks, then claimed that Adkins had made improper advances to a young female relative of Adams, thereby transforming his act from a grudge killing or political assassination to a matter of "honor." A local gossip told the *New York Times* that Adkins was "a notorious debaucher. His negro [*sic*] *amours* are more numerous than his years." The Shreveport *South-Western*, meanwhile, called Adkins "a habitual inmate of negro brothels. . . . He was among the most degraded of the scalawags." Detractors claimed to possess a "love letter" written by Adkins—a gospel minister, then in his sixties—to the young woman in question, but it was never produced and likely never existed.

U.S. general Alfred Terry, based in Atlanta, sent two companies of infantry to Warren County on May 13, 1869. They camped outside Warrenton and tried to suppress local violence, with mixed results. No charges were filed against Ellis Adams, and he died in a shoot-out that December. Troops sought to arrest a second murder suspect in March 1870, but he was warned in advance and fled the county. The case remains officially unsolved.

AGNEW, Barbara See "VALLEY KILLER"

AIRCRAFT crashes: accidents or murder?

Over the past nine decades, various fatal air crashes have spawned conspiracy theories that linger as haunting historical mysteries. Five cases produced official verdicts of criminal activity, but no suspects were ever indicted. The remainder are listed as accidents, but nagging doubts remain. The cases include:

- *July 4, 1923* Actor-pilot Beverly "B. H." DeLay and passenger R. I. Short (president of the Essandee Corporation) died while performing aerial acrobatics at Venice Beach, California. *Time* magazine reported that half-inch bolts in the wings of DeLay's aircraft had been switched for smaller bolts, causing the wings to collapse during flight. Gunshots of unknown origin had also been fired at DeLay days earlier, during a performance in Santa Monica. Journalists linked the crash to bitter litigation between DeLay and C. E. Frey, a rival who claimed ownership of an airstrip purchased by DeLay in 1919. Several Frey employees were jailed for sabotaging that airfield, but no one was indicted for DeLay's murder.

- *October 10, 1933* A United Airlines Boeing 247 aircraft traveling from Cleveland to Chicago crashed near Chesterton, Indiana, killing all seven persons aboard. Witnesses reported hearing a midair explosion at 9:15 P.M. and watching the plane plummet in flames from 1,000 feet. Investigators from Northwestern University and the Chicago FBI office concluded that a bomb had detonated in the plane's baggage compartment, but no suspects were ever identified.

- *March 29, 1959* Barthélemy Boganda, first prime minister of the Central African Republic (C.A.R.) and presumed to win election as president when France released control of his nation in 1960, died with all others aboard when his plane crashed 99 miles west of Bangui. No cause of the crash was officially determined, but suspicion of sabotage persists. On May 7, 1959, the Paris weekly *L'Express* reported discovery of explosive residue in the plane's wreckage, whereupon the French high commissioner banned sale of that issue in the C.A.R. In 1997 author Brian Titley suggested that Boganda's wife, Michelle Jourdain, may have killed him to avert divorce and collect a large insurance policy.

- *November 16, 1959* National Airlines Flight 967 vanished over the Gulf of Mexico with 42 persons aboard while en route from Tampa, Florida, to New Orleans. The final radar contact with Flight 967 was recorded at 12:46 A.M. Searchers found scattered wreckage and corpses near that point, but most of the aircraft was never recovered. Suspicion focused on passenger William Taylor, who boarded the plane with a ticket issued to ex-convict Robert Vernon Spears. Authorities surmised that Spears had tricked Taylor, a friend from prison, into boarding the plane with a bomb, thus permitting Spears to collect on a life insurance policy purchased in his name. Police later arrested Spears in Phoenix, driving a car registered 'to Taylor, but he subsequently vanished and was never charged with any crime pertaining to the crash.

- *September 18, 1961* Dag Hammarskjöld, second secretary-general of the United Nations, died with 15 others when his plane crashed near Ndola, Northern Rhodesia (now Zambia), during a diplomatic tour of the strife-torn Congo. Security was tight during the tour, including use of a decoy aircraft, and Hammarskjöld's pilot filed no flight plans on the trip. Officially, the crash resulted from a pilot's error in approach-

ing Ndola's airfield at the wrong altitude after nightfall. Many observers suspected a bomb or rocket attack. In August 1998, Archbishop Desmond Tutu, chairman of South Africa's Truth and Reconciliation Commission, announced that recently uncovered letters implicated South African intelligence officers, Britain's MI5, and the American CIA in Hammarskjöld's death. One letter claimed that a bomb in the plane's wheel bay was set to explode on landing. In July 2005, Norwegian major general Björn Egge told the newspaper *Aftenposten* that an apparent bullet hole in Hammarskjöld's forehead was airbrushed out of photos later published showing his corpse.

- *October 16, 1972* House majority leader Thomas Hale Boggs, Sr., was campaigning for Representative Nick Begich when their airplane vanished during a flight from Anchorage to Juneau, Alaska. Also aboard were pilot Don Jonz and Begich aide Russell Brown. The plane was never found. Begich won November's election with a 56-percent margin, but his presumed death left GOP rival Don Young running unopposed in a special election to fill Begich's vacant seat in Congress. Some conspiracy theorists link the disappearance to Boggs's outspoken criticism of FBI director J. Edgar Hoover (who died in May 1972), but Begich's children blamed President Richard Nixon, claiming that the crash was staged in a vain attempt to thwart congressional investigation of the unfolding Watergate scandal.

- *August 1, 1981* Brigadier General Omar Torrijos Herrera, "Supreme Chief of Government" for Panama since 1968, died with several others when his plane exploded in midair during a storm. Slipshod radio coverage delayed the report of his plane's disappearance for nearly a day, and several more days elapsed before soldiers found the wreckage. Florencio Flores succeeded Torrijos as commander of Panama's National Guard and de facto ruler of the country.

- *October 19, 1986* Samora Moisés Machel, president of Mozambique and a leading critic of South Africa's racist apartheid system, died with all aboard when his plane crashed near Mbuzini, in South Africa's Lebombo Mountains. At the time, Machel was returning home from an international conference in Zambia. The Margo Commission, an investigative panel including representatives from several nations, blamed the crash on pilot error—a verdict flatly rejected by the governments of Mozambique and the Soviet Union. Russian members of the commission filed a minority report claiming that Machel's plane was lured off-course by a decoy radio beacon, set up by South African intelligence officers. Machel's widow, Graça, remains convinced that he was murdered. In 1998 she married then-South African president Nelson Mandela.

- *August 17, 1989* General Muhammad Zia-ul-Haq, ruler of Pakistan since he overthrew predecessor Zulfikar Ali Bhutto in 1977, died with several other generals and U.S. ambassador Arnold Raphel when their plane crashed shortly after takeoff from Bahawalpur, Pakistan. Witnesses reported a smooth liftoff, followed by erratic flying and a steep nosedive. FBI agents called the crash accidental, but persistent conspiracy theories blame a wide range of suspects, including the CIA, Russia's KGB, Israel's Mossad, India's RAW intelligence agency, Afghan communists, and Shi'ite Muslim separatists.

- *April 6, 1994* Unknown snipers shot down a government aircraft at Rwanda's Kigali airport, killing Rwandan president Juvénal Habyarimana, President Cyprien Ntaryamira of Burundi, and all others aboard. The resultant political chaos led to full-scale genocide in Rwanda, where ruling Hutu tribesmen slaughtered rival Tutsis, and sparked civil war in Burundi.

- *July 19, 1994* Alas Chiricanas Flight 901 exploded while en route from Colón, Panama, to Panama City, killing all 21 persons aboard. Authorities found evidence of a bomb, blaming the crime on terrorists. Suspicion focused on Jamal Lya, the only passenger whose corpse remained unclaimed after the bombing. Soon afterward, an unknown spokesperson for a group calling itself Ansar Allah ("Followers of God") claimed credit for the attack, but investigators could find no other trace of the organization.

- *July 17, 1996* Trans World Airlines Flight 800 left New York's JFK Airport, bound for Paris, at 10:19 P.M. Twelve minutes later it exploded in midair, killing all 230 persons aboard and littering the ocean with wreckage offshore from East Moriches, New York. Despite initial speculation of a terrorist attack, the National Transportation Safety Board issued a final report in August 2000, blaming the explosion on a presumed electrical short circuit that ignited fumes in the aircraft's center wing fuel tank. Meanwhile, multiple eyewitnesses on land reported seeing "a streak of light" rising from sea level toward the airliner before it exploded. Initial examination of the wreckage revealed apparent residue from three different explosive compounds—PETN, RDX, and nitroglycerin—but authorities claimed to find no evidence of impact from a rocket or missile. Some conspiracy theorists maintain that Flight 800 was shot down by terrorists, while others suggest a disastrous mistake during an offshore U.S. Navy training exercise involving surface-to-air missiles. The case is officially closed.

- *October 25, 2002* Minnesota senator Paul Wellstone died with seven others, including his wife and three children, when his aircraft crashed near Eveleth, Minnesota. Wellstone was near the end of his campaign for a third Senate term, his death coming 11 days before the scheduled balloting. Initial reports blamed icing of the aircraft's wing, but that suggestion was later rejected. Federal investigators finally named pilot error as the "likely" cause of the crash, claiming that deceased First Officer Michael Guess was "below average" in proficiency. In fact, Guess had been fired from two previous flying jobs for incompetence. Jim Fetzer, a philosophy professor at the University of Minnesota Duluth, published a book in 2004, blaming Wellstone's death on unnamed members of President George W. Bush's administration.

- *July 30, 2005* Dr. John Garang De Mabior, vice president of Sudan and former head of the rebel Sudan People's Liberation Army, died when his helicopter crashed in southern Sudan. Circumstances of the crash remain unclear, and Ugandan president Yoweri Museveni blamed "external factors" for the incident. Foreign observers note that Garang's death helped bring an end to Sudan's long-running civil war.

ALAMEDA County, California unsolved murders (1983–84)
In the 12-month period between December 1983 and November 1984, four teenage girls were murdered in northern California's Alameda County. Fourteen-year-old Kelly Jean Poppleton was the first victim. Tina Faelz, also 14, was stabbed to death on April 5, 1984, while taking a popular shortcut under a freeway, near the county fairgrounds. Later in April, 18-year-old Julie Connell vanished from a local park; her lifeless body was found six days later, dumped in a nearby field. Lisa Monzo, age 18, was last seen alive on November 27, 1984, walking in the rain near Nimitz Freeway. She was reported missing the following day, then found strangled on December 2, 1984. At press time, more than 20 years after the final killing in the series, authorities still have no suspect.

ALLAN, Jane See "BABYSITTER"

ALLEN, Kim See "OCCULT MURDERS"

ALLEN, Louis murder victim (1964)
A native of Amite County, Mississippi, born in 1922, Louis Allen dropped out of school in the seventh grade to become a logger and part-time farmer. Drafted by the U.S. Army in January 1943, he served 19 months in uniform, including combat duty in New Guinea. Upon discharge from service, he returned to his wife and two young children, the beginning of a family that soon increased to six. Although a proud African American, Allen had no part in the civil rights movement that challenged Mississippi's pervasive system of racial segregation in 1961. He would become a martyr to that movement by coincidence, strictly against his will.

One who joined the Amite County movement willingly was 50-year-old Herbert Lee, a member of the National Association for the Advancement of Colored People (NAACP) and a participant in the 1961 voter-registration drive by Robert Moses of the Student Nonviolent Coordinating Committee. Blacks who sought to vote in Amite County faced intimidation and worse, from racist vigilantes and from Sheriff E. L. Caston Jr., whose deputies raided NAACP meetings and confiscated membership lists. A neighbor of Lee's, farmer E. W. Steptoe, led the local NAACP chapter and complained to the U.S. Depart-

ment of Justice about Caston's harassment. On September 24, 1961, Justice attorney John Doar visited Amite County with Robert Moses, interviewing Steptoe and requesting names of any other blacks who had suffered harassment. Herbert Lee's name was first on the list, but Doar missed him that afternoon, as Lee was called away from home on business.

There would never be another chance for them to meet.

Early on September 25, the day after Doar returned to Washington, Lee drove a truckload of cotton to the gin near Liberty, Mississippi. Behind him, as he pulled into the parking lot, was another vehicle occupied by state legislator E. H. Hurst and his son-in-law, Billy Caston. An argument ensued between Hurst and Lee and climaxed when Hurst drew a pistol and shot Lee once in the head, killing him instantly. Robert Moses later described the event and its aftermath to journalist Howard Zinn.

Lee's body lay on the ground that morning for two hours, uncovered, until they finally got a funeral home in McComb to take it in. Nobody in Liberty would touch it. They had a coroner's jury that very same afternoon. Hurst was acquitted. He never spent a moment in jail. . . . I remember reading very bitterly in the papers the next morning, a little item on the front page of the McComb Enterprise-Journal said that a Negro had been shot as he was trying to attack E. H. Hurst. And that was it. Might have thought he'd been a bum. There was no mention that Lee was a farmer, that he had a family, nine kids, beautiful kids, and that he had farmed all his life in Amite County.

One witness to the shooting was Louis Allen, who arrived at the cotton gin moments before Lee was killed. He watched Lee die, then saw a second white man lead E. H. Hurst to a nearby vehicle, whereupon they departed from the scene. Allen retreated to a nearby garage, where one of Liberty's white residents located him and walked him back to the cotton gin. En route to the crime scene, Allen's escort told him, "They found a tire iron in that nigger's hand. They found a piece of iron, you hear?"

Allen knew better, but he had a wife and four children to consider. Within the hour, he found himself at the county courthouse, where a coroner's hearing had been hastily convened. White men armed with pistols packed the hearing room, glaring at Allen as he took the witness stand and lied under oath, confirming the tale that Herbert Allen had been armed, assaulting E. H. Hurst when he was shot. The jury wasted no time in returning a verdict of "justifiable homicide." Hurst subsequently told the *New York Times* that he had quarreled with Lee over a $500 debt, which Lee refused to pay. When Lee attacked him with the tire iron, Hurst declared, "I didn't run. I got no rabbit in me." Instead, he had struck Lee with his pistol, then shot him: "I must have pulled the trigger unconsciously." Hurst denied Lee's civil rights activity, dubbing his victim "a smart nigger" who normally avoided conflict with whites.

Guilt-ridden by his false testimony, Allen confessed the lie to his wife and to Robert Moses. Elizabeth Allen described the conversation in a 1964 affidavit, as follows:

The day Herbert Lee was killed, Louis came home and said that they wanted him to testify that Herbert Lee had a piece of iron. He said that Herbert Lee didn't have no iron. But he said for his family and for his life he had to tell that he had an iron. Louis told me that he didn't want to tell no story about the dead, because he couldn't ask them for forgiveness. They had two courts about Herbert Lee's killing. When they had the second court, Louis did not want to testify. He said he didn't want to go back and testify no more that a man had a piece of iron when he didn't have it, but he said he didn't have no choice, he was there and he had to go to court. He said he told the FBI the truth, that Herbert Lee didn't have a piece of iron when he was shot.

The "second court" was a state grand jury hearing, convened in Amite County a month after Lee was shot. Allen approached Robert Moses, reporting that he had told his story to FBI agents, suggesting that if he could get protection with the Justice Department he would testify truthfully and "let the hide go with the hair." Moses then telephoned Washington, and heard from Justice that "there was no way possible to provide protection for a witness at such a hearing." (In fact, such protection is routinely offered to witnesses in organized crime cases and similar matters.) Allen went on to repeat his false story before the grand jury, which returned no indictments.

Things went from bad to worse for Allen after that, as Amite County whites apparently learned of his abortive effort to tell the truth. Strangers visited Allen's home and accosted his children, threatening his life. In June 1962 Allen was arrested on trumped-up charges of "interfering with the law"; he spent three weeks in jail, was threatened with lynching, and suffered a broken jaw after one of Sheriff Caston's deputies struck him with a flashlight. White customers stopped buying logs from Allen, and local merchants cut off his credit at various stores. Only his ailing mother kept Allen from leaving Amite County, but her death in late 1963 freed him at last. Eagerly, Allen made plans to leave Mississippi for Milwaukee, where his brother lived.

Unfortunately, he had already waited too long.

On January 1, 1964, one of Allen's white creditors stopped at the house to collect a bill payment. While Allen counted out the money, his visitor pointed to Allen's three-year-old daughter playing nearby, and remarked, "It would be mighty bad if she turned up burnt, wouldn't it? She's an innocent baby, but she could get burnt up just like that. I could tell you more, but I'm not. If I was you I would get my rags together in a bundle and leave here."

Resolved to do exactly that, on January 31, 1964, Allen sought work references from some of his former clients. The first, Melvin Blalock, declined to provide a letter, concerned that he "might be helping a communist." Another, Lloyd King, later recalled speaking to Allen around 8:10 P.M. Two cars were seen trailing Allen's pickup when he left King's farm, driving home. At the foot of his long gravel driveway, Allen left his truck to open the gate, then apparently threw himself under the vehicle. The move failed to save him, as two shotgun blasts ripped into his face. Son Henry Allen found his father's body hours later, when he returned from a dance.

No suspects in Louis Allen's murder were ever identified, but Robert Moses placed partial blame for the slaying on the FBI's doorstep. Moses and other activists believed that G-men routinely leaked the contents of confidential statements to local police in civil rights cases, thus leaving witnesses vulnerable to attack by racist authorities or the vigilante Ku Klux Klan. The segregationist McComb *Enterprise-Journal* seemed to confirm at least some measure of that theory in its description of the murder, noting that "Strictly non-documented rumors have been current in and around Liberty since the Lee case of 1961 that Allen may have become a 'tip-off man' for the integration-minded Justice Department. Similarly, there was at one time a belief that the logger was one of the spearheads of a reported complaint that 'economic pressure' being applied against some Amite County Negroes."

ALLEN, Mary   See "TOLEDO CLUBBER"

"ALPHABET Murders" Rochester, New York (1971–73)

This troubling case draws its popular nickname from the matched initials of three young victims raped and murdered over a three-year period. Eleven-year-old Carmen Colon was the first to die, in 1971. Wanda Walkowicz, age 10, followed a year later, and 10-year-old Michelle Maenza was the last. The "alphabet" angle was further emphasized when the killer dumped each Rochester victim in a nearby town whose name began with the same letter as the murdered girl's first and last names: Colon in Churchville, Walkowicz in Webster, and Maenza in Macedon. Police note that aside from the similarity in age, all three girls came from poor Catholic families and each had recently suffered from trouble at school. Detectives thus suspected a killer employed by some social service agency, whose job gave him access to such information, but interviews with 800 potential suspects led nowhere.

In 1979 Rochester police named former resident Kenneth Bianchi as a suspect in the murder series. Better known to Californians as the "Hillside Strangler," the confessed slayer (with cousin Angelo Buono) of 10 young women in Los Angeles, Bianchi was serving life for two more murders in Bellingham, Washington, and thus was unlikely to sue for slander. Authorities note that Bianchi left Rochester in January 1976, driving a car that resembled a vehicle seen near the site of one "alphabet" slaying. Bianchi has not been charged in the case, and the waters were muddied further in December 1995, when an imprisoned killer claimed to know the "alphabet" murderer's name. That tip, like the Bianchi lead before it, has thus far failed to solve the case.

AL SANE, Adnan Abdul Hameed murder victim (1993)

A 46-year-old Kuwaiti banker who retired from the business and moved to London in 1986, Adnan al Sane dined with a business acquaintance on the evening of December 16, 1993, at the Britannia Hotel in Grosvenor Square. No one admits to seeing him alive after that meeting, but his headless and partly burned body, nude but for underpants, was found on December 17 beneath a railway arch near Piccadilly Station, in Manchester. His severed, mutilated head was found six weeks later and 70 miles away by a man walking his dog along the M6 motorway at Cannock, Staffordshire. Blows from a machete had disfigured al Sane's face beyond recognition, but he was identified on the basis of bridgework including a rare metal alloy. Police believe he had made it home after dinner on December 16 and was later abducted from his apartment, but no suspects have yet been identified in the grisly case.

AMTRAK derailment Arizona (1995)

Sleeping passengers aboard Amtrak's Sunset Limited were jolted awake in the predawn hours of October 9, 1995, when eight cars derailed and four plunged 30 feet from a trestle into a dry gulch near Hyder, in Yuma County. One person was killed, with 78 others injured in the crash. Authorities discovered that 29 spikes had been pulled from the track and the rails forced apart, in a deliberate and deadly act of sabotage. A jumper wire was used to bypass a computer system that warned engineers of track failures ahead, and a metal plate had been installed with spikes to prevent the separated tracks from reconnecting accidentally. A note left at the scene, signed "Sons of the Gestapo," condemned federal agents for their actions in confrontations with the Randy Weaver family at Ruby Ridge, Idaho (1992), and the Branch Davidian religious sect at Waco, Texas (1993).

FBI agents assigned to the case remain baffled, since no organization called Sons of the Gestapo is known to exist in the United States (or anywhere else, for that matter). The note's signature is thought to be a crude diversionary tactic, and the crime is generally blamed on unknown members of the far-right "patriot militia" movement, but no suspects have been named to date. In October 1998 investigators plumbed the depths of an abandoned Arizona mine, descending 160 feet into the Earth on a tip that corpses, stolen cars, and evidence related to the Amtrak case might be found there. They emerged with five vehicles, but no bodies or other significant evidence. Dozens of searches and hundreds of interviews were conducted in what G-men called "one of the most intensive investigations on record," but all in vain. Several suspects passed polygraph tests and were thereby cleared of suspicion. Despite the "Gestapo" message, authorities suspect the crime was committed "by someone with a grudge against

Targets of alleged anarchist bombings in 1919 included the Washington home of U.S. attorney general A. Mitchell Palmer. (Library of Congress)

the railroad." A $320,000 reward remains outstanding for information leading to arrest and conviction of those responsible.

ANARCHIST Bombings (1919)

Throughout the early decades of the 20th century, conservative American leaders lived in constant fear of revolution. Radical violence had swept Europe in waves for the past 40 years, and President William McKinley was assassinated by a self-proclaimed anarchist, Leon Czolgosz, in 1901. Anarchists—opponents of any and all organized government—were the usual culprits prior to 1917, when Russia's Bolshevik revolution raised the new specter of a global communist threat. By 1919, when members of radical labor unions such as the Industrial Workers of the World (IWW) engaged in 3,600 strikes from coast to coast, some businessmen and politicians believed the revolution was finally at hand.

Those fears were exacerbated in April 1919, when 29 bombs were sent through the mail to various prominent targets around the United States. The first was detected and disarmed on April 28, at the home of Seattle mayor Ole Hanson (who had recently used troops to crush a strike by 60,000 shipyard workers). The next day, in Atlanta, a parcel bomb exploded at the home of former U.S. senator Thomas Hardwick, maiming one of his servants. Over the next week, 34 more bombs were intercepted and defused without further injury. Their targets included Frederick Howe (commissioner of immigration at Ellis Island); Senator Lee Overman (chairman of recent hearings on the Bolshevik menace); Supreme Court Justice Oliver Wendell Holmes Jr.; U.S. Postmaster General Albert Burlson; Secretary of Labor William Wilson; Attorney General A. Mitchell Palmer; federal judge Kenesaw Landis (who had sentenced IWW leaders to prison); and two living symbols of unfettered capitalism, J. P. Morgan and John D. Rockefeller.

The bombers tried again on the night of June 3, 1919. This time they delivered their "infernal devices" by hand and all detonated, but the only casualties were two of the bombers themselves. In Washington, D.C., a blast outside the home of Attorney General Palmer damaged houses within a two-block radius, shredding the bodies of two clumsy saboteurs who would remain forever unidentified. Other bombs rocked targets in Boston; Cleveland; New York City; Newtonville, Massachusetts; Paterson, New Jersey; Philadelphia; and Pittsburgh, without further injury. Handbills were found at most of the bombing scenes, signed by the "Anarchist Fighters." They read, in part:

Plain Words

The powers that be make no secret of their will to stop here in America the worldwide spread of revolution. The powers that be must reckon that they will have to accept the fight they have provoked. A time has come when the social question's solution can be delayed no longer; class war is on, and cannot cease but with a complete victory for the international proletariat.

Attorney General Palmer and young associate J. Edgar Hoover struck back with a vengeance between November 1919 and January 1920, with a series of coordinated dragnet raids designed to capture and deport alleged "enemy aliens." Thousands were arrested without warrants or specific charges from coast to coast, but fewer than 600 were finally deported, while most were released without so much as an apology for their detention and occasional subjection to brutal "third-degree" tactics in custody. The sweeping "Palmer raids" produced no suspects in the 1919 bombing, and publicity surrounding the fiasco boomeranged against Attorney General Palmer in Congress, where exposure of his vigilante tactics doomed his presidential ambitions and soon drove him from office in disgrace. (J. Edgar Hoover dodged the axe and lived to raid another day, concocting fables that he had "deplored" the raids, although surviving documents prove that he personally organized and supervised every aspect of the events.)

Two months after the last Palmer raids, on March 7, 1920, FBI agents in New York City arrested Andrea Salsedo, an immigrant printer known for his sympathy to anarchist causes. At some point over the next two months, while he was held incommunicado and without legal counsel, Salsedo allegedly confessed to printing the "Anarchist Fighters" handbills of June 1919. Unfortunately for the government's case, Salsedo "committed suicide" on May 3, 1920, allegedly leaping from a window of Bureau headquarters before he could confirm his confession in court. Richard Rohman, a reporter for the *New York Call,* was present in the FBI office moments before Salsedo plunged to his death, and he described the scene for his readers as follows:

I became aware of cries coming from an inner office. As I walked on, I could hear these terrible cries, subhuman cries of a man in terrible pain. Suddenly I barged into an inner room from which the cries were coming. Salsedo was slumped in a chair, and he looked as if every bone in his body had been broken. Two or three agents were standing over him, hitting him with blackjacks.

When they heard me, they whirled around, and they recognized me, of course. One of them shouted, "There's that SOB from that Socialist rag, the Call. *Let's get him." They came for me, and I turned and dashed down some 14 or 15 flights of stairs, with them at my heels. I finally outdistanced them, jumped into the subway, and got back to my office, where I wrote the story.*

Salsedo's "confession" notwithstanding, no suspects were ever charged with the spate of bombings and bombing attempts in 1919. Authorities later speculated on an anarchist link to the catastrophic WALL STREET BOMBING of 1920 (also unsolved), but critics of federal conduct in America's first red scare have suggested an alternative scenario. Mindful of illegal FBI tactics documented during the 1950s and 1960s, including frequent use of agents provocateurs to entrap alleged radicals in bomb plots and similar crimes, skeptics suggest that the 1919 bombings may have been perpetrated by right-wing conspirators (or by unscrupulous G-men themselves) to justify the roundup of anarchists and "Bolsheviks." Eighty years and counting after the events, it is unlikely that the controversy will ever be resolved.

ANASTASIA, Albert mobster and murder victim (1957)

A native Italian, born Umberto Anastasio in 1903, Albert Anastasia entered the United States illegally sometime between 1917 and 1920 (reports vary). With brother Anthony ("Tough Tony") Anastasio, he soon muscled his way into labor activities on the Brooklyn docks and rose to a leadership position in

Albert Anastasia was known as the Lord High Executioner of the underworld hit team dubbed "Murder, Inc." (Library of Congress)

the longshoreman's union. Anastasia committed his first known murder—of a fellow longshoremen—in the early 1920s and was sentenced to die in the electric chair at Sing Sing, but a new trial was granted on appeal and Anastasia was acquitted after four key witnesses vanished without a trace.

That pattern of eradicating witnesses became Anastasia's trademark, expressed to underworld cohorts as a simple motto: "If you ain't got no witness, you ain't got no case." In the late 1920s Anastasia aligned himself with up-and-coming mobsters Charles ("Lucky") Luciano and Frank Costello, soon emerging as their primary hit man in the war between Mafia bosses Joe Masseria and Salvatore Maranzano. Luciano's group first betrayed Masseria (shot while dining with Luciano on April 15, 1931), and then eliminated Maranzano (killed in his office on September 10, 1931) to consolidate their rule over the New York City underworld.

Luciano's victory placed Anastasia in charge (with Mafia ally Louis Buchalter) of a Brooklyn-based hit team later nicknamed "Murder Incorporated" by sensational journalists. The same reporters dubbed Anastasia the "Lord High Executioner," while some who knew him better spoke of him (behind his back) as "The Mad Hatter." Psychotic rages notwithstanding, Anastasia served the syndicate loyally for decades, and he was duly rewarded. In 1951, with Luciano deported to Italy and Costello trapped in the spotlight of televised hearings on organized crime, Anastasia was elevated to lead his own "family," formerly led by Vincent Mangano (another permanently missing person).

Anastasia survived only six years as one of the Big Apple's five Mafia bosses. With virtual absolute power in hand, he became too aggressive and erratic for the other mob leaders to trust or tolerate. On the morning of October 25, 1957, two masked gunmen entered the Park Sheraton Hotel's barbershop, where Anastasia was getting a shave, and killed him in a blaze of pistol fire. Underworld rumors named the shooters as JOSEPH GALLO and his brother Larry, but no suspects were ever formally identified.

Suggested motives for the Anastasia rubout are diverse. Some authors believe he was killed by rival mob boss Vito Genovese, while others blame Anastasia's first lieutenant (and successor) Carlo Gambino. Yet another theory has both mobsters collaborating against Anastasia for mutual benefit. A fourth theory contends that Florida mobster Santos Trafficante teamed with Jewish gangsters Meyer Lansky and Moe Dalitz to eliminate Anastasia, after Anastasia demanded a share of their gambling interests in Cuba. Whatever the truth, it is known that a national conclave of Mafia bosses was scheduled for November 14, 1957, with an explanation for Anastasia's murder topping the agenda. (He was accused, among other things, of selling Mafia memberships to "undesirable" subjects.) New York state police raided the meeting at Apalachin and jailed 58 mobsters on various charges (mostly dismissed), while dozens more escaped the dragnet. The raid and attendant publicity finally forced J. Edgar Hoover's FBI to acknowledge the existence of organized crime in America.

ANDERSON, Angela See PORTLAND, OREGON, MURDERS

ANDERSON, Judith See CHICAGO CHILD MURDERS

ANDREWS, Jack See CASTRATION MURDERS

ANN Arbor, Michigan hospital murders (1975)

Over a six-week period in July and August 1975, 27 patients at the Veterans Administration hospital in Ann Arbor, Michigan, were stricken with unexplained respiratory arrests that left them unable to breathe without mechanical aid. Some patients suffered more than one attack, and 11 died before doctors admitted that the incidents could not be explained as natural phenomena. Investigations proved that 18 of the patients, including nine who died, had received unprescribed injections of Pavulon, a synthetic form of curare sometimes used by anesthetists as a muscle relaxant.

Federal Bureau of Investigation agents sent to investigate the case reported that most of the respiratory failures had occurred on the afternoon shift, in the hospital's intensive care unit. All victims had been fed intravenously, and G-men concluded that Pavulon had been injected into the plastic feeding tubes. A review of work schedules focused suspicion on two Filipina nurses, 31-year-old Leonora Perez and 29-year-old Filipina Narciso. Both protested their innocence, though Perez was identified by a surviving victim, 61-year-old Richard Neely, as the nurse who entered his room moments before the onset of a near-fatal respiratory attack—and who then ran away as he cried out for help.

Perez and Narciso were indicted on five counts of murder and convicted at trial in July 1977. Their verdicts were overturned on appeal, in December 1977, and charges were dismissed in February 1978. No other suspects have been named, despite the FBI's insistence that at least five patients (and perhaps as many as 11) were murdered by some unknown member of the VA hospital's staff. No motive was suggested for the slayings, although various nurses convicted in similar cases, have described their crimes as "mercy" killings.

ANSTEY, Marie See "ASTROLOGICAL MURDERS"

ANTHRAX murders (2001)

On September 18, 2001—one week after the 9/11 terrorist attacks in New York City and Washington, D.C.—five letters containing deadly anthrax bacteria were mailed from Trenton, New Jersey. Four went to New York, addressed to the corporate offices of ABC News, CBS News, NBC News, and the *New York Post*; the fifth went to Boca Raton, Florida, addressed to the *National Enquirer* tabloid newspaper at American Media, Inc. (AMI). In New York, only two of the letters—those addressed to NBC and the *Post*—were actually found. Existence of the other three was surmised when employees of ABC, AMI, and CBS contracted anthrax.

The NBC and *New York Post* envelopes contained identical notes, sprinkled with anthrax. They read:

09-11-01
THIS IS NEXT
TAKE PENACILIN NOW
DEATH TO AMERICA
DEATH TO ISRAEL
ALLAH IS GREAT

Nine victims contracted anthrax between September 22 and October 1, but they were incorrectly diagnosed. AMI employee Ernesto Blanco was hospitalized for "pneumonia" on October 1, while coworker Robert Stevens entered a Florida hospital the following day, diagnosed with anthrax infection on October 4. Stevens died on October 5, and anthrax spores were found on his computer keyboard two days later, prompting closure of AMI's office and testing of all employees. NBC's letter, already opened, was delivered to FBI agents on October 12 and tested positive for anthrax. The *Post*'s letter was found, unopened, on October 19.

Meanwhile, two more contaminated letters left Trenton on October 9, 2001, addressed to Senator Tom Daschle of South Dakota and Senator Patrick Leahy of Vermont, both identified in media reports as opposing various provisions of the new USA PATRIOT Act before Congress. Those identical letters read:

09-11-01
YOU CAN NOT STOP US.
WE HAVE THIS ANTHRAX.
YOU DIE NOW.
ARE YOU AFRAID?
DEATH TO AMERICA.
DEATH TO ISRAEL.
ALLAH IS GREAT.

One of Daschle's aides opened his letter on October 15, causing a shutdown of mail delivery to government offices. Leahy's envelope was initially misdirected to the State Department's mail annex at Sterling, Virginia, where it lay unopened with impounded mail until November 16. Both letters bore fictitious return addresses for a nonexistent "Greendale School" in Franklin Park, New Jersey, with the zip code for nearby Monmouth Junction.

Tom Ridge, director of Homeland Security, went public with the anthrax attacks on October 19, two days after five Senate staffers tested positive for infection. Washington postal employee Thomas Morris died from anthrax on October 21, followed by coworker Joseph Curseen on October 22. In all, 23 victims were diagnosed as suffering from anthrax by November 14, including eight in New York City, six

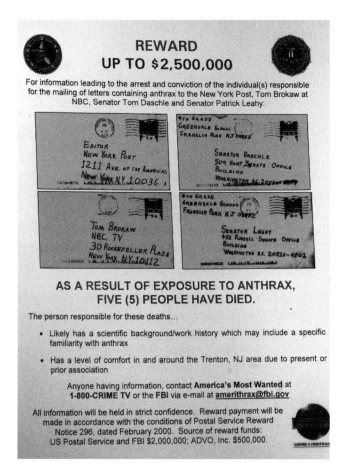

AS A RESULT OF EXPOSURE TO ANTHRAX, FIVE (5) PEOPLE HAVE DIED.

The FBI and U.S. Postal Service released this reward flyer for up to $2.5 million for information leading to the arrest and conviction of the individuals responsible for mailing anthrax-tainted letters in September 2001. (AP Photo/Brian Branch-Price, file)

in New Jersey, five in Washington, five in Florida, and one in Connecticut. Other fatalities included New York hospital worker Kathy Nguyen (October 31) and 94-year-old Ottilie Lundgren of Oxford, Connecticut. Authorities found no anthrax in Lundgren's home, and the source of her infection remains unknown.

So, too, does the identity of those responsible for mailing the anthrax-contaminated letters in 2001. Despite a sweeping FBI investigation, dubbed "Amerithrax," the crimes remain unpunished today.

Forensic study of the anthrax samples identified two different strains, with experts stating that the Senate samples were more potent than those sent to media outlets. Still, DNA sequencing revealed that both preparations derived from the same bacterial strain—specifically the "Ames strain," first researched by the U.S. Army Medical Research Institute of Infectious Diseases at Fort Detrick, Maryland. Radiocarbon dating of the samples proved that the anthrax was cultured no earlier than 2000. Another report, issued in October 2006, traced water used in processing the anthrax to the northeastern United States—and there the trail ended.

Failure to solve the "Amerithrax" case, despite an outstanding $2.5 million reward, ranks among the modern FBI's greatest embarrassments. In 2002, Attorney General John Ashcroft named virologist Steven Hatfill as "a person of interest" in the case, but no evidence suggesting his guilt was ever produced. Hatfill filed libel suits against Ashcroft, the FBI, and the *New York Times* during 2003–04. The *Times* won a summary judgment dismissing its case in 2006, while Hatfill's libel case against Ashcroft and the FBI proceeded toward trial. Forensic linguistics expert Donald Foster, who advised the FBI on various hoaxed anthrax threats in 2001–02 and linked Hatfill to those letters in a 2003 article for *Vanity Fair,* reportedly settled a $10 million libel action filed by Hatfill in February 2007. On June 27, 2008, the Justice Department paid Hatfill $5.85 million to settle his claim out of court.

Various media sources also named Dr. Philip Zack, formerly employed at Fort Detrick, as an alternative "person of interest." According to published reports, Zack had access to "Ames strain" anthrax and allegedly displayed motive for the attacks by "exhibiting hostile behavior" toward a coworker Dr. Ayaad Assaad. Security cameras allegedly caught Zack during an unauthorized visit to the fort's anthrax lab, from which the samples were presumably stolen, and while G-men have reportedly interrogated all concerned, no charges were filed.

On August 1, 2008, FBI spokesmen announced a break in the case, declaring that new suspect Bruce Ivins, a 62-year-old microbiologist who helped G-men analyze anthrax samples mailed in 2001, had committed suicide "just as the Justice Department was about to file criminal charges against him for the attacks." As revealed in the media, Ivins had worked since 1990 at the U.S. Army Medical Research Institute of Infectious Diseases at Fort Detrick. He died on July 29, reportedly after ingesting a large dose of Tylenol mixed with codeine.

Ivins's death came one month after Justice Department officials settled a lawsuit filed by former "suspect" Steven Hatfill, and some found the timing suspicious. Ivins had never been named as a suspect or "person of interest" in the case, but following his death G-men claimed that the apparent suicide occurred after they informed his lawyer that criminal charges would be filed "related to the [anthrax] mailings."

Was it true? And if so, did that make Ivins the anthrax killer?

Agents now claimed that they had focused on Ivins in early 2007, after FBI director Robert Mueller III replaced the original investigation's leaders with fresh talent, adding that "significant progress" was made, six years after the fact, in analyzing genetic properties of anthrax spores mailed to the U.S. Senate. Army spokesmen added that Ivins had "erred" by decontaminating areas of anthrax spillage in his lab but failed to formally report the incident for several months during the winter of 2001–02. Strangely, in light of later accusations, he was neither disciplined nor even censured for those failures at the time. In retrospect, the feds could only say that those unpunished incidents belatedly "raised serious questions about his veracity and his intentions."

Furthermore, agents claimed that Ivins "began showing signs of serious strain" after Justice settled the Hatfill lawsuit. Their "evidence": Ivins sought treatment for clinical depression at a Maryland facility operated by the Sheppard Pratt Health System. He was released, presumably improved, on July 24—five days before his suicide. The *Los Angeles Times* reported that Ivins faced mandatory retirement in September 2008, a circumstance that has depressed thousands of persons who were not involved in any criminal activity.

Was Ivins the anthrax killer?

On August 2, 2008, the *Los Angeles Times* reported that he "stood to gain financially from massive federal spending in the fear-filled aftermath of those killings." Specifically, federal records named him as coinventor on two patents for a genetically engineered anthrax vaccine and on a patent application for "an additive to various biodefense vaccines." VaxGen, a California-based biotechnology firm, holds the first contract issued under Project BioShield, to produce the vaccine at a cost of $877.5 million to American taxpayers. While the amount of royalties due to Ivins is unknown, the FBI suggests that profit "may have been a motive" for his alleged role in the anthrax murders—whatever *that* was.

No one has yet claimed that Ivins personally mailed anthrax to any of the victims targeted in 2001, but G-men claim that DNA from spores found in a flask from Ivins's lab, laboratory grown in 1999, reveal "a perfect match" to those from some of the letters mailed two years later. Having said that, they confessed that "it was unclear how many others at Fort Detrick had access to the flask." News reports described FBI headquarters "bracing for the possibility of a skeptical reception from scientists," and it was not long in coming. Colleagues of Ivins at Fort Detrick proclaimed his innocence, telling reporters that he had neither the motive nor the means to create the fine lethal powder used in the attacks. To them, at least, federal claims that Ivins was "homicidal and obsessed with the notion of revenge" proved distinctly unconvincing.

Jeffrey Adamovicz, former director of the lab where Ivins spent two decades, said, "I really don't think he's the guy. I say to the FBI, 'Show me your evidence.' A lot of the tactics they used were designed to isolate him from his support. The FBI just continued to push his buttons." Bureau critics note that similar tactics were used, without success, against Steven Hatfill, 1999 espionage suspect Dr. Wen Ho Lee, 1996 Centennial Olympic Park bombing suspect Richard Jewell, and many others throughout the FBI's 100-year history. Thus far, conclusive proof of guilt—against Ivins or any other suspect in the case—remains classified and unavailable for public scrutiny.

APULIA, Italy unsolved serial murders (1997)

In 1997 the Apulia district, located in the "heel" of the Italian "boot," was terrorized by a serial killer who preyed on elderly women, invariably committing his murders on Wednesdays and Thursdays. At the time police announced the crimes with an appeal for help, the unknown killer had already claimed six widows and one spinster. Each of the victims lived alone in ground-floor lodgings, and all apparently opened their doors voluntarily, leading police to suggest that "the assailant could be a priest or another woman." Each victim was stabbed repeatedly in the throat, their wounds inflicted variously with a knife, an ice pick, or a screwdriver. Police also noted, for what it may be worth, that a soccer game was playing on television at the time of each murder. Authorities vaguely profile their quarry as "a person 25 or 40 years of age, who as a small child may have been maltreated by his grandmother." Thus far, no suspects have been named and no further slayings have been added to the official body count.

AQUASH, Anna Mae Pictou murder victim

A Canadian-born member of the American Indian Movement (AIM), Anna Aquash traveled to the Pine Ridge (South Dakota) reservation in March 1975, with other AIM members. She was arrested by FBI agents on September 5, 1975, reportedly on weapons charges, and was questioned concerning the June 1975 shoot-out that killed two G-men at Pine Ridge. When she declined to answer, agents allegedly warned Aquash that they would "see her dead within a year."

Released on bond a few days after the interrogation, Aquash fled to Oregon, but she was traced and arrested there on November 14, 1975, then returned to South Dakota for trial on the pending weapons charges. On November 24 Judge Robert Merhige freed Aquash on her own recognizance, her trial scheduled for the following day, but Aquash never returned to court. Her corpse was found at Pine Ridge on February 24, 1976, near the site where a victimless hit-and-run accident had been reported one week earlier. FBI agents photographed the death scene but failed to identify Aquash, an oversight repeated when G-men observed her autopsy. Dr. W. O. Brown, coroner for the Bureau of Indian Affairs, blamed the death on alcohol and exposure, sending Aquash's severed hands to the FBI Crime Lab in Washington for fingerprint identification. By the time she was identified, on March 3, 1976, Aquash had already been buried in an unmarked grave.

Upon receiving notice of Aquash's death, her family demanded an independent review of the case. Aquash was exhumed on March 11, 1976, the second autopsy disclosing an obvious close-range bullet wound in the back of her neck. A bullet was extracted from her left temple, variously described in published reports as a .32- or .38-caliber pistol slug. Dr. Brown grudgingly admitted that "the bullet may have initiated or set in progress the mechanism of death, the proximate cause of which was frostbite." A report by the U.S. Commission on Civil Rights described the FBI's handling of Aquash's murder as "at the very least [an] extremely indifferent and careless investigation." Surviving relatives spoke more bluntly, one declaring: "The FBI wanted the investigation to go cold because they thought it would lead them somewhere that they didn't want to go." More specifically, Aquash's relatives and AIM supporters blamed her murder on a vigilante group called Guardians of the Oglalla Nation (GOON), which was allegedly supported and protected by the FBI at Pine Ridge. The case remains unsolved today.

ARLOSOROFF, Vitaly murder victim (1933)

Vitaly Viktor Haim Arlosoroff was born to Jewish parents in Romny, Ukraine, in 1899. Six years later, anti-Semitic pogroms forced his family to emigrate, settling in Berlin, where Arlosoroff earned a doctorate in economics. As a college student, he also immersed himself in Zionist politics, becoming one of Germany's best-known proponents of establishing a Jewish state of Israel in Palestine. Ironically, his lover during those years was Magda Rietschel, who joined the Nazi Party in 1930 and subsequently married Propaganda Minister Joseph Goebbels, becoming known as the "First Lady of the Third Reich."

Before that happened, in 1924, Arlosoroff left Germany for the British Mandate of Palestine. Two years later, he was chosen to represent the Yishuv (Jewish settlers in Palestine) before the League of Nations. Arlosoroff returned to Nazi Germany in 1933 to negotiate the Ha'avara ("transfer") agreement, permitting Jewish immigration to Palestine. Confronted with Nazi demands that Jewish emigrants must leave all property behind in Germany, Arlosoroff negotiated a trade-off by which Jewish funds would purchase German goods for export to Palestine and other countries, with proceeds from their sale abroad paid to Jews on arrival in the Holy Land.

Arlosoroff returned to Tel Aviv on June 14, 1933. Two days later, he was shot and killed while walking with his wife, Sima, on a local beach. British police arrested Abba Ahimeir, head of the Zionist revisionist group Brit HaBirionim, as the mastermind of Arlosoroff's murder, while Sima Arlosoroff identified Brit HaBirionim members Zevi Rosenblatt and Abraham Stavsky as the triggermen. Defense attorneys accused police of manipulating Sima's testimony and rigging other evidence for political reasons. The court acquitted Ahimeir and Rosenblatt, while convicting Stavsky—but he was later acquitted by the Supreme Court for lack of evidence corroborating Sima's testimony.

Arlosoroff's murder remains officially unsolved, but conspiracy theories persist. Some historians blame militant Zionists, noting that Abraham Stavsky later became a high-ranking officer in the Irgun ("National Military Organization in the Land of Israel") and was killed while smuggling weapons to Zionist guerrillas in Palestine. An alternative theory suggests that Joseph Goebbels learned of his wife's affair with a prominent Jew and ordered the slaying as a hedge against personal embarrassment. An Israeli investigative panel, belatedly formed in March 1982, exonerated Rosenblatt and Stavsky of Arlosoroff's slaying, but failed to name any other suspects.

ARMSTRONG, Emily murder victim (1949)

A 69-year-old resident of London, England, Emily Armstrong was beaten to death on the afternoon of April 14, 1949, in the dry-cleaning shop she managed on St. John's Wood High Street. Police determined that she was killed sometime during the hour before her corpse was found, at 4:00 P.M. Postmortem examination revealed that her skull had been shattered by no fewer than 22 blows from some rigid, heavy object. The murder weapon was never found, but authorities believed it to be a claw hammer. Also missing from the crime scene was Armstrong's handbag. Patrolmen found a bloody handkerchief nearby, bearing laundry mark H-612, but it never led to a viable suspect.

Authorities pursued various theories in their futile effort to solve the case. Witnesses reported a "suspicious" man lurking near the shop, described as 30 years old and 5-feet-5- or 5-feet-6-inches tall, but he was never identified. An escapee from Broadmoor prison, child-killer John Allen, was one of those briefly sus-

pected, but neighborhood witnesses failed to pick him from a police lineup. Several army deserters were questioned as possible suspects, but none was ever charged. Another theory linked Armstrong's murder to the slaying of 65-year-old Gertrude O'Leary on June 30, 1939, but no connection between the two crimes was ever proved. Frustrated authorities finally concluded that Armstrong's slayer was a transient "or a man who had fled to Ireland."

ARNE, Peter murder victim (1983)

A British subject, born in 1921, Peter Arne served as a Royal Air Force pilot in the Battle of Britain at age 19. Following the end of World War II, he pursued an acting career that included roles in such films as *Straw Dogs* (1971) and *The Return of the Pink Panther* (1975). In early August 1983 Arne was scheduled to film an episode of the British Broadcasting Company's *Dr. Who* television series, but he never made it to the set.

On August 1, 1983, London police were summoned to Arne's Knightsbridge apartment building, after a neighbor found a bloodstained fireplace log in the hallway. Inside Arne's flat officers found the 62-year-old actor dead from blunt trauma and slashing wounds to his throat. A medical examiner, Dr. Ian West, reported that the throat wounds had produced "a torrential hemorrhage" resulting in rapid death. Investigation of Arne's background revealed that he was in the habit of soliciting sex from young homeless men around London's Charing Cross railway station.

On August 3, 1983, authorities found bloodstained clothing and the passport of a 32-year-old Italian immigrant, one Giuseppi Perusi, on the banks of the River Thames. Perusi's nude body was pulled from the water a short time later. Police discovered that Perusi had been an active member of the Communist Party in his native Verona, and that he had served as a teacher for handicapped children. "Sexual identity problems" had driven him to London, where he had run out of money and taken to sleeping in parks. Witnesses reported seeing Perusi in Knightsbridge on July 31, 1983, asking for "Peter," and a note in Arne's diary suggested a meeting with Perusi. A bloody handprint in Arne's apartment was also identified as that of Perusi. A coroner's verdict subsequently blamed Perusi for Arne's murder, followed by remorseful suicide, but the case remains officially unsolved since no charges were filed.

ARNOLD, Maxine, and Gooderham, Terry murder victims (1989)

On December 22, 1989, 32-year-old Maxine Arnold and her boyfriend of the moment, Terry Gooderham, were found shot to death in Gooderham's black Mercedes Benz, parked beside a popular lover's lane in Epping Forest, outside London. Police discovered that Gooderham was an accountant who divided his romantic time between Arnold and another pretty blonde in Chingford. Speculation on a motive for the double murder began with potential jealous lovers, but a lack of evidence in that direction led detectives to search farther afield, delving into the murky realm of London's underworld.

Investigators learned that Arnold had spoken to a friend on the telephone, around 7:00 P.M. on December 21, remarking that she had a date with Gooderham and that she would call again later. Arnold's mother had visited the Walthamstow apartment soon after that call, finding the lights on and the front door locked. Police found Arnold's clothes laid out on the bed as if she had been choosing outfits for the evening. Her purse was still in the apartment, as were Gooderham's wallet and wristwatch.

Authorities soon discovered that in addition to his bookkeeping duties, Gooderham had lately involved himself in the business of various London pubs and wine bars. Rumors circulated that he may have been involved in selling drugs, or that he tried to "muscle in" on the lucrative Spanish ice-cream market controlled by London gangsters. One story from the streets described a £50,000 murder contract taken out on Gooderham by angry ice-cream mobsters; another claimed that he had embezzled £150,000 from a client linked to organized crime. Yet another tale alleged that Gooderham had uncovered a major fraud in the course of his work and was killed to keep him from talking. As one friend of Gooderham's told the police, "It is nothing to do with his love life or his own business, but a lot of money is involved."

London authorities finally concluded that Gooderham was the target of a gangland murder, ordered for reasons unknown, and that Maxine Arnold was eliminated incidentally, as an inconvenient witness. No suspects have been named, and no charges have been filed to date.

ARON, Edith See JOHANNESBURG "MUTI" MURDERS

ARZT, Emma See RIVERDELL HOSPITAL MURDERS

ASHBURN, George W. murder victim (1868)

As a prominent Republican in Columbus, Georgia, George Ashburn was treated to the general public derision, scorn, and threats reserved for Southern members of the Grand Old Party during Reconstruction (1865–77). As a white man who rejected the Confederate cause and slavery, he was also reviled as a "traitor" to his race, earmarked for murder by the vigilante Ku Klux Klan. In early 1868 Ashburn had the dubious honor of becoming the first person murdered by Klansmen outside the KKK's home state of Tennessee.

Columbus Democrats—or "Conservatives," as they preferred to call themselves—mounted a campaign of character assassination against Ashburn while he was absent from home in March 1868, attending the state constitutional convention in Atlanta. Democratic mouthpiece Benjamin Hill branded Ashburn "a man of very low morals," while newspaper editorials called him "a man utterly destitute of principle." Upon his return to Columbus, Ashburn found the town's white boardinghouses closed to him, and he was forced to rent rooms in a black widow's home (later described in Conservative editorials as "a negro [sic] brothel of the lowest order."

As luck would have it, the Klan had organized its first "den" in Columbus a week before Ashburn returned from Atlanta, its advent hailed with a glowing editorial in the Columbus *Sun*. Shortly after midnight on March 30, 1868, 30 or 40 Klansmen invaded the house where Ashburn had quarters and shot him to death. Klan apologists called it "self-defense," claiming the night riders simply meant to frighten Ashburn, who provoked his own death by drawing a pistol. The *Sun* went even further, changing its editorial tune to dismiss the KKK as a "wholly imaginary organization." The *Sun* further deemed it inconceivable "that respectable white men should as a body plan murder." A local whispering campaign suggested that Ashburn's killers, in fact, were fellow Republicans inflamed by jealousy of his renown.

General George Meade, commanding the military district that included Georgia, Florida, and Alabama, issued an order on April 4, 1868, forbidding any further efforts at Klan intimidation via posted notices or newspaper articles. The state's "grand dragon," allegedly disturbed by his organization's resort to random violence, issued a similar order, without any visible result. Terrorism continued in Georgia through the November presidential election and beyond. No suspects in the Ashburn case were ever publicly identified.

ASHMOLEAN Museum art theft (2000)

The crime scene resembled a Hollywood sound stage, recalling sequences from such films as *Entrapment* (1999) and *The Thomas Crown Affair* (1999). Unfortunately, though, the action did not unfold on a sound stage, but rather within the "secure" confines of the Ashmolean Museum at Britain's Oxford University.

Unseen by security guards or bystanders, a daring burglar took advantage of the fireworks display scheduled to mark the onset of a new millennium, starting at midnight on January 1, 2000. The thief approached through a construction site adjoining the museum, then scaled an outer wall and made his (or her) way across the roof. Smashing through a glass skylight, the prowler dropped a smoke grenade that achieved the double benefit of blinding museum security cameras and triggering fire alarms to create more confusion. Within 10 minutes, the burglar escaped with one painting, a Paul Cézanne landscape titled *Auvers-sur-Oise,* valued at £3 million (approximately $4.5 million). Museum security personnel only discovered the theft after firefighters had searched the facility and found the smoke grenade.

Cézanne's masterpiece remains missing today, and no suspects have yet been named in the case that journalists quickly dubbed the "Y2Kaper." Authorities suspect that the painting was "stolen to order" for some illicit collector who derives satisfaction from possessing a stolen treasure, even when it cannot be displayed outside a tight circle of intimate friends.

"ASTROLOGICAL Murders" California (1969–73)

Between December 1969 and November 1970, California authorities identified nine unsolved murders as the work of a single predator. A common bond was seen in the killer's disposal technique, discarding corpses in wooded ravines, and in a hypothetical connection to astrology: Seven of the victims died in fair proximity to a seasonal solstice or equinox, while two were killed on Friday the 13th. Unofficial research suggests that the crimes may have claimed six more victims, continuing through December 1973.

The official victim list begins with Leona Roberts, found in December 1969, 10 days before the winter sol-

stice. Her case was treated as a homicide, although the medical examiner blamed her death on exposure to the elements. Five victims were killed in March 1970, over a span of 17 days leading up to the vernal equinox. Collette Ellison's nude body was found on March 3, cause of death undetermined. Patricia King was strangled and discarded in a gully two days later. Nurse Judith Hakari disappeared on March 7, found nude and bludgeoned in an overgrown ravine on April 26. Marie Anstey was kidnapped from Vallejo on Friday the 13th, stunned by a blow to the head, and then drowned. Her corpse was recovered from rural Lake County nine days later, an autopsy revealing traces of mescaline in her blood. Celebrating the equinox itself, on March 20, the killer clubbed Eva Blau to death and left her body in a roadside gully. Once again, the presence of drugs was noted in the coroner's report.

Nurse Donna Lass, official victim number seven, was abducted from Lake Tahoe following the autumnal equinox, on September 26, 1970. Her body has not been recovered. Nancy Bennallack appeared to break the killer's pattern, dying of a slashed throat in her Sacramento apartment, on October 26, but she remains on the official list of victims. Number nine was a Sacramento X-ray technician, Carol Hilburn, found beaten to death and dumped in a ravine on Friday, November 13, 1970. She had been stripped except for one boot and panties, which her killer left around her knees.

The tally might end there, but author Robert Graysmith proposed six more additions to the list in his book *Zodiac* (1986). The supplementary victims include: 21-year-old Betty Cloer, beaten and shot in June 1971, found two days before the summer solstice; 19-year-old Linda Ohlig, found bludgeoned at Half Moon Bay on March 26, 1972, six days after the vernal equinox; Alexandra Clery, stripped and beaten to death in Oakland, 18 days before the autumnal equinox in September 1972; 19-year-old Susan McLaughlin, stabbed and discarded in March 1973, 18 days before the vernal equinox; and double-murder victims Michael Shane and Cathy Fechtel, shot and left beside a road in Livermore, in December 1973, 18 days before the winter solstice.

Mere coincidence? Graysmith proposes a total of 49 victims for the elusive "ZODIAC" killer, whose official tally nonetheless stands at seven dead and one wounded. Critics respond that Graysmith has been overzealous in blaming the Zodiac for various California homicides where no scientific links exist. The 17-year argument will doubtless continue, but one fact remains indisputable: All the murders cited above are still unsolved.

ATHERSTON, Thomas Weldon murder victim (1910)

A minor British actor, born in 1863, Thomas Atherston was murdered in Battersea, London, on July 16, 1910. A chauffeur, one Edward Noice, was driving along Rosenau Road at 9:30 P.M. when he heard two gunshots and saw a man scaling the garden wall at 17 Clifton Gardens, fleeing on foot toward the River Thames. Noice drove on to the nearest police station and reported the incident. An officer was dispatched to the scene and spoke with the tenant, Elizabeth Earl (or Earle, accounts vary). Earl and her dinner guest, 21-year-old Thomas Frederick Anderson, confirmed hearing gunshots and glimpsing a prowler as he fled over the garden wall.

Searching the grounds outside, the officer heard heavy breathing and followed the sound to the foot of a staircase behind Earl's home. There he found Thomas Atherston, wearing bedroom slippers, dying from a gunshot wound to the face. A calling card in Atherston's pocket identified the victim, but it failed to explain the "rudimentary form of life-preserver" he carried in his pocket, described in reports as a piece of insulated electric cable wrapped in paper and wool, with a loop to pass over the wrist.

Police returned to Earl's flat and asked Thomas Anderson if he knew a man named Atherston. Anderson replied that Atherston was his father's stage name, but then curiously added that the dead man could not be his father, "as his father did not wear a moustache." Informed that the murder victim was clean-shaven, Anderson then broke down in tears and sobbed, "I saw my father die!"

London reporters had a field day with the case, reporting that Elizabeth Earl was Atherston's one-time mistress, speculating on a possible romantic triangle that pitted father against son for the woman's affection. Questions abounded, most of them still unanswered after nearly a century. Why was Atherston lurking outside Earl's home in slippers, with a "life-preserver" in his pocket? What business did Anderson have with his father's ex-mistress? Did Earl and Anderson conspire to murder Atherston? Who was the gunman seen fleeing Earl's garden after the fatal shots were fired?

Police finally abandoned any conspiracy theories in favor of a more mundane explanation. They reported that Earl had "been like a mother" to Atherston's sons, and that she dined with Anderson frequently. Battersea residents, meanwhile, had suffered a series of recent burglaries committed by persons unknown. Authorities speculated that Atherston, turned increasingly paranoid since receiving a head injury in 1908, may have lurked outside Earl's flat in hopes of catching her with another lover. While waiting in the shadows, police suggested, he may have surprised the neighborhood burglar and thus received his mortal wound. In any case, no charges were filed, and the crime remains unsolved today.

ATLANTA, Georgia "child murders" miscarriage of justice (1979–82)

The kidnap-murder of a child is every parent's nightmare. The specter of a psychopath at large and killing children by the dozens goes beyond that primal fear, to traumatize entire communities. It is the kind of panic that turns peaceful neighbors into vigilantes, searching for a monster to eradicate.

Atlanta, Georgia, lived with that oppressive fear for two long years, between July 1979 and June 1981. The nightmare was exacerbated by issues of race and politics that threatened to set "the South's most liberal city" on fire. When a solution was finally offered, weary citizens and career-minded politicians embraced it with near-hysterical relief. There was only one problem.

The "solution" solved nothing.

The nightmare endures.

Officially, the Atlanta "child murders" case began on July 28, 1979. That afternoon, a woman hunting for empty bottles and cans along Niskey Lake Road, in southwest Atlanta, stumbled on a pair of corpses carelessly concealed in roadside undergrowth. One victim, shot with a .22-caliber weapon, was identified as 14-year-old Edward Smith, reported missing on July 21. The other was 13-year-old Alfred Evans, last seen alive on July 25. Pathologists attributed his death to "probable" asphyxiation. Both dead boys, like all of those to come, were African American.

On September 4, 1979, 14-year-old Milton Harvey vanished during a neighborhood bike ride. His body was recovered three weeks later, but the cause of death remains undetermined. Nine-year-old Yusef Bell was last seen alive when his mother sent him on a shopping errand, on October 21. He was found dead in an abandoned schoolhouse on November 8, 1979, manually strangled by a powerful assailant.

Twelve-year-old Angel Lenair was the first recognized victim in 1980. Reported missing on March 4, she was found six days later, tied to a tree with her hands bound behind her. The first female victim, Lenair had been sexually assaulted and strangled; pathologists found a pair of panties, not her own, lodged in the girl's throat.

One day after Lenair's body was recovered, Jeffrey Mathis vanished on an errand to the store. Eleven months would pass before his skeletal remains were found, advanced decomposition ruling out a declaration on the cause of death. Fourteen-year-old Eric Middlebrooks left home on May 18, 1980, after receiving a telephone call from persons unknown. He was found the next day, bludgeoned to death with a blunt instrument.

The terror escalated into summer 1980. On June 9, 12-year-old Christopher Richardson vanished en route to a neighborhood swimming pool. Latonya Wilson was kidnapped from her home on June 22, the night before her seventh birthday, prompting FBI agents to assert federal jurisdiction. Ten-year-old Aaron Wyche was reported missing by his family on June 23. Searchers found his body the next afternoon, lying beside a railroad trestle, his neck broken. Originally classified as an accident, Wyche's death was subsequently added to Atlanta's list of murdered and missing black children.

The killer's pace slowed in July, but he did not abandon the hunt. Nine-year-old Anthony Carter disappeared while playing near his home on July 6; found the next day, he was dead from multiple stab wounds. Earl Terrell joined the list on July 30, when he disappeared from a public swimming pool. His skeletal remains, recovered on January 9, 1981, would yield no clues about the cause of death.

Next on the list was 12-year-old Clifford Jones, sodomized and strangled on August 20, 1980. Eyewitness Freddie Cosby told Atlanta police that he saw a white man, Jamie Brooks, rape and strangle Jones in the back room of a laundromat Brooks managed. Four other witnesses confirmed Cosby's account of watching Brooks carry a corpse to the trash Dumpster behind his laundromat. Under police questioning, Brooks admitted various sexual encounters with young boys, some in the laundromat's back room. He denied killing Jones, but failed several polygraph tests. Nonetheless, Atlanta detectives ignored the five eyewitness statements, listing Jones with other victims of the "unknown" murderer. (In 1981 Jamie

Brooks was convicted and imprisoned for aggravated assault and sodomy on a young boy, in an unrelated case.)

Eleven-year-old Darren Glass vanished near his Atlanta home on September 14, 1980. He was never found, and joined the growing list primarily because authorities could do nothing else with his case. Charles Stephens was reported missing on October 9 and found the next day, his life extinguished by asphyxiation; two Caucasian hairs were reportedly found on the body. Authorities found the skeletal remains of Latonya Wilson on October 18, 1980, but they never could determine how she died. Two weeks later, on November 1, Aaron Jackson's frantic parents reported him missing; he was found one day later, another victim of asphyxiation. Fifteen-year-old Patrick Rogers disappeared on November 10, 1980. His pitiful remains, skull crushed by heavy blows, were not recovered until February 1981.

Two days after New Year's 1981, the elusive slayer picked off Lubie Geter, strangling the 14-year-old and dumping his corpse where it would not be found until February 5. Witness Ruth Warren told police that she had seen Geter enter a car driven by a scar-faced white man on the day he vanished, but she had not noted the license number. Fifteen-year-old Terry Pue disappeared on January 22 and was found the next day, a victim of ligature strangulation. This time, police told the press that special chemicals enabled them to lift a suspect's fingerprints from the corpse. Unfortunately, they were not on file with any law enforcement agency in the United States. Twelve-year-old Patrick Baltazar vanished the day after Lubie Geter's body was recovered. Another victim of ligature strangulation, Baltazar was found a week later, along with the skeletal remains of Jeffrey Mathis. Thirteen-year-old Curtis Walker was strangled on February 19 and found the same day.

The case took another strange turn on March 2, 1981, when 16-year-old Joseph ("Jo Jo") Bell dropped out of sight. The next evening, Bell telephoned the Atlanta restaurant where he worked part-time and told the assistant manager, "This is Jo Jo. They're about to kill me. I'm about dead. They are about to kill me. Jerry, they're about to kill me." With that, the line went dead. A friend of Bell's, Timothy Hill, disappeared on March 14, and the same restaurant received another call the following night. This time, the caller was an anonymous woman whose voice "sounded white." She told the café manager "her man" was dangerous—a killer, in fact. She said Jo Jo Bell was "different from the other murdered kids," a friend of hers, and she was trying to negotiate his safe release. Before hanging up, the woman warned that "they" would kill Bell if police were informed of her call. Both Bell and Hill were subsequently pulled from local rivers, their deaths ascribed respectively to asphyxiation and drowning.

On March 30, 1981, Atlanta police added the first adult victim to their list of murdered and missing children. He was 20-year-old Larry Rogers, linked to several younger victims solely by the fact that he had been asphyxiated. No cause of death was determined for 21-year-old Eddie Duncan, but he made the list anyway, when his corpse was discovered on March 21. Michael McIntosh, a 23-year-old ex-convict, was added to the list on April Fool's Day, another victim of asphyxiation.

By April 1981 it seemed apparent that the Atlanta "child murders" case was getting out of hand. Community critics denounced the official victims list as incomplete and arbitrary, citing such cases as the January 1981 murder of Faye Yerby to prove their point. Yerby, like "official" victim Angel Lenair, had been bound to a tree by her killer, hands behind her back; she had been stabbed to death, like four acknowledged victims on the list. Despite those similarities, police rejected Yerby's case on grounds that she was a female (as were victims Wilson and Lenair), and that she was "too old" at age 22 (although the latest victim listed had been 23). Ex-cop and author Dave Dettlinger, examining police malfeasance in the case, suggests that 63 potential "pattern" victims were capriciously omitted from the official roster, 25 of them *after* a suspect's arrest supposedly ended the killing.

In April 1981 FBI spokesmen declared that several of the Atlanta crimes were "substantially solved," outraging the black community with suggestions that some of the victims (unnamed) had been slain by their own parents. While that storm was raging, Roy Innis, head of the Congress of Racial Equality, went public with the story of a female witness who described the murders as sacrifices committed by a cult involved with drugs, pornography, and Satanism. (The woman, unlike murder suspect Jamie Brooks, passed two polygraph tests.) Innis led reporters to an apparent ritual site, complete with large inverted crosses, but police by that time had focused on another suspect, narrowing their scrutiny to the exclusion of all other possibilities.

On April 21, 1981, 21-year-old ex-convict Jimmy Payne was reported missing from Atlanta. Six days later, when his body was recovered, death was publicly attributed to suffocation, and Payne's name was added to the list of murdered "children." Seventeen-year-old William Barrett disappeared on May 11; he was found the next day, another victim of asphyxiation.

Several bodies had by now been pulled from local rivers, and police were staking out the waterways by night. In the predawn hours of May 22, 1981, a rookie officer stationed under a bridge on the Chattahoochee reported hearing a splash in the river nearby. Above him, a car rumbled past and officers manning the bridge were alerted. Police and FBI agents halted a vehicle driven by Wayne Bertram Williams, searching his car and grilling him for two hours before they released him. Two days later, the corpse of Nathaniel Cater, a 27-year-old ex-convict, was pulled from the river downstream. Authorities connected the dots and thereafter focused their probe on Wayne Williams to the exclusion of all other suspects.

From day one, he made a most unlikely suspect. The only child of two Atlanta schoolteachers, Williams still lived with his parents at age 23. A college dropout, he cherished ambitions of earning fame and fortune as a music promoter. In younger days he had constructed a functional radio station in the basement of the family home. Still, he was young and black, as predicted in the FBI's profile of the "Atlanta child killer," and a black suspect was required to cool simmering racial tension in Atlanta.

Williams was arrested on June 21, 1981, charged with killing Nathaniel Cater—this despite testimony from two witnesses, known to police, who recalled seeing Cater alive on May 22 and 23, *after* the infamous Chattahoochee "splash." Authorities formally indicted Williams for two murders, of adult victims Cater and Payne, on July 17, 1981, while newspapers trumpeted the capture of Atlanta's "child killer."

At his trial, convened on December 28, 1981, the prosecution painted Williams as a violent homosexual and bigot, so disgusted with his own race that he hatched a harebrained plot to wipe out future generations by killing black children before they could breed. Direct evidence was as flimsy as the alleged motive. Witness Robert Henry, himself once imprisoned for sexual assault, claimed he had seen Nathaniel Cater "holding hands" with Williams a few hours before Williams was stopped on the Chattahoochee bridge, but he later recanted that testimony in a sworn affidavit. A 15-year-old witness told the court that Williams had once paid him two dollars for the privilege of fondling his genitals. Meanwhile, police added a final victim, 28-year-old John Porter, to the official list of Atlanta's dead and missing "children."

Defense attorneys tried to balance the scales with testimony from a woman who admitted having "normal sex" with Williams, but the prosecution won a crucial victory when Judge Clarence Cooper (a longtime friend of District Attorney Lewis Slaton) permitted introduction of evidence concerning 10 "pattern" murders, though Williams was charged with none of those crimes. The additional victims included Alfred Evans, Eric Middlebrooks, Charles Stephens, William Barrett, Terry Pue, John Porter, Lubie Geter, Joseph Bell, Patrick Baltazar, and Larry Rogers. The "pattern," as described in court, included 15 separate elements:

1. All victims were black males.
2. All came from poor families.
3. All were raised in broken homes.
4. None of the victims owned a car.
5. All were deemed "street hustlers" by the state.
6. None showed evidence of forcible abduction.
7. All died by strangulation or asphyxiation.
8. All were transported after death.
9. All were dumped near "major arteries" of travel.
10. Bodies were disposed of in "unusual" fashions.
11. Clothing was absent from the murder scenes.
12. No valuables were found with any of the bodies.
13. Similar fibers were found on several victims.
14. No motive was apparent for any of the crimes.
15. Williams denied contact with any of the victims.

Discounting the last two points (which are equally consistent with Williams's claim of innocence) and number 12 (with its contradictory suggestion of robbery as a motive in the slayings), prosecutors still had glaring problems with their "pattern." Seven of the 10 were too young to drive, so their lack of cars was superfluous. Victims Rogers and Middlebrooks were beaten to death, not strangled or asphyxiated. Edward Smith, a gunshot victim, was excluded from the "pattern" list although his corpse was found with that of Alfred Evans. Prosecutors likewise ignored

the strange phone calls that followed Joseph Bell's abduction (referring to multiple abductors) and their own reported discovery of unidentified fingerprints on Terry Pue's corpse. A witness who described glancing out the window of his workplace, seeing Williams and Lubie Geter together on the day Geter disappeared, was found to be lying; his manager testified that the "witness" had not worked on the day in question. A second witness, Ruth Warren, changed her original story of seeing Geter with a scar-faced white man the day he vanished; in court she described an African-American suspect "resembling" Wayne Williams.

The most impressive evidence of guilt was offered by a team of scientific experts, dealing with assorted hairs and fibers found on certain "pattern" victims. Testimony indicated that some fibers from a brand of carpet found inside the Williams home (and countless other homes, as well) had been identified on several bodies. Furthermore, victims Middlebrooks, Wyche, Carter, Terrell, and Stephens all supposedly bore fibers from the trunk liner of a 1979 Ford automobile owned by the Williams family. The clothes of victim Stephens also allegedly yielded fibers from a second car—a 1970 Chevrolet—owned by Wayne's parents. Curiously, jurors were not advised of a critical gap in the state's fiber case.

Specifically, Wayne Williams had no access to the vehicles in question at the times when three of the five "fiber" victims were killed. Wayne's father took the Ford in for repairs at 9:00 A.M. on July 30, 1980, some five hours before Earl Terrell vanished that afternoon. Terrell was long dead before Williams got the car back on August 7, 1980, and it was returned to the shop on August 8, still refusing to start. A new estimate on repair costs was so expensive that Wayne's father refused to pay, and the family never again had access to the vehicle. As for Charles Stephens, kidnapped on October 9, 1980, Wayne's family did not purchase the 1970 Chevrolet until October 21, 12 days after Stephens's death. At trial, no mention was made of the two Caucasian hairs recovered from Stephens's body.

Wayne Williams was convicted of two murder counts in January 1982 and received a double life sentence on February 27. Two days later, the Atlanta "child murders" task force disbanded, announcing that 23 of 30 official "List" cases were considered closed with Williams's conviction, although he had never been charged. (One of the cases thus "solved" was that of Clifford Jones, excluded from trial testimony to avoid introduction of eyewitness statements blaming another suspect for his death.) The remaining seven cases, still open, reverted to Atlanta's normal homicide detail and remain unsolved today.

Georgia's Supreme Court reviewed the Williams case in 1983, with Justice Richard Bell assigned to draft the court's opinion. Bell, a former prosecutor, criticized Judge Cooper for admitting prosecution "pattern" evidence, specifically in regard to victims Baltazar, Evans, Middlebrooks, Porter, and Stephens. As Bell explained in his draft, "There was no evidence placing Williams with those five victims before their murders, and as in all the murders linked to Williams, there were no eyewitnesses, no confession, no murder weapons and no established motive. Also, the five deaths, while somewhat similar to each other in technique, were unlike the two for which Williams was tried." After a review of Bell's draft, as detailed in the *Washington Post* two years later, Bell was pressured to change his opinion and finally lent his name to a majority ruling *upholding* the Williams verdict.

In November 1985 a new team of defense lawyers uncovered once-classified documents concerning an investigation of the Ku Klux Klan, conducted during 1980 and 1981 by the Georgia Bureau of Investigation. A spy inside the Klan told GBI agents that Klansmen were "killing the children" in Atlanta, hoping to ignite a race war that would turn into a statewide purge of blacks. One Klansman in particular, 30-year-old Charles Sanders, allegedly boasted of murdering "List" victim Lubie Geter following a personal altercation. Geter reportedly struck Sanders's car with a go-cart, prompting Sanders to tell the GBI informant, "I'm gonna kill him. I'm gonna choke that black bastard to death." Geter was in fact strangled, some three months after the incident in question. Carlton Sanders, father of Charles and subject of 35 arrests since 1951 (including one for molestation, case dismissed), matched Ruth Warren's original description of the scar-faced white man seen with Geter on the day he vanished. Another "List" victim, Charles Stephens (found with Caucasian hairs on his underclothes), was dumped near a trailer park frequented by brothers Charles, Don, and Terry Sanders.

Based on reports from their informant, GBI agents obtained warrants for wiretaps on the various Sanders telephones. On April 1, 1981, the taps recorded a conversation between brothers Don and Terry Sand-

ers (themselves both Klansmen). The transcript read in part:

> *Don: Is Ricky around?*
> *Terry: Well, he just left with Kenneth.*
> *Don: Did he?*
> *Terry: Yeah.*
> *Don: Where's he headed?*
> *Terry: To his apartment or something.*
> *Don: Do you think he'll be back?*
> *Terry: Oh yeah.*
> *Don: After a while.*
> *Terry: Yeah.*
> *Don: I'll just give a buzz back, and I might get out and ride around a little bit, and I might come by there.*
> *Terry: Go find you another little kid, another little kid?*
> *Don: Yeah, scope out some places. We'll see you later.*

The GBI informant also recounted another conversation with one of the Sanders brothers from early 1981, warning authorities that "after 20 black-child killings they, the Klan, were going to start killing black women." Perhaps coincidentally, police records document the unsolved murders of several black women in Atlanta in 1980–82, with most of the victims strangled.

Armed with the new information, Williams and his attorneys continued their battle in court. On July 10, 1988, Butts County superior court judge Hal Craig rejected an appeal based on charges of prosecutorial misconduct (specifically suppression of exculpatory evidence by D.A. Lewis Slaton) and claims of ineffective representation at trial. A year later, on July 8, 1999, the State Supreme Court reversed that decision on a 4-to-3 vote and sent the case back to Judge Craig for further study. A further 11 months passed before Craig rejected the new-trial motion a second time, on June 15, 2000. Four years and counting since defense attorney Lynn Whatley called for DNA testing of the state's forensic evidence, vowing to "show there is no linkage in Wayne Williams," no apparent progress has been made toward scientific resolution of the case.

Was Williams framed?

There is no doubt that certain evidence—the Pue fingerprint, eyewitnesses to the Jones murder, apparent Klan links to the Geter case, etc.—were withheld from the defense and from the jury in 1981. Whether or not suppression of that evidence qualifies as criminal misconduct, its introduction at trial would have shattered the state's "pattern" case and might have provided sufficient reasonable doubt for an acquittal.

Is the Klan conspiracy plausible? We know that Klansmen have committed thousands of atrocities since their organization was founded in 1866. Collusion with racist police to obstruct prosecution has been documented since the days of Reconstruction, and Atlanta has been the Klan's national Mecca since defrocked preacher William Simmons revived the order in 1915. The KKK's grand dragon, one Samuel Roper, led the Georgia Bureau of Investigation in the 1940s, and Klan membership was a virtual prerequisite for Atlanta police recruits through the early 1950s.

As far as plotting "race war" goes, the theme has recurred among Klansmen and affiliated neo-Nazi groups since the mid-1960s, when long hot summers of ghetto rebellion produced the first echoes of "white backlash" against the civil rights movement. One fascist cult, the World Church of the Creator (WCC), uses "RAHOWA!"—*Racial Holy War*—as its motto, while other cliques have progressed from fighting words to action. The most recent example, reported from straitlaced Boston in July 2002, involves the alleged plot by white supremacist (and alleged WCC associate) Leo Felton to bomb prominent black and Jewish targets (Jesse Jackson, Al Sharpton, Steven Spielberg, the Holocaust Museum) to ignite a wave of ethnic cleansing in America, driving Jews and nonwhite "mud people" from the nation.

Preposterous? Of course. But to extremists of the Klan-Creator sort, absurd conspiracies are day-to-day reality, and nonetheless deadly to innocent victims simply because they spring from addled minds.

More to the point, a race war in Atlanta was a pervasive fear during the "child killer's" reign of terror. One month to the day before Edward Smith and Alfred Evans were found dead in Atlanta, on June 28, 1979, a young white physician was killed by black muggers while attending a medical convention. Four months later, a white legal secretary was killed on her birthday by a mentally unbalanced black assailant. Atlanta's black mayor and police commissioner heard the calls for a crackdown on street crime, along with rumors that a white conspiracy lay behind the murders of young blacks. Indictment of a white suspect, much less an outspoken racist with ties to militant terrorist groups, risked igniting the powder keg. Official Atlanta *needed* a black "child killer," both to defuse the conspiracy talk and to demonstrate for the record that black officials were doing their job without fear or favor.

Would the FBI collaborate to frame an innocent man? The question seems ludicrous today, after exposure of the bureau's collusion with New England mobsters to convict various patsies for murders committed by active-duty FBI informers. Peter Limone and John Salvati were sentenced to die in Massachusetts for a 1965 gangland slaying they did not commit; their sentences were later commuted to life in prison, and both served 30-plus years before they were finally exonerated. Today, one of the FBI agents responsible is himself imprisoned for accepting Mafia bribes, while the man behind the slayings—gangster James ("Whitey") Bulger—is a fugitive on the bureau's Ten Most Wanted list.

In 1933 FBI agents framed bootlegger Roger Touhy for a kidnapping in St. Paul, Minnesota (actually committed by "Ma" Barker's gang); when jurors acquitted Touhy of that charge, the feds collaborated with rival Chicago mobsters to convict Touhy of a second kidnapping that never occurred. (Touhy was exonerated by a federal court in 1946, then murdered by former bootleg competitors soon after his release from prison.) Another case from 1933 saw G-men frame the wife of George (Machine Gun) Kelly for an Oklahoma kidnapping; 26 years later, a federal court exonerated Kathryn Kelly, when the FBI refused to disclose exculpatory evidence suppressed for over a quarter century. Elmer ("Geronimo") Pratt, a onetime member of the Black Panther Party, spent nearly three decades in a California prison after FBI agents and local police conspired to frame him for murder in the early 1970s.

Those cases, and the belated exoneration of their innocent defendants, are a matter of public record. Others including the highly suspicious convictions of alleged cop-killers Leonard Peltier and Mumia Abu-Jamal, invite closer scrutiny in light of the FBI's demonstrated propensity for fabricated evidence and perjured testimony. To be sure, Wayne Williams was neither a notorious "public enemy" nor a "radical" minority activist at the time of his arrest, but he was what the doctor ordered for Atlanta in its time of racial crisis.

As for the FBI, its current spokesmen have forgotten the April 1981 statements of their predecessors, blaming black parents for the murder of their own children in Atlanta. Today, retired agents (John Douglas, Robert Ressler, Roy Hazelwood, et al.) tout the Williams case in their memoirs as a marvel of psychological profiling, one more instance where G-men worked their magic and inexorably ran their prey to ground.

If only it were true.

ATLANTA, Georgia "Lover's Lane" murders (1977)

While detectives in New York City were stalking the elusive gunman known as Son of Sam, their counterparts in Georgia tried to identify a killer with a similar modus operandi, who preyed on couples parked on darkened streets, striking from the shadows, interrupting passion with point-blank gunshots. Manhattan officers eventually bagged their quarry by means of a parking ticket, but Atlanta's manhunters have thus far been stumped in their search.

The murders began on January 16, 1977, when police were summoned to the scene of an unusual auto accident. The vehicle had veered across an intersection, out of control, to collide with a traffic sign. Behind the steering wheel, a naked man lay slumped, covered with blood. A woman, also nude and bloody, sprawled across the backseat, partly covered by a coat. The driver was identified as 26-year-old LaBrian Lovett; his passenger was 20-year-old Veronica Hill. Lovett had been shot four times (in the head, stomach, left arm, and right leg), while Hill was shot twice (in the left leg and abdomen). Both died from their wounds at a local hospital.

Police determined that the shooting occurred in nearby Adams Park, presumably while Lovett and Hill were engaged in sex. Officers were searching for a jealous former boy- or girlfriend when the shooter struck again, at 2:45 A.M. on February 12, 1977. This time, his target was a teenage couple necking in West Manor Park, three miles northwest of Adams Park. He fired six shots into the car, inflicting nonfatal chest wounds on both victims, then fled when he was unable to open the car's locked doors. Both victims survived and described their assailant as a large African-American male. Traditional motives were discarded when ballistics tests revealed that the same .38-caliber weapon had been used in both shootings.

On the night of March 12, 1977, 20-year-old Diane Collins was parked with her fiancé in Adams Park. Distracted, neither saw the gunman as he approached their car and fired six rounds through the passenger's window, killing Collins instantly. Though wounded in the head, her fiancé managed to start the car and instinctively drove home before calling police. Authorities were baffled, but at least they had a semblance of a pattern in the shootings. Twenty-seven days had elapsed between the first and second attacks, 28 days between the second and third. If the shooter operated on a four-week schedule, police rea-soned, they had a fair chance of catching him if they staked out local parks on the nights of April 6–8.

It was a logical plan, but nothing came of it. Detectives manned their posts, but the gunman had abandoned his crusade. Weeks stretched into months without another shooting, climaxed by a March 1979 admission that police had no suspects or leads in the case. There the matter rests, a quarter century and counting since the Lover's Lane killer made his last appearance in Atlanta.

ATLANTA, Georgia serial murders of women (1980–82)

On May 18, 1982, less than three months after dissolving a task force created to solve a series of grisly ATLANTA "CHILD MURDERS," homicide detectives announced that another serial killer was at large in their city. They noted "strong similarities" in the recent deaths of three black women, and four other victims were also linked to the series, their murders dating back to June 18, 1980. (One account referred to 27 murders, but no details were provided.)

According to official statements, the most recent victim was 29-year-old Lillian Lawrence, found in a vacant lot on May 15, 1982. Like six others before her, all in their twenties, Lawrence had died from multiple stab wounds to the neck and chest. Two of the most recent victims were nude when discovered, a third partly disrobed, and police spokesmen noted "evidence to suggest sexual activity" in all seven cases. Attempting to forestall another panic, Mayor Andrew Young acknowledged "a normal paranoia" in the city, while refusing to discuss the crimes in any detail, reminding journalists that sensational publicity might thwart the investigation.

From all appearances, the silent treatment fared no better, since the crimes remain unsolved. In 1988 attorneys for alleged Atlanta child-killer Wayne Williams uncovered reports from the Georgia Bureau of Investigation, suppressed for nearly a decade, which implicated members of the Ku Klux Klan in the slayings. According to an informer's report, Klansmen had murdered several black children in Atlanta and planned on killing women next, in the hope of fomenting a "race war." The key suspect was dead by 1988, and nothing suggests that the KKK leads were pursued.

"ATLAS Vampire" unknown killer (1932)

Vasastaden is a 1.2-square-mile district in central Stockholm, Sweden, today ranked as the city's second most populous quarter, with some 52,000 residents. Its central feature, in turn, is Sankt Eriksplan (Saint Erik's Plaza), named in honor of King Erik IX (1120–60), who serves as Stockholm's patron saint and is depicted on the city's coat of arms.

In 1932, Sankt Eriksplan was also a popular prostitute's "stroll," where commercial liaisons were easily arranged. On May 4 of that year, a 32-year-old streetwalker was found dead in her apartment in the Atlas neighborhood adjoining Saint Erik's Plaza. Authorities determined that she was killed two days earlier, by crushing blows to her skull, and police spokesmen claimed that the slayer drank some of her blood. Newspapers trumpeted the case of the "Atlas Vampire," but no suspect was ever identified and the crime remains unsolved today.

"ATTERIDGEVILLE Mutilator" unknown serial killer (1956)

South Africa has suffered a veritable plague of serial murders since the fall of apartheid in 1990, but this unidentified slayer anticipated the national trend by more than three decades. His victims, all young boys, were killed in the small Pretoria township of Atteridgeville, found with their tongues and genitals cut away during a five-month period in 1956. No clue to the killer's identity has yet been uncovered, and barring a deathbed confession, solution of the case seems unlikely.

Strangely, the Mutilator's crimes seem to have set a bloody pattern in Atteridgeville, with the settlement spawning at least five more serial killers in recent times. Their number includes strangler Moses Sithole, convicted of 38 murders in December 1997, and four others still unidentified. The latter group includes killers nicknamed "Axeman," "Beastman," "IRONMAN," and "Kgabi." Fear is so pervasive in Atteridgeville, these days, that some locals suggest the township may be cursed, haunted by some evil spirit that possesses ordinary people and transforms them into monsters.

AUSTIN, Annie murder victim (1901)

The vice-ridden Spitalfields district of London became globally infamous in 1888, when "JACK THE RIPPER" murdered local prostitutes and taunted authorities with mocking letters. Thirteen years later, in May 1901, police were confronted with another murder mystery from the same neighborhood—and this one, like Jack's slayings, would also remain unsolved.

The latest Spitalfields victim was Annie Austin, a 28-year-old slum resident separated from her husband for the past 10 days. At 7:30 A.M. on May 26, 1901, a tenant of a rundown lodging house at 35 Dorset Street heard moaning from one of the occupied cubicles and glanced inside to find Austin sprawled on the bed, covered in blood. Transported to London Hospital, she was examined by doctors who found deep stab wounds in her rectum and vagina. Police were summoned, but in their leisurely response none had arrived to question Austin by the time she died on May 30. Instead, one of the hospital's physicians related her account of the attack. As described to the doctor by Austin, she had brought a strange man home to her tiny room for sex on the night of May 25. Sometime in the predawn hours, Austin heard her guest preparing to leave, then felt the sharp pains of a knife blade piercing her body. She had never asked the stranger's name, but described him as a short man of "Jewish appearance," with dark hair and moustache.

At the subsequent inquest, a police pathologist reported no signs of a struggle in Austin's bedroom. The victim had been generally healthy, he declared, except for an advanced case of syphilis. Austin's estranged husband had an unbreakable alibi for the time of the murder. Flophouse proprietor Henry Moore and his brother-in-law, Daniel Sullivan were briefly suspected of the murder since they had given police the wrong number for Austin's room, initially sending officers to Room 44 instead of Room 15. Both presented alibis that were accepted by the coroner's jury, however, and the case remains unsolved. Inspector Thomas Divall described the general air of official frustration in his final report on the case.

From the first to the last we have to deal with a class of witnesses that are as low as they can possibly be and it is difficult to know when they are speaking the truth. In some instances they lie without any apparent motive. Although we never despair I fear that nothing further can be done to elucidate this mystery and the perpetrator of this crime unfortunately goes unpunished as a result of the scandalous conduct of nearly the whole of the witnesses in this case.

AVILA, Robert, and Davis, Raymond murder victims (1982)

On the afternoon of July 30, 1982, the corpses of two boys were found within 100 yards of each other, on an embankment of the Hollywood Freeway in

Los Angeles. Three weeks passed before the youths were identified as 16-year-old Robert Avila, of Los Angeles, and 13-year-old Raymond Davis, from Pittsburg, California. Davis had vanished while visiting his mother in the neighborhood of Echo Park, and his death was attributed to strangulation. Avila lived 12 blocks from the home of Davis's mother, but the boys had not known each other in life. No cause of death was determined in Avila's case, and while the boys had died roughly a month apart, disposal of their bodies in such close proximity suggested a single killer. So far, neither crime has been attributed to Southern California "freeway killers" William Bonin (executed for 10 homosexual murders on February 23, 1996) or Randy Kraft (awaiting execution for the murders of 16 young men, suspected of 51 more).

AYER, Dr. Benjamin assassination victim (1869)

A 70-year-old member of the Georgia state legislature, elected from Jefferson County during Reconstruction (1865–77), Dr. Benjamin Ayer lost most of his personal property during the Civil War because of his outspoken support for the Union. He was also a Republican, elected chiefly with black votes, which guaranteed ostracism by local white Democrats (a.k.a. "Conservatives") and death threats from the terrorist Ku Klux Klan. In the spring of 1869 Dr. Ayer accompanied state senator JOSEPH ADKINS and other Georgia Republicans on a pilgrimage to Washington, D.C., seeking restoration of military rule to suppress Klan violence. The delegation returned in April, with Ayer traveling by train through Augusta and on to his Louisville home. One day after his return, Ayer was ambushed and fatally shot while walking near his house.

Local Democrats maintained consistency by mounting a posthumous campaign of character assassination against Ayer. In addition to various slanders about his public and private life, Ayer's detractors denied the existence of a Klan in Jefferson County (or in Georgia, for that matter) and claimed Ayer had been shot by black outlaws. More than two years later, in testimony before a committee of the House of Representatives, Georgia political kingpin Benjamin Hill repeated the fiction that Ayer had been killed "by a negro [sic] for money." No suspects in his murder, black or white, were ever publicly identified.

AZZAM, Abdullah Yusuf unsolved murder (1989)

Sunni Muslim theologian Abdullah Azzam was born in 1941, in the British Mandate of Palestine. The creation of Israel, seven years later, embittered his family and encouraged Azzam to complete his secondary education in Syria. He joined the Palestinian Muslim Brotherhood in 1967 and participated in guerrilla activities against Israeli troops in the West Bank region. Disillusioned by Marxist elements within the Palestine Liberation Organization, Azzam moved to Egypt in 1970, pursuing graduate studies at Cairo's Al-Azhar University, where he obtained a Ph.D. in the Principles of Islamic Jurisprudence.

Armed with that degree, Azzam went to teach in Jordan. His "radical" views drew flack from authorities, and he soon moved to Saudi Arabia, where King Faisal welcomed exiled academics. While teaching at King Abdul Aziz University, during 1976–79, Azzam met future terrorist leader Osama bin Laden. By 1981 both men were in Pakistan, directing the Islamic jihad against Soviet occupation troops in neighboring Afghanistan. Azzam served chiefly as a fund-raiser and propagandist for that effort, while bin Laden worked more directly with Afghanistan's mujahideen and their covert supporters from the American Central Intelligence Agency.

Russian troops left Afghanistan in February 1989, whereupon Azzam and bin Laden turned their energies toward global jihad against Israel and all her supporters, demanding "no negotiations, no conferences, and no dialogues." Nine years later, that movement became al-Qaeda (the "Base"), but Azzam would not live to witness its terrorist raids on the West.

Soon after the Russian pullout from Afghanistan, Azzam narrowly escaped death when a bomb, planted in the pulpit of a mosque in Peshawar, Pakistan, failed to explode during one of his lectures. A second attempt at the same mosque proved successful on November 24, 1989, when a remote-controlled car bomb killed Azzam, his two sons, and various bystanders.

Suspects in the still-unsolved assassination include Osama bin Laden (who, some say, might have killed his mentor to gain control of their movement); competing Islamic militia leaders in Pakistan or Afghanistan; members of Ayman al-Zawahiri's militant Egyptian Islamic Jihad, who had suffered a falling-out with Azzam; Pakistan's secretive Interservices Intelligence Agency; Israel's Mossad; and the American CIA.

B

"BABYSITTER" unidentified serial killer (1976–77)

Between January 1976 and March 1977, an unknown killer or killers murdered seven children in Oakland County, Michigan, a region of affluent "bedroom" communities located northwest of Detroit. The dread engendered by those crimes lingers yet in some parts of the county, since the homicides were never solved.

Sixteen-year-old Cynthia Cadieux was the first to die, kidnapped from Roseville on January 15, 1976. She was found the next morning, naked and dead, lying beside a rural road in Bloomfield Township. Postmortem tests revealed that she had been raped and bludgeoned, her body dragged for some distance over snow-covered pavement. Her clothing was found discarded in a pile, 15 feet from the corpse.

Four days later, 14-year-old Sheila Shrock was raped and shot to death in her Birmingham home. Police made the discovery while checking out reports of a prowler in the neighborhood. Two blocks away, John McAuliffe had been terrorized, bound and robbed of five dollars by a gunman who invaded his house. Police had a description of the robber, but it led nowhere.

Shortly after noon on February 13, 12-year-old Mark Stebbins left the American Legion hall in Ferndale, walking homeward. He never made it, and his lifeless body was found in Southfield six days later, lying in the snowy parking lot behind an office building. Sexually assaulted, then smothered, Stebbins had been dead at least 36 hours when his body was

found. The killer had cleaned his corpse with meticulous care before it was laid out in the snow.

The slayer's pattern seemed to break with 13-year-old Jane Allan, kidnapped while hitchhiking through Royal Oak on August 8, 1976. Her body was found three days later at Miamisburg, Ohio, the cause of death listed as carbon monoxide poisoning. Detectives saw no evidence, yet, to connect the four murders, nor could they link any of the recent deaths to the still-unsolved September 1972 strangulation of teenager Donna Serra in Ray Township. Different killing techniques and disposal methods, coupled with sexual assaults on victims of both genders, suggested at least two killers, perhaps as many as four.

Twelve-year-old Jill Robinson was next, reported missing from Royal Oak on December 22, 1976. She was found four days later near Troy, in southern Oakland County, her body neatly laid out on a roadside snowbank. The cause of death had been a close-range shotgun blast—another deviation—but Robinson had been bathed prior to death, as had Mark Stebbins. The coroner found no evidence of sexual assault.

On January 2, 1977, 10-year-old Kristine Mihelich left her Berkley home to buy a magazine and vanished on the three-block stroll. She was found in Franklin Village on January 21, near the spot where Cynthia Cadieux had been dumped one year earlier. Unlike Cadieux, however, Mihelich had not been raped or beaten; instead, she had been suffocated, her body washed and laid out in a funereal position, as with victims Stebbins and Robinson.

Homicide investigators were convinced of a link between three cases now, and they did not have long to wait for a fourth. On March 16, 1977, 11-year-old Timothy King vanished from Birmingham, his case igniting a general panic throughout Oakland County. Witnesses reported seeing King with a shaggy-haired man, chatting beside a blue Gremlin compact car, but no one remembered the auto's license number. Appearing on local television, King's mother pleaded for his safe return, promising that his favorite fried-chicken dinner would be waiting when he came home.

The search ended on March 23, with discovery of King's body in a roadside ditch near Livonia. Suffocated like victims Stebbins and Mihelich, King had been scrubbed and manicured after death, with his clothes washed and pressed. Medical examiners confirmed a sexual assault, but they "detected no proof that the killer was a male." Examination of stomach contents showed that King had been allowed one final chicken dinner prior to death, perhaps in response to his mother's televised comments.

Reporters dubbed their elusive quarry the "Babysitter," after the apparent care lavished on his victims while he held them captive. Authorities disagreed on the killer's motives, some suggesting that he scrubbed the bodies to eliminate trace evidence, others reading the act as a ritual exorcism of guilt. The molestation of male victims pointed to a homosexual killer, but if that were true, why had two of the victims been female? The shooting death of Jill Robinson was another riddle. One theory suggested that she had survived attempted suffocation, suddenly reviving on the roadside; another noted that she had begun to menstruate, hypothesizing that the killer had altered his pattern to cope with his only "adult" victim.

On March 27, 1977, Detroit psychiatrist Bruce Danto published an open letter to the killer, speculating on his motives and pleading with the Babysitter to surrender or call for help. Among the predictable rash of crank calls, one stood out. The male caller told Danto, "The article was wrong. You better hope it doesn't snow anymore." Soon, Danto began receiving calls and letters from a man who called himself "Allen," claiming to be the killer's roommate. According to Allen, he and the Babysitter had served together in Vietnam, his roommate returning home with a deep bitterness toward affluent America. Suburban children were chosen as victims, he said, in an effort to "bring the war home" and teach wealthy slackers how much combat veterans had suffered. Once, Allen scheduled a meeting with Danto, but he never appeared, and the calls ceased thereafter.

Spring and summer passed without another death in Oakland County, but parental anxiety worsened with the onset of winter. Aside from cleanliness, fresh snow seemed to be the Babysitter's chief obsession. Safety programs instituted the previous winter were revived and police patrols multiplied countywide, but the Babysitter and roommate Allen were gone without a trace. To date, no suspects have been named and no charges filed in any of the county's unsolved homicides.

BACON, David murder victim (1943)

Massachusetts native Gaspar Griswold Bacon, Jr., born in 1914, was the scion of a politically powerful family. His father served on the board of Harvard University before his election as president of the state senate (1929–32) and lieutenant governor (1933–35). Gaspar Jr. summered with his family on Cape Cod, where he joined a theater troupe called the "University Players," including then unknown actors Henry Fonda and James Stewart. While they advanced to Hollywood stardom, success eluded Bacon, reducing him to the role of a gigolo in New York City. Later, as "David" Bacon, he moved to Los Angeles and married Austrian singer Greta Keller. Years later, Keller revealed that Bacon was gay and she was a lesbian, their masquerade marriage contrived to advance careers in Hollywood.

Bacon met billionaire Howard Hughes in 1942 and signed a contract to portray Billy the Kid in a forthcoming Western, *The Outlaw,* which Hughes was producing. Before filming began, Hughes replaced Bacon with actor Jack Buetel, but Hughes still held Bacon to his exclusive contract, casting him in smaller roles for six films during 1942–43. Greta Keller subsequently claimed that Bacon engaged in a homosexual affair with Hughes, which led to his replacement in *The Outlaw,* but no Hughes biographer to date has found any evidence supporting that allegation.

On September 13, 1943, Bacon crashed his car against a curb in Santa Monica, California, then staggered from the vehicle and collapsed. Bystanders found him wearing only a swimsuit, with a knife protruding from his back. Its blade had pierced a lung, delivering a fatal wound. Greta Keller—eight months pregnant when the murder occurred—delivered a stillborn child and soon returned to Europe, where she pursued an active singing career until her death in November 1977, at age 74.

Police found a wallet and a camera in Bacon's car after the crash. The wallet's owner remains unidentified, and the camera's film contained only one image—of Bacon nude and smiling on a beach. Detectives surmised that the killer snapped that picture shortly before stabbing Bacon, but despite persistent rumors of gay affairs with Howard Hughes and various actors, no suspect was ever named. Bacon's best-known Hollywood production, the *Masked Marvel* serial, premiered two months after his death, on November 6, 1943.

BACON, Francis stolen portrait (1988)

Born in Dublin, Ireland, on October 28, 1909, Francis Bacon became one of the 20th century's most commercially successful artists, earning more than £14 million from sale of his paintings prior to his death, in Spain, on April 28, 1992. In 1951 Bacon sat for a portrait by fellow artist Lucian Freud, a grandson of psychotherapist Sigmund Freud, who moved to England with his parents in 1931 and acquired British citizenship eight years later. The portrait of Bacon was valued at £1.4 million when it was stolen in May 1988, in broad daylight, from Berlin's Neue Nationalgalerie. Thirteen years after the theft, in June 2001, the British Council persuaded Freud—then 79 years old—to prepare a special "Wanted" poster of the missing portrait, offering a reward of 300,000 German marks (£100,000) for its safe return. Andrea Rose, the council's art director, told reporters the painting was sought for a major Freud retrospective exhibition, planned by London's Tate Britain Gallery for 2002. "This is an extraordinary painting, a portrait of one national icon by another," Rose said. "I would dearly like to see it back where it belongs."

Despite international publicity, the reward offer failed to recover Freud's portrait of Bacon. The painting is still missing, and while the statute of limitations for criminal prosecution has expired, authorities remind the public that the painting is considered stolen property. As such, possession or sale of it constitutes a separate felony, for which offenders may still face trial.

BAGNOLS sur Ceze art theft (1972)

On November 12, 1972, an unknown thief (or thieves) looted the town hall at Bagnols sur Ceze, France, and removed nine impressionist paintings valued conservatively in the millions of U.S. dollars. The stolen works included:

Pierre Bonnard's *Le Petit Café*
Eugene Boudin's *Cows in a Pasture*
Raoul Dufy's *Composition* and *Orchestre avec nu*
Albert Marquet's *View of the Port of Marseille*
Henri Matisse's *View of Saint Tropez*
Pierre Renoir's *Roses in a Vase* and *Portrait of Madame Albert André*
Édouard Vuillard's *Pot de Honfleur*

No trace of the stolen paintings has been found since their disappearance in 1972, and no suspects have been named in the case. The statute of limitations for criminal prosecution has expired, but French authorities continue to remind the public that the paintings are considered stolen property, and that possession or exchange of stolen items is a separate criminal offense. Police presume that the paintings were purchased by one or more rogue collectors who cherish such items as personal treasures, without a need to display them publicly.

BAILES, Marie murder victim (1908)

On May 30, 1908, a "nervous" man entered a public lavatory located on St. George's Road in Islington, London. He carried a large parcel wrapped in brown paper, handling it with evident difficulty, and he left the package behind when exiting the facility. A curious lavatory attendant waited briefly for the stranger to return, then opened the parcel to satisfy his curiosity. Inside, wrapped in a blanket and dusted with sand as if lately disinterred from a shallow grave, lay the corpse of a young girl.

Police were summoned, and they identified the child as six-year-old Marie Bailes, last seen alive on the previous afternoon, when she left St. John's Roman Catholic School with a classmate. After a block or so, the girls had separated and Marie had disappeared. Police scoured the neighborhood and detained two male suspects, one of them a fugitive from a Wandsworth workhouse, but both were cleared after the lavatory attendant viewed them in custody. At a coroner's inquest, on June 22, a member of the audience rose to shout that six clues proved a woman was the killer, but he failed to enumerate the points, and police dismissed him as a crank. The coroner's jury returned a verdict of willful murder by person or persons unknown, and the case was never solved.

BAKER, Catherine   See NEW JERSEY MURDERS

BALCHIN, Olive   murder victim (1946)

A resident of Manchester, England, born in 1906, Olive Balchin was found beaten to death at a World War II bomb site on October 20, 1946. Police discovered a bloodstained hammer near her corpse, presumed to be the murder weapon. Suspicion soon focused on 39-year-old Walter Rowlands, previously convicted of killing his own daughter in 1934, later reprieved and released in 1940. Manchester merchant Edward Macdonald identified Rowlands as the recent purchaser of a hammer resembling the Balchin murder weapon. Forensic evidence collected by police included hair and dust from Rowlands's shoes, together with a small bloodstain on one shoe that matched Balchin's blood type. At his arrest in a local hotel, Rowlands asked the officers, "You don't want me for the murder of that woman do you?"

They did, indeed. Rowlands pled not guilty, but a jury disbelieved him, and he was convicted of the crime, later sentenced to hang. That verdict had barely been recorded, however, when a prisoner awaiting trial in Liverpool, one David John Ware, confessed to Balchin's murder. Rowlands's attorney raised the issue of Ware's confession on appeal, but the appellate court refused to question Ware. "It is not an unusual thing," the lord chief justice declared, "for all sorts of confessions to be made by people who have nothing to do with a crime." As bailiffs led him from the court, Rowlands shouted, "I am an innocent man! This is the grossest injustice which has ever occurred in an English court. Why did you not have in court the man who confessed to the crime? I am not having justice because of my past. I am innocent before God!"

King's Counsel J. C. Jolly was appointed to investigate the case on behalf of the British home secretary's office. When interviewed by Jolly, David Ware recanted his confession, declaring his previous statement "absolutely untrue. I have never seen the woman Balchin, who was murdered, in my life. I did not murder her and had nothing to do whatsoever with the murder. I made these statements out of swank more than anything." Edward Macdonald and other witnesses viewed Ware in a police lineup, unanimously denying that he was the man they had seen in October 1946.

Walter Rowlands's appeal was finally dismissed on February 10, 1947, and he was hanged on February 27. Doubts concerning his guilt were rekindled in November 1951, when David Ware was jailed in Bristol for attempted murder. In custody, Ware told police, "I have killed a woman. I keep having an urge to hit women on the head." He was convicted of the latest charge and confined to a hospital for the criminally insane.

BALDI, Stefano   See "MONSTER OF FLORENCE"

BANKER, Jaylene   See RAWLINS, WYOMING, RODEO MURDERS

BARCOMB, Jill, and Robinson, Kathleen   murder victims (1977)

A native of Syracuse, New York, born in 1959, Jill T. Barcomb moved to Los Angeles at age 18. Her departure from Syracuse was encouraged by two prostitution arrests, in January and September 1977, resulting in a sentence of one year's probation. Last seen alive in L.A. on November 9, 1977, Barcomb was found the next day in Franklin Canyon, north of Beverly Hills. She had been stripped, sexually assaulted, then beaten and strangled to death. Police initially linked Barcomb's death to the ongoing series of Hillside Strangler murders, a theory encouraged by reports that Barcomb was acquainted with 15-year-old Hollywood victim Judith Miller, found murdered in La Crescenta on October 31, 1977.

The next apparent victim in the murder series, 17-year-old Kathleen K. Robinson, was a Hollywood high school student who lived with her mother and frequently hitchhiked around Los Angeles. Robinson disappeared from a Santa Monica beach on November 17, 1977, her strangled corpse recovered the following day from a parking lot on Pico Boulevard, in the Wilshire district. According to police reports, no evidence of sexual assault was found. Robinson's name was added to the Hillside Strangler victims list, despite misgivings on the part of some investigators.

The case broke in January 1979, after two young women were murdered in Bellingham, Washington. Former Los Angeles resident Kenneth Bianchi confessed to those crimes, and in June 1979 admitted participating in the Hillside murders with his cousin, Angelo Buono. Bianchi pled guilty in five of the Los Angeles slayings, but reneged on a promise to testify against Buono at trial. Bianchi was consigned to Washington's state prison for life, while Buono's California trial dragged on. Convicted on nine murder counts in November 1983, Buono was sentenced to life imprisonment and subsequently died in custody. Bianchi remains confined in Washington at this writing (in December 2008).

By the time the Hillside Stranglers faced justice in court, Jill Barcomb and Kathleen Robinson had been removed from the list of presumed series victims. George Shamshak, a Massachusetts prison inmate serving time for armed robbery, subsequently told authorities that he had committed the murders with an accomplice, one Peter M. Jones. On the strength of Shamshak's statement alone, police arrested Jones—a licensed maintenance engineer for a medical office building in Beverly Hills—on suspicion of murder, but their investigation failed to support the charge, and Jones was never charged. In fact, detectives learned that Jones knew Shamshak only slightly, through Shamshak's brother, and that he (Jones) had never met the murdered women. (Shamshak was never charged with either crime.) Exoneration notwithstanding, Jones suffered such adverse publicity that he lost his job and moved to Maine. Even there, harassment continued in the form of death threats and a drive-by shooting that shattered his apartment windows. A public apology from LAPD Chief Darryl Gates provided some relief, but Jones received more satisfaction from his successful libel suit against a Boston television station that named him as a suspect in the case.

Despite his vindication in the double-murder case, Jones could not shake his reluctant interest in victims Barcomb and Robinson. In 1995 he contacted the Los Angeles Police Department and was told the crimes remain unsolved, with records of both cases "destroyed in an earthquake." Jones has offered a $10,000 reward for information leading to the arrest and conviction of the killer(s), but so far the offer has produced no leads.

BARHAM, Harry murder victim (1972)

A London bookmaker, 50-year-old Harry Barham was sitting in his car on Windmill Lane, in Stratford, East London, when an unknown gunman approached him at 6:30 P.M. on February 14, 1972. Three shots were fired at close range from a .45-caliber pistol, two bullets striking Barham in the back, while a third pierced his skull and killed him instantly.

Police assigned to the case learned that Barham had fallen on hard times of late. Losses at his betting shops in Holborn and Islington had cost him £50,000 in recent months, and he was awaiting trial at the Old Bailey on charges of evading £160,000 in gambling taxes. In an effort to pay off his debts, Barham had begun to purchase jewelry at bargain rates and resell it for a profit, collecting some £40,000 in all by the day he was killed. Authorities suspected that some malefactor knew Barham was carrying substantial sums of cash and had arranged a meeting that turned into a fatal ambush. (No money was found in his car.)

An alternative theory, floated on the streets without substantiating evidence, maintained that Barham had uncovered evidence of some major crime in progress and tried to blackmail the gang responsible. Informers named a London underworld character, one Edward (Teddy) Machin, as the triggerman, but by the time his name surfaced in the investigation Machin had passed beyond reach of the law, gunned down near his Forest Gate home on May 23, 1973. An associate of Machin's, Alan Mackenzie, pled guilty to manslaughter in that case on December 6, 1973, but the Barham homicide remains unsolved today.

BARMORE, Seymour murder victim (1868)

A one-time agent of the U.S. Treasury Department, later a private detective, Seymour Barmore was hired by Tennessee Republicans in 1867 to investigate criminal activities by the Ku Klux Klan. The KKK had initially been organized as a social club in 1866, but it was revamped in early 1867 as a vehicle of armed resistance to congressional Reconstruction following the Civil War. By the time Barmore was hired, Klan members had been linked to lynchings, floggings, and other acts of terrorism directed at black freedmen and white Republicans alike.

Operating from a Nashville office, Barmore had no difficulty obtaining information from talkative (sometimes drunken) Klansmen. One report, never confirmed, alleged that Barmore joined the KKK himself, to learn its inmost secrets and identify members responsible for various crimes around the group's birthplace at Pulaski, Tennessee. Sometime before year's end, Barmore's KKK informers warned him that he had fallen under suspicion, but the investigator persisted, heedless of the danger to himself.

On January 11, 1868, after transporting a black prisoner to Pulaski for trial and lingering for a nocturnal Klan meeting, Barmore boarded a late train back to Nashville. It would be his last ride, as the train crew and telegrapher that night were all Klan members or collaborators pledged to eliminate the spy. Shortly after midnight the train stopped at Columbia, Tennessee, and a dozen masked men boarded Barmore's car. They swiftly overpowered Barmore and dragged him from the train, conveying him to a wood four miles distant, where he was hanged and riddled with bullets. That accomplished, the raiders cut him down and dumped his body in the Duck River, a frequent repository for Klan victims, where it was found weeks later.

In the wake of Barmore's murder, rumors circulated that he had obtained a full list of Tennessee Klansmen and had carried it with him on the night he died. If so, the list was taken by his killers, and Barmore's police contacts never learned the names of those included on the roster. The only legacy of Barmore's last assignment was a Klan robe and mask, found among his personal effects after his death. No suspects were ever named in the case.

BARNES, Angela Denise See "FREEWAY PHANTOM"

BARNES, Anthony See MARYLAND GAY MURDERS

BARTHELEMY, Helen See "JACK THE STRIPPER"

BATES, Cheri Jo See "ZODIAC"

BATTLE Creek, Michigan unsolved murders (1982–83)
Between August 1982 and March 1983, residents of Battle Creek, Michigan, were shocked by the brutal murders of three young women. Authorities

suggested possible satanic motives in the case, and while no link to devil worship was ever proved, the mere suggestion was enough to spread a pall of fear through the community.

The first to die was 20-year-old Margaret Hume, an ex-cheerleader and National Honor Society member, found strangled in the closet of her own apartment on August 18, 1982. Hume had been living in the flat for just three months before she died, her corpse hidden by a pile of clothes and bedding.

Patricia Rosansky, age 17, was walking to school on the morning of February 3, 1983, when she disappeared within two blocks of campus. Hikers found her body outside town on April 6, concealed by leaves and branches in a shallow gully. Heavy blows had crushed Rosansky's skull. "Street talk" linked her death to a satanic cult, and while no charges have been filed, police once described their prime suspect as a self-styled Satanist who boasted of leading black masses at Kalamazoo, Michigan.

On March 13, 1983, 17-year-old Karry Evans disappeared from rural Bellevue, 13 miles east of Battle Creek. Last seen walking near her grandparents' home, Evans was found by mushroom hunters on May 10. She had been strangled, her body concealed by brush in a swampy region south of town. Once again there were rumors of demonic involvement: Evans had described her own occult beliefs in letters to friends, and she allegedly sported a jacket with the satanic emblem "666."

No suspects have been publicly identified or prosecuted for the homicides at Battle Creek. More than two decades after the crimes, it seems unlikely that the case will now be solved, but homicide investigators still invite new leads, in the hope that someone, somewhere, may provide a crucial piece of evidence to break the stalemate.

BAUERDORF, Georgette Elise murder victim (1944)
The daughter of a Nevada oilman, born in May 1924, Georgette Bauerdorf was educated in a convent on New York's Long Island, but religious instruction could not curb her desire to become a film star. She pursued that dream by moving west at age 19, in the midst of World War II, and volunteering as a junior hostess at the Hollywood Canteen, where she danced with numerous servicemen. Supported chiefly by her father, Bauerdorf had a small apartment on Fountain Avenue, in West Hollywood, where she sometimes entertained male visitors.

On October 10, 1944, Bauerdorf cashed a check for $175 and bought a $90 airline ticket to El Paso, Texas, telling friends that she planned to visit a "soldier boyfriend." The following day, she lunched and went shopping with her father's secretary, Rose Gilbert, seeming in good spirits at the time. Bauerdorf worked at the Hollywood Canteen that evening, leaving for home at 11:15 P.M. Around midnight, Fred Atwood—the janitor at Bauerdorf's apartment house—was roused from sleep by a crashing sound from Bauerdorf's apartment, but he soon went back to sleep. So did a neighbor, who recalled a woman screaming, "Stop! Stop, you're killing me!" around 2:30 A.M. on October 12.

Atwood and his wife entered Bauerdorf's apartment at 11:10 A.M., discovering her half-nude body in the bathtub. Pathologist Frank Webb discovered that Bauerdorf was strangled by means of a towel jammed into her throat. Bruising on the right side of her face and abdomen suggested powerful blows with a fist, while the knuckles on her own right hand were bruised from fighting back. On Bauerdorf's right thigh, Webb found the markings of a hand, complete "even to the fingernail marks piercing the skin."

Investigators from the Los Angeles County Sheriff's Department found that the bulb of an automatic night-light outside Bauerdorf's apartment door had been deliberately loosened to prevent it from working. Fingerprints were lifted from the lightbulb, but were never linked to a suspect. Robbery was dismissed as a motive, despite the theft of nearly $100 from Bauerdorf's purse, since a large roll of cash and silver items worth several thousand dollars remained in plain sight at her dwelling. A 1936 Pontiac coupe, registered to Bauerdorf's older sister, Connie, was found abandoned in Los Angeles, where it had run out of gas. A new dent in the fender led police nowhere.

Detectives theorized that Bauerdorf was surprised by someone who entered her flat, perhaps with a passkey, while she was getting ready for bed. Rose Gilbert, speaking for the Bauerdorf family, refuted suggestions that Georgette may have dabbled in prostitution. She told reporters, "Perhaps, on occasion, one of her gentlemen friends might stop in for a moment or two, but she never asked them to remain." Georgette, she insisted, "had very definite ideas of propriety."

Still, investigators had Bauerdorf's airplane ticket to El Paso, her date book filled with names of servicemen, and a diary entry from October 10, reading: "Call to Jerry at 6:30 A.M. came thru—Jerry's a lamb. Letter from Dud and Jerry—wrote Jerry."

"Jerry," they learned, was Private Jerome Brown, a Chicago native stationed at Fort Bliss, outside El Paso, for training as an antiaircraft gunner. Brown admitted meeting Bauerdorf at the Hollywood Canteen in June 1944, shortly before his transfer from Camp Callan, San Diego, to Fort Bliss. He gave six letters from the heiress to police. Brown quickly proved that he had been in Texas when Bauerdorf died, and authorities moved on to other suspects.

One was a "swarthy" soldier who aggressively cut in on Bauerdorf's dance partners at the Hollywood Canteen on the night she was killed. Officers identified the G.I. in question as Cosmo Volpe—but, like Brown, he had an ironclad alibi, having checked into his barracks at the Lockheed Air Terminal at 11 P.M. on October 11.

A third exonerated suspect, never publicly identified, was a soldier described as 6 feet 4 inches tall, whom Bauerdorf had briefly dated, and who a friend of Bauerdorf's, June Ziegler, said was "very much taken" with Georgette. Bauerdorf had dumped him nonetheless, and detectives satisfied themselves that he was innocent.

One suspect not in uniform was 20-year-old Robert George Pollock White. A short time after Bauerdorf's slaying, San Diego police jailed him for raping an elderly woman, whom White first gagged by shoving a towel in her mouth. White admitted being in Los Angeles when Bauerdorf was slain, but he denied the crime and no proof against him was found in that case.

Meanwhile, publicity surrounding Bauerdorf's death produced a false confession in December 1944 from suspect John Lehman Sumter. A 22-year-old double-reject from military service, discharged by the navy and court-martialed out of the army, Sumter claimed credit for Bauerdorf's death, but discrepancies in his confession betrayed him. Finally admitting his lie, he told police, "I wanted to die in the chair because I had nothing to live for."

In September 1945 the *Los Angeles Examiner* received and printed a taunting note, purportedly written by Bauerdorf's murderer, which described her slaying as an act of "retribution." The author of that note remains officially unknown, although speculation concerning his identity appeared in certain true-crime books published long after the fact.

Long after detectives stopped looking for Bauerdorf's killer, speculation linked her death to other unsolved slayings in Los Angeles, including the 1947 murder of "BLACK DAHLIA" Elizabeth Short. Thus far, four books have linked Bauerdorf's murder to Short's. Authors John Gilmore (1993) and Donald Wolfe (2005) blame both crimes on deceased suspect Jack Anderson Wilson—with Wolfe adding other killers to the Short case, including notorious mobster Benjamin "Bugsy" Siegel. Janice Knowlton posthumously accused her father, George Knowlton, of these murders and others in 1994, while ex-policeman Steve Hodel did likewise with his late father, Dr. George Hodel, in 2003. Spokesmen for the Los Angeles Police Department still deny that either slaying has been solved, or the killers identified.

BAY Area child murders California (1983–91)

No murder case is more disturbing to authorities than one in which they are convinced they know the killer, but sufficient evidence is lacking to support a formal charge. The frustration is worse yet with multiple victims and a suspect who flaunts himself to the media. Such has been the protracted dilemma of police in Northern California—until new leads convinced some investigators that they may have been mistaken all along.

The nightmare began on November 19, 1983, when five-year-old Angela Bugay vanished within 50 feet of her Antioch, California, home. Her corpse was found seven days later, autopsy results disclosing that the girl had been sexually assaulted, then smothered by her kidnapper. The investigation proved fruitless, and it was hopelessly stalled by June 3, 1988, when seven-year-old Amber Swartz disappeared from a quiet residential street in Pinole, a few miles west of Antioch.

Amber had been missing for three days when a stranger turned up on her mother's doorstep, introduced himself as Tim Binder, and explained that he had been out searching for the missing girl. Clearly distraught, tears brimming in his eyes, he told Kim Swartz, "I tried to save her. I couldn't. I looked everywhere. I did everything I could to save Amber." Before leaving, the stranger somberly proclaimed, "You realize that we're looking for a dead body."

The visit was eerie enough to interest police. A background check identified the stranger as Timothy James Binder, born February 26, 1948, the son of a career military officer and a former army nurse. An Indiana native, Binder had married his high school sweetheart in 1968, but they divorced 11 years later. Meanwhile, in 1975, he had settled in Oakland and gone to work as a claims adjuster for the Social Security Administration. Binder was promoted in 1979, then abruptly fired in 1985. The reason: His superiors had learned that he was using government computers to identify young girls in Colorado, recording their addresses and birth dates, sending $50 to each—nearly $2,000 in all—on her birthday. In his own defense, Binder claimed he got the idea from a 1950s television show, *The Millionaire*, about a wealthy eccentric who bestows financial rewards on deserving strangers. Binder's boss didn't buy it, and Tim found himself unemployed.

Detectives interviewed Binder soon after his talk with Kim Swartz, and they brought along a bloodhound that reacted strongly—so they later said—to the scent of Amber Swartz in Binder's van. A search of the van revealed photos of several young girls taped to the dashboard, sun visors, and windshield, but Amber Swartz was not among them, and the searchers found no evidence of any crime. Questioned repeatedly by local officers and Federal Bureau of Investigation agents, Binder professed his love for children, manifested in compulsive urges to search for kidnap victims. He also kept a file of news clippings on the Bugay case and had mailed a letter to Angela's mother on June 2, 1988—one day before Amber Swartz disappeared. In passing, Binder predicted to authorities that the next child kidnapped in the area would be nine or 10 years old.

A month after his first uninvited visit, Binder telephoned Kim Swartz to report his "progress"—none—and to admit that he was now a suspect in the case. "But of course, they're never going to find anything," he said, "because there's nothing to find." It was the start of a bizarre, long-running correspondence between Binder and Kim Swartz, his obsessive behavior swiftly convincing Amber's mother that he was, indeed, responsible for the girl's disappearance.

Police, meanwhile, hit another macabre detour in the case on June 15, 1988, when their bloodhounds tracked Amber's scent to the grave of Angela Bugay. They already knew that Tim Binder visited the cemetery often, sometimes reclining on Angela's grave to drink a beer, other times leaving coins behind when he departed. As for the scent traces of Amber Swartz in Binder's van and at the cemetery, they were inadmissible in court. So, too, were the results of three FBI polygraph tests administered to Binder in June 1988. Two of the tests were "inconclusive," G-men said, while the third "clearly indicated deception" in Binder's denial of guilt.

On November 14, 1988, Binder wrote a cryptic letter to Kim Swartz. It read: "I have learned many valuable lessons and made some decisions in the past few months. One of the lessons is that only I can decide what is the proper course of action for me to take, and one of the decisions is that I must not let the fear of possible consequences ever deter me from actions conceived in love and compassion and a desire to help." Uncertain what to make of the note, Mrs. Swartz turned it over to police.

Five days later, Binder failed a firefighter's agility test in Hayward, California, south of Oakland. That same afternoon, nine-year-old Hayward resident Michaela Joy Garecht vanished on an errand to the grocery store. Early the next morning, November 20, Binder launched a two-week private search, which failed to turn up any traces of the missing girl. Investigators found it more than coincidental that Garecht's age matched that predicted by their leading suspect for the next kidnap victim. Questioned by police concerning his latest search, Binder described a "mental picture" of Garecht's kidnapping, but no evidence was found to support a criminal charge.

On January 6, 1989, Binder was briefly detained and questioned by police in San Pablo, California, after they found him sitting in his van, illegally parked on the sidewalk, talking to a group of children. Inside the van, officers found an open beer bottle and the names of missing Bay Area girls, written in crayon. A search of Binder's pockets revealed a chunk of stone. Binder explained, "It's a broken angel's wing from a young girl's marble headstone. I didn't know her, but I would have liked to." Despite his claim that he was "just making friends," the officers arrested Binder on a misdemeanor charge of "annoying and disturbing children," after two 12-year-old girls described his persistent efforts to offer them a ride. At his booking, a note was found in Binder's wallet. It read:

I love you Amber. You are my first, and I tried for you. Tried + cried and still ache in my heart. They will always try to pull me back, but I never will. They don't know about us. They never heard of us.

Binder spent the night in jail, and while the charges were later dismissed without trial, Bay Area authorities resolved to keep an even closer watch on him. His whereabouts were unknown for January 20, 1989, when 13-year-old Ilene Misheloff vanished from Dublin, midway between Hayward and Antioch, but Binder was soon on the hunt, launching another unsolicited one-man search for the third missing child in eight months. On February 11, Binder later claimed, he was accosted by FBI agents while "searching" a half mile from Misheloff's house, and "they scared me off," prompting him to withdraw from the case.

On May 23, 1991, young Sheila Cosgrove received a peculiar letter at her home in Fairfield, north of Antioch. The note, signed "TJB," was written backward, so that it had to be read in a mirror, and the envelope contained two coins: a silver dollar and an Indian-head penny. The letter was postmarked from Oakland, and a second backward message followed two days later, signed, "Your friend, Tim."

While the first note simply related the history of the 1921 silver dollar, number two closed on a more intimate tone: "I dare not send you a hug and a kiss, so instead I send you one-third of a hug, and two-millionth of a kiss, and thirteen dodecillian dreams." A third letter included Binder's return address, and police dropped by to discuss his interest in underage girls. That visit prompted yet another mailing to Sheila, Binder advising the girl that "I am not a threat to you and never will be." He signed off, "Love to you all, Tim."

On December 27, 1991, 14-year-old Amanda (Nikki) Campbell vanished within a few yards of her Fairfield, California, home. By that time, no one was surprised when Tim Binder telephoned the hotline, on December 30, and offered to help in the search. On a hunch, detectives took their bloodhounds back to Oakmont Cemetery on New Year's Day, and the dogs tracked Campbell's scent to the grave of Angela Bugay. Six days later, in a second test, the dogs "indicated strongly" that Campbell's scent was found in Binder's van. For his part, Binder called the test harassment, explaining to police, "I was picking up cans out there while I was searching for her. That's probably how her scent could have gotten in my car." He also penned another note to Sheila Cosgrove, expressing "shock and sadness" that Campbell had lived near Sheila's home.

In his spare time Binder also mailed a steady stream of letters to Fairfield detective Harry Sagan, an investigator on the Campbell case who had researched Binder's background the previous spring, after Binder started sending his unwelcome notes to Sheila Cosgrove. In one typical letter, discussing the area's several missing girls, Binder wrote, "I will always love them. Will you?" By March 1992 Binder was literally sending chess moves to Sagan—i.e., "pawn to king four," "bishop to rook." The odd behavior boomeranged nine months later, when police secured a warrant to search Binder's home on December 9, 1992. No incriminating evidence was found, but the press had Binder's story now, complete with all the tales of strange behavior. He was publicly named as a suspect in Nikki Campbell's disappearance, his name inevitably linked to the four other dead or missing girls.

Binder responded to the adverse exposure with a publicity campaign of his own, granting press interviews and volunteering for a spot on Jane Whitney's TV talk show in January 1993. Six months later, Binder filed a $25 million harassment claim against Detective Sagan and the city of Fairfield. The press conference included a statement from Binder, denying any part in Campbell's abduction and claiming he was "40 miles away from Fairfield" when she disappeared. The damage claim was formally rejected in August 1993, whereupon Binder's lawyer proceeded with civil litigation. A federal court dismissed the lawsuit in May 1995, remanding it to state court for a hearing.

The case of Northern California's missing girls, meanwhile, had taken yet another bizarre turn. On February 14, 1995, a spokesman for the FBI's San Francisco field office informed Detective Sagan that Binder "has been eliminated as a suspect" in the Bugay murder. The G-men refused to say more, since the Antioch case was at "a very sensitive stage, and any information is closely guarded," but another 14 months would pass before the arrest of murder suspect Larry Graham, on April 24, 1996. (Graham had once dated Bugay's mother, and his DNA matched semen traces found on the child's body. Graham was convicted of murder and sentenced to die for Angela's slaying in February 2003. He remains on death row as this book goes to press.)

The announcement confused local investigators, and no charges were filed against Graham in the four unsolved kidnappings. In March 1996 police used a voice stress analyzer—a kind of long-distance "lie detector," inadmissible in court—to analyze Binder's recorded statement from June 1993, concluding that his denials of involvement in the Campbell kidnapping were false. Fourteen months later, the city of Fairfield settled Binder's lawsuit out of court with a $90,000 payment, and he remains at large today.

Another strange twist in the case was reported on March 29, 2000, when a young woman in San Jose identified herself as Amber Swartz. Questioned by police, she provided alleged details of the 1988 kidnapping and permitted herself to be fingerprinted. By April Fool's Day authorities had identified the impostor as 21-year-old Amber Marie Pattee. No motive for the cruel hoax was suggested, but Pattee was held on an outstanding $15,000 misdemeanor warrant from another jurisdiction.

On June 6, 2002, newspapers reported that police were searching the Truckee, California, home of a defrocked Catholic priest, 55-year-old Stephen Kiesle, for remains of Amber Swartz and other missing children. Kiesle already faced criminal charges of molesting children (now adult women) in his Alameda County parish between 1969 and 1971. Excavation of his yard began after police cadaver dogs "hit" on suspected remains underground, and authorities noted that Kiesle lived in Swartz's Pinole neighborhood when Amber disappeared, in 1988. Arrested for "annoying" children in 1978, Kiesle left the priesthood three years later and faced no more serious charges until April 2001, when his now-adult accusers came forward. The ex-priest was free on $180,000 bond when police began digging up his yard and using radar to look for bodies beneath the concrete floor of his garage.

In addition to Amber Swartz, search warrants entitled police to search Kiesle's property for remains of 11-year-old Jaycee Lee Duggard, missing since she left her South Lake Tahoe home for school one morning in 1991. Affidavits supporting the warrants also referred to 11-year-old Tony Franko, missing from Washoe County, Nevada, since 1983, and an 11-year-old girl reported missing in June 1987. The first dig produced "several individual hairs and a bag of dirt containing possible decomposed clothing," but no conclusive evidence of homicide or any other crime had been reported as of early August 2002.

While no new slayings have been linked to the Bay Area child murders, police scrutiny of suspects continues. In May 2006 they considered Sebastian Alexander Shaw, a 37-year-old confessed serial killer condemned for one Oregon slaying and sentenced to life imprisonment for two others. In custody, Shaw admitted slaying 10 or 12 victims in the 1990s. In

California, Alameda County sheriff's officers considered Shaw a suspect in the May 1994 slaying of 14-year-old Jennifer Lynn, but no charges have been filed in that case thus far, and attempts to link Shaw with other Bay Area child murders have proved fruitless.

August 2006 brought another fleeting surge of hope to police, when John Mark Karr allegedly confessed involvement in the 1996 Boulder, Colorado, murder of JONBENÉT RAMSEY. Karr had also lived in Los Angeles, where police held warrants charging him with possession of child pornography. In fact, however, Karr's supposed confession in the Ramsey case proved to be false, and L.A. investigators somehow managed to "lose" his computer with its alleged stash of illicit photographs, leaving Karr cleared of all charges. No evidence was found connecting Karr to any other slayings.

BEARDSLEY, John   See NEW YORK CITY GAY MURDERS (1973)

BECKER, Michelle   See GRAND RAPIDS, MICHIGAN, MURDERS

BELL, California transient murders (1987–88)
This intriguing case involves the shooting deaths of five homeless transients, all white males in their fifties and sixties, around Bell, California (southeast of Los Angeles) between December 1987 and April 1988. Authorities acknowledge investigation of "a possible relationship" among the slayings, but no suspect has been identified.

The first known victim of Bell's phantom gunman, 52-year-old James Stout, was killed on December 21, 1987, along a local railroad right of way. The next to die, 66-year-old Eric Ford, was found in front of the town's public library on March 14, 1988. Number three, 66-year-old Dennis Lynch, was discovered inside an abandoned building on April 7. The last two victims were found on April 10, 1988, lying 80 feet apart on the same railroad right of way where James Stout was killed, 16 weeks earlier. One of the pair was 62-year-old Jack Horn; his companion in death was described as a 57-year-old man, whose name was withheld by police. To date, more than 15 years after the last of the shootings, no solution to the case has been revealed.

BELL, Frankie   See "SOUTHSIDE SLAYER"

BENDA, Paul   See NEW JERSEY MURDERS

BENDER family serial killers who eluded capture (1872–73)
Nothing is known of the Bender family's origins, except that all four members spoke with varying degrees of a German accent. Whether or not they were actually European immigrants is now impossible to learn, an aspect of the killer brood that shall, like so much else about their lives, remain forever wrapped in mystery.

The Benders enter recorded history in 1872, as new arrivals in the small community of Cherryvale, Kansas. William Bender was the patriarch, a bearded hulk whose age was estimated in the neighborhood of 60 years. No given name has been recorded for his wife, "Ma" Bender, some 10 years her husband's junior. Their elder child was John, a brawny simpleton given to odd fits of giggling. The baby and star of the family was daughter, Kate, an attractive blonde in her early 20s who quickly emerged as the family's spokesperson—and, some said, the brains behind their infamous career in homicide.

Soon after their arrival in Montgomery County, the Benders built a one-room cabin on the road between Cherryvale and Thayer. A sheet of canvas cut the room in half, with private living quarters on one side and a public room on the other. Travelers could buy a home-cooked meal or rent a cot from the Benders, but some paid for the rest stop with their lives.

In practice, transient groups and hard-luck drifters had nothing to fear from the Bender clan; a solitary traveler with cash or valuables in hand was something else again. The chosen mark was seated at a table, with the canvas curtain at his back. Kate Bender served his meal, distracting him with conversation or a bit of cleavage while her brother or the old man crept up on the victim's blind side and dispatched him with a crushing hammer blow. That done, the corpse was lowered through a trapdoor to the cellar, stripped and looted, finally buried on the grounds outside. Ma Bender did her part by planting flowers to conceal the graves.

When travelers were scarce, Kate Bender did her part to keep the family business going. On her own, she toured southeastern Kansas, billing herself as "Professor Miss Kate Bender," a psychic medium with contacts in the spirit world. Her public séances earned money for the family, and young male members of the audience were sometimes more impressed with Kate's appearance than her ESP. A number of those would-be suitors made the trip to Cherryvale and wound up in Ma Bender's flower bed.

The family's last known victim was Dr. William York, from Fort Scott, Kansas. Passing through Cherryvale in March 1873, York asked about overnight lodging and was pointed toward the Bender spread. He never made it home, and it was May before his brother, Col. A. M. York, arrived in search of explanations. Questioning the Benders, York received denials. He declined their hospitality and cautioned them that he would soon return if he could not pick up his brother's trail.

Next morning, on May 5, 1873, a passing neighbor saw the front door of the Bender cabin standing open, the family team and wagon missing. Stepping inside, he found the place deserted. Fresh dirt in the cellar marked the grave of Dr. York, and 10 more bodies were unearthed around the cabin, all with shattered skulls. By then, the Benders had a two-day lead. Colonel York led a posse in pursuit, but they returned at length with word that no trace of their quarry could be found.

And there the matter rested—for a while.

In 1884 an old man matching William Bender's description was arrested in Montana for a homicide committed near Salmon, Idaho. The victim's skull had been crushed with a sledgehammer in that case, and a message was wired to Cherryvale, seeking positive identification of the suspect. That night, the prisoner severed his own foot to escape from leg irons, and he was dead from loss of blood when his breakfast arrived in the morning. By the time a deputy arrived from Kansas, advanced decomposition had destroyed any hope of identifying the corpse. (Even so, the "Bender skull" was publicly displayed in Salmon's Buckthorn Saloon until 1920, when Prohibition closed the tavern and the relic disappeared.)

Five years after the bizarre events in Idaho, Cherryvale resident Leroy Dick paid a visit to Michigan, where he identified Mrs. Almira Griffith and her daughter, Mrs. Sarah Davis, as Ma and Kate Bender. The suspects were extradited to Kansas, where seven members of a 13-man panel agreed with Dick's identification. Then, on the eve of trial, a Michigan marriage license was produced for one of the women, dated 1872, and all charges were dropped.

In 1909 George Downer, dying in Chicago, told his attorney that he had ridden with Colonel York's posse in 1873. Far from coming up empty, he said, they had captured the "Hell Benders" and meted out brutal vigilante justice, saving Kate for last and burning her alive. The bodies were consigned to an abandoned well, and posse members swore among themselves that they would take the secret to their graves. In 1910, before Downer's statement was widely aired, a similar deathbed confession emerged from New Mexico. The source, a man named Harker, admitted taking several thousand dollars from the Bender corpses before they went into the well. A search for the burial site proved fruitless, the well—if it ever existed—long since vanished in a sea of cultivated corn, but the lynching tale resurfaced in 1940, published by the son of an alleged posse member named Stark.

Did vigilante justice overtake the Benders on a lonely stretch of Kansas prairie in 1873? Or did the lethal clan escape, perhaps to build another roadside lair and kill again? How many victims did they claim *before* they moved to Cherryvale? More than 130 years beyond their crimes, the only answer to those nagging questions is the silence of the grave.

BENNALLACK,   Nancy See "ASTROLOGICAL MURDERS"

BERMÚDEZ Varela, Enrique murder victim (1991)
A Nicaragua native, born in December 1932, Enrique Bermúdez Varela was the son of a mechanical engineer who followed in his father's footsteps, graduating from Nicaragua's military academy in 1952 and joining the engineer corps of the Nicaraguan National Guard. By 1979, he held the rank of lieutenant colonel and served as President Anastasio Somoza Debayle's military attaché to the United States.

Sandinista rebels overthrew Somoza's military dictatorship in July 1979, driving the president into exile. Enemies tracked Somoza to Paraguay, where he was assassinated in September 1980, while Bermúdez emerged as a leader of the contra resistance to Sandinista rule in Nicaragua. With comrade Ricardo Lau, Bermúdez first organized the 15th of September Legion to wage guerrilla warfare in Nicaragua, then returned from exile to personally lead the so-called Nicaraguan Democratic Force as "Comandante 380."

Enrique Bermúdez Varela stands in front of his contra troops in 1985. (Time & Life Pictures/Getty Images)

President Ronald Reagan supported the contra war against Nicaragua's elected government, comparing Bermúdez and his men to America's founding fathers and using the contras as surrogate soldiers in a bid to drive supposed agents of Russia's "evil empire" from the Western Hemisphere. The resultant Nicaraguan civil war claimed at least 30,000 lives (some reports say 50,000), while graphic reports of contra atrocities and illicit cocaine smuggling drove Congress to ban U.S. support for the rebels in early 1988. Reagan and successor George H. W. Bush defied that ban, continuing covert support for the contras through the Central Intelligence Agency. Exposure of those crimes sparked scandal in the States and led to conviction of several Reagan-Bush aides (all of whom were pardoned by Bush before he left office in January 1993).

Meanwhile, Bermúdez pursued his military campaign in Nicaragua, climaxed with the electoral defeat of Sandinista leaders in February 1990. President-elect Violetta Chamorro was supported by the Bush White House, which promised withdrawal of U.S. economic sanctions against Nicaragua if she was elected.

One year after that apparent victory for contra ideology, on February 16, 1991, gunmen ambushed Bermúdez and killed him outside Managua's Inter-Continental Hotel. Some observers believe that a meeting he planned to attend, scheduled to occur at the hotel, was in fact simply bait in the trap that claimed his life. In 1994, Bermúdez's daughter Claudia told the *Miami Herald*, "There were a lot of people who would have benefited from having my dad put away—the Sandinistas, the Chamorro government, the United States. My dad died with a lot of information." Despite investigation of the murder by Chamorro's police, the Bermúdez gunmen remain unidentified today.

BERNAS, Melanie   See BROSSO, ANGELA

BHUTTO, Benazir assassination victim (2007)
Benazir Bhutto was born in Karachi, Pakistan, on June 21, 1953. Her father, Zulfikar Ali Bhutto,

founded the Pakistan Peoples Party (PPP) and served as president of Pakistan from 1971 to 1973, then as prime minister from 1973 to 1977, when he was deposed in a military coup. His successor, General Muhammad Zia-ul-Haq, imposed martial law and charged Zulfikar Ali Bhutto with conspiracy to kill a rival politician. Zulfikar was convicted and, despite widespread suspicion of a frame-up, he was hanged on April 4, 1979. His eldest son, Shahnawaz, died under mysterious circumstances in France in July 1985.

Educated at Harvard and in England, Benazir Bhutto won election as Pakistan's prime minister in November 1988, taking office on December 2. She won the Liberal International's Prize for Freedom in 1989, but her crusade for modernization of Pakistan angered Muslim fundamentalists. President Ghulam Ishaq Khan removed her from office in 1990, citing allegations of corruption, but Bhutto never faced trial. Voters reelected her as prime minister in 1993, but stiff opposition persisted. Bhutto's brother, Mir

Murtaza, was murdered in 1996, even as fresh corruption charges surfaced.

Bhutto entered self-imposed exile that year, after President Farooq Leghari removed her from office. Investigators filed charges of money-laundering and other improprieties, but a report from Pakistan's auditor general supported Bhutto's claim that the charges were purely political. In 2002, President Pervez Musharraf amended Pakistan's constitution, limiting prime ministers to two terms in office, whereupon Bhutto determined to seek the presidency. Her path to that office was cleared in 2007, when Musharraf granted amnesty to Bhutto and dismissed all pending charges against her.

Bhutto returned to Pakistan on October 18, 2007. That very day, suicide bombers killed 139 persons and injured 450 more at Jinnah International Airport. The bombers missed Bhutto's family, but killed 50 of her personal PPP bodyguards. Security was tightened for Bhutto's family, including mercenary gunmen from the U.S.-based Blackwater firm and

Mourners carry the coffin of assassination victim Benazir Bhutto, Pakistan's former prime minister, in December 2007. (AP Photo/Anjum Naveed)

ArmorGroup. Subsequent revelations demonstrated that Bhutto also sought protection from the CIA, Scotland Yard, and Israel's Mossad.

None of it helped.

On December 27, 2007, Bhutto addressed a PPP rally in Rawalpindi. As she prepared to leave the rally in a "bulletproof" car, gunmen fired on the vehicle and a suicide bomber detonated his charges nearby. Bhutto—standing erect with her head and shoulders outside the car's sunroof—suffered fatal wounds, while 23 other persons also died. Government pathologists blamed Bhutto's death on a skull fracture resulting from the explosion, while friends insisted she was shot before the blast. Scotland Yard's investigation affirmed the official verdict, but controversy persists. A report published by the PPP, signed by seven physicians, states that Bhutto died from "a laser beam shot." Specifically, the doctors said, "There were two to three tiny radio densities under each fractured segments on both projections which were in fact invisible electromagnetic radiations."

Whatever the immediate cause of Bhutto's death, the aftermath was cataclysmic. Widespread rioting followed the murder, with protesters burning Musharraf campaign billboards and attacking police. At least 47 persons died in the resultant turmoil, while rioters destroyed 176 banks, 34 gasoline stations, and hundreds of shops and cars. January's scheduled election was delayed, prompting one of Bhutto's top aides, Senator Latif Khosa, to charge that "state agencies are manipulating the whole process, there is rigging by the ISI [Pakistan's Inter-Services Intelligence], the Election Commission and the previous government, which is still continuing to hold influence. They were on the rampage."

Bhutto's assassination remains officially unsolved today. On December 27, 2007, al-Qaeda terrorist commander Mustafa Abu al-Yazid claimed credit for the murder, telling journalists, "We terminated the most precious American asset which vowed to defeat [the] mujahideen." Meanwhile, Pakistan's Interior Ministry claimed to have intercepted a message from Baitullah Mehsud, an independent rebel leader in Waziristan (a Pakistani state on the Afghan border), congratulating his disciples for Bhutto's slaying. Mehsud issued a public statement on December 29, saying, "I strongly deny it. Tribal people have their own customs. We don't strike women. It is a conspiracy by government, military and intelligence agencies." CIA spokesmen supported the al-Qaeda scenario, but their credibility had suffered grievous wounds over depiction of nonexistent Iraqi weapons of mass destruction four years earlier. Farhatullah Babar, a PPP spokesman, subsequently told the media, "The story that al-Qaeda or Baitullah Mehsud did it appears to us to be a planted story, an incorrect story, because they want to divert the attention."

BIBBENS, Dolly See SAN DIEGO MURDERS (1931–36)

"BIBLE John" unknown serial killer (1968–69)

On Friday morning, February 23, 1968, a resident of Glasgow, Scotland, found a naked, lifeless woman sprawled in the alley behind his apartment building. Police recorded that the woman lay spread-eagled on her back, with no sign of any clothing at the scene. The victim, raped and strangled, was identified as 25-year-old Patricia Docker, employed as an auxiliary nurse at Glasgow Hospital. Last seen by her parents on Thursday night, when she left home to go dancing, Docker had worn a light-orange dress and gray coat, with a brown purse and matching shoes. No trace of her missing bag or garments was ever found.

Eighteen months elapsed before the killer struck again, on August 16, 1969. That Sunday night, 32-year-old Mima MacDonald went dancing at the Barrowland Ballroom and never returned. Her seminude corpse was found on Monday morning in a vacant apartment on Mackeith Street, a few blocks from her home. MacDonald had been raped, then strangled with her own stockings, which the killer left knotted around her neck. Police noted that both victims were petite, both had spent their last hours at a dance hall, and both were menstruating when they were murdered. The last point, if not pure coincidence, suggested the possibility of some private sexual obsession on the killer's part, but it brought detectives no closer to their quarry.

Patrons of the Barrowland Ballroom helped piece together Mima MacDonald's last evening alive. She had left around midnight, in the company of a tall, slender man, a redhead with his hair cut short, wearing a stylish suit. Observers placed the man's age between 25 and 35 years, but no one who had seen him knew his name. MacDonald and her date were last seen walking in the general direction of Mackeith Street, less than a mile from the dance hall. A sketch of the suspect was published, but it produced no worthwhile leads.

Eleven weeks later, on the night of October 30, 1969, sisters Helen and Jeannie Puttock dropped by the Barrowland Ballroom. Both wound up dancing with men who called themselves "John," although neither was further identified. Helen's John was 5-feet-10-inches, a redhead in his early thirties, whose courtesy and custom-tailored suit convinced Jeannie Puttock that he "wasn't the Barrowland type"—a reference to the working-class types who normally patronized the club. Still, despite "John's" seeming courtesy, he underwent a rapid mood swing at one point, causing an angry scene with the manager over some pocket change lost to a defective cigarette machine.

When time came to leave, red-haired John shared a taxi with the sisters, Jeannie afterward recalling his comments on the subject of religion. The man described himself as a teetotaler and avid Bible student who knew the scriptures by heart, priding himself on his ability to quote verses from memory. The taxi dropped Jeannie off first, and she waved good-bye to her sister from the curb, unaware that it would be the last time she ever saw Helen alive.

Around 7:00 A.M. on October 31, a woman walking her dog found 29-year-old Helen Puttock's strangled corpse, clothing torn and disarrayed, not far from Puttock's Glasgow apartment. As with Mima MacDonald, the murder weapon was one of Puttock's own stockings, left coiled around her neck. And like the strangler's two previous victims, Puttock had been menstruating on the night she died.

Police questioned hundreds of men who resembled the elusive killer, now dubbed "Bible John" by tabloid journalists. One innocent local, Norman Mac-Donald—no relation to Mima—was hauled in so often that detectives finally issued him a special pass to avert further harassment. Aside from grilling look-alikes, Glasgow detectives also visited 240 tailors, seeking one who might recall a particular red-haired customer . . . but all in vain.

In 1970, still clueless and bereft of suspects, police consulted a forensic psychiatrist, Dr. Robert Brittain, to obtain a "profile" of their subject. Brittain guessed that Bible John was under 35 years old, an introspective man who shied away from social contacts, sexually dysfunctional and suffering an ambivalent love/hate relationship with his mother. In fact, Brittain suggested, he might be a latent homosexual, perhaps a closet transvestite. He might

also be obsessed with weapons, though none had been used in his crimes.

It seems that Bible John may have "retired" after the Puttock homicide in 1969, although one published report mentions another spate of unsolved Scottish murders in 1977–78, briefly prompting rumors that the strangler had returned to active duty. No more details were forthcoming on the later crimes, and Glasgow police still peg the slayer's body count at three victims. Forensic science took a stab at the case in 1996, with exhumation of an unnamed suspect's corpse at Lanarkshire, for DNA comparison with a semen stain found on Helen Puttock's clothing, but the test results were inconclusive, and the case remains officially unsolved.

BIGGS, Frank   See RIVERDELL HOSPITAL MURDERS

BIGGS, Mikelle missing person (1999)
An 11-year-old resident of Mesa, Arizona, Mikelle Biggs left home to purchase ice cream from a passing truck at 6:00 P.M. on January 2, 1999. She rode her sister's bicycle to catch the familiar vehicle, which had moved beyond her street by the time she borrowed money from her mother for an ice-cream bar. She never returned from her quest, though searchers found the bike and two borrowed quarters lying in the middle of the street. Mikelle and the ice-cream truck were gone.

Police found no useful leads in their search for Biggs, and interviews with self-styled psychics failed to crack the case. Officers scoured 35 abandoned mine shafts in the nearby Santan Mountains, swept the surrounding desert, distributed thousands of posters, and traced every known ice-cream vendor in the state of Arizona—all in vain. More than 9,500 fruitless leads have been received to date by Mesa detectives, the paperwork filling more than 70 loose-leaf binders, each four inches thick. Investigators have tracked futile tips from Mexico to Pennsylvania, chasing tales of drug-related kidnapping, child pornography, and predatory pedophiles. Thus far, their efforts have yielded no results.

BINGHAM family murders England (1911)
Historically, members of the Bingham family have been the official custodians of Lancaster Castle, in Lancashire County, England. William Hodges Bingham,

patriarch of the clan, served as chief caretaker for three decades before his death, in January 1911. Son James succeeded William, and he soon brought a sister, Margaret, to work as a housekeeper in the castle, but her stay was brief, ending with her untimely death a few weeks later. Margaret, in turn, was replaced by half sister Edith Agnes Bingham, a shrewish backbiter who quickly alienated James. They quarreled incessantly, and James made plans to ease her out of her job. A replacement was scheduled to start work on August 14, 1911, but the plan abruptly changed on August 12, when James collapsed and died after dinner.

Police discovered that his last meal had been steak, prepared by Edith, and an autopsy listed the cause of death as arsenic poisoning. William and Margaret Bingham were then exhumed, more arsenic was found in their remains, and Edith faced a charge of triple murder, based on a theory that she killed her relatives to gain a small inheritance. At trial her barrister reminded jurors that there was no evidence of Edith possessing arsenic at any time, and she was acquitted after 20 minutes of deliberation, leaving the case forever unsolved.

BIOFF, Willie Morris gangland murder victim (1955)

It is difficult to improve on Willie Bioff's self-description, offered under oath from a Chicago witness stand in 1943. On that occasion Bioff told the court, "I am just a low, uncouth person. I'm a low-type sort of man." Some might suggest, all things considered, that the self-assessment stopped short of defining his loathsome character.

A Russian native, born in 1900, Bioff immigrated to Chicago with his family, as a child. By age 10 he was already pimping girls from his slum neighborhood; at 16 he was associated with brothers Jake and Harry Guzik, later high-ranking members of Al Capone's criminal syndicate. Bioff's natural sadism kept his streetwalkers in line, and later served him well as a slugger in various labor rackets. One of his mob assignments in the 1930s was muscling club owners who balked at booking entertainers represented by the Music Corporation of America (MCA); another was collaborating with like-minded felon George Browne in a scheme conceived by Capone successor Frank (The Enforcer) Nitti, to seize control of the International Alliance of Theatrical Stage Employees and Motion Picture Operators (IATSE). With Bioff at his side, treating the opposition to displays of brute force, Browne

easily captured the IATSE's presidency and prepared for an all-out attack on the movie industry at large.

Step one was consolidation of the union's grip on theaters from coast to coast, including a contract provision that required employment of a second, superfluous projectionist in every movie house. Bioff later described the means by which he persuaded theater owner Jack Miller to cooperate: "I told Miller the exhibitors would have to pay two operators for each booth. Miller said, 'My God! That will close up all my shows.' I said, 'If that will kill grandma, then grandma must die.' Miller said that two men in each booth would cost about $500,000 a year. So I said, why don't you make a deal? And we finally agreed on $60,000. You see, if they wouldn't pay, we'd give them lots of trouble. We'd put them out of business—and I mean out."

Bioff and Browne soon took their campaign to Hollywood and New York, where Willie demanded a $2 million payoff from Nick Schenck, the CEO of Loew's Incorporated. Schenck bargained the squeeze

Before his murder, mobster Willie Bioff made some influential friends, including Arizona senator Barry Goldwater (pictured here). (Library of Congress)

down to $1 million, payable over four years, but it was all gravy for Bioff and Browne. Together, they initially split 50 percent of the kickbacks, while sending the rest to Chicago. Nitti and company soon demanded 75 percent of the take for themselves, but by then the cash flow was so massive that Bioff and Browne had no grounds for complaint.

Trouble began for the mob's top extortionists when Bioff encountered right-wing columnist Westbrook Pegler at a Hollywood party. Bioff's "low, uncouth" manners irked Pegler, and distaste turned to hunger as Pegler uncovered tales of Bioff's syndicate connections. Unaided by friend and frequent source J. Edgar Hoover (whose FBI staunchly denied the existence of organized crime until 1961), Pegler dug into Bioff's background and uncovered multiple convictions for beating his girls in Chicago. The six-month sentence for one such conviction, levied in 1922, had never been served, and Pegler harped on the subject in print until Chicago authorities finally issued a warrant for Bioff's arrest in November 1939. Willie served five months, beginning on April 15, 1940, and while friendly guards made his confinement as pleasant as possible (including daily deliveries of iced beer by the tubful), Bioff emerged to find new problems waiting for him.

In Bioff's absence the Internal Revenue Service had noted a $69,000 omission from his declared income for 1937. Digging a little deeper, agents uncovered Bioff's Hollywood extortion scam and followed the trail to George Browne. On May 23, 1941, both men were indicted on racketeering and tax evasion charges. Their trial opened on October 6, 1941, and both were convicted three weeks later; Bioff received a 10-year sentence, while Browne was slapped with an eight-year term. Desperate for leniency, the pair "rolled over" on their Chicago sponsors, providing testimony that secured racketeering indictments against Nitti and six top-ranked associates, including Paul (The Waiter) Ricca, Phil D'Andrea, Charles (Cherry Nose) Gioe, Lou Kaufman, and Johnny Roselli. Nitti was found shot to death in Chicago on March 19, 1943, allegedly a suicide. The trial of his surviving codefendants opened on October 5, 1943, with Browne and Bioff as the prosecution's star witnesses. All six of the accused were convicted on November 31, 1943, and sentenced to varying prison terms.

Bioff and Browne were rewarded for their testimony with early release in December 1944. Browne promptly disappeared as if the Earth had swallowed him, while Bioff made his way to Phoenix, settling there under the pseudonym of William Nelson. In 1952 he donated $5,000 to the senatorial campaign of department store magnate Barry Goldwater, thus earning himself an influential friend. Bioff shared Goldwater's fondness for the gambling dens of Las Vegas, Nevada, and soon went to work part-time for GUS GREENBAUM, syndicate manager of the Riviera Hotel and Casino. Perhaps unknown to Bioff-Nelson, the Riviera was bankrolled by Chicago mobsters—none of whom, despite the passage of a decade, had forgotten Bioff's treachery. On November 4, 1955, Bioff climbed into his pickup truck at home, waved farewell to his wife, and pressed the truck's starter. A powerful bomb exploded beneath the hood, demolishing the vehicle and killing Bioff instantly. After his death "Nelson's" identity was revealed in lurid press reports that embarrassed Senator Goldwater (but which failed to stop him from associating with other known mobsters in Nevada and Arizona). The bombing, like so many other "hits" ordered from the Windy City, remains unsolved today.

BISSITT, Carol See NEW ORLEANS MURDERS (1987–88)

"BLACK Dahlia" Murder Los Angeles (1947)

On the morning of January 15, 1947, Los Angeles police were summoned to a vacant lot at 39th and Norton Streets by reports of a body lying in the weeds. They expected another routine drunk arrest, but instead found a woman's naked corpse—and the beginning of their city's most enduring mystery.

The victim was identified from fingerprints as Elizabeth Ann Short, born July 29, 1924, in Hyde Park, Massachusetts. A would-be actress, Short had migrated to California in 1942 and was briefly jailed the following year, in Santa Barbara, for underage drinking. A penchant for black clothing to match her raven hair had earned Short a nickname among her friends: They called her the "Black Dahlia." Dr. Frederick Newbarr's autopsy report describes her ghastly fate.

OFFICE OF THE COUNTY CORONER

I performed an autopsy on Elizabeth Short on January 16, 1947, at the Los Angeles County Coroner's mortuary and found the immediate cause of death: hemor-

rhage and shock due to concussion of the brain and lacerations of the face.

EXAMINATION

The body is that of a female about 15 to 20 years of age, measuring 5'5" in height and weighing 115 lbs.

There are multiple lacerations to the midfore-head, in the right forehead, and at the top of the head in the midline. There are multiple tiny abrasions, linear in shape, on the right face and forehead. There are two small lacerations, 1/4" each in length, on each side of the nose near the bridge. There is a deep laceration on the face 3" long which extends laterally from the right corner of the mouth. The surrounding tissues are ecchymotic and bluish purple in color. There is a deep laceration 2½" long extending laterally from the left corner of the mouth. The surrounding tissues are bluish purple in color. There are five linear lacerations in the right upper lip which extend into the soft tissues for a distance of 1/8". The teeth are in a state of advanced decay. The two upper central incisors are loose, and one lower incisor is loose. The rest of the teeth show cavities.

Upon reflecting the scalp there is ecchymosis in the right and upper frontal area. There are localized areas of subarachnoid hemorrhage on the right side and small hemorrhagic areas in the corpus callosum. No fracture of the skull is visible.

There is a depressed ridge on both sides and in the anterior portion of the neck, which is light brown in color. There is an abrasion, irregular in outline, in the skin of the neck in the anterior midline. There are two linear abrasions in the left anterior neck. There are two depressed ridges in the posterior neck, pale brown in color. The lower ridge has an abrasion in the skin at each extremity.

The pharynx and larynx are intact. There is no evidence of trauma to the hyoid bone, thyroid or cricoid cartilages, or tracheal rings. There is a small area of ecchymosis in the soft tissues of the right neck at the level of the upper tracheal rings. There is no obstruction in the laryngotracheal passage.

There is an irregular laceration with superficial tissue loss in the skin of the right breast. The tissue loss is more or less square in outline and measured 3¼" transversely and 2½" longitudinally; extending toward the midline from this irregular laceration are several superficial lacerations in the skin. There is an elliptical opening in the skin located ¾" to the left of the left nipple. The opening measures 2¾" in a transverse direction and 1¼" in a longitudinal direction in its midportion. The margins of these wounds show no appreciable discolorations. There are multiple superficial scratches in the skin of the left chest on the anterior wall. There is a

Aspiring actress Elizabeth Short, the "Black Dahlia," poses for a head shot. (Bettman/Corbis)

healed scar in the skin of the right lower posterior chest at the level of the ninth rib which measures 3¼" in length and its direction is diagonally to the right. Crossing this scar are three scars which appear to be healed suture scars. There are four small superficial lacerations in the skin of the lower chest on the left side close to the midline. There is no discoloration at the margins. There are superficial linear lacerations in the skin of the left upper arm on its external aspect. There is a double ridge around the left wrist close to the hand. The fingernails are very short, the thumbnail measuring 5/16" in length and the fingernails measuring 3/16" in length. There are superficial lacerations and scratches in the skin of the external surface of the right forearm. There is a double ridge depressed around the right wrist. The fingernails are very short, the thumbnail measuring 3/16" in length and the others 1/8" in length. The palmar surfaces of both hands are somewhat roughened but no firm calluses are seen.

The organs of the chest are in normal position. The left lung is pink in color and well aerated. The right

This envelope, containing the birth certificate, address book, and personal papers of 22-year-old Elizabeth Short, was received at the Los Angeles post office on January 24, 1947, and turned over to police. (AP Photo)

lung is somewhat adherent due to fairly firm pleural adhesions. The lung is pink in color and well aerated. There is a calcified thickening of the ninth rib on the right side in the midscapular line. The heart shows no gross pathology.

The trunk is completely severed by an incision which is almost straight through the abdomen severing the intestine at the duodenum and through the soft tissue of the abdomen, passing through the intervertebral disk between the second and third lumbar vertebrae. There is very little ecchymosis along the track of the incision. There is a gaping laceration 4¼" long which extends longitudinally from the umbilicus to the supra-pubic region. On both sides of this laceration there are multiple crisscross lacerations in the suprapubic area which extend through the skin and soft tissues. No ecchymosis is seen.

There is a square pattern of superficial lacerations in the skin of the right hip. The organs of the abdomen are entirely exposed. There are lacerations of the intestine and both kidneys. The uterus is small, and no pregnancy is apparent. The tubes, ovaries, and cul-de-sac are intact. The labia majora are intact. There is an abrasion which extends through the lower half of the labia minora and the margin shows some bluish discoloration. Within the vagina and higher up there is lying loose a piece of skin with fat and subcutaneous tissue attached. On this piece of loose skin there are several crisscrossing lacerations. Smears for spermatozoa have been taken.

The anal opening is markedly dilated and the opening measures 1¼" in diameter. The mucous membrane is brown throughout the circumference of the opening. There are multiple abrasions, and a small amount of ecchymosis is seen at the margin. The laceration of the mucous membrane extends upward for a distance of ½". At a point about 1" up from the anal opening there is a tuft of brown curly hair lying loose in the anal canal. The hair corresponds in appearance to the pubic hair. Smear for spermatozoa has been taken.

There is an irregular opening in the skin on the anterior surface of the left thigh with tissue loss. The opening measures 3½" transversely at the base and 4" from the base longitudinally to the upper back. The laceration extends into the subcutaneous soft tissue and muscle. No ecchymosis is seen. There is a ridge in the skin of the lower right thigh, anterior surface, located 5" above the knee. There is a diagonal ridge in the skin of the upper third of the right leg which is light brown in color; extending down from this point there are three light brown depressed ridges. There is a circular ridge around the left lower leg and also a diagonal depression ridge just below this area. The skin of the plantar surface of the feet is stained brown.

The stomach is filled with greenish brown granular matter, mostly feces and other particles which could not be identified. All smears for spermatozoa were negative.

The references to lack of ecchymosis—i.e., bruising—demonstrate that only Short's head and facial wounds were inflicted while she lived, and those are listed as the cause of death. What followed afterward, as grisly as it was, did not amount to torture (as described in many popular accounts of the crime), since the victim was already dead. The autopsy also debunks a host of other myths about Short's death. Her teeth were not punched out or broken off. Her skin displayed no burns from cigarettes or any other source. Her breasts were not sliced off, nor did the killer clip one earlobe as a grisly souvenir. No words or cryptic letters were carved into her flesh. Her genitals were not deformed or "infantile," incapable of normal intercourse, as later claimed in one "solution" to the case.

Detectives questioned Short's relatives and acquaintances, ex-boyfriends, and a steady parade of cranks (some reports say "more than 50," others claim 500) who were driven to confess the crime for twisted reasons of their own. None were responsible, as far as the police could tell. The killer had eluded them, but he was not done yet.

On January 22, 1947, an unknown man telephoned editor James Richardson of the Los Angeles *Examiner.* The caller congratulated Richardson on his coverage of the Short case and offered to "send you some of the things she had with her when she . . . shall we say . . . disappeared?" Three days later, postal inspectors intercepted a package addressed to the *Examiner* with a cut-and-paste message: "Here is Dahlia's belongings. Letter to follow." The parcel had been wiped with gasoline to eradicate fingerprints. Inside were photographs, newspaper clippings, and an address book with one page conspicuously missing. Police chased the new leads in vain, gathering more details on Short's chaotic life but finding no leads to her killer.

On Sunday, January 26, 1947, a hand-printed letter was mailed to the *Examiner*. It read: "Here it is. Turning in Wed., Jan. 29, 10 A.M. Had my fun at police. Black Dahlia Avenger." Detectives surrounded the newspaper's office on the appointed day, but their quarry never appeared. Instead, at 1:00 P.M., another paste-up message was delivered: "Have changed my mind. You would not give me a square deal. Dahlia killing was justified."

Another half dozen unsolved murders of women occurred in Los Angeles during the six months following Short's death, prompting some reporters to suspect a serial killer at large (and to write in the plural of "Black Dahlia murders"). Interrogation of suspects continued for a decade after the initial crime, but none produced sufficient evidence to file a murder charge. The better part of half a century would pass before two very different solutions to the case appeared in print—neither acknowledged to this day by the Los Angeles Police Department.

In January 1987, on the 40th anniversary of Short's death, media reports proclaimed that Hollywood author John Gilmore had cracked the Dahlia case. Unfortunately, the reports of his "solution" were confused and contradictory: One claimed the killer—identified as "Arnold Smith"—lived in Indianapolis, where Gilmore had "watched" him without making personal contact; another placed the slayer in Reno, Nevada, operating a saloon. A book was forthcoming, the stories agreed, but there was still no sign of it in 1990, when Gilmore sat for a televised interview in Los Angeles. This time he told reporters that he had interviewed "Mr. Smith"—by then incinerated in a flophouse fire—and that the suspect "all but confessed" to the crime. When Gilmore's book was finally published (*Severed*, 1998), it identified "Smith" as Jack Anderson Wilson, allegedly suspected in Short's death and another murder by legendary L.A. homicide detective "Jigsaw John" St. John. A lack of evidence prevented Wilson's arrest in either case, Gilmore reported, but there was another problem with the theory. When interviewed by this author in 1993, Detective St. John (now also

deceased) flatly rejected Gilmore's theory as inaccurate and claimed Short's murder was still a subject of active investigation.

In April 1989, meanwhile, California resident Janice Knowlton—in the midst of psychotherapy related to severe depression—recovered memories of violent events involving her father, the late George Frederick Knowlton. By November 1989 Janice had recalled enough details to identify one of her father's several victims as Elizabeth Short. Police were apathetic and suggested that she investigate the matter herself. Knowlton followed their advice and launched a marathon investigation that uncovered circumstantial links between her father and a string of unsolved murders spanning the nation, from California to the original family home in Massachusetts. Relatives acknowledged George Knowlton's boasts of unprosecuted homicides; others bore witness to his brutal treatment of his wife and children. As with suspect Jack Wilson, however, George Knowlton was beyond the reach of living investigators, killed with his youngest son in a 1962 car crash near Claremore, Oklahoma.

Jan Knowlton's recollections, while partly validated by another living sister, invited scathing criticism from strangers who blamed her reports on "false memory syndrome." Various survivors of childhood abuse were generally more receptive to her account, published in 1995 as *Daddy Was the Black Dahlia Killer*.

In 1996, the *Los Angeles Times* writer Larry Harnisch named Dr. Walter Alonzo Bayley as a suspect in Short's murder. Until October 1946, when he separated from his wife, Bayley occupied a home one block south of the lot where Short's body was dumped. Bayley's wife still lived in that house, and Harnisch claims that Bayley's daughter was a friend of Short's sister and brother-in-law, having served as matron of honor at their wedding. Dr. Bayley died a year after Short's murder, at age 67, and his autopsy revealed evidence of degenerative brain disease. While that proves nothing, and police never considered Bayley a suspect, the doctor's estranged wife claimed that Bayley's mistress knew an unspecified "terrible secret" about Bayley. Other researchers suggest that the secret involved Bayley's hypothetical involvement with then-illegal abortions. Harnisch theorizes, without any proof, that Bayley's brain disease prompted him to kill Short, and that Bayley cut her body in half for easier transport. The novelist James Ellroy endorsed Harnisch's theory in a 2001 film, *James Ellroy's Feast of Death*, but no proof was forthcoming.

In 2003, an ex–LAPD homicide detective Steve Hodel published a book naming his late father, Dr. George Hodel, as a serial killer who murdered Short and other victims previously linked to the Black Dahlia slaying in Jan Knowlton's 1995 autobiography. In fact, aside from his father's medical degree, the case presented by Hodel in *Black Dahlia Avenger* was strongly reminiscent of Knowlton's account. Police accused George Hodel of molesting his 14-year-old daughter in October 1949, but jurors acquitted him two months later. Detectives subsequently placed Dr. Hodel under surveillance as a Dahlia suspect, during February and March 1950, and Lieutenant Frank Jemisen of the L.A. County District Attorney's office filed the following report with a grand jury in February 1951:

Doctor George Hodel, M.D. 5121 Fountain [Franklin] Avenue, at the time of this murder had a clinic at East First Street near Alameda. Lillian DeNorak who lived with this doctor said he spent some time around the Biltmore Hotel and identified the photo of victim Short as a photo of one of the doctor's girl friends. Tamar Hodel, fifteen year old daughter, stated that her mother, Dorothy Hodel, has told her that her father had been out all night on a party the night of the murder and said, "They'll never be able to prove I did that murder." Two microphones were placed in this suspect's home (see the log and recordings made over approximately three weeks time which tend to prove his innocence. See statement of Dorothy Hodel, former wife). Informant Lillian DeNorak has been committed to the State Mental Institution at Camarillo. Joe Barrett, a roomer at the Hodel residence cooperated as an informant. A photograph of the suspect in the nude with a nude identified colored model was secured from his personal effects. Undersigned identified this model as Mattie Comfort, 3423½ South Arlington, Republic 4953. She said that she was with Doctor Hodel sometime prior to the murder and that she knew nothing about his being associated with the victim. Rudolph Walthers, known to have been acquainted with victim and also with suspect Hodel, claimed he had not seen victim in the presence of Hodel and did not believe that the doctor had ever met the victim. The following acquaintances of Hodel were questioned and none were able to connect the suspect with murder: Fred Sexton, 1020 White Knoll Drive; Nita Moladero, 1617½ North Normandy; Ellen Taylor, 5121 Fountain Avenue; Finlay Thomas, 616½ South Normandy; Mildred B. Colby, 4029 Vista Del Monte Street, Sherman Oaks (this witness was a girlfriend of Charles Smith, abortionist friend of Hodel); Turin Gilkey, 1025 North Wilcox; Irene Summerset, 1236¼ North Edgemont; Norman Beckett, 1025 North Wilcox; Ethel Kane, 1033 North Wilcox; Annette Chase, 1039 North Wilcox; Dorothy Royer, 1636 North Beverly Glenn. See supplemental reports, long sheets and hear recordings, all of which tend to eliminate this suspect.

Dr. Hodel died in 1999, and his son Steve published his posthumous murder accusation four years later, driven by examination of two photographs of a young woman "resembling" Short found in Dr. Hodel's photo album. Steve's book also accuses his father of various other slayings cited in Knowlton's book as the work of *her* father, including the 1958 murder of future novelist James Ellroy's mother. Perhaps coincidentally, Steve Hodel's sister—whom father George allegedly molested in 1949—was also a friend of Jan Knowlton. James Ellroy wrote a laudatory foreword for the paperback edition of Hodel's book, then waffled in 2006 and announced that he would never henceforth discuss the Dahlia case.

Donald Wolfe is the latest author to tackle Short's case, with his volume *The Black Dahlia Files* published in 2005. Wolfe, whose previous work includes *The Assassination of Marilyn Monroe* (1999), is a former screenwriter and film editor, who has contributed articles to the *New York Times* and *Paris Match*. He claims that five slayers participated in Short's murder and mutilation, including Jack Wilson (formerly named by John Gilmore), Dr. Leslie Audrain (alleged leader of an L.A. abortion ring), Maurice Clement (a pimp and supposed driver of the getaway car), local gangster Albert Louis Greenberg, and transplanted New York mobster BENJAMIN "BUGSY" SIEGEL. According to Wolfe, Short died because she was impregnated by Norman Chandler, publisher of the *Los Angeles Times*, and threatened to blackmail him. Siegel's gang carried out the murder contract as a favor to Chandler and dumped the corpse near the home of rival mob leader Jack Dragna as a gesture of intimidation. Many researchers dispute that theory, and Larry Harnisch has accused Wolfe of plagiarizing text from his (Harnisch's) Internet Web site to produce *The Black Dahlia Files*.

Controversy continues in the Dahlia case, in which only one thing appears certain: Despite their perennial claims of "ongoing investigation," Los Angeles police will likely never book their man.

BLAU, Eva   See "ASTROLOGICAL MURDERS"

BLESSING, Sarah   See "I-70/I-35 MURDERS"

BLOCKER, Lateashia See Washington, D.C., murders (1996–97)

BOHN, Amy See St. Louis child murders

BOHN, Martine See "Butcher of Mons"

BOLLINGER, Loren See Columbus, Ohio, murders

BOMPENSIERO, Frank mobster and murder victim (1977)
Born in 1905, Frank Bompensiero grew up tough and crafty, earning a reputation as a fearsome killer that served him well after his initiation to the Mafia. "Bomp" was said to favor a strangling technique nicknamed the "Italian rope trick," but he was not above shooting his victims, stabbing them with ice picks, or using any other means at hand to fulfill a murder contract. While operating chiefly from Southern California, with his home base in San Diego, Bompensiero handled "hits" as far east as Detroit when duty called—and the price was right.

In 1967, following a federal conspiracy indictment, Bompensiero chose indiscretion as the better part of valor and became an informant for the Federal Bureau of Investigation. His charges were dismissed in return for covert information on the daily workings of Los Angeles mobster Jack Dragna's crime family—dubbed the "Mickey Mouse Mafia" by some eastern hoodlums—but collaboration with G-men never cramped Bompensiero's style. He continued his criminal activities without respite, including the 1975 contract murder of San Diego real estate broker Tamara Rand (carried out on behalf of Las Vegas associates).

Around the same time, Bompensiero maneuvered several Los Angeles mobsters into contact with a pornography firm that was actually the front for an FBI sting operation. Several of his cronies were arrested, and they had no doubt who was to blame for their embarrassment. Bompensiero did his best to keep a low profile thereafter, sticking close to his Pacific Beach apartment except for short hikes to neighborhood phone booths. He avoided trouble for a while, but one night in February 1977 Bompensiero was ambushed outside his apartment, shot four times in the head by an unknown gunman. The crime remains unsolved today.

BOOKER, Betty Jo See Texarkana "Phantom Gunman"

BORDEN, Andrew and Abby murder victims (1892)
Today we know her chiefly through a bit of childish verse, composed more than a century ago:

Lizzie Borden took an axe
And gave her mother forty whacks.
And when she saw what she had done,
She gave her father forty-one.

But *did* she? Despite the passage of time and reams of commentary on the case, Lizzie Andrew Borden's guilt in the brutal hatchet slayings of her father and stepmother is no more certain today than it was in 1892. She was in fact acquitted by a jury of her peers, and the double homicide remains officially unsolved.

Seventy-year-old Andrew Borden ranked among the wealthiest men in Fall River, Massachusetts, in August 1892, a landlord with extensive holdings who also served as a director on the boards of several banks. Success had not improved his dour temperament, however, and he was known as a virtual miser. Abby Borden, six years her husband's junior, was his second wife. They shared a home at 92 Second Street in Fall River with Andrew's spinster daughters from his first marriage, 43-year-old Emma and 32-year-old Lizzie. Also in residence when disaster struck were John Vinnicum Morse (a maternal uncle of Lizzie and Emma), and 26-year-old housemaid Bridget Sullivan (called Maggie by the Borden sisters).

At 11:10 A.M. on August 4, 1892, Lizzie summoned Sullivan to the home's first-floor sitting room with a cry of "Father's dead! Somebody's come in and killed him!" Sullivan arrived to find Andrew Borden sprawled on the couch, his face and head savaged with deep hacking wounds. Dispatched to fetch the family physician, Dr. Seabury Bowen, Sullivan crossed Second Street to the doctor's nearby home but found him absent. After telling Mrs. Bowen of the murder, Sullivan returned home and was sent out again, this time to fetch Alice Russell, a friend of the family who lived several blocks away.

While Sullivan was out, Lizzie Borden called to a neighbor, Adelaide Churchill, from her back porch, reporting her father's death. Churchill inquired about Abby, whereupon Lizzie replied that her stepmother had gone out that morning to visit a sick friend. Upon

The trial of alleged murderer Lizzie Borden attracted international attention. (Library of Congress)

Over the next few weeks, investigators prepared a rough time line of events preceding the murders and built a circumstantial case against prime suspect Lizzie Borden. Unfortunately for prosecutors Hosea Knowlton and William Moody (later U.S. attorney general), the state had no clearly identified murder weapon, no forensic evidence of guilt, no compelling motive for murder, and no clear demonstration of opportunity. Still, authorities felt they had enough information to hold Lizzie over for trial.

Researching events prior to the murders, police learned that Abby Borden had approached Dr. Bowen early on August 3, complaining that she, Andrew, and Bridget Sullivan had been violently ill overnight. Andrew, for his part, denied any illness and refused to pay Bowen for an unsolicited house call. Later the same day, Lizzie had tried to purchase deadly prussic acid from a local pharmacy, allegedly to kill some household vermin, but clerk Eli Bence refused to sell it without a prescription. (Lizzie denied visiting the pharmacy on August 3, although two other witnesses placed her there.) Alice Russell spoke to Lizzie on the night of August 3 and found her agitated by some unspecified threat to Andrew Borden. John Morse left the Borden house around 8:45 A.M. on August 4, to visit friends across town. Andrew left on his business rounds 15 minutes later, returning home around 10:45 A.M. Despite Lizzie's tale of her stepmother being called away by a sick friend, Abby Borden never left the house and no note from the friend was found. (Lizzie later told police she might have inadvertently burned it.) Police determined that Abby was murdered around 9:30 A.M., with her husband killed sometime between 10:55 and 11:10.

Lizzie told detectives she had gone out to a barn behind the house when her father came home, to find some fishing sinkers. Bridget Sullivan, meanwhile, said she had gone upstairs for a rest at 10:55—without glimpsing Abby's corpse or any signs of violence. When police asked Lizzie if there were any hatchets in the house, she replied, "They are everywhere." A search of the basement revealed four hatchets, including one smeared with blood and hair (from a cow, it turned out) and another with no handle, its head covered with ash. Police believed the hatchet handle had been snapped off recently, selecting the charred head as their probable murder weapon. The autopsies on Andrew and Abby Borden were performed on their own dining table; both corpses still lying there at 7:00 P.M., when Emma Borden returned from an overnight visit

learning that Dr. Bowen was unavailable, Churchill sent a handyman to notify police and find another physician. Officers at Fall River's police station, situated some 400 yards from the Borden home, received word of Andrew's murder at 11:15 A.M. Still, Dr. Bowen arrived before the police and briefly examined Andrew's corpse. Bridget Sullivan returned around the same time, and Lizzie sent her upstairs to see if Abby Borden had returned from her morning excursion. Joined by Mrs. Churchill, Sullivan ascended to the second floor and found Abby sprawled on the floor of a guest room, hacked to death like her husband. (An autopsy report found 19 hatchet wounds—not 40—all delivered to the back of her head and neck.) By 11:45 A.M. police and Fall River's medical examiner, Dr. William Dolan, were on the scene and starting their investigation.

to Fairhaven. Bridget Sullivan spent the night with a neighbor, while Alice Russell slept in the Borden house with Lizzie, Emma, and John Morse. Sullivan returned for her belongings next morning and left the household again, never to return.

On Sunday, August 7, Russell observed Lizzie burning a dress in the kitchen stove. She remarked, "If I were, I wouldn't let anybody see me do that," whereupon Lizzie told her the dress was stained with paint beyond repair. Russell's description of the incident at a subsequent inquest prompted Judge Josiah Blaisdell to charge Lizzie with murder on August 11, 1892. She was formally arraigned the next day and entered a not-guilty plea. Lizzie did not testify at the preliminary hearing, convened on August 22, but her testimony from the inquest was placed in evidence by family attorney Andrew Jennings, whereupon Judge Blaisdell tearfully proclaimed her probable guilt and bound her over for a grand jury. That panel convened on November 7, 1892, and issued a curious three-count murder indictment against Lizzie on December 2. (She was charged with killing her father, her stepmother, and both of them together.)

Lizzie Borden's trial opened on June 5, 1893, and spanned the next two weeks. Prosecutor Moody's opening statement claimed that Lizzie was "predisposed" to kill her parents, that she planned the murder in advance, and that her subsequent contradictory statements were proof of guilt. In regard to motive, the state presented evidence that Andrew Borden had planned to draft a "new" will—the "old" one was never discovered—leaving all but $50,000 of his $500,000 estate to Abby. Introduction of Lizzie's inquest testimony was barred on a defense objection, as was testimony concerning her alleged attempts to buy poison on August 3, 1892. Defense attorneys called several witnesses to confirm the presence of an unidentified young man near the Borden home on August 4, and sister, Emma, testified that Lizzie had no motive to kill either victim. Closing arguments were delivered on June 19, and the all-male jury deliberated for 68 minutes before acquitting Lizzie on all counts.

Five weeks after the verdict, Lizzie and Emma purchased a large home—which they called Maplecroft—on The Hill, Fall River's most fashionable neighborhood. Lizzie Borden, henceforth known as "Lizbeth" at her own insistence, was charged in 1897 with stealing two paintings from a Fall River shop. The works were valued below $100, and the matter was settled out of court. In 1904 she met a young actress

named Nance O'Neil, and they became inseparable companions, prompting Emma to leave Maplecroft (and later Massachusetts). Lizzie died on June 1, 1927, following a long illness, and Emma followed her on June 10, tumbling down the back stairs of her home in Newmarket, New Hampshire. They were buried together in the family plot at Fall River, leaving their estates to charity.

Theories abound in this still-unsolved slaying from America's Gilded Age. The most prominent of them include:

1. *Lizzie did it.* Most reporters prior to World War II accepted some version of this theory, although their individual takes on the killings varied considerably. Edwin Porter (1893) settled for a dispassionate analysis of the known evidence. Only five copies of his book are known to exist, prompting (unsubstantiated) rumors that Lizzie Borden bought and burned the rest to keep them out of circulation. Some believers in Lizzie's guilt presume she plotted the death of both victims to reap her inheritance; others maintain that she despised her stepmother to the point of homicide and killed her father as an unlucky witness to the crime. Author Victoria Lincoln (1967) blames the slaughter on "spells" Lizzie allegedly suffered during her menstrual period—in effect, exonerating her on grounds of temporary insanity.

2. *Emma did it.* Author Frank Spiering (1984) fingered Emma Borden as the murderer, with sister, Lizzie, as her fainthearted accomplice. In this scenario Emma's trip to Fairhaven—some 15 miles from Fall River—was simply an alibi, granting her time to return in a buggy and commit the crimes, then flee once more and thus preserve her façade of innocence.

3. *Bridget Sullivan did it.* Author Edwin Radin (1961) hypothesized that the Borden's maid was driven mad by Abby forcing her to wash windows on the hottest day of the year. After killing Abby, Sullivan slew Andrew Borden to prevent him from disclosing an earlier argument about the window-cleaning assignment. A variant of this theory fingers Sullivan as Lizzie's lesbian lover, presumably enraged by Lizzie's suffering at the hands of her cruel stepmother. A compromise theory proposed by Gerald Gross (1963) casts Lizzie as the killer with Sullivan as her accomplice, smuggling the murder weapon and a

bloody dress out of the house on her various runs around town. (After a brief return to her native Ireland, Sullivan came back to the United States and settled in Montana, where she died in 1948.)

4. *William Borden did it.* The weakest case to date, proposed by Arnold Brown in 1992, blames the murders on a mentally retarded Fall River resident alleged to be Andrew Borden's illegitimate son. In this scenario the crimes were a product of mental imbalance, but the cover-up involved a conspiracy by the Borden sisters, John Morse, Dr. Bowen, and attorney Jennings to preserve Andrew's estate against possible future claims by son William.

Whatever the truth, the Borden case maintains a sturdy grip on the American consciousness. In Fall River Lizzie's former home on Second Street is now a bed-and-breakfast, with a small museum devoted to the case. Her final legacy is best summarized in another poem, written by A. L. Bixley and published during the 1892 murder trial.

> *There's no evidence of guilt,*
> *Lizzie Borden,*
> *That should make your spirit wilt,*
> *Lizzie Borden;*
> *Many do not think that you*
> *Chopped your father's head in two,*
> *It's so hard a thing to do,*
> *Lizzie Borden.*
>
> *You have borne up under all,*
> *Lizzie Borden.*
> *With a mighty show of gall,*
> *Lizzie Borden;*
> *But because your nerve is stout*
> *Does not prove beyond a doubt*
> *That you knocked the old folks out,*
> *Lizzie Borden.*

BORRERO, Robben See NEW YORK CITY GAY MURDERS (1973)

"BOSTON strangler" reopened serial murder case (1963–64)
Ten years before the term *serial killer* entered popular usage, Boston was terrorized by an elusive predator who raped and strangled women in their homes, slaying 11 between June 1962 and July 1964. In every case

the victims had been raped—sometimes with a foreign object—and their bodies laid out nude, as if on display for a pornographic snapshot. Death was always caused by strangulation, though the killer sometimes also used a knife. The ligature—a stocking, pillow case, whatever—was invariably left around the victim's neck, tied with an exaggerated, ornamental bow.

Anna Slessers, 55 years old, had been the first to die, strangled with the cord of her bathrobe on June 14, 1962. A nylon stocking was used to kill 68-year-old Nina Nichols on June 30, and 65-year-old Helen Blake was found the same day, with a stocking and bra knotted around her neck. On August 19, 75-year-old Ida Irga was manually strangled in her home, "decorated" with a knotted pillowcase. Sixty-seven-year-old Jane Sullivan had been dead a week when she was found on August 20, 1962, strangled with her own stockings, slumped over the edge of the bathtub with her face submerged.

The killer seemed to break his pattern on December 5, 1962, when he murdered Sophie Clark, a 20-year-old African American. Another shift was seen with 23-year-old Patricia Bissette, strangled on her bed and covered to her chin with a blanket, in place of the usual graphic display. With 23-year-old Beverly Samans, killed on May 6, 1963, the slayer used a knife for the first time, stabbing his victim 22 times before looping the traditional stocking around her neck. Evelyn Corbin, 58, seemed to restore the original pattern on September 8, 1963, strangled and violated in an "unnatural" assault, but the killer went back to young victims on November 23, strangling 23-year-old Joann Graff and leaving bite marks on her breast. The final victim, 19-year-old Mary Sullivan, was found on January 4, 1964, strangled with a scarf.

Ten months later, 33-year-old Albert Henry DeSalvo was detained for questioning in an unrelated case, suspected in a two-year series of rapes committed by a prowler called the Green Man, after the green work clothes he wore while assaulting victims in Massachusetts, Connecticut, and Rhode Island. In custody, DeSalvo confessed to those rapes and hundreds more, dating back to his molestation of a nine-year-old girl in 1955, while DeSalvo was a soldier stationed at Fort Dix, New Jersey. The marathon confession landed DeSalvo in Bridgewater State Hospital, committed for psychiatric evaluation, and there he met George Nasser, a convicted murderer facing trial for his second known slaying since 1948. Their private conversations were interspersed with visits from police, climaxed by DeSalvo's full confession to the Boston Strangler homicides.

In his statement, DeSalvo added two "new" victims, never previously linked by the authorities. One, 85-year-old Mary Mullen, was found dead at her home on June 28, 1962, her passing attributed to simple heart failure. DeSalvo claimed that Mullen had collapsed from shock when he invaded her apartment, whereupon he left her body on the couch without continuing his usual assault. Mary Brown, age 69, was stabbed and beaten to death at her home on March 9, 1963, again without a showing of the famous "strangler's knot."

It seemed like an open-and-shut case, but numerous problems remained. The strangler's sole surviving victim, assaulted in February 1963, could not pick DeSalvo out of a lineup. Neither could witnesses who glimpsed a suspect near the Graff and Sullivan murder scenes. Several detectives had focused their aim on another suspect, fingered by "psychic" Peter Hurkos, but their man had voluntarily committed himself to an asylum soon after the last murder. Finally, if DeSalvo was driven by a mother fixation, as psychiatrists claimed, why had he chosen young women (including one African American) as five of his last seven victims?

Some students of the case believe the answer may be found at Bridgewater, where killer George Nasser conferred with DeSalvo through long days and nights. It is possible, critics maintain, that Nasser may have been the strangler, briefing DeSalvo on the details of his crimes in hope of sending authorities off on a wild-goose chase. DeSalvo, already facing life imprisonment for countless rapes, admittedly struck a cash bargain with Nasser, whereby Nasser would pocket part of the outstanding reward for turning DeSalvo in, afterward passing most of the cash to DeSalvo's wife. As a clincher, the strangler's lone survivor favored Nasser as a suspect, rather than DeSalvo. Other theories postulate the existence of *two* Boston Stranglers, one each for the young and the elderly victims. Journalist Hank Messick added a new twist in the early 1970s, quoting Mafia hit man Vincent Barbosa (now deceased) to the effect that DeSalvo had been paid, presumably by organized crime, to "take a fall" for the actual, unidentified Boston Strangler.

Be that as it may, DeSalvo never went to trial for murder in Boston. Lawyer F. Lee Bailey managed to negotiate a deal in 1967, whereby DeSalvo drew a term of life imprisonment for crimes committed as the Green Man. Never formally charged with the Boston stranglings, DeSalvo was stabbed to death by a fellow inmate at Walpole Prison in November 1973.

And there the matter rested . . . for a while.

More than a quarter century after DeSalvo's murder in prison, forensic scientists revisited the Boston Strangler case in an effort to determine whether or not DeSalvo committed the murders to which he confessed. His body was exhumed in October 2001, for extraction of DNA material unknown to pathologists at the time of the original murders. The material was slated for comparison with evidence collected in the case of 19-year-old Mary Sullivan, the strangler's last victim, found dead on January 4, 1964.

Announcements of "new evidence" in the Boston case were made on December 6, 2001, with James Starrs—a professor of law and forensic science at George Washington University—promising "blockbuster results." Another GWU spokesman, Paul Fucito, said of the DNA findings: "Whether they announce one way or another whether [DeSalvo] did it or not, I think that will be a fairly conclusive announcement." He added that the DNA report would "be revealing enough that it will give the Boston authorities the incentive to look at their evidence and their findings and maybe compare notes and maybe bring the investigation forward."

In fact, by December 2001, neither DeSalvo's family nor Mary Sullivan's believed DeSalvo was the Boston Strangler. That opinion was apparently supported on December 6 by reports that Prof. Starrs's "All-Star Forensic Science Team" had discovered foreign DNA from *two* individuals on Sullivan's body and clothing, neither of the samples linked to DeSalvo. As Prof. Starrs told the press, "It's indicative, strongly indicative, of the fact that Albert DeSalvo was not the rape-murderer of Mary Sullivan. If I was a juror, I would acquit him with no questions asked." Sullivan's nephew, Casey Sherman, had an even more emphatic statement for the press. "If he didn't kill Mary Sullivan, yet he confessed to it in glaring detail, he didn't kill any of these women."

Retired Massachusetts prosecutor Julian Soshnick disagreed, retorting, "It doesn't prove anything except that they found another person's DNA on a part of Miss Sullivan's body." Seeming to ignore that neither donor was DeSalvo, Soshnick stood firm: "I believe that Albert was the Boston Strangler." Another retired investigator, former Boston homicide detective Jack Barry, stood firm on DeSalvo's detailed confessions. "He just knew so much," Barry said, "things that were never in the paper. He could describe the wallpaper in their rooms." Dr. Ames Robey, Bridgewater's supervisor in the 1960s and the chief psychiatrist who evaluated DeSalvo, found the confessions less persuasive. "He was a boaster," Dr. Robey told reporters. "I never believed it for a minute."

In any case, the DNA discovery still stopped short of solving Boston's most famous murder case. Prof. Starrs believes at least one of the DNA samples recovered from Sullivan's body belongs to her killer, but as he admitted in December 2001, "We cannot tell you the $64,000 question as to whose it is." Casey Sherman, a nephew of victim Mary Sullivan, announced his plan to crack the case in August 2002.

In 2003, Boston telejournalist Casey Sherman published a book dissecting evidence in the 1964 slaying of victim Mary Sullivan (Sherman's aunt). Collaborating with members of the DeSalvo family, Sherman revealed discrepancies in DeSalvo's confession to the Sullivan slaying and secured DNA test results that cleared DeSalvo of that crime, at least. Sherman's series on the case, aired by WBZ-TV in Boston, earned him an Emmy nomination, but no new charges have been filed to date and the Boston Strangler case remains hauntingly unsolved.

BOTELHO, Sandra   See NEW BEDFORD, MASSACHUSETTS, MURDERS

BOTHELL, Washington unsolved murders (1995–97)

King County, Washington, has long been infamous as the hunting ground of the elusive "Green River Killer," but it seems that elusive predator (finally identified in 2001, some 17 years after his last-known murder) may not be the region's only serial killer. In February 1998 multiple human remains were unearthed near Bothell, a Seattle suburb, apparently unrelated to the Green River slayings of 1982–84. Captain Bob Woolvert, of the Bothell Police Department, told reporters on February 12, 1998, that there was a "strong indication" of at least two corpses buried at the site. While declining to furnish much detail on the remains, initial reports state that one of the fragmentary skeletons belonged to a person below the age of 20, apparently dead for less than three years.

A team of 70 investigators, including police detectives, lab technicians from the King County Medical Examiner's office, and volunteer search-and-rescue workers, labored in pouring rain to seek more remains of the unidentified victims. Bothell police chief Mark Ericks told the press, "This is as bad as it could get. The rain and mud is horrible, and it's making our job harder and harder. We could use 30 more people to help." Authorities from both King and Snohomish Counties were represented in the dig, concerned that the skeletons might represent new victims for one or another of the area's unidentified serial killers.

According to media reports, the first set of bones was found by a transient on Tuesday, February 10, 1998, lying atop straw that was scattered over a newly graded construction site. Police were notified and commenced to dig at the scene, suggesting to reporters that the first bones had been unearthed and scattered by animals. At this writing the victims remain unidentified, and no further corpses have been found.

BOWKER, Sarah Jane   See FORT WAYNE CHILD MURDERS

BOYD, Alexander assassination victim (1870)

A native of South Carolina, raised in Greene County, Alabama, Alexander Boyd was 19 years old in 1856, when he killed a young man named Brown in a personal quarrel. Convicted of second-degree murder at trial, he received a 10-year prison term, but Alabama's governor reviewed the case on a plea for executive clemency and reduced Boyd's sentence to one year in county jail. Upon release, Boyd left Alabama for Arkansas, remaining away from his childhood home until the latter part of 1867.

By the time he returned to his hometown of Eutaw, Alabama was a defeated member of the Confederate States of America, its former white ruling class seething in the grip of congressional Reconstruction. Boyd joined the then-dominant Republican Party and despite his criminal record won election as Greene County's solicitor. His duties included prosecution of violent felons, and there was no shortage of suspects in those days, as the terrorist Ku Klux Klan waged brutal guerrilla warfare against black freedmen and their Republican benefactors. Boyd soon earned a reputation as a vigorous prosecutor and enemy of the KKK, securing indictments against several night riders who had flogged blacks after a political meeting at nearby Union, Alabama. At the same time, he also pressed an investigation into the lynching of one Samuel Colvin, a black man taken from Eutaw's jail by Klansmen and killed on an accusation of murder.

A reign of terror against blacks and Republicans, including the murder of Alexander Boyd, inspired this view of the South during Reconstruction. (Florida State Archives)

Shortly after 11:00 P.M. on March 31, 1870, a party of 20 to 30 masked men invaded the Eutaw tavern where Boyd rented rooms, bursting into his flat and dragging Boyd from bed, firing two point-blank pistol shots into his forehead. Reports of the Thursday night murder brought several hundred armed and outraged freedmen into Eutaw on Saturday, April 2, calling for retaliation against the night riders. One member of that mob spoke for all when he complained that local Confederates "have never surrendered yet, and the only way to stop this is to burn them out." A store in Eutaw, owned by a prominent white Democrat, was burned a few days after Boyd's murder, and several barns were also reportedly torched over the next month.

Lieutenant Charles Harkins, commanding a U.S. 2nd Infantry detachment sent to restore order in Greene County, reported his findings on April 13, 1870. "Civil affairs are in a very disturbed and agitated condition," Harkins wrote. "Seven murders have been committed in this county within the past three months, and but little effort made to arrest and bring to justice the perpetrators of these crimes; the civil officers seem powerless to restore and maintain law and order." Troops on the scene made no great improvement, and the terrorism continued until Alabama threw off control by "carpet-

bag" Republicans. No suspects were ever indicted for Boyd's murder.

"BOY in the Box" Philadelphia murder (1957)

Philadelphia's most enduring mystery began on the evening of February 23, 1957, when a La Salle College student parked his car off Susquehanna Road, in the Fox Chase district, and began to hike across a vacant lot in drizzling rain. The young man—various reports peg his age between 18 and 26 years—was an habitual voyeur, en route to spy on inmates of the nearby Good Shepherd Home, a Catholic residence for "wayward" girls. Instead of getting lucky, though, he stumbled on a cardboard box, observed the small corpse wedged inside, and retreated swiftly to his vehicle. Frightened and embarrassed, the man confessed his discovery to a priest on February 24 and was told to call the police. He complied the next day, after concocting a tale that he had found the box while chasing a rabbit through the weeds.

Patrolmen arriving on the scene found a large cardboard carton lying on its side and open at one end. Inside lay the body of a small Caucasian boy, his nude body wrapped in two segments of a cheap blanket printed with designs reminiscent of American Indian artwork. Seventeen feet from the box, police found a man's Ivy League cap, size seven and one-eighth, made from royal blue corduroy with a leather strap and buckle at the back. Coincidentally or otherwise, a beaten path through weeds and underbrush led directly from the cap to the makeshift cardboard coffin.

Philadelphia's medical examiner, Dr. Joseph Spelman, performed an autopsy on the young victim. His report pegged the boy's age between four and six years; he had blue eyes and blond hair cut in an amateurish style. The boy was 41 inches tall and weighed a pathetic 30 pounds at death. Malnourishment was evident, but Dr. Spelman blamed the child's death on a savage beating that left his face and body mottled with fresh bruises. Older marks included a small L-shaped scar on the boy's chin; a 1.5-inch surgical scar on the left side of his chest; a round, irregular scar on the left elbow; a well-healed scar at the groin, apparently from surgery to mend a hernia; and a scar on the left ankle resembling a "cut-down" incision used to expose veins for a medical infusion or transfusion. The boy was circumcised but bore no vaccination marks, suggesting that he had not been enrolled in public school.

Dr. Spelman's report contained other intriguing details, as well. The victim's right palm and the soles of both feet were rough and wrinkled, presenting the "washerwoman" effect that indicates extended submersion in water, immediately before or after death. When exposed to ultraviolet light, the boy's left eye also fluoresced a brilliant shade of blue, indicating recent treatment with a special diagnostic dye used in treatment of chronic ocular diseases. Spelman attributed death to head trauma, probably inflicted with a blunt instrument, but he could not rule out damage by "pressure"—a circumstance that prompted some investigators to suggest the fatal damage was inflicted by someone squeezing his head when he got his last haircut. Detectives clothed the child and photographed his battered face, in hopes that they could thereby learn his name.

Their hope was sadly premature.

Investigators learned that their victim's makeshift casket had originally held a bassinet sold by a JC Penney store. The bassinet in question was one of a dozen received on November 27, 1956, and sold for $7.50 sometime between December 3, 1956, and February 16, 1957, from a Penney outlet in Upper Darby, Pennsylvania, perhaps as recently as a week before the boy died. The store kept no records of individual sales, but the other 11 bassinets were eventually located by detectives. FBI fingerprint technicians found no useful latent prints on the carton recovered from Susquehanna Road.

Examination of the blanket proved equally frustrating. The blanket was made of cheap cotton flannel, recently washed and mended with poor-grade cotton thread. It had been cut in half, one section measuring 33 by 76 inches, while the other (with a piece missing) measured 31 by 51 inches. Analysis at the Philadelphia Textile Institute determined that the blanket had been manufactured either at Swannanoa, North Carolina, or at Granby, Quebec. Unfortunately, it was turned out by the thousands and police never identified a likely point of sale.

A label inside the discarded cap led police to Philadelphia's Robbins Bald Eagle Hat & Cap Company, where proprietor Hannah Robbins described it as one of 12 made from corduroy remnants sometime prior to May 1956. Robbins recalled the particular cap because it was made without a leather strap, but its purchaser—a blond man in his late twenties—had returned a few months later to have a strap sewn on. Robbins described her customer as resembling photo-

graphs of the "Boy in the Box," but she had no record of his name or address.

Philadelphia police circulated more than 10,000 flyers, bearing the child's photograph, to police departments throughout eastern Pennsylvania and southern New Jersey, all without result. The Philadelphia Gas Works mailed 200,000 flyers to its customers with their monthly bills, while more were circulated by the Philadelphia Electric Company, grocery stores, insurance agents, and a pharmacists' association—some 300,000 flyers in all. An article on the case was also published in the FBI's monthly *Law Enforcement Bulletin*, again without producing any worthwhile leads. Five months after the boy was found, authorities buried him in Philadelphia's potter's field, near the Byberry state hospital. Detectives on the case collected money to erect the seedy graveyard's only headstone. Its inscription: "Heavenly Father, Bless This Unknown Boy."

There the matter rested until November 4, 1998, when the "Boy in the Box" was exhumed for extraction of DNA samples, collected for future comparison with any suspected relatives. A year elapsed before authorities admitted that no satisfactory DNA profile could be obtained from the child's degraded remains. An attempt to glean mitochondrial DNA from the core of the boy's teeth likewise failed in February 2000, but a second attempt was reported as successful in April 2001. Granted, discovery of living relatives at this point seems unlikely in the extreme, but various investigators remain cautiously hopeful. Frank Bender, a forensic artist and active member of the VIDOCQ SOCIETY, sculpted a bust which he believes may bear a strong resemblance to the dead boy's father. *America's Most Wanted* profiled the case for a national television audience on January 16, 1999, and efforts to identify the child continue, albeit with decreasing energy as each new day brings other cases forward to command police attention.

In June 2002 Philadelphia homicide investigator Tom Augustine visited Cincinnati with a pair of Vidocq Society members, there to interview a woman who claimed knowledge of the case. The alleged witness, never publicly identified, called the dead boy "Jonathan," claiming that she had lived with him in the affluent Philadelphia suburb of Lower Merion. She described Jonathan as mentally handicapped, reporting that he was fatally injured after he vomited in the bathtub and an abusive, enraged female caretaker hurled him to the bathroom floor. The incident allegedly climaxed a life of brutal physical and sexual abuse, with Jonathan forced to live in a cellar and sleep in an old refrigerator box. According to the witness, Jonathan's biological parents had sold him to his killer and her husband, some two years before he died. As of press time for this volume, none of the reported information has been verified by police.

BRACEWELL, Brooks See TEXAS TRI-COUNTY MURDERS (1971–75)

BRADSHAW, Hazel See SAN DIEGO MURDERS (1931–36)

BRAUN, Donna See "OCCULT MURDERS"

BRAZEAU, Pauline See "HIGHWAY KILLER"

BRAZELL, Rashawn murder victim (2005)
An African-American resident of Brooklyn, New York, born in April 1985, Rashawn Brazell was a popular college student whose murder ranks among New York City's most gruesome unsolved crimes. The case began on February 14, 2005, when Brazell missed an appointment with his personal accountant and a lunch date with his mother in Manhattan. Relatives reported him missing, but the police response was sluggish, since Brazell was a legal adult and an acknowledged homosexual, once arrested for possession of marijuana.

At 3:00 A.M. on February 17, city transit workers found two suspicious bags beside subway tracks at Brooklyn's Nostrand Avenue station. Persistent fear of terrorist attacks prompted a closer look, revealing that one bag—a black plastic trash bag with a blue trash bag inside it—contained the dismembered remains of a young black male. The second bag—beige and black, with wheels and a "Rooster" logo on one side—contained bloody drill bits and other tools. More body parts surfaced on February 23, at New York City's Humboldt Street recycling plant. Still more remains were found at the recycling plant on February 24. In both cases, the body parts were double-bagged, in blue and black plastic.

Pathologists reported that the corpse was carefully dismembered, each joint cut with some unknown sharp instrument, before dismemberment was com-

pleted with an electric chainsaw. No cause of death was determined, despite a stab wound on one side of the torso, since the head remains missing, but fingerprints identified the victim as Rashawn Brazell. New York's medical examiner opined that Brazell was alive for two days between his disappearance and his murder.

Investigation revealed that a still-unknown person rang the buzzer at Brazell's apartment at 7:30 A.M. on February 14, drawing him downstairs. Witnesses saw Brazell meet a man outside his apartment house, then enter the Gates Avenue J line subway station with his unidentified companion. Other witnesses claimed sightings of the two men exiting the Nostrand Avenue A line station in the Bedford-Stuyvesant neighborhood. Detectives learned that the "Rooster" bag found on February 17 was one of only 15 made as prototypes and sold exclusively to the Metropolitan Transportation Authority in 2001—but there, the trail ended.

Many mainstream media outlets ignored Brazell's story at first, prompting black activists and Internet bloggers to charge that reporters automatically dismiss attacks on working-class African Americans. The TV show *America's Most Wanted* subsequently profiled Brazell's case on September 24, 2005, on April 1, 2006, December 9, 2006, December 22, 2007, and August 16, 2008, but no new leads emerged.

While acknowledging Brazell's gay lifestyle, detectives found no evidence that his slaying was a hate crime. Likewise, despite one drug arrest, nothing linked Brazell to any other form of criminal activity. He worked four jobs, had tried his hand at fashion modeling, and hoped to become a professional Web page designer. Nothing, in short, suggested why Brazell was killed.

Police suspect his slayer may have been a transit worker, both from access to the limited-edition "Rooster" bag and because of where the first batch of remains was found. NYPD detective Anthony Baker told *America's Most Wanted*, "The killer or killers knew the layout. These tracks are two flights down, which leads me to believe they had some knowledge of the tracks, because nobody really goes to the unknown to dispose of something like that unless they have been there before." Retired detective Ray Pierce speculated that Brazell's slayer might be an unrecognized serial killer, saying, "He's had a violent history in the past and this is culminated in this homicide and perhaps other homicides." Thus far, no suspects have been named.

BRESCIANO, Adolfo murder victim (1993)

An Italian native, born in August 1949, Bresciano emigrated to Canada and began wrestling professionally in 1970. He adopted the ring name "Dino Bravo" from an early 1960s wrestler who had teamed with partner Dominic DeNucci as "the Bravo brothers." Bresciano learned the grappling trade from mentor Gino Brito, who also worked as Bresciano's tag team partner and billed "Bravo" as his cousin. When that team broke up, Bresciano partnered first with Tim "Mr. Wrestling" Woods, then with Dominic DeNucci himself. Together, Bresciano and DeNucci won the World Wide Wrestling Federation's World Tag Team Championship.

By the late 1970s, "Bravo" was popular enough with fans to do a solo wrestling act, advertised on various occasions as "Canada's strongest man." In December 1978 he beat Gene Kiniski in Toronto to win Canada's heavyweight wrestling title. In the early 1980s, Bresciano joined Vince McMahon's World Wrestling Federation (WWF), briefly teamed with "King Tonga" Fifiti, then resumed solo wrestling. He quit the WWF in 1986, after federation officials canceled a Montreal match against Terry "Hulk" Hogan—allegedly worried that Canadians would cheer their native favorite over the WWF's reigning champion.

Bresciano's rift with the WWF was short-lived, and he returned to the fold with bleached hair in 1987, as part of the "Dream Team" managed by ex-wrestler John Sullivan (a.k.a. "Luscious Johnny Valiant"). Bresciano replaced Edward "Brutus Beefcake" Leslie in Sullivan's stable, with others including Greg "The Hammer" Valentine, Tito Santana, and Sylvester "Junkyard Dog" Ritter. In 1988, Bresciano once again resumed his solo career and his strongman shtick, billing himself as "the world's strongest man." Cast as a villain, who entered the ring bearing a sign that read "USA is Not OK," Bresciano gravitated to manager Jimmy Hart's stable and subsequently teamed with John "Earthquake" Tenta for tag team matches.

On March 24, 1991, at Wrestlemania VII in Los Angeles, Bresciano lost a match to Kerry Von Erich, then vanished from the WWF for several months. He resurfaced in Canada, as a mock-heroic "babyface" wrestler matched against Jacques "The Mountie" Rougeau, then retired from wrestling in April 1992, after a tour of Britain. Bresciano's new career as a wrestling trainer in Montreal was cut short on March 11, 1993, when police found him shot to death at his home in the Vimont section of Laval, Québec.

That crime remains unsolved today, despite intense police investigation. Rumors persist that Bresciano had become involved in a cigarette-smuggling ring linked to organized crime, but no evidence proving that connection ever surfaced.

BREST, Belarus taxicab murders (1996–97)

Taxi drivers in Brest, near the Belarussian border with Poland, were terrorized in the winter of 1996–97 by a serial killer blamed for the murders of three cabbies and a gas station attendant over four months' time. After the final slaying, reported in January 1997, angry drivers staged a protest demonstration, surrounding the latest murder scene with their taxis and honking their horns nonstop for half an hour. Despite the public outcry, police at last report still had no suspect in the murders, and the case remains unsolved.

BREWER, Theresa See SAN DIEGO MURDERS (1985–88)

BRIDGEWATER, Carl murder victim (1978)

Carl Bridgewater was a British newspaper delivery boy, shot to death at age 13 on September 19, 1978, while delivering a paper to an isolated farmhouse at Yew Tree Farm, three miles northwest of Stourbridge, in Staffordshire, England. The fatal shot was fired into his head at point-blank range when Bridgewater apparently surprised burglars ransacking the house. The home's elderly owners were off on vacation, but a family friend found Bridgewater's corpse at 5:30 P.M., less than an hour after he was killed.

Fifty detectives were assigned to the case, which shocked British civilians and hardened policemen alike. Detective Chief Superintendent Bob Stewart, commanding the investigation, suggested that Bridgewater was killed because he recognized one or more of the thieves, adding, "Every police officer on this inquiry is appalled by the viciousness of this unmerciful killing." Bridgewater's slayers had dragged him into the home's sitting room before shooting him. Police announced their interest in tracing a blue estate car seen near the crime scene around the same time.

Suspicion ultimately focused on four suspects who became known as "the Bridgewater Four": Michael Hickey, his cousin Vincent Hickey, Patrick Molloy, and Jim Robinson. Detectives claimed that "members of the criminal fraternity" broke their traditional code of silence to finger the killers, but all four suspects initially denied the charges. Fifty-year-old Pat Molloy later changed his story and confessed to burglarizing Yew Tree Farm, but denied any part in Bridgewater's slaying. Molloy claimed that he was upstairs, heard a "bang," and descended to find Bridgewater dead in the sitting room. Apparently, the boy had entered through an unlocked door and caught the burglars red-handed. Jim Robinson allegedly told Molloy that his pistol "went off accidentally."

At trial, in 1979, the judge praised "thorough" detective work for capturing Bridgewater's slayers, but Molloy's confession remained the only substantial prosecution evidence. On November 9, jurors convicted all four defendants. Robinson and the Hickeys were found guilty of murder and aggravated burglary. Robinson and 25-year-old Vincent Hickey received life prison terms with 25-year minimums, while 17-year-old Michael Hickey was sentenced to detention "at Her Majesty's pleasure." Molloy, thanks to his confession, was convicted on a lesser count of manslaughter and received a 12-year-prison term. He died in prison, from a heart attack, in 1991.

Meanwhile, the surviving "Bridgewater Three" continued to insist that they were innocent of any crime. Three legal appeals and six separate police inquiries climaxed on February 21, 1997, when Robinson and the Hickeys were exonerated and released from custody. Defense attorneys proved, by means of electrostatic document analysis, that four Staffordshire policemen forged Vincent Hickey's signature on a false confession, then showed that spurious statement to Pat Molloy, who confessed in turn to escape a life sentence. Hickey's "confession" was not introduced at trial, and Crown attorneys reluctantly admitted that Molloy's confession should have been suppressed at trial. The guilty officers were threatened with trial for falsifying evidence, but that case was dropped in December 1998 and they remain unpunished for their crime.

Likewise, prosecutors dropped their plan to pursue unrelated armed robbery charges against Vincent Hickey, held pending since his murder conviction. "My conviction has been quashed," Hickey told reporters, "so I am absolved and as far as I'm concerned that's the end of it." Jim Robinson died of lung cancer on September 1, 2007. The true slayer (or slayers) of Charles Bridgewater remains unidentified.

BRITISH child murders (1978–84)

On April 21, 1986, detectives from Scotland Yard held a conference to examine evidence and discuss possible links in the deaths and disappearances of 16 British minors in the past eight years. The victims ranged in age from five to 16 years, with officers reporting that at least seven cases seemed connected through a close proximity to fairs and circuses. In several other cases links were theorized for the homicides and nearby streams or lakes habitually frequented by anglers.

Three of the murders under consideration—those of 11-year-old Susan Maxwell, five-year-old Caroline Hogg, and 10-year-old Sarah Harper—were ultimately solved with the conviction of a predatory pedophile. That defendant, however, was cleared in the remaining 13 cases on Scotland Yard's list. Those victims include: Genette Tate, 13, missing from Ayelsbeare, in Devon, since August 19, 1978; Sean McGaun, 15, murdered on April 7, 1979; 15-year-old Marion Crofts, murdered at Fleet, in Hampshire, on June 9, 1981; eight-year-old Vishal Mehrota, slain in Putney, West London, on July 29, 1981; Jason Swift, 14, murdered at Hackney, East London, on July 11, 1983; nine-year-old Imnan Voha, killed the same day as Jason Swift, at Preston, in Lancashire; Collette Aram, 16, murdered at Keyworth, in Nottinghamshire, on October 30, 1983; 15-year-old Lynda Mann, killed at Narborogh, Leicestershire, on November 21, 1983; nine-year-old Chris Laverack, murdered in Hull on March 9, 1984; Mark Teldesley, seven, missing from Workingham, Berkshire, since June 1, 1984; and six-year-old Barry Lewis, murdered at Walworth, South London, on September 15, 1984.

To date, despite interrogation of numerous suspects and pursuit of countless futile leads, the homicides and disappearances remain unsolved. Police can only speculate on how many of the crimes may be the work of a single, elusive killer, but in any case—one slayer or many—the nightmare of grieving parents endures.

BROOKLYN, New York unsolved murders (1989)

Murders are so common in New York City that they often receive short shrift in the local press. Many slayings are ignored completely by the august *New York Times*, while others rate a mention in the tabloids only if they are particularly gruesome or the victims are celebrities. One such case, briefly mentioned in passing by New York reporters and then forgotten, involved a series of home invasions during 1989.

On July 22, 1989, spokesmen for the New York City Police Department published a sketch of an unidentified black male, suspected in a series of daylight robberies reported from Brooklyn's Parkville district. The unnamed victims were all senior citizens, apparently followed home by a lurking predator who then forced his way inside their apartments, beating and terrorizing his prey before he looted their homes. Two female victims died from their injuries, on July 9 and 14, before police made their announcement and published the sketch. The most recent robbery in the series had been reported on July 17. Judging by the stony silence since that first press conference, it appears that New York's finest never caught the man responsible.

BROOKS, Virginia See SAN DIEGO MURDERS (1931–36)

BROSSO, Angela murder victim (1992)

Angela Brosso was one day short of her 22nd birthday on November 8, 1992, when she left her apartment in northwest Phoenix, Arizona, for a nocturnal bike ride through nearby Cave Creek Park. The ride was a nightly routine, never previously interrupted, but this time Brosso did not return. The next day her headless corpse was found on a bike trail near Cactus Road and Interstate Highway 17, disemboweled by a ragged slash that opened her chest and abdomen. Brosso's severed head was found on November 20, in the Arizona Canal. Her purple 21-speed Diamondback racing bicycle remains missing to this day.

Authorities believe Brosso's murder to be the work of a still-unidentified serial killer. Ten months after her slaying, in September 1993, 17-year-old Melanie Bernas was ambushed and murdered in Phoenix, her body dragged from the Arizona Canal near the spot where Brosso's head had been found. Bernas suffered no mutilations, but her green SPC Hardrock Sport mountain bike was missing from the scene and has not been found to date. A discarded turquoise bodysuit lay nearby, described by police as a clue to the murder. In March 1994 DNA testing of unspecified "biological evidence" found on both corpses linked a single unknown slayer to both crimes. The fugitive's DNA profile has been entered into a national database, waiting to snare him if he is tested for any reason in the future. Until that day, the Phoenix homicides remain hauntingly unsolved.

BROWN, Ben murder victim (1868)

Political activity was perilous for an African American in the South during Reconstruction (1865–77), when white Democrats (or "Conservatives") joined forces with the terrorist Ku Klux Klan and similar groups to overthrow Republican rule in the wake of the Civil War. Ben Brown, a former slave, faced greater risks than most when he assumed the presidency of the Republican Grant and Colfax Club in Sumter County, Alabama. Pledged to the election of Republican presidential candidate Ulysses Grant and running mate Schuyler Colfax, the club was a lightning rod for threats and violence in a district largely controlled by the KKK.

Brown was warned repeatedly by local whites to cease and desist holding black political meetings in Sumter County. By late September 1868 he was virtually besieged, dwelling on the plantation owned by a white Republican, Dr. Gerard Choutteau (himself a target of numerous threats and assaults). On the night of October 2, 1868, a band of 25 to 30 terrorists raided Brown's home and shot him to death. County authorities declined to investigate the crime, and no suspects were ever publicly identified. Nocturnal raiders subsequently returned and set fire to Dr. Choutteau's home, another crime that remained forever unpunished.

BROWN, Carline See RAWLINS, WYOMING, RODEO MURDERS

BROWN, Vivian See GOOD SAMARITAN HOSPITAL MURDERS

BUFFALO, New York taxi murders (1980)

In October 1980 residents of Buffalo, New York, were stunned by the grisly murders of two black taxi drivers on successive nights, details of the crime suggesting human sacrifice or worse. The first victim, 71-year-old Parker Edwards, was found in the trunk of his cab on October 8, his skull crushed with a blunt instrument, his heart cut out and missing from the murder scene. One day later 40-year-old Ernest Jones was found beside the Niagara River in Tonawanda, New York, likewise bludgeoned to death, with his heart carved from his chest. Jones's blood-spattered taxi was retrieved by police in Buffalo, three miles from the site where his body was found. After the second slaying,

Erie County district attorney Edward Cosgrove told reporters, "This is the most bizarre thing I have ever seen in my life. Any word I reach for to describe it is inadequate."

Worse yet, from the standpoint of racial harmony, four other Buffalo blacks had been killed in the past 18 days, all gunned down with the same .22-caliber weapon. Then, barely 24 hours after the murder of Ernest Jones, 37-year-old Colin Cole was assaulted in his Buffalo hospital room by a white man who told him, "I hate niggers." A nurse's arrival saved Cole from death by strangulation, but he sustained severe injuries to his neck. Descriptions of the would-be strangler roughly matched eyewitness reports of Buffalo's elusive ".22-caliber killer."

Some authorities believed the mystery was solved three months later, with the arrest of army private Joseph Christopher at Fort Benning, Georgia, charged with stabbing a black fellow soldier. A search of Christopher's former residence, near Buffalo, revealed quantities of .22-caliber ammunition, a gun barrel, and two sawed-off rifle stocks. Police also learned that Christopher had joined the army on November 13, 1980, arriving at Fort Benning six days later. He was absent without leave from December 19, 1980, through January 4, 1981, with a bus ticket recording his arrival in Manhattan on December 20—just two days before five blacks and one Hispanic victim were stabbed there, four victims fatally, in random street attacks.

Hospitalized following a suicide attempt on May 6, 1981, Christopher bragged to a nurse of his involvement in the September shootings around Buffalo. Four days later, he was charged with three of the ".22-caliber" slayings, a fourth murder charge added to the list on June 29, 1981, plus further counts related to nonfatal Buffalo stabbings in December 1980 and January 1981. In New York City indictments were returned in two of the December 1980 stabbings.

Joseph Christopher was ruled incompetent for trial in December 1981, but that verdict was reversed four months later. On April 27, 1982, after 12 days of testimony, Christopher was convicted on three counts of first-degree murder in Buffalo, drawing a prison term of 60 years to life. Seventeen months later, in September 1983, he sat for an interview with Buffalo reporters, boasting that his murder spree had claimed a minimum of 13 lives. Journalists noted that he "did not deny" the Jones-Edwards "heart murders" of October 1980, but neither did he confess to the crimes, and no charges were filed in those cases. Christopher's Buffalo conviction was overturned in July 1985 on grounds that the judge improperly barred testimony pointing toward mental incompetence. Three months later, in Manhattan, a jury rejected Christopher's insanity plea, convicting him on one count of murder and another of attempted murder. The murders of Parker Edwards and Ernest Jones remain officially unsolved.

BUGAY, Angela   See BAY AREA CHILD MURDERS

BULL, Gerald Victor murder victim (1990)
An American citizen born at North Bay, Ontario, in 1928, Gerald Bull suffered a loveless childhood, raised by an aunt after his mother died and his father left for parts unknown. Still, he excelled in school and was rated a virtual genius, earning his Ph.D. from the University of Toronto at age 23. By that time, he was already obsessed with the idea of building giant guns that could propel satellites into outer space, a vision fueled in equal parts by childhood readings of Jules Verne and study of the giant field guns used by Germany to bombard Paris during World War I.

Bull took the first step toward realizing his vision when he joined the Canadian Armament and Research Development Establishment (CARDE), involved throughout the 1950s with problems of supersonic aerodynamics for aircraft and missiles. Supersonic wind tunnels were expensive to build, so Bull devised an alternative method of testing: In lieu of constructing vast tunnels, he proposed using cannon to fire models down a test range at supersonic speed. The early tests were successful, and at age 31 Bull was promoted to lead CARDE's aerophysics department. A loathing for bureaucratic red tape drove Bull to a series of unapproved media interviews, which in turn alienated his superiors, and he was dismissed from CARDE two years later, in 1961.

Briefly adrift in private life, Bull soon found support from the Pentagon, the CIA, and the Canadian Defense Department for a new experimental program dubbed Project HARP (High-Altitude Research Program), created to study large guns and high-altitude ballistics. Initial testing was done in subterranean tunnels, on land Bull purchased along the Vermont-Quebec border. Free-flight tests were later conducted on the island of Barbados, where giant projectiles were lobbed over the Atlantic, peaking at an altitude of 108 miles.

Diversion of military funds for the ongoing Vietnam War doomed Bull's project and once again left him without official sponsors. Before the bitter end, Bull transferred HARP's assets to his own company—Space Research Corporation (SRC)—operating from an 8,000-acre spread in rural Vermont. By the 1970s CIA contacts had placed Bull in touch with government representatives from South Africa, China, and Iraq, but those connections ultimately landed Bull in jail. American relations with South Africa's racist apartheid regime were severed in the latter 1970s, and U.S. corporations were banned from doing business with Johannesburg. Bull ignored the restrictions until he was arrested for smuggling 30,000 artillery shells to South Africa via the West Indies. A guilty plea on that charge brought Bull a six-month jail term, despite a federal prosecutor's recommendation that Bull serve no time in custody. The conviction left Bull bankrupt and desperate. Upon release from prison, he moved to Brussels, seeking any clients who would keep his dream afloat financially.

By 1981 Bull had a new deal with Iraq, by then immersed in a marathon war with neighboring Iran. Rumors persist that Bull met personally with Saddam Hussein, then a favorite client of the Pentagon and Reagan-Bush White House for his opposition to Iran. According to journalist David Silverberg, Hussein was so taken with Bull's presentation that he "downed a bottle of Johnnie Walker Red and called up his cronies in the middle of the night, insisting that they rush right over to hear Bull." Be that as it may, Bull soon found himself at the helm of Project Babylon, designing a "supergun" for Iraq that would sport a 120-meter barrel and tip the scales around 4.2 million pounds. A model of the giant weapon was displayed in May 1989 at the Baghdad International Exhibition for Military Production. On the side, Bull also helped Iraq design a multistage missile that would have permitted long-range strikes against Hussein's enemies.

At 6:20 P.M. on March 22, 1990, as Bull paused to unlock the door of his sixth-floor apartment in Brussels, an unknown assassin shot him three times in the back with a silencer-equipped pistol. Bull collapsed to the floor, where two more shots were fired into the back of his head at close range. Killed instantly, he lay bleeding on the floor for 20 minutes before police arrived. Bull's briefcase lay untouched nearby, containing various papers, financial documents, and close to $20,000 in cash. Within days of the murder, Saddam Hussein declared in a speech from Baghdad, "A Canadian citizen with U.S. nationality came to Iraq. He might have benefited Iraq. I don't know. They say

the Iraq intelligence service is spread over Europe, but nobody spoke of human rights of the Canadian citizen of U.S. nationality. After he came to Iraq, they killed him."

Israel was the immediate prime suspect in Bull's murder, committed to retarding weapons-development programs in Iraq and other hostile Arab states. Alternative scenarios blame the Iranian government (known enemies of Iraq), British intelligence, and the CIA. The British theory, advanced by journalist Walter De Bock in 1998, claims that Prime Minister Margaret Thatcher ordered Bull's murder because he was taking lucrative Iraqi arms contracts away from British firms. (As support for his claim, De Bock noted that reporter Jonathan Moyle was murdered in Chile on March 31, 1990—eight days after Bull's assassination—while investigating claims of secret British military trading with Iraq.) American involvement in the murder was suggested by Canadian journalist Dale Grant, reporting that Michael Bull "broached the idea that the CIA did it, because his father was applying for a U.S. pardon of his arms-smuggling conviction." Two years later, former SRC employee Christopher Cowley told the House of Commons that he and Bull had briefed the CIA and Britain's MI5 on the progress of Project Babylon as it proceeded. While convinced that Israel was responsible for killing Bull, Cowley "speculated that the CIA must have been tipped off by the Mossad [Israeli intelligence] and thus had acquiesced in the assassination."

Project Babylon disintegrated after Bull's death, which was doubtless the intention of his killer or killers. SRC immediately closed its doors and the employees scattered. Iraqi forces invaded neighboring Kuwait on August 2, 1990, and U.S.-led forces responded with aerial attacks in January 1991, climaxed by a swift land offensive the following month. Bull's superguns were located and destroyed by United Nations weapons inspectors in the wake of the Gulf War. No suspects have yet been identified in Dr. Bull's murder.

BURGHARD, Paul See NEW YORK CITY TAXI MURDERS

BURK, William murder victim (1868)
A former slave in Marshall County, Tennessee, William Burk risked his life to become a Republican Party activist during the violent Reconstruction era (1865–77).

His work was particularly dangerous since Cornersville, his hometown, lay less than 20 miles northeast of Pulaski, birthplace of the terrorist Ku Klux Klan. A band of masked Klansmen raided Burk's home on the night of July 4, 1868, and left him dying from multiple gunshot wounds. Pulaski's Democratic newspaper, the *Citizen,* responded to the murder by branding Burk "a vicious and dangerous negro [*sic*]." On the night Burk died, an editorial maintained, he "was waited upon by some gentlemen, who approached him to talk the matter over in a civil way. He wouldn't listen to a word, but immediately began firing at the party. The gentlemen, who were said to be Kuklux, were compelled to shoot him down in self-defense." If true, it seems odd that the gunmen took pains to conceal their identities after the shooting. In any case, they were never publicly named and the murder remains unsolved.

BURKE, Richard assassination victim (1870)

A black Republican in Reconstruction-era Greene County, Alabama, Richard Burke was elected to the state legislature in 1870, when his white successor panicked in the face of threats from the Ku Klux Klan and refused to fill his post. Political activity was a virtual death sentence for Southern blacks in those years, but Burke—an older man and former slave—disdained all efforts at intimidation. By the time Burke returned from Montgomery to the Greene County seat at Livingston, in early August 1870, Klan members had decided he must die.

The trigger incident occurred on August 13, when rumors spread that 100 armed freedmen were descending on Livingston, prepared to massacre white residents. The county sheriff led 200 armed men to intercept the guerrillas, but he found only

A raid like this one, by the Ku Klux Klan, claimed the life of the black activist Richard Burke. (Library of Congress)

40 blacks bound for a Republican political meeting. The peaceable crowd was dispersed with warnings to stay out of trouble—defined in that time and place as any assertion of personal rights—but nightfall found a new rumor in circulation. According to the latest story, Richard Burke had confronted stragglers from the band and denounced them as cowards for dispersing in the face of superior force. "You go back and shoot out your last load of ammunition," he allegedly declared, "and then club your guns and fight to the last."

While none of the freedmen took that advice—and Burke probably never spoke the words at all—Klansmen were moved to proceed with his elimination. On the night of August 18, 1870, a band of 20-odd riders stopped at the home of Judge Turner Reavis, abducting one of the judge's black servants and compelling him at gunpoint to show them Burke's house. Burke saw the mob coming and leapt from a second-story window, fleeing on foot until they overtook him some 50 yards from the house. Judge Reavis recalled hearing gunfire and later found Burke "shot all to pieces." When questioned later by congressional investigators, Reavis denied any knowledge of other violence in the neighborhood or of "any permanent organization for political or other purposes, called Ku-Klux, or anything else."

Gainesville Klansman Edward Clement Sanders cast doubt on that testimony when he told the same panel of his personal experiences with the Greene County Klan. Judge Reavis had been present on the night he was initiated, Sanders swore under oath, and while the question of Reavis's Klan membership remained open, it seems unlikely that outsiders would be welcomed to clandestine meetings of the order.

Greene County Republicans were shocked by Burke's murder. They postponed a county-wide convention, scheduled for August 27, until U.S. troops arrived to protect them four days later. The convention then proceeded under armed guard, but it was a wasted effort. In time Klan terrorism would "redeem" Alabama and the rest of the South for white Democrats, instituting seven decades of virtual one-party rule.

BURKS, Diane   See DETROIT MURDERS

BURNHAM, A. J.   See COLORADO MURDERS (1911–12)

BURROUGHS, Krystal   See NEW ORLEANS MURDERS (1987–88)

"BUTCHER of Mons" Belgian serial killer (1997)
Police in Mons, near Belgium's border with France, blame one unknown killer for the murders of four women, whose dismembered bodies were retrieved from roadside ditches and riverbanks in 1997. The first discovery, in March, revealed the severed limbs of three different victims, wrapped in trash bags and dumped beside a highway on the outskirts of Mons. One day later, another trash bag was found, this one containing a woman's "surgically dissected" torso. Some of the limbs appeared to match, while others remained without bodies. Postmortem tests revealed that one victim had been killed within a week of discovery; the other two, with limbs apparently frozen at some time, may have been killed as early as 1995.

Authorities immediately discounted any speculative link between the dismemberment slayings and killer pedophile Marc Dutroux, whose recently exposed child pornography ring had slain at least four children. The latest Belgian stalker clearly preferred adult victims, and he also seemed to possess a macabre sense of humor, discarding body parts at sites with such names as Rue du Depot (Dump Street), Chemin de l'Inquietude (the Path of Worry), or beside the Rivers Haine (Hate) and Trouille (Jitters).

As far as technique was concerned, detectives initially said the killer's victims were dismembered with "remarkable precision," prompting speculation that their man might be a surgeon or a butcher. The disposal of remains on weekends pointed to a subject gainfully employed, a weekday nine-to-fiver, but further details of an FBI profile prepared on the killer remain under wraps.

The Butcher's fourth victim surfaced in June 1997, bagged in plastic like the others, dropped along Rue St. Symphorien (named for a beheaded third century martyr, whose remains are entombed at a nearby church). On June 3, 1997, a report was broadcast that authorities were investigating possible religious motives for the murders, perhaps satanic in nature, since "the treatment of the bodies is very methodical, which is often the case with satanics involved in ritualistic killings." That report also dismissed prior claims of the killer's surgical skill, noting that his latest victim had been chopped into numerous pieces, none more than 12 inches long.

Two of the Butcher's victims have thus far been identified. Martine Bohn, a 43-year-old French transsexual and retired prostitute, had disappeared in July 1996, her bagged remains found floating in the Haine, both breasts removed. The second positive I.D. was that of 21-year-old Nathalie Godart. A third presumed victim, 33-year-old Jacqueline Leclercq, was last seen alive on January 23, 1997. Study of an unknown woman's pelvis, found across the border in France, has so far failed to confirm a link with the murders in Mons.

Belgian psychiatrists describe their faceless killer as a meticulous anal retentive whose murders are committed "very neatly, very precisely, the work of an obsessive." The only suspect named to date was cleared upon substantiation of his alibi and subsequently left Belgium. Police have no leads to the killer (or killers), waiting grimly to see if he (or they) strike again, perhaps leaving clues that may lead to an arrest. Eleven years of inactivity and counting suggest that their wait may be in vain.

A possible break in the Butcher case occurred on February 17, 2007, when police in Podgorica, Montenegro, arrested 66-year-old Smailj Tulja as a suspect in the slaying of Mary Beal, a 61-year-old New York resident found dismembered and stuffed into trash bags left near the Brooklyn Bridge in September 1990. At the time, Tulja was living in New York City, working as a taxi driver. Police learned that Beal had loaned $10,000 to Tulja—a fellow Yugoslav immigrant—for the purchase of a home. They also discovered that since his immigration in 1961, Tulja had compiled a record of arrests for violent crimes, including one charge of attempted murder. Officers found traces of

blood inside Tulja's home, despite recent sanding of the wood floors, but Tulja and his taxi vanished, eluding authorities for the next 17 years.

His capture resulted from a chain reaction of coincidence. Detective James Osorio, a member of the NYPD's Cold Case Squad, had visited the FBI Academy in Quantico, Virginia, where G-men mentioned the dismemberment slayings of two women in Albania. Osorio made the link to Tulja, who had identified himself as a butcher on his original application for a U.S. visa. In addition to his versatile employment (including work as a court translator in New York), Tulja also adopted various pseudonyms. NYPD documents referred to him as Smajo Dzurlic, while an FBI affidavit from February 2007 called him Smajo Djurlric.

By any name, he was a wanted man. Brooklyn's district attorney issued a warrant for Tulja's arrest in 1994 and passed an extradition request on to authorities in Belgium, where he allegedly settled after fleeing New York. Belgian police had no luck finding him, although they listed him as "a person of interest" in the Mons Butcher slayings. No details are available about the Albanian slayings, aside from the fact that both victims were killed in 2006. After Tulja's arrest in Montenegro, the *New York Times* reported that FBI agents had watched him for several weeks, finally matching his fingerprints through Interpol with records from a 1974 arrest in New York.

But is Smailj Tulja the Butcher of Mons? Police would like to think so, and while Claude Michaux, the King's Solicitor in Mons, describes the FBI's information as "serious," he also states that "for now, there is not enough objective evidence to make a connection" between Tulja and the Butcher's crimes. The case remains officially unsolved.

CABO, Ronald See New York City gay murders (1973)

CADIEUX, Cynthia See "Babysitter"

CAIN, Jessica See "I-45 murders"

CALVI, Roberto murder victim (1992)
A native of Milan, Roberto Calvi was the chairman of Banco Ambrosiano, a Roman Catholic bank founded in 1896 and named for Saint Ambrose, Milan's fourth-century Catholic archbishop. Founder Giuseppe Tovini created the bank to offset Italy's secular banks and, more specifically, to serve "moral organisations, pious works, and religious bodies set up for charitable aims." One chairman was a nephew of Pope Pius XI, and Banco Ambrosiano (or B.A.) soon became known as the priests' bank. The Vatican Bank was Banco Ambrosiano's primary shareholder.

B.A. director (later chairman) Carlo Canesi brought Calvi into the bank in 1947. Calvi expanded the bank's interests, including creation of offshore firms in South America and the Bahamas, acquisition of a controlling interest in the Banca Cattolica del Veneto, and financing of the newspaper *Corriere della Sera*. Behind the scenes, Calvi was very active in the Masonic lodge known as Propaganda Due or P2, implicated in many conspiracy theories involving the Mafia, Third World military juntas, and ter-

rorist groups. By 1971, when Calvi became Banco Ambrosiano's chairman, he was widely known as God's banker.

In 1978 the Bank of Italy produced a report on Banco Ambrosiano, predicting disaster for it from its issuance of unsecured loans and widespread involvement with suspect organizations. That prediction initially rebounded on its authors—Milanese magistrate Emilio Alessandrini was assassinated by leftist guerrillas, while Bank of Italy inspector Mario Sarcinelli was briefly jailed on charges later dismissed—but the report did prove prophetic.

In 1981 Italian police raided P2's headquarters and arrested "Worshipful Master" Licio Gelli. Financial ledgers and other evidence seized in that raid led to Calvi's arrest and conviction for violating Italian currency laws. Specifically, prosecutors charged that he had shipped $27 million out of Italy without official sanction. Calvi received a four-year prison term and a $19.8 million fine, attempting suicide in jail before he was released on bond, pending disposition of his appeal. Despite his conviction, Calvi retained his position with Banco Ambrosiano.

In spring 1982 auditors discovered that Banco Ambrosiano had somehow misplaced $1.287 billion. Calvi wrote a letter to Pope John Paul II on June 5, warning of the B.A.'s imminent collapse, which would "provoke a catastrophe of unimaginable proportions in which the Church will suffer the gravest damage." Five days later, Calvi fled the country, traveling to London on a false passport in the name of Gian Roberto Calvini. His secretary, Graziella Corrocher, left a suicide note denouncing Calvi, before plunging from her fifth-floor office window. Despite suggestions of foul play, her death was ruled a suicide.

Banco Ambrosiano did collapse, in fact, amid published reports that $700 million to $1.5 billion had been siphoned off by embezzlers through Vatican bank accounts. B.A. executives belatedly stripped Calvi of his office on June 17, 1982. One day later, at 7:30 A.M. on June 18, a postman found Calvi's body hanging beneath Blackfriars Railway Bridge in London's financial district. His pockets were weighted with bricks and $15,000 in three different currencies.

As in Corrocher's case, the first inquest on Calvi's death, convened in July 1982, listed the cause as suicide. A second official inquest, one year later, recorded an "open" verdict that left the case in limbo. In 1984 the Vatican Bank agreed to reimburse 120 Banco Ambrosiano creditors for a total of $224 million, in "recognition of moral involvement" in B.A.'s collapse.

Surviving members of Calvi's family rejected the suicide hypothesis. His corpse was exhumed in December 1998, and an independent forensic report published in October 2002 pronounced his death a homicide. Specifically, the examiners found that injuries to Calvi's neck were inconsistent with suicide by hanging, that he had not touched the bricks retrieved from his pockets, and that his shoes displayed none of the rust or flaking paint that should have transferred to their soles as Calvi climbed the scaffold from which he was hanged. Furthermore, while Calvi was found at low tide, dangling well above the River Thames, he had died at *high tide,* when the scaffold was easily accessible by boat.

There was no shortage of suspects in Calvi's slaying. One theory involved the P2 lodge, whose members called themselves *frati neri* ("black friars"), thus linking the group symbolically to Blackfriars Bridge. Jeff Katz, a private investigator hired by Calvi's family in 1991, blamed unnamed "senior figures in the Italian establishment" for Calvi's slaying. Other theories involve the Mafia and the Vatican Bank, whose covert dealings inspired a subplot of the 1990 film *The Godfather: Part III.*

In July 1991 Mafia informer Francesco Mannoia told Italian police that Calvi was killed for losing syndicate funds when the B.A. collapsed. Mannoia named the killer as Francesco Di Carlo (who lived in London at the time) and said the order came from bosses Giuseppe Calò and Licio Gelli. Di Carlo himself turned informer in 1996, denying participation in Calvi's murder, but he admitted that Calò had asked him to handle the job. Di Carlo named the killers as Vincenzo Casillo and Sergio Vaccari, members of the Neapolitan Camorra gang, who had been murdered in the meantime.

In 1997 Italian prosecutors accused Calò and Sardinian businessman Flavio Carboni of the murder. The charges also implicated Di Carlo and Ernesto Diotallevi, alleged leader of a Roman crime syndicate called the Banda della Magliana. Six years later, officials declared that the Mafia had not acted alone in Calvi's murder, but had killed him to prevent Calvi from blackmailing "politico-institutional figures and [members] of freemasonry, the P2 lodge, and the Institute of Religious Works with whom he had invested substantial sums of money, some of it from Cosa Nostra and Italian public corporations."

Two year later, in April 2005, prosecutors indicted four suspects in Calvi's slaying. They included Calò, Ernesto Diotallevi, Flavio Carboni, and Manuela Kleinszig (Carboni's former girlfriend). The indictment charged that they killed Calvi to stop him "from using blackmail power against his political and institutional sponsors from the world of Masonry, belonging to the P2 lodge, or to the Institute for Religious Works [the Vatican Bank] with whom he had managed investments and financing with conspicuous sums of money, some of it coming from Cosa Nostra and public agencies." On July 19, 2005, authorities formally notified P2 leader Licio Gelli that he was under investigation as the instigator of Calvi's murder. Also charged in a later indictment was Calvi's former bodyguard and chauffeur, Silvano Vittor.

A trial convened in Rome on October 5, 2005, for defendants Calò, Carboni, Diotallevi, Kleinszig, and Vittor. Judge Mario d'Andria, presiding over a fortified courtroom in Rome's Rebibbia prison, dismissed all charges on June 6, 2007, citing "insufficient evidence." At the same time, d'Andria declared that Calvi's death *had* been a murder, committed by persons unknown.

CAMBI, Susanna   See "MONSTER OF FLORENCE"

CAMPBELL, Amanda   See BAY AREA CHILD MURDERS

CAMPBELL, Howard See Los Angeles drive-by murders

CAPIOLA, Debra See Washington, Pennsylvania, murders

CARFANO, Anthony gangland murder victim (1959)
Little is known about the early life of mobster Anthony Carfano, better known to police and his Mafia associates as "Little Augie Pisano." Author Carl Sifakis reports that Carfano, raised in New York City, borrowed his sobriquet from a dead East Side gangster, but the other details of his childhood (including date of birth) remain obscure. We know Carfano was arrested several times for carrying concealed weapons, and that while he was once charged with murder, the case never went to trial. That fact was likely due in large part to Carfano's mob connections, including FRANKIE YALE, Frank Costello, Joseph ("Joe Adonis") Doto, Anthony ("Tony Bender") Stralla, Mike Miranda, and super-bookie Frank Erickson. Carfano also achieved a measure of faux respectability from his marriage to the daughter of John DiSalvio (a.k.a. Jimmy Kelly), a Greenwich Village nightclub owner and Tammany Hall election captain in the Second Assembly District.

In June 1928, after Frankie Yale fell prey to the Big Apple's first machine-gun drive-by shooting, Carfano was chosen to administer the late mobster's Brooklyn rackets for Joe Adonis. Three years later, he attended an organizational meeting of the national crime syndicate at New York's Waldorf-Astoria Hotel, mingling with mob leaders whose number included Charles ("Lucky") Luciano, Meyer Lansky, BENJAMIN ("BUGSY") SIEGEL, Moe Dalitz, and ALBERT ANASTASIA. Luciano was subsequently convicted of "white slavery" and sentenced to prison, then deported to his native Italy, but Carfano was among those present for a lavish welcome home party thrown for Luciano in Havana, Cuba, on December 22, 1946. (Frank Sinatra provided the entertainment, while assembled mob leaders discussed the growth of Las Vegas and voted to eliminate Ben Siegel for skimming syndicate funds.)

In the late 1950s Carfano moved to Miami, Florida, and sought to establish himself as a big fish in a relatively small pond. Miami had been deemed an "open city" by the syndicate, theoretically meaning that any mobster was free to operate there, as long as he inconvenienced no one else. In fact, however, Miami gambling was dominated by Lansky and other members of the so-called Jewish Mafia—Moe Dalitz, Sam Tucker, Morris Kleinman—and the Mafia was ably represented by Santo Tràfficante. Still, Carfano reasoned, there should be loot enough to go around.

On the night of September 29, 1959, Carfano was in New York, dining at the Copacabana nightclub with Mrs. Janice Drake. A former beauty queen, Drake was the wife of comedian Alan Drake, whose career had received a boost from Carfano's mob influence. Carfano's relationship to Mrs. Drake remains speculative: She called him "Uncle Gus" and may have simply been a platonic friend, as Carfano maintained. On the night in question, they were joined for dinner by four companions, including Tony Bender, Vincent Mauro, ex-convict Al Segal, and Segal's wife. In the middle of dinner, around 9:45 P.M., Carfano received a phone call and left the restaurant with Drake. At 10:30 they were found in Queens, parked on a residential street near La Guardia Airport in Carfano's black 1959 Cadillac. Both had been shot in the back of the head, by one or more gunmen seated behind them. Police speculated that the killer (or killers) had been waiting in Carfano's car when he left the restaurant, forcing him to serve as their chauffeur on Little Augie's last ride.

Detectives thought Mrs. Drake had been killed as an unlucky eyewitness to murder, but the motive for Carfano's death remains a subject of debate among mob-watchers. Some observers believe he was killed on orders from Lansky and/or Trafficante, for invading their Miami turf without permission. Others maintain that Carfano fell prey to the same late-Fifties underworld that claimed the lives of Albert Anastasia and ABNER ("LONGY") ZWILLMAN. A long-shot third scenario involves Carfano's dubious relationship with Janice Drake, although the method of his death (and hers) clearly suggests the work of a professional killer.

CARLSZEN, Signe See Colorado murders (1911–12)

CARROLL, Anna See "Frankford Slasher"

CARTER, Diane   See Detroit murders

CARTER, Gloria   See Washington, D.C., murders (1988)

CARTER, Leroy murder victim (1981)
Shortly after noon on February 8, 1981, San Francisco police received complaints of a transient sleeping near Alvord Lake in Golden Gate Park. The report was not unusual, by any means. A verbal warning would suffice, perhaps a trip downtown in handcuffs if the subject was disorderly or drunk. Patrolmen answering the call were ill prepared for an excursion through the twilight zone of cults and human sacrifice that waited for them in the park.

Arriving at the scene, two officers were met by a complaining witness who led them to a clump of bushes where a sleeping bag was partially concealed. A nightstick drew the top flap of the sleeping bag aside, revealing a decapitated human body with a chicken wing and two kernels of corn where the missing head should be. Detectives were summoned, and a search of the area turned up several mutilated chickens in a cardboard box, some 50 yards distant from the corpse. No trace of the victim's head could be found.

Fingerprints identified the dead man as 29-year-old Leroy Carter, a black petty criminal whose record included arrests for trespassing, auto theft, assault, and battery. A canvass of his known associates produced no motive for the slaying, but Coroner Boyd Stevens publicly described the murder as a ritual homicide.

With that in mind, the case was referred to the San Francisco Police Department's resident "cult expert," Detective Sandi Gallant. She, in turn, placed a call to Charles Wetli, coroner of Dade County, Florida, and the nation's top expert on Santeria. Wetli noted that chickens are routinely sacrificed to various *orishas* (gods) in the Afro-Caribbean religion, but corn is specifically sacred to the god Eleggua, ruler of gates and crossroads. Based on evidence from cases in Miami, Wetli advised that the missing head would be buried for 21 days, then unearthed by the killers and kept for another three weeks to extract psychic powers, before it was returned to the murder scene.

Det. Gallant relayed Wetli's information to homicide investigators, facing ridicule for her efforts and becoming the subject of countless "chicken jokes" around the squad room. The laughter stopped abruptly when a new report came in from Golden Gate Park on March 22, 1981. A black man's severed head had been discovered close to Alvord Lake, exactly 42 days from the date Carter's body was found.

Unfortunately, proof of Santeria cult involvement in the case brought police no closer to a suspect. More than two decades after the fact, the murder of Leroy Carter remains unsolved.

CARTWRIGHT, Una   See "West Side Rapist"

CASTRATION murders U.S. serial killings (1981–86)
Around 7:00 a.m. on June 14, 1982, sheriff's deputies in Wasatch County, Utah, were summoned to the banks of Daniels Creek, where a fly fisherman had reported a grisly discovery. On arrival, they found a man's nude body lying on its back, knees raised, with the genitals severed and missing from the scene. Autopsy results disclosed that the castration had occurred postmortem, after the victim was shot once in the back of the head with a .38-caliber pistol. On October 11, 1983, the victim was identified from fingerprints as Marty Shook, age 21, from Truckee, California. He had last been seen alive on June 12, 1982, leaving his mother's home on a hitchhiking trip to Colorado.

Another four years and seven months elapsed before Utah authorities submitted details of Shook's murder to the FBI's National Center for the Analysis of Violent Crime, for comparison to other crimes reported from around the country. The marvels of computer science notwithstanding, it was May 1989, nearly seven years after the slaying, when G-men reported back on a strikingly similar case from Pennsylvania. There, six miles north of Williamsburg, another young man had been found on August 19, 1981, nude and emasculated, shot in the back of the head. The Pennsylvania victim was identified as 30-year-old Wayne Rifendifer, a North Carolina native with a record of arrests for larceny. Ballistics tests proved that Shook and Rifendifer had been shot with the same gun.

Authorities suspect the same killer is responsible for the November 1986 murder of 26-year-old Jack Andrews, an Oklahoma native with a criminal record, found nude and wrapped in a blanket at a highway rest stop near Litchfield, Connecticut. In addition to the standard missing genitals, Andrews's nipples were also cut off and both legs were severed at mid-thigh. None of the missing parts were found, and cause of death was not determined in the Litchfield case. Andrews had not been shot.

No progress has been publicly reported on these crimes since 1989, and while investigators theorize about a transient killer—possibly a long-haul trucker who preys on hitchhikers—they are no closer to a suspect now, than back in 1981. Barring spontaneous confession by the killer (or killers) or coincidental matchup of a gun recovered by police, there is no prospect for solution of the mystery.

"CHAIN murders" Iranian political homicides (1988–99)
"Chain murders" is the popular label applied to a series of deaths and disappearances occurring in Iran since the late 1980s. In all cases the victims or missing persons were dissidents who criticized the Islamic Republic established by fundamentalist Ayatollah Khomeini in 1979. Surviving critics of the Iranian government believe the deaths were staged in various ways—including faked robberies, car "accidents," and heart attacks induced by lethal injections—to divert international protest.

Observers of the "chain murder" series list 107 victims since 1988, including political activists, writers and poets, translators, and various ordinary citizens. Forty-four of the dead belonged to the Kurdistan Democratic Party of Iran (KDP), a Kurdish opposition group in Iranian Kurdistan that champions Kurdish rights within a democratic federal republic.

Victims identified by full names and dates of their deaths include:

- Zahra Eftekhari, a newly released political prisoner, kidnapped and murdered in February 1988;

- Ebrahim Zalzadeh, a writer stabbed 15 times in March 1988;

- Kazem Sami, Iran's first postrevolution health minister, fatally stabbed by an attacker posing as a clinic patient in November 1988;

- Ata Rezapour, a KDP member killed in Saghez, in August 1990;

- Othman Zurai', killed at Sardasht in 1991;

- Kamal Ghaderzadeh, a KDP member murdered in Marivan in 1991;

- Khaled Saghezi, a KDP activist killed in Saghez in 1991;

- Hassan Alipour and Mohammad Jalil, KDP members killed in Piranshahr during September 1991;

- Almas Khedr, a KDP member killed at Oshnavieh in September 1991;

- Kamran Shafai', a KDP activist murdered in Mehabad in 1992;

- Hossein Sarshar, an opera singer, killed in an April 1992 auto accident in Abadan;

- Mahmud Rahmani, KDP member, slain in Piranshahr, June 1992;

- Hadi Mahmudi, KDP leader, killed in Urumanat, in June 1992;

- Ali Taludeh, killed in Marivan, June 1992;

- Ebrahim Sheikhi, KDP member, slain in Bukan, July 1992;

- Shahpour Firuzi, a KDP recruiter, killed in Kamyaran, July 1992;

- Ahmad Fatemi, murdered in Sardasht during August 1992;

- Mohammad-Amin Makruli, KDP member, killed in Piranshahr, September 1992;

- Salar Jajlai, KDP organizer, slain in Nowsud, September 1992;

- Mohammad Nazari, a member of the dissident Ranjbaran Party, killed in December 1992;

- Pour-Mohammad Sheikheh, a KDP activist killed at Sangsar in December 1992;

- Taher Manuchehri and Rashir Rostami, KDP members murdered in Band-Khan, December 1992;

- Mohammad Mehrabani, KDP member, killed at Barikeh in 1993;

- Mahmud Mojahedi, KDP leader, slain in Haji-Abad, November 1993;

- Shahu Moradi, a KDP member, killed at Band-Khan, November 1993;

- Abdollah Rabbani, KDP activist, murdered in the Labbankan Valley in 1994;

- Zohreh Izadi, a medical student, killed in Tehran, 1994;

- Mohammad-Pour, a KDP activist killed in Bazian, 1994;

- Abdolkarim Jalali, KDP member, slain at Kooye Sanjagh in March 1994;

- Kalleh Mameh, KDP member, murdered in Sardasht during June 1994;

- Morad Mohammad Zadeh, KDP activist, killed in Urumieh, June 1994;

- Mehdi Dibaj, a Christian convert from Sunni Islam, convicted of apostasy, abruptly released from prison in July 1994, kidnapped and murdered days later;

- Ahmad Ruin-Tan, a KDP member killed in Urumieh, July 1994;

- Hassan Shah-Jamali, another Christian convert slain in July 1994;

- Shamseddin Mir Alai', former Iranian ambassador to France, killed in a staged auto accident, July 1994;

- Haik Hovseppian, Dibaj, and Mikhailian, three Christian priests killed in Karaj, August 1994;

- Esfandyar and Mehran Taheri, related KDP activists, slain in Urumieh, August 1994;

- Ghafur Mehdizadeh, KDP member, killed at Kooye Sanjagh, August 1994;

- Sarajeddin Jajuri and Behruz Taghizadeh, a KDP member and one of his friends, killed at Urumieh in August 1994;

- Ali Akbar Sai'di Sirjani, a dissident journalist arrested for criticizing Iran's theocracy, found dead in jail under mysterious circumstances, November 1994;

- Mohamad Said Jaderi, KDP member, killed at Kooye Sanjagh, December 1994;

- Mohammad Sheikheh, KDP activist, slain at Saghez in December 1994;

- Hossein Barazandeh, an engineer and friend of exiled Iranian sociologist Dr. Ali Shariati, vanished from his Mashad home on January 2, 1995. Police found his corpse near the local prison and blamed his death on a heart attack, but independent examiners say he was smothered;

- Mohammad Nanvai', killed in Bazian, January 1995;

- Mohammad Abdollahi and Jakardeh, KDP members murdered in Basermeh, April 1995;

- Ebrahim Rahmani, KDP member, killed in Kamyaran, July 1995;

- Abdollah Bak and Ali Zekateh, KDP sympathizers murdered in Bukan during July 1995;

- Asghar Rostami, KDP member, killed in Vilaj Rostam, August 1995;

- Ahmad Mir-Alai', a writer/translator who left his Isfahan home at 8:00 A.M., October 24, 1995, and never returned. Police announced discovery of his corpse at 11:00 P.M., blaming cardiac arrest, but postmortem examination revealed that his heart had been stopped by a potassium injection;

- Sadegh Abdoltahu, KDP member, killed at Kooye Sanjagh, December 1995;

- Mohammad Babai', killed in Saghez during 1996;

- Reza Sharifi, KDP activist, killed in Saghez, September 1996;

- Mohammad Ravanbakhsh, a Christian priest, murdered in Sari, September 1996;

- Siamak Sanjari, a government critic slain on his wedding night, in November 1996;

- Ghaffar Hossenini, a writer, murdered at Isfahan, November 1996;

- Mohammad-Rasul Ghaderzadeh and Ja'far Omarbil, KDP members killed in Kooye Sanjagh, November 1996;

- Alian Najafabadi, vanished in January 1997;

- Dr. Ahmad Tafazzoli, a professor of ancient Iranian literature and culture, found with his skull crushed in January 1997;

- Amir Ghaffuri, disappeared in March 1997;

- Ebrahim Zalzadeh, editor of *Me'yar* magazine and director of the Ebtekar publishing house, kidnapped en route from his office to home and found stabbed to death on March 29, 1997;

- Farzineh Maghsud and her nephew, stabbed a total of 75 times in March 1997;

- Seyed Mahmoud Meidami, disappeared in April 1997;
- Said Moradi, KDP member, killed at Bukan in August 1997;
- Ra'fat Hoseini, Seid Mansur Naseri, and Yadolay Shirin-Shukhan, KDP members murdered in Kooye Sanjagh, December 1997;
- Fatemeh Ghaem-Maghami, murdered in December 1997, allegedly on orders from fugitive Iranian Intelligence Minister Hojjatoleslam Ali Fallahian;
- Hamid Haji Zadeh and her 9-year-old son, killed at their home in Kerman during 1998;
- Firuzeh Kalantari and Manuchehr Sanei', victims of multiple stab wounds in February 1998;
- Majid Sharif, a writer who contributed to the banned periodical *Iran-e Farda*, found dead beside a road in Tehran on November 18, 1998;
- Dariush Foruhar and Parvaneh Eskandari, a dissident politician and his wife, found dead in Tehran on November 21, 1998. Authorities first blamed their deaths on "heart failure," then admitted that Foruhar had been stabbed 11 times, and Eskandari 24 times, while the house was ransacked;
- Mohammad Mokhtari, a writer, left his Tehran home on December 2, 1998, and was found strangled on December 8;
- Mohammad Jafar Pouyandeh, author and translator, vanished after leaving his Tehran office on December 8, 1998, and was found strangled on December 12, near the site where Mohammad Mokhtari's corpse was dumped;
- Mohamad-Taghi Zehtabi, a historian and linguist, murdered in December 1998;
- Mohammad Ziai', an imam in Bandar Abbas, killed in January 1999;
- Ahmad Mirin Sayyad, a scholar slain in January 1999;
- Piruz Davani, a writer, killed in January 1999;
- Karim Jalli and Fatemeh Eslami, an engineer and his wife, murdered at home in Tehran, January 1999;
- Javad Emami and Sonya Ale-Yasin, a Tehran jurist and his wife, killed at home in January 1999;
- Dr. Jamshid Partovi, the cardiologist of Ahmad Khomeini (son of Ayatollah Khomeini, who died from apparent heart failure in March 1995), murdered at his home in January 1999;
- Hossein Fattapour, killed outside his Tehran home in November 1999.

Suspects abound in the Iranian "chain murders." Ayatollah Khomeini blamed foreign powers, claiming that "the enemy" was "creating insecurity to try to block the progress of Iran's Islamic system." Fundamentalist newspapers echoed that theme, blaming "foreign sources"—more specifically, the Iraq-based Mojahedin-e-Khalq terrorist group—for generating "an environment of insecurity and instability in the country."

On December 20, 1998, a group calling itself "pure Mohammadan Islam devotees of Mostafa Navvab" issued a statement claiming credit for several recent slayings. That statement read, in part:

Now than domestic politicians, through negligence and leniency, and under slogan of rule of law, support the masked poisonous vipers of the aliens, and brand the decisive approaches of the Islamic system, judiciary and responsible press and advocates of the revolution as monopolistic and extremist spread of violence and threats to the freedom, the brave and zealous children of the Iranian Muslim nation took action and by revolutionary execution of dirty and sold-out elements who were behind nationalistic movements and other poisonous moves in universities, took the second practical step in defending the great achievements of the Islamic Revolution.... The revolutionary execution of Dariush Forouhar, Parvaneh Eskandari, Mohammad Mokhtari and Mohammad Jafar Pouyandeh is a warning to all mercenary writers and their counter-value supporters who are cherishing the idea of spreading corruption and promiscuity in the country and bringing back foreign domination over Iran.

On January 4, 1999, Iran's Ministry of Information issued a press release admitting that "staff within" its own headquarters had "committed these criminal activities . . . under the influence of undercover rogue agents." The bulletin went on to say:

The despicable and abhorring recent murders in Tehran are a sign of chronic conspiracy and a threat to the national security. The Information Ministry based on their legal obligations and following clear directives issued by the Supreme Leader and the President, made the discovery and uprooting of this sinister and threatening event the priority action for the Ministry. With the cooperation of the specially appointed Investigatory Committee of the President, the Ministry has succeeded to identify the group responsible for the killings, has arrested them and processed their cases through the judicial system. Unfortunately a small number of irresponsible, misguided, headstrong and obstinate staff within the Ministry of Information who are no doubt under the influence of undercover rogue agents and act towards the objectives of foreign and estranged sources committed these criminal activities.

On June 3, 1999, prosecutors accused Saeed Emami, deputy security chief for the Ministry of Information, with ordering the murders. Also charged were three subordinates: Mehrdad Alikhani, Khosro Basati, and Mostafa Kazemi. Strangely, the press reported that Emami had committed suicide by drinking hair remover six months *before* his arrest was announced. Emami was secretly buried, and autopsy reports on his case have not been released.

Other defendants soon joined the list and began to confess. Ali Rowshani admitted killing victims Mohammad Mokhtari and Mohammad Pouyandeh, on orders from Alikhani and Kazemi. Three other prisoners confessed slaying Dariush Foruhar and his wife on orders from Alikhani and Kazemi.

Defendants Alikhani and Kazemi were sentenced to die on four counts of murder, in December 2000, but the Iranian Supreme Court commuted their sentenced to life imprisonment in January 2003. Two agents accused of conducting the actual murders received 10-year terms, while seven accomplices drew terms ranging from 30 months to 10 years. Most of the "chain murders" still remain officially unsolved, and the near-slaying of newspaper editor Saeed Hajjarian—shot and paralyzed for life on March 12, 2000—suggests that the Iranian housecleaning was unsuccessful.

CHANEY, Trina See "SOUTHSIDE SLAYER"

CHAPMAN, Annie See "JACK THE RIPPER" (1888)

CHARLTON, Judge assassination victim (1870)
A prominent Republican in Summerville, Alabama, during Reconstruction (1865–77), Judge Charlton suffered the double misfortune of being slain for his political beliefs and losing his first name entirely to the tides of history. Military and congressional investigators who reviewed his case in 1870–71 knew him simply by the title of his office, and so he is identified today.

Judge Charlton's trouble began in the wake of America's bitter Civil War, when he switched allegiance from the white-supremacist Democratic Party to campaign for Republicans and establishment of black civil rights in Alabama. As if that were not bad enough, in the eyes of Confederate neighbors who dubbed him a crass "scalawag," Charlton also served as foreman for a federal grand jury based at Huntsville, which returned multiple indictments against members of the Ku Klux Klan and other racial terrorists. Few of those charged were ever arrested, but dodging the police and U.S. troops was still an inconvenience. Inevitably, the Morgan County Klan swore vengeance against Charlton.

The night riders made their first attempt in October 1868, shortly before the upcoming presidential election. A gang of masked Klansmen spent the night terrorizing local Republicans, including a deputy sheriff and circuit court clerk, but they hit a snag when they reached Judge Charlton's home. The raiders kicked in his front door, but were surprised when a visitor—one Bob Gardner—rushed past them and into the night. While the Klansmen unloaded their weapons at Gardner, without effect, Charlton's son opened fire from the house and scattered them into the night. Rumors spread that one raider succumbed to his wounds, but if so he was secretly buried, leaving no record behind.

In the wake of the raid on his home, Judge Charlton joined other Republicans and disgruntled ex-Klansmen to organize an "Anti-Ku-Klux" band in Morgan County. The group quelled terrorism by visiting known Klansmen at home, warning them that any future violence would be answered in kind. Acknowledged members of the Anti-Klan later denied any mayhem on their own part, and perhaps threats were enough to discourage local raiders—but they would not save Judge Charlton.

On March 18, 1870—soon after the grand jury's session ended with 33 new indictments, including seven for murder and manslaughter—Charlton went to visit a friend in Decatur, Alabama. A gunman lay in wait for the judge near his destination, firing a shotgun blast that killed Charlton outright. Alabama Governor

William H. Smith promised "a vigorous and determined policy" to suppress terrorism, but his words had little effect in the hinterlands, and Charlton's killer was never identified. Local Democrats blamed a personal feud for the murder, thereby absolving the Klan, and Lieutenant Charles Harkins could not prove them wrong when he led a detachment of the 2nd Infantry to garrison the district. As Harkins reported on March 5, 1870: "Family, political, and personal quarrels have been so blended and mixed that it is very difficult to ascertain where one commences and the others end. These, and other conflicting interests, have kept the spirit of discord and animosity alive, and have engendered such deadly feuds to such an extent that at the present time law and order are set at defiance." So it would remain, throughout the state, until white terror "redeemed" Alabama from Republican rule and Reconstruction came to an end.

CHASE, Richard and Russell murder victims (1976)

For one brief day the savage murder of three young boys on Gila River Indian Reservation, southeast of Phoenix, ranked among the most sensational homicide cases in Arizona history. Twenty-four hours later, it was eclipsed and driven from the headlines by an even more sensational crime—and so it remains unsolved today, after more than a quarter century. Critics suggest that racism may be one reason why there have been no arrests in what became known as the case of the boys on the tracks.

Eleven-year-old Richard Chase, Jr., was the oldest victim, murdered with his nine-year-old brother Russell and their 10-year-old cousin David Johns. All three boys were stabbed repeatedly by an unknown assailant, a total of 39 knife wounds in all. When they were dead or dying, the killer laid his victims out across the Southern Pacific Railroad's tracks and left them for the next train passing through to mutilate their bodies. Medical examiners had grisly work ahead of them after the boys were run over by seven locomotives and 20 railroad cars, but they still determined stabbing as the cause of death for all three boys.

No murder weapon was found, and authorities concluded that the boys were slain elsewhere, at some site still unknown, then carried to the tracks where they were found. Authorities were barely starting their investigation when a Phoenix car bombing claimed the life of newsman Don Bolles the next day, and reporters inflamed by the murder of a colleague virtu-

ally abandoned the Gila River story to pursue Bolles's killers. (Unlike the reservation slayer, they were soon identified.) Back on the reservation, meanwhile, police chased reports of a man in a cape, reportedly seen near the point where the three boys were found. Investigators speculate (without proof) that the mystery man may have been Gerald Ray White, a rail-riding mental patient later detained for questioning in the Oklahoma stabbing murder of another Native American boy. In May 2002 an investigator told the *Arizona Republic,* "In the interview with [White], we felt maybe he had multiple personalities, but we never could get him into [the] right personality to talk to us."

Alternative suspicion focused on relatives of the victims, as in all cases where a child is murdered, but again, no evidence has been produced against any family member. Georgette Chase, mother of the slain brothers, complained to the *Republic* in 2002 that the murders had blocked her campaigns to be elected tribal governor. "They say, 'Oh, she killed her kids, anyway,'" Chase told reporter Charles Kelly. "I wish it could get resolved so it wouldn't be a political football."

CHASE, Valentine, and Pope, Henry assassinated (1868)

Autumn 1868 was a chaotic season in Louisiana. Recently defeated in the Civil War, most ex-Confederates still refused to acknowledge Union authority or the victorious Republican Party. Southern Democrats—lately christened Conservatives—were committed to "redeeming" Dixie by any means available. In 1868, with state and presidential elections looming in early November, the means had largely been reduced to terrorism, spearheaded by members of the Ku Klux Klan. In Louisiana the Klan's efforts were supplemented by another paramilitary organization, the Knights of the White Camellia. Together, those groups and various local lynch mobs would slay more than 1,800 victims in the two weeks prior to November's election, while wounding, flogging, and otherwise intimidating thousands more.

Two of the most prominent victims were Judge Valentine Chase of St. Mary's Parish and Sheriff Henry H. Pope. Both were active Republicans, and Sheriff Pope compounded that offense by his recent wartime service in the United States Army. On October 17, 1868, a band of armed men confronted Pope and Valentine on a public street in Franklin, Louisiana, and riddled both victims with bullets, afterward escaping without difficulty. The killers were never charged, and

Pope's Republican successor as sheriff was chased from the parish a short time later, before the election. Statewide, such violence had the desired effect: The total of Republican ballots cast in Louisiana dropped from 61,152 in the April primary elections to 34,859 in November, while Democratic votes increased from 43,739 to 88,225.

CHIANG, Joyce murder victim (1999)

Joyce Chiang was the daughter of Taiwanese immigrants, born in Chicago on December 7, 1970. She graduated from Smith College in 1992, after serving as student body president in her senior year, then moved to Washington, D.C. Chiang first worked as an intern for California congressman Howard Berman, then became a legislative aide on Berman's staff while attending classes at Georgetown University Law Center. She completed her legal studies in 1995 and went to work as an attorney with the Immigration and Naturalization Service (now U.S. Citizenship and Immigration Services).

On the evening of January 9, 1999, Chiang met several friends for dinner and a movie. One of the friends offered to drive her home and, while Chiang accepted the ride, she asked her friend to drop her at a Starbucks coffee shop four blocks from her home, at the corner of Connecticut Avenue NW and R Street NW. She planned to walk home from there, but never reached her apartment.

A couple strolling in Anacostia Park found Chiang's wallet on January 10 and delivered it to the park's lost-and-found office. On January 14, the couple saw Chiang's photo on television, accompanied by a missing person bulletin, and telephoned the FBI. G-men searched the park as part of their duty to investigate any disappearance of a federal government employee. They found Chiang's jacket, torn down the back, along with her keys, gloves, and two credit cards. In May 1999 a canoeist on the Potomac River found a decomposed corpse, eight miles from Anacostia Park. DNA testing identified the body as Joyce Chiang's.

The homicide remains unsolved today, but it received national attention in 2001, following the disappearance of CHANDRA LEVY. Authorities noted that both women were young, petite brunettes with an ethnic appearance (Levy was Jewish), both had worked as congressional interns, their apartments stood four blocks apart, and Levy frequented the same Starbucks where Chiang stopped on the night of her murder.

Those similarities fueled speculation concerning a serial killer at large, but despite the best efforts of investigators and Chiang's brother—a former Democratic Party officer—the killer remains unidentified.

CHICAGO, Illinois child murders (1956–57)

Within an eight-month period in 1956–57, three Chicago teenage girls were slain in a grisly string of homicides that have remained unsolved for nearly half a century. Police stop short of blaming one killer for all three deaths, but in the absence of any real evidence, theorists are free to speculate.

On December 28, 1956, 15-year-old Barbara Grimes and her 13-year-old sister Patricia failed to come home from a neighborhood theater. Reminded of an October 1955 triple murder involving three young boys (solved 40 years later, by chance), Chicago panicked. Singer Elvis Presley, star of the last movie seen by the sisters, issued a public appeal for the girls to come home and be "good Presley fans." Columnist Ann Landers received an anonymous letter, allegedly written by a girl who had seen a young man force the Grimes sisters into his car. A partial license number was provided, but it led police nowhere, and the letter's author was never identified.

On January 22, 1957, a motorist in Du Page County spotted the missing girls in a roadside ditch, their naked, frozen bodies laid out side by side. Both sisters had been raped and beaten, but the coroner attributed their deaths to hypothermia. Homicide investigators refused to comment on rumors that the victims had been mutilated, their lips sliced away.

Seven months later, on August 15, 1957, 15-year-old Judith Anderson disappeared on the one-mile walk between her home and a friend's house. A week later, her dismembered remains surfaced in two 55-gallon oil drums, found floating together in Montrose Harbor. One barrel contained the girl's severed head, with four .32-caliber slugs in the brain. Police learned that Anderson had received threatening calls at her workplace, a Chicago modeling agency, but the male caller remains anonymous.

A short time after Anderson's murder, police detained teenager Barry Cook, suspected of strangling a middle-aged victim, one Margaret Gallagher, on Foster Beach. The evidence was flimsy, and Cook was acquitted of murder at trial, but he subsequently drew an 11-year sentence for aggravated assault and attempted rape in an unrelated case. Speculation was rampant concerning Cook's possible guilt in the three unsolved murders, but no evidence was ever found to link him with those crimes.

CHICAGO, Illinois holdup murders (1971–72)

Initially described in media reports as the murders of six black "businessmen," Chicago's string of brutal homicides in 1971–72 had several things in common: All the victims were indeed black males; each was shot in the back of the head, execution-style; and all were dumped in the muddy South Branch of the Chicago River. Those points aside, the crimes share one more similarity: All six remain unsolved today.

Lee Wilson was the first to die, in September 1971. Employed as a laborer in a meatpacking plant, Wilson worked a shift from 4:00 P.M. to midnight. After driving a coworker home around 1:00 A.M. on September 2, Wilson started for home but never arrived. His car was recovered later that day; Wilson's body, with hands bound and a bullet in his brain, was dragged from the river four days later. Robbery was suggested as a possible motive, though Wilson carried no more than three dollars on the night he died.

William Thomas, a baggage handler at O'Hare Airport, habitually traveled with $200 or $300 in his pocket, to cope with "emergencies." On the night of November 4, 1971, he called home and told his wife he would be working late. Around 9:30 P.M. Thomas picked up an employee's airline pass to Florida . . . and disappeared. The pass was in his car when police found it abandoned, on November 7. Thomas, bound and shot like Lee Wilson before him, was pulled from the Chicago River on December 12, 1971.

Meanwhile, the elusive killer had found his third victim. A cab driver with his own taxi, 47-year-old Albert Shorter was off duty and cruising the bars when he vanished on November 17, 1971. The victim's Cadillac was found the next day; his lifeless body was pulled from the river on November 21.

Vernell Lollar, though unemployed, was flush with $900 from a recent insurance settlement when he disappeared on November 26, 1971. His body, sans cash, was retrieved from the Chicago River on December 13, one day after Lee Wilson surfaced.

Lieutenant Scott (his name, not a military rank) was the first victim to actually qualify by normal standards as a businessman. A partner in a local snack shop, he withdrew $2,000 from a pension fund on the afternoon of December 13, 1971, and vanished the same evening. Scott's car was found on December 14, his body hauled ashore on New Year's Day.

The final victim in the murder series was 28-year-old Richard Stean, a partner in a television sales and service business. He left home around midnight on January 2, 1972, carrying $2,000 earmarked for a building contractor he was scheduled to meet the next morning. Stean missed that appointment, and his car was recovered on January 6, near Chicago's notorious Cabrini Green housing project. FBI agents entered the case when an anonymous caller demanded $11,000 ransom from Stean's father, but no one showed up to collect the payoff, and Stean's corpse was pulled from the river on February 5, 1972.

A special task force was created to investigate the murders, but after several weeks of fruitless effort police could only say, "The trail is cold." So it remains, almost four decades after the last acknowledged murder in the series.

CHICAGO, Illinois holdup murders (1992)

In the summer of 1992 Chicago's mostly black Chatham and Avalon Park neighborhoods were terrorized by a gunman who killed at least four victims and robbed an estimated 20 others. The killer's victims of preference were elderly residents, generally accosted in their own yards or driveways while returning home from some errand. According to eyewitness statements, the shooter was a light-skinned African-American male in his twenties, 5-feet-11-inches tall, weighing between 150 and 170 pounds. He frequently wore sunglasses and had a fondness for black clothing, offset on occasion with a loud purple shirt.

By Labor Day 1992 residents of the beleaguered neighborhoods were complaining to the press about police inaction on the case. Authorities responded with denials of any negligence, claiming that they had expended their best efforts to solve the crimes and would continue to do so. Ironically, press coverage of the controversy named only one of those slain by the gunman: Thomas Hodges, shot down in his own garage on July 22, 1992, was said to be the second of four persons killed in the holdup series. The rest remained anonymous to most Chicagoans and to the world at large, but their loss was keenly felt in neighborhoods where their killer was still at large.

Thus far, despite the self-described best efforts of Chicago police, there have been no reports of any major clues or suspects in the case. Perhaps the sudden fanfare of publicity drove Chicago's stalker to another hunting ground, or maybe he was taken into custody on unrelated charges. It seems doubtful that authorities will ever know the truth.

CHILD Abductions

A child's kidnapping sparks anxiety and outrage in society beyond the scope of any other crime except political assassination. Every parent knows the fear and shares the nightmare of a missing child. From America's first reported child snatching for ransom (victim Charles Ross, 1874) to the Lindbergh case (1932) to the murder of Adam Walsh, whole communities are convulsed by panic at the news of an abduction, while Amber Alerts now warn the nation at large of another tragedy in progress.

It is ironic, therefore, that despite those spasmodic outpourings of emotion, no consistent effort is made by any government agency in the United States to determine how many American children are missing at any given moment. Sporadic efforts to compile such data in the past 20 years have produced confused and contradictory reports that fuel debate without providing reliable answers, much less a proposed solution to the problem.

In 1984 the U.S. Department of Health and Human Resources estimated that 1.8 million children vanish from home every year. Ninety-five percent were listed as runaways, and 90 percent of those returned home within two weeks, leaving about 171,000 children unaccounted for. Five percent of the missing (about 90,000) were formally termed abductees, with 72,000 of those kidnapped by parents in custodial disputes. The other 18,000 children were simply gone.

Six years after that report was issued, the U.S. Justice Department banished runaways from consideration and surveyed the number of children abducted in 1988 (reputedly the last year with "complete figures") in 1990. The list included 354,100 cases in which "victims" were not returned promptly to their custodial parents after court-approved overnight visits and 163,200 longer-term parental abductions. (Ninety percent saw the child returned within a week; 10 percent were protracted for a month or more; in 1 percent of the cases children were still missing after two years.) During the same year 114,600 "broadly defined" stranger abductions of children were attempted across the United States,

with 3,200 to 6,400 succeeding. (The vague statistics are routine in government reports.) The "good news," apparently, was that only 200 or 300 abductions in 1988 fit the FBI's definition of "stereotypical kidnapping," wherein victims were gone overnight, carried 50 miles or more from home, with evidence of an intent to kill or permanently keep the child. Of the "stereotypical" abductions, between 43 and 147 had ended in murder. (The strange imprecision remains unexplained.)

Federal Bureau of Investigation spokespersons, regarded in some quarters as having the last word on crime statistics, have only succeeded in further confusing the issue with contradictory reports. In 1988, stung by media accounts of epidemic child abductions, G-men declared that only 150 "stranger abductions" were logged in the United States between 1984 and 1986. By 1995, however, the bureau admitted receiving complaints of some 300 stranger abductions *per year*—for an average of one every 29 hours, nationwide. Even then the numbers were suspect, since FBI agents involve themselves only in selected kidnappings, and no consistent, mandatory system of reporting currently exists in the United States.

In August 2000 an "unprecedented analysis" of FBI data from 1997 confirmed what criminologists have known for decades—namely, that most American children who suffer abduction are kidnapped by someone they know. The study concluded that (in 1997, at least) 24 percent of kidnapped children were taken by strangers, while 27 percent were snatched by acquaintances and 49 percent were abducted by relatives. Unspecified injury to the victims was reported in 16 percent of all stranger abductions, in "nearly a quarter" of kidnappings by acquaintances, and in 4 percent of parental kidnappings. Today the FBI still keeps no running tabulation of children kidnapped in the United States.

CIUDAD Juárez, Mexico unsolved murders (1993–??)

Alva Chavira Farel probably was not the first to die, but she appears to be the first young woman listed on a grim roster of death maintained by police in Ciudad Juárez, across the border from El Paso, Texas. Her body—beaten, raped, and strangled—was found on January 23, 1993. Before year's end, another 16 murders would be added to the list. Of those, four cases would be solved by the arrest of lovers, "friends," or relatives. Five of those remaining on the list for 1993 have yet to be identified. The victims had been variously shot, stabbed, strangled, beaten, and in one case set afire. Another 13 female victims, six of them still unidentified, were murdered in Ciudad Juárez during 1994. Oscar Maynez Grijalva, a criminologist for the state of Chihuahua, told police a serial killer might be responsible for the crimes, but his warning was ignored. At least 18 more (nine unidentified) were killed between February and September 1995, before police arrested their first suspect in the case.

That suspect was Abdul (or Abdel) Latif Sharif, an Egyptian national born in 1947, who immigrated to the United States in 1970. Based on geographical coincidence and charges filed in Mexico, New Jersey authorities would name him as a suspect in the January 1977 kidnap-murder of airline flight attendant Sandra Miller. (No charges were filed in that case.) Sharif was fired from a New Jersey job for fraud in 1978 and moved to Florida three years later. Two Palm Beach women accused him of rape in 1981; Sharif received probation for one incident, and served 45 days in jail for the other. In 1983, charged with another rape in Florida, Sharif escaped from jail but was recaptured and convicted, receiving a 12-year prison term in January 1984. Despite threats of deportation to Egypt upon his release, Sharif was paroled in 1989 and moved to Texas, where he logged multiple arrests for drunk driving. Immigration officers started deportation proceedings in 1992, but Sharif was still at large (and suspected of another rape) when he moved to Ciudad Juárez in May 1994. Satisfied with his departure, U.S. authorities dismissed all charges against him three months later.

In October 1995 a female resident of Ciudad Juárez accused Sharif of holding her captive at his home and raping her repeatedly over a three-day period. Police investigating that charge soon discovered that Sharif had been seen frequently with 17-year-old Elizabeth Castro Garcia, found raped and murdered on August 19, 1995. Sharif was jailed for that slaying and named as a suspect in 17 others, while staunchly proclaiming his innocence. Unfortunately for authorities and for the women of Ciudad Juárez, the slayings continued while Sharif sat in jail, five more before year's end and another 10 in the first four months of 1996.

While reporters speculated on "copycat" killers imitating Sharif's alleged crimes and women lived in fear of the killer dubbed "El Depredador Psicópata," police in Ciudad Juárez devised a unique explanation for their ongoing problem. Abdul Sharif, they declared, was directing the murders from jail, paying members of a street gang called *Los Rebeldes* to slaughter fresh victims, thereby supporting Sharif's claim of innocence. In April 1996 Chihuahua state police raided several downtown nightclubs in Ciudad Juárez, detaining 300 persons and charging several members of *Los Rebeldes* with conspiracy to free Sharif. (The gang members denied all charges, claiming they were tortured by police, and none were ever brought to trial for the alleged conspiracy.)

Despite the raids and fruitless indictments, the slaughter continued in Ciudad Juárez. Police recorded 16 more unsolved murders of women in the last six months of 1996, 20 in 1997, 21 in 1998, eight in the first three months of 1999. Mexico's Human Rights Commission issued a scathing report on the stalled investigation during 1998, but Chihuahua politicians managed to delay publication of the report until after state elections were completed, thereby sparing incumbent officials from criticism in the media. Abdul Sharif was convicted of Elizabeth Castro Garcia's murder on March 3, 1999, and sentenced to a term of 30 years' imprisonment (the maximum sentence available under Mexican law). Chihuahua authorities promptly announced that unnamed Federal Bureau of Investigation profilers agreed with their conclusion that Sharif was the primary killer in Ciudad Juárez, but spokesmen for the Bureau's El Paso field office denied that report.

That controversy was still reverberating in the media when Mexican police identified another suspect, bus driver and convicted rapist Jesús Manuel Guardado Márquez, as a possible participant in the slayings. Known to selected friends as "El Dracula" and "El Tolteca," Guardado was accused of raping a 14-year-old girl on March 18, 1999, but he fled Ciudad Juárez with his pregnant wife before police could arrest him. Captured in Durango, Guardado allegedly confessed to police and implicated four other bus drivers in the city's murder spree. Again, police maintained that the gang—dubbed "Los Choferes," The Drivers—were bribed by Abdul Sharif to kill two women per month as part of his legal defense strategy.

Again police in Ciudad Juárez claimed they had cracked the case, and again their latest crop of suspects would never face trial. The lagging homicide investigation drew sharp criticism at the United Nations in June 2000, with reference to 13 unsolved murders for the year to date. By February 23, 2001, when yet another suspect was identified, media reports spoke of "more than 200 women" murdered in Ciudad Juárez since 1993. The latest accused, 24-year-old Jose Juárez Rosales, was arrested in Dallas, Texas, for skipping bond on a drunk-driving charge. In custody, his fingerprints were matched to a 1996 arrest warrant in the murder of Rosario Garcia Leal. Mexican authorities named Juárez as a member of Los Rebeldes and told reporters, "When he arrives in Mexico he will be a suspect in many crimes."

Grim news continued from Ciudad Juárez despite the latest arrest. On November 6 and 7, 2001, the corpses of eight women were found on a vacant lot near a busy downtown intersection, discarded as if in a gesture of contempt for the authorities. (The victims, identified by DNA profiles, ranged in age from 15 to 20; they had disappeared between December 2000 and October 2001.) Three days later, police announced the arrest and confessions of two more bus drivers, but the suspects—Javier Garcia Uribe and Gustavo Gonzalez Meza—insisted they were tortured into making false statements. Attorneys for Garcia and Gonzalez reported death threats; one of them, Mario Escobedo Jr., was killed in a high-speed chase with police on February 5, 2002, but officers explained the "accident" by claiming they mistook Escobedo for a fugitive. Six days later, representatives of the Inter-American Commission for Human Rights began interviewing residents of Ciudad Juárez who claim they were harassed by police for organizing protests against the murders. Texas residents joined a protest march in Ciudad Juárez on March 9, 2002, and Lone Star legislators called for a binational investigation of the case. FBI spokesmen joined the call for a collaborative effort in July 2002, while relatives of the victims blamed an official cover-up for the ongoing crimes.

Reliable information on the murders is now nearly as difficult to find as a viable suspect. On July 21, 2002, an article in the *El Paso Times* referred to "325 girls and women slain [in Ciudad Juárez] since 1993," at least 60 of them employees from various *maquiladoras* (factories) where workers earn $6 per day producing goods for export. Critics of the sluggish investigation claim some of the victims were killed by drug-dealing gangsters who pay police to look the other way. The dead so far include at least six women from Texas and New Mexico whose remains, like the rest, have been discarded in or near Ciudad Juárez. The murders sparked a protest by two dozen black-garbed women in Washington, D.C., on August 15, 2002, and Mexican officials formally requested FBI assistance three weeks later. In September 2002, when activists sought to erect a memorial for the victims, members of the Association of Business Owners and Professionals of Juárez Avenue complained to Mayor Jesus Delgado about the "horrible image for tourism."

Yet another female victim was discovered in the desert outside Ciudad Juárez on October 5, 2002, inspiring media reports that "about 340 women" had thus far been slain. Meanwhile, renewed DNA testing cast doubt on the published identification of seven victims found in November 2001, thereby jeopardizing the prosecution's case against suspects Garcia and Gonzales. Mexico's first lady called for an end to the murders in November 2002, as 1,000 women paraded through Mexico City in protest. And still the crimes continue, with another corpse discovered in Ciudad Juárez on November 21, 2002. With authorities unable to agree on suspects, motives, or a body count, prospects for a definitive solution to the long-running crime spree are bleak.

Nothing has changed for the better in Ciudad Juárez since the first edition of this book was published. Various sources disagree on the latest body count of slaughtered women and girls, but all concur that the toll is steadily rising. In February 2005, Amnesty International reported that 370 bodies had been recovered so far, with "over 400 women" still missing. Seven months later, a report from the Latin American Working Group Education Fund claimed 410 murders since 1993, with suspects named or detained in 189 cases. In November 2005, Mexican human rights ombudsman José Luis Soberanes reported 28 slayings for that year alone. In June 2007, other activists claimed "more than 475 women killed violently" since 1993. California representative Hilda Solis, addressing Congress on September 4, 2007, cited a figure of "well over 400 women" dead or missing. A media report published in January 2008 claimed 393 murders between 1993 and 2007.

Mexican police continue to arrest suspects in some of the slayings, and U.S. authorities cooperate on occasion, as in the December 2003 extradition of alleged drug smuggler Felipe de Jesus Machado Reyes from Texas to face trial on charges of killing three women in Ciudad Juárez. Still, the official efforts are haphazard at best, marred by recurring charges of cover-up and corruption. According to the Latin American Working Group Education Fund's report of September 2005, "In at least 30 of the 189 murders where a suspect has been detained, officials have created a second class of victim—scapegoats who are falsely imprisoned and often tortured into confessing to crimes they did not commit."

The global media remains fascinated by the ongoing slaughter in Ciudad Juárez. In 2003, Polish journalists Eliza Kowalewska and Grzegorz Madej produced a series on the murders for Poland's TVN network, while cyberjournalist Max Blumenthal won the Online News Association's independent feature award for his "Day of the Dead" article on Salon.com. In 2004 the Greek documentary team Exandas released a film titled *Juárez, City of the Dead*. During the same year, American musician Bugs Salcido released a thematic album titled *The Juárez Murders*, while the Mexican group Los Tigres del Norte recorded their song "Las Mujeres de Juárez." The year 2006 saw publication of *The Killing Fields: Harvest of Women* by Diana Washington Valdez and production of two films on the Juárez murders: *Border Echoes*, directed by Lorena Mendez, and *Bordertown*, directed by Gregory Nava, with Antonio Banderas and Jennifer Lopez starring. Emmy-winning journalist Teresa Rodriguez published her book *The Daughters of Juárez* in 2007, while Canadian filmmakers Alex Flores and Lorena Vassolo produced another documentary on the case.

In June 2007, human rights activists charged Mexican officials with promoting a news blackout on the 1998 murder of Dutch tourist Hester Suzanne Van Nierop. Her slaying was atypical, with her corpse found underneath a bed at the downtown Hotel Plaza, but the claims of official malfeasance kept a global spotlight on the continuing crimes.

The latest victims, at this writing, are a 45-year-old woman and a girl age 12 or 13, found raped and murdered in Ciudad Juárez during July 2008. Their deaths brought the year's total to 17 murders, by official tabulation. Upon discovery of the corpses, journalists Julia Monarrez and Maria Tabuenca wrote, "Women murders are a sad reality and go unpunished. There's no indication so far of any commitment from federal or state governments to solve these murders."

CLAREMONT Murders unsolved serial homicides (1988–97)
Claremont is a suburb of Perth, in Western Australia, located on the north bank of the Swan River.

Founded as a trading post in 1830, 20 years before British authorities began transporting convicts to Australia, the town today has roughly 7,000 residents. Large homes predominate along Agett Road and Richardson Avenue, but most of Claremont's citizens reside in apartments or townhouses.

During 1996–97, a still-unidentified serial killer visited Claremont, slaying two young women and receiving credit for the disappearance of a third who is still missing, but some researchers believe that the murders actually began eight years earlier.

The Claremont killer's theoretical first victim was 22-year-old Julie Cutler, a university student from Fremantle (12 miles southwest of Perth), who vanished after leaving a party at Perth's Parmelia Hilton Hotel, at 12:30 A.M. on June 20, 1988. Two days later, Cutler's car was found in the surf at Cottesloe Beach, but her body has not been recovered. Australian journalist Liam Bartlett reports that police have told Cutler's father she was "probably" the Claremont killer's first victim.

The first "official" murder in the series occurred on Australia Day (January 26) in 1996. The victim, 18-year-old secretary Sarah Spiers, left the Club Bay View bar in Claremont's business district around 2:00 A.M. and walked to a nearby intersection, where pay phone records indicate that she called for a taxi. When the cab arrived, Spiers had vanished, and she has not been seen since.

On June 9, 1996, 23-year-old Jane Louise Rimmer went drinking with friends at Claremont's Continental Hotel (now the Redrock). She never made it home, and her decomposed remains were found in August, in scrubland south of Perth.

Ciara Glennon, a 27-year-old lawyer, also made her last stop with friends at the Continental Hotel, before she disappeared on March 14, 1997. Her body was recovered from bushland north of Perth on April 3, prompting police to acknowledge a serial killer at large.

A special task force established by the Western Australia Police—code-named "Macro"—initially believed that the slayer was a taxi driver, since Sarah Spiers and the other victims were last seen alive in circumstances where they may have sought a cab. Complaints of certain taxi drivers behaving inappropriately with female fares, logged in the latter part of 1995, also increased the focus of suspicion. As a result of the manhunt—including DNA testing of all 2,000 cabbies in Western Australia, sweeping background checks that led to dismissal of drivers with criminal records, and strict new guidelines for screening job applicants—taxi service in the district was improved... but police did not find the killer.

Aside from grilling cabbies, police commanders used female officers as decoys in various Claremont nightclubs, distributed questionnaires to "persons of interest," and sometimes confronted individuals at large to ask, "Are you the killer?" That tactic backfired when officers targeted Peter Weygers, mayor of Claremont during 1985–97 and a prominent civil libertarian. Police may have targeted Weygers for his public criticism of their reaction to the slayings, but he also rented rooms to a cab driver who claimed to have transported Sarah Spiers shortly before her disappearance. Officers raided Weygers's rental property and obtained DNA samples from the cabbie, but the investigation hit another dead end.

Several suspects have been identified in the Claremont serial murders. They include:

- Bradley John Murdoch, convicted in 2005 for the July 2001 murder of Peter Falconio and assault-related charges concerning Falconio's girlfriend. That crime occurred in the remote Northern Territory, but Murdoch previously lived in Western Australia. The theory hit a snag when police learned that he had been jailed for 15 months in 1995–97 for shooting at participants in a Kimberly soccer match. His release in February 2007 made Murdoch eligible for Ciara Glennon's murder, but he could not have killed Sarah Spiers or Jane Rimmer.

- Mark Phillip Dixie (a.k.a. "Shane Turner"), who murdered 18-year-old model Sally Anne Bowman in Surrey, England, after she spent a night out with friends on September 25, 2005. Jurors convicted Dixie in February 2008 and he received a life sentence. DNA samples from Dixie and semen samples recovered from Bowman's body were sent to the Macro Task Force in October 2006 for comparison with evidence collected in the Claremont case, but no match was announced.

- "Lance," a middle-aged junior officer of the Western Australian Public Service who lived with his parents in a suburb adjoining Claremont, targeted by police after he drew their attention during a decoy operation on April 3, 1999. Officers initially detained him for questioning at 3:00 A.M., then mounted 24-hour surveillance on him, lasting through October 1999. The investigation included forensic examination of Lance's car, two searches of his home, a polygraph test, and two days of voluntary psychological assessment—none of which developed any links to the crimes.

- A former boyfriend of Western Australian journalist Estelle Blackburn; Blackburn speculated on his guilt in her 2007 memoir, *The End of Innocence*. According to Blackburn, the man in question repeatedly beat and threatened to kill her. She also claims that he did maintenance work on taxis and had access to the vehicles at night. No charges have been filed against the suspect.

Twelve years after Jane Rimmer's slaying, in August 2008, police acknowledged the existence of video footage revealing her in conversation with an unnamed man at 12:04 A.M. on the night she disappeared. Authorities initially planned to air the tape on pay TV on August 28, but word of its existence leaked to the media 10 days ahead of schedule, prompting Deputy Police Commissioner Chris Dawson to admit that it "could have been handled better." The 12-year delay was occasioned, Dawson said, by scientific efforts to enhance the blurry tape, a goal finally achieved with aid from experts at the University of Western Australia and the National Aeronautics and Space Administration (NASA). Even then, Dawson acknowledged that the timing of its release was "stage managed," in hopes of "a controlled release."

As he explained that choice, "You don't play all your cards and put it out into the public domain. The primary reason we are releasing it (the video) now is that we want people to come forward who may never have come forward before. The investigators made the decision that once they decided to participate in a one-hour documentary they wanted to optimize the coverage that that documentary be shown and in that opportunity is an opportunity to put forward this vision. We want to stimulate any interest from any person that has never come forward before." Prior to enhancement of the tape, Dawson said, "People couldn't even recognize themselves. That's how poor these images are."

Who is the man on tape? Sadly, the camera only caught the back of his head, and its black-and-white tape makes identification of clothing dubious, at best. Meanwhile, detectives had spent 12 months surveilling a suspect whom they identified only as "an information technology expert." He is *not* the man on the videotape, they admit, but he attracted official attention in 2007 by attempting to lure a young woman into his car at Mosman Park. Despite exoneration as the man on tape, the anonymous suspect could present no alibi for any of the Claremont slayings and therefore police "have been unable to rule him out of the inquiry."

A media review of the enhanced videotape says that the unknown man "is seen approaching Jane at one minute after midnight on the morning of Sunday, June 9, 1996, there appears to be some interaction between Jane and this man, in the next vision 28 seconds later Jane is still there, but the man cannot be seen." As this book went to press, the Claremont murders remained unsolved.

CLAYTON, John Middleton murder victim (1889)

John Clayton was one of 10 children born on a farm outside Chester, Pennsylvania. In 1861, at age 20, he joined the Army of the Potomac and fought in various eastern campaigns of the Civil War. In 1867, Clayton moved with his wife and six children to Arkansas, where his older brother Powell Clayton became the state's governor on July 2, 1868.

During Reconstruction, white Democrats condemned the Yankee Republican Claytons as "carpetbaggers," and Powell Clayton waged guerrilla warfare against the terroristic Ku Klux Klan throughout his gubernatorial administration. In 1871, John Clayton was elected to the Arkansas House of Representatives from Jefferson County, while brother Powell advanced to the U.S. Senate. John served on the first board of trustees for Arkansas Industrial University (now the University of Arkansas) in 1871, and two years later helped to found Branch Normal College in Pine Bluff (now the University of Arkansas–Pine Bluff). That same year, 1873, saw John elected to the state senate, where he spent part of his term as Speaker pro tempore.

Spring of 1874 found Clayton embroiled in the Brooks-Baxter War, fought around Little Rock between the rival "Brindletail" and "Minstrel" Republican factions. "Brindletail" gubernatorial can-

didate Joseph Brooks was a "radical" carpetbagger, while opponent Elisha Baxter of the "Minstrels" was marked as a "scalawag" (a native southerner who opposed secession and favored civil rights for African Americans). Despite the similarity of their platforms, Brooks and Baxter were deadly enemies, and Brooks refused to accept the tabulations presented by Baxter's vote-counters. Clayton supported Brooks, leading troops against Baxter's faction, but weeks of violence left Baxter in charge as governor.

Black Republican votes made John Clayton the sheriff of Jefferson County in 1876 and reelected him for five successive two-year terms. In 1888, he lost a race for U.S. Congress to Democrat Clifton Breckenridge, in an election marked by rampant fraud. White terrorism kept many black voters from the polls that year, but Breckenridge still won by the narrowest of margins: 846 votes out of 34,000 ballots. Noting that armed racists had stolen ballot boxes in Conway County, where Clayton enjoyed widespread popularity, Clayton challenged the election results—and thereby sealed his fate.

On January 29, 1889, while personally leading an investigation of vote fraud in Plumerville, Clayton was shot through the window of his room at a local boardinghouse. The bullet killed him instantly, and while the sniper was never identified, Clayton enjoyed a triumph of sorts in death. He was officially declared the winner of his last election contest, Breckenridge was ousted from Congress, and the seat was declared vacant.

CLERY, Alexandra See "Astrological Murders"

CLEVELAND, Ohio "Torso" murders (1934–??)

The gully known as Kingsbury Run looks like a scar across the face of downtown Cleveland. Sixty feet deep in places, the ancient creek bed is lined with 30-odd pairs of railroad tracks serving local factories and distant cities, bearing cargo to Pittsburgh, Chicago, or Youngstown, whisking commuters to posh bedroom communities like Shaker Heights. During the Great Depression, Kingsbury Run was also a favorite camp for hoboes and a playground for children with time to kill. In the latter 1930s it became the focal point of America's most fascinating murder mystery—a puzzle that endures to this day—though in fact the case had its origins elsewhere, on the shores of Lake Erie.

On September 5, 1934, a driftwood hunter found the lower portion of a woman's torso buried in sand at Euclid Beach, eight miles east of downtown Cleveland. The victim's legs were severed at the knees, her skin discolored by application of a chemical preservative. The coroner extrapolated height and age from the meager evidence available, but the resultant portrait resembled none of Cleveland's known missing women. The "Lady of the Lake" was never identified, police adding insult to injury with their stubborn refusal to count her as an "official" victim once a pattern of crime was revealed.

A year later, on September 23, 1935, boys playing in Kingsbury Run found two headless male corpses, nude but for the stockings worn by the younger victim. Both had been emasculated, and their severed heads were found nearby. Pathologists determined that the older victim, unidentified, was killed at least five days before the other, and his skin bore a reddish tinge from treatment with a chemical preservative. The younger man, identified as 29-year-old Edward Andrassy, was a bisexual ex-convict with a long record of petty arrests in Cleveland. Retraction of the neck muscles on both corpses indicated that the men had been alive when their heads were severed.

On January 26, 1936, a Cleveland butcher was alerted to the presence of "some meat in a basket" behind his shop. Investigating, he was shocked to find two human thighs, one arm, and the lower half of a woman's torso. The upper torso, lower legs, and missing arm were found 12 days later, behind a vacant house, but fingerprints had already identified the victim as Florence Polillo, a 41-year-old prostitute. Her severed head was never found.

Four months later, on June 5, 1936, two boys traversing Kingsbury Run found a man's head wrapped in dirty trousers, a mile from the spot where Edward Andrassy and his nameless companion were dumped in September 1935. Railroad workers found the victim's body on June 6, but victim number five remained nameless, despite publication of his numerous distinctive tattoos and a plaster death mask displayed for all comers at the 1936 World's Fair in Cleveland.

On July 22, 1936, the nude, headless body of an unknown man was found beside Big Creek, in the suburb of Brooklyn, across town from Kingsbury Run. The only victim killed on Cleveland's west side, this "John Doe" would also be the only victim killed where he was found, as demonstrated by the blood-soaked earth beneath him. Decomposition foiled all efforts to identify the corpse.

A hobo spotted victim number seven—or part of him, at least—in Kingsbury Run on September 10, 1936. The dismembered remains were floating in a stagnant pond, and police divers were called to retrieve two halves of a torso, plus the lower legs and thighs. The severed head, arms, and genitalia were never found.

Soon after that discovery, Detectives Peter Merylo and Martin Zalewski were assigned full-time to the "torso murders" case, tracking the elusive killer whom newspapers variously dubbed "The Mad Butcher of Kingsbury Run," "The Headhunter," or simply "The Unknown." Over the next two years Merylo and Zalewski investigated hundreds of leads, cleared scores of innocent suspects, and jailed dozens more on a wide variety of charges—all without bagging their primary target. Newspapers, meanwhile, had a field day with the murders, speculating endlessly on motives, the identity of the victims, and the slayer's supposed surgical skill.

On February 23, 1937, the upper half of a woman's torso was found at Euclid Beach, almost precisely where the first (still unacknowledged) victim had been found in September 1934. The lower trunk surfaced in Lake Erie, off East 30th Street, on May 5, 1937, while the head, arms, and legs remained forever missing.

On June 6, 1937, the skeleton of a black woman, missing the limbs and one rib, was found beneath the Lorain-Carnegie Bridge. As in every other case, the victim was decapitated. Coroner Samuel Gerber dated her death from early June 1936. In April 1938 the son of vanished Rose Wallace "identified" the remains as his mother's, based on dental work, but problems remained. Wallace had disappeared in August 1936, two months after the victim's estimated date of death, and her Cincinnati dentist was deceased, his files destroyed, thus ruling out a positive identification. Detective Merylo accepted the shaky I.D., but it brought him no closer to the killer.

Exactly one month after number nine was found, the lower torso of a man was sighted in the Cuyahoga River, underneath the Third Street Bridge. Police retrieved the upper trunk and severed thighs that afternoon, but other pieces surfaced over the next week. By July 14, 1937, authorities had everything except the latest victim's head and name.

On April 8, 1938, a woman's lower left leg was fished out of the Cuyahoga River, behind Public Square. The missing left foot, both thighs, and two halves of the bisected torso were hauled ashore, wrapped in burlap, on May 2, but the victim's head, right leg, and arms were never found. Like most of the others, she remains unidentified today.

The last "official" victims—male and female, killed at different times—were found on August 16, 1938, by workmen at a lakeside rubbish dump. The new "John Doe" was nothing but a skeleton, decapitated in familiar style, missing two ribs, both hands, and feet. Coroner Gerber placed his death somewhere between December 1937 and February 1938. The female victim was cut into nine pieces, all accounted for. She was killed, Gerber said, sometime between February and April 1938, her identity forever obscured by advanced decomposition.

In January 1939, the Cleveland *Press* printed the following letter, mailed from Los Angeles:

> *Chief of Police Matowitz:*
> *You can rest easy now, as I have come to sunny California for the winter. I felt bad operating on those people, but science must advance. I shall astound the medical profession, a man with only a D.C.*
>
> *What did their lives mean in comparison to hundreds of sick and disease-twisted bodies? Just laboratory guinea pigs found on any public street. No one missed them when I failed. My last case was successful. I know now the feeling of Pasteur, Thoreau and other pioneers.*
>
> *Right now I have a volunteer who will absolutely prove my theory. They call me mad and a butcher, but the truth will come out.*
>
> *I have failed but once here. The body has not been found and never will be, but the head, minus the features, is buried on Century Boulevard, between Western and Crenshaw. I feel it my duty to dispose of the bodies as I do. It is God's will not to let them suffer.*
> *"X"*

No buried heads were found in Los Angeles, and the manhunt shifted back to Cleveland. On July 5, 1939, sheriff's deputies arrested a Slavic immigrant, 52-year-old Frank Dolezal, and launched a marathon interrogation at the county jail. Dolezal eventually confessed to the Andrassy and Polillo murders, flubbing many details that were "corrected" in subsequent statements. He finally recanted all confessions, charging detectives with third-degree tactics, and suspicious stains found in his flat were identi-

fied as animal blood. On August 24, 1939, Dolezal "committed suicide" in his cell, allegedly hanging himself from a wall hook shorter than he was, and the autopsy revealed four ribs broken in jailhouse beatings. Today, no one regards Dolezal as a serious suspect in the torso case.

On May 3, 1940, three male corpses were discovered in abandoned box cars at McKees Rocks, Pennsylvania, outside Pittsburgh. All had been decapitated and the heads were missing; one victim was otherwise intact, while two had been dissected at the hips and shoulders. Killed in the cars where they lay, the men had been dead from three to six months, and all three bodies had been scorched by fire. The most complete victim was identified as 30-year-old James Nicholson, a homosexual ex-convict from Wisconsin. The killer had carved the word *NAZI* on Nicholson's chest, inverting the *Z* by accident or by design. Authorities unanimously blamed the crimes on Cleveland's headhunter, tracing the box cars to pinpoint the murders at Youngstown, Ohio, in December 1939.

Journalist Oscar Fraley, in his book *4 Against the Mob* (1961), contends that Cleveland public safety director Eliot Ness not only identified the torso killer in 1938, but also brought him to a semblance of justice. Tagged with the pseudonym of "Gaylord Sundheim" in Fraley's account, the suspect was described as a homosexual premed student and member of a prominent Cleveland family. Interrogated by Ness in autumn 1938, "Sundheim" allegedly escaped prosecution by committing himself to a mental hospital, where he died in 1940 or 1941. In the interim, he tormented Ness with a series of obscene, menacing notes, which terminated with his death.

The tale deserves consideration, inasmuch as Ness preserved the "greeting cards"—all carefully anonymous—and they are viewable in Cleveland archives, but do the taunting notes provide a viable solution to the mystery? Why did experts on the case insist the Butcher claimed three victims in December 1939, when "Sundheim" had been out of circulation for a year or more? If Ness was certain of the killer's identity, why did he allow suspect Frank Dolezal to be tortured (and possibly murdered) by sheriff's officers in 1939? If the case was solved in 1938, why did Detective Merylo pursue the Mad Butcher into retirement, blaming his elusive quarry for 50-odd murders by 1947?

Professor James Badal answered some of those questions, while raising new ones, 40 years after Fraley's account was published. His definitive study of the torso case, *In the Wake of the Butcher* (2001), identifies Ness's suspect by name, but discredits much of Fraley's account in the process. Subject Francis Edward Sweeney was not a medical student, but rather a licensed physician, with a history of psychiatric treatments dating from December 1933 (and possibly much earlier). A veteran of World War I, Dr. Sweeney entered the Sandusky (Ohio) Soldiers and Sailors Home on August 25, 1938, nine days after the last official torso victims were found in Cleveland. Contrary to Fraley's report, Sweeney outlived Eliot Ness by seven years, his death reported on July 9, 1964. The murders after 1938 are theoretically explained by Sweeney's *voluntary* self-commitment to the hospital, which left him free to come and go at will, without restraint, but Professor Badal concedes that the case against Sweeney is not definitively proved.

There is a grisly postscript to the Mad Butcher's story. On July 22, 1950, a man's headless body, emasculated and dismembered, was found at a Cleveland lumber yard, a few miles from Kingsbury Run. The severed head turned up four days later, and the victim was identified as 40-year-old Robert Robertson, an alcoholic with a dozen arrests for public drunkenness during his last year alive. Coroner Gerber, still on the job in Cleveland, reported that "the work resembles exactly that of the torso murderer."

In retrospect, it seems clear that the Mad Butcher killed at least 16 victims between 1934 and 1939. He may have slaughtered Robert Robertson, as well, and speculation links the same elusive suspect to a series of "headless murders" around NEW CASTLE, PENNSYLVANIA between 1925 and 1939. No firm connection was established in that case, and the number of New Castle victims has been wildly inflated by sensational journalists, but the crimes *were* committed in proximity to rail lines between Cleveland and Youngstown, Ohio. None of the New Castle victims were ever identified, and Professor Badal notes that Francis Sweeney "is not a likely suspect" in the Pennsylvania crimes. The identity of that killer, like the whereabouts of the Cleveland Butcher's eight trophy heads, remains a mystery.

CLIFFORD, Rochelle See NEW BEDFORD, MASSACHUSETTS, MURDERS

CLOER, Betty See "ASTROLOGICAL MURDERS"

COCHRAN, Frances Marie murder victim (1941)

A friend of Frances Cochran once described the 19-year-old bookkeeper as "death on auto rides." Cochran had a passion for cars and never missed an opportunity to ride in one. She took the bus each morning from her parents' home on Webster Street in Lynn, Massachusetts, to the Dudley Leather Company. Each evening after work the same bus brought her back, and Frances walked the few blocks from the bus stop to her door.

Unless she got a lift along the way.

A 6:00 P.M. on Thursday, July 17, 1941, Cochran disembarked from her bus at the corner of Chatham and Marianna Streets. She dropped a letter in the corner mailbox and began to walk down Marianna toward her home on Webster. Coming from the opposite direction was a square-backed car, described in later press reports as "ancient," black with yellow trim and wooden spokes on its wheels. The driver noticed Cochran, slowed to make a U-turn in the middle of the street, and pulled up beside her. Bystanders saw her smile, approach the car, climb in, and close the door. The car turned onto Chatham Street, away from Webster and her home.

Cochran was never seen alive again.

Descriptions of the driver were inconsistent, and no one got a clear look at his face, but there was general agreement that he was a "dark" or "swarthy" man with "slicked-back hair." His age was anybody's guess.

Cochran's parents were worried by 7:00 P.M. and frantic by 9:30 when police arrived at their home. Their daughter, a 1940 graduate of Lynn English High School, was a person of regular hours and habits. Her reputation was "beyond even the whisper of reproach." A fraction over five feet tall, she tipped the scales at a petite 100 pounds. Most men, detectives knew, would have no difficulty overpowering a girl her size.

Harold Cochran was still sitting up, waiting for his daughter at 3:00 A.M. on Friday when a car pulled up outside the house. He went to have a closer look and found two men in the vehicle, one behind the steering wheel, the other seated in the rear. As Harold approached the car, the driver told him, "She's in back." The second man replied, "No, Frances is in front." With that, the car sped off, and while police turned out to mount a guard on Webster Street, the strangers were content to play their eerie little joke and slip away unrecognized. If Harold described the car or visitors in any detail the descriptions have been lost with time.

At 1:00 P.M. on Sunday, July 20, a local radio station aired an appeal from Cochran's parents to their missing daughter: "If you hear this broadcast, Frances, come home or telephone at once. If there are any explanations, do not hesitate." Forty minutes later, an unknown man telephoned the station. "If you want the body," he declared, "it's off the Danvers Road, off Highland Avenue, at the Swampscott line." The caller left no name, and all police could say about the man was that he spoke "better than passable English."

Two Swampscott patrolmen drove out to the site, a kind of lover's lane almost directly opposite the Moose Lodge at the corner of Highland Avenue and Swampscott Road. They found a woman's shoe beside the road and spent the best part of an hour searching the adjacent field before they found what they were looking for.

The corpse was concealed within a thicket, lying on its back, a stone beneath the battered skull. The woman's face was beaten to a pulp, bone showing through a pair of gashes in her forehead just above the eyes. Several of her teeth were broken, and an inch-thick swamp alder stick protruded from her mouth, shoved deep into her throat. Her open jacket was pulled up beneath her armpits and her blouse was torn, exposing bruised and lacerated flesh. Her skirt and slip were bunched around her hips; grass and twigs had been stuffed into her vagina. Scorch marks on the victim's shoulders, neck, and chest suggested an attempt to burn the body. Every inch of skin the officers could see bore witness to "a furious assault." A quantity of sand, identified as foreign to the dump site, had been sprinkled over Cochran's face and breasts. Police identified the body from initials engraved inside her class ring.

The coroner first said Cochran had been suffocated, possibly by choking on the stick, but he later agreed that she could have died from the ferocious beating. In fact, she had been dead a day or two when found. No precise time of death was determined, but the slow rate of decomposition convinced authorities the body had been stored in a cool place, perhaps a refrigerator, while the killer planned his next move.

Police Chief Edward Callahan predicted an early arrest. "No stone must be unturned," he told the press, "to bring the perpetrators of this foul deed to justice." The first of many suspects in the case, described in media reports as a Lynn resident in his thirties, was found at 8:30 A.M. on July 21, 1941, sleeping in his car 100 yards from the old field artillery stables on Highland Avenue. Under questioning, he told police that he had spent the weekend with a couple in New Hampshire and had parked along the road when he became too tired to drive. Authorities reviewed his story and released him. Neither he nor his New Hampshire friends were ever publicly identified.

Another suspect was a young married man who had given Cochran a ride home from her bus stop several days before she disappeared. Police were fishing, though; he did not match the vague description of the driver glimpsed by witnesses on July 17. In fact, detectives never came close to finding the killer despite several arrests, some 1,900 interviews, and more than 20 false confessions to the crime. Chief Callahan's determination notwithstanding, the case remains unsolved.

COHN, Lenora   See "JACK THE RIPPER" (1915)

COLBY, Barbara   murder victim (1975)
The actress Barbara Colby was born in New York City on July 2, 1940, and launched her professional career in 1964 with a performance in *Six Characters in Search of an Author*. She made the leap to Broadway a year later, debuting in *The Devils*, and impressed critics in 1965–67 with roles in *Under Milkwood*, *Murder in the Cathedral*, *Dear Liar*, and *Julius Caesar*. Her first feature film role cast Colby as an uncredited character in *Petulia* (1968).

Colby made the switch to television in 1969, with an appearance on *N.Y.P.D.*, and seemed to realize that she had found her niche. Although cast in three subsequent Hollywood films—*Memory of Us* (1974), *California Split* (1974), and *Rafferty and the Gold Dust Twins* (1975)—the rest of her work would be done for the small screen. During 1971–74 Colby appeared on television series including *The Odd Couple*, *The FBI*, *McMillan & Wife*, *ABC Afterschool Specials*, *Medical Center*, *Kung Fu*, and *Gunsmoke*. During the same period, her made-for-TV movies included *Columbo: Murder by the Book* (1971), *Look Homeward, Angel* (1972), *A Brand New Life* (1973), and *Judgment: The Trial of Julius and Ethel Rosenberg* (1974).

Colby struck career gold in 1974, with a guest appearance on the *Mary Tyler Moore Show*, portraying a smart-mouthed hooker in a scene where lead character Mary Richards (Moore) is briefly jailed. That episode won an Emmy Award for Outstanding Writing in a Comedy Series, and the show's producers recalled Colby for a second episode in 1975, then offered her the prized "second-banana" role behind Cloris Leachman in *Phyllis*, an *MTM* spin-off premiering in 1975.

Colby completed taping of the *Phyllis* pilot and two subsequent episodes, but she would not live to see Leachman collect her Golden Globe for that series. On July 24, 1975, Colby left an acting class in Venice, California, with fellow TV actor James Kiernan. As they neared their car, two unknown gunmen shot them in the parking lot. Colby died instantly, while Kiernan (whose sole screen credit was an episode of *Rhoda*) lived long enough to describe the unprovoked shooting.

Police noted that neither victim was robbed, and, since Kiernan did not recognize either shooter, authorities classified the double murder as a random "thrill" killing. No suspects were identified. Barbara Colby's final made-for-TV film, *The Ashes of Mrs. Reasoner*, aired the year after her death.

COLE, Jessica   See WASHINGTON, D.C., MURDERS (1996–97)

COLEMAN, Eloise   See FORT LAUDERDALE MURDERS

COLEMAN, Guilford   murder victim (1870)

A former slave and Republican Party activist in Reconstruction-era Alabama, Guilford Coleman was one of two freedmen from Greene County who attended district and state political conventions despite threats and warnings from the Ku Klux Klan. Witnesses before a subsequent congressional investigating panel recalled Coleman as "a very good old negro [*sic*] . . . and . . . not a noisy man in politics," but terrorists seeking to recapture the state for one-party Democratic rule were immune to such fine distinctions. In their view any black political involvement was a capital offense against tradition and the "Southern Way of Life."

One night in September 1870 a band of masked Klansmen raided Coleman's home and dragged him out, leaving two of their number behind to guard his wife and prevent her from summoning help. The execution party returned after an uncertain interval, whistling for their rear-guard comrades to rejoin them. After the raiders were gone, Coleman's wife and neigh-

bors set out to find him, tracking a blood trail through the woods without result. Historian Allen Trelease, in his classic history of the Reconstruction KKK (*White Terror*, 1971), reports that Coleman's abductors "mutilated his body almost beyond recognition," but testimony received in 1871 indicated that his corpse had not been found. In either case, the crime remained officially unsolved.

COLEMAN, Patricia   See "SOUTHSIDE SLAYER"

COLES, Frances   murder victim (1891)

London police constable Ernest Thompson was completing his first night on foot patrol when he entered Swallow Gardens at 2:20 A.M. on February 13, 1891. Despite its lyrical name, Swallow Gardens was a squalid alley underneath a railroad arch, connecting Chambers Street to Rosemary Lane (modern Royal Mint Street). As Thompson entered the alley, his lantern beam picked out a woman's prostrate form. A closer look showed him the bloody gash across her throat.

Though mortally wounded, the woman was still alive when Thompson found her, staring at him with terrified eyes. Thompson heard footsteps retreating toward Rosemary Lane, but standing orders for discovery of bodies required him to stay with the woman while his shrill whistle summoned help. Acquaintances later reported that Thompson regretted his choice— and the probable killer's escape—to the end of his life. (Nine years later, Thompson was stabbed to death on duty while trying to arrest a rowdy street brawler.) At that, his efforts to save the woman were wasted. She died on a stretcher, en route to London Hospital.

Detectives identified the dead woman as 26-year-old Frances Coles, a prostitute otherwise known as Frances Coleman, Frances Hawkins, and "Carroty Nell." A bootmaker's daughter, Coles had worked as a wholesale chemist's packer until 1884, when she left that job to try her luck on London's streets. Investigators at the murder scene found her nightly earnings, about two shillings, concealed behind a gutter pipe at one end of the alley. A black crepe bonnet lay where she had fallen, and morgue attendants found a second hat pinned underneath her dress.

The victim's occupation and the cause of death prompted suspicion that Coles might have been killed by "JACK THE RIPPER," London's elusive serial killer who had claimed no verified victims since November 1888. Dr. Bagster Phillips, in his autopsy report, found that Coles had been killed by a right-handed man who passed a knife three times across her throat from left to right, while she lay on the ground. None of the Ripper's characteristic abdominal mutilations were present, but detectives and reporters thought the killer was disturbed by Constable Thompson before he could complete his ghastly work.

Inquiries produced a witness, one William (Jumbo) Friday, who had seen a man and woman talking together near Swallow Gardens in the early-morning hours of February 13. Friday believed the woman had been Frances Coles; her male companion was stocky, with a "foreign" appearance that somehow suggested employment as a ship's fireman. Further investigation led police to James Thomas Sadler, recently a fireman on the SS *Fez,* moored at the London docks. Discharged from the ship on February 11, Sadler had found his way to the Princess Alice pub on Commercial Street and there renewed a former acquaintance with Frances Coles. They spent that night together, and Sadler had given Coles the money to purchase the second-hand bonnet found beside her body. Still together on February 12, they spent the day drinking Sadler's paycheck, until he was mugged on Thrawl Street and Coles abandoned him to find a man with money. Sadler had visited her White's Row lodging house around 11:30 P.M., and they had argued for the best part of an hour. Sadler left at 12:30 A.M. on February 13, followed by Coles five minutes later. Fifty minutes before Constable Thompson found her dying, Coles met prostitute Ellen Callagher on Commercial Street, then went on a "date" (against Callagher's advice) with a man who had assaulted Callagher several days earlier. Nothing more is known of her movements until she was found with her throat slashed in Swallow Gardens.

Police arrested Sadler for murder on February 14, and while he made no great protest at first, that changed when Sadler found he was suspected of the Ripper crimes. The Seamen's Union provided attorneys for the inquest, and the lawyers in turn produced seven witnesses to Sadler's movements on the night Coles was slain. Blood on his clothing was explained by a series of drunken brawls with dock workers and inhabitants of a Spitalfields rooming house that finally sent Sadler to London Hospital at 5:00 A.M. on February 13. Before that trip, Sadler had sold his knife for a shilling to another sailor, Duncan Campbell, who found it too dull to cut meat when he sat down to din-

ner. Dr. F. J. Oxley, the first physician to examine Coles at Swallow Gardens, testified that "If a man were incapably drunk and the knife blunt I don't think he could have produced the wound [that killed Coles]." The prosecution's case collapsed entirely when witnesses Kate McCarthy and Thomas Fowled identified themselves as the couple seen by Jumbo Friday near Swallow Gardens the night Coles died. Sadler was discharged on February 27, 1891, with a coroner's verdict of "murder by a person or persons unknown."

That ruling did not exonerate him in the minds of London detectives, however. Any link to the Ripper crimes was disproved when officers learned that Sadler had shipped out for the Mediterranean on August 17, 1888, and returned to London on October 1, thereby missing four of Jack's five homicides, but some still believed he had killed Frances Coles. Sir Melville Macnaghten, chief constable of Scotland Yard's Criminal Investigation Division from 1890 to 1903, said as much in 1894, but no serious evidence supports that contention, and the case remains officially unsolved today.

COLGROVE, O. R. assassination victim (1869)

The brothers Colgrove were atypical "carpetbaggers" in 1869, having left their northern home to settle in North Carolina before secession and the later Civil War. Still, they were Unionists and proud Republicans, which marked them for harassment and worse during the tumultuous Reconstruction era (1865–77). Worse yet, the brothers sought and won public office under the Grand Old Party's banner, O. R. Colgrove elected to serve as sheriff of Jones County, while brother D. R. Colgrove filled a seat in the state senate.

Election of outside Republicans was bad enough, but Sheriff Colgrove compounded the insult by taking his duties seriously, pursuing and arresting racial terrorists from the Constitutional Union Guard (widely regarded as a front group for the Ku Klux Klan). Fearing more arrests, Jones County militants recruited gunmen from the Lenoir County Klan to eliminate Colgrove. On May 28, 1869, the killers ambushed their quarry on a rural road, killing the sheriff and a black traveling companion. Democratic newspapers celebrated the event with a campaign of posthumous character assassination, meanwhile ignoring the Klan's reign of terror.

Governor William Holden, himself a Republican, dispatched 25 state militiamen to Jones County in

June 1869, but they returned to Raleigh in August and the bloodshed resumed immediately. Holden also employed a private detective, one L. H. Mowers, to investigate Colgrove's murder, but no suspects were ever publicly identified. By year's end, D. R. Colgrove and other prominent Republicans were forced to flee Jones County in fear of their lives. It would require federal troops to suppress the Klan in North Carolina, and even that would not prevent "redemption" of the state for white dominance after 1877.

COLLIER, Myrtle   See "Southside Slayer"

COLLINS, Diane   See Atlanta "Lover's Lane" murders

COLLINS, Kevin Andrew missing person (1984)
Born on January 24, 1974, Kevin Collins lived with his parents and eight siblings in San Francisco's Western Addition neighborhood, between Golden Gate Park and Pacific Heights. He attended St. Agnes School in the Haight district and vanished after leaving basketball practice at the school's gymnasium on February 10, 1984.

Coaches recalled that Kevin left the gym between 6:00 and 6:30 P.M., walking home alone since his older brother Gary was ill at home. Witnesses saw him around 7:55 P.M. at the intersection of Masonic Avenue and Oak Street, waiting for a bus to take him home. Some recalled him talking to a tall blond man accompanied by a large black dog.

Kevin never made it home, and he has not been found. The trauma of his disappearance ultimately led his parents to divorce, but not before their missing son literally became a poster child for vanished children nationwide. The search began with posting of his photograph in shop windows and on telephone poles, then expanded to billboards, "Have-You-Seen-Me?" milk cartons, and coverage in national magazines including *Newsweek.*

None of it helped.

Detectives chased various leads and investigated hundreds of individuals, ranging from family friends and acquaintances to complete strangers. Officers hoped for a break in the case in 1988, when San Mateo resident John Dunkle was arrested for the murders of three boys ages 12–15 during 1981–85, but while Dunkle confessed and was sentenced to die, no evidence linking him to Kevin's disappearance was uncovered.

Collins remains missing and, while he is now presumed dead by the law and his loved ones, no proof of his murder has ever been found.

A strange footnote to this unsolved case emerged in 2005, when a would-be identity thief used Kevin's name in an attempt to procure a fraudulent passport. California resident Behzad Mofrad, age 39, believed the case was "cold" enough that Kevin's name would not be recognized, but a State Department clerk saw through the scam and alerted authorities. On November 15, 2005, Mofrad pled guilty in federal court. He received a 33-month prison term in February 2006.

COLON, Carmen   See "Alphabet Murders"

COLORADO unsolved murders (1911–12)
A puzzling case from the Centennial State made headlines during August 1911, when music teacher Signe Carlszen was reported slain in Denver. On the night of August 9 she left a student's home at nine o'clock, hiking across a lonely, open field to reach the streetcar that would take her home. When she had not arrived by 2:00 A.M., her father launched a search, but seven hours passed before a farmer found her body in the field.

According to published reports, Carlszen was found with a scarf wound tightly around her neck, skull fractured by at least six heavy blows. Some of the head wounds measured three inches across, and local newspapers reported that "the blows caused her eyes to bulge from their sockets." One article also claimed that Carlszen's body had been mutilated with a knife.

Confusion still surrounds the other victims in this case, with Signe Carlszen seemingly the last to die. On August 11, 1912, the *New York Times* reported that authorities were studying "a half-dozen similar crimes" in Denver and its suburbs, spanning the past six months. Local reports, meanwhile, linked Carlszen's death to a triple murder reported from Colorado Springs on September 17, 1911. The victims in that case were named as Mr. and Mrs. H. F. Wayne and a female houseguest, Mrs. A. J. Burnham. Homicide investigators labored long and hard to solve the case, but all in vain. Their search was fruitless, and no suspects were ever charged or publicly identified.

COLUMBUS, Ohio serial murders (1965–66)

On May 23, 1966, an unknown gunman ambushed Loren Bollinger, a 40-year-old rocket scientist at Ohio State University, outside his office in downtown Columbus. Five bullets were extracted from Bollinger's corpse, including one that pierced his brain. Ballistics tests linked the .25-caliber pistol to the earlier murders of two gas station attendants in or near Columbus, since September 1965. The same weapon was also linked to fourth crime, in which another service station employee was robbed, then shot and left for dead by a white male assailant. Motive remains obscure in the Bollinger case, in which no attempt at robbery was evident. Despite a fair description of the gunman from his sole surviving victim, Columbus detectives are no closer to solving the case at present than they were in 1966.

COMPOS, Sonyia   See GRAND RAPIDS MURDERS

CONNELL, Julie   See ALAMEDA COUNTY MURDERS

CONNIFF, Helen   See DETROIT MURDERS

COOK, Gale   See GRAND RAPIDS MURDERS

COOK, Justin   See HOSPITAL FOR SICK CHILDREN MURDERS

COOK, Kelly   See "HIGHWAY KILLER"

COOKE, Linda   See WILTSHIRE, ENGLAND, MURDERS

"COOPER, D. B." unidentified skyjacker (1971)

On November 24, 1971, a passenger using the name Dan Cooper boarded Northwest Orient Airlines Flight 305 at Oregon's Portland International Airport, bound for Seattle. He was assigned to seat 18C, at the rear of the Boeing 727–100 aircraft. Subsequent descriptions portray a man in his mid-40s, between five feet 10 inches and six feet tall. He carried a briefcase and wore black sunglasses, with a black raincoat over a dark suit, white shirt, and a black necktie with a mother-of-pearl tie tack.

After takeoff, Cooper handed an envelope to flight attendant Florence Schaffner, seated in a nearby jump seat. Schaffner, an attractive young woman accustomed to "passes" from male passengers, assumed the envelope contained Cooper's telephone number. She put it in her pocket, unopened, whereupon Cooper leaned close and said, "Miss, you'd better look at that note. I have a bomb."

Inside the envelope, Schaffner found a message reading: "I have a bomb in my briefcase. I will use it if necessary. I want you to sit next to me. You are being hijacked." The message also demanded $200,000 in unmarked $20 bills, and two sets of parachutes including two main chutes and two emergency chest packs. Written instructions demanded delivery of the cash and parachutes upon arrival at Seattle-Tacoma Airport.

Schaffner informed pilot William Scott of the threat, whereupon Scott radioed Seattle to alert authorities. Acting in concert with FBI agents, Northwest Orient president Donald Nyrop ordered Scott to cooperate with the hijacker. Scott sent Schaffner to confirm that Cooper had a bomb. Cooper opened his briefcase long enough for her to see red cylinders resembling dynamite, a battery, and various wires. At the same time, Cooper issued instructions that the jet must stay aloft until his ransom and parachutes were ready at Seattle-Tacoma.

While the aircraft circled over Puget Sound, G-men plotted a means of trapping Cooper without endangering innocent persons. They complied with his request for unmarked bills, but chose twenties printed in 1969, issued by the Federal Reserve Bank of San Francisco, whose serial numbers began with the letter *L*. Each of the 10,000 bills was then photographed before packing. Seattle police complied with Cooper's demand for civilian-type parachutes with manually operated ripcords, bypassing McChord Air Force Base to use chutes from a local skydiving school.

Controversy surrounds Cooper's onboard behavior prior to touchdown at Seattle-Tacoma. Flight attendant Tina Mucklow, who spent most of the flight beside Cooper, said that the hijacker "seemed rather nice." He was considerate enough, in fact, to demand meals for the crew after landing. G-men, on the other hand, filed unsupported claims that Cooper was "obscene" and used "filthy language." In retrospect, those reports smack of the hyperbole that dominated FBI publicity releases under J. Edgar Hoover.

At 5:24 P.M., traffic controllers radioed word that Cooper's demands had been met. The jet landed 15 minutes later and taxied to a distant runway, with interior lights dimmed on Cooper's order to frustrate police sharpshooters. A Northwest Orient employee delivered the money and parachutes, whereupon Cooper released Florence Schaffner and his 36 fellow passengers. Pilot Scott, copilot Bob Rataczak, flight engineer H. E. Anderson, and Tina Mucklow were forced to remain aboard. Cooper examined the ransom while mechanics refueled the airliner, and the plane took off again at 7:40 P.M., ordered to set a course for Mexico City and proceed with the landing gear down, flying at the comparatively slow speed of 196 miles per hour and an altitude of 10,000 feet (20,000 feet below normal cruising altitude for the 727).

Copilot Rataczak told Cooper that the plane could only travel for 1,000 miles at the designated speed and altitude, so Cooper ordered a detour for refueling at Reno, Nevada. He also directed that the cabin be unpressurized, which would marginally increase his chances of a successful parachute jump. Cooper ordered Tina Mucklow to the cockpit, and moments later—at 8:13 P.M.—he lowered the jet's aft stairway and jumped from the plane, concealed by clouds from U.S. Air Force jet fighters assigned to track the Northwest Orient flight.

"Dan Cooper" has not been seen since. A search of the aircraft in Reno recovered the hijacker's tie and tie tack, two of his four parachutes, and various unidentified fingerprints. Missing with Cooper were two parachutes, the bag of cash, and his briefcase. Passengers and crew helped forensic artists create drawings of Cooper, which FBI headquarters still regard as accurate. Soon after the hijacking, G-men questioned and released a Portland resident named D. B. Cooper, who was never a serious suspect. Careless reporters substituted *that* Cooper's initials for "Dan Cooper's" false first name, and the erroneous label was soon established in print.

Authorities first believed Cooper might have landed near Lake Merwin, Washington, 30 miles north of Portland, Oregon, but details belatedly elicited from Captain Scott in 1980 moved the presumptive jump site 20 miles farther east. Precise calculation of the landing zone was by the jet's airspeed and 200-mile-per-hour winds aloft at the time Cooper jumped. Searchers combed the rural district for 18 days in 1971 and returned with 400 soldiers from Fort Lewis for a six-week search in spring 1972, but neither effort revealed any useful evidence.

G-men staked their hopes for an arrest on a search for the ransom bills, sending lists of the 10,000 serial numbers to banks and other commercial institutions, as well as to law enforcement agencies around the world. Northwest Orient offered a $25,000 reward for information leading to Cooper's arrest and conviction, but it drew no takers and the offer was later rescinded. In November 1973, the *Oregon Journal* offered a $1,000 reward to the first person reporting discovery of a verified ransom bill—but, again, no hits were verified.

Late in 1978, a hunter found a placard, which included directions for lowering a 727's aft staircase, in the woods a short flight distance north of Cooper's presumed jump zone. On February 10, 1980, picnickers found 294 of the ransom bills submerged in the Columbia River, five miles northwest of Vancouver, Washington. The $20 bills were still wrapped in rubber bands, prompting FBI spokesman Ralph Himmelsbach to speculate that the currency "must have been deposited within a couple of years after the hijacking," since "rubber bands deteriorate rapidly and could not have held the bundles together for very long."

Independent scientists disagreed, opining that the cash had reached its final resting place due to a dredging operation conducted by the Army Corps of Engineers in 1974. Another dissenter, geologist Leonard Palmer of Portland State University, dismissed that claim, noting that the money was found *above* clay deposits dredged up by the army engineers. FBI headquarters now maintains that the cash reached its final resting place at least three years after the hijacking, washed into the Columbia from some tributary within Cooper's drop zone. Discovery of the cash in 1980 fueled rumors that Cooper was dead, based on his presumed reluctance to leave any of the hard-earned ransom behind.

Investigators waffled on their opinion of Cooper's skills as a parachutist. Based on comments Cooper made aboard the aircraft, including a reference to the location of McChord Air Force Base, G-men initially suspected he might be a member of the Air Force, either active or retired. That theory and an alternate scenario, involving a professional skydiver, were discarded when agents decided that no truly experienced jumper would leap from 10,000 feet without protective clothing or an oxygen tank to avert blacking out.

Agents involved in the Cooper manhunt scrutinized more than 1,000 potential suspects. The most notorious include:

- *John Emil List,* a New Jersey resident who murdered five members of his family in November 1971, then vanished for almost 18 years, living under the pseudonym "Robert Peter Clark." List generally matched Cooper's description, and Agent Himmelsbach once called him a "viable suspect." List was captured in June 1989, after his ancient case was profiled on *America's Most Wanted,* and although he was imprisoned for murder (dying in custody on March 21, 2008), no evidence ever linked him to the Northwest Orient hijacking.

- *Richard Floyd McCoy Jr.,* who used the alias "James Johnson" to board a United Airlines flight at Denver on April 7, 1972. Once airborne, McCoy presented a flight attendant with an envelope labeled "Hijack Instructions," containing a demand for $500,000 and four parachutes. McCoy directed the Boeing 727 to San Francisco International Airport for refueling. Armed with an empty pistol and a dummy paperweight hand grenade, McCoy received the cash and leapt from the plane, landing safely. FBI agents identified him from fingerprints on the ransom note, which he left behind in the plane, and arrested him on April 9. G-men found $499,970 of the ransom at his Utah home, and, while McCoy claimed innocence, he received a 45-year prison term. In August 1974 he escaped with other inmates and remained at large for three months. G-men traced him to his most recent residence on November 9 and killed him when he threatened them with a shotgun. The G-man who shot McCoy allegedly said, "When I shot Richard McCoy, I shot D. B. Cooper at the same time."

But was it true? Proponents of the theory base their belief on the similarity of hijack techniques (which McCoy could have learned from media reports) and on a Brigham Young medallion found on the Northwest Orient flight in 1971, allegedly bearing McCoy's initials on the back. McCoy, a Mormon Sunday school teacher, had briefly attended Brigham Young University before joining the U.S. Army and serving in Vietnam as a helicopter pilot. In 1991 his widow sued the authors and publisher of a book that claimed McCoy was D. B. Cooper. She received an undisclosed out-of-court settlement in 1994.

- *Duane L. Weber,* born in 1924, who was accused by his widow following his death on March 28, 1995. Jo Weber waited another five years to break the story in July 2000, claiming that shortly before his death in Florida, Duane told her, "I'm Dan Cooper." Weber had served prison time in Oregon after World War II, but a comparison of his fingerprints to those recovered from the Northwest Orient flight produced no matches. Beyond Weber's alleged confession, his widow's "evidence" was vague, at best. She claimed that Duane once took her on "a sentimental journey" to Seattle and the Columbia River in 1979, that he once had a nightmare about leaping from an aircraft, and that he claimed an old knee injury was caused by "jumping out of a plane." She also claimed that a book on Cooper's crime, found at a local library, contained marginal notes in Duane's handwriting. Agent Himmelsbach—who earlier suspected John List—referred to Weber as "one of the best suspects he had come across."

- *Kenneth P. Christiansen,* named as a suspect in the October 29, 2007, issue of *New York* magazine. That article described him as a former army paratrooper and airline employee, who lived in Washington near Cooper's jump site and thus knew the terrain. The story also claimed that Christiansen resembled Cooper, but G-men disagreed, reporting that his height, weight, eye color, and complexion deviated from their unknown subject's.

Before the Christiansen snafu, in February 2007, radio producers of Florida's *MJ Morning Show* published photos of a deceased man they believed to be D. B. Cooper. Relatives of the still-unnamed suspect are reportedly collaborating with the FBI and private attorney Galen Cook to uncover any evidence related to the hijacking. Cook speculates that the new suspect "might have known" Richard McCoy Jr., but no further information is presently available.

On November 1, 2007, the FBI released evidence from its D. B. Cooper file that had previously been closed to public scrutiny, including Cooper's $18.52 plane ticket and a "partial DNA profile" on Cooper derived from his necktie. Two months later, on December 31, G-men placed photos and fact sheets online in a bid to trigger old memories of the case. On March 24, 2008, the FBI acknowledged possession of a parachute unearthed near Amboy, Washington, by a farmer bulldozing his field. Earl Cossey, who provided Cooper's chutes in 1971, examined the relic and announced on April 1, 2008, that it "absolutely, for sure" was not one of those given to Cooper.

COTA, Celia   See SAN DIEGO MURDERS (1931–36)

COURTEMANCHE, Bernice   See "VALLEY KILLER"

CRANE, Bob   murder victim (1978)

Robert Edward Crane was a Connecticut native, born July 13, 1928. He quit high school in 1946 to become a professional drummer, then switched careers in 1950 to work as a radio disc jockey. Early jobs in Hornell, New York, and Bridgeport, Connecticut, led Crane to employment with the CBS radio network in 1956. Transferred to a CBS radio station in Hollywood, California, Crane was soon known as the "King of the Los Angeles Airwaves," recruiting on-air guests including Frank Sinatra, Bob Hope, and Marilyn Monroe.

Living in Hollywood sparked Crane's ambition to become an actor. During 1961, he debuted on television with appearances on *The Twilight Zone* and *General Electric Theater,* while landing uncredited roles in the feature films *Return to Peyton Place* and *Man-Trap.* Crane's performance in a 1962 episode of *The Dick Van Dyke Show* landed Crane the continuing role of "Dr. David Kelsey" on *The Donna Reed Show* during 1963–65. During those same years he appeared on the TV series *Channing* and *The Alfred Hitchcock Hour,* while making another uncredited big-screen appearance in *The New Interns.*

In 1965, Crane was chosen to star in *Hogan's Heroes,* a new TV series set in a German POW camp during World War II. Despite the odd premise for a comedy, Crane and his cast mates made it work. The show finished in TV's top 10 for 1965–66 and ran through 1971, earning Emmy nominations for Crane in 1966 and 1967. In the course of that run, Crane joined fellow *Hogan's Heroes* actors Leon Askin, John Banner, and Werner Klemperer in a feature film, *The Wicked Dreams of Paula Schultz* (1968). The following year, Crane filmed a made-for-TV version of *Arsenic and Old Lace.*

Romance found Crane on the set of *Hogan's Heroes* in the person of guest star Patricia Olsen. Smitten, Crane divorced his wife of 20 years and married Olsen on the show's set in 1970. When *Hogan's Heroes* folded, Crane maintained a busy acting schedule, with appearances on TV series including *The Doris Day Show, Night Gallery,* and *Love, American Style* in 1971; *Tenafly* and *Police Woman* in 1974; *Joe Forrester, Ellery Queen, Spencer's Pilots,* and *Gibbsville* in 1976; and *Quincy M.E.* and *The Hardy Boys/Nancy Drew Mysteries* in 1977. A new star vehicle, *The Bob Crane Show,* failed to interest viewers and was canceled by NBC after three months in 1975. Still, Crane found work in feature-length films including *The Delphi Bureau, Gus,* and as the title character in *Superdad.*

There was a dark side to Bob Crane, behind his smiling public face. A longtime photography enthusiast and sex addict, Crane had produced homemade pornographic films since 1956. During the run of *Hogan's Heroes,* costar Richard Dawson introduced Crane to electronics expert John Carpenter (unrelated to the Hollywood director of the same name), and Carpenter provided Crane with video equipment, joining Crane and various women in group sex on camera at Crane's home in Scottsdale, Arizona. Crane's second wife filed for divorce in early 1978.

On the evening of June 26, 1978, Crane and Carpenter attended a barbecue at the Scottsdale home of actress Victoria Berry. The men posed for photos together, then Crane met a woman and left the party with her, leaving Carpenter behind. Crane and Carpenter hooked up again the following day, visiting an electronics store together and sitting for portraits at a photographic studio. That evening, they went out to dinner with two women, then left their dates and moved on to a bar at 11:00 P.M. Cocktail waitress Linda Robertson later recalled that Crane and Carpenter "were tense toward each other. It was nothing that other people noticed. I noticed it because business was slow."

Crane soon left the tavern, returning around 11:35 with his date from earlier in the evening, and the trio ultimately left together. They had breakfast together, then Crane dropped Carpenter at a car-rental office and took his date home. At 5:00 A.M. he was seen alone at Scottsdale's Safari Coffee Shop. Sometime later, Crane retrieved a pair of eyeglasses from a girlfriend's home, then rendezvoused with Carpenter to hit another portrait studio. They lunched with Frank Grabiec and Ralph Tirrell, owner of Dyna-Tronics (an electronics shop). Crane borrowed a video recorder from Grabiec and eventually went home.

Actress Ronni Richards called Crane from New York at 5:30 P.M. on June 28, 1978. Carpenter answered Crane's home phone and told Richards that Crane was out. Five hours later, Crane quarreled with his estranged wife on the phone, then joined Carpenter at a local bar. Crane called his date from the previous night, and she met both men at the Safari, where Crane told her that "his wife was extremely distraught, anxious over the breakup, and that she was overly jealous of him and even his relationship with their children." From all apparent evidence, Crane finally went home alone.

Crane missed a local Television Academy luncheon at noon on June 29, where he and Victoria Berry were scheduled for interviews. Berry drove to Crane's home at 2:00 P.M. and tried the door when no one answered her knock. She moved through the apartment, calling Crane's name, and found Crane in bed, bludgeoned and strangled. A postmortem examination revealed that Crane died from blunt-trauma wounds to the skull, before a video cable was cinched around his neck.

Medical examiner Heinz Karnitschnig believed that Crane's killer was male, judging that only a "very strong man" could have inflicted the actor's head wounds. Dr. Karnitschnig said, "The killer's first blow laid open Crane's scalp, covering the weapon with blood. The second blow was delivered with a short arc, slinging only a couple of droplets onto the ceiling and table near the bed."

Still, some investigators speculated that a woman could have killed Crane… or, perhaps, induced a man to do the job. Crane's sexual adventures and his huge porn collection—including films made surreptitiously, without the knowledge of his female partners—suggested possible motives of jealousy or revenge. Had Crane been killed by a former lover? By someone he had filmed secretly? By an outraged spouse or boyfriend?

Suspicion focused on John Carpenter as friends described the recent souring of his relationship with Crane. Some claimed that Carpenter was bisexual, suggesting that he was attracted to Crane and may have been enraged if the hyper-heterosexual Crane rejected his advances. Police learned that Carpenter had flown from Scottsdale to Los Angeles at 11:00 A.M. on June 29, then phoned a Scottsdale woman from L.A. at 2:30 P.M. to report "some problem at Bob Crane's apartment, that the police were investigating the incident." Moments later, Carpenter phoned another Scottsdale friend and asked for Crane, then left a message: "Tell him I arrived in town OK." Finally, at 3:00 P.M.,

Carpenter called Crane's apartment. Victoria Berry answered the phone and passed it to a policeman.

Carpenter introduced himself, but did not ask why the police were at Crane's home. He told the officer in charge, "I was with Bob Crane last night. I called him at one this morning to tell him I was preparing to return to California. He told me he was going to be sleeping late in the morning."

Detective's examined Carpenter's rented car in Scottsdale, locating traces of human blood inside the passenger door. The blood was type B, the same as Crane's, but DNA testing was unavailable in 1978, and some 10 percent of the U.S. population shares type B. In a subsequent interview, Carpenter denied any role in Crane's death. Police declined to charge him, based on insufficient evidence.

Detectives reopened their investigation of Crane's case in 1989, with DNA testing of the blood from Carpenter's vehicle, but the results were inconclusive. Another three years passed before Carpenter was finally charged with Crane's murder, based on new evidence—specifically, a photograph of the rented car's door panel, revealing a speck of alleged brain tissue one-sixteenth of an inch in diameter. The tissue itself no longer existed, but prosecutor Bob Shutts proceeded to trial, telling jurors that Carpenter "fed off the fame and energy of the actor. Bob Crane became a source of women that [Carpenter] could never obtain for himself." Unconvinced, the panel acquitted Carpenter, who died from a heart attack on September 4, 1998.

CRATER, Joseph Force missing person (1930)

A native of Easton, Pennsylvania, born in 1889, Joseph Crater graduated from Lafayette College in his hometown (1910) and from New York's Columbia Law School (1913). While engaged in private practice, Crater launched a secondary career in Democratic Party politics, then controlled in New York by the bosses of Tammany Hall. By 1929, he served as president of the 19th Assembly District's Democratic Club of Manhattan, known citywide as a man who enjoyed the high life. In April 1930 his connections paid off with an appointment to fill a vacancy on the New York State Supreme Court. Clearly ambitious (if not avaricious), Crater seemed to have the whole world in front of him—or at least a major piece of the Empire State.

August 1930 found Judge Crater vacationing with his wife of 14 years at Belgrade Lakes, Maine. On August 5, he returned alone to New York City, visiting his official chambers on Fifth Avenue and spending the night at his apartment on 45th Street. The next day, on a second visit to his office, Crater filled several valises with unknown documents and sent them on by courier to his apartment, then he cashed two personal checks for a total of $5,150. He next purchased a single ticket for a new Broadway production, *Dancing Partner*, playing at the Belasco Theater. En route to the play that night, he stopped at the Billy Haas restaurant on West 45th Street. There Crater met an attorney and a showgirl who asked him to join them. The play was already in progress at 9:15 P.M., when Judge Crater hailed a taxi outside the restaurant, bid his friends good night—and vanished forever.

Crater's wife grew concerned when he failed to rejoin her or call from the city, but no alarm was raised until August 25, when Crater missed a business appointment in Manhattan. Fellow jurists launched a private search, hoping to solve the riddle without involving the authorities, but police were finally notified, and the story made front-page news on August 26, 1930. Nearly 100 witnesses were called during the inquest into Crater's disappearance, but none shed any useful light on the matter. Investigation revealed that his office safe and bank deposit box were empty, but no final inventory of their missing contents was ever compiled. Investigators learned that Crater had withdrawn $7,500 from his bank and sold securities worth $15,779 in June 1930, suggesting to critics of New York's judicial corruption that Crater had paid the traditional one year's salary in advance to obtain his State Supreme Court seat. Before his judicial appointment, Crater had also served as referee for the sale of the Libby Hotel on Manhattan's Lower East Side. Initially appraised at $1.2 million, the hotel was sold on June 27, 1929, for a mere $75,000 to the American Bond and Mortgage Company. Six weeks later, it sold for $2,850,000—a tidy profit of $2,775,000 for American Bond on the original investment.

Such indications of corruption notwithstanding, the inquest discovered no proof that Crater had met with foul play. As revealed in the panel's final verdict, "The evidence is insufficient to warrant any expression of opinion as to whether Crater is alive or dead, or as to whether he has absented himself voluntarily, or is a sufferer from disease in the nature of amnesia, or is the victim of a crime." Mrs. Crater, for her part, believed her husband was murdered "because of a sin-ister something that was connected with politics" and Tammany Hall.

Emil Ellis, a New York attorney and friend of Judge Crater, proposed an alternative scenario. While representing Mrs. Crater in a lawsuit against her husband's insurance carrier, Ellis suggested that Crater had been blackmailed by a Broadway showgirl and was murdered by the unnamed woman's gangster boyfriend while delivering a payoff. No evidence was produced to support that contention, and nine years passed before Crater was declared legally dead on June 6, 1939. Eight years later, Crater's case inspired a comic film, *The Judge Steps Out*, starring Alexander Knox as a distinguished jurist who embarks on an unscheduled road trip. Unlike the cinematic version, though, Judge Crater's vanishing act would have no resolution in the final reel. He remains missing today, his case unsolved.

CRITCHLEY, Elizabeth See "VALLEY KILLER"

CROCKETT, Brenda See "FREEWAY PHANTOM"

CROSSLAND, M. P. assassination victim (1868)
A prominent Republican in Tuscaloosa County, Alabama, M. P. Crossland found himself subjected to "a great deal of threatening and prejudice" in 1868, as his state seethed in the grip of Reconstruction following the Civil War. Crossland had supported the late Confederacy and actively recruited soldiers for its lost cause, but he later abandoned the all-white Democratic Party and thereby earned derision from "loyal" Alabamians as a traitorous "scalawag." He was also litigious, frequently taking his neighbors to court, and it did not help Crossland's case that some of those he sued were members of the Sipsey Swamp gang, widely regarded as a front for the local Ku Klux Klan.

Crossland's problems came to a head in 1868, when he was elected as a member of Alabama's first state legislature since the war. One afternoon in September he left home in company with Simeon Brunson, the elected representative from Pickens County, and Brunson's teenage stepson. The two legislators were bound for Tuscaloosa, there to catch a train for the state capital at Montgomery; Brunson's stepson had been drafted to take their horses home from the depot. As the party approached Moor's Bridge, spanning the Sipsey River 12 miles east of Tuscaloosa, gunfire rang out from a roadside thicket. Crossland was killed instantly, and Brunson's stepson pitched from his saddle, critically wounded. Brunson rode on to the county seat and alerted Sheriff Tom Lewis, but the lawman was afraid to investigate. By the time a posse was organized, the killers had fled, leaving no useful clues in their wake.

Brunson's stepson survived his wounds, but he could offer no description of the gunmen. Brunson, likewise, had been more intent upon survival than identifying his assailants. No suspects were identified, and local residents were still debating the killers' motive three years later, when congressional investigators probed the crime. Some blamed the Klan, while others accused "one McGee, who was sort of a desperado before the war came out." Various stories had Crossland embroiled in a lawsuit with McGee, or else defending McGee's battered wife from domestic abuse. Few Republicans doubted a political motive in the murder, noting that a rash of homicides and other terrorist crimes soon followed Crossland's death in Tuscaloosa County. Simeon Brunson was driven from Alabama by Klan threats in December 1870 and resettled in Mississippi.

CROY, Lily   See "TOLEDO CLUBBER"

CULIANU, Ioan Petru   murder victim (1991)

A Romanian national, born at Iaşi in January 1950, Ioan Culianu studied at the University of Bucharest and later sought political asylum from his homeland's communist regime while traveling in Italy in July 1972. He subsequently graduated from Milan's Università Cattolica del Sacro Cuore. After residing briefly in France and the Netherlands, Culianu emigrated to the United States and became a professor of history and religion at the University of Chicago. He completed his doctoral studies through the University of Paris in January 1987, with a thesis titled "Research into Western Dualisms: An Analysis of Their Major Myths."

Culianu was a disciple of Mircea Eliade, an exiled Romanian philosopher, religious historian, novelist, and covert neo-fascist activist who died at Chicago's Bernard Mitchell Hospital in April 1986. Culianu's studies included gnosticism and Renaissance magic, examining "the interrelation of the occult, Eros, magic, physics, and history." He was also an outspoken critic of Romanian dictator Nicolae Ceauşescu, denouncing Ceauşescu's secret police—the Securitate, or State Security Department—as a body "of epochal stupidity." Nonetheless, when revolutionaries overthrew Ceauşescu's government in 1989, Culianu almost instantly became a leading critic of replacement Ion Iliescu and his National Salvation Front.

On May 21, 1991, an unknown assailant killed Culianu in a restroom at Swift Hall, the University of Chicago's divinity school, by firing a single shot into the back of his head. Authorities learned that Culianu had received a series of threatening telephone calls before his murder, but they never identified the callers or the shooter.

Suspects fell into four broad categories, including:

- Former Securitate agents, seeking revenge for Culianu's criticism of the deposed Ceauşescu regime. A built-in weakness of this theory is the fact that Culianu's murder came 18 months *after* Ceauşescu was deposed and executed, rather than during his reign.

- Agents of the present-day Romanian Intelligence Service (SRI) or Foreign Intelligence Service (SIE), incensed by Culianu's attacks on the new government. Private researchers claim that certain unspecified pages of Culianu's Securitate/SRI dossier are "missing without reason."

- Occultists, investigated by the FBI on grounds that Culianu's research frequently explored the realms of myth, magic, and witchcraft. Various occult-satanic groups have been involved in crimes, including murder, but no present evidence exists linking any such group to Culianu's slaying.

- Ultranationalists and neo-fascists linked to postrevolutionary Romania's far-right România Mare and Vatra Românească parties, described by some observers as a second coming of the Iron Guard that collaborated with Adolf Hitler's SS to exterminate Romanian Jews during World War II. One motivation for a far-right plot against Culianu is Culianu's rift with mentor Mircea Eliade in the mid-1980s, and his role in exposing Eliade's ties to Romanian neo-fascist groups. Some biographers believe that the embarrassment of those revelations hastened Eliade's death. Furthermore, shortly before his murder, Culianu became engaged to marry a Jewish graduate of Harvard University's divinity school, which may have angered anti-Semites.

CUMMINSVILLE, Ohio "mad killer" at large (1904–10)
The Cincinnati suburb of Cumminsville, Ohio, is normally a peaceful place, but in the six-year period from 1904 to 1910 it earned the grisly reputation of a "murder zone" where women walked in fear and dreaded riding streetcars after dark. A ferocious "mad killer" was on the loose, claiming five victims within a mile of the point where Winton Road meets Spring Grove Avenue, eluding police and neighborhood vigilante patrols to leave a nagging mystery behind.

Thirty-one-year-old Mary McDonald had "been around" before she met her killer in the predawn hours of May 4, 1904. An ill-fated love affair with her sister's husband had driven her to find solace in whiskey, but things were looking up that spring, with her engagement to be married. Shortly after 1:30 A.M., she left a local tavern in the company of her fiancé, and he watched her safely board an "owl car," homeward bound. Near daybreak the switchman on a passing train saw Mary sprawled beside the tracks, near Ludlow Avenue, and summoned help. She was alive but incoherent, with a fractured skull and one leg severed. McDonald died hours later, and police initially dismissed her death as accidental, later shifting to the view that she was beaten and pushed in front of a train in a deliberate act of murder.

Louise Mueller, age 21, was the next to die. She left home for a stroll on October 1, 1904, and never returned. Her body was found the next morning, her skull hammered to pulp, in a gully beside some abandoned railroad tracks. Her killer had scooped a shallow grave from the soft earth nearby, but Mueller's corpse lay above ground, as if some passerby had disturbed the hasty burial.

At 9:00 P.M. on November 2, 1904, 18-year-old Alma Steinigewig left her job as an operator at the local telephone exchange, vanishing before she reached her home. The next morning a streetcar conductor spotted her corpse in a nearby vacant lot, skull crushed by savage blows. The victim's clothes were muddy, indicating that she had been dragged across the lot, and while police found footprints near the body, they ran out a few yards later and were never matched to any suspect. Clutched in Alma's hand, detectives found a streetcar transfer punched at 9:40 the previous night.

An ugly pattern was forming, and homicide investigators questioned suspects by the dozen, ultimately forced to free them all for lack of evidence. One who eluded them, a stocky man remembered for his heavy beard, had shown up at the Mueller death scene, wringing his hands and crying out, "It was an accident!" Other witnesses placed the same man (or his twin) at the scene of Alma Steinigewig's murder, but he was never identified, and his link to the case—if any—remains open to conjecture.

Six years passed before the killer struck again, claiming 43-year-old Anna Lloyd on December 31, 1909. Employed as a secretary at a Cumminsville lumber yard, Lloyd worked until 5:30 P.M. that New Year's Eve, her body found hours later, a short walk from the office. She had been gagged with a cheap black muffler, throat slashed, leaving signs of a fierce fight for life. A single strand of black hair was clutched in one fist, but primitive forensic tests of the day made it useless as evidence. Police initially called the slaying a contract murder, but no suspect or credible motive was ever identified.

The Cumminsville stalker claimed his last victim on October 25, 1910, when 26-year-old Mary Hackney was found dead in her cottage on Dane Street, her skull crushed and throat slashed. Suspicion briefly focused on her husband, but police proved that Mary was still alive when he reported for work on October 25. A series of letters were mailed by someone claiming knowledge of the Hackney murder, signed with the initials "S. D. M.," but authorities finally dismissed them as a hoax, and the author was never located.

Fading memories of murder were rekindled in December 1913 by investigators of the Burns Detective Agency, hired to find the persons responsible for unsolved acts of violence in a recent streetcar strike. The private eyes told Cincinnati's mayor that they had discovered an "indefinite" solution to Anna Lloyd's murder, pointing the finger of suspicion at a onetime streetcar conductor later confined to a lunatic asylum. A search of the suspect's former lodgings had turned up a threatening letter, addressed (but never sent) to persons "who saw him in the act of December 31," and police leapt to a theoretical connection with the three-year-old slaying. Ultimately fruitless, the investigation petered out a few days later, and the Cumminsville murders remain unsolved.

CUSTER, Linda See "INDEPENDENCE AVENUE KILLER"

D

DANIELS, Jonathan Myrick civil rights martyr (1965)
A native of Keene, New Hampshire, born March 20, 1939, Jonathan Daniels emerged from a brief period of teenage rebellion to graduate with top honors from Virginia Military Institute, moving on from there to postgraduate study at Harvard University. He planned to teach English, but a religious epiphany at Easter 1962 changed his mind, prompting Daniels to abandon Harvard and enroll at an Episcopal seminary in Cambridge, Massachusetts. It was there, on March 8, 1965, that he heard Dr. Martin Luther King's televised plea for clergy of all denominations to join in the ongoing civil rights struggle at Selma, Alabama. Daniels answered the call and flew south the next day, on the same plane that carried Rev. James Reeb to his death.

Instantly captivated by the struggle in Alabama, Daniels returned to Cambridge on March 18 and secured permission to finish the school year in Selma. He returned to the Cotton State as an official representative of the Episcopal Society for Cultural and Racial Unity, his ESCRU lapel button and clerical collar marking him as an "outside agitator" for any local whites who passed him on the street. One of his letters home described an encounter at the Selma post office.

In the line next to me a redneck turned and stared: at my seminarian's collar, at my ESCRU button, at my face. He turned to a friend. "Know what he is? . . . Why he's a white niggah." I was not happy thus to become the object of every gaze. And yet deep within me rose an affirmation and a tenderness and a joy that wanted to shout, Yes! If pride were appropriate in the ambiguities of my presence in Selma, I should be unspeakably proud of my title. . . . As I type now, my hands are hopelessly white. "But my heart is black . . . " Hear, O Israel: given an irony or two in the holy mystery of His economy, I am indeed "a white nigger." I wouldn't swap the blessings He has given me. But black would be a very wonderful, a very beautiful color to be."

Protests that summer were not confined to Selma. On August 14, 1965, a mixed group of civil rights activists picketed whites-only stores at Fort Deposit, in neighboring Lowndes County. "Bloody Lowndes" was a stronghold of the Ku Klux Klan, where activist Viola Gregg Liuzzo had been murdered five months earlier. Following acquittal of her killers by an all-white jury, local Klansmen plastered bumper stickers on their cars that bore the message: OPEN SEASON. Law enforcement officers in Lowndes County were widely recognized as friends or active members of the terrorist KKK.

That Saturday morning Jon Daniels and a white Catholic priest, 27-year-old Rev. Richard Morrisroe, were among 30 demonstrators arrested in Fort Deposit, transported to jail at the county seat in Hayneville. Most of the others detained were black teenagers. The group spent six days in custody, before they were released without warning at 3:00 P.M. on

Police violence against civil rights demonstrators in Selma, Alabama, inspired Jon Daniels to join the crusade that cost him his life. (Library of Congress)

Friday, August 20. The release smacked of a setup: Jailers demanded no bail, refused to offer the party protection, and denied all requests for transportation back to Fort Deposit. If the plan was not designed to facilitate murder, it nonetheless had that effect.

While two youths went to find a telephone and call for rides, Daniels and Rev. Morrisroe escorted black teenagers Ruby Sales and Joyce Bailey to a nearby store to purchase soft drinks. Their destination, Varner's Grocery Store, served a predominantly black clientele. Ruby Sales describes what happened next.

We walked over to this store down the street. I was walking in front. Reverend Daniels was behind me. Joyce Bailey was behind him and Father Morrisroe was behind Joyce. . . . I was up on the steps of the store, halfway, when this Mr. Coleman comes out pointing a gun at us and screaming about niggers on the property.

"Goddam niggers, get off this property before I blow your damn brains out," he yelled. Before I knew what happened someone yanked me off the steps and I heard a shot. I saw Reverend Daniels fall to the ground holding his stomach and all bloody. I heard another shot and Father Richard fell down. Then I began to scream and saw all that blood.

"This Mr. Coleman" was 55-year-old Tom Lemuel Coleman, the alcoholic son of a former state legislator, employee of the state highway department, part-time "special" deputy sheriff, and a member of the Ku Klux Klan who was, in the words of one acquaintance, "maddened by the prospect of Negroes voting in Lowndes County." Coleman had committed his first known homicide in August 1959, shooting a black inmate who had assaulted a guard at the Greenville prison camp. (Coleman was not a prison guard, but he was in the neighborhood, armed with his trusty shotgun, and a hasty inquest accepted his claim of self-defense.) Since then, Coleman's son had become a state trooper and personal bodyguard for Colonel Al Lingo, commander of the state police and a self-proclaimed "good friend" of the KKK. Lingo was also a friend of Tom Coleman; so was Sheriff Jim Clark from Selma, whose "special posse" included numerous Klansmen. Ten days before the shooting, Coleman had confronted state attorney general Richmond Flowers at the Hayneville post office, warning Flowers to "get off the Ku Klux Klan and get on these outfits down here trying to get these niggers registered. If you don't get off this Klan investigation, we'll get you off!"

Jon Daniels was killed instantly by the shotgun blast to his abdomen. Rev. Morrisroe lay in the street for an hour, critically wounded, before an ambulance arrived and carried him 20 miles north to a Montgomery hospital. Coleman, meanwhile, strolled back to the courthouse. Sheriff Frank Ryals was out of town, so Coleman sat down and himself answered the first phone call reporting the shootings. That done, Coleman called Al Lingo and told Alabama's top lawman, "I just shot two preachers. You'd better get on down here." Lingo, in turn, alerted Coleman's son and picked up a bail bondsman identified as a member of the KKK before he drove to Hayneville. Sheriff Clark popped over from Selma to offer moral support, and three attorneys soon arrived from Montgomery to safeguard Coleman's civil rights. Sheriff Ryals returned in time to tell reporters that Coleman had been acting as a deputy, responding to reports of "a disturbance" at Varner's Grocery, when the shooting occurred. Al Lingo, for his part, preferred stonewalling the press, answering all questions with a terse, "It's none of your damn business!"

By midnight on Friday, County Solicitor Carlton Perdue had decided to charge Coleman with first-degree murder, but he made the move with obvious reluctance, telling reporters that if Daniels and Morrisroe "had been minding their own business like I tend to mine, they'd be living and enjoying themselves today." Richmond Flowers sent assistant Joe Gantt from Montgomery to supervise the investigation, accusing Lingo of a cover-up and calling Coleman's act "another Ku Klux Klan murder." Coleman was arraigned on Saturday morning, August 21, in a hearing that lasted all of 15 minutes. Bond was set at $10,000 on the murder charge, with another $2,300

on a second count of assault with intent to murder. A grand jury session was scheduled for September 13, 1965. Local whites rallied to Coleman's defense, one Lowndes County deputy sheriff speaking candidly of Rev. Morrisroe to visiting reporters: "I hope the son of a bitch dies. That'll give us two, instead of one."

The state's case against Coleman was prepared by Carlton Perdue, assisted by Circuit Solicitor Arthur Gamble. Richmond Flowers challenged Perdue's fitness to try the case, based on early statements to the press, and a group calling itself Concerned White Citizens of Alabama echoed that opinion, declaring that Perdue "could not possibly execute justice impartially," and that "there is no doubt about the immaturity and incapability of a county solicitor who implies that emotional outrage is justification for killing." The group's leader asked Flowers to remove Perdue as prosecutor, but Flowers demurred on grounds that such a move "would ruin any chance you might have for a conviction." Grasping at straws, Flowers expressed his hope that Perdue "would not let his personal beliefs interfere with his prosecution of the case."

That hope was in vain.

On September 13, 1965, a grand jury composed of 17 whites and one African American reduced Coleman's murder charge to first-degree manslaughter (defined in Alabama law as a killing performed "intentionally but without malice"). The charge of assault with intent to murder was likewise reduced to assault and battery. As explained by Carlton Perdue, the panel believed Coleman acted "spasmodically," in defense of the grocery's female proprietor, rather than as a cold, calculating murderer. Richmond Flowers, professing himself "shocked and amazed," used his power as attorney general to relieve Perdue and Gamble, assigning Joe Gantt to try the state's case.

The trial, beginning on September 27, was a predictable fiasco. Coleman's name appeared on the jury list, prompting laughter from the court, and Judge T. Werth Thagard denied a motion for postponement until Rev. Morrisroe could leave the hospital to testify. When Joe Gantt pressed the point, Judge Thagard accused him of "trifling with the court" and returned the case to Carlton Perdue. Testimony included a deputy sheriff's memory of Jon Daniels kissing "a nigger girl," while coroner C. J. Rehling noted that Daniels wore shoes "such as no man of God in Lowndes County ever wears," while his underpants "smelled of urine." Friends of Coleman described

Daniels carrying "some kind of knife," while Morrisroe allegedly held something "that looked like a gun barrel." The disappearance of those mythical weapons was explained by testimony that an unidentified "colored boy" had "picked up something from the ground" and "stuck it in his britches."

Arthur Gamble's summation sounded more like a brief for the defense than for the prosecution, replete with references to "that knife" and Jon Daniels "attempting to force his way" into the store. "There is no evidence here at all that Jonathan Daniels made any attempt to actually cut [Coleman] with that knife," Gamble acknowledged, but he never challenged the weapon's existence. Coleman's lawyer, meanwhile, told jurors, "You can believe that knife was there or not. I believe it was there whether it was or not." More to the point, he said, "I think we ought to thank Almighty God that we have got such a man as Tom Coleman in our midst." The panel agreed, requiring less than two hours to acquit Coleman of manslaughter, with jurors lining up to shake his hand on their way out of court.

Coleman's second trial, for wounding Rev. Morrisroe, was scheduled for May 1966, but Judge Thagard postponed it until such time as the victim was fit to travel. Richmond Flowers asked the grand jury to reinstate a charge of assault with intent to murder, but his motion was refused. Next, he asked Judge Thagard to nol-pros (nolle prosequi—waive the original indictment) the case, thus clearing the way for a new indictment, but Thagard chose to dismiss the case "with prejudice," precluding any future trial for Morrisroe's shooting. Coleman, thus cleared of all charges, remained with the highway department until 1977. He was a fixture at the Lowndes County courthouse until his death, at age 86, on June 13, 1997.

DARLINGTON, Pamela See "HIGHWAY KILLER"

"DARTMAN" New York (1975–76)

Between February 28, 1975, and May 13, 1976, at least 23 female residents of New York's Westchester County were wounded by one-inch steel darts, fired by an unknown assailant armed with an air gun. All the victims lived in ground-floor apartments, and each was wounded in the head, neck, or chest by the projectiles fired through windows. No suspect was identified in the case, and police lost interest two months after the final attack in Nanuet, New York, when a gunman calling himself the "Son of Sam" brought lethal terror to New York City after dark. The Westchester "Dartman" remained at large.

Journalist Maury Terry, investigating alleged satanic connections in the "Sam" case, discovered that the Dartman was a symbol of death in 15th-century Europe. It made a tantalizing lead, combined with reports of cult gatherings, canine sacrifice, and ritual gang rapes in Westchester County, but without a suspect or a solid lead the trail went cold. A similar series of woundings, blamed on an unknown blowgun sniper, were reported from Washington, D.C., in the spring of 2002. That case also remains unsolved.

DAVIS, Caroline See "OCCULT MURDERS"

DAVIS, Cindy See FORTH WORTH MURDERS

DAVIS, Emile See WASHINGTON, D.C., MURDERS (1996–97)

DAVIS, Raymond See AVILA, ROBERT

DAYS Inn murders Indiana (1989)

A transient gunman with a grudge against the Days Inn motel chain was apparently responsible for the murder of two desk clerks in separate Indiana towns, on March 3, 1989. Slain that day were 24-year-old Marty Gill, at the Days Inn in Merrillville, and 34-year-old Jeanne Gilbert, at the chain's motel in Remington. Robbery was suspected as a motive in both cases. A surprising two years elapsed before Merrillville police chief Jerry McCory announced a description of the suspect: a white male in his late thirties or early forties, six feet tall, about 180 pounds, with graying "salt-and-pepper" hair. The description was vague enough to fit millions of men across the United States, and no further leads have been announced to date. Authorities have not commented on the similarity between victim surnames, and it may be mere coincidence. Barring death or conviction on unrelated charges, the gunman remains at large.

DEACON, Beryl See WILTSHIRE, ENGLAND, MURDERS

DEASON, Mat assassination victim (1871)

Mat Deason was the sheriff of Wilkinson County, Georgia, during that state's violent Reconstruction era, following the Civil War. He was a Georgia native but flouted the state's most hallowed traditions of racial separation, supremacy, and Democratic Party rule. Elected to office as a "radical" Republican, Sheriff Deason actively pursued racist members of the Ku Klux Klan and Constitutional Union Guard (a Klan front group) who flogged and murdered numerous freedmen within his jurisdiction. On top of those offenses, he also flouted convention by taking a black woman as his common-law wife.

Deason's perilous domestic arrangement actually dated from 1859, when his (white) legal spouse was committed to an asylum for the mentally deranged. Over the next 12 years, Deason shared quarters with his black lover and their union produced five children. Local bigots ignored that indiscretion until Reconstruction, when Deason's politics and his threats to kill any person who bothered his family proved intolerable for Georgia Klansmen.

On the night of August 27, 1871, a masked party of night riders stormed Deason's home, crushing the back of his skull with a club, then pumping five pistol shots into his forehead as a gruesome coup de grâce. Deason's lover was killed at the same time, her death afterward described to congressional investigators by a witness who said Klansmen "caught her, tied a bar of iron to her, and threw her in the creek." Klan historian Allen Trelease, in his book *White Terror* (1971), reports that Deason and his consort were roped together and thus consigned to a watery grave. No suspects were ever publicly identified.

"DEATH Angels" violent U.S. religious cult (1969–??)

A fanatical offshoot of the Nation of Islam (Black Muslims), the Death Angels cult was apparently founded in California, in late 1969 or early 1970. Members adhere to the Black Muslim dogma that whites are "beasts" and "grafted devils" spawned from ancient genetic experiments, but members of the new cult carried their beliefs into action, pur-

posefully striving to exterminate Caucasians. On joining the cult, new recruits were photographed, afterward earning their "wings" (drawn on the snapshot in ink) by killing a specified number of whites. The mandatory body count was based on a point system geared to emotional difficulty, with prospects required to kill four white children, five women, or nine men. Murders were verified through media reports, eyewitness accounts from fellow cultists, and/or Polaroid snapshots of the dead. (As reported by author Clark Howard in *Zebra* [1980], one Death Angel candidate flew to Chicago—"New Mecca" in Black Muslim parlance—with a collection of photos, seeking promotion to the nonexistent cult rank of lieutenant. His unexpected visit puzzled members of the headquarters staff and might have been disastrous, had he not been intercepted by the leader of the secret group, who "counseled" him and sent him home.)

By October 1973, the cult reportedly had at least 15 accredited members, their winged photographs displayed on an easel at covert gatherings in Northern California. Together, those 15 were theoretically responsible for killing 135 men, 75 women, 60 children, or some combination of victims sufficient to earn their "wings." The California state attorney general's office had compiled a list of 45 similar murders, committed at random with cleavers, machetes, or close-range gunshots, all involving white victims and black assailants, wherein identified suspects were invariably linked to the Nation of Islam. Thus far, attacks have been recorded in Berkeley, Long Beach, Los Angeles, Oakland, Pacifica, Palo Alto, San Diego, San Francisco, and Santa Barbara, plus rural areas in the counties of Alameda, Contra Costa, Los Angeles, San Mateo, Santa Clara, and Ventura.

By January 28, 1974, when California law enforcement officers convened a secret conference on the problem, 64 persons were known to have died in ritualistic racist attacks, and three more deaths were recorded by late March. A rare survivor, Thomas Bates, was thumbing rides near the Bay Bridge at Emeryville, south of Oakland, when two black men pulled up in an old-model Cadillac. Rolling down his window, the passenger grinned at Bates and said, "Hello, devil," then opened fire with a pistol at point-blank range. Although bleeding profusely from wounds to the arm, hip, and stomach, Bates managed to reach a nearby motel, where employees phoned for police and paramedics.

San Francisco was paralyzed with fear in 1974, as a sudden rash of "Zebra" murders—so dubbed by police for the races of victims and assailants—left 15 persons dead and eight wounded over a six-month period. Eight alleged Death Angel prospects were finally arrested in that crime spree; four were convicted of murder and sentenced to life imprisonment, while the rest were acquitted. According to Clark Howard, none of those accused were bona fide Death Angels in possession of their "wings."

California police have released no further information on this troubling case, but the Death Angel cult name resurfaced a decade later, on the far side of the continent. This time, the label was applied to armed enforcers of a sect ironically called the Temple of Love or Hebrew Israelites, founded in 1978 by ex-Muslim Hulon Mitchell, Jr. (a.k.a. "Yahweh Ben Yahweh," literally "God, son of God.") By October 1986 various Hebrew Israelites had been linked to four Miami slayings and one in Chicago, but the most shocking news was yet to come. Self-described cult killer Neariah Israel (born Robert Rozier) issued a jailhouse confession describing a cult-within-a-cult, dubbed the Sons of Yahweh or Death Angels, whose members were required to "show thyselves" by murdering "white devils" and presenting severed ears as trophies of the hunt. Miami homicide investigators believe that 17 white victims, mostly homeless "street people," were dispatched in a series of Hebrew Israelite "ear murders" dating from April 1986. Rozier/Israel himself pled guilty to four slayings, thus avoiding death row, and he later added two more victims to the tally during unexpected courtroom testimony.

According to Rozier, Yahweh's orders were specific: "Kill me a white devil and bring me an ear." His hit team delivered one such keepsake in September 1986, Rozier testified, making Yahweh so happy that "we got the day off and went to the movies." Tried with 14 associates on various felony charges, Yahweh was convicted of conspiracy and drew a 20-year prison sentence. Six other defendants were likewise convicted of conspiracy in May 1992, but acquitted on more serious racketeering charges; seven were acquitted on all counts, while jurors deadlocked on the final two defendants. A second jury acquitted Yahweh of murder in November 1992, and most of the grisly "ear" slayings (except those confessed by Robert Rozier) remain officially unsolved.

DELEON, Gloria   See New York City strangulation murders

DELISLE, Judy   See Toronto rape-murders

DEMELLO, Deborah   See New Bedford, Massachusetts, murders

DENEVEU, Leslie   See Oakland torso murders

DENNIS, Patricia   See "Southside Slayer"

DENNIS, William murder victim (1871)
As a prominent black Republican in Meridian, Mississippi, William Dennis was subject to numerous threats and insults during Reconstruction, following the Civil War. His stance in favor of black civil rights made life perilous in those days, when the local Ku Klux Klan was powerful enough to strike by night or day, secure in the protection of the all-white Democratic Party. In early 1871 he led a delegation to the state capital at Jackson, asking Governor James Alcorn to suppress Klan terrorism in Lauderdale County, but Alcorn feared political retaliation and refused to intervene.

Dennis called a public meeting in Meridian on March 4, 1871, to report the mission's failure and call for local blacks to rally in self-defense. Speakers at the gathering, aside from Dennis, included black state legislator Aaron Moore, with Warren Tyler and Daniel Price, employed as teachers at the county's first black school. All featured prominently on the Klan's hit list, and their call for armed resistance to white violence did not improve their prospects for longevity. Freedmen paraded through Meridian that night with fife and drum, in a demonstration of racial solidarity, but white terrorists preferred to strike in the dark, torching a local Republican's store. Both sides quickly mobilized for battle. Dennis survived a clumsy attempt on his life, but authorities jailed him that night (March 4) on charges of making "incendiary" speeches. By March 6 Moore and Tyler were jailed on similar charges, while Price fled the county in fear.

Monday morning (March 6) witnessed a rally of white racists in Meridian, described by historian

Allen Trelease as "part of a white coup d'état, aimed at seizing control of the city" from Republican mayor William Sturgis and his subordinates. Many of those present were Alabama Klansmen, described by Trelease as "professional rioters," veterans of numerous clashes on both sides of the Mississippi border. While speakers called for replacement of Meridian's current leaders, whites in the crowd checked their pistols and knives, waiting for their cue to run amok.

Their opportunity arrived on Monday afternoon, during a preliminary hearing for the three defendants. Armed Klansmen packed the courtroom, muttering among themselves as each new charge was read. When Warren Tyler called for witnesses to challenge the testimony of white accuser, James Brantley, Brantley charged at Tyler with a raised walking stick. Before he could strike, a shot rang out from the audience and chaos erupted. When the pistol smoke cleared, four men lay dead, including the judge, presiding officer, and two black spectators. Tyler was wounded (along with several others), but he escaped from the courthouse to a nearby store. Friends tried to hide him there, but a rampaging lynch mob broke in and riddled him with bullets. William Dennis, also wounded in the courtroom melee, was taken into "protective custody," but his guards vanished that night, permitting Klansmen to invade his cell and slash his throat.

The Klan rioters, meanwhile, organized into squads and scoured Meridian's black community, confiscating any weapons found and lynching three more victims before dawn on Tuesday. Mayor Sturgis fled in the confusion and never returned. Defendant Aaron Moore initially played dead in the courtroom, then slipped out of town and made his way on foot to Jackson, hiking more than 60 miles through swamps and forests. Frustrated lynchers commandeered a train and rode it 50 miles west, but they failed to sight Moore and retreated before reaching the state capital. Murders and mutilation of blacks continued for several days around Meridian, until the Klansmen got tired and went home.

Six rioters were subsequently arrested on charges of assault, unlawful assembly, and intent to kill, but the Lauderdale County grand jury refused to indict them at its April session and none were brought to trial. One visitor from Alabama was convicted of raping a black woman during the riot, but he served no prison time. The Meridian massacre ranks among the most spectacular of Mississippi's countless unsolved racial crimes.

DENUCCIO, Carmela See "MONSTER OF FLORENCE"

"DEPREDADOR Psicópata" See CIUDAD JUÁREZ, MEXICO

DETROIT, Michigan suspected serial murders (1980)
Detroit has seen its share of mayhem, from the bootleg wars of Prohibition to the catastrophic riots of the 1960s, fueled by street gangs, racist groups, and drug rings. But by any estimation, 1980 was a special year. From January through December, 18 women were killed in similar brutal fashion, 12 of them strangled, all but one discarded outdoors, with little or no effort made to hide their remains. The murders spanned Detroit, without apparent pattern until they were plotted on a map, drawing a narrow corridor of death northwestward from the Detroit River at Belle Isle to Eight Mile Road, then westward to the city limits. Despite the arrest of two separate suspects and the conviction of one, at least 13 of the slayings remain unsolved today.

The first victim was Lois Johnson, a 31-year-old alcoholic barmaid killed on January 12, 1980. Her frozen body was found early the next morning, torn by 26 stab wounds to the neck, chest, and abdomen. Blood tests revealed that Johnson was falling-down drunk when she died.

A month later, on February 16, 26-year-old prostitute Patricia Real was shot on a public street, her death causing barely a ripple in greater Detroit. The death of 23-year-old Helen Conniff was a different story. A devout born-again Christian and student at Oakland University, Conniff left class early to visit her boyfriend on the night of March 10, 1980. She never reached her destination, but the boyfriend's roommate found Conniff at 10:30 P.M., hanging from a nearby fence with a dog leash wrapped around her neck.

Days later, 20-year-old Cecilia Jacobs was the next to die, found strangled in a Detroit alley, still fully clothed, with no apparent evidence of sexual assault. The same lack of motive was evident on March 31, when 26-year-old Denise Dunmore was strangled in the parking lot of her apartment complex: She had not been raped, and her expensive jewelry was undisturbed. Arlette McQueen, age 21, had been working the night shift at an Oak Park supermarket for over four months, but April 9, 1980, marked the first night she took a bus home. Her strangled body was found the next morning, dumped between houses a block from her intended destination.

Nine days after McQueen's murder, known prostitute Jeanette Woods took a break from business to meet her boyfriend at 9:00 P.M. She missed the rendezvous, and a pedestrian found her body at 1:30 A.M.—battered, raped, and strangled, throat slashed in an ugly coup de grâce. Two weeks later, 20-year-old Etta Frazier was found dead in an old garage behind a burned-out house. Nude, bound hand and foot, she had been beaten about the face, tortured with lit cigarettes, and sexually abused before she was strangled. While not a prostitute, the victim had a record of arrests for disorderly conduct and neglecting her son. Rosemary Frazier was unrelated to Etta, but her death bore striking similarities to that of her predecessor. An epileptic and longtime mental patient, Rosemary was found nude, beaten, and strangled on a grassy slope near Rosedale Park Community House. In the wake of her death, relatives staunchly denied police reports characterizing Rosemary as a streetwalker.

On May 31, 1980, Linda Monteiro was murdered four blocks from the Conniff crime scene, in nearly identical style: strangled in her own driveway as she returned home from a nightclub. Two days later, Diane Burks made the list, found with hands tied behind her back, nude but for slacks and panties lowered to her knees. The 22-year-old drug-addicted prostitute had been strangled with an intertwined chain and telephone cord.

Cassandra Johnson, described by police as a 17-year-old prostitute, was bludgeoned to death on the night of July 1, 1980, found just before noon the next day. Another working girl, 23-year-old Delores Willis, was last seen with a john on August 26, found strangled the next morning, with her scalp laid open to the bone by heavy blows. On September 29, 19-year-old Paulette Woodward phoned her mother from business school, around 5:00 P.M., to say she was on her way home. Anxious relatives were still waiting the next morning, when police reported the discovery of Woodward's body. Beaten and strangled to death, she had not been sexually assaulted. Twenty-six-year-old Betty Rembert was found beneath a hedge on October 8, legs protruding toward the sidewalk, with her skull crushed and a stab wound to the neck. Diane Carter, a 30-year-old prostitute, was last seen alive at 3:00 A.M. on December 17, 1980, found lying on a vacant lot eight hours later, shot once at the base of the skull.

By then, police had two suspects in custody, charged with a total of five homicides. One of them, 23-year-old David Payton, was locally famous for high school athletics, employed since graduation from college as a girl's basketball coach. Arrested on November 17, Payton was grilled for 84 hours prior to arraignment, ultimately confessing to four of the recent murders. According to his signed statements, Payton killed Jeanette Woods, Rosemary Frazier, Diane Burks, and Betty Rembert in arguments over the price of oral sex, when they scornfully rejected his low-ball offers. It seemed to be a solid case, but problems soon developed. On December 15, 1980, detectives jailed Donald Murphy, charged with murdering two Detroit prostitutes in October and November. While confessing those crimes, Murphy also admitted to murdering Woods, Burks, and Rembert, providing enough details that several investigators found themselves "absolutely convinced" of his guilt.

Despite the flagrant contradictory evidence, prosecutors pressed forward in both cases. Payton was charged with four murders, while Murphy faced trial on the original two. A Detroit judge dismissed Payton's charges on March 20, 1981, finding that a previous magistrate had "abused judicial discretion" by admitting Payton's confessions as evidence. Prosecutor William Cahalan vowed to appeal that ruling, insisting that "We have the right man charged with the right crimes," but the murder counts were not reinstated. Separately charged with raping and robbing two other prostitutes, Payton was acquitted at trial and sued Detroit police for coercing his worthless confessions. In 1991 he was awarded $8 million in damages for his ordeal.

Donald Murphy, meanwhile, was tried and convicted only in the original prostitute murders charged against him. He is presumed innocent of any other charges, but even if his guilt is assumed (as confessed) in the Woods, Burks, and Rembert slayings, 13 of Detroit's 1980 victims remain unaccounted for, their killer still at large.

DIAMOND, John, Jr. ("Legs") gangland murder victim (1931)

A Philadelphia native, born in 1897, Jack Diamond was 16 years old when his mother died and his father moved the small family—himself, with sons John Jr. and Edward—to Brooklyn. The Diamond brothers grew up as street hoodlums, members of the notorious Hudson Dusters gang, and Jack reportedly earned his famous nickname for his skill in outrunning police in a series of thefts from delivery trucks. (An alternative, more fanciful story refers to his reputation as an expert ballroom dancer.) Drafted by the army in 1918, Diamond soon went AWOL and served 366 days of a five-year sentence for desertion. Upon release, he went to work as a bodyguard for New York gambler Arnold Rothstein, then for one of Rothstein's partners, labor racketeer Jacob (Little Augie) Orgen.

By the time gangland killers caught up with Orgen on October 15, 1927, also wounding Diamond in a drive-by shooting, Legs was overseeing Little Augie's bootlegging and narcotics rackets. Diamond emerged from the hospital to proclaim himself the new boss. Violence flared anew in 1928, when rival mobster Dutch Schultz invaded Diamond's territory,

and a two-year shooting war erupted. Diamond was wounded in three separate ambushes, surviving each time, and journalists thereafter dubbed him the "clay pigeon of the underworld." Emboldened by his own resilience, Diamond carried the war to Schultz and expanded his frontiers with raids into the territory held by rival Irving Wexler (a.k.a. Waxey Gordon). More powerful mobsters, including Charles (Lucky) Luciano and Meyer Lansky, may have feared they were next on the reckless Irishman's hit parade. By 1931 the heat in Manhattan was too intense, and Diamond moved to Albany, New York, in hopes of improving his luck.

In fact, it had the opposite effect.

Diamond's first move in Albany was a bid to persuade two local bootleggers, James Duncan and Grover Parks, that they should make him a partner in their thriving liquor business. When they refused, Duncan and Parks were kidnapped, held captive, and tortured until they relented. The pair surprised Diamond, however, by filing a complaint with the police as soon as they were freed. Diamond and associate Garry Saccio were held on kidnapping charges, with Saccio convicted and sentenced to 10 years in Sing Sing prison. Diamond was acquitted and

"Legs" Diamond (second from left) appears in a New York police lineup. Charles "Lucky" Luciano is on the far right. (Library of Congress)

Police escort Legs Diamond's casket, following his gangland murder in 1931. (Library of Congress)

released from custody on December 17, 1931, to celebrate with his wife and mobster friends at an Albany speakeasy.

Midway through the victory celebration, Diamond slipped away from the bar, allegedly to visit a group of friendly reporters. In truth, however, he had a rendezvous with showgirl-mistress Kiki Roberts. After three torrid hours in bed, he hailed a cab and returned to one of his Albany hideouts, a shabby rooming house on Dove Street. Diamond was drunk on arrival, but cabbie Jack Storer helped him unlock the front door. A short time later, with Diamond sprawled unconscious on the bed, two gunmen entered and fired three shots into his head at point-blank range. Landlady Laura Wood heard the killers afterward, arguing on the stairs about whether they should return to Diamond's room and "finish

the job." One shooter complained, "That guy ain't human and it will take a lot to get him for sure." The other replied, "Oh hell, that's enough."

It was. The clay pigeon of gangland was finally dead, on the sixth attempt.

But who killed him?

Longtime underworld attorney Dixie Davis later gave credit for Diamond's murder to Abraham (Bo) Weinberg, top gun for the Dutch Schultz syndicate, but other candidates included past or potential enemies Waxey Gordon, Vincent (Mad Dog) Coll, Owen (The Killer) Madden, Lucky Luciano, and Meyer Lansky. Gangsters Salvatore Spitale and Irving (Bitsy) Bitz also harbored a grudge against Diamond, for absconding with $200,000 they had given him as start-up money for a heroin pipeline from Europe. A dark horse suspect was Alice Diamond, long aware of her husband's flagrant infidelity, but her grief at his passing appeared genuine. Indeed, upon viewing her husband's remains, Alice had the presence of mind to tell detectives at the scene, "I didn't do it."

DICKERSON, Elinor See PRINCE GEORGES HOSPITAL MURDERS

DICKINSON, John Q. assassination victim (1871)

Jackson County, Florida, was among the South's most violent districts during the chaotic Reconstruction era (1865–77), described by former slaves and white Republicans as the place "where Satan has his seat." Official estimates of racist murders committed in Jackson County during that period ranged from 153 to 179, exceeding the death toll for all other Florida counties combined. A militant Ku Klux Klan unit, led by merchant James Coker and his trigger-happy son, vowed to "kill the last damned Republican in the place," and it proved to be no idle threat.

By early 1871 John Dickinson *was* the last Republican, employed as court clerk in the county seat at Marianna, hanging onto his principles and his job despite years of harassment and threats on his life. Dickinson's predecessor, Dr. JOHN FINLAYSON, had been murdered by the Klan in 1869; since then, every other Republican official in Jackson County had either resigned, shifted party allegiance, or fallen before KKK guns. Dickinson described the local situation in a letter of February 23, 1871, addressed to Florida's secretary of state in Tallahassee. It read:

Sir:

Your letter of the 14th instant, requesting certain information as to outrages committed in this county since reconstruction, as to the spirit of the press, &c., &c., was received last night; the high water on the Apalachicola River delayed the mails.

I regret the fact that outrages upon loyalty in this county are always so vivid a reality of the present and so fearful a probability of the future that we have failed to think of the past. I cannot, without considerable time and research, give you any history of the different terrible scenes through which I have passed here.

You intimate that your information must be immediate, and I will give you the best views of the situation

I can under the circumstances. Since reconstruction there have been about seventy-five persons violently killed in this county; and more than nine-tenths were republicans, and nearly nine-tenths colored.

Practically the civil rights of the colored man are subordinate to those of the white man. The press has been and is disgustingly uncandid, abusive of everything republican, and at times openly seditious.

Human life is counted cheap when passion or politics call for its sacrifice, and the frequency and cold blood which have characterized our murders has not been to me so fearful a fact as the carelessness with which the public learn a new outrage.

Public sentiment is terribly demoralized in this direction. Within the last few days our sheriff has been shamefully beaten on the public streets and two colored men fatally assaulted. Neither of them are yet dead, but I believe no hopes are entertained of their recovery. For myself, I blush to say that for nearly three years I have managed to live here only by dexterously compromising the expression of my opinions, and by a circumspect walk. To say that the colored man here has, through my agency, uniformly obtained even-handed justice would be a lie!

To say that I have striven, even to a loss of self-respect, to do the best thing under the circumstances, is but to tell the whole truth. If some particular information is required, I shall require time to prepare it.

Very respectfully,
J.Q. Dickinson

P.S.—One of the colored men I mentioned died last night, and I have held an inquest to-day. Verdict, Unknown! Everybody in the county knows the murderer; he has left for Alabama. I learn just now that the other man is dead, and I also hear it disputed.

I shall immediately investigate.

In haste,
J.Q. Dickinson

Dickinson's luck ran out on the night of April 3, 1871. While walking home from his Marianna office at 10:00 P.M., he was ambushed and killed within a few yards of the spot where Dr. Finlayson was murdered two years earlier. Local Democrats celebrated the assassination, while their official organ—the *Marianna Courier*—attributed the slaying to an unnamed black husband, allegedly resulting from an interracial love affair. Circuit Judge T. T. Long repeated that fable when he testified before congressional investigators in November 1871, blaming the homicide on a black fugitive named

Homer Bryant. The crime, Long assured his audience, had occurred in "connection with some family matters, with some colored woman that [Dickinson] kept." Unfortunately, Bryant mimicked Jackson County's Klan assassins by eluding capture and the case remained unsolved.

DIGGS, Frank murder victim (1870)

A former slave, employed as a mail agent on the Selma and Meridian Railroad, Frank Diggs faced double danger in Reconstruction-era Alabama. He was black, first of all, in a time and place where contention over slavery and civil rights placed every African American at risk; and he was an employee of the federal government, despised below the Mason-Dixon line for its efforts (however short-lived) to eradicate the white-supremacist "Southern Way of Life" that had prevailed before the Civil War. Sadly for Diggs, his normal route required him to travel daily between Selma, Alabama, and Meridian, Mississippi, two cauldrons of virulent Ku Klux Klan activity with a world of grief in between.

Masked Klansmen had raided the Selma and Meridian trains periodically since 1868, dragging black firemen from their cars and flogging them beside the tracks, while threatening the engineers who carried them. Some of the line's white employees were no better, including brakeman Robert Eustick, who while on duty assaulted and pistol-whipped a black man in October 1870. Frank Diggs reported the incident to Selma authorities and offered to testify against Eustick at trial. The same day, Eustick was fired by conductor William English after threatening to murder Diggs. Unfortunately, English saw no need to warn Diggs personally, as he "did not think the threat was serious."

The conductor was forced to reconsider that judgment on November 1, 1870, when the train stopped for firewood at Kewaunee, just across the Mississippi line in Lauderdale County. The train's baggage master described a masked man's approach to the mail car, pushing a double-barreled shotgun through the open window and leveling Diggs with a blast to the torso. Several witnesses watched the gunman flee, but none could afterward identify him. William English claimed that Robert Eustick confronted him three days after the murder, bragging that he had killed Diggs, but a report to postal authorities and the U.S. deputy marshal in Selma produced no arrest.

Despite the private quarrel with Eustick, Klansmen were still widely suspected of playing some role in the Diggs homicide, and the victim's white replacement, John Coleman, was accosted by night riders in February 1871, warned to stay east of Sumter County, Alabama, if he valued his life. (Coleman also taught a school for blacks in his spare time, a sore point for bigots statewide.) Edmund Pettus, a prominent Klansman from Selma, took pains to disassociate the KKK from Diggs's murder when he testified before congressional investigators in October 1871. Pettus blamed Eustick—"a terribly mean and vicious boy"—for the murder, while proclaiming Diggs "a well-behaved man and a man of good character" who was "a popular man with the white people, and also with the negroes [sic]." Pettus called the murder "one of the worst cases that I ever heard of"—but like other influential white residents in those days, he did nothing to see the crime solved.

DIXON, Charlye See WAYCROSS, GEORGIA, MURDERS

DOCKER, Patricia See "BIBLE JOHN"

DOLLAR, William assassination victim (1868)

As a Republican deputy sheriff in Drew County, Arkansas, William Dollar was particularly vulnerable during the chaotic Reconstruction era following the Civil War. Arkansas was a hotbed of Ku Klux Klan activity, amounting to a guerrilla war against radical Republicans and newly enfranchised blacks, with the worst violence occurring prior to the presidential election of 1868.

William Dollar fell prey to that racist frenzy in October 1868, when a gang of 15 masked Klansmen stormed his home one night, dragging Dollar and a black visitor, one Fred Reeves, from the house. The raiders tied one end of a rope around each captive's neck and led them 300 yards from Dollar's home, where both were cut down in a hail of gunfire. Neighbors left the corpses in the road for two more days, as a kind of ghoulish tourist attraction. No suspects were identified in the double murder, but Klansmen remained active in Drew County. On the weekend before the election they flogged two black ministers, inflicting 400 lashes on one of the victims. White residents of Monticello, the county seat, were threatened with death if they voted Republican, and Democratic candidate Horatio Seymour logged 1,292 votes as a result, Ulysses Grant trailing in the county with a mere 33 ballots.

"DOODLER, The" California serial killer (1974–75)

Years before the advent of AIDS, the gay community of San Francisco was confronted with another lethal menace, wrought in human form. Between January 1974 and September 1975, a knife-wielding stalker was responsible for 17 attacks, 14 of them fatal, which left police bitterly frustrated.

When the murders began, based on discrepancies in choice of victims, authorities believed they were tracking three different serial killers. Five of the victims were Tenderloin drag queens, mutilated by a slasher who apparently despised transvestites. Six others (including high-profile attorney George Gilbert) were selected from the sadomasochistic world of leather bars, clubs with names like Ramrod, Fe-Be's, and Folsom Prison. The last six were middle-class businessmen, slain by an assailant who picked them up in Castro Village bars, wooing his prey with cartoon sketches of themselves. Three of the latter victims survived the attacks, and the killer's taste for comic artwork gave the "Doodler" his nickname.

Over time, as leads were run down and eliminated, police realized they were searching for a single killer in their string of unsolved homicides. In 1976 suspicion focused on a suspect described by authorities as a mental patient with a history of treatment for sex-related problems. Questioned repeatedly, the suspect spoke freely to police, but he always stopped short of a confession. Meanwhile, the three surviving victims refused to identify their attacker, afraid of ruining their lives by "coming out" in court. On July 8, 1977, frustrated investigators announced that an unnamed suspect had been linked to 14 murders and three assaults in 1974–75. Indictment was impossible, they said, without cooperation from survivors of the Doodler's attacks. Thirty years after the fact, the case remains a stalemate, officially unsolved, with the suspect—if he still survives—presumably under ongoing surveillance.

DOWD, Carol   See "FRANKFORD SLASHER"

DOWLER, Amanda Jane murder victim (2002)

Amanda Dowler, known to family and friends as "Milly," was a 13-year-old student at Heathside School in Walton-on-Thames, Surrey, England, when she disappeared on March 21, 2002. Witnesses reported that she left campus at 3:00 P.M. and caught the usual train for home, but she got off with friends at the Walton-on-Thames railway station, rather than riding as usual to her stop in Hersham. Dowler and her friends went to a local café, and she phoned home at 3:47 P.M., telling her father that she would be home within half an hour. She was last seen alive about 4:00 P.M., walking along Station Approach.

Amanda's disappearance prompted a local search that later spread nationwide. Around Hersham, 100 police officers searched yards, fields, and rivers, with airborne help from helicopters. Public appeals for information included a recreation of Amanda's presumed abduction on the TV show *Crimewatch,* and pop star Will Young made a special televized appeal after learning that Amanda had attended one of his concerts on the day before she vanished. On March 28, police spokesmen declared that Amanda had probably not been taken by force, since no witnesses had reported seeing a struggle along Station Approach.

On April 23, 2002, police pulled a decomposed corpse from the Thames. Although initially believed to be Amanda Dowler, the body was identified on April 24 as Maisie Thomas, a 73-year-old woman who disappeared in 2001. Authorities denied any evidence of foul play in that case and continued their search for Dowler. A London tabloid newspaper the *Sun* offered a £100,000 reward for solution of the case in June 2002, while Amanda's parents kept dialing her cell-phone number, in futile hope that she or someone else would answer.

That hope was dashed on September 18, 2002, with discovery of Dowler's skeletal remains in Yately Heath Forest, near Fleet, in Hampshire. None of Amanda's clothes or personal belongings—purse, cell phone, or backpack—were recovered.

Dowler's murder remains unsolved today, but three persons landed in jail on charges related to the case. They include:

- *Paul Hughes,* a sex offender already imprisoned for molesting a 12-year-old girl, who sent Dowler's mother a series of letters threatening to kill her and claiming credit for Amanda's death. Prison authorities apologized for failing to screen Hughes's outgoing mail and added five years to his sentence.

- *Lianne Newman* of Tewksbury, Gloucestershire, who made numerous phone calls to Dowler's family, her school, and the police, posing as Amanda. She received a five-month jail sentence in April 2003, upon pleading guilty to telephone harassment.

- *Gary Farr,* a schizophrenic mental patient in Retford, Nottinghamshire, who sent a blizzard of e-mails to Dowler's family and friends, her school, and police assigned to her case, claiming that Amanda had been kidnapped and smuggled into Poland to work as a stripper and prostitute. Her death was faked, Farr claimed, to cover up the kidnapping. In October 2006, Farr was confined indefinitely under Britain's Mental Health Act, as a serious risk to the public.

On February 25, 2008, police named their prime suspect in the Dowler case as Levi Bellfield. That announcement came on the day of Bellfield's conviction for murdering two young women and trying to kill a third. Detective Chief Inspector Colin Sutton, with London's Metropolitan Police, described the former nightclub bouncer as a sexual predator.

"He has a massive ego to feed," Sutton said. "He thinks he's God's gift to everyone. He drives around in his car, feels a bit 'whatever' and sees some young blonde girl. Young blonde girl says, 'Go away,' and he thinks, 'You dare to turn down Levi Bellfield, you're worth nothing,' and then she gets a whack over the head. It is shown in the case of [surviving third victim] Kate Sheedy. She was smart enough to think she didn't like the look of his car and crosses the road. He thinks. 'You think you're so clever' and whoosh, he runs her over."

At press time for this volume, no charges have been filed against Bellfield in Amanda Dowler's case. He is serving a life term in prison for the February 2008 conviction.

DOWNS, Janine See "Operation Enigma"

DUBBS, Sandra See "I-35 murders"

DUFF, Edmond See South Croydon murders

DUFF, Susan See "Highway Killer"

DUNMORE, Denise See Detroit murders

DUPREE, Jack murder victim (1871)

Mississippi has a reputation as the most intransigent of American states in regard to improvement of conditions for racial minorities. That was certainly true in the violent Reconstruction era (1865–77), when newly freed ex-slaves were allowed to vote for the first time in history and they cast their ballots overwhelmingly for the party of Abraham Lincoln, ensuring that white-supremacist Democrats loyal to the late Confederacy would be driven from office. The bitter "outs" retaliated with a brutal guerrilla campaign of murder and mayhem designed to "redeem" their state for white Democratic control.

Monroe County ranked among Mississippi's most violent districts, inhabited by a band of sadistic Klansmen who tortured and mutilated their victims prior to death, sometimes forcing black Republicans to accompany the raiding parties in disguise, as a form of psychological warfare. One of their primary targets in early 1871 was Jack Dupree, a "boisterous" freedman who led the county's Republican club. On the night of February 10, 1871, a band of 50 or 60 masked Klansmen (including five or six black hostages riding under the gun) surrounded Dupree's home, 10 miles southeast of Aberdeen. Joseph Davis, one of the freedmen forced to ride with the terrorists, described what happened next in his November 1871 testimony before congressional investigators.

They called him to come out, and he didn't come out; but he got up and opened the door, and went back and got into bed; and then they came in and asked him to get up; and he didn't get right up out of bed, but he began to fight them; and they jumped on him, some five or six of them, and began to knock him with guns and sticks; and his wife was hollowing [sic], and they drew their pistols on her, and told her if she hollowed, or said another word, they would blow her up, or they'd kill her and then they taken him out, and carried him down the road, down below Ross's Mill, somewhere in the swamp, and they whipped him; they whipped him until—well, they whipped him an hour or more, until he hollowed and went on so he could scarcely hollow; you could scarcely discern him hollow, so they said; and when they came back to where we were and the horses, they said they had cut his damned guts out.

Davis subsequently surrendered and turned state's evidence against the night riders, telling authorities at Oxford, Mississippi, how the Klansmen had abducted Dupree, flogged him unmercifully, and "then cut him open from the throat to the straddle, took out all his insides, and then threw his body into McKinley's Creek." A visit to the reported crime scene proved fruitless, and while Dupree's body was never found, six Klansmen were indicted for his kidnapping and for the murder of a second freedman, Aleck Page, also witnessed by Davis. The defendants included Klansmen William Butler, Dudley Hutchinson, Barbour Quarles, John Roberts, William Walton, and Plummer Willis. (Davis also identified four other Klansmen who compelled him at knifepoint to join in the raid on Dupree, but no charges were filed against them.)

Aberdeen attorney Reuben Reynolds was hired to represent five of the defendants, and in the atmosphere of the time he had no difficulty recruiting alibi witnesses. At a hearing in which he sought release of his clients under a writ of habeas corpus, Reynolds paraded several of these—"both respectable white and colored citizens of the county"—to swear that the accused were gathered for a party at William Walton's home on the night Dupree vanished, and that they jointly watched the band of masked riders gallop past on their grisly errand. (No one in authority questioned the impossible notion of blacks and whites mingling at a "social gathering" in Reconstruction-era Mississippi.) As to Page's murder, a black witness was found to swear that Davis had been mowing grass with her on the night in question, miles from the scene of the crime. The suspects were accordingly released and never brought to trial. Both crimes remain officially unsolved today.

DURKIN, Jeanne   See "FRANKFORD SLASHER"

E

EBOLI, Thomas gangland murder victim (1972)

A native of New York City, born in 1911, Thomas Eboli—better known as Tommy Ryan—was a professional prizefighter before he joined the Vito Genovese Mafia family as a strong-arm enforcer. While not the brightest of Genovese's subordinates, Eboli proved himself both loyal and ruthless (suspected in at least 20 homicides). Thus he rose through the ranks, maintaining his sporting interest as a boxing promoter until he was barred from the fight game for assaulting a referee. When Genovese was imprisoned for narcotics smuggling in 1959, nominal control of the family passed to co-captains Eboli and Gerardo Catena. Genovese called the shots until his death in 1969, and Catena was jailed the following year, leaving Eboli in full control for the first time.

He proved unequal to the task, despite some notable success at muscling into the entertainment industry and Greenwich Village gay bars. In 1972 Eboli borrowed $4 million from the Carlo Gambino crime family to finance a drug deal with importer Louis Cirillo. The scheme fell apart when federal agents arrested Cirillo and sent him to prison for 25 years. Gambino demanded a refund, and Eboli made the mistake of his life by refusing to pay.

On July 1, 1972, Eboli visited one of his several mistresses at her apartment in Brooklyn's Crown Heights district. Bodyguard-chauffeur Joseph Sternfeld saw his employer emerge and opened the back door of Eboli's black Cadillac. At that moment a red-and-yellow van swerved in to the curb and one of its occupants strafed Eboli with a burst of submachine-gunfire. Five .45-caliber bullets smashed into the mobster's face and throat, killing him instantly. Sternfeld, who had dived for cover when the shooting started, professed himself unable to describe the killer. A perjury indictment failed to refresh his memory, and the charge was subsequently dropped.

Carlo Gambino was the prime suspect in Eboli's murder, though no one accused him of pulling the trigger himself. A secondary suspect, perhaps in league with Gambino, was Eboli's successor as head of the Genovese family, Frank (Funzi) Tieri. Eboli's murder came in the midst of a New York gangland upheaval that began with the June 1971 shooting of Joseph Colombo Sr. and continued with the death of JOSEPH GALLO in April 1972. Lesser Mafiosi fell along the way, but their deaths shared one thing in common with Eboli's: the majority remain officially unsolved today.

EDDOWES, Catharine See "JACK THE RIPPER"

EDWARDS, Parker See BUFFALO, NEW YORK, TAXI MURDERS

ELAM, Roberta See WASHINGTON, PENNSYLVANIA, MURDERS

ELLISON, Collette See "Astrological Murders"

ELLROY, Geneva murder victim (1958)

The last thing anyone expects to find at baseball practice is a woman's corpse. A few skinned knees and elbows are the norm, sore feelings on the losing team, perhaps a fistfight now and then. But the three coaches from California's Babe Ruth League were looking forward to a normal practice session on June 22, 1958, as they trudged along King's Row, a private access road that served Arroyo High School's athletic field in the Los Angeles suburb of El Monte, California. Burdened with equipment, they were talking shop when one of them stopped dead in his tracks, pointing to the base of an acacia thicket on the left side of the road.

The glitter of a broken necklace caught his eye, pearls scattered in the dust, and then he saw the woman's supine body lying with her skirt bunched up around her waist. She wore no slip or panties and her shoes were missing. Her right stocking was in place; police would find the left one wrapped tightly around her neck, together with a cotton cord.

There was no question of an accidental death or suicide. The woman's purse was missing from the scene. A coat that seemed to match her dress was spread beneath the body, almost as a courtesy, to spare her flesh from contact with the soil. The victim was completely naked underneath her dress, but homicide detectives later found a bra beneath her body. El Monte police captain Orval Davis told the press she had been murdered elsewhere and transported to King's Row, 150 feet due east of Tyler Avenue.

The red-haired, blue-eyed victim was a nurse, Geneva Ellroy, though the press and medical examiner would stubbornly refer to her as Jean. Newspapers also shaved six years from Ellroy's age, reporting her as 37, but that hardly mattered in the circumstances. At five feet five and busty, she could have passed for a younger woman.

Dr. Gerald Ridge, deputy medical examiner for Los Angeles County, performed the autopsy on Monday, June 23. The cause of death was listed as strangulation with "intense paratracheal soft tissue hematoma, level of ligature." Ellroy had also been beaten over the head, as evidenced by multiple "deep scalp focal ecchymoses." Lesser injuries included a bruised right eyelid, superficial abrasions on the left hip and both knees, and deep purple bruising on the inside of both thighs. The victim had been menstruating when she died, and Dr. Ridge found a tampon in place, along with quantities of semen. (Curiously, despite disarrayed clothing, bruising, and presence of semen, the *Los Angeles Times* declared that Ellroy's autopsy revealed no evidence of sexual assault.) Ellroy's blood-alcohol level of .08 was slightly below the legal limit for intoxication.

Aside from the semen—still decades away from the science of DNA "fingerprints"—and a few streaks of "apparent dried blood" on Ellroy's right palm, there was nothing left to help police identify her killer. Subsequent reports made much of skin and tiny hairs allegedly recovered from beneath her fingernails, but Dr. Ridge's autopsy report is unequivocal: "The spaces beneath the fingernails, which are rather long, are grossly clean in appearance, with no visible debris."

Divorced with a son to support, Geneva Ellroy had been on her own that weekend, while 10-year-old James spent time with his father. James learned of the murder when a taxi dropped him off in El Monte on Sunday afternoon. The yard at home was jammed with detectives, and patrol cars were lined up at the curb. It was a tragedy, of course, but James was not exactly prostrate with grief. He would have preferred to live with his father, but a divorce court had decreed otherwise, leaving James with the woman he described as "sharp-tongued" and "bad-tempered," "a boozer, lazy, and semipromiscuous." "I found her in bed with men," he recalled, years later. "I had lots of uncles." On hearing the news of her death, James says, "I felt relieved. I remember forcing myself to cry crocodile tears on the bus going back to L.A."

Police, meanwhile, were busy looking for Geneva's killer. They had nothing of substance to work with, but an informant seemed to recall seeing the victim on Saturday night, June 21. She had been drinking at a bar on Valley Boulevard, and he had seen her "for a short time" with a couple who might or might not have escorted her out. The male half of the nameless duo was described as swarthy, dark-haired, 40-something, wearing a dark suit with a sport shirt open at the neck. His female companion was blonde, age 35 to 40, five feet six, 135 pounds, and wearing her hair in a ponytail.

The crime was never solved, but it left an indelible mark on James Ellroy. Decades later, as a best-selling crime novelist, he would memorialize his mother's death in a novel about another unsolved Los Angeles murder, the 1947 slaying of "BLACK DAHLIA" Elizabeth Short. Later still, Ellroy penned a nonfiction volume on his effort to solve the case (*My Dark Places,* 1996), but he fared no better after 38 years than police had in 1958.

ESPLER, Bill See NAHANNI VALLEY MURDERS

ETHIER, Michel See MONTREAL CHILD MURDERS

EVANGELISTA murders Detroit (1929)
A native Italian who immigrated to the United States near the turn of the last century, Benjamino Evangelista settled first in Philadelphia, where he worked on a railroad crew. Although a practicing Roman Catholic, he was also fascinated—some said obsessed—with the occult sciences, sharing his passion with coworker Aurelius Angelino. Together, the men practiced various mystic rituals, sometimes joined by Evangelista's wife, but their studies were interrupted in 1919, when Angelino ran amok and killed two of his own children with an axe, afterward committed to a state asylum for the criminally insane.

Shaken by the grim turn of evens, Evangelista moved his family to Detroit and invested his savings in real estate, soon emerging as a prosperous realtor and landlord. On the side, he earned a supplemental tax-free income from the sale of hexes, herbs, and "spiritual remedies" in Little Italy, often performing chants, dances, and chicken sacrifices to "cure" his ailing customers. The basement of Evangelista's home, on St. Aubin Avenue, contained an occult ritual chamber, complete with a crude altar,

with "evil eye" and "divine" figurines dangling on strings from the ceiling. In his spare time, Evangelista penned a manuscript titled *The Oldest History of the World, Discovered by Occult Science in Detroit,* that detailed workings of a mythical cult, the Great Union Federation of America.

On the morning of July 3, 1929, another realtor stopped by to visit Evangelista at his office, attached to the family home. The caller was stunned to find Evangelista slumped behind his desk, his severed head reposing on the floor beside his chair. Police were summoned, and they found Evangelista's wife in bed, also decapitated. All four of Evangelista's children had been murdered while they slept, and then dismembered. The only clue, a single bloody thumbprint from the back door of the house, would never be identified.

Police briefly suspected one of Evangelista's tenants, posthumously accused of the murders by a vengeful ex-wife, but the dead man's thumbprint did not match. Another possible solution involved Aurelius Angelino, who escaped from the Pennsylvania asylum in 1923 and was never recaptured. Unfortunately, Angelino's fingerprints were not on file, so his involvement in the massacre could neither be eliminated nor confirmed.

EVANS, Karry See BATTLE CREEK, MICHIGAN, MURDERS

EWELL, Shari Dee See YAKIMA, WASHINGTON, MURDERS

EYERLY, Sherry See SALEM, OREGON, MURDERS

FAELZ, Tina See ALAMEDA COUNTY MURDERS

FAGER, Phillip murder victim (1987)
Mary Fager had no intimation of disaster when she returned to her Wichita, Kansas, home on December 31, 1987, following a three-day trip to visit relatives. She was stunned to find her husband Phillip shot twice in the back, her two daughters—10-year-old Sherri and 16-year-old Kelli—strangled in the family's basement hot tub. Kelli Fager was nude; her sister's hands had been bound with black electrical tape that loosened in the water after she was dead.

Police had barely launched their fruitless search for suspects in the triple slaying when Mary Fager received a letter purportedly written by Wichita's notorious "BTK Strangler," blamed for six unsolved murders between 1974 and 1977. Investigators disagree on whether the note was an authentic BTK correspondence, but they ultimately dismissed the still-unidentified serial killer as a suspect in the Fager massacre.

Instead, Wichita police focused their attention on William Butterworth, a local contractor arrested in Florida on January 2, 1988, while driving Phillip Fager's car. In custody, Butterworth told detectives that he had gone to the Fager home, where he was making renovations, and found Phillip dead on the floor. Exploring further, he had heard suspicious noises in the house and fled in panic—strangely tak-

ing the family car instead of his own vehicle. Butterworth had been reported missing two days before Mary Fager returned to find her family dead, and he claimed amnesia surrounding the event. Butterworth was charged with three counts of murder, but a jury acquitted him at trial. Wichita police still consider him the only suspect, and they have not officially closed the case despite his acquittal. William Butterworth's present whereabouts are unknown.

FANTAZIER, Joanne See NEW JERSEY MURDERS (1965–66)

FARADAY, David See "ZODIAC"

FARROKHZAD, Fereydoun murder victim (1992)
An Iranian native, born in 1936, Fereydoun Farrokhzad was a famous poet and singer-songwriter. Prior to 1979, he focused primarily on romantic songs and poetry, but the Islamic revolution prompted a shift to political subjects that drove him into exile. His public performances diversified to include lectures criticizing Iran's Ayatollah Khomeini and thus placed his life at risk from Muslim extremists.

On August 9, 1992, unknown intruders stabbed and beheaded Farrokhzad at his home in Bonn, Germany. The crime remains officially unsolved, but no one seriously doubts the involvement of Iranian intelligence agents or terrorists loyal to Khomeini. Some reports link Farrokhzad's death to the "CHAIN MURDERS" of dissidents within Iran during 1988–99, but no solid evidence has thus far been presented.

FECHTEL, Cathy See "ASTROLOGICAL MURDERS"

FERRIN, Darlene See "ZODIAC"

FEUSI, Nancy See "OCCULT MURDERS"

FIGG, Elizabeth See "JACK THE STRIPPER"

FINLAYSON, John assassination victim (1869)
A native of Jackson County, Florida, during the state's unsettled Reconstruction era (1865–77), Dr. John Finlayson placed himself at risk by supporting black civil rights and the Republican Party in a region dominated by white-supremacist Democrats. Death threats from the local Ku Klux Klan were taken seriously in those days, when Jackson County boasted more racist murders than all other Florida counties combined. Still, Dr. Finlayson remained active in liberal politics while serving as clerk of the county's court at Marianna.

On the night of February 26, 1869, Finlayson attended a public concert with Republican state senator William Purman, a "carpetbagger" from Pennsylvania. As the two men walked home, sometime after 10:00 P.M., a single shot was fired at them from ambush, drilling Purman's neck before it struck Finlayson in the temple and killed him instantly. Purman spent five weeks recuperating from his wound, then fled the county, dogged by reports that the KKK had placed a thousand-dollar bounty on his head.

Rumors named Finlayson's killer as a disreputable Jackson County thug, one Thomas Barnes, and a reward was offered for his capture. Two black officers surprised him later in the year, at a girlfriend's home near Chattahoochee, but Barnes killed them both and escaped once more, this time for good. In his absence, the *Tallahassee Democrat* attributed Finlayson's mur-

John Finlayson was murdered by Florida terrorists for holding office as a member of the "radical" Republican Party. (Florida State Archives)

der to a personal feud, entirely divorced from politics. It remains one of Jackson County's 179 unsolved murders from the Reconstruction era.

FINN, Shirley murder victim (1975)
Born in 1951, Shirley Finn was a flamboyant mother of three who ran a brothel in Perth, Western Australia. On June 23, 1975, authorities found her corpse, shot twice in the head, in a car parked on Labouchere Road, near the Royal Perth Golf Club in South Perth. While ranked as one of Western Australia's most notorious crimes, it remains unsolved today.

Public speculation naturally linked Finn's death to her career as a whorehouse madam, but despite inquiries by a royal commission, a dearth of evidence frustrated the investigation. Had Finn been killed by an unhappy client? By one of her girls or a jealous boyfriend? By members of organized crime? Or, as some alleged, was the shooter a policeman?

On the 30th anniversary of Finn's slaying, police announced a cold-case review of the crime. Acting Assistant Commissioner Jeff Byleveld advised reporters, "People may have been to the police and may not have divulged all the information. They may have reconsidered over the years and with the passage of time they may feel inclined to come forward and let us know what's going on." Concerning charges of police complicity, he added, "I am aware of the speculation but with the passage of time we're able to apply fresh minds to it now and we'll take that as it comes. And if the information comes to hand [that police were involved] we'll deal with it. As police we're not afraid to open our investigations. I think Mrs. Finn's lifestyle and occupation certainly attributed to those rumors and innuendoes and I'm not sure that they can take us anywhere but we will have an open and frank review of this."

Byleveld was optimistic concerning his chances of solving the case. He said, "Our methodologies are as far advanced as every agency that has advanced in technology; we're exactly the same and our ability to investigate I'd say is much improved from 1975." While that is certainly true, three years and counting have passed since announcement of the new investigation and no useful leads have emerged.

FISCHER, Yukon See Nahanni Valley murders

FLAT-TIRE murders Florida (1975)

On August 29, 1975, Dade County's assistant medical examiner announced his belief that one man was responsible for five recent murders of women in southern Florida. Homicide investigators were convinced of a connection in the July slayings of 27-year-old Ronnie Gorlin and 21-year-old Elyse Napp, while the pathologist's report named three other victims. Barbara Stephens, age 23, had been kidnapped from a South Dade shopping mall and stabbed to death in February 1975, while a pair of 14-year-old high school classmates, Barbara Schreiber and Belinda Zeterower, had been killed at Hollywood in June 1975.

On hearing the Florida announcement, Sgt. Erwin Carlstedt of the Sonoma County (California) Sheriff's Department chimed in with his theory of a single killer, moving coast to coast with more than 30 murders to his credit—probably a reference to serial slayer Ted Bundy, before he was publicly identified

as a suspect in murders spanning the United States. Florida detectives offered no comment on Carlstedt's hypothesis, concentrating on their search for an elusive killer who deflated his victims' tires in commercial parking lots, then lured them to their deaths with an offer of assistance. None of the "flat-tire" victims were included in Bundy's 1989 confession of 30 murders, and the case remains open today, with no further victims publicly listed.

FLEISHMAN, Samuel murder victim (1869)

A native of Ohio, Samuel Fleishman left the Buckeye State in 1851 and settled in Marianna, Florida, the seat of Jackson County. By all accounts, the region was among Florida's most peaceful and prosperous in that decade before the Civil War, and Fleishman prospered, apparently spared any overt prejudice based on the fact that he was Jewish. That placid picture changed, however, with war's end and the onset of Reconstruction. Jackson County soon emerged as a hotbed of violent Ku Klux Klan activity, described by former slaves and "radical" Republicans as the place "where Satan has his seat."

Fleishman played no active role in politics, but he was outraged by the abuse of African Americans he witnessed every day around Marianna. In early October 1871 rumors spread that he had urged black patrons of his store to arm and retaliate for any future atrocities. "If the colored people are to be murdered in this way," he declared, "for every black man that is murdered there should be three white people killed." Fleishman later admitted the statement to a friend, recalling that he was "greatly excited" at the time. News of his comment soon reached fellow merchant and local Klan leader James Coker. An affidavit sworn by Fleishman on October 5, 1869, describes what happened next.

James P. Coker, on Sunday, the 3rd of October, came to the store of Altman & Bro., in Marianna, of which firm I am the authorized agent, and asked for all the guns and pistols I had in the store. He said they were wanted for the men in defense of the town during the present excitement, and that they should all be returned, and that he would be responsible for their return. He took five guns worth $20 each, and three guns worth $25 each. Eleven pistols worth $18 each. Powder, shot, and caps worth about $20. The key was delivered up to James P. Coker by Wilbur F. Jennings, who was acting as my clerk.

Although effectively disarmed, Fleishman had not heard the last of Coker and the Klan. His affidavit continues:

Yesterday, the 4th day of October, A.D. 1869, about 4 o'clock p.m., or a little later, I was visited by Arthur A. Calhoun and John R. Ely, at my boarding-place in Marianna . . . and Ely informed me that James P. Coker, William D. Barnes, and John R. Ely wished to see me at the store of James P. Coker on particular business. I immediately repaired there. I waited there, in company with John R. Ely and James P. Coker, till nearly dark, when Coker told me that as Barnes had failed to come I need not wait longer, and asked me if I would come up again the next morning. I again went there this morning, and found several persons of influence in the county assembled. . . . Thomas M. Clark informed me of the general object of the meeting, while we were waiting outside. James P. Coker and others stated to me that they represented a committee that represented the whole community, and that it was the general desire of the community that I should leave for the good of said community; that they were confident that if I remained I should be killed on account of certain expressions made by me, as alleged, on Tuesday last; that if I were killed they feared twenty or thirty others might be killed on account of it, and to save bloodshed I ought to leave. I refused and stated that my business was such that it would damage me twenty thousand dollars. They gave me at first two hours to arrange my business to get out of town; afterwards till 5 o'clock p.m.; afterwards till sundown. I told them if I had committed some crime I was willing to be tried and punished for it, but that it was impossible to arrange my business to leave before January 1, 1870; that I would rather die than leave. They informed me that they would take me off at sundown, willing or unwilling. They stated that they had no desire to take my life, but, on the contrary, wished to save it, and to do the best thing they could for the safety of the community. They then dismissed me, saying I could go and attend to my business until sundown, at which time they should come after me, and take me away.

Fleishman filed that affidavit with county clerk JOHN DICKINSON at 1:00 P.M. on October 5, 1869. Coker's gang of Klansmen came for him at sundown, as threatened, and removed him from his home by force, transporting Fleishman to the Georgia state border. He spent the night in Bainbridge, Georgia, then returned to Florida next morning, stopping near Chattahoochee to seek assistance from a friend, Malachi Martin. At the time, Mar-

tin was serving as warden of the state penitentiary, and he was not fully cognizant of the ongoing terrorism in Jackson County. Two of his own guards had recently been killed while trying to arrest the suspected slayer of DR. JOHN FINLAYSON, the late county clerk, and Martin warned Fleishman against returning to Marianna.

"I advised him not to go there," Martin told congressional investigators in November 1871, "but he said he was compelled to go; that all he had in the world was there; that he had a large amount out; that he had trusted the planters a great deal, I do not recollect the amount, but he said they would gather their crop and sell it, and he would not be able to collect his money unless he was there; that his family was there; that his store and stock of goods and all his interests were there, and he must go back. I went down to Chattahoochee with him, and met several persons there and asked them if they had heard anything from Jackson [County]; if they knew whether there was a sheriff there, and what condition things were in. They could not tell me anything about it; communication was stopped; every one was afraid to go there, and no person would go except some one who supposed he would be safe, who was one of the white people who belonged to the party there; some such person as that might go, but no person who was a republican would go."

Fleishman proceeded on his way alone, and met a former employee along the way. The other traveler, a white Democrat named Sims who later fled to Texas after murdering a freedman, warned Fleishman to turn back, but the merchant paid no mind. A few miles outside Marianna he was ambushed and killed by unknown gunmen, thus entering history as the Florida Klan's first Jewish victim. Democratic spokesmen did their best to blacken Fleishman's character, thereby excusing his murder, and that process was still ongoing seven decades later. Historian Stanley Horn, in his book-length defense of the KKK (*The Invisible Empire* 1939), ignored Fleishman's 20-year residence in Florida and his frequent dealings with white planters, branding him "a carpetbagger who . . . catered especially to the black trade."

No investigation of Fleishman's murder was ever conducted, but a local grand jury addressed the issue of his October abduction in December 1869. The panel's report, signed by foreman J. Widgeon three days before Christmas, dismissed the event in a single line: "We, the grand jury, have examined diligently into [*sic*] the within case, and cannot find it a case of kidnapping."

FLEMING, Mary   See "JACK THE STRIPPER"

FOGGI, Giovanni   See "MONSTER OF FLORENCE"

FORBES, Dennis   See NEW YORK CITY TAXI MURDERS

FORD, Eric   See BELL, CALIFORNIA, MURDERS

FORT Lauderdale, Florida unsolved murders (1981)

On February 17, 1981, the body of a young, unidentified African-American woman was found on the outskirts of Fort Lauderdale's ghetto. The medical examiner's report described her death as a homicide committed by "unspecified means." The skeletal remains of a second black female, approximately 13 years old, were discovered in the same vacant field on June 1, 1981; once again, authorities could not identify the victim or the cause of death. Victim number three, found in the same field nine days later, was identified as 30-year-old Eloise Coleman, a neighborhood resident last seen alive on June 7. Death was attributed to head wounds from a heavy, blunt object.

More than two decades after the crimes, police remain baffled by the Fort Lauderdale slayings, unwilling to call the crimes a "series," but unable to deny the similarities and geographical relationship. The killer (or killers) remains unidentified.

FORT Wayne, Indiana child murders (1988–90)

Police in Fort Wayne cite FBI psychological profiles as the basis for their declaration that two "identical" rape-murders of young girls, committed 26 months apart, "are actually separate cases and will be pursued individually." Some local residents regard that decision as a critical mistake, and while neither side can prove its case definitively in the absence of a suspect, the fact remains that both slayings—plus 10 more attempted kidnappings of children in the same area—remain unsolved today.

The first victim, eight-year-old April Marie Tinsley, was abducted near her Fort Wayne home on April 1, 1988, snatched by the driver of a blue pickup truck. Found three days later in a DeKalb County ditch, she had been raped and suffocated, then redressed before her body was discarded. A pathologist's report suggests that Tinsley was killed 24 to 48 hours before her body was recovered.

Police had no leads in that case two years later, when seven-year-old Sarah Jean Bowker was kidnapped from a residential street on June 13, 1990, found dead the next day in a shallow creek near her home. Like April Tinsley, Bowker had been sexually assaulted, then smothered to death. Authorities described the crimes as "identical," until members of the FBI's Behavioral Science Unit at Quantico, Virginia, provided their insight. The resultant profiles, as described by Fort Wayne police in their statements to the media, "strongly indicate that the killings, though similar, are not related."

And still, no suspect could be found, though someone clearly harbored an unhealthy interest in Fort Wayne's children. Following Sarah Bowker's murder, 10 more abduction attempts were reported to police. The last attempt publicized occurred on March 25, 1991, when a 12-year-old girl narrowly avoided being dragged into a stranger's car. Allen County sheriff's lieutenant Ed Tutwiler acknowledged "a certain amount of paranoia running in this," and planned a meeting with parents "to try to quell some of the rumors that are running wild out there."

The murders of two children were no rumors, though, and the formation of a task force meant to solve the case—ironically announced on the day of the last attempted kidnapping—has thus far shed no new light on the crimes. Fort Wayne's child killer (or killers) presumably remains at large.

In 2004, Fort Wayne police identified mysterious notes left at area residences as possibly having been written by the same person who scrawled a message claiming responsibility for April Tinsley's death across a barn door in 1990. They called on the public for help in identifying the writer of the notes. To date, no one has done so.

FORT Worth, Texas unsolved murders (1984–85)

Between September 1984 and January 1985 a string of brutal homicides and disappearances spread fear among the female residents of Tarrant County, Texas. Four young women and a teenage girl would lose their lives before the crime spree ended, as mysteriously as it had begun. Police have yet to name a suspect in the case.

On the night of September 30, 1984, firefighters were called to an apartment occupied by 23-year-old Cindy Davis, on the city's southwest side. They extinguished a small fire, traced to a cigarette dropped on the bed, but there was no sign of Davis, an aspiring model. Neighbors reported the sound of voices raised in anger and a car racing away from the scene, shortly before the blaze erupted, but their statements gave police no further leads.

Three weeks later, on October 22, 23-year-old Cindy Heller stopped to help stranded motorist Kazumi Gillespie on Fort Worth's southwest side. Though the women were strangers, they spent the next two hours in a tavern, while Gillespie tried in vain to telephone a friend. When they at last split up, Gillespie remained at the bar, while Heller agreed to drive by the friend's house and leave a note on his door. The note was waiting when he came home at midnight, but Cindy Heller had vanished. Her car was found the next morning, its interior gutted by fire, with dry blood smeared on one door handle. No trace could be found of its owner, a two-time contestant in local beauty pageants.

Police noted striking similarities in the two apparent kidnappings—victims of identical age and given names, missing in circumstances that included suspicious fires—but they were not prepared to link the cases yet. Shortly after midnight on December 10, 1984, Angela Ewart left her fiancé's home in the Wedgewood section of southwest Fort Worth, stopping for gas at a station nearby. From there, the 21-year-old model and one-time beauty contestant vanished into limbo, her car discovered the next morning, doors locked, with a broken knife lying nearby. A flat tire, reported to police by a passing motorist, had been switched with a spare by the time patrolmen arrived on the scene.

On December 30, 1984, 15-year-old Sara Kashka left her home in Denton, Texas, for a party in Fort Worth, arriving to find the festivities canceled. Sarah's date dropped her off at a Wedgewood apartment, near the gas station where Angela Ewart was last seen alive, but Kashka's bad luck continued. The friends she intended to visit were out for the evening, and Sarah had vanished before they came home. Two days later, her corpse—torn by stab wounds—was found in a marshy area near Mountain Creek, in southwest Dallas. Police initially

treated her murder as a separate case from the three disappearances, citing "a difference we really can't talk about," but they later hedged their bets. As Detective Ben Dumas told reporters, "We can't establish any thread, because we only have one girl found."

That changed on January 5, 1985, when children playing on the campus of Texas Christian University stumbled over Cindy Heller's decomposing body. She had been tortured, strangled, and beheaded, her skull retrieved from a nearby lake four days later. That same day, January 9, 20-year-old Lisa Griffin was found shot to death, execution-style, in southwest Fort Worth. Sheriff's investigators charged a former mental patient with that murder, but he was released when his fingerprints failed to match others lifted from Griffin's abandoned car.

A final, grisly twist was added to the case on January 23, 1985, when construction workers uncovered human bones beside some railroad tracks, 10 miles south of the Wedgewood "murder zone." The skeletal remains were identified as those of Cindy Davis, missing since September, but the find brought authorities no closer to a suspect in the case. Angela Ewart and Sarah Kashka remain missing, the five crimes still unsolved.

FOSSEY, Dian murder victim (1985)

Dian Fossey was born in San Francisco on January 16, 1932. After graduating from Lowell High School, she defied her father's wish that she pursue a business career and, instead, pursued her love of animals by enrolling in pre-veterinary courses at the University of California, Davis. Fossey supported herself and her studies by clerking at a department store and working as a factory machinist, but she had difficulty with courses in chemistry and physics, prompting a change of majors and schools. In 1954 Fossey received a bachelor's degree in occupational therapy from San Jose State College, subsequently serving as director of the occupational therapy department at Kosair Children's Hospital in Louisville, Kentucky.

Fossey's fascination with Africa began in Louisville, where she attended a lecture by archaeologist and naturalist Louis Leakey. In 1963, she borrowed money for a trip to Africa, meeting Dr. Leakey and his wife, Mary, at their permanent worksite on Olduvai Gorge in Tanzania. The Leakeys briefed Fossey on colleague Jane Goodall's groundbreaking work with chimpanzees. After leaving Olduvai, Fossey visited Uganda and experienced her first encounter with wild mountain gorillas.

Supported by Louis Leakey, Fossey returned to Africa in December 1966 to undertake long-term study of gorillas. She established her first base of operations at Kabara, in Zaire (now the Democratic Republic of Congo), but ongoing political instability prompted a move to Rwanda in 1967. With a $30,000 contribution from the Rwandan government, Fossey established a headquarters in the Virunga Mountains of Ruhengeri Province. She merged the names of two nearby volcanoes, Mount Karisimi and Mount Visoke, to christen her Karisoke Research Center.

Fossey became an international celebrity in January 1970 after her photo appeared on the cover of *National Geographic* magazine. Inside that issue, Bob Campbell's photographs of Fossey interacting with gorillas in the wild dispelled long-standing fictional images of great apes as vicious man-killers and abductors of women. Financed by grants and increased public donations, Fossey championed a program of "active conservation" that combined preservation of gorilla habitats with aggressive patrols against poachers.

Fossey also opposed collection of gorillas for zoos, which generally involves killing adults and snatching young ones from their natural habitat. In a single case involving young gorillas "Coco" and "Pucker," earmarked for export to Germany, Fossey proved that 20 adult gorillas had been slain to secure the two captives. The collectors in that case permitted Fossey to treat Coco and Pucker for injuries suffered during capture, then shipped them off to Germany, where they both died in the same month, nine years later. In the wild, unmolested mountain gorillas may live 50 years or more.

Fossey earned a doctorate in animal behavior from Darwin College, Cambridge, in 1974, thus enhancing

Murder victim Dian Fossey plays with a group of young mountain gorillas in Rwanda's Virunga Mountains in central Africa in October 1982. (AP Photo)

her scientific credentials. Three years later, after poachers killed and mutilated "Digit," one of her favorite gorillas, she created the Digit Fund (now the Dian Fossey Gorilla Fund International) to fund gorilla conservation. In 1980, Fossey accepted a post as visiting professor at Cornell University and there completed her book, *Gorillas in the Mist* (1983), which remains the best-selling book on the great apes.

Fossey's good work did not go unopposed. Rwanda's office of tourism (ORTPN) resented her opposition to "theoretical" conservation—that is, collection of tourist income without actually using the money to help save gorillas—and the ORTPN's director refused to renew Fossey's visa in autumn 1985. Fossey's letters to friends also claim that the African Wildlife Foundation, Fauna Protection League, Mountain Gorilla Project, World Wildlife Fund, and some of her own former students all tried to seize control of her Karisoke Research Center. In particular, Fossey charged that the Mountain Gorilla Project covered up deaths of gorillas on their Mount Sabyinyo preserve to bolster donations, while Fossey herself prevented any poaching of gorillas in her territory during 1983–85. She angered rivals by suggesting that donations to their organizations were used primarily "to pay the airfare of so-called conservationists who will never go on anti-poaching patrols in their life."

In 1985 Fossey signed a $1 million contract with Warner Brothers for a movie adaptation of *Gorillas in the Mist*. At the same time, she secured a two-year visa extension from Augustin Nduwayezu, Rwanda's secretary-general in charge of immigration. The long-term future of her research center was assured—or would have been, if Fossey had survived.

On December 26, 1985, Fossey was murdered in her cabin at the Karisoke Research Center, her skull split by a machete she had confiscated from poachers years earlier, which hung on a wall of her adjacent living room. Investigators found her sprawled beside her bed, near a hole that had been cut in the cabin's wall that day. Investigators noted the relatively light bleeding from Fossey's massive head wound, speculating that she may have been killed by some other means before she was struck with the machete.

Early suspicion focused on gorilla poachers, but police observed that the killer had entered Fossey's cabin by removing metal sheathing from a corner of her bedroom, in the only place where furniture would not obstruct entry. That pointed to an inside job. Officers also noted that while Fossey's home was ransacked, thousands of dollars in cash, traveler's checks, and photographic equipment were left at the crime scene. Likewise, Fossey's gun was found beside her body, but its ammunition had been switched to an incorrect caliber, thus rendering the weapon useless.

Police arrested all of Fossey's staff, along with Rwelekana, a native tracker she had fired months earlier. All were released after questioning, except Rwelekana, who supposedly hanged himself in jail. No one was ever charged with Fossey's murder, but conspiracy theories abound.

The author Farley Mowat believes the killing was ordered by Rwandan officials who sought to exploit gorilla conservation for personal profit. Poachers, Mowat says, would most likely have ambushed Fossey in the forest. Linda Malvern's book *Conspiracy to Murder* implicates Protais ("Mr. Z") Zigiranyirazo, brother-in-law of former Rwandan president Juvénal Habyarimana and governor of Ruhengeri Province during 1974–89. A third author, Nick Gordon, writes that "Another reason why she might have been murdered is that she knew too much about the illegal trafficking by Rwanda's ruling clique." Gordon also points a finger at "Mr. Z," who has been publicly accused of promoting genocide of Tutsi tribesmen during 1994. When *Gorillas in the Mist* was finally filmed, the ORTPN's director demanded minimal treatment of Fossey's death scene.

A solution of sorts to Fossey's murder emerged in December 1986, with the indictment in absentia of Wayne Richard McGuire, a doctoral student who worked with Fossey at the Karisoke Research Center. A three-judge panel convicted McGuire and sentenced him to death by firing squad, but the verdict had no binding effect outside of Rwanda. McGuire proclaimed his innocence, and most observers regard his trial as a face-saving exercise by the Rwandan government, but notoriety surrounding the case did cost McGuire his job as director of a state mental health office in Nebraska.

Fossey's treasured research center is no more. She left the $1 million from the Warner Brothers film to finance Karisoke, but Fossey's mother contested the will in court and won the money for herself. Meanwhile, students who had objected to Fossey's methods and philosophy took control of Karisoke at her death and ran the center until 1994, when the camp was looted and demolished by terrorists engaged in the Tutsi genocide and the Virunga parks were swamped with refugees. Today, a remnant of her cabin stands as a museum for tourists, but the slaughter of mountain gorillas continues.

FOUNTAIN, Albert Jennings murder victim (1896)

A New York native, born on Staten Island in October 1838, Albert Jennings was the son of Solomon Jennings and Catherine de la Fontaine. He emigrated to California as a young man and there adopted an Anglicized version of his mother's surname for reasons still unclear. As Albert Fountain, he studied law but never took the California bar exam.

Four months after the August 1861 Confederate attack on Fort Sumter, Fountain joined the Union army as a junior officer and helped defeat rebel sympathizers in the Arizona Territory. Discharged as a captain in 1865, Fountain took his wife and growing brood of children to El Paso, Texas, where he served the U.S. Property Commission by assessing and selling off former Confederate property. Fountain's performance in that post was impressive enough to rate him appointment as customs collector in El Paso, then as an election judge, and finally as assessor and collector of revenue for western Texas.

As a Republican and "Yankee carpetbagger," Fountain was elected to the state senate in the 12th Texas legislature (February 8, 1870–December 2, 1871), serving as president pro tempore of the senate and briefly as lieutenant governor ex officio. Despite strident opposition from Democrats, the Ku Klux Klan, and other vigilante groups, Fountain was reelected to the 13th Texas legislature (January 14–June 14, 1873). During his tenure, Fountain was challenged to several duels and killed at least one man, opponent Frank Williams, in a classic showdown.

In 1873 Fountain emigrated to his wife's hometown of Mesilla, New Mexico, opening a private law practice. Success as a litigator won him appointment as assistant district attorney for Doña Ana County, later serving as a probate judge and deputy court clerk. During the 1880s, Fountain fought Apaches as a colonel in the state militia. After Geronimo surrendered in September 1886, Fountain returned to civilian life as a prominent leader of New Mexico's Republican Party.

As in Texas, however, Fountain had made enemies during his tenure in the Land of Enchantment. Resuming his prosecutor's role in the 1890s, he pursued cattle rustlers and corrupt land-grabbers. Chief among his targets was Oliver Milton Lee, a rancher, part-time deputy U.S. marshal, gunfighter, and suspected rustler whose attorney—Kentucky native Albert Bacon Fall—managed to keep him out of jail.

On February 1, 1896, Fountain and his eight-year-old son Henry vanished near White Sands, New Mexico, while traveling by buckboard from Lincoln to their home in Mesilla. Investigators found Fountain's buckboard and cravat, some of his legal papers, several spent cartridges, two pools of blood, and a bloody knotted handkerchief. Forever missing were the bodies, a blanket and quilt from the buckboard, and Fountain's rifle.

Suspicion quickly focused on Oliver Lee and more specifically on two of his quick-triggered employees, Jim Gililland and William McNew. Both were deputy sheriffs, but their guilt seemed certain when they fled the county, pursued by Sheriff Pat Garrett. Garrett's posse overtook the fugitives near Alamagordo, but Gililland and McNew fought their way out of the trap, killing a deputy in the process. They subsequently surrendered for trial on charges of murdering Fountain, joined by Lee as a defendant, but Albert Fall persuaded jurors to acquit all three suspects.

In the wake of that verdict, Fall and Lee resumed their thriving career in land fraud and political corruption. Fountain's still-unsolved slaying ranked as New Mexico's most famous murder until February 1908, when Pat Garrett was ambushed and slain near Las Cruces. Ironically—or, perhaps, predictably—Albert Fall also defended the primary suspect in Garrett's murder and won acquittal for his client.

Fall's political connections and his reputation for lax ethics led President-elect Warren Harding to appoint Fall as Secretary of the Interior in 1921. Fall stood out in an administration rife with corruption, negotiating the illegal sale of stockpiled government oil that finally produced the Teapot Dome scandal of 1923. Fall received a one-year prison term for accepting $385,000 in bribes, although jurors acquitted the oilman accused of bribing him. Upon release from prison, Fall retired to El Paso, Texas, where he died in 1944. At his death, one critic joked that Fall was "so crooked they had to screw him into the ground."

Oliver Lee faced no such setbacks in his life after the Fountain murder trial. He served a term in New Mexico's state senate and continued operating various ranches until his death at Alamagordo in

December 1941. Oliver Lee Memorial State Park is named in his honor.

"FRANKFORD Slasher" Philadelphia serial killer (1985–90)
Philadelphia's Frankford district is the hardscrabble neighborhood chosen by Sylvester Stallone as the setting for his first *Rocky* film, in 1976. Stallone and his fictional hero had gone on to bigger, better things by the mid-1980s, however, when Frankford earned a new and unwelcome celebrity, this time as the hunting ground of a vicious serial killer who slaughtered at least seven women.

The carnage began at 8:30 A.M. on August 28, 1985, when two transit workers reported to work at a Frankford Avenue maintenance yard. Within moments, they found a woman's lifeless body sprawled between two stacks of railroad ties. She was nude from the waist down, legs spread, blouse lifted to expose her breasts. A pathologist's report counted 19 stab wounds, plus a gaping slash between the victim's navel and vagina, nearly disemboweling her. The woman was identified as 52-year-old Helen Patent, well known in many of the bars on Frankford Avenue.

On January 3, 1986, a second mutilated corpse was found on Ritner Street, in South Philadelphia, 10 miles from the first murder site. Neighbors were surprised to find the door of 68-year-old Anna Carroll's apartment standing open, and they found her dead in the bedroom. Like Helen Patent, Carroll was nude below the waist, her blouse pushed up. She had been stabbed six times, and her abdomen was slit from sternum to pubis.

No more was heard from the slasher for nearly a year, until December 25, 1986, when victim number three was found on Richmond Street, in the Bridesburg district, three miles from the Patent murder scene. Once again, worried neighbors found the corpse, investigating an open apartment door to find 74-year-old Susan Olzef stabbed six times in the back. Like Helen Patent, Olzef was a familiar figure on Frankford Avenue, police speculating that her killer may have known her from the neighborhood.

Thus far, authorities had little in the way of evidence, and they resisted the notion of a serial killer at large in their city. As Lt. Joe Washlick later told reporters, in an effort to explain the oversight, "The first three slayings happened in different parts of the city. We could almost give you a different suspect for each job."

Almost, but not quite.

In fact, no suspects had been identified by January 8, 1987, when two Frankford Avenue fruit vendors found a woman's corpse stuffed underneath their stand, around 7:30 A.M. The latest victim, 28-year-old Jeanne Durkin, lay facedown, nude below the waist, legs splayed. She had been stabbed no less than 74 times, with several wounds gashing her buttocks.

At last, with four victims and no end in sight, police officially linked the Patent and Durkin murders, later connecting all four and creating a special task force to hunt the man Philadelphia journalists were already calling the "Frankford Slasher." The task force spun its wheels for nearly two years, making no apparent progress until November 11, 1988. That morning, 66-year-old Marge Vaughn was found dead on Penn Avenue, stabbed 29 times in the vestibule of an apartment building from which she had been evicted the previous day. She died less than three blocks from the Durkin murder scene, half a mile from the spot where Helen Patent had been found.

And this time there was a witness of sorts.

A Frankford Avenue barmaid recalled seeing Vaughn around 6:30 P.M. the previous day, drinking with a round-faced, middle-aged white man who wore glasses and limped when he walked. Several sketches of the suspect were prepared and published, but despite a flurry of false leads, police seemed no closer to their quarry than they had been in August 1985.

Two months later, on January 19, 1989, 30-year-old Theresa Sciortino left a Frankford Avenue bar at 6:00 P.M. She was last seen alive moments later, walking down the street with an unidentified middle-aged man. Around 6:45, Sciortino's neighbors heard sounds of an apparent struggle inside her apartment, followed shortly by footsteps on the stairs, but they did not call police, and it was 9:00 P.M. before they notified the building's manager. He, in turn, waited past midnight to check on Sciortino, then found her sprawled in her kitchen, nude but for stockings, stabbed 25 times. A bloody footprint at the scene provided homicide investigators with their best lead yet, and while they initially considered Sciortino's boyfriend "a good suspect," he was finally cleared when police checked his shoes, pronouncing them "similar, but not identical" to the killer's.

Any Information Regarding The Identities Of The Above
CONTACT HOMICIDE 592-5859 • 592-5860

Philadelphia police circulated these sketches of the still-unidentified Frankford Slasher. (Author's collection)

Another 15 months elapsed before the slasher struck again. Patrolman Dan Johnson was cruising his beat in the predawn hours of April 28, 1990, when he saw a woman's nude, eviscerated corpse in the alley behind a Frankford Avenue fish market. The latest victim had been stabbed 36 times, slashed open from navel to vagina, with her left nipple severed. A handbag found nearby identified the woman as 45-year-old Carol Dowd, and a preliminary canvass of the neighborhood located a witness who had seen her walking along Frankford Avenue with a middle-aged white man several hours before Patrolman Johnson found her body.

It seemed like another dead end until detectives questioned employees of the fish market several days later. One of them, 39-year-old Leonard Christopher, had already spoken to reporters about Dowd's murder, calling the alley behind his workplace a "hooker's paradise" and frequent scene of drug deals. Questioned by police about his movements on the night Dowd was murdered, Christopher replied that he

had spent the evening with his girlfriend. The lady in question denied it, however, insisting that she spent the night alone. Suspicious now, investigators took a closer look at Christopher. A mail carrier reported seeing Christopher and Dowd together at a bar on the night she died. Another witness, this one a convicted prostitute, allegedly saw Christopher and Dowd walking together, near the murder site. A second hooker told police she saw Christopher emerge from the alley around 1:00 A.M. on April 28, insisting that he was "sweating profusely, had his shirt over his arm, and a 'Rambo knife' was tucked into his belt."

On the strength of those statements, police arrested Christopher—an African American who bore no resemblance to the Frankford Slasher sketches or the middle-aged white man seen walking with Dowd the night she died. Police searched Christopher's home, but found nothing of value: one pair of slacks bore a tiny bloodstain, but it was too small to be typed, much less tested for a DNA profile.

While Christopher sat in jail, denied bond pending trial in December, the Frankford Slasher struck again. It was 1:00 A.M. on September 8, 1990, when tenants of an Arrott Street apartment house complained of rancid odors emanating from the flat occupied by 30-year-old Michelle Martin. The manager used his passkey and found Martin dead, nude from the waist down, blouse pushed up to expose her breasts and 23 stab wounds. She had last been seen alive on September 6, drinking with a middle-aged white man in a bar on Frankford Avenue.

Ignoring their obvious dilemma, prosecutors pressed ahead with Christopher's trial on schedule, in December 1990. The case was admittedly weak—no motive or weapon, no witness to the crime, no forensic evidence linking Christopher to the victim or the murder scene—but jurors were persuaded by testimony describing Christopher's "strange" behavior and lies to police. On December 12 he was convicted of Carol Dowd's murder, later sentenced to life imprisonment. From his cell Christopher still insists, "I was railroaded."

And what of the Frankford Slasher, described for years as a middle-aged white man? What of the near-identical murder committed while Leonard Christopher sat in jail, awaiting trial? Lt. Washlick shrugged off such questions, telling reporters, "Surprisingly, we still get phone calls. Leonard Christopher is a suspect in some of the killings, and we have additional suspects as well. Last year, we had 481 homicides in the city, and we solved 82 percent of them."

But not the Frankford Slasher case. The perpetrator of those crimes is still at large.

FRAZIER, Etta   See DETROIT MURDERS (1980)

FRAZIER, Rosemary   See DETROIT MURDERS (1980)

"FREEWAY Phantom" Washington, D.C. (1971–72)
A puzzling case recorded from the nation's capital, this murder series stands officially unsolved despite the conviction of two defendants in one of seven similar slayings. Authorities have speculated on solutions to the case, asserting that "justice was served" by the roundup of suspects on unrelated charges, but

their faith was shaken by an outbreak of look-alike murders in nearby Prince Georges County, Maryland, in 1987. Today, some students of the case believe the "Freeway Phantom" has eluded homicide detectives altogether, shifting his field of operations to a more fertile hunting ground.

The capital stalker's first victim was 13-year-old Carole Denise Sparks, kidnapped on April 25, 1971, while en route to a neighborhood store in southeast Washington. Her body, raped and strangled, was found six days later, a mile and a half from home, lying on the shoulder of Interstate Highway 295, one of several freeways passing through Washington east of the Anacostia River.

Ten weeks passed before 16-year-old Darlenia Denise Johnson disappeared, on July 8, from the same street where Sparks was abducted. She was found on July 19, strangled and dumped within 15 feet of the spot where Sparks was discovered on May 1. In the meantime, a third victim—14-year-old Angela Denise Barnes—had been snatched from southeast Washington on July 13, shot to death, and dumped at Waldorf, Maryland, the same day. Brenda Crockett, age 10, disappeared two weeks later, her strangled corpse recovered on July 28 near an underpass on U.S. Highway 50.

The killer took a two-month break in August and September 1971, returning with the kidnap of 12-year-old Nenomoshia Yates on October 1. Familiar marks of strangulation were apparent when police found her body six days later, discarded on Pennsylvania Avenue near the Maryland state line. Brenda Denise Woodward, age 18, was the oldest victim to date, abducted from a Washington bus stop on November 15, stabbed to death and dumped the next day on an access road leading to PRINCE GEORGES HOSPITAL. A mocking note, its contents still unpublished, was discovered near the body, signed "The Freeway Phantom" in accordance with the nickname coined by journalists. In a macabre twist FBI handwriting analysts claimed Woodward had written the note herself, in a steady hand, betraying no hint of fear.

Police now had ample evidence of a pattern, from the victims' race—all were African American—to the fact that four were named Denise. There also seemed to be a geographical pattern, both in abduction of victims and disposal of remains, but speculation brought authorities no closer to their goal of an arrest. Black Washington was up in arms, demanding a solution to the case, many intent on proving that a white racist killer was responsible, but angry rhetoric did nothing to advance the murder probe.

Ten months elapsed before the Phantom claimed his final victim, abducting 17-year-old Diane Williams on September 5, 1972. Her body was found the next day beside I-295, five miles from the place where Carole Sparks had been dumped in May 1971. Again, police noted striking similarities with the other crimes—and again, they found no evidence that would identify a suspect in the case.

In late March 1973 Maryland state police arrested two black suspects, 30-year-old Edward Leon Sellman and 26-year-old Tommie Bernard Simmons, on charges of murdering Angela Barnes. Both defendants were ex-policemen from Washington, and both had resigned in early 1971, before completion of their mandatory probation periods. Investigators now divorced the Barnes murder from the other Freeway Phantom cases, filing additional charges against their suspects in the February 1971 abduction and rape of a Maryland waitress. Convicted of murder in 1974, Sellman and Simmons were sentenced to life in prison.

Meanwhile, a federal grand jury probing the Phantom murders focused its spotlight on "a loosely knit group of persons" suspected of luring girls into cars, sometimes rented for the hunt, then raping and/or killing them for sport. Two suspects, 28-year-old John N. Davis and 27-year-old Morris Warren, were already serving life terms on conviction for previous rapes when new indictments were returned in December 1974. Warren received a grant of limited immunity in return for his testimony against Davis and another defendant, 27-year-old Melvyn Sylvester Gray. As a government spokesman explained, "The ends of justice can be served just as well if the person is convicted and sentenced to life for kidnapping, than if he is jailed for the same term for murder."

Critics questioned the wisdom of that judgment 13 years later, when a new series of unsolved murders was reported from neighboring Maryland. Again, the female victims were young African Americans, abducted and discarded in a manner reminiscent of the Freeway Phantom's style. Authorities refused to speculate on a link between the crimes, and so both cases are considered open, still officially unsolved.

FRENCH, Jeanne Thomas murder victim (1947)

At 9:30 A.M. on February 10, 1947, a coroner's wagon was summoned to retrieve the body of a female murder victim, found on Grandview Street in West Los Angeles. A bulldozer operator had found the body, lying in a vacant lot described in press reports as "a sort of lovers' lane." Barely four weeks had passed since the gruesome discovery of "BLACK DAHLIA" victim Elizabeth Short, found seven miles away from the present crime scene, and newspapers drew the inevitable comparison. A *Daily News* report described what ambulance attendants found:

> The body, while not sliced up as was the Dahlia's, was viciously mutilated. One side of her face had been torn open from the lip almost to her ear. One breast was slashed by some instrument which detectives thought was a tire iron or heavy wrench. Part of her hair had been cropped, as in the case of the Dahlia. And the obscenity written on her dead body led police to believe it could have been the maniacal boasting of the Dahlia's mad killer.

The slayer had scrawled a message in lipstick on his victim's torso. Press photographer Joe Jasgur, recording the grim scene for posterity, recalled the message: "Fuck you—B.D. Killer." Below the infamous "B.D." initials, according to press reports, was written "what appeared to be 'Tex' and 'O.'" Years later, a retired detective told author James Ellroy that the word *cocksucker* was also printed on the corpse.

The Grandview victim was identified as Jeanne French, a 45-year-old former actress, aviatrix, airline hostess, and army nurse. The cause of death was listed as "hemorrhage and shock due to fractured ribs and multiple injuries"—in other words, a savage beating. News reports state that the killer not only bludgeoned French, but also "stamped with heavy shoes on her breast, hands and face."

The victim had a checkered past, including three arrests for public drunkenness. Her blood-alcohol level was .30, three times the legal limit for intoxication, at the time she died. Some of her clothing—a burgundy dress, brassiere, and fur-trimmed coat—was dumped atop her body in the field where she was found. No panties or stockings remained, but French's shoes had been "carefully arranged" on either side of her head, 10 feet from the body. Also recovered at the scene was French's black plastic purse, described by reporters as "almost identical with one Elizabeth Short carried."

Detectives guessed that French had been dead some two hours when found, at 8:30 A.M., but the coroner was more cautious, placing the time of death within 24 hours. As with Short's murder, there were no significant traces of blood at the scene, prompting investigators to surmise that French was stripped and beaten in a car but managed to escape, whereupon the killer followed, clubbed her repeatedly with a blunt instrument, then finished the job with his feet.

Jeanne's husband, 47-year-old Frank French, was a natural suspect, already on probation for a wife-beating incident in December 1946. He staunchly denied the murder, and plaster casts of footprints found around the corpse did not appear to match his shoes. Frank's landlady confirmed that he was home during the presumed time of the murder, and he passed a polygraph test administered by police.

French's car was found abandoned at Washington and Sepulveda on the night of February 10, but there were no incriminating bloodstains in the vehicle, no fingerprints police were able to identify. Detectives calculated that a chrome-plated wrench, perhaps the murder weapon, was missing from the car, but it never surfaced. There were vague reports of French dining with "a dark-haired man" at a West L.A. hamburger stand sometime after midnight on February 9–10, but there the trail went cold. The case remains unsolved today.

FRIED, Ellen   See "VALLEY KILLER"

FUGATE, Christy   See "INDEPENDENCE AVENUE KILLER"

G

GALANTE, Carmine gangland murder victim (1979)

The son of a Sicilian fisherman who immigrated to New York, born in 1910, Carmine Galante logged his first arrest at age 11 and may have committed his first murder around the same time. As leader of a brutal street gang on New York's Lower East Side, he soon became friendly with members of the Mafia and established himself as a ruthless contract killer. In 1930 he led several cronies in the attempted robbery of a truck in Brooklyn's Williamsburg district. The holdup went sour and ended in a shoot-out with police, leaving a patrolman and a six-year-old girl gravely wounded. Galante drew a 12-year prison term and was paroled in 1939, to join the Vito Genovese Mafia family. Genovese was hiding in Italy, a fugitive from murder charges since 1937, but he trusted Galante to carry out one of his most important murder contracts, gunning down newspaper editor Carlo Tresca in Manhattan, on January 11, 1943.

Galante later defected to join the crime family run by Joseph Bonnano, rising to serve as underboss of that gang in the 1950s. Though generally loyal, Galante defied Bonnano's orders in 1954 by traveling to Italy with Canadian mobster Frank Petrula, where they met with exiled crime lord Charles (Lucky) Luciano and established the infamous French Connection drug network, smuggling heroin from Marseilles to the United States and Montreal. The venture was lucrative but ultimately doomed. Indicted with Genovese and 22 others in 1958, Galante was convicted on narcotics charges and received a 20-year sentence in 1962. An acquaintance at the federal lockup in Atlanta later described his perverse character: "If he was walking with one person, you'd learn not to join him as a third. He'd pick a fight with the third person and force the second to become his ally."

Paroled on November 23, 1974, Galante returned to New York and launched a bloody campaign to recapture lost drug territories from black and Hispanic street gangs. Federal agents nabbed him for parole violation in 1978, charging that Galante had violated terms of his conditional release by associating with known criminals, but he soon won his freedom again with help from high-powered lawyer Roy Cohn. Within a matter of weeks, eight high-ranking members of the Genovese crime family were murdered in New York, while Galante demanded that leaders of the city's five Mafia families fall in line behind his leadership as Boss of Bosses.

It was not to be.

On July 12, 1979, Galante stopped for lunch at Joe and Mary's Restaurant, in Brooklyn's Bushwick section. The "Joe" in Joe and Mary was Galante's cousin, Joseph Turano, preparing for an extended trip to Italy. During the meal one of Galante's guests departed with a plea of illness, while two others left to make telephone calls. Galante was alone at the outdoor table when three masked men appeared, one of them carrying a sawed-off shotgun. Galante

Carmine Galante was a candidate for "Boss of Bosses" in the New York Mafia. (Library of Congress)

was helpless as the shooter stepped forward and fired both barrels into his face and chest. He died with a trademark cigar still clenched in his teeth.

No one was ever charged for the Galante slaying. Rumor has it that a secret meeting of rival New York bosses was held at Boca Raton, Florida, in June 1979 to plot Galante's murder. Participants in that gathering allegedly included mobsters Santo Trafficante, Gerardo Catena, Frank (Funzi) Tieri, and Paul Castellano (himself later murdered on orders from rival John Gotti). With Galante's fate decided, the plotters reportedly telephoned Mafia bosses around the country and secured unanimous approval for elimination of the rogue in their midst.

GALLO, Joseph gangland murder victim (1972)

The oldest of three Mafia brothers, born in 1929, Joseph Gallo earned the nickname Crazy Joe from his penchant for reckless acts of violence. By the 1950s, with brothers Lawrence and Albert (Kid Blast), Gallo was a recognized member of the New York crime family led by Joseph Profaci. The Gallos specialized in "protection" rackets, selling

neighborhood merchants "insurance" against their own mayhem, but they were also dependable contract killers. While they were never charged, Crazy Joe and his siblings remain primary suspects in the October 1957 barbershop slaying of Mafia boss ALBERT ANASTASIA.

By 1960 the Gallos and a group of allied "Young Turks" were chafing under Profaci's conservative leadership. They demanded a larger piece of the action, and when Profaci refused them a gang war erupted, claiming more than a dozen lives around New York. Profaci died of natural causes on June 6, 1962, with the issue unresolved, and the Gallos continued their feud with his successor, Joseph Colombo Sr. The conflict ended, at least temporarily, when Crazy Joe was convicted of extortion and packed off to Attica prison. There, he broke with Mafia tradition once again by befriending black inmates and winning their confidence, looking ahead to the day when much of New York's street action would be controlled by nonwhite minorities. The Gallo-Profaci war, meanwhile, was reduced to a subject of humor by Jimmy Breslin's novel (and subsequent movie) *The Gang That Couldn't Shoot Straight.*

While Gallo sat in prison, brooding and biding his time, Joe Colombo consolidated his hold on the Profaci family. In 1970, after his son's indictment on federal charges, he launched the Italian-American Civil Rights League and picketed FBI headquarters, drawing enough public support for his claims of "discrimination" that 50,000 persons gathered for an Italian-American Unity Day rally in June 1970. An even larger rally was planned for the following year, but New York's mob bosses were tired of the constant publicity—and by that time, Crazy Joe Gallo was back on the street.

When Colombo mounted the stage to address his second mass audience, on June 28, 1971, a black man named Jerome Johnson shot him three times in the back of the head. Bodyguards killed Johnson as he turned to flee, but the damage was done. Colombo survived his wounds, after a fashion, but he never regained consciousness and later died, still comatose, in 1978. Joe Gallo was an immediate suspect, considering his long feud with Colombo and his friendship with black hoodlums, but detectives never succeeded in linking Gallo to gunman Jerome Johnson. (Three years after the shooting, FBI agents learned that rival boss Carlo Gambino had confronted Colombo in May 1971 and ordered him to abandon his "civil rights" work, whereupon Colombo spat in Gambino's face.)

Joe Gallo kept a low profile around New York until January 1972, when he suddenly emerged from hiding in a fanfare of publicity, courting local celebrities who included playwright Neil Simon, actress Joan Hackett, and actor Jerry Orbach. There was talk of "going straight," but it was all for show. Behind the scenes he teamed with black allies to poach on Gambino's drug turf in East Harlem, precipitating a showdown with Don Carlo in March 1972. At that meeting, as later reported in *Time* magazine, Gallo insulted Gambino with a torrent of obscenities and repeated Joe Colombo's fatal error by spitting in the old man's face.

On April 7, 1972, Gallo celebrated his 43rd birthday at the Copacabana nightclub, accompanied by his wife, his sister, bodyguard Pete (The Greek) Diapoulas, and assorted celebrities. Around 4 A.M., Gallo entered Umberto's Clam House, on the border between Chinatown and Little Italy, to enjoy an early breakfast with Diapoulas, his wife, and sister. Gallo and his bodyguard sat with their backs to the door, unaware of the gunmen who came in behind them and triggered an estimated dozen pistol shots. Gallo was dying as he staggered to the street outside and collapsed a few feet from his car.

Survivors of the Gallo family apparently blamed Colombo loyalists for the murder, and Gallo's sister, standing by his casket at the funeral three days later, wailed, "The streets are going to run red with blood, Joey!" A spate of killings followed, climaxed by the death of mob boss THOMAS EBOLI in July. Throughout the carnage, Carlo Gambino remained aloof, quietly consolidating his power within the New York Mafia. No one was ever charged with Joey Gallo's slaying, and "experts" still debate over who gave the final orders for his death.

GARCIA, Cheryl See JACKSON, MISSISSIPPI, MURDERS

GARECHT, Michaela Joy See BAY AREA CHILD MURDERS

GARNETT, Kevin See HOSPITAL FOR SICK CHILDREN MURDERS

GASTON, April See JESSUP, GEORGIA, CHILD DEATHS

GEDALICIA, Sara See SAN DIEGO MURDERS

GENCY, Mary See WASHINGTON, PENNSYLVANIA, MURDERS

GENTILCORE, Pasquale See "MONSTER OF FLORENCE"

GENTILE, Donna See SAN DIEGO MURDERS

GIDLEY, Nancy See "OCCULT MURDERS"

GILBERT, George See "Doodler"

GILBERT, Jeanne See Days Inn murders

GILL, Mary See Days Inn murders

GILMORE Lane Convalescent Hospital (1984–85)

On December 23, 1985, California state authorities announced that an investigation was under way in the cases of 11 "suspicious" deaths at the Gilmore Lane Convalescent Hospital in Oroville. (Several more patients reportedly died after being transferred to Oroville Hospital for emergency treatment.) The deaths, attributed to unknown "illness," all occurred in January 1985, at a time when Justice Department officials were already investigating the cases of 38 other elderly patients, lost between January and April 1984. Health officials reportedly failed to perform autopsies in the 49 cases, leaving prosecutors to start from scratch with bodies already buried or cremated. At this writing, no final result of the investigation has been published.

GLASSCOCK, Mary Ann See "I-70/I-35 Murders"

GLENNON, Ciara See Perth, Australia, murders

GLICO-MORINAGA Case extortion (1984–85)

This strange case of industrial extortion, known officially to Japanese authorities as Metropolitan Designated Case 114, involved two major confectionery firms: Osaka-based Ezaki Glico, founded in 1922, and Tokyo-based Morinaga & Company, founded in 1899.

The case began at 9:00 P.M. on March 18, 1984, when two masked gunmen invaded the home of Glico president Katsuhisa Ezaki's mother, tied her up, and stole a key to her son's home next door. Using that key, they burst into Ezaki's home, cut telephone lines, and bound Ezaki's wife and daughter, while Ezaki and two other children locked themselves in a bathroom. Death threats finally brought Ezaki out to face them, whereupon he was abducted.

On March 19 the kidnappers phoned Glico's director, demanding 1 billion yen ($9.3 million) and 220 pounds of gold bullion for Ezaki's safe return. Before that ransom was paid, however, Ezaki escaped on March 21 from the warehouse where he was held in Ibaraki.

If Glico executives thought their problem was solved, they were sadly mistaken. On April 10, arsonists torched three cars in a parking lot at the firm's trial production building. Six days later, Ibaraki police found a plastic jug of hydrochloric acid bearing a note that threatened the company. May 10 brought a letter signed by "The Monster with 21 Faces," claiming that Glico candies laced with cyanide had been distributed in stores. Glico issued a sweeping product recall, while police noted that the threat had been written using hiragana (one of three Japanese syllabaries), with a dialect peculiar to Osaka.

That lead had produced no suspects when "The Monster with 21 Faces" (borrowed from a fictional villain in detective novels written by author Rampo Edogawa) began taunting authorities. One letter to detectives read in part: "Dear dumb police officers. Don't tell a lie. All crimes begin with a lie as we say in Japan. Don't you know that?" Another, addressed to officers at the Koshien station, read: "You seem to be at a loss. So why not let us help you? We'll give you a clue. We entered the factory by the front gate. The typewriter we used is Panwriter. The plastic container used was a piece of street garbage. Monster with 21 Faces."

The harassment campaign shifted toward a new target on June 26, with a "Monster" note announcing, "We forgive Glico!" A new rash of threatening letters bombarded Morinaga & Company, along with two Japanese food producers: the House Food Corporation and Marudai Ham. Marudai executives agreed to a payment of 50 million yen, but dispatched a policeman disguised as a company employee to deliver the ransom on June 28.

The extortionist's orders were simple: Toss a sack of cash from a train bound for Kyoto, at the point where a white flag was displayed at trackside. The officer boarded his train on schedule and observed a suspicious man shadowing him. He later described the individual as large, with short, permed hair and glasses framing "eyes like those of a fox." For reasons still unknown, no white flag appeared along the railroad tracks. Arriving in Kyoto, the detective and his "fox-eyed" shadow disembarked, dawdled around the depot, then boarded another train back to Osaka. A second officer was waiting for their train on arrival, but he lost the suspect when the suspect boarded another train to Kyoto.

In October 1984, "The Monster with 21 Faces" sent letters to various Osaka news agencies. Addressed to "Moms of the Nation," the notes warned that 20 packages of Morinaga candy had been spiked with cyanide and placed in various stores nationwide. Searches ensued, recovering 21 packages of poisoned sweets by February 1985. No one was injured by the candy, which in fact bore labels warning: "Danger: Contains Toxins."

Meanwhile, on November 14, 1984, House Food executives scheduled a payment of 100 million yen to "The Monster with 21 Faces." Delivery was planned at a rest stop on the Meishin Expressway, outside Ōtsu, in Shiga Prefecture, and police staked out the drop. From hiding, they observed a suspect thought to be the "fox-eyed man," although he wore sunglasses, but another comedy of errors ensued. Officers pursued the suspect's car, but he eluded them and dumped the stolen vehicle at the Kusatsu railroad station. Inside the car, officers found a police radio scanner, with which the "fox-eyed man" had monitored their calls and movements, thus effecting his escape.

In January 1985, police published a composite sketch of the still-unidentified "fox-eyed man." Days later, Tokyo police identified the man as Miyazaki Manabu, recognized in 1975–76 as a whistle-blower who exposed Glico's dumping of industrial waste into rivers around Osaka. Company executives blamed Manabu for forcing the resignation of a corrupt union boss, and police claimed that one of his audiotapes, issued in 1976, echoed wording from subsequent letters penned by "The Monster with 21 Faces." Be that as it may, police checked Manabu's alibis for the dates of various crimes during 1984–85 and formally exonerated him.

On August 7, 1985, with no new suspects in sight, Superintendent Yamamoto of the Shiga Prefecture police committed suicide by setting himself on fire. Five days later, "The Monster with 21 Faces" sent his last message, reading:

Yamamoto of Shiga Prefecture Police died. How stupid of him! We've got no friends or secret hiding place in Shiga. It's Yoshino or Shikata who should have died. What have they been doing for as long as one year and

five months? Don't let bad guys like us get away with it. There are many more fools who want to copy us. No-career Yamamoto died like a man. So we decided to give our condolence. We decided to forget about torturing food-making companies. If anyone blackmails any of the food-making companies, it's not us but someone copying us. We are bad guys. That means we've got more to do other than bullying companies. It's fun to lead a bad man's life. Monster with 21 Faces.

Subsequent theories attribute the "Monster's" crimes to members of the Yakuza crime syndicate or to communist agents from North Korea. In any case, it no longer matters. The statute of limitations on Katsuhisa Ezaki's kidnapping expired in June 1995, while the legal deadline for prosecuting attempted murder in the product-tampering case lapsed in February 2000. Even if identified today, "The Monster with 21 Faces" and his various accomplices could not be charged or tried.

GODART, Nathalie   See "Butcher of Mons"

GODFREY, Sir Edmund Berry   murder victim (1678)

Edmund Godfrey was born in the British district of Swale, Kent, on December 23, 1612. As the scion of an established, wealthy family, he attended Westminster School and studied at Christ Church, Oxford, subsequently establishing himself as a prominent coal and wood merchant. He also served as justice of the peace at Westminster and was knighted in September 1666 for remaining at his post during a bubonic plague epidemic. Three years later, he was briefly imprisoned by King Charles II after having the royal physician Sir Alexander Frazier jailed for unpaid debts.

In 1678, Godfrey became embroiled with the "Popish Plot" hysteria sparked by anti-Catholic activist Titus Oates (1649–1705). The affair began in August, when chemist Christopher Kirkby and author Israel Tonge warned Charles II of a supposed Roman Catholic revolutionary plot. Oates approached Godfrey on September 6, claiming he had proof of the conspiracy, subsequently accusing various religious orders and numerous individuals of treason. Godfrey collected depositions from Tonge and Oates on September 28, then warned one of the accused suspects—queen's physician Edward Coleman—of the charges filed against him.

On October 12, 1678, Godfrey failed to return home from his normal duties in Westminster. Five days later, he was found dead in a ditch on Primrose Hill, run through with his own sword. His body bore various bruises, including one around his neck, which—with the fact that his sword wound had not bled—suggested that Godfrey was strangled, then stabbed. His purse and jewelry were still intact on his body, eliminating robbery as a motive.

Authorities posted a £500 reward for solution of Godfrey's murder, but two separate committees failed to crack the case, collecting contradictory descriptions of Godfrey's movements on his last day alive. Titus Oates exploited Godfrey's slaying, citing it as further evidence of the Popish Plot, while "reformed" conspirator William Bedloe claimed he had been taken to Somerset House to view Godfrey's corpse on October 14. One of those present, Bedloe said, was Samuel Atkins, secretary to M.P. Samuel Pepys. Despite several telling variations in that story, Bedloe was secured by the House of Lords as a prosecution witness.

Edward Coleman was convicted of treason and sentenced to die on December 3, 1678. On December 21, authorities jailed Miles Prance, a Catholic servant of Queen consort Catherine of Braganza, based on accusations from Bedloe. Two days later, Prance confessed to participating in Godfrey's murder and named three priests—Henry Berry, Robert Green, and Lawrence Hill—as the instigators. All three were arrested, while Prance waffled on his story, recanting then reaffirming it several times. Despite that shaky evidence, the three priests were condemned on February 5, 1679, and subsequently hanged.

Too late to save them, Prance recanted his testimony once more and pled guilty to perjury. Titus Oates enjoyed his new celebrity until August 1681, when he was charged with sedition, imprisoned, and fined £100,000. He served three years, then was pardoned by King William III and received a pension of £5 per week.

The perjury confession from Miles Prance left Godfrey's murder unsolved. Many theories were proposed over the next three centuries, none supported by any hard evidence. In 1687, British pamphleteer Roger L'Estrange opined that Godfrey hanged himself in a fit of melancholy, whereupon his brothers staged the murder scene to avert legal forfeiture of Godfrey's estate. Other theories blame Catholic assassins; supporters of Oates, who feared that Godfrey would expose Oates as a liar; Protestant extremists who hoped Godfrey's death would incriminate Catholics (as it did, however briefly); or random thugs who met Godfrey by chance and killed him on a whim. In 1936, novelist John Dickson Carr suggested that Godfrey was killed by Philip Herbert, whom Godfrey convicted of murder in 1677. A pardon from the House of Lords spared Herbert's life and left him free to plot revenge, but he faced a second charge of murder in 1680, for killing London Officer of the Watch William Smeethe.

GOLETA Murders serial killings (1979–81)

Goleta is a pleasant suburb of Santa Barbara, California, which claimed 29,000 inhabitants in 2006. Its most notorious crime occurred on January 30, 2006, when ex-postal worker Jennifer San Marco shot and killed seven former colleagues, then turned the gun on herself.

Nearly three decades before that incident, however, a serial killer stalked Goleta's streets by night, attacking couples in their homes. Although the crimes are nearly forgotten today, they sparked panic at the time—and they remain unsolved.

The first attack occurred on October 1, 1979, when an intruder approached a home on Queen Anne Lane. He rode a stolen bicycle, snatched moments earlier from an open garage a quarter-mile from his chosen target. Several windows were open, granting the prowler access. He took a knife from the kitchen, roused his sleeping victims in their bedroom, then bound them and proceeded to roam through the house. In his absence, both captives freed themselves and escaped, fleeing in different directions. Unable to pursue both, the invader abandoned his bike and ran, briefly pursued by an off-duty FBI agent who lived nearby and heard the commotion.

The stalker struck again on December 30, 1979, invading a condominium occupied by Dr. Robert Offerman and Debra Manning on Avenida Pequena. This time, he brought a gun and took no chances, binding both victims, then shooting them while they sat upright in bed. Neighbors heard the shots but ignored them, while the killer fed leftover Christmas turkey to his companion—a white-haired German shepherd with a toe missing from one paw.

The dog was present again when the killer staged his next known raid on the night of July 26–27, 1981. This time, he broke into a house on Toltec

Way, several blocks from the second crime scene, using a tool obtained from a backyard shed. Inside the home, he shot Gregory Sanchez, then bound Cheri Domingo and bludgeoned both victims to death with the stolen tool. As in the Offerman-Manning case, neighbors heard the gunshot but paid no attention.

Evidence linking the crimes includes identical footprints found in the first and second cases, German shepherd hairs and identical paw prints found at the second and third scenes, plus identical twine used to bind victims in the first two attacks. None of the killer's victims were raped. All three target dwellings were one-story homes, located within blocks of one another and close to San Jose Creek. Police also noticed, perhaps coincidentally, that none of the couples selected were married.

While the case remains unsolved, police and journalists have naturally speculated on possible links to other cases. One suspect often proposed is the still-unknown serial killer nicknamed the "ORIGINAL NIGHT STALKER," to distinguish him from California death-row inmate Richard "Night Stalker" Ramirez. The Original Night Stalker staged lethal home invasions in several southern California towns during 1980–86, and DNA from those attacks was later matched to crimes committed by northern California's "East Area Rapist" during 1976–79. While that proposed solution was enticing, a spokesman for the Santa Barbara County Sheriff's Department stated in 2000 that DNA recovered from a Goleta crime scene did not match that of the Original Night Stalker.

GONZALEZ, Pedro   See NEW YORK CITY GAY MURDERS (1985–86)

GOOD, Danielle   See SALEM, OREGON, MURDERS

GOOD Samaritan Hospital Illinois (1979–80)
Ninety-two-year-old Ellen O'Hara was awaiting surgery at Good Samaritan Hospital, in the Chicago suburb of Downers Grove, when she suddenly died on October 19, 1979. Autopsy results blamed her death on hypoglycemia (abnormally low blood sugar) induced by unknown causes. O'Hara's body was routinely cremated, but hospital administrators

were startled when patient Vivian Brown died with identical symptoms on February 8, 1980. Neither patient had a prior history of hypoglycemia, and the police chief of Downers Grove called Brown's death "highly suspicious." Physicians agreed, concluding in May 1980 that her death was caused by an "externally administered dose of insulin." In retrospect, they thought it likely that Ellen O'Hara had been the victim of a similar lethal injection.

In early June 1980 hospital administrators suspended 24-year-old Linda Kurle from her post as a night-shift nurse at Good Samaritan. Patients O'Hara and Brown had both shown their first symptoms of hypoglycemia during Kurle's shift, and while Kurle professed no memory of Ellen O'Hara, she recalled finding Vivian Brown in "serious straits" in the predawn hours of February 8, 1980. Her treatment of the patient, Kurle insisted, had been by the book. No charges were filed, and the case of the mysterious insulin injections at Good Samaritan Hospital remained open at press time.

GORLIN, Ronnie   See "FLAT-TIRE MURDERS"

GORMAN, Ken murder victim (2007)
A Denver native, born in July 1946, Ken Gorman graduated from high school in 1964 and followed his father's lead by joining the U.S. Air Force as an air traffic controller. In that capacity, he worked in Vietnam and Japan before leaving the service for employment as a civilian air traffic controller with the Federal Aviation Administration. In August 1981, Gorman was one of 11,358 members of the Professional Air Traffic Controllers Organization fired by President Ronald Reagan for going on strike.

Gorman's first wife introduced him to marijuana in 1969, and, while Gorman later said, "It has been a friend to me ever since," he did not immediately pursue the advocacy of legalization that ultimately made him famous. Instead, after the PATCO strike, he settled in Papua New Guinea, befriended impoverished natives, and published many articles supporting expansion of their civil rights. Papuan officials jailed him several times on trumped-up charges, then finally convicted him of possessing pornography (a *Playboy* magazine) and sent him to the Philippines. There, Gorman agitated against the corrupt regime of dictator Ferdinand Marcos and was deported to the United States in 1985, one year before Marcos fled into exile with his wife and stolen millions.

Back in the States, while employed as a commercial salesman for Video Professor, Gorman read Jack Herer's book *The Emperor Has No Clothes* (1985) and found himself enraged by details of the U.S. government's long campaign to ban marijuana. Thereafter, Gorman devoted his life to legalizing cannabis, launched a company that sold hemp products, and advertised "free delivery" of marijuana through Denver's alternative newspaper *Westword*. By year's end, he was staging "smoke-ins" at Colorado's state capital.

From public advocacy, it was a short step into politics. Gorman ran for governor in 1994 and 1998, but lost both races. In 1999, he was arrested for selling three pounds of marijuana to a police informant who posed as a medical patient. Convicted in that case, Gorman served 22 months in jail, another 18 months at a halfway house, and two years of remote supervision via an electronic ankle bracelet. However, largely as a result of his efforts, in 2000 Colorado ratified a constitutional amendment authorizing distribution and use of medicinal marijuana.

Gorman followed up that victory by recruiting suppliers to provide high-quality medicinal pot for registered Colorado patients. He also campaigned for Libertarian Party candidates who supported legalization of marijuana, including Senate hopeful Rick Stanley and gubernatorial candidate Ralph Shnelvar (both running in 2002). Despite ongoing official harassment under new federal legislation passed by the George W. Bush administration in 2002–03, Gorman continued to hold rallies and served as a speaker for the Colorado Compassion Club in 2004–05.

On February 17, 2007, an unknown gunman murdered Gorman at his home on South Decatur Street in Denver. Police report that the slayer broke into Gorman's home and shot him in the living room, suggesting that the crime occurred during an attempted drug theft. Friend and fellow activist Timothy Tipton told the *New York Times*, "Ken was really fed up with the barrage of robberies and he told me it would never happen again." Two months before the murder, Gorman showed a gun to Tipton, but he never had a chance to reach it on the night he died. To date, no suspects have been named by Denver authorities.

GOSCH, John David missing person (1982)

Johnny Gosch was born in Des Moines, Iowa, on November 12, 1969. On September 5, 1982, he left his home in suburban West Des Moines before dawn to deliver newspapers. Gosch's father normally assisted him, but that morning Johnny went out on his bike with only the family's dachshund for company. Other paper carriers saw Gosch at the usual drop, collecting his newspapers—then he vanished into limbo.

Later that morning, Gosch's parents received several calls from newspaper subscribers, complaining that their papers had not been delivered. Gosch's father went looking for Johnny and found the boy's wagon, still filled with newspapers, two blocks from their home. A phone call to police received a slow response: Officers reached the Gosch home 45 minutes later, then told Johnny's parents they could not accept a missing-person report for 72 hours. Meanwhile, the family's dachshund came home without Johnny.

After initially dismissing Johnny as a runaway, police became convinced that he was kidnapped. Their only witness, another newsboy, said that he and Gosch were approached at the corner of Marcourt Lane and 42nd Street by a stocky man driving a two-toned Ford Fairlane with Iowa license plates. The man asked directions, then left, but Gosch allegedly remarked on his suspicious behavior. Some accounts claim that the same witness saw *another* man following Gosch, but details are vague. The lead went nowhere, police identified no suspect or motive, and the case remained unsolved.

A year later, on September 18, 1983, 13-year-old paper boy Danny Joe Eberle was snatched from his route and murdered in Bellevue, Nebraska, 124 miles west of Des Moines. FBI agent Robert Ressler noted the similarity in victims and suspected that the crimes might be linked. Serial killer John Joubert later confessed to Eberle's slaying and to the August 1982 murder of 11-year-old Richard Stetson in Maine, but he denied involvement in the Gosch case and was executed in July 1996 without changing his story.

Meanwhile, Johnny became a literal poster child for missing children in the 1980s. His mother, Noreen, established the Johnny Gosch Foundation in 1982 and gave seminars at public schools on recognition and avoidance of sexual predators. In 1984—the same year Johnny's photo first appeared on milk cartons nationwide—Noreen secured passage of the "Johnny Gosch Bill," mandating immediate police reports of missing Iowa children. That August, she testified at U.S. Senate hearings on organized crime, suggesting that "organized pedophilia" played a part in Johnny's abduction. As if to confirm that opinion, Noreen Gosch began receiving anonymous death threats.

On August 12, 1984, another Des Moines newspaper boy—13-year-old Eugene Wade Martin—vanished from his delivery route on the city's south side. Like Gosch, Martin normally covered his route with a companion, his older stepbrother, who failed to join him on the day he disappeared. Speculation on a link between the kidnappings proved fruitless, but Noreen Gosch claimed that a private investigator hired to find her son had predicted the second abduction weeks in advance.

On June 29, 1989, the *Washington Times* ran a front-page story headlined: "Homosexual Prostitution Inquiry Ensnares VIPs with Reagan, Bush." Reporters George Archibald and Paul Rodriguez claimed that President Ronald Reagan and Vice President George H. W. Bush were linked to a male prostitution ring that engaged in "abduction and use of minors for sexual perversion." The chief source of those charges was Paul Bonacci, a young sex offender jailed in Nebraska, who told attorney John DeCamp that he (Bonacci) had been kidnapped and forced into sexual slavery, attending orgies where Bush and other highly placed officials molested children. Bonacci named the gang's leaders as Lawrence E. King (director of the Franklin Credit Union in Omaha) and Craig Spence (a Republican lobbyist who committed suicide in 1989, following arrest on drug and weapons charges).

Nebraska's Douglas County grand jury considered those charges in July 1990, hearing testimony from Bonacci and another self-described victim, Alisha Owen. The panel dismissed the sex charges as a "carefully crafted hoax," and while the authors of that hoax went unidentified, both Bonacci and Owen faced perjury charges. Despite that brush-off, Bonacci sued King for $1 million in damages, alleging King's involvement in kidnapping, sexual abuse, and various other crimes. Bonacci won a default judgment in February 1999, when King failed to appear in court to answer the charges. King's excuse: He was in prison, serving a 15-year term imposed in 1991 for embezzling $38

million from the Franklin Credit Union. King initially appealed the civil judgment, then dropped his appeal in January 2000.

Noreen Gosch testified in Bonacci's lawsuit against King. Specifically, she said that Johnny had come to her home in March 1997, accompanied by a male stranger. Noreen did not recognize her 27-year-old son at first, but he opened his shirt to reveal a familiar birthmark. The second man never identified himself during their 90-minute conversation. According to Noreen's sworn testimony, Johnny said he had escaped from his captors—whom he named—and said that he was living under an assumed identity to protect himself. He confirmed Paul Bonacci's statements about the child-sex ring and asked Noreen to keep the information secret. Throughout their conversation, she said, "Johnny would look over to the other person for approval to speak. He didn't say where he is living or where he was going."

In fact, reporters learned that Noreen had kept news of Johnny's visit secret even from her ex-husband, whom she divorced in 1993. Asked for comment by the media, Johnny's father questioned Noreen's credibility. In 2000, Noreen self-published an exposé on the case, titled *Why Johnny Can't Come Home,* including information gathered over the years by various private investigators.

There matters rested until September 1, 2006, when CNN reported that Noreen had found several photographs on her doorstep and had posted them to her Internet Web site. One color photo depicts three boys bound and gagged, Noreen claiming that one is her son. A black-and-white photo appears to show Johnny soon after his abduction, lying bound and gagged on a bed, shirtless but wearing sweatpants which Noreen says he wore on the day he vanished. An apparent brand marks his bare left shoulder. Oddly, a color version of the same photo, reportedly found on "a Russian pedophile Web site around Thanksgiving 2007" and posted on Noreen's site in February 2008, reveals no brand on Johnny's shoulder. Other photos of Johnny in bondage, wearing different pants and pajama bottoms, were added to Noreen's Web site over time, through incoming e-mails.

While the global traffic in sex slaves is well established, victimizing both children and adults, some critics dismiss Noreen Gosch's specific allegations as products of fantasy. On September 13, 2006, soon after Noreen announced receipt of the photos at her home, Des Moines police received an anonymous letter that read:

> Gentlemen,
> Someone has played a reprehensible joke on a grieving mother. The photo in question is not one of her son but of three boys in Tampa, Florida, about 1979–80, challenging each other to an escape contest. There was an investigation concerning that picture, made by the Hillsborough County (FL) Sheriff's Office. No charges were filed, and no wrongdoing was established. The lead detective on the case was named Zalva. This allegation should be easy enough to check out.

Nelson Zalva, formerly employed as a Hillsborough County sheriff's deputy, confirmed as much to journalists, saying he investigated the photo in "1978 or 1979," years before Johnny Gosch disappeared. "I interviewed the kids," he said, "and they said there was no coercion or touching. . . . I could never prove a crime." Florida officials tried to find the file in question, but failed. On September 21, Zalva told reporters, "It's been like searching for a needle in a haystack."

Unimpressed, Noreen Gosch insisted that "one of the photos is definitely Johnny." On September 18 she received another anonymous death threat. One month later, on October 17, WOI-TV in West Des Moines announced that the photos in question do not, in fact, depict Johnny Gosch. Noreen remains convinced that her son is still alive, in hiding as a fugitive from would-be murderers.

GOUDREAU, Marie   See "Highway Killer"

GOULET, Diane   See Woonsocket, Rhode Island, murders

GRAND Rapids, Michigan serial murders (1994–96)
Authorities in Kent County, Michigan hesitate to blame a serial killer for the murders of 11 women—eight of them known prostitutes—since early 1994, but Lt. Carol Price, spokesperson for a 15-member task force assigned to solve the case, has told reporters: "We're not denying it's a possibility. But we don't concentrate on that theory to the exclusion of others." Thus far, sadly, no theory has brought

police any closer to a solution in the case that has Grand Rapids residents glancing over their shoulders in grim apprehension.

The first known victim, 25-year-old prostitute Lesa Otberg, was abducted from Grand Rapids on March 28, 1994, her corpse discarded in Muskegon, 40 miles to the northwest. Seven months later, on November 6, a second body was found in neighboring Ottawa County, to the west. That victim remains unidentified, listed on the record as a "Jane Doe," age 35 to 50 years. Authorities believe she was murdered in the spring or early summer of 1994. Pamela Verile, a 33-year-old prostitute and drug addict, was next, found beaten to death on June 1, 1995, in a thicket near Walker, on the western outskirts of Grand Rapids. Thirty-seven-year-old Gale Cook, a convicted drug user and fugitive from a prison work-release program, was found strangled in Grand Rapids Township on October 4, 1995. Local prostitute Dawn Shaver, 25 years old, was beaten and strangled before she was dumped in a creek north of town, her body recovered on November 21. No cause of death was determined for Michelle Becker, a 36-year-old convicted streetwalker found dead in downtown Grand Rapids on August 9, 1996. The same was true for 27-year-old Sonyia Compos, a prostitute found in Walker on September 21, and for the "Jane Doe" victim found in Plainfield Township 10 days later. Thirty-year-old Sharon Hammack, another addict-prostitute, was killed on October 3, 1996, discarded on the fringes of suburban Kentwood.

A task force was organized to investigate the murders on October 10, 1996. Three days later, an anonymous telephone call led police to a 10th victim—yet another "Jane Doe," 40 to 55 years old—in a field behind a south Grand Rapids factory. The 11th victim, 29-year-old Victoria Moore, was found two weeks later, on October 27, her decomposing body dumped beside a country road, 20 miles north of Grand Rapids. By that time, a pattern of sorts had emerged, police acknowledging that Moore and at least four other victims had spent time at Rose Haven Ministry, a local sanctuary for prostitutes. Rose Haven's director, Brenda Dalecke, told reporters, "I'd be really surprised if it wasn't a serial killer. It's too much of a coincidence."

The authorities, for their part, were less certain. "We're not ready to use the big 'S' word yet," said Walker police chief Walter Sprenger. "So far, we haven't found the common thread that links all these victims together." Of course, police were not discounting the theory, either. Capt. Kevin Belk, chief of detectives for the Grand Rapids Police Department, conceded to reporters that "There are enough similarities to lead us to believe that a majority or all of these homicides are related." Still, he added, "We're not prepared to say any one person was responsible. We have several tips and leads, but we're not focusing on any prime suspect."

Nothing has changed, apparently, with the passage of time. Police are no closer to an arrest in Grand Rapids today than they were in 1996. The killer (or killers) of at least 11 women there remains at large.

GRANT, Lucy   See "WEST SIDE RAPIST"

GREAT Basin   dumping ground for unknown murderers

The Great Basin is a huge, arid depression bounded by the Rocky Mountains on the east and the Sierra Nevada on the west. It encompasses all of Nevada, plus parts of California, Utah, Idaho, and Wyoming. It is an unforgiving land, mostly desert, where water and shade remain precious commodities for travelers. Its highways stretch for barren miles between small towns. Rainfall is sparse, and rivers find no outlet to the sea. In the 19th century it was littered with the bones of hapless prospectors and pilgrims. Today, the victims are more likely to be women killed and dumped by unknown human predators.

Authorities stop short of blaming a single killer for the string of female victims found scattered over three Great Basin states between 1983 and 1997, typically raped and murdered in grisly examples of overkill, but they have attempted to coordinate investigation through a special unit, the Utah Criminal Tracking Analysis Project (UCTAP). In fact, collaborating officers believe they are dealing with the handiwork of more than one serial slayer, experienced stalkers who used the Great Basin as a dumping ground, trusting the desert and its scavengers to eradicate trace evidence. The list of victims includes:

Janelle Johnson, found raped and murdered in Fremont County, Wyoming, on March 1, 1983. Investigators say the case is unlikely to be solved, after more than two decades, and vital DNA evidence was lost when a police refrigera-

tor lost power, thereby spoiling a semen sample recovered from Johnson's body. In August 1999 Detective Roger Rizor of the Fremont County Sheriff's Department told APB News that the crime's only suspect—once a cook at a local supper club—"has never been cleared," but neither can he now be charged with the crime.

Lisa Marie Kimmell, found on April 2, 1988, in Natrona County, Wyoming. A semen sample survives in this case, but police remain baffled, regarding both the identity of Kimmell's killer and the whereabouts of her missing car. Lt. Chuck Lauderdale told APB News in August 1999 that the Natrona County Sheriff's Department still received "two or three leads a week [on the case], but nothing ever pans out. The same names keep popping up here and there, but they've all been pretty much cleared."

Vikki Perkins, found in Emery County, Utah, on May 13, 1999. No clues presently exist in the murder of this Portland, Oregon, native, who sometimes used the pseudonym Victoria Lynnette Lapauno. At last report, authorities were unable even to state a cause of death for Perkins, since her decomposed remains had been partially devoured by coyotes prior to discovery. Investigators cannot rule out sexual assault, but no semen traces or other DNA evidence was found that might identify the killer(s) at some future date.

Jane Doe #1, discovered in Millard County, Utah, on October 26, 1990. Failure to identify a victim makes the tracing of her killer doubly difficult, sometimes impossible. Utah authorities worked overtime to link suspect Howard Williams to this case, after he was charged with killing his wife in neighboring Juab County, but Williams staunchly denied involvement in the second murder and sheriff's lieutenant John Kimball told APB News in August 1999 that detectives are "half-convinced that he's telling the truth." Kimball added, ruefully, "I think I'm going to retire and I'll never solve this." So far, his prediction has been accurate.

Ermilinda Garza, killed near St. George, Utah, on April 2, 1991. Like Vikki Perkins, this victim also used an alias from time to time, representing herself as Linda Sherman. Her corpse was still warm when a landscaper found it beside Interstate Highway 15, but authorities have had no luck solving the case. One suspect, imprisoned in Utah for an unrelated homicide, predictably denied involvement in Garza's death, and his DNA profile failed to match that of semen recovered from Garza's body.

Jane Doe #2, found in Sweetwater County, Wyoming, on March 1, 1992. Police believe the slayer in this case to be a truck driver, although their reasons for holding that opinion remain undisclosed. The victim's fingerprints have thus far failed to match any records held by the FBI or various state and local law enforcement agencies. Again, without the victim's name or some other basic knowledge of her life and habits, identification of her killer remains virtually impossible.

Jane Doe #3, found near Elko, Nevada, on November 16, 1993. No new information has been uncovered in the decade since discovery of the victim's decomposed remains, and her case appears likely to remain in the unsolved file.

Tonya Teske, found dead in Bonneville County, Idaho, on August 15, 1997. Police were hopeful when a shopping bag filled with Teske's clothes was found near the loading dock of the Southern Post Company, a fence post manufacturer in Brigham City, Utah (90 miles south of the crime scene), but the new evidence produced no useful leads. Authorities suspect Teske was killed by a trucker, who then dropped her clothing off in Brigham City as he traveled south.

APB News reported on August 26, 1999, that tri-state authorities believe that "certain of these . . . slayings may be linked," and that "the killers . . . may have killed before—or since." That said, until all of the victims are finally identified and police find some concrete forensic evidence linking two or more cases, the theory remains simply that. Homicide detectives deem the first 48 hours of any investigation critical to success or failure, and cases protracted for years, much less decades, are rarely solved short of a confession—or a miracle.

GREEN, Howard, and Marron, Carol murder victims (1979)

At 7:00 P.M. on Sunday, December 16, 1979, a motorist in West Paterson, New Jersey, sighted the bodies of a man and woman lying on the grassy shoulder of Route 80. Authorities were summoned,

and both victims were pronounced dead at the scene. Each had been clubbed on the left side of the head and stabbed in the right eye; a clump of hair was also found clutched in each victim's hand. Autopsy reports showed that both corpses were completely drained of blood, with the killers apparently using a large veterinarian's syringe.

Police identified the victims as 53-year-old Howard Green and 33-year-old Carol Marron, residents of Brooklyn, New York. Green was a cab driver and part-time artist, while Marron held a secretarial position at Brooklyn's Pratt Institute, designing clothes in her spare time. They shared a basement flat on DeKalb Avenue, where a police search uncovered various items of occult paraphernalia. The couple had last been seen alive in the early evening of December 15, by a friend who met them briefly on a Manhattan subway train.

While motive and suspects remained elusive in the case, New York detective Jim Devereaux told reporters, "It was definitely a satanic murder. And it wasn't a one-man job. In all my years in this business, I've never seen anything like this." Independent confirmation of that analysis came from journalist Maury Terry, who received an anonymous letter, later published in his book *The Ultimate Evil* (1987). It read:

> *Dear Maury Terry. Please look into this double killing. Carol was asking people about the OTO a year prior to the murders. I can't accept that the people responsible for this are still walking around free. I am afraid that the problem will not go away and that minds this unbalanced may perpetrate additional horrors. Forgive me for not signing my name. I haven't gotten over the fear.*

Terry's anonymous correspondent was never identified, and despite that pointer to the Ordo Templi Orientis—a ritual magic society once led by self-styled "Great Beast 666" Aleister Crowley—police have made no further progress on the case since 1979.

GREENBAUM, Gus gangland murder victim (1958)

A native of New York City's Lower East Side, born in 1894, Gus Greenbaum was an early associate of Meyer Lansky and BENJAMIN (BUGSY) SIEGEL during Prohibition. With repeal of the "noble experiment" in 1933, he turned his full attention to gambling, managing the syndicate's illicit casinos and bookmaking parlors. When Siegel went west to establish Las Vegas, Nevada, as the mob's ultimate gold mine,

Gus Greenbaum (second from left) was a major power in Las Vegas until drug addiction made him unreliable. (Library of Congress)

Greenbaum detoured to Phoenix and organized Arizona's bookies for his pals back east. Twenty minutes after Siegel was murdered in Beverly Hills, on June 20, 1947, Greenbaum arrived at Bugsy's Flamingo Hotel and Casino in Las Vegas to announce that he was taking over.

All went well at first—so well, in fact, that Greenbaum was promoted to manage the new $10 million Riviera in Vegas in 1955. He still officially resided in Phoenix, where a friendship had blossomed with Senator Barry Goldwater, but Greenbaum spent an increasing amount of time in Las Vegas and suburban Paradise—where he took the unusual step (for a mobster) of running for mayor. His sponsors in Chicago were not pleased when Gus won the election, but they let it slide—until word came that he was hooked on heroin, losing heavily at craps, and cavorting night after night with expensive call girls. Even that might have been forgiven, before the normally profitable Riviera began losing money. Mob investors took it as a sign that Greenbaum was skimming the till to support his drug and gambling habits.

At Thanksgiving 1958 a mob summit conference convened at the Arizona home of transplanted Detroit gangster Peter (Horse Face) Licavoli. Federal agents later dubbed it the meeting of the "Four Joes": Chicago's Joe (Big Tuna) Accardo, plus New York mobsters Joe Profaci, Joe Bonnano, and Joe Magliocco. No FBI bugs were installed in Licavoli's home at the time, but subsequent rumors contended that the Four Joes spent their holiday deciding the fate of Gus Greenbaum.

Five days later, on December 3, 1958, Greenbaum and his wife were murdered at their Phoenix home. A housekeeper found Gus sprawled across his bed, nearly decapitated with a butcher knife. Bess Greenbaum lay on a sofa in the nearby den, slain in identical fashion. The gruesome murder of a spouse departed from Mafia tradition. Some mob-watchers believe Bess was killed as an object lesson to future embezzlers, while others maintain that the killer (or killers) were simply overzealous or decided to eliminate the only living witness. There is even doubt as to the source of Greenbaum's death sentence. While most authors blame the Four Joes or Chicago alone, FBI informer Jimmy Fratianno fingered Meyer Lansky for the murder, insisting that Greenbaum's death was "Meyer's contract." No one was ever charged in the double slaying, and the truth remains unknown today.

GREEN Bicycle Case murder (1919)

British subject Bella Wright was born in 1898, the oldest of seven children sired by an illiterate herdsman living near Leicester, England. She quit school at age 12 to work as a domestic servant, then secured full-time work at a factory in Bates, five miles from her home. At the premature end of her life, she was dating Archie Ward, a stoker in the Royal Navy, and at least one other man who remains unidentified today.

On July 5, 1919, Wright rode her bicycle from home to the house of an uncle, George Measures, in nearby Gaulby. She arrived with a man unknown to her relatives, explaining that he was a stranger that she had met on the road from Leicester. She lingered at the house, saying she hoped the man would leave without her, but he waited for her in the yard. James Evans, husband of Wright's cousin Margaret, spoke to the man and noted "some unusual features" on his bike. Wright and the stranger left between 8:45 and 9:00 P.M., pedaling back toward Leicester along Wright's normal route.

At 9:20 P.M. a local farmer found Wright sprawled on the road in a pool of blood, lifeless. A physician summoned to the scene examined Wright's body in near-darkness, assuming that she was struck by an automobile. Police subsequently viewed the body at a nearby chapel and discovered a bullet hole in Wright's left cheek, with an exit wound at the top of her skull. A belated search of the murder scene disclosed unexpected bloodstains on a field gate near where Wright's body was found—and bird tracks from the pool of blood around her body, which led searchers to a dead bird in a nearby field. Searchers also found "recent" human footprints and a spent .455-caliber bullet, lying in the middle of the road some 17 feet from where Wright had collapsed.

A second, more thorough postmortem examination revealed that Wright had indeed been shot through the head, with a firearm discharged at a range of six or seven feet from her face. Despite further searches, no weapon was found at the scene.

Witnesses described Wright's mystery companion as 35–40 years old, average height, with a high-pitched voice. His bicycle was green, with an "unusual" shape to the handlebars and a braking system that involved pedaling backward. James Evans also thought it had been recently repaired. On July 10, in response to police inquiries, Leicester repairman Harry Cox announced that he had recently worked on a similar bike.

The green bicycle surfaced, literally, on February 23, 1920, when part of it snagged on a canal boat's tow-rope. Police determined that the bike had been dismantled and thrown into the canal piecemeal, with its identification marks filed off, but investigators found one small mark still intact and traced it to Ronald Vivian Light, a mathematics teacher who purchased it in 1910. Light had lived in Leicester at the time of Wright's murder, subsequently finding work at the Dean Close School in Cheltenham.

Police investigated Light's background, discovering that he was born in 1885 and was expelled from school at 17 for "lifting a little girl's clothes over her head." In 1914, Light was fired from his job with a British railroad for writing obscene graffiti in a men's room and allegedly setting fire to an office cupboard. A farmer that he subsequently worked for also fired Light for allegedly torching haystacks. He joined the British army as a second lieutenant during World War I, but was discharged for unspecified reasons, then reenlisted as a private and suffered "shell shock" on the Western Front. Light's father, a successful inventor, killed himself in 1916, and Light's mother blamed the suicide in part on her husband's concerns for their son.

Back in civilian life and in his 30s, Light supposedly "attempted to make love to a girl 15 years of age," and in October 1919 he supposedly confessed "improper conduct" with an eight-year-old, but no charges were filed in either case. Police found two girls, ages 12 and 14, who claimed Light had pur-

sued them on his bicycle the same day Bella Wright was killed.

Officers arrested Light for Bella Wright's murder on March 4, 1920. Two weeks later, canal workers dredged up an army pistol holster and a dozen live .455-caliber cartridges which "precisely matched" the bullet found at Wright's death scene. In fact, however, the Webley .455-caliber revolver had been Britain's standard military and police sidearm since 1887. Thousands of the weapons were in circulation by 1919, with millions of cartridges.

On advice from his attorney, Sir Edward Marshall Hall, Light admitted meeting Wright on the day she was killed but denied committing the murder. He claimed that Wright had stopped him on the road around 6:45 P.M. and asked him for a wrench to tighten a loose freewheel mechanism on her bike. He did not have one, but offered to accompany her to her uncle's house and admitted remaining in Wright's company during that visit. He denied being the anonymous "officer" whom Bella claimed had a crush on her, but Light acknowledged concealing his bike after the murder, purportedly to spare his mother from worry. He also admitted owning the holster and ammunition found in the canal, but once again denied any part in Wright's slaying.

Light's trial opened in Leicester on July 9, 1920, before Judge Thomas Gardner Horridge. On the witness stand, Light admitted most of the prosecution's contentions, even granting that he had once owned a .455-caliber pistol, but steadfastly denied the murder. Defense attorney Hall focused chiefly on technical matters and drew an admission from the crown's ballistics expert that Wright may have been shot with a rifle, suggesting that her death was a long-distance accident. Hall also emphasized his client's lack of motive, asserting that Light and Bella had never met before the day she was slain. Jurors deliberated for three hours, then acquitted Light of all charges.

Following his acquittal, Light returned to live with his mother, then moved to Kent and married under an assumed name in 1934, maintaining the alias for another 11 years. He died in 1975, at age 89, still considered by many the prime suspect in Bella Wright's murder.

From 1930 onward, various authors have studied the green bicycle case, reaching divergent verdicts on Light's guilt or innocence. H. R. Wakefield defended Light, while Wendy East deemed him guilty as charged. An intermediate theory, claiming that Light shot Bella accidentally while showing her his pistol, rests on a note supposedly written by Leicester police superintendent Levi Bowley three days after Light's acquittal. That note, still unauthenticated, claims that Light confessed the accidental shooting to Bowley *before* Light was tried. Why Bowley would have kept such information secret—if, in fact, the jailhouse conversation ever happened—is anyone's guess.

GREER, Georgia See TEXAS TRI-COUNTY MURDERS (1971–75)

GREIVE, Emily See ZEPHYRHILLS, FLORIDA, MURDERS

GRICAR, Ray Frank missing person (2005)

Ohio native Ray Gricar was born in October 1945. He graduated from Cleveland's Gilmour Academy, then from the University of Dayton and Case-Western Reserve Law School. He spent 10 years as an assistant prosecutor in Cleveland, before relocating to Centre County, Pennsylvania, as an assistant district attorney. Gricar was elected to serve as the county's part-time D.A. in 1985 and lobbied to make the post a full-time position, which it became in 1996. In January 2004, Gricar announced plans to retire and declared that he would not seek reelection when his current term expired.

On the morning of April 15, 2005, Gricar told Patty Fornicola—his live-in girlfriend and a clerk in Gricar's office—that he planned to take the day off. Fornicola praised his decision and left for work at her regular time. At 11:30 A.M., Gricar phoned Fornicola to say that he was driving on Highway 92, from Bellefonte to Lewisburg, and "wouldn't make it back to take care of Honey," the couple's dog.

In fact, he never made it back at all.

Fornicola reported Gricar missing when he had not returned home by 11:30 P.M. on April 15. The next day, police found his car in a Lewisburg parking lot across the street from an antique market where he sometimes shopped. Officers who opened the vehicle noted a smell of tobacco smoke, though Gricar was not a smoker, and forensic examiners found traces of ash on the car's floorboard, as if a smoker had leaned through the open window to speak with Gricar. Investigators found no sign of foul play, and Gricar's

assistant district attorney, Mark Smith, told reporters, "There is no evidence of any medical, physical, or mental condition whatsoever."

Searchers fanned out through a wooded area near the point where Gricar's vehicle was found, abutting the Susquehanna River. Bloodhounds were deployed in a futile effort to trace Gricar's steps, and a state police helicopter followed the river in vain. One witness from the antique store described Gricar speaking to an attractive brunette, age 30–40 years, but there the trail ended.

Police scrutiny of the Susquehanna River was not coincidental. Gricar's younger brother Roy had vanished from home in West Chester, Ohio, in May 1996, after telling his wife he was going out for a walk. Police found his corpse in the Great Miami River two days later and pronounced the death a suicidal drowning. Still, Ray Gricar's friends and relatives denied any significant problems in his personal or professional life.

Investigators noted that Gricar's laptop computer, issued to him by the county, was missing at the time he disappeared. It was pulled from the Susquehanna on September 30, with the hard drive missing. Two months later, the hard drive surfaced but was damaged beyond the point of retrieving any data. Meanwhile, a surveillance videotape from April 14, 2005, showed Gricar leaving Centre County's administrative building without the laptop.

FBI agents joined in the search for Gricar, but accomplished nothing. Bellefonte's police chief, Duane Dixon, told reporters, "I don't have a logical theory at this point." Assistant D.A. Mark Smith agreed, saying, "We are just baffled by his absence."

Gricar was still missing as this work went to press. Court TV featured his case on its *Haunting Evidence* program, on June 21, 2006, followed by coverage on the CBS program *Without a Trace*, on March 25, 2007. Despite that national publicity, no useful leads have been developed in Gricar's case and his disappearance remains unexplained.

GRIFFIN, Canoscha See "SOUTHSIDE SLAYER"

GRIFFIN, Lisa See FORT WORTH MURDERS

GRIFFIN, Richard See TEXARKANA "PHANTOM GUNMAN"

GRIMES, Barbara and Patricia See CHICAGO CHILD MURDERS

GROSS, Christy See RAWLINS, WYOMING, RODEO MURDERS

"GUANGZHOU Ripper" serial murderer (1991–92)
Hard-line communist societies once faced a self-imposed disability in dealing with serial killers, since state propaganda organs routinely denied the existence of serious crime in a "workers' paradise." Authorities in the former USSR learned the grim truth over a span of two decades, from butchers like Gennadiy Mikhasevich (36 victims), Andrei Chikatilo (52 dead), Nikolai Dzhumagliev ("at least 100" slain), and Anatoly Onoprienko (51 victims), but the notion of serial murder was still new to the People's Republic of China in 1991, when an unknown stalker surfaced in Guangzhou (formerly Canton).

The slasher's first victim was reportedly found on February 22, 1991, vaguely described as a woman in her early 20s. Her genitals were excised with a knife, but the injury did not prevent police from finding unspecified "evidence of sexual intercourse." Five more slayings followed in the next six months, each victim reportedly subjected to a sexual assault, then smothered, stabbed, or strangled, after which the bodies were dismembered, stuffed into rice bags, and dumped on rubbish heaps in the bleak suburbs where Guangzhou's "floating population" lives in dismal squalor. And then, the murders stopped.

Thus far, there had been no press coverage of the crimes in China, marking the case as a "success" in terms of propaganda, even though the murderer remained at large. Chinese authorities ran out of luck in March 1992, when a seventh victim washed ashore in the nearby British colony of Hong Kong. As described in the *South China Morning Post,* number seven had been slit from throat to stomach, then crudely stitched shut again, her finger severed almost as an afterthought. Because no women were reported missing from Hong Kong, it was assumed the corpse had floated in from mainland China, and so the "Guangzhou Ripper" was belatedly exposed.

Even then, it was impossible for mainland homicide investigators, reared from childhood under communism, to believe that their system would spawn such a monster. Zhu Minjian, head of Guangzhou's provincial Criminal Investigation Department, told reporters, "In all my thirty years with the force, I have never come across anything like this. Perhaps he copied from the West." Zhu said there had been "progress" on the case, but he was not prepared to share details. "We're putting a lot of effort into this case," he declared. "We've got to solve it."

Or, perhaps not. More than a decade after the first press report of the crimes, Chinese authorities have yet to name a suspect in the string of murders they found so shocking. Unless the killer has been secretly detained—unlikely on its face, considering the rash of prior publicity—we must assume that Guangzhou's Ripper has performed a successful disappearing act.

GUIDA, Sheryl See NEW YORK CITY STRANGULATION MURDERS

GUIHARD, Paul murder victim (1962)
A French journalist, born in 1932, Paul Guihard was working on assignment in New York at age 30, when a federal court ordered the University of Mississippi to accept James Meredith as its first black student. Governor Ross Barnett had exhausted his legal remedies in the fight to keep "Ole Miss" lily-white, and the task of preventing Meredith's enrollment now fell to a ragtag army of racist students, professional bigots, and assorted mental misfits. Members of the Ku Klux Klan and neo-Nazi National States Rights Party flocked to Oxford, Mississippi, from surrounding states, rallied to the banner of resistance raised by former U.S. Army general Edwin Walker. Violence was anticipated, and Guihard was one of several hundred journalists who flew south to cover the action on September 30, 1962.

Meredith arrived on schedule at Ole Miss, protected by a force of 300 armed U.S. marshals. That force soon found itself besieged by a mob of several thousand screaming white supremacists who surrounded the main administration building, pelting it with stones and scattered gunfire. White policemen gave the rioters advice on vandalizing federal cars, while caravans and busloads of redneck reinforcements came to join the action. The U.S. marshals, reinforced by army troops and National Guardsmen, fought a desperate holding action against rioters who tried to storm the building on foot, then sought to crash the barricades with a stolen fire truck and bulldozer. When the smoke cleared next morning, 158 of the 300 marshals were wounded, 58 of them by bullets. At least 130 other persons had been injured, with nearly 200 (including Edwin Walker) arrested. More than 50 guns were confiscated from the rioters, along with heaps of knives, blackjacks, and other weapons. A white man, Ray Gunter, was killed in the midst of the action, when a stray shot drilled his skull.

The other fatality was Paul Guihard, and his death was clearly no accident. Authorities found him sprawled outside a women's dormitory shortly before 9:00 P.M., executed by a close-range pistol shot to the back. As investigators later reconstructed the crime, someone in the racist mob had singled out the bearded newsman as a "Yankee" or "outsider" and marched him away from the main riot scene, to kill him in relative privacy. Without a weapon for comparison, it was impossible to trace the fatal bullet. No suspect was ever identified in the slaying. Guihard was buried at Saint Malo, on October 5, 1962, following a memorial service in New York attended by French and U.S. officials. President John Kennedy wired a personal apology to the French press agency, while the student newspaper at Ole Miss established a scholarship fund in Guihard's name.

A force of 23,000 federal troops was quartered in Oxford to prevent further violence, living in tents that they labeled "Andersonville" and "KKK HQ," while the latrine bore a sign reading "Governor's Mansion." Despite a false alarm on October 11, 1962—10,000 troops responding to a riot call found themselves confronted with a fraternity "pinning" ceremony—the action at Ole Miss subsided to a numbing routine of nonviolent harassment and insults. Meredith graduated on schedule in 1964 and later published an account of the experience (*Three Years in Mississippi*, 1966). On June 5, 1966, he was wounded by a roadside sniper near Hernando, Mississippi, while conducting a one-man "march against fear" through the Magnolia State. The hospital that treated Meredith received a bomb threat from a caller who identified himself as a member of the Ku Klux Klan.

GUNNESS, Belle serial killer who eluded capture

America's first "black widow" serial killer was born Brynhild Paulsdatter Storset, on November 11, 1859, in the fishing hamlet of Selbu, Norway. The daughter of an unsuccessful merchant, she immigrated to the United States in 1881; three years later she settled in Chicago, Americanizing her name to Belle or Bella. In 1884, at age 25, she married Mads Sorenson, a Norwegian immigrant.

The couple opened a confectioner's shop in 1896, but the business was wiped out by fire the following year. Belle told her insurance agents that a kerosene lamp had exploded, and the company paid off on her policy, although no lamp was found in the wreckage. The Sorensons used their windfall to purchase a home, but fire leveled the house in 1898, bringing further insurance payments. Bad luck dogged the couple, and a second house burned down before they found a home that suited them on Alma Street.

As everything Belle touched was soon reduced to ashes, so her family began to dwindle in the latter 1890s. Daughter Caroline, her oldest child, went

Suspected murderer Belle Gunness poses in a photo with her children. Gunness is suspected of killing up to 15 men for their insurance. (Bettmann/Corbis)

first, in 1896. Two years later, Axel, Belle's first son, was laid to rest. In each case the children were diagnosed as victims of "acute colitis," demonstrating symptoms which (in hindsight) may have indicated they were poisoned.

Mads Sorenson died at home on July 30, 1900, exhibiting the classic symptoms of strychnine poisoning. Belle admitted giving her husband "a powder," but the family's physician did not request an autopsy. With Mads under treatment for an enlarged heart, his death was automatically attributed to natural causes. The widow Sorenson collected her insurance money and departed from Chicago, settling outside La Porte, Indiana, with three children under her wing. Two were her natural daughters: Myrtle, born in 1897, and Lucy, born in 1899. The new addition, Jennie Olsen, was a foster daughter passed along to Belle by parents who, apparently, were tired of dealing with the child.

In April 1902 Belle married a Norwegian farmer named Peter Gunness. Less durable than Sorenson before him, Gunness lasted only eight months after his trip to the altar. On December 16, 1902, he was killed when a heavy sausage grinder fell from its place on a shelf, crushing his skull. A son named Philip was born of the brief union, in 1903, and Jennie Olsen vanished from the Gunness farm three years later. When neighbors inquired, Belle explained that her foster child had been sent "to a finishing school in California."

Widowed for the second time, with only children to assist her on the farm, Belle started hiring drifters who would work a while and then, apparently, move on. She also started placing "lonely-hearts" ads in Norwegian-language newspapers across the Midwest, entertaining a series of prospective husbands at her farm. Somehow, none of them measured up to her standards—and none of them were ever seen again.

On April 28, 1908, the Gunness homestead was leveled by fire. Searchers digging through the rubble found a quartet of incinerated bodies in the basement. Three were clearly children, while the fourth—a woman's headless corpse, without a skull in evidence—was taken for the last remains of Mrs. Gunness. The local sheriff arrested handyman Ray Lamphere, employed by Belle from 1906 until his dismissal in February 1908, on charges of arson and murder.

The case became more complicated on May 5, when searchers started finding *other* bodies on the Gunness farm. Dismembered, wrapped in gunnysacks and doused with lye, a few reduced to skeletons, the corpses told a graphic tale of wholesale slaughter spanning years. The final body count has been a subject of enduring controversy. Without citing its source, the *Guiness Book of World Records* credited Belle with 16 known victims and another 12 "possibles." The local coroner's office was more conservative, listing (in addition to the basement bodies) 10 male victims, two females, and an unspecified quantity of human bone fragments. Belle's suitors were buried together in the muck of a hog pen, while her female victims had been planted in a nearby garden patch.

Only six of the victims were positively identified. Jennie Olsen was there, far removed from the mythical finishing school. Farmhands Eric Gurhold and Olaf Lindholm had ended their days in the hog pen, beside farmers John Moo (of Elbow Lake, Minnesota) and Ole Budsburg (from Iola, Wisconsin). Both of the latter had answered Belle's newspaper ads, and so presumably had their six anonymous companions in death. The single Jane Doe, buried beside Jennie Olsen, remains an anomaly, unexplained to this day.

A coroner's inquest was launched on April 29, 1908, and witness depositions taken through May 1 reflect a standard heading: "Over the dead body of Belle Gunness." After May 5, with the discovery of new corpses, official documents began describing the headless woman as "an unidentified adult female," assuming that Belle must have faked her own death to escape punishment. A futile search for the missing skull began on May 19, resulting in discovery of Belle's dental bridge, complete with anchor teeth attached. Ignoring the various unanswered questions, the coroner issued his final report on May 20, 1908, declaring that Belle Gunness had died "at the hands of persons unknown."

Ray Lamphere, from his jail cell, was adamant in claiming Belle was still alive. On April 28, he said, after Belle had set the house afire, he drove her to the railway station at nearby Stillwell, Indiana. Police initially took his story at face value and arrested an innocent widow, Flora Heerin, en route from Chicago to visit relatives in New York City. Hauled off the train at Syracuse and briefly detained as Belle Gunness, Mrs. Heerin retaliated with a lawsuit for false arrest.

Charged with four counts of murder and one count of arson, Ray Lamphere went to trial in November 1908. On November 26, he was convicted of arson alone, suggesting that the jurors felt Belle's death had not been proved beyond a reasonable doubt. Lamphere survived for two years in prison, talking endlessly about the case, crediting Belle with 49 murders and theft of more than $100,000 between 1903 and 1908. The basement victim, he contended, had been found in a saloon and hired for the evening, murdered to serve as a stand-in. Belle had promised she would get in touch with Lamphere after she was settled elsewhere, but it seemed that she had changed her plans.

The first reported sighting of a resurrected Belle was logged on April 29, 1908, six days before new bodies were discovered at her farm. Railroad conductor Jesse Hurst was certain Mrs. Gunness had boarded his train at Decatur, Indiana. She was bundled on a stretcher, he recalled, and seemed quite ill.

Perhaps, but what are we to make of the reported sighting at La Porte on April 30, 1908? While visiting Belle's closest friend, Almetta Hay, a local farmer claimed he saw the missing woman sitting down to coffee. When Almetta died in 1916, neighbors picking through the litter in her crowded shack retrieved a woman's skull, found wedged between two mattresses. In spite of speculation that it might belong to the decapitated basement victim, the intriguing lead was not pursued.

More "sightings" of Belle Gunness were recorded through the years. In 1917 a childhood neighbor recognized Belle on admission as a patient to the South Bend, Indiana, hospital where he was working as a student nurse. He called police, but Belle had slipped away before detectives reached the scene. In 1931 a Los Angeles prosecutor wrote to La Porte's sheriff, claiming that murder defendant Esther Carlson—charged with poisoning 81-year-old August Lindstrom for his money—might be Belle Gunness. Carlton carried photographs of three children resembling Belle's, but La Porte could not afford to send its sheriff west in those Depression days, and the suspect died of tuberculosis prior to trial, leaving the question forever open.

As late as 1935, subscribers to a popular magazine allegedly recognized Belle's photo as the likeness of a brothel madam in Ohio. Confronting the old woman and addressing her as "Belle," one amateur detective was impressed with the vehemence of her reaction. Pursuing the investigation through friends, he was urgently warned to let the matter rest—and so it did, for another 73 years.

In 2007, La Porte's Gunness 100th Anniversary Committee, chaired by Bruce Johnson, unofficially reopened the mysterious case. Forensic anthropologist Andrea Simmons joined the team, recalling childhood stories of Indiana's notorious black widow.

"There was always a sense of, what if she's still out there? What if she's lurking around," Simmons told reporter Tom Coyne. She also marveled at the fact that Gunness was largely forgotten, among America's more recent serial slayers. "When you look at the numbers [of victims]," she said, "she should be a household name."

Simmons exhumed the corpse presumed to be Belle's in November 2007 and discovered that her casket contained body parts from two unidentified children. Forensic tests proved that the youngsters in question were not foster children presumed to have died when Belle's home burned in 1908, but their identity remained unknown at press time for this volume. The remains may have come from Belle's basement, carelessly scooped up at the time of the fire, but Simmons admitted, "We don't know whether we're adding two more people to our body count." Thus far, attempts to finally identify Belle's headless corpse through DNA testing have not borne results.

If Gunness did, in fact, survive her "death," she stands with BELA KISS and members of the BENDER FAMILY in that elite society of serial killers who, although identified, still manage to escape arrest and so live out their lives in anonymity. Her legacy is rumor and a snatch of tawdry rhyme that reads, in part:

> *There's red upon the Hoosier moon*
> *For Belle was strong and full of doom;*
> *And think of all those Norska men*
> *Who'll never see St. Paul again.*

GUSHROWSKI, Carol See SAN DIEGO MURDERS (1985–88)

GUSTAVSON, Cathy See "SOUTHSIDE SLAYER"

HA, Oanh   See "HIGHWAY KILLER"

HACKNEY, Mary   See CUMMINSVILLE MURDERS

HAGERMAN, Amber Renee murder victim (1996)
Nine-year-old Amber Hagerman was riding her bicycle in the parking lot of an Arlington, Texas, supermarket when a stranger snatched her on January 17, 1996. Only her younger brother witnessed the abduction, and police had no useful leads when Amber's nude corpse was found on January 21, in a creek bed near the Forest Hollow apartment complex in north Arlington. She had been raped before her throat was cut. A neighbor supplied police with a vague description of a possible suspect—male, Caucasian or Hispanic, driving a black pickup truck—but the tip led nowhere.

As a result of Hagerman's slaying, Texas inaugurated a system of "Amber Alerts" to notify potential witnesses of child abductions. In October 2000, the U.S. House of Representatives adopted House Resolution 605, encouraging cities nationwide to adopt the "Amber Plan." Federal legislation followed, signed by President George W. Bush in April 2003, which made Amber Alerts mandatory throughout the United States. Despite that legislation, however, several states are still bogged down in implementation of the program, squabbling over varied activa-

tion criteria and hampered by outdated Emergency Alert System guidelines.

While Amber's slaying remains unsolved, detectives have announced that suspect Terapon Adhahn of Tacoma, Washington, is under investigation for the crime. Washington police arrested Adhahn on July 9, 2007, for the kidnap-slaying of 12-year-old Zina Linnik, abducted on July 4 and found murdered on July 12 in Pierce County. Charged with murder, kidnapping, and rape in that case, Adhahn is also considered a "person of interest" in the 2005 murder of 10-year-old Adre'Anna Jackson in Tillicum, Washington. An additional indictment charges Adhahn with raping two other girls.

HALEY, Lesa   See "I-35 MURDERS"

HALL, Edward, and Mills, Eleanor murder victims (1922)
At 10:00 A.M. on September 16, 1922, 23-year-old Raymond Schneider was strolling with 15-year-old Pearl Bahmer on a country lane outside New Brunswick, New Jersey, when they found two bodies lying on the grassy shoulder of the road. They ran to the home of a neighbor, Edward Stryker, and police were summoned to the scene. Patrolman Edward Garrigan was first on the scene, examining the fully clothed corpses of a man and woman. Both had been shot

in the head at close range, the male victim once, his companion three times; the woman's throat was also cut from ear to ear. Her head lay on the man's right arm, her left hand on his knee, as if they had been posed in death. The man's pale face was covered by a Panama hat. A business card was propped up against the heel of the dead man's left shoe. Scattered around the corpses were torn shreds of paper, a .32-caliber cartridge, and a two-foot piece of iron pipe. A man's wallet lay open nearby, revealing a driver's license in the name of 41-year-old Edward Wheeler Hall, a New Brunswick resident.

In fact, Hall was more than that: He was the pastor of New Brunswick's Episcopal Church of St. John the Evangelist. The business card placed at his foot was Hall's, apparently the killer's way of making sure the victim was identified. The woman was 34-year-old Eleanor Mills, wife of the sexton at Rev. Hall's church and a member of the choir. The papers strewn around the corpses proved to be cards and love letters exchanged by the pair, charting the course of a torrid four-year romance. "Oh, honey," Mills had written in one letter, "I am fiery today. Burning, flaming love." And in another: "I know there are girls with more shapely bodies, but I do not care what they have. I have the greatest of all blessings, the deep, true, and eternal love of a noble man. My heart is his, my life is his, all that I have is his . . . I am his forever."

As it turned out, the adulterous affair had been no secret to most of Hall's parishioners. Forty-five-year-old James Mills knew of his wife's dalliance, although he initially denied it in his first statement to police. Frances Hall, seven years her late husband's senior, likewise denied any knowledge of the romance, but authorities were naturally suspicious. She had taken three calls from Eleanor Mills on September 14, the last around 8:00 P.M., and Rev. Hall had gone out moments later, explaining that he needed to speak with Mills about the cost of her recent surgery. (Hall had agreed to pay for the operation because James Mills could not afford it.) When he failed to return by 2:30 A.M., Mrs. Hall had gone searching for him with her brother, William Stevens, who resided with the family. They found the church and Mills, apartment dark, but had resumed their search the next morning, in vain. James Mills had likewise gone looking for his wife that night, but gave up the hunt when he failed to find her by 2:00 A.M. He had reported her missing on September 15 and then went to work at a local school, where he was employed as a janitor.

An autopsy revealed that Hall and Mills had been killed about 36 hours before they were found—i.e., around 10:00 P.M. on September 14. When Hall was undressed at the morgue, a bullet fell out of his clothing. By the time James Mills and Frances Hall allegedly began to search for their respective spouses, the lovers were already dead. Forensic evidence indicated that Rev. Hall had been shot by someone standing above him, as he lay on the ground.

In addition to Mills and Mrs. Hall, police also suspected the widow's two brothers. William Stevens was mentally disabled, known for his explosive temperament. He admitted owning a .32-caliber revolver but claimed he had not fired it in more than a decade. (Police examined the weapon, pronounced it incapable of firing, and returned it to Stevens.) An older brother, Henry Stevens, was a retired exhibition marksman and expert with firearms. He lived at Lavallette, New Jersey, some 50 miles from New Brunswick, but a witness later placed him near the murder scene. Several witnesses reported seeing Eleanor Mills on the night of September 14, walking near the spot where her corpse was later found, and one recalled lights in the windows of Rev. Hall's church around 1:15 A.M. on September 15. A sharp-eyed neighbor of the Millses, Millie Opie, told police that Eleanor and Hall met almost every day at Eleanor's apartment, while her husband was at work.

On September 17, 1922, prosecutors publicly blamed "a jealous couple" for the murders, but no charges were filed. Grand juries convened in New Brunswick and Middlesex Counties without filing indictments, and a $1,000 reward for information on the case went unclaimed. Mrs. Hall hired a private investigator, Timothy Pfeiffer, to investigate the murder, but his search for evidence was still continuing on October 9, 1922, when police announced the arrest of suspect Clifford Hayes.

According to the prosecutor's office, Hayes had been in love with Pearl Bahmer, and he was enraged at seeing her with Raymond Schneider, whom Hayes regarded as a friend. Another acquaintance, 16-year-old Leon Kaufman, told police that Hayes was carrying a gun on the night of September 14, when they saw Bahmer with "another man" and followed the couple, then lost them in the darkness. Detectives theorized that Hayes had stumbled upon Hall and Mills, shooting them both in a case of mistaken identity, but the story failed to explain Eleanor's slashed throat, the posed corpses, and the shredded love letters. It all came to nothing a short time later, when Kaufman recanted his story and Hayes was released.

Suspicion then shifted back to Frances Hall, her brothers, James Mills, and 16-year-old daughter Charlotte Mills, who had recently sold a packet of her late mother's love letters to the *New York American* for $500. All were questioned anew, but once more no charges were filed. Around the same time a new witness was identified, one Jane Gibson, who claimed to have heard gunshots and screams near her hog farm on the night of September 14. Dubbed the "Pig Woman" in newspaper accounts, Gibson said she was first alerted by her barking dogs around 9:00 P.M., then saw a figure skulking in her cornfield. Mounting a mule, she rode off in pursuit of the prowler and glimpsed four persons standing at the murder scene. She heard a shot and saw one figure fall, as a woman cried, "Don't! Don't!" Turning to flee, Gibson heard more gunshots and glimpsed a second victim falling, as a woman shouted, "Henry!" Gibson had approached police when Clifford Hayes was arrested, but officers had been "too busy to listen."

They listened now, but Gibson's testimony conflicted with the evidence that Hall was shot while lying down. When pressed for further details, Gibson recalled an open touring car parked near the murder scene, and she claimed that the headlights of a second vehicle had briefly given her a clear view of the night's combatants. One had been a woman in a long gray coat; another was a man with bushy hair and a dark mustache. Gibson now recalled that one of the women had asked, "How do you explain these notes?" She also added a new twist to the murders: Mrs. Mills had tried to run, Gibson said, but the killers had dragged her back to the killing ground and shot her three times. In a third interview Gibson added yet *another* piece of crucial information: She had gone back to the murder site at 1:00 A.M., Gibson now claimed, and had seen Mrs. Hall—a "big lady" with "white hair"—sobbing as she knelt beside her husband's corpse.

Gibson's story soon came under fire. A neighbor, awake on the night of the slayings, recalled none of the shouting and gunfire described so vividly by Gibson. The neighbor had spoken to Gibson on September 15 and recalled no mention of the crimes. Other acquaintances also described Gibson as a notorious liar. Reporters learned that Gibson had lied about her own marital status, describing herself as a minister's widow, when in fact her husband—toolmaker William Easton—was still alive and well. Defiant, Gibson declared that she had told reporters and detectives different stories of the crime, but that she would reveal the truth in court. In November she identified the triggerman as Henry Carpender, a cousin of Frances Hall and her brothers, but Carpender presented a solid alibi. On the night of the slaying he had dined with his wife and some friends until 10:30 P.M. A third grand jury convened on November 20, 1922, hearing 67 witnesses before it adjourned five days later, without indictments.

There the matter rested until July 3, 1926, when Arthur Riehl filed a petition for annulment of his 10-month marriage to Louise Geist, a former maid at the Hall residence in New Brunswick. Riehl wanted out of the union, he said, because his bride had lied to him about her knowledge of the Hall-Mills murders. Specifically, Riehl claimed that Geist had warned Frances Hall of her husband's plan to elope with Eleanor Mills, then accompanied Mrs. Hall and Willie Stevens to the murder scene, driven by the Halls' chauffeur. After the slayings, Riehl declared, Geist had been paid $5,000 to ensure her silence. Geist denied the story, echoed by the chauffeur, but newspapers ran with the story and Governor A. Harry Moore ordered a review of the case. Frances Hall was arrested for murder on July 28, while special prosecutor Alexander Simpson, a flamboyant state senator from Hudson County, reviewed the available evidence. Much of the evidence collected in 1922 was missing, but a grand jury still saw fit to indict Mrs. Hall, along with her two brothers and Henry Carpender. All pled not guilty, and Carpender filed a successful motion to have his trial held separately. A new autopsy was ordered for both victims, revealing that Eleanor Mills's tongue and larynx had been cut out by her killer.

Mrs. Hall and her brothers faced trial on November 3, 1926, before Judges Charles Parker and Frank Cleary. The state's primary evidence included a fingerprint from William Stevens, reportedly found on the business card left with Rev. Hall; the fact that Mrs. Hall had dyed a brown coat black after the murders; and a claim that her private detective had tried to bribe a key witness. Charlotte Mills, loving the limelight, was called to identify her mother's love letters. Witness Ralph Gosline claimed he had seen Henry

Stevens near the murder scene on September 14, 1922, and that Stevens had fired two warning shots to scare him away (thus contradicting the Pig Woman and others, who heard only four shots). Three fingerprint experts identified William Stevens's print from the business card, while defense experts refuted the identification. A former state trooper, Henry Dickman, claimed he left New Jersey in the midst of the original investigation after Henry Carpender paid him $2,500 to drop the case, but cross-examination revealed his recent incarceration at Alcatraz as a military deserter. Jane Gibson arrived in court on a stretcher, pleading ill health, but her testimony—yet another contradictory version of events—was interrupted when her own mother rose from the gallery and shouted, "She's a liar! Liar, liar, liar! That's what she is and what she's always been!"

Defense witnesses substantiated Henry Stevens's alibi for the night of the murder, while brother William and Frances Hall took the stand to deny any role in the crime. Testimony revealed that Jane Gibson had been unable to pick out the suspects upon her first viewing, and a neighbor, George Sipel, testified that Gibson had offered him cash to support her version of events. In all, jurors listened to 157 witnesses, then deliberated for five hours on December 3, 1926, before acquitting all three defendants. Prosecutor Simpson took the unusual step of calling for a mistrial on grounds of "jury misconduct," but his motion was denied. Henry Carpender was never tried, but he joined the other defendants in suing the *New York Daily Mirror* for libel. The case was settled out of court with an undisclosed payment.

Theories abound in the Hall-Mills murders, with suspects including the original defendants, James Mills, early suspect Clifford Hayes, or a professional assassin hired by Frances Hall. Long-shot candidates include an unnamed rival of Eleanor Mills for Rev. Hall's affections, an ex-lover of the slain adulteress (perhaps trial witness Ralph Gosline), or random highwaymen who may have surprised the lovers and killed them in a holdup gone wrong. Jane Gibson's many contradictory statements cast her as another dark-horse suspect, although she lacked any motive for killing the victims, and no evidence linking her to the crime was ever discovered. In 1964 author-attorney William Kunstler blamed Ku Klux Klan vigilantes for the slaying, presumably a part of the Klan's long campaign for "Christian morality," but once again no evidence or suspects were identified.

HALL, Edwin See NAHANNI VALLEY MURDERS

HAMMACK, Sharon See GRAND RAPIDS MURDERS

HAMPTON, Jason See WAYCROSS, GEORGIA, MURDERS

HAMPTON Rapist See MR. CRUEL

HARPER, Olga See "WEST SIDE RAPIST"

HARRY, Tonja See PORTLAND, OREGON, MURDERS

HARYONO, Martadinata murder victim (1998)
Martadinata Haryono, known to family and friends as "Ita," was the daughter of an Indonesian human rights activist, residing in Jakarta. She was 17 years old and still in high school in May 1998, when brutal riots left 1,200 victims dead and at least 168 ethnic Chinese women victimized by gang rape. That violence forced President Mohammed Suharto's resignation, but government aid for rape victims was not forthcoming. Ita Haryono was one of those who filled the gap, volunteering as a counselor for riot victims and pleading their case before the international community.

On October 6, 1998, Haryono's organization—the Volunteer Team for Humanity—held a press conference in Jakarta to announce that its members had received anonymous death threats. Ita and her mother were supposed to leave for the United States the following week, accompanying four riot victims to testify before Congress, but they never made it. On October 9, an intruder murdered Ita in her home, slashing her throat and inflicting 10 stab wounds in her chest, stomach, and right arm. Dr. Mun'im Idris told the state Antara news agency, "Her head was almost cut off at the throat."

Despite the previous death threats, Indonesian police declared that Ita's slaying was an "ordinary crime," committed by a drug addict whom she caught in the act of robbing her home. At the same time, authorities mounted a campaign of character assassination against Haryono, accusing her of sodomy and drug addiction, denying that the murder had any link to May's riots or Ita's work as a human rights advocate. The net result, according to civil rights campaigner Ester Indahyani Jusuf Lubis, was that "people will now be afraid to tell anyone what happened during the riots. This is terrorizing Indonesia's ethnic Chinese."

Albert Hasibuan, a leader of Indonesia's National Commission on Human Rights, agreed with that judgment when he publicly blamed Ita's murder on "the government and other parties" anxious to suppress reports of mass rapes in Jakarta. Subsequently, Lieutenant Colonel Imam Haryatna, head of Jakarta's central police precinct, reversed his department's original statement, announcing that robbery had been ruled out as a motive for Ita's slaying.

The ink was barely dry on that press release when officers arrested a neighbor of Ita's, a young man named Suryadi, who allegedly was found in possession of Ita's jewelry and some of her blood-stained clothing. Waffling once again, Major General Noegroho Djajoesman of the Indonesian army announced that Suryadi was a drug addict who "had planned the robbery long beforehand." Djajoesman's statement flatly contradicted those of Albert Hasibuan and Lieutenant Colonel Haryatna, denying any political motive for Haryono's death.

Virtually no one appears to believe the latest government story. Muslim opposition leaders in Jakarta now describe Haryono's slaying as a sign of the government's fatal decadence. Abdurrahman Wahid, head of the Nadhlatul Ulama Muslim group, told reporters and mourners, "The Indonesian nation is heading toward destruction, with all the rapes and the killing of a child." At press time for this volume, officials in Jakarta showed no further inclination to review the case.

HAUSER, Kaspar possible murder victim (1833)

The streets of Nuremberg, Germany, were nearly empty on May 26, 1828, as churchgoers celebrated the day after Pentecost. Georg Weickmann, a shoemaker residing in Unschlitt Square, immediately noticed the teenaged boy dressed in peasant garb who staggered past his home, appearing drunk or ill. Weickmann approached the youth, who offered him a sealed envelope addressed "To the Honourable Captain of the Cavalry of the Fourth Squadron, of the Sixth Regiment of the Light Cavalry in Nuremberg."

Surprised and impressed, Weickmann escorted the boy to the home of Captain von Wessenig, at the local guard tower. Servants informed him that the captain was out and asked him to wait. They offered Weickmann and the boy refreshments, but the youth spat out his beer and sausage, finally wolfing down a meal of black bread and water. Despite his healthy appetite, the youth wept miserably and pointed to his feet, as if they pained him. In response to varied questions, he said only, "I don't know," and "I would like to be a rider the way my father was." Finally, he was shown to the stables, where he lay down and went to sleep.

Upon returning home, Captain von Wessenig received word of his visitor and went to see the boy. Unable to communicate with him in words, von Wessenig opened the envelope addressed to him and found two letters inside. The first read:

From the Bavarian border, the place is not named, 1828
Honoured Captain,

I send you a lad who wishes to serve his king in the Army. He was brought to me on October 7th, 1812. I am but a poor laborer with children of my own to rear. His mother asked me to bring up the boy, and so I thought I would rear him as my own son. Since then, I have never let him go one step outside the house, so no one knows where he was reared. He, himself, does not know the name of the place or where it is.

You may question him, Honoured Captain, but he will not be able to tell you where I live. I brought him out at night. He cannot find his way back. He has not a penny, for I have nothing myself. If you do not keep him, you must strike him dead or hang him.

The second letter, dated 1812, allegedly came from the boy's anonymous mother. It read: "This child has been baptized. His name is Kaspar; you must give him his second name yourself. I ask you to take care of him. His father was a cavalry soldier. When he is seventeen, take him to Nuremberg, to the Sixth Cavalry Regiment: his father belonged to it. I beg you to keep him until he is seventeen. He was born on April 30th, 1812. I am a poor girl; I can't take care of him. His father is dead."

Captain von Wessenig took "Kaspar" to the Nuremberg police station, where officers recorded his description: 4 feet 9 inches tall, with curly brown hair, "fair and delicate" skin, soft hands, and badly blistered feet inside a pair of ill-fitting boots. Despite his peasant garb, one arm bore an apparent vaccination mark, rare enough in those days to suggest upper-class origins. The boy played with a coin he was given, repeatedly saying, "Horse! Horse!" When handed pen and paper, though, he wrote the name Kaspar Hauser "in firm, legible letters." Aside from the cryptic letters, he carried a handkerchief embroidered with the initials "H. K.," prayer beads, a key of unknown origin, a small envelope containing gold dust, and several religious tracts, including a pamphlet titled *The Art of Replacing Lost Time and Years Badly Spent.*

Uncertain what to do with him, police confined Kaspar in a jail in the Vestner Gate Tower for two months, while they attempted to research his background. In custody, he welcomed visitors but spurned all food aside from black bread and water. His reaction to simple objects such as candles and mirrors revealed near total ignorance of normal daily life. He distinguished men from women only by their clothing and referred to all species of animals as horse. Analysts determined that the two letters he carried had been written by the same hand, but beyond that point the trail went cold.

Judge Paul Johann Ritter von Feuerbach visited Kaspar on June 11, 1828, and subsequently provided a tutor, George Friedrich Daumer, the following month. Daumer commenced instruction in various subjects and also subjected Hauser to simple experiments. Feuerbach described one test: "When Professor Daumer held the north pole towards him, Kaspar put his hand to the pit of his stomach, and, drawing his waistcoat in an outward direction, said that it drew him thus; and that a current of air seemed to proceed from him. The south pole affected him less powerfully; and he said that it blew upon him."

Hauser's communication skills improved with practice, though he spoke German with an unspecified "foreign accent," while habitually referring to himself and others in the third person. He swiftly mastered horseback riding, but loud noises sent him into convulsions. Strong odors nauseated him, and the mere scent of wine proved intoxicating. Strong sensitivity to metals and magnets persisted, while static electricity from thunderstorms left Hauser writhing in pain. Against those handicaps, the youth displayed abnormally keen hearing and acute night-vision, sometimes reading the Bible aloud in a pitch-black room.

In 1829, Hauser wrote a personal memoir, claiming that he had been raised in a "cage" of some 120 cubic feet, within a closed room or shed where he never saw sunlight, surviving on a bread-and-water diet furnished by a keeper—known as "The Man"— who only approached him in darkness, insisting that Hauser keep his back turned. Sometimes he was drugged, waking to find his clothes changed, his hair and nails trimmed. His toys consisted of two wooden horses, a wooden dog, and red ribbons. On one occasion, when he proved too noisy, Hauser's jailer struck him with a stick, inflicting permanent scars on his right elbow. Of his release, Hauser remembered only being drugged and carried from his prison by The Man, dumped on the outskirts of Nuremberg.

On October 17, 1829, soon after local newspapers covered his autobiography, a stranger invaded George Daumer's home in the teacher's absence, slashing Hauser's forehead with a butcher knife. A blood trail marked Hauser's flight through the house, and Daumer found him in the cellar, muttering deliriously, "Why you kill me? I never did you anything. Not kill me! I beg not to be locked up. Never let me out of my prison—not kill me! You kill me before I understand what life is. You must tell me why you locked me up!"

Upon regaining his senses, Hauser described his assailant as a man with a black hat and black silk scarf hiding his face. He had recognized his former jailer's voice, when the man informed him, "You must die before you leave the city of Nuremberg." Neighbors recalled a man of similar description washing his hands in a water trough near Daumer's home. On October 21, a similar man returned to the neighborhood, asking questions about Hauser's condition, but he fled before police arrived.

In January 1830, Daumer's failing health and fears for Hauser's safety prompted a move to the home of Professor Johann Biberbach, where Hauser lived under police guard. On April 3 a pistol shot brought the guards to his room, where they found Hauser bleeding from another head wound. Hauser claimed that he had fallen from a chair while reaching for books on a high shelf, dislodging a pistol mounted on the wall that fell and accidentally discharged. Skeptics noted a recent quarrel between Hauser and Professor Biberbach's wife, who had complained of Kaspar's "horrendous mendacity" and "art of dissimulation," calling him "full of vanity and spite."

In May 1830, Hauser moved to the home of a Baron von Tucher, who sheltered him for the next 12 months, despite more complaints of Hauser's habitual lying. In May 1831, Hauser received a visit from a British aristocrat—Philip Henry, Lord Stanhope—who apparently believed that Hauser was the hereditary prince of Baden, born on September 29, 1812, who reportedly died after 18 days. Stanhope lavished gifts on Hauser, furnished money for his upkeep, and successfully applied for guardianship. Despite public promises that he would move Hauser to England, however, Stanhope soon lost interest in his charge, and in December 1831 left Hauser at Ansbach, 50 miles from Nuremberg, with tutor Johann Georg Meyer. Stanhope left Germany on January 9, 1832, and never saw Hauser again, although he continued financial support.

The change was not a happy one. Acquaintances described Dr. Meyer as a strict, mean-spirited man who seemed obsessed with Hauser's conversion to Meyer's brand of straitlaced Christianity. Hauser submitted to baptism, but never matched Meyer's religious zeal. He found work as a clerk in a local law office, but his relationship with Meyer suffered from incessant arguments.

Meanwhile, rumors of Hauser's supposed royal origins proliferated, spawning tales of intrigue and infants switched at birth. The stories intrigued Judge Feuerbach, who resumed his personal investigation of Hauser. Feuerbach came to believe that Hauser was the legitimate heir of the duke of Baden, son of Stéphanie de Beauharnais, the adopted daughter of Napoléon. In May 1832, Feuerbach wrote to Lord Stanhope, claiming that he possessed proof of that theory. A year later, on May 29, 1833, Feuerbach died while en route to discuss the matter with an informant named Klüber in Frankfurt. On his deathbed, he claimed that he had been poisoned on orders from Baden's royal family. Feuerbach's grandson later claimed that three more relatives were poisoned in similar fashion by royal assassins. Strangely, some sources claim that Feuerbach also left a note reading: "Kaspar Hauser is a smart scheming codger, a rogue, a good-for-nothing that ought to be killed."

On December 9, 1833, Hauser had one last raging quarrel with Johann Meyer. Five days later, Hauser lurched home with a wound in his chest, gasping, "Man . . . stabbed . . . knife . . . Hofgarten . . . gave purse . . . Go look quickly." Suspecting deception, Meyer delayed calling a doctor. By the time one was summoned and found that the wound had punctured Hauser's lung and liver, Hauser could not be saved.

Police went to the Hofgarten and found a single set of footprints in the snow. There was no murder weapon, but a black purse on the ground contained a note in *Spiegelschrift*, backward writing that could only be read with a mirror. It said: "Hauser will be able to tell you quite precisely how I look and from where I am. To spare him from this task I will tell you myself. I am from . . . on the Bavarian border . . . on the river . . . I even want to tell you the name: M.L.Ö."

Prior to his death on December 17, Hauser described the fateful afternoon. He had left work at noon, ate lunch, then visited a minister who had become his spiritual adviser. From there, Hauser told the minister that he was going to meet a young lady, but instead he went to the Hofgarten, lured by a stranger's promise of information about Hauser's mother. There, a bearded man in a black cloak had offered the purse, then drew a knife and attacked.

Hauser was buried in a rural cemetery, beneath a headstone reading: "Here lies Kaspar Hauser, riddle of his time. His birth was unknown, his death mysterious." A monument at the Hofgarten bore the legend: "Here a mysterious one was killed in a mysterious manner."

Some observers, however, dismissed any mystery, calling Hauser's death an "accidental suicide." They noted that grammatical errors in the *Spiegelschrift* note mirrored those common to Hauser's writing and cited deathbed statements that referred to "writing with a pencil." In his final moments, Hauser also muttered, "Many cats are the death of the mouse," and, "Tired, very tired, still have to take a long trip." Hauser's autopsy surgeon, Dr. Friedrich Wilhelm Heidenreich, disagreed, stating that Hauser's mortal wound was too large and deep to be self-inflicted. That postmortem also revealed signs of cerebral atrophy, though its significance remains unclear.

Following Hauser's death, Lord Stanhope mounted a campaign to discredit his own former claims about Kaspar's royal lineage. On December 26, 1833, Stanhope visited the prince of Öttingen-Wallerstein, Bavaria's minister of the interior, to argue that Hauser was a fraud. Subsequently, Stanhope also interviewed everyone still living in Nuremberg who had met Hauser, asking them to endorse his new theory. Finally, Stanhope embarked on an expensive—and seemingly pointless—tour of Europe, haranguing various public figures with his depiction of Hauser as a suicidal hoaxer. Predictably, those efforts only deepened the mystery surrounding Hauser's case.

Modern science took a crack at the enigma in 1996, when editors of the German magazine *Der Spiegel* acquired blood samples from clothing worn by Hauser on the day he was stabbed. DNA analysis was performed by experts at the University of Munich's Institute of Legal Medicine and Forensic Science Service in Birmingham, England. Comparison of Hauser's supposed DNA failed to match samples obtained from members of Baden's royal family, but the case still was not closed.

In 2002, the University of Münster's Institute of Legal Medicine procured locks of Hauser's hair and skin cells from his clothing, subjecting them to further DNA analysis. Six different samples proved to be identical—but all differed significantly from those tested in 1996. Results of that examination revealed a 95-percent match to the DNA of Astrid von Medinger, a known descendant of Stéphanie de Beauharnais, thus apparently confirming Hauser's royal ancestry.

HAWKINS, John Edward murder victim (2006)

A Houston, Texas, native born in November 1969, John Hawkins achieved fame as a rap singer under the stage names "Big Hawk" and "H.A.W.K." In 1994, with brother PATRICK HAWKINS (a.k.a. "Fat Pat") and fellow artist Robert Earl Davis Jr. (a.k.a. "DJ Screw"), Hawkins created the group D.E.A. and Dead End Records, named for the dead-end block of Houston's Martin Luther King Boulevard where the Hawkins brothers were raised. Also known collectively as the Screwed Up Click, D.E.A. released the rap album *Screwed for Life* in 1995.

Tragedy followed, beginning with the still-unsolved murder of "Fat Pat" in 1998 and DJ Screw's death from a drug overdose two years later. Between those events, other members of the Screwed Up Click were jailed on various charges, leaving Big Hawk alone to pursue what he called his "Ghetto Dream." His solo album, *Under Hawk's Wings*, was released in 2000, enhancing his local reputation while he collaborated with other rap artists for various concerts and recordings. In 2002, he released the self-titled *HAWK* album, from Game Face Records, with the single "U Already Know" premiering at number 45 on Billboard's list of top R&B and Rap Albums. Switching to Presidential Records thereafter, Hawkins released *A Bad Azz Mix Tape Vol. II* in 2003 and *Wreckin 2K4* in 2004.

In April 2006, Hawkins married longtime girlfriend Meshah Writa Ayana Henderson, with whom he already had two sons. Less than one month later, at 10:30 P.M. on May 1, he was gunned down on a Houston street by unknown assailants. Rumors persist that Hawkins was slain over a debt owed by his late brother, but police have not identified a suspect and the case remains unsolved.

HAWKINS, Patrick Lamont murder victim (1998)

Born in 1970, Texas rap singer Patrick "Fat Pat" Hawkins was the younger brother of JOHN EDWARD HAWKINS, known in the trade as "Big Hawk." They frequently performed together and were cofounders, with Robert "DJ Screw" Davis, of the Houston rap group Screwed Up Click. When not performing with his brother and Screwed Up Click, Hawkins appeared with fellow artists Willie D, Scarface, Lil' Keke, the Botany Boys, and South Park Mexican. Critics opined that Fat Pat would be the first Screwed Up Click member to enjoy national success, but his career was cut short at age 27—by murder.

On February 3, 1998, Hawkins went to collect an appearance fee from a Houston promoter's apartment. The man he meant to see was not at home, but someone else met Pat, shooting him dead in the hallway outside. Rumors suggest that he was slain over an unpaid debt—and that the same elusive cash may have resulted in his brother's unsolved slaying eight years later. Houston police spokesmen have no public opinion on the matter.

Wreckshop Records released Fat Pat's first solo album, *Ghetto Dreams*, two weeks after his death. A second album, *Throwed in Tha Game*, followed in June 2008. Fellow Texas rapper Paul Wall named his firstborn son in Fat Pat's honor, and lyrics by Hawkins still surface occasionally in recordings by other artists, such as Frazier "Trae" Thompson's hit single "Swang."

HAYNES, A. J. murder victim (1869)

A. J. Haynes served as a captain of the Arkansas state militia during that state's troubled Reconstruction era, following the Civil War. Violence by the Ku Klux Klan was so extreme in the Razorback State during the 1868 presidential campaign that Governor Powell Clayton declared martial law in the worst counties, thereby removing authority from local officials who were either allied with, or cowed by, the KKK. Capt. Haynes served in Crittenden County, under Col. E. M. Main, until martial law was lifted by executive order, on March 21, 1869. Shortly thereafter, pro-Klan Democrats announced their intent to file murder charges against Haynes and Main, relating to the deaths of several night riders killed during terrorist raids.

Legal maneuvers stalled the threatened indictments, and Haynes was soon beyond the reach of any earthly authority. One afternoon in July 1869 he was ambushed on a street corner in Marion, Arkansas, by 21-year-old Klansman Clarence Collier. Collier had fled Crittenden County to avoid arrest under martial law, but now he was back with a vengeance. Before Haynes recognized his danger, Collier shot him in the back with a double-barreled shotgun, then stood over his prostrate form and fired six shots from a revolver at close range. That done, Collier retrieved his coat from a nearby restaurant, mounted a horse tied outside, and rode out of town at a leisurely pace, unimpeded.

Collier was right not to fear arrest. While Marion authorities pretended to be baffled by the crime, the Memphis *Public Ledger* rhapsodized about the murder in an editorial published on July 21, 1869: "Gallant Clarence Collier! The blessings of an oppressed people go with you, and whenever the clouds lift you shall be known and honored throughout the lands [*sic*] as the William Tell of Crittenden County, Arkansas." It never came to that, in fact, but Collier was never arrested or charged with the crime. The public murder of Capt. Haynes is still officially unsolved in Arkansas.

HAYS, Andy   See NAHANNI VALLEY MURDERS

HELLER, Cindy   See FORT WORTH MURDERS

HELSEL, Chandra   See "INDEPENDENCE AVENUE KILLER"

HENDERSON, Cheryl   See MARYLAND MURDERS (1986–87)

HENDERSON, Margaret   See RIVERDELL HOSPITAL MURDERS

"HIGHWAY Killer(s)" Canada (1973–81)

For the best part of a decade, between 1973 and 1981, Canadian authorities were baffled by a series of unsolved sex-murders along the Trans-Canada Highway, spanning the provinces of Alberta and British Columbia. Victims ranged in age from 12 to 35, and while published sources could never agree on a body count (citing various totals from 11 to 33 victims), the most frequent tally lists 28 slayings spread over eight years. Many of the victims were apparently hitchhikers, sexually assaulted before they were beaten, strangled, or stabbed to death, with some of the bodies revealing postmortem mutilations.

Generally acknowledged as the first "highway" victim, 19-year-old Gale Weys was thumbing her way home to Kamloops, from a job in Clearwater, when she met her killer on October 19, 1973. Her nude, decomposing corpse was found a few miles south of Clearwater on April 6, 1974. By that time the killer had already claimed another victim, picking off 19-year-old Pamela Darlington at Kamloops, on November 6, 1973. Her body was fished out of the Thompson River the next day, and crewmen on a passing train reported sighting a man with "messy blonde hair" near the scene of the crime, but the vague description led detectives nowhere.

Colleen McMillan, age 16, was last seen alive on August 9, 1974, thumbing rides near Lake La Hache. A month later, her nude, decomposed remains were found some 35 miles away. Police suspected a drug addict, who confessed to the slaying and then recanted before committing suicide. The case remains officially unsolved.

On January 9, 1976, 16-year-old Pauline Brazeau was found stabbed to death, outside Calgary. Six months later, on July 1, 19-year-old Tera White disappeared from Banff, her skeletal remains discovered near Calgary in March 1981. Marie Goudreau, age 17, was murdered near Devon on August 2, 1976, and 20-year-old Melissa Rehorek was killed near Calgary on September 15, her body discarded 12 miles from the spot where Pauline Brazeau had been discovered.

Barbara McLean, age 26, traveled all the way from Nova Scotia to meet her death near Calgary, strangled by persons unknown on February 26, 1977. Fourteen-year-old Monica Jack disappeared while bicycling near Merritt, on May 6, 1978, and she has not been seen since, though her bike was found at the bottom of a highway embankment. On September 26, 1979, 12-year-old Susan Duff went biking near Pinticton and never returned, her body recovered from the outskirts of town on October 21. Marie Jamieson, age 17, vanished while hitchhiking near Davis Bay, on August 7, 1980; nine days later, when her body was discovered in some nearby woods, the cause of death was listed as asphyxiation. Victim Oanh Ha, a 19-year-old Vietnamese immigrant, was raped and strangled near Golden on February 28, 1981, her body mutilated posthumously. Two months later, on April 22, 15-year-old Kelly Cook was reported missing, her body found near Taber, Alberta, on June 29. The only male victim in the murder series, transvestite Frederick Savoy, was parading in drag when the killer apparently mistook him for a woman, knifing him to death in a Vancouver parking lot. Maureen Mosie, generally described as the last "highway" victim, was beaten to death at Kamloops on May 8, 1981.

Six months later, authorities convened a special summit meeting to discuss 33 of Canada's 200 unsolved murders, and while they generally agreed that they were seeking several killers—possibly as many as 18—in the "highway" series, no prime suspects were identified. A ray of hope broke through in 1983, with the marathon confessions of American serial killers Ottis Toole and Henry Lee Lucas, but no charges were filed against either, and both are now deceased. The long series of slayings in Canada remains unsolved.

HIGHWAY Murders Germany (1935)

In September 1935 authorities in Berlin were plagued by a sudden rash of unexplained violent crimes. While firefighters were kept busy with an outbreak of arson incidents, blamed on "malignant maniacs," other culprits were stretching taut wires across rural highways by night, wrecking cars and killing or injuring their occupants. Robbery was suspected in one or two of the cases, but for the most part victims were left unmolested after their vehicles crashed. According to newspaper reports, "The similarity of the method of fastening the wires leads the police to believe a maniac is the chief culprit."

Without motives or suspects, though, investigators could do little but stand by and watch as the body count rose. Berlin auto dealers were more resourceful,

cashing in on the panic while it lasted by offering their customers saw-toothed attachments for the front of their cars, designed to clip cables on impact. It is not recorded whether the devices worked or not, since the crimes apparently ended as suddenly as they began. No final body count was ever published, and the case was never solved.

HIKARI, Judith See "Astrological Murders"

HILBURN, Carol See "Astrological Murders"

HILL, Veronica See Atlanta "Lover's Lane" murders

HILLIARD, Derrick See Maryland gay murders (1996–97)

HINDMAN, Thomas Carmichael, Jr. murder victim (1868)

Thomas Hindman, Jr., personified America's antebellum southern gentry. His maternal ancestors included Major Robert Holt, a wealthy planter and member of Virginia's House of Burgesses in 1655. His paternal forebears were Scotsmen who fought at the Battle of Culloden in 1746, then emigrated to North America and settled at Knoxville, Tennessee. Hindman's father, Thomas Sr., served as a naval officer in the War of 1812 and fought at the Battle of New Orleans in 1815. Four years later, he married Sallie Holt, whose family he moved to Tennessee from Virginia, and their first son, Thomas Jr., was born in January 1828.

The family subsequently moved to Alabama, where Thomas Sr. earned a reputation for dealing fairly with Cherokee tribesmen and was named U.S. Agent for the Cherokee Nation by President James Monroe. In 1841, Thomas Sr. bought a Mississippi plantation and moved his family once more, while Thomas Jr. attended boarding schools in New York and New Jersey. By the time Thomas Jr. graduated with honors, in September 1843, his father was immersed in Mississippi politics as leader of the state's Whig Party.

During the Mexican-American War of 1846–48, Thomas Jr. joined the U.S. Army as a member of the

Second Mississippi Infantry. He missed the Battle of Buena Vista by one day in February 1847, then joined the long march into Mexico that saw 167 members of his troop die from disease or guerrilla attacks, while 38 others deserted. Hindman's brother Robert was discharged after contracting smallpox, but Thomas, Jr., stayed on to the end, released from service in 1848 with the rank of lieutenant and post adjutant.

Back in Mississippi, Hindman studied law, but his family's luck had soured. Brother Robert died in a duel with opponent William Falkner, who had blackballed Robert from membership in the local Sons of Temperance. Jurors acquitted Falkner of murder in that case and again after he killed a friend of the Hindman family. Thomas, Jr., subsequently faced Falkner in a shootout that left both men unscathed. With that feud behind him, Hindman served briefly in Mississippi's state legislature (1853–54), then moved to Helena, Arkansas, to practice law and pursue a political career.

A radical for his time, Hindman stood in opposition to the violently xenophobic Know-Nothing movement, whose members he publicly condemned as "pestilent fanatics." With law partner John Palmer, Hindman established a local Democratic association to oppose Know-Nothing bigotry. He also joined with colleagues Patrick Cleburne and William Weatherly to buy and run a newspaper, the *Democratic Star,* which roundly criticized Know-Nothings. That campaign led to a street fight that left both Hindman and Cleburne wounded by gunfire, but they survived and were cleared of all charges. Democratic triumph in the 1856 elections spelled the temporary end of Know-Nothing agitation in Arkansas.

By 1857, Hindman was the undisputed leader of the Arkansas Democratic Party and editor of the *Helena States-Rights Democrat.* Voters sent him to Congress in 1858, where he served until Arkansas seceded from the Union. Hindman zealously advocated secession and attended the state convention in May 1861 where Arkansas delegates approved departure from the Union by a vote of 65 to 5. By June, Hindman had organized 10 companies of rebel troops, but lost five of them when the recruits refused to fight outside of Arkansas. Hindman subsequently reported to General Robert E. Lee's command in Richmond, Virginia, and was promoted to the rank of brigadier general in September 1861.

His career as a rebel commander began badly, with the disastrous Kentucky campaign of early 1862, then suffered interruption with his wounding at the Battle of Shiloh. Upon recovery, Hindman was named commander of the Confederacy's Trans-Mississippi Department, seeking to forestall a Union invasion through harsh measures including conscription, guerrilla warfare, and requisition of supplies from southern farmers. Those measures angered many residents of Arkansas, who joined forces with Hindman's prewar political rivals to agitate for his replacement. Confederate president Jefferson Davis bowed to that pressure, replacing Hindman with incompetent successor Theophilus Holmes, while Hindman was posted to a field command in northern Arkansas. Wounded twice more, at the battles of Chickamauga (September 1863) and Kennesaw Mountain (June 1864), Hindman was incapacitated as a field commander and retired with his family to Texas.

At war's end, in April 1865, Hindman refused to surrender and led an exodus of Confederate refugees into Mexico, where he remained in exile for two years. April 1867 found him back in Arkansas, where he petitioned President Andrew Johnson for a pardon and was refused. Despite that setback, Hindman tried to resume his antebellum political career, opposing the measures of Radical Reconstruction that granted citizenship to former slaves. Others would triumph with that posture of defiance in the next decade, but for Hindman it proved an unfortunate choice.

At 9:30 P.M. on September 27, 1868, as Hindman sat reading a newspaper to his children in their Helena home, a volley of gunfire smashed the parlor window. Musket balls struck Hindman in the jaw, throat, and both hands, inflicting wounds that claimed his life through loss of blood eight hours later. Despite his mortal injuries, Hindman delivered a farewell speech to his neighbors with "perfect composure," admonishing them to "unite their courage and determination to bring peace to the people." As for his slaying, Hindman said, "I do not know who killed me; but I can say, whoever it was, I forgive him."

Hindman's killers were never identified, despite rumors linking his death to a recent debate against radical Arkansas governor Powell Clayton. In 1869, a white inmate in the Phillips County jail told police that he had heard two black prisoners—Sip Cameron and Heyward Grant—discussing Hindman's murder. According to the informant, Grant confessed participation in the slaying and described it as revenge for the Ku Klux Klan's lynching of black activist Lee Morrison in Helena, on the day Hindman was shot. White authorities investigated the claim and declined to charge Grant—proof positive, in that time and place, that the accusation carried no weight.

HINDS, James M. assassination victim (1868)

The presidential campaign of 1868 witnessed unprecedented violence in Reconstruction-era Arkansas, as members of the all-white Democratic Party teamed with night-riding terrorists of the Ku Klux Klan to "redeem" their state from the control of "radical" Republicans who favored equal rights for blacks. Conditions were such that Governor Powell Clayton felt obliged to declare martial law in several counties, replacing civil authorities with officers of the new state militia. Even then, mayhem continued nearly unabated in some districts, with more than 200 murders recorded in the three months preceding Election Day.

One of those victims was James Hinds, a native of Washington County, New York, born December

This *Harper's Weekly* cartoon depicts a Northern view of Southern politics, sparked by crimes like the murder of James Hinds. (Florida State Archives)

5, 1833. Hinds had migrated to Little Rock after the Civil War and won election to the U.S. House of Representatives. He was therefore doubly despised by Arkansas Klansmen as a Republican and a "carpetbagger." On October 22, 1868, while traveling to keep a political speaking engagement, Hinds was ambushed by assassins near Indian Bay in Monroe County. The burst of gunfire killed him instantly and injured a traveling companion, James Brooks, who managed to survive his wounds. White Democrats congratulated themselves on removing one more rival, and no suspects were ever identified in the slaying.

HINTERKAIFECK Murders (1922)

In 1922, a farm called Hinterkaifeck lay between the German towns of Ingolstadt and Schrobenhausen, 43 miles north of Munich. Sixty-three-year-old Andreas Gruber occupied the property with his 72-year-old wife Cäzilia; their widowed 35-year-old daughter Viktoria Gabriel; her children Cäzilia (age 7) and Josef (age 2); and Maria Baumgartner, a maid who joined the family on March 31, mere hours before grisly tragedy struck the homestead.

Andreas Gruber was unpopular with his neighbors, who regarded him as greedy and cantankerous. That reputation worsened when neighbors accused Gruber and daughter Viktoria of incest, speculating that Andreas had sired his own grandson, Josef. Josef's birth certificate named a neighbor, dubbed "L.S.," as his father, but the document failed to suppress local gossip.

The Grubers dropped from sight without explanation on Saturday, April 1, 1922. Young Cäzilia missed school that day, and none of the family attended church the following day, as was their habit. Cäzilia missed school again on April 3, while the local postman noted that Saturday's mail was still in the family's mailbox. He left new mail on a windowsill, when no one answered his knock. On April 4, a mechanic named Albert Hofner spent five hours at the Gruber farm, repairing a feeding machine, and left without seeing any member of the household.

Later on April 4, three neighbors visited the Gruber farm to see if something was amiss. They found the barn doors locked, and broke in to discover four bludgeoned corpses—Gruber, his wife, Viktoria, and daughter Cäzilia—hidden under straw and an old door. Josef Gruber and Maria Baumgartner lay dead in the farmhouse. A boy was dispatched on his bicycle, to the nearby village of Wangen, where he alerted the mayor. Police summoned from Munich reached the farm to find dozens of curiosity seekers milling around the property, contaminating the crime scene, even making snacks in the kitchen.

Despite that interference, and the primitive state of forensic science in 1922, investigators made certain conclusions about the murders. A court physician, Dr. Johann Baptist Aumüller, performed his autopsies in the Gruber barn on April 5, reporting that all six victims were slain with a pickaxe on the night of March 31–April 1. Young Cäzilia had survived for several hours after being wounded, tearing clumps of hair from her scalp as she lay dying in the barn, beside other corpses. Dr. Aumüller removed all six heads and sent them to Munich for further study—including an alleged examination by clairvoyants—but no further information was deduced.

Authorities surmised that the barn victims were lured to their deaths one by one, after which the slayer invaded the house to dispatch Josef and the maid. While robbery was first suspected, police changed their mind after finding large sums of cash undisturbed in the house. Neighbors also reported smoke rising from the Gruber chimney at various times after the victims were slain, and crime scene evidence suggested that their killer had remained at the farm for several days, eating Gruber's food, feeding his animals, and milking his cows.

While frightened villagers scoured the countryside with axes and pitchforks, seeking suspicious strangers, police collected information about the victims. Inspector Georg Reingruber, from Munich, learned that Andreas Gruber had complained to neighbors of mysterious events around the farm for weeks before the massacre. Maria Baumgartner's predecessor had quit her job six months earlier, saying that the Gruber farm was haunted, while Andreas spoke of footsteps in the attic, unfamiliar footprints in the snow, a strange newspaper left at the farm, and the disappearance of his keys. A neighbor offered his revolver to Andreas, for defense against intruders, but Gruber declined.

Inspector Reingruber's detectives questioned more than 100 suspects in the Hinterkaifeck slayings, both local residents and transients, but they charged no one. For reasons still unclear, mechanic Albert Hofner was not questioned until 1933. The last interrogation occurred in 1986, based on supposed new leads, but it also proved fruitless. An elderly woman approached police in 1999, claiming that her ex-landlord had claimed knowledge of the crimes in 1935, but without a live suspect the lead went nowhere.

The Hinterkaifeck victims were buried at Waidhofen, minus their heads, which remained in Munich as evidence and later vanished in the chaos of World War II. Gruber's farm buildings were leveled in 1923 and replaced with a memorial shrine. Reports that a pickaxe was found in the attic remain unverified.

Three published theories suggest solutions to the Hinterkaifeck slayings. One blames neighbor "L.S." for the crimes, noting that he allegedly sired Josef Gabriel, was the neighbor who offered Andreas Gruber a pistol during the weeks before murders, and was present at discovery of the corpses. Another tale theorizes that Viktoria's late husband, Karl Gabriel—reportedly killed on the Western Front in 1914, but never found—actually survived World War I and returned to slaughter the family upon finding that his wife had borne another man's child.

The last theory involves political extremists of the right or left, whose violence racked Germany from 1921 until 1933, when Adolf Hitler seized power and suppressed all opposition nationwide. Both Nazis and communists participated in 12 years of bloody guerrilla warfare, street fighting and assassination, including the murder of Foreign Minister Walter Rathenau in June 1922. No evidence links Andreas Gruber to either political wing, but theorists speculate that his isolated farm may have been an ideal hideout, meeting place, or arms repository for some militant group, prompting reprisals by opponents.

HODGES, Thomas See CHICAGO HOLDUP MURDERS (1992)

HOEY, Evelyn suspicious death (1935)

Minneapolis native Evelyn Hoey was born on December 15, 1910, and launched her hometown singing career at age 10. In 1928 she appeared on Broadway with Australian-born actor/comedian Leon Errol in *Yours Truly*, crossed the Atlantic to appear in the London production of *Good News*, and played Paris nightclubs in 1929. There, she met composer E. Ray Goetz, who signed her to play the torch singer in Cole Porter's musical comedy "Fifty Million Frenchmen." Hoey's other stage roles included performances in the

Vanderbilt Revue and S. J. Perelman's *Walk a Little Faster.* In 1930, Hoey appeared in the film *Leave It to Lester,* directed by Frank Cambria, costarring Lester Allen and Hal Thompson.

Hoey's promising career ended abruptly on September 11, 1935, when she was shot and killed at the Dowington, Pennsylvania, home of millionaire Henry Rogers III, grandson of former Standard Oil senior director Henry Rogers, Sr. Also present in the house when a single .45-caliber bullet drilled Hoey's skull were cinematographer William J. Kelley, chauffeur Frank Catalano, Japanese cook George Yamada, and a farmer who had come to collect his wages from Rogers. Hoey was shot in the bedroom where she had spent a week as Rogers's guest, then her corpse was transported to Dowington's morgue, and from there to West Chester's county hospital for postmortem examination.

Police initially held Rogers and Kelley under $2,500 bond on suspicion of murder, but a coroner's inquest discharged them after Catalano, Yamada, and the farmer corroborated claims that both men were in the mansion's living room when the fatal shot was fired upstairs. The coroner's jury returned an open verdict of suicide, but District Attorney William Parke was unsatisfied with that, convening a grand jury to examine the case in November 1935. Expanding beyond the mere facts of the crime, Parke charged the 22-member panel to investigate members of the original coroner's jury and their relationship with journalists who had covered Hoey's death.

The grand jury met on November 12 and questioned various witnesses, including Victor Andoga, Hoey's former singing coach from New York City. Andoga opined that Hoey had killed herself in a fit of depression over her failed love affair with a New York actor, coupled with fears that her voice was failing. He further claimed that she had traveled to Bermuda in 1934, planning to leap from the cruise ship and drown herself at sea, but subsequently lost her nerve.

The grand jury returned a verdict of suicide on November 18, 1935, but suspicion of foul play persists in Hoey's death, with Rogers and Kelley regarded as suspects by some theorists. Rogers had married a Cleveland physician's daughter in 1929, but he was estranged from his wife by 1935 and Hoey's presence in his home inspired rumors of an adulterous relationship leading to tragedy.

HOFFA, James Riddle   presumed murder victim (1975)

A native of Brazil, Indiana, born February 14, 1913, Jimmy Hoffa lost his father at age seven, whereupon his mother moved the family to Detroit. Hoffa dropped out of elementary school to work in a Kroger Company warehouse, and he led his first strike there at age 17. The labor action brought him into contact with Detroit racketeers, including members of the Mafia and future Las Vegas gambling mogul Moe Dalitz (with whom Hoffa reportedly shared a mistress). By 1933, when he became the business agent for Detroit Local 299 of the mob-dominated Teamster's Union, Hoffa was well acquainted with violence, kickbacks, payoffs, and sweetheart contracts. Underworld connections and a rough charisma helped Hoffa advance through the Teamster ranks. In the early 1940s he organized and led the Michigan Conference of Teamsters. In 1952 he was elected international vice presi-

Former union boss Jimmy Hoffa pulled a famous disappearing act in 1975. (Library of Congress)

166

President Richard Nixon released Hoffa from prison with the provision that he was barred from holding union office. (Library of Congress)

A year later, Teamsters renewed a longtime friendship with presidential candidate Richard Nixon. Heavy campaign contributions swayed Nixon toward leniency for Hoffa, but new Teamster president Frank Fitzsimmons feared loss of power when Hoffa returned to free society. Nixon, looking forward to his reelection campaign in 1972, struck a bargain with union leaders: He commuted Hoffa's prison term on Christmas Eve 1971, but the terms of Hoffa's release barred him holding any union office for the next 10 years. Furious, Hoffa filed lawsuits to invalidate the stipulation while working tirelessly behind the scenes, intent on seizing effective control of the union from Fitzsimmons.

On July 30, 1975, Hoffa went to lunch at the Machus Red Fox restaurant in Bloomfield Hills, a suburb of Detroit. He was expecting company—specifically Detroit mobster Anthony (Tony Jack) Giacalone and New Jersey Teamster boss Anthony (Tony Pro) Provenzano, another syndicate thug who had served time with Hoffa in federal prison. Hoffa telephoned his wife around 2:15 P.M. to report that his guests were late. Witnesses recall him sitting in a car outside the restaurant, but they were vague on times and whether Hoffa was alone. His car was found unlocked in the restaurant parking lot on July

dent of the union, and five years later he took control from disgraced Teamster president Dave Beck (imprisoned for skimming $370,000 from the Western Conference of Teamsters).

Promotion made Hoffa a prime target for investigators, chief among them ROBERT KENNEDY, head counsel for the U.S. Senate Select Committee on Improper Activities in the Labor or Management Field. Hoffa and Kennedy publicly clashed for the first time in 1957, igniting a blood feud that may have climaxed six years later, with the murder of President JOHN KENNEDY in Dallas. Upon becoming U.S. attorney general in 1961, Robert Kennedy created a special "Get Hoffa" squad in the Justice Department, sparing no effort to convict the Teamster president. Hoffa was indicted for extortion, but the case ended with a hung jury in 1962. Kennedy next charged Hoffa with jury tampering in that case, with additional charges of embezzling $1.7 million in union funds. Conviction on those charges earned Hoffa an eight-year prison term in 1964, but appeals stalled his incarceration until 1967.

Teamsters boss Frank Fitzsimmons made the deal with Nixon to protect himself from Hoffa's return to power in the union. (Library of Congress)

31, and relatives filed a missing-person report with the Bloomfield police. FBI agents took charge of the case two days later and obtained a search warrant for Hoffa's car on August 8, 1975. That search revealed fingerprints from Hoffa's "foster son," Teamster Charles O'Brien, on a soda bottle under the passenger's seat and on papers found in the glove compartment. Two weeks later, tracking dogs allegedly found Hoffa's scent in the backseat of a car O'Brien had borrowed from Joe Giacalone (son of Tony Pro). A grand jury convened on September 2, 1975, but failed to indict any suspects in Hoffa's disappearance.

Over the next decade 200 G-men were assigned to Hoffa's case, filing some 16,000 pages of reports. Six suspects in the disappearance were convicted on unrelated charges, including Tony Giacalone and Provenzano (who died in prison while serving time for another murder). Hoffa was declared legally dead in 1982, around the same time that self-described contract killer Charles Allen told Senate investigators that Hoffa was killed on Provenzano's orders, his corpse "ground up in little pieces, shipped to Florida and thrown into a swamp." Seven years later, another confessed hit man, Donald (Tony the Greek) Frankos, claimed Hoffa was buried under Giants Stadium in East Rutherford, New Jersey, but G-men checked the lead and pronounced it false. Kenneth Walton, head of the FBI's Detroit field office from 1985 to 1988, told reporters in 1989, "I'm comfortable I know who did it, but it's never going to be prosecuted because . . . we would have to divulge informants, confidential sources."

That judgment seemed to be reversed in November 2000, when past and present FBI agents met with U.S. attorneys in Detroit to discuss prosecutorial strategies and the state of the bureau's investigation. A second meeting was convened in March 2001, after DNA tests matched hairs from Hoffa's hairbrush to a hair found in the backseat of Charles O'Brien's car. Agent John Bell, head of the FBI's Detroit office, referred the case to Oakland County prosecutors for possible action in March 2002, but the results were disappointing. On August 29, 2002, prosecutor David Gorcyca announced that the DNA evidence found in O'Brien's car was insufficient to support criminal charges. A 2004 book *I Heard You Paint Houses* by Charles Brandt claimed to solve the Hoffa mystery based on the "deathbed" confession of Hoffa friend Frank "The Irishman" Sheeran.

HOLLIS, Jimmy See Texarkana "Phantom Gunman"

HOLLOWAY, Natalee Ann missing person (2005)

Natalee Holloway was born in Mississippi on October 21, 1986, but her family later moved to Mountain Brook, Alabama, where she attended high school. She graduated on May 24, 2005, and embarked with 124 classmates on an unofficial senior class graduation trip to the Caribbean island of Aruba, off the northern coast of Venezuela. She was last seen around 1:30 A.M. on May 30, in the town of Oranjestad, leaving the Carlos'n Charlie's nightclub with three young men: 17-year-old Dutch student Joran Van der Sloot and two brothers from Suriname, Deepak and Satish Kalpoe. A witness watched the four climb into Deepak Kalpoe's car, and Natalee was never seen again.

Holloway missed her return flight to the United States later in the morning of May 30, and a search of her hotel room revealed her passport and packed luggage. When Natalee failed to arrive or call home, Natalee's mother and stepfather, Beth and George Twitty, chartered a jet to Aruba the same day. Within four hours of arrival on the island, they identified Joran Van der Sloot, supplying police with his name and address. Confronted by detectives, Van der Sloot initially denied knowing Natalee, then changed his story and joined Deepak Kalpoe to make a joint statement.

Van der Sloot and Kalpoe claimed that they drove Natalee from Carlos'n Charlie's to Arashi Beach at her request to look for sharks, then dropped her back at her hotel around 2:00 A.M. on May 30. Both claimed that she fell while stepping from the car, but refused Van der Sloot's assistance. Driving away, the pair said they had seen a man in a black shirt, resembling a security guard's uniform, approach Natalee on the sidewalk.

Over the next few days, thousands of volunteers joined in the search for Natalee, including 50 Dutch marines and countless Arubans granted time off from work to join in the sweep. Aruban banks donated $20,000 to support the effort, while Beth Twitty received free lodging in Natalee's room at the Holiday Inn, subsequently upgraded to the Wyndam Hotel's presidential suite. Police examined a suspected bloodstain in Deepak Kalpoe's car, then reported that it was not blood.

On June 2, Beth Twitty received a telephone call from a woman who refused to identify herself, claim-

KIDNAPPED

LAST SEEN AT CARLOS & CHARLIES
MONDAY, MAY 29, 2005 1:30AM
NATALEE HOLLOWAY
CAUCASIAN AMERICAN FEMALE
BLUE EYES / LONG BLOND HAIR
5'4" 110 LBS.   18 YEARS OLD

ANY INFORMATION
PLEASE CALL 587-6222
OR CALL POLICE STATION 100

This poster, prepared and released by the Holloway family, was part of a massive search effort for Natalee Holloway, who went missing in Aruba in May 2005. (AP Photo/Holloway Family)

ing knowledge of Natalee's whereabouts, stating that Natalee was well but refused to speak with her mother. The caller claimed that Natalee was hiding in a local drug house, but demanded $4,000 for further details. Julia Renfro, American owner of the newspaper *Aruba Today,* visited the drug house but later told *Vanity Fair* that George Twitty had been there before her, creating "uproar and panic" that spoiled any chance of finding Natalee.

On June 5, Aruban police detained two security guards from the Allegro Hotel, located close to the Holiday Inn. Suspects Antonius John and Abraham Jones allegedly spent their time "trolling" hotels for women, but both were released on June 13, with no charges filed. Meanwhile, on June 9, Joran Van der Sloot and the Kalpoe brothers were jailed on suspicion of murdering Natalee. Two days later, David Cruz, a spokesman for Aruba's Minister of Justice, announced that Natalee was dead and that police knew where to find her body. Within hours, Cruz recanted that

statement, complaining that he had fallen prey to a "misinformation campaign." That same night, Police Commissioner Gerold Dompig told reporters that one of the suspects in custody had confessed that "something bad" happened to Natalee after their drive to Arashi Beach. Dompig said the unnamed man was leading officers to the crime scene, but Justice Minister Rudy Croes contradicted that claim on June 12, dismissing claims of a confession as a rumor.

On June 17, 2005, police jailed a fourth man, disc jockey Steve Croes (no relation to Aruba's Justice Minister), "based on information from one of the other three detainees." Five days later, officers arrested lawyer Paulus Van der Sloot, Joran's father, then released him and Steve Croes without charges on June 26. During that flurry of arrests, the Kalpoes and Joran Van der Sloot changed their stories, now claiming that the brothers had dropped Joran and Natalee at a beach near the Marriott Hotel. Joran added that he had left Natalee there, unharmed, and walked home alone, receiving a text message from Natalee 40 minutes later.

As if that switch were not confusing enough, Van der Sloot offered police a *third* tale, claiming that the Kalpoes had driven him home, then drove off together with Natalee. Commissioner Dompig dismissed that statement, telling reporters, "This latest story [came] when he saw the other guys, the Kalpoes, were kind of finger-pointing in his direction, and he wanted to screw them also, by saying he was dropped off. But that story doesn't check out at all. He just wanted to screw Deepak. They had great arguments about this in front of the judge. Because their stories didn't match. This girl, she was from Alabama, she's not going to stay in the car with two black kids. We believe the second story, that they were dropped off by the Marriott."

The judge in question released both Kalpoes on July 4, while ordering Van der Sloot held for another 60 days. That same morning, three Dutch fighter planes fitted with infrared sensors joined the search for Holloway, but found nothing. Employing every high-tech tool at their disposal, police also reviewed satellite photos of Aruba, seeking potential grave sites, but the effort produced no results.

Beth Twitty condemned the Kalpoes' release, stating that both were "involved in a violent crime against my daughter." Her remarks sparked protest demonstrations and a threat of litigation from Satish Kalpoe's lawyer, whereupon Twitty apologized "to the Aruban people and to the Aruban authorities if I or my family offended you in any way." Twitty later said that her accusation was based, in part, on a videotaped interview with Deepak Kalpoe, conducted by private investigator Jamie Skeeters. In that conversation, Skeeters asked Kalpoe if Natalee had engaged in sex with the three suspects, whereupon Kalpoe replied, "She did. You'd be surprised how easy it was."

By July 25, 2005, rewards for solution of Natalee's disappearance totaled $1 million, with $100,000 offered for recovery of her remains (increased to $250,000 the following month). On July 27, police began draining a pond at the Aruba Racquet Club, near the Marriott beach, after an informant dubbed "the gardener" claimed he had seen Joran Van der Sloot and the Kalpoes on the property between 2:30 and 3:00 A.M. on May 30. Simultaneously, another witness ("the jogger") directed officers to landfill where he allegedly saw three men planting a blond-haired corpse the same night. Despite assistance from FBI agents and specially trained cadaver dogs, neither search produced any useful evidence.

On August 26, police rearrested the Kalpoes, along with new suspect Freddy Arambatzis, a friend of the brothers and Van der Sloot. Officers suspected Arambatzis of molesting and photographing an unnamed female minor prior to Holloway's disappearance, suggesting that Van der Sloot and the Kalpoes were somehow involved. Van der Sloot's mother called the arrests "a desperate attempt to get the boys to talk," and Commissioner Dompig later admitted as much. No confessions were forthcoming. A judge released all four prisoners on September 3, over objections from the prosecution. On September 14, the Combined Appeals Court of the Netherlands Antilles and Aruba removed all travel restrictions on Van der Sloot and the Kalpoes.

One day later, on September 15, TV's syndicated *Dr. Phil* show featured Holloway's case and aired the supposed Skeeters videotape indicating that Natalee had sex with the three suspects in her disappearance. Dutch forensics experts subsequently charged that the tape had been "manipulated" to misrepresent Deepak Kalpoe's remarks to Skeeter. In fact, the authorities said, Kalpoe had answered Skeeter's question by saying: "No, she didn't. You'd be surprised how simple it would have been."

On November 8, 2005, the Twittys joined Alabama governor Bob Riley for a press conference urging all citizens of the state to boycott Aruba. The governors of Arkansas and Georgia joined in that campaign, as did Alabama's senators, a congressman, and the city council of Philadelphia, Pennsylvania. Aruban officials and leaders of the tourist industry retaliated with formation of an "Aruba Strategic Communications Task Force" to combat the bad publicity. Two days after the Alabama press conference, Paulus Van der Sloot won a judgment for unjust detention against Aruban police. His claim for monetary damages, while initially successful, was quashed on appeal by the government.

Back in the United States, G-men began the laborious process of questioning Natalee's classmates in January 2006, while Aruban police continued their fruitless search for her corpse. Joran Van der Sloot granted television interviews in March, claiming that Natalee had asked him for sex on the night of May 30, but he declined for lack of a condom and left her alone on the Marriott beach. On March 25, Commissioner Dompig told CBS News that he believed Natalee had died from a self-inflicted overdose of drugs or liquor, and that someone had concealed her body later, to avoid trouble.

On April 15, 2006, Aruban police jailed new suspect Geoffrey von Cromvoirt on charges of selling illegal drugs, which prosecutors claimed "might be" related to Holloway's disappearance. Another alleged suspect, identified only as "A.B.," was arrested on April 22, then released the same day. Von Cromvoirt was freed without charges on April 25. May 17 found yet another suspect—Guido Wever, son of a retired Aruban politician—detained in Holland as a suspected accomplice in Natalee's kidnap-murder. Police in Utrecht questioned him for six days, then released him without filing any charges.

At the request of Aruban authorities, officers of the Dutch National Police Agency assumed command of the Holloway case in September 2006. Three months later, the Kalpoe brothers sued Dr. Phil McGraw and Jamie Skeeters for libel and slander, in Los Angeles. Beth Twitty and ex-husband Dave Holloway fired back with a wrongful-death case against the Kalpoes, also in L.A. (dismissed in June 2007 for improper jurisdiction). Skeeters died in January 2007, but the case against Dr. Phil remained pending at press time for this book.

Natalee Holloway remained missing, but the case continued to spark controversy during 2007. Joran Van der Sloot published a book, *The Case of Natalee Holloway,* in April, apologizing for various false statements but reaffirming his innocence. Beth Twitty and husband George divorced in that same month, while

Dutch National Police began their formal investigation on Aruba. On April 27 detectives searched the Van der Sloots' home on the island, seizing diaries and a personal computer, which were later returned. Next, searchers visited the Kalpoe brothers on May 12, saying that their purpose was to "get a better image of the place or circumstances where an offense may have been committed and to understand the chain of events leading to the offense."

On November 21, 2007, citing unspecified new evidence, officers rearrested Joran Van der Sloot and the Kalpoe brothers on suspicion of "manslaughter and causing serious bodily harm that resulted in the death of Holloway." Dutch police returned Van der Sloot to Aruba, where he was jailed with the brothers already held there. Nine days later, in a familiar scene, the court ordered jailers to release the Kalpoes, once again over objections from the prosecution. The state's appeal of that ruling was denied on December 5, with the court opining that "the file against the suspect [sic] does not contain direct indications that Natalee passed away due to a violent crime." Van der Sloot was freed once again on December 7, for lack of evidence that any crime had been committed. Prosecutor Hans Mos officially closed the Holloway case on December 18, 2007, while proclaiming that authorities had "a continuing" interest in the Kalpoes and Van der Sloot.

On January 31, 2008, Dutch journalist Peter de Vries announced that he had solved the case and would "tell all" for TV cameras in three days. Other reporters scooped him on February 1, writing that Joran Van der Sloot had issued a "confession" in Natalee's case. Van der Sloot fired back with claims that he had been secretly filmed while telling some person "what he wanted to hear," but insisted once more that he had no knowledge of Natalee's fate. Back in Aruba, that same day, prosecutors declared that they had reopened the case.

The de Vries exposé, aired on February 3, featured videotape of Van der Sloot talking to ex-convict Patrick van der Eem while they smoked marijuana. On that tape, Van der Sloot said that Natalee had passed out in his presence, on May 30, 2005, and he had been unable to revive her. The suspect claimed that a friend, called "Daury," had helped him dispose of Natalee's corpse. Daury, in turn, denied any part in the crime, saying that he had been at school in Rotterdam when Holloway vanished.

Van der Sloot met with Aruban prosecutors in the Netherlands, on February 8, after an Aruban judge denied pleas for a new arrest warrant. Van der Sloot admitted making the recent videotape, but once more dismissed his comments as lies. Prosecutors lost their appeal for a new arrest warrant on February 14. Days later, Aruban TV reporters secretly taped Patrick van der Eem's admission that he hoped to become a millionaire by tricking Van der Sloot into confessing.

As this work went to press, Natalee Holloway remained missing and presumed dead. Her case is still officially unsolved.

HOLSTER, Ira   See RIVERDELL HOSPITAL MURDERS

"HONOLULU Strangler" serial murderer (1985–86)

It was perhaps inevitable that America's vacation paradise should ultimately share the notoriety of other states where random killers have made headlines, claiming one innocent victim after another while police stand baffled on the sidelines. Still, Hawaii avoided the plague longer than most states, perhaps due in part to its geographic isolation from the mainland. Unfortunately, unlike their fictional counterparts on *Hawaii Five-O*, detectives in Honolulu have yet to identify the slayer in their midst, nearly two decades later.

Twenty-five-year-old Vicky Purdy was the first to die. A twice-married housewife, employed at a local video shop, she was kidnapped and strangled by persons unknown on May 29, 1985. When found, Purdy still wore her jumpsuit and jewelry, with no indications of robbery or sexual assault.

On January 15, 1986, 17-year-old Regina Sakamoto vanished on her way to school, moments after phoning her boyfriend to say she had just missed her bus. Strangled and raped, her partially nude body was fished out of Keehi Lagoon a month later.

Denise Hughes, a 21-year-old navy wife, failed to report for her regular job on January 30, 1986. Listed as a missing person, she was found in a drainage canal on February 1, strangled to death, hands bound behind her, her body wrapped in a blue plastic tarp.

Two months later, on March 26, the killer claimed 25-year-old Louise Medeiros, a single mother three months pregnant at the time she died. Ambushed en route to her boyfriend's apartment, Medeiros was found dead on April 2, hands tied behind her back, wearing only a blouse. Authorities have not released the cause of death.

Linda Pesce, age 36, was last seen alive on April 29, 1986, reported missing by her roommate the following day. On May 3 her body was found at Sand Island, arms bound behind her back, the cause of death once more remaining secret at the wish of homicide investigators who insist one killer is responsible for all five murders.

A profile of the unknown slayer, prepared by FBI agents, describes him as a white man in his late thirties or early forties, driving a light-colored cargo van. Six days after Linda Pesce's body was found, Honolulu officers detained a 43-year-old suspect for questioning, but he was released without charges after 10 hours of interrogation. At press time, the case remains open, with no arrest in sight.

HOPE, Edward   See San Diego gay murders

HORN, Jack   See Bell, California, murders

HORSE mutilations

Since the early 19th century, farmers in Great Britain and the United States have reported strange cases of livestock deaths and mutilations, often occurring in waves that claim dozens of animals under mysterious circumstances. Sheep were the most common victims in Britain and Ireland between 1810 and 1905, with dogs or wolves typically blamed (even though woolly victims were often drained of blood but otherwise uninjured). In the 1960s and 1970s hundreds of U.S. cattle mutilations were reported, with ranchers again citing evidence of bloodless corpses, some with the eyes, udders, and genitalia cleanly excised. While frightened locals spoke of UFOs, black helicopters, and satanic cults, an official report from New Mexico district attorney Ken Rommel blamed most of the mutilations on natural predators.

The same cannot be said in England, where a disturbing series of horse mutilations has been documented over the past century. According to Fort's *Wild Talents,* the earliest known attacks occurred in 1903, blamed on a Hindu attorney named George Edalji, who received a seven-year prison sentence for the crimes. (Today it appears that Edalji was probably an innocent victim of racial prejudice.) Four more horses were slashed around Wyrley and Breenwood in 1907, with the culprit (or culprits) unidentified, and similar crimes have continued throughout the United Kingdom to the present day.

Fortean Times, a journal of the unexplained named in honor of Charles Fort, published a four-year tabulation of British horse "rippings" in January 1997. The tally for 1993–96 included 131 animals attacked with knives; 73 killed in arson incidents; seven assaulted with blunt instruments; six sexually assaulted by humans; five smeared with paint; three poisoned; two shot; and one each injured or killed in incidents of stoning, strangling, acid hurling, and assault by crossbow. A total of five suspects were identified in the four-year string of incidents targeting 231 horses.

No more recent tabulation is available for horse mutilations in Britain, but similar attacks for the same period were reported in the United States (six cases in Maryland between June and October 1993, with more reported from Virginia; two horses with their tongues cut out at Redmond, Washington, in October 1994); at Canberra, Australia (a bisected horse carcass found in an abandoned laboratory building, surrounded by occult graffiti, in November 1995); at Pisa, Italy (four horses, February 1996); and in Germany (89 animals killed and 229 injured by "horse rippers" between 1992 and 1996). Attacks around the world continue to the present day, with multiple incidents reported from Calgary, Alberta, in April 2001 and around Melbourne, Australia, two months later.

HOSPITAL for Sick Children Canada (1980–83)

Between June 1980 and March 1981 the cardiac ward at Toronto's Hospital for Sick Children experienced a traumatic 616 percent leap in infant mortality, with the number of actual deaths pegged between 21 and 43 babies in various police and media reports. The first suspicious death was that of 18-day-old Laura Woodstock, lost on June 30, 1980. Two months later, after 20 deaths, a group of nurses on the ward voiced their concern to resident cardiologists, and a fruitless investigation was launched on September 5 in the interest of resolving "morale problems."

Still the deaths continued, and a staff physician aired his personal suspicions in a conversation with Toronto's coroner, on March 12, 1981. An autopsy of the latest victim, 27-day-old Kevin Garnett, found 13 times the normal level of digoxin, a drug used to regulate heart rhythm (itself fatal if taken in too large a dose). On March 21, after more deaths and discovery of elevated digoxin levels in two more corpses, the coroner met with police and hospital administrators in an emergency session. Members of the cardiac nursing team were placed on three days' leave while officers began to search their lockers, comparing work schedules to the dates and times of suspicious deaths.

On March 22, 1981, with the locker searches under way, another baby died on the cardiac ward at Sick Children. Justin Cook is generally named as the last victim in a bizarre string of slayings, his death attributed to a massive digoxin overdose inflicted by persons unknown. Three days later, police arrested nurse Susan Nelles on one count of murder, adding three identical charges to the list on March 27. As evidence of her involvement in the crimes, officers referred to certain "odd" remarks and facial expressions mentioned by other nurses, further noting that 24 of the suspicious deaths occurred on Nelles's shift, between 1:00 and 5:00 A.M.

With Nelles on leave pending trial, bizarre events continued at the hospital. In September 1981, nurse Phyllis Trayner found capsules of propranolol (another heart regulator) in her salad, at the hospital cafeteria, and a second nurse spooned more capsules out of her soup. Administrators had no explanations for those incidents, and rumors flourished of a "phantom" or a "maniac" stalking the hospital corridors.

A preliminary hearing in the case of Susan Nelles opened on January 11, 1982, with prosecutors citing 16 other carbon copy murders in addition to the four already charged. Four months later, on May 21, the pending charges were unconditionally dismissed, the presiding judge describing Nelles as "an excellent nurse" with "an excellent record." At the same time, he noted that five of the hospital deaths were apparently murders, committed by persons unknown.

Fresh out of suspects, the state launched its first judicial probe of the case on May 25, 1982, requesting assistance from the Atlanta-based Centers for Disease Control four months later. The CDC's report on 36 submitted cases called 18 of the deaths "suspicious," with seven listed as probable homicides; another 10 cases were deemed "consistent" with deliberate digoxin poisoning, but there was insufficient evidence for a definitive conclusion.

A new judicial inquiry was ordered on April 21, 1983, and six-month-old Gary Murphy died on the cardiac ward two days later, his passing notable for "elevated digoxin levels" found in postmortem testing. Murphy's death was excluded from the "official" victims' list when hearings began on June 21, 1983, with testimony pointing vaguely toward a different suspect on the hospital staff. By February 1984 cardiac

nurses were voicing suspicions against Phyllis Trayner, one reporting that she saw Trayner inject infant Allana Miller's I.V. bottle with an unknown drug three hours before the girl died, on March 21, 1981. Trayner flatly denied all charges of impropriety, and the commission left her denials unchallenged, refusing to name a suspect in its January 1985 report. That document described eight infant deaths as murders, while another 13 were listed as "highly suspicious" or merely "suspicious." A quarter century later, a solution in the case seems improbable at best.

HOUSMAN, Angie   See ST. LOUIS MURDERS

HOUSTON, Texas decapitation murders (1979)
Residents of Houston, Texas, are accustomed to reports of violent death, but nothing in their past experience prepared them for the string of crimes that dominated headlines in the latter part of 1979. Between the last week of July and first week of October, four lives were extinguished by a killer who seemed bent on claiming human heads as trophies of the hunt. Despite sensational publicity surrounding the attacks, the case remains unsolved today.

The first slaying occurred in southwest Houston, with a female victim beheaded in her own apartment on July 27, 1979. Investigators had not found her head by August 10, when yet another victim was discovered, spared complete decapitation when her killer was disturbed and frightened from the scene.

Five blocks away from the last murder site, residents of the neighborhood adjoining Freed Park were roused from sleep by screams and gunshots in the late-night hours of October 3, 1979. Police responded to the call but found no evidence of any crime in progress. Daylight on October 4 would lead them to the body of 16-year-old Jean Huffman, shot to death and dumped beside a picnic table with her jeans unzipped. Nearby, her boyfriend's car was found abandoned on a used-car lot, the headless body of its owner, 18-year-old Robert Spangenberger, locked inside the trunk.

No trace of either missing head has yet been found in Houston, and police hesitate to link the unsolved slayings, despite the geographic and forensic similarities. The killer's motive and identity remain unknown.

HUFFMAN, Jean   See HOUSTON DECAPITATION MURDERS

HUGHES, Denise See "Honolulu Strangler"

HUISENTRUIT, Jodi Sue missing person (1995)

Minnesota native Jodi Huisentruit was born at Long Prairie on June 5, 1968. She excelled at golf in high school, winning statewide Class A tournaments in 1985 and 1986, then moved on to St. Cloud State University. In 1990, Huisentruit earned her bachelor's degree in television broadcasting and speech communication, working briefly for Northwest Airlines before she took a job at KGAN-TV, Channel 2, in Cedar Rapids, Iowa. She subsequently worked for KSAX-TV in Alexandria, Minnesota, then for KIMT-TV, Channel 3, in Mason City, Iowa.

Huisentruit was employed as KIMT's news anchor when she vanished on her way to work, in the pre-dawn hours of June 27, 1995. Before leaving home that morning, she spoke by telephone with KIMT producer Amy Kuns, at 4:00 A.M. When Huisentruit had not reached the station two hours later, Kuns filled in for her on the station's *Daybreak* show, then called police when the program ended at 7:00 A.M. Officers drove to Huisentruit's apartment, where they found her car still in the parking lot. Scattered around the vehicle lay car keys, earrings, a woman's red dress shoes, a blow drier and a bottle of hair spray. Neighbors recalled hearing an early-morning scream, but had not bothered to investigate. Detectives subsequently announced their search for a white Ford Econoline van, mid-1980s vintage, but did not reveal their source of information.

Exhaustive searches failed to uncover any further trace of Jodi Huisentruit. Occasional discovery of decomposed remains over the next year sparked renewed interest in the case, but some of those remains belonged to animals and none of the human corpses was Huisentruit's. In December 2006 a woman told KIMT that she had witnessed Huisentruit's murder by six unknown men in 1995, when she (the witness) was a 13-year-old runaway. Mason City police questioned the woman, who recanted her statement.

In June 2008, the Mason City *Globe Gazette* received Huisentruit's 84-page diary in the mail. The envelope was postmarked from Waterloo, Iowa, on June 4 and bore no return address. Detectives jumped on the lead, and soon identified the sender as Cheryl Ellingson, wife of ex-police chief David Ellingson. Cheryl admitted mailing the diary, saying that she found it at home while preparing to move and "decided to share it with the *Globe Gazette*." While disconcerted by the leak, police declared that Ellingson had committed no crime by mailing the diary. Department spokesmen issued a release, reading: "The primary concern over the release of the diary has continued to be the compromising of the investigation into the disappearance of Jodi Huisentruit. Regardless of Cheryl Ellingson's motive or the *Globe Gazette's* interest in printing the diary, no credible leads have yet resulted." Officers searched Ellingson's home and found "no other reports or records which could further compromise the Huisentruit investigation or any other police investigation."

Jodi Huisentruit remained missing as this book went to press. No suspects in her case have been identified.

HUME, Margaret See Battle Creek murders

HUMPHRIES, Ban murder victim (1868)

A former slave and post-Civil War Republican activist in Reconstruction-era White County, Arkansas, Ban Humphries was one of 200-plus victims murdered by terrorists during the three months prior to 1868's presidential election. Governor Powell Clayton, despised as a "radical" Republican by the state's white-supremacist Democrats, employed private investigator Albert Parker to investigate the Humphries murder and the attempted assassination of State Senator Stephen Wheeler. Parker suspected members of the Searcy, Arkansas, Ku Klux Klan chapter led by "cyclops" John McCauley, but he (Parker) was murdered before he could collect evidence against specific individuals. The Democratic Press blamed members of the Republican Loyal League for killing Humphries, but they were unable to concoct a logical motive. No one was ever charged in the case.

I

I-35 murders Texas (1976–81)

Interstate Highway 35 traverses some 740 miles between Salina, Kansas, in the north and Laredo, Texas, on the Mexican border. More than half the journey's length, in excess of 420 miles, runs north-south across the Lone Star State, past Gainesville and Denton, splitting to accommodate the twin giants of Dallas–Fort Worth, reuniting above Hillsboro for the long run south through Waco, Temple, Austin, and San Antonio. Between 1976 and 1981 the Texas stretch of I-35 was the hunting ground for a killer (or killers) who preyed on hitchhikers and stranded motorists, claiming at least 22 victims in five years' time. Some officers believe the stalker is still at large today.

The first "official" I-35 victim was 21-year-old Lesa Haley, found two miles north of Waxahatchie, Texas, on August 23, 1976. Bound for Oklahoma City, traveling by thumb, she was last seen climbing into a van at Waco. Haley was stabbed in the neck with an awl before she was dumped on the highway's gravel shoulder.

On the night of November 5, 1978, 19-year-old Frank Key and 18-year-old Rita Salazar ran out of gas on a date in Austin. Next morning, Key was found north of Georgetown, shot nine times with a .22-caliber pistol, including four postmortem shots in the back of the head. Salazar's body, shot six times with the same gun, was found on a frontage road near Waco.

Sharon Schilling, age 27, was found on a street in San Marcos, Texas, on Labor Day 1979, a few blocks from I-35. Shot once in the abdomen with a .410-gauge shotgun, she died on September 13 without regaining consciousness. Less than a month later, Sandra Dubbs was kidnapped after her car broke down on the drive from St. Louis to San Antonio. Her body, stabbed 35 times, was found in Travis County, Texas. On Halloween 1979 the strangled body of a "Jane Doe" victim, nude except for a pair of orange socks, was found in a highway culvert near Georgetown.

On June 23, 1980, victim Rodney Massey, shot four times, was discovered in a field near Temple, Texas, 70 miles north of Austin. On July 9, 1980, a Hispanic "Jane Doe" was found near Pflugerville, stabbed 27 times with a screwdriver; her pants had been pulled down, although there was no evidence of sexual assault. Yet another "Jane Doe" was found near New Braunfels in May 1981, shot six times in the head with a .25-caliber pistol.

Authorities convened in Austin to discuss the murders on October 30, 1981, but their review of the cases produced no results. Two years later, serial slayers Henry Lee Lucas and Ottis Toole confessed to most of the I-35 murders, and Lucas was sentenced to death in the "orange socks" case, but Lucas later recanted his statements and produced Florida payroll records suggesting that he was not in Texas when the crime occurred. (Governor George W. Bush eventually commuted Lucas's death sentence to life imprisonment, a strange compromise if he truly believed Lucas innocent of the murder.) Texas authorities remain divided on the subject of Lucas and Toole's confessions in the other I-35 cases, and both suspects are now deceased, making further investigation of their claims impossible.

I-45 murders Texas (1982–97)

Between 1982 and 1997 42 teenage girls and young women were kidnapped from small towns and suburbs along Interstate Highway 45, between Houston and Galveston, Texas. Many of those were later found dead, described by Federal Bureau of Investigation (FBI) agents and local authorities as victims of one or more serial killers prowling the 50 miles of wide-open highway. Despite the four-year focus of attention on a single suspect, no evidence has been found to support an indictment, and by early 1998 it appeared that authorities had been mistaken in their choice of targets all along.

The most recent "official" victim in the murder series was 17-year-old Jessica Cain, last seen alive while performing with a community theater group, one night in August 1997. Following the show, Cain left for home, driving alone down I-45, but she never reached her destination. Cain's father found her pickup truck abandoned on the highway's shoulder, and her name was added to the ever-growing victims list.

By that time police believed they knew the man responsible. Their suspect, Robert William Abel, was a former NASA engineer and operator of a horseback riding ranch near League City, in Brazoria County. Abel first came under suspicion in 1993, when the corpses of four missing girls were found in the desert, near his property. FBI agents spent a grand total of two hours with League City police, sketching a psychological profile of the unknown killer based on such traits as "intelligence level" and assumed proximity to the crime scene. Abel's ex-wife pitched in with tales of alleged domestic abuse ("externalized anger" in FBI parlance) and claims that Abel sometimes beat his horses (a charge that he staunchly denies). The punch line of the federal profile was direct and to the point—"Serial sexual offender: Robert William Abel."

That profile alone was deemed sufficient to support a search warrant, and police moved in, seeking evidence that included a cache of nude photos described by Abel's ex-wife. In fact, they *did* find photographs, some 6,000 in all, of which precisely two depicted naked women (neither of them victims in the murder spree). No evidence was found at Abel's ranch connecting him with any sort of criminal activity, including cruelty to animals.

Frustrated in their search for clues, League City police took the unusual step of naming Abel publicly as a suspect in the I-45 murder case. He was "innocent until proven guilty," of course, but in the absence of alternative suspects his life became a waking Hell on Earth, with death threats pouring in from neighbors and the relatives of sundry victims. One such, Tim Miller, having lost his daughter Laura to the unknown killer, launched a personal crusade of daily "reminders" to Abel, including armed visits to his home and threats of murder recorded on Abel's answering machine. League City's finest, still convinced that Abel was their man, took no steps to halt the harassment and stalled when Abel volunteered to take a polygraph test. In fact, while League City's assistant police chief publicly "welcomed" Abel's cooperation in the case, said cooperation only made matters worse, since such behavior is common among serial killers.

It was early 1998 before Robert Abel got to take his long-sought polygraph, courtesy of the *20/20* television program. In fact, two tests were administered by a retired FBI agent, with Abel denying any knowledge of the four victims found near his ranch in 1993. He hesitated in responding to one surprise question, dealing with rumors of a young victim's drug use, and was rated "untruthful" in respect to that answer, but a second test administered without trick questions found him to be truthful on all counts. FBI agents in Houston called the *20/20* tests "extremely significant," admitting that the four-year-old profile of Abel was "poor quality" work on the part of their colleagues. In fact, they told the world, Robert Abel had been eliminated as a suspect in their eyes, and even Tim Miller appeared to relent in his harassment of Abel, with a televised apology.

Not so the lawmen in League City. Abel may indeed be innocent, they say, but since they have no solid evidence to clear him by their own exacting standards, Abel "is still swimming in the pool of suspects." One is tempted to to ask *what* pool, since vague local references to "other suspects" always stop short of naming alternative candidates. Texas courts have barred Abel from filing a lawsuit to clear his name, ruling that League City police are within their rights to publicize him as a suspect, even when the original FBI profile has been retracted. The real I-45 killer, meanwhile, remains unidentified and presumably still at large. Critics of police performance in the case note that unsolved murders and disappearances of women in the region have continued while Abel was under surveillance. Thirty-nine-year-old Jo Ann Sendejas vanished from San Leon in December 1999 and remains missing today; 57-year-old Tot Tran Harriman disappeared (with her car) in July 2001, while visiting friends in League City; and 23-year-old Sarah Trusty was kidnapped while bicycling at Texas City, found dead at a nearby reservoir in July 2002.

I-70/I-35 murders United States (1992–94)

In the spring of 1992, midwestern merchants were briefly terrorized by a killer who roamed across three states, striking randomly at small "specialty shops" near Interstate Highway 70, stealing small amounts of cash and executing shop proprietors or employees. The murder spree ended as suddenly and mysteriously as it began, only to resume (some authorities say) a year later, in a different part of the country. Six murders are definitely linked to one unknown subject by ballistics evidence, while police suspect the same man (using different weapons) in at least four other homicides.

The first definite victim was 26-year-old Robin Fuldauer, gunned down on the job at an Indianapolis shoe store on April 8, 1992. Three days later, in Wichita, Kansas, the same .22-caliber weapon was used to kill proprietor Patricia Magers, age 26, and 23-year-old employee Patricia Smith at a small bridal shop. The shooter was seen by at least one witness, who assisted in the preparation of a published sketch, but all in vain. On April 27 the only male victim in the series, Michael McCown, was shot and killed in a Terre Haute, Indiana, ceramics shop. Six days later, on May 3, Nancy Kitzmiller was slain in St. Charles, Missouri, at a shop specializing in western boots. The last "official" victim, 37-year-old Sarah Blessing, was killed in a Raytown, Missouri, video store on May 7, 1992. Once again there was a witness, who confirmed descriptions of the gunman seen in Wichita.

According to police in the five cities where the gunman struck, their suspect was a white male in his twenties or thirties, 5-feet-6 or 7 inches, with sandy blond or reddish hair, sometimes sporting a day's worth of beard stubble. Ballistics tests confirmed a single weapon used

in all six murders, and the small amounts of cash stolen in each case—never more than $400 from any one shop—convinced authorities that they were dealing with a killer who "cased" his targets in advance, seeking attractive brunet victims. (Police speculated that Michael McCown, who wore long hair and earrings, may have been mistaken for a woman as the killer watched him from a distance, through the windows of his shop.) In each case the victims were found in the rear of their stores, shot in the back of the head, with no signs of a struggle. Though all but one of the victims were attractive females, there was never any sign of an attempted sexual assault.

The murders were a nine-day wonder across the Midwest, but public interest faded when the killing stopped. Within a week of the final murder, police in St. Charles disbanded their task force, with Raytown authorities following suit on May 21, 1992. Officially, law enforcement spokesmen promised that the crimes would be investigated "at nearly the same level" by individual detectives, but in fact they had no leads, admitting for the record that solution of the mystery would probably rely on some fatal mistake by the killer, rather than any great detective work.

A brief ray of hope was seen in early June 1992, when authorities in Dyersburg, Tennessee, announced a "possible link" between the I-70 murders and a pair of local homicides. Suspect Donnie Waterhouse, age 37, had been sought for questioning since February 1992, when his mother and stepfather were found shot to death in their home. A trail of blood at the scene and more stains in an abandoned pickup suggested Waterhouse may have wounded himself while killing his parents. Dyersburg authorities noted Waterhouse's resemblance to the I-70 gunman—5-feet-6, 145–155 pounds, blond, and balding—but there was nothing else to link him with the Midwest slayings, and the slim lead ultimately came to naught.

By the first anniversary of the I-70 murders, police across the Midwest started to relax, indulging in the wishful notion that their subject might be dead or locked up on some unrelated charge. By summer's end, however, they had started hearing rumbles from the state of Texas, where another unknown gunman had begun to prey on look-alike victims in strikingly similar settings.

The first to die in Texas was 51-year-old Mary Ann Glasscock, shot execution-style in her Fort Worth antique shop on September 25, 1993. On November 1, after Amy Vess was killed in an Arlington dancewear shop, Texas authorities described a link to the I-70 murder series as "definitely possible." Before the month was out, a Dallas shop clerk was killed in similar circumstances, and January 15, 1994, witnessed the murder of a fourth Texas victim, this time in Houston.

Supporters of the linkage theory had no solid evidence of a connection in the later crimes; ballistics did not match the Midwest homicides. Still, they pointed to the similarity of victims and targets: dark-haired women killed in shops adjacent to Interstate Highways 35 and 45, which in turn leads back to I-70 at Salina, Kansas. Capt. Chris Dahlke, with the Indianapolis Police Department, was one who saw the connection, citing a "strong possibility" that the Texas murders were committed by the unnamed I-70 gunman.

Perhaps.

If police in Texas and Indiana are correct, their quarry is responsible for at least 10 murders—and he has dropped out of sight once again, with no new crimes added to the hypothetical roster since January 1994. If they are wrong about the link, then Texas has a random killer all its own, a circumstance that would be no surprise in one of the nation's five worst states for incidence of serial murder. Either way, the cases have remained unsolved, and barring a spontaneous confession from the killer (or killers), no solution is anticipated.

"INDEPENDENCE Avenue Killer" serial murderer (1996–97)

Named by journalists after the street where most of his victims plied their trade as streetwalkers, this unidentified killer is blamed for 10 known murders and the disappearances of three more women since October 1996. All victims found so far have been dragged from the Missouri River, downstream from Kansas City, leading police to suspect their corpses may have been dropped from various bridges.

The slayer's first acknowledged victim was 21-year-old Christy Fugate, last seen alive on October 3, 1996, her corpse pulled from the river 12 days later in neighboring Lafayette County. The only African-American victim in the series, 20-year-old Connie Wallace-Byas, worked Independence Avenue for the last time on November 19, 1996; she was missing five months before her body surfaced in Boone County, 90 miles east of Kansas City, in April 1997. Her killer had been

busy in the interim, new victims including: 26-year-old Sherri Livingston, vanished on February 14, 1997, pulled from the river in Lafayette County on March 29; 41-year-old Linda Custer, missing since February 27, found on April 23, 1997, near Dover, in Lafayette County; and 30-year-old Chandra Helsel, last seen alive on April 5, dragged from the river near Booneville, in Cooper County, on May 8, 1997. Tammy Smith, age 30, vanished from Independence Avenue on December 20, 1997; her corpse was found in the river near Silby, Missouri, on April 2, 1998.

When the case was featured on *America's Most Wanted,* in the spring of 1998, police said four more women's bodies had been found along the Missouri's banks, all counted as probable victims of the Independence Avenue Killer. None were identified, but authorities described them as alleged or convicted prostitutes, similar in height and weight. Advanced decomposition and submersion in the river have thus far cheated forensic experts in their search for scientific evidence, and the cause of death has not been publicly declared in any case.

Besides the 10 officially acknowledged dead, police fear that three missing women may also have fallen prey to Kansas City's stalker. Alleged prostitute Connie Williams, age 32, was last seen at her mother's home, but authorities say she was known to look for "tricks" on Independence Avenue. If she was murdered, as police presume, her disappearance two day's prior to Christy Fugate's would make Williams the killer's first known victim. Forty-year-old Jamie Pankey disappeared on November 1, 1996, while the youngest apparent victim, 19-year-old Cheresa Lordi, was last seen alive on February 24, 1997. At press time police remain baffled by the string of murders, with nothing to suggest an imminent arrest.

INDIANAPOLIS, Indiana taxi murders (1993)

Cab drivers in Indianapolis, as in any other city, face predictable risks on the job from armed robbers and random psychopaths. They suffer fewer casualties per year than cabbies in New York, Chicago, or Los Angeles, but there is no safe-conduct pass from danger, even when they travel armed.

On February 5, 1993, 57-year-old Samuel Smith was found dead in his taxi, parked in an alley near the 400 block of North Concord Street. He had been shot several times in the back of the head and apparently robbed. Police still had no leads in that case five months later, on July 12, when 50-year-old Charles Nixon drove his cab up to a fire station on East 34th Street, then staggered out and collapsed on the floor, dying from a gunshot in the back that pierced his heart.

Authorities could only speculate on the motive for Nixon's murder, since he still had his wallet and cash, but the presumption was attempted robbery. Dispatchers noted that Nixon had been sent to the 3700 block of North Bancroft Street around 1:15 A.M., to pick up a fare known only as "John." Company records show that Nixon turned his meter on three minutes later, bound for some unknown destination. Police reported his shooting to dispatchers at 1:30 A.M. Ironically, Nixon had carried a pistol for self-defense on the job until the previous week, when it was confiscated by police for lack of a legal permit. Armed or not, however, Nixon's girlfriend told reporters, "He wasn't going to give up nothing without a fight."

At last report, Indianapolis homicide detectives were "looking at the possibility that Nixon and Smith were killed by the same person," but no suspects have been identified in either case. Unless deceased or jailed on unrelated charges in the meantime, the killer (or killers) remains at large.

INTURRISI, Louis   See ITALY GAY MURDERS

"IRONMAN" serial murderer (1970s)

Time and distance make the details sketchy in this case from South Africa, involving a still-unidentified killer who ambushed late-night strollers in the small township of Atteridgeville, near Pretoria. Before the murders ceased, at least seven victims were beaten to death with an iron bar, their corpses robbed before the slayer fled. The grisly crimes exacerbated paranoia in a region that has seen more than its share of serial murders, beginning with the depredations of the "ATTERIDGEVILLE MUTILATOR" in 1956. Like that stalker before him, "Ironman" has apparently retired, his crime spree ended, but police still have no clue to his identity, and no solution to the murders is now anticipated.

ISABELLA Stewart Gardner Museum art theft (1990)

At 1:45 A.M. on March 18, 1990, two men dressed in police uniforms presented themselves at the Isabella Stewart Gardner Museum, in Boston, Massachusetts.

The men verbally identified themselves as Boston police officers, claiming they had been dispatched to investigate reports of "a disturbance" within the museum compound. Security personnel admitted the two strangers and were swiftly overpowered, handcuffed, and gagged with duct tape. Over the next hour and 20 minutes, the intruders proceeded to remove 12 art objects valued by experts at $300 million. Their haul included the following treasures:

From the museum's Dutch Room Gallery:
Jan Vermeer's oil painting *The Concert*
Two Rembrandt oils, *A Lady and Gentleman in Black* and *The Storm on the Sea of Galilee*
Rembrandt's *Self Portrait,* an etching the size of a postage stamp
Govaert Flinck's oil painting *Landscape with an Obelisk*
A Chinese bronze beaker dating from the Shang Dynasty, circa 1200–1100 B.C.

From the Short Gallery:
Five drawings by Edgar Degas, including *La Sortie de Pelage, Cortege aux Environs de Florence, Three Mounted Jockeys,* and two different versions of *Program for an Artistic Soiree*

From the Blue Room Gallery:
Édouard Manet's oil painting *Chez Tortini*

The thieves were assisted by an oversight in the museum's security preparations. Aside from a panic button linked to Boston police headquarters—which security personnel had no chance to utilize during the robbery—all alarm systems within the Isabella Stewart Gardner Museum were strictly internal, designed to alert on-site security personnel without summoning authorities. The thieves were thus uninterrupted, and completed their sweep by removing video surveillance film from the museum's cameras upon departure.

Museum security officers described the robbers as two white males in their thirties, both with black hair and wearing false mustaches. The shorter of the pair wore square-rimmed, gold-framed spectacles and spoke with an apparent Boston accent. Neither has been identified to date, nor have the stolen treasures been recovered. The Federal Bureau of Investigation offers a $5 million reward for information leading to the recovery (undamaged) of all 12 missing items;

unspecified smaller rewards are offered for the recovery of individual items from the robbery.

ISFORD, Jennifer   See Toronto rape-murders

ITALY gay murders (1997)

In August 1997 Italian police announced that a serial killer might be at large in their country, targeting older gay men. That declaration followed the bludgeon slayings of two prominent homosexuals, one each in Rome and Florence. The first victim, 56-year-old Louis Inturrisi, was an American who divided his time between teaching university classes and writing for the *New York Times*. Police found him beaten to death in his own apartment, in Rome. The killer's second target was an Italian nobleman and former managing director of Sotheby's Italia, 72-year-old Count Alvise di Robilant. Authorities report that Robilant was bludgeoned in his Renaissance home, in Florence, under circumstances "similar" to Inturrisi's death. While famous for his female conquests, the count reportedly began a homosexual love affair shortly before he was killed. No suspects have been charged or publicly identified in either case.

IVERS, Peter Scott murder victim (1983)

A native of Brookline, Illinois, born in September 1946, Peter Ivers moved with his family, as a small child, to the Boston suburb of Brookline, Massachusetts. There, he attended the Roxbury Latin School, followed by study of classical languages at Harvard University. Close friends included comedian John Belushi and Harvard classmate Douglas Kenney, founder of *National Lampoon* magazine.

Midway through his Harvard studies, however, he became enthralled by music and began performing on harmonica with a Boston musical group, Beacon Street Union. Ivers went solo in 1969, with his album *Knight of the Blue Communion* from Epic Records, but he switched to Warner Brothers after Epic shelved his second album, *Take It Out on Me*. Warner released his eponymous *Peter Ivers* album in 1976, the same year film director David Lynch signed Ivers to write a song ("In Heaven," a.k.a. "The Lady in the Radiator Song") for his cult-classic movie *Eraserhead*.

In 1981, producer David Jove hired Ivers to host *New Wave Theater* on Los Angeles television station KSCI-TV, subsequently syndicated on weekend broadcasts from the USA Network. In that post, Ivers introduced America to various alternative bands, including the Angry Samoans, Black Flag, the Circle Jerks, the Dead Kennedys, Fear, 45 Grave, and the Plugz. The program drew mixed reviews, citing Ivers's "manic" style of presentation and the "frantic cacophony" of music, comedy, and theatrical sketches.

On March 3, 1983, an unknown assailant beat Ivers to death in his small apartment on L.A.'s Skid Row. No suspect or motive was identified for his still-unsolved slaying. Harvard University subsequently honored Ivers with creation of the Peter Ivers Visiting Artist Program, while two more of his albums were released posthumously, *Nirvana Cuba* and *Terminal Love* (both in 2001).

J

JACK, Monica See "Highway Killer"

JACKSON, Essie See Portland, Oregon, murders

JACKSON, Mississippi unsolved murders (1994–95)
Mishandling of critical evidence by the Federal Bureau of Investigation's (FBI) crime lab in Washington, D.C., is blamed by local authorities for their failure to solve the murders of four alleged prostitutes in Jackson, Mississippi. All four women were strangled after having sex, with the latest victim, Cheryl Garcia, killed in January 1995. Nine months later Jackson police packed up DNA samples from all four crime scenes, plus samples taken from a suspect, and shipped the lot off to Washington for examination by FBI experts. No results were forthcoming by August 1996, when police told Virginia Swann (Garcia's mother) that the suspect in her daughter's slaying "had been turned loose because there wasn't enough evidence." Disgusted by the news, Swann told reporters, "I just don't understand it. I don't feel good about this at all."

Neither did Jackson police detective Ned Garner, admitting that the case had stalled with their best suspect at liberty. Until the DNA results came back, Garner told the media, "we have nothing to show he committed all those" murders. As far as the

delay went, police spokesman Lee Vance reported, "The only explanation I've ever been given is that they have a lot of cases." Jay Miller, then chief of the FBI's forensic science lab, confirmed that grim assessment. "We can't service all the requests that we get," he told *USA Today,* adding that delays of a year or more in processing evidence were not unusual. With or without the elusive test results, however, there has still been no report of a solution in the Jackson homicides.

JACKSON, Wharlest civil rights martyr (1967)
A native of Adams County, Mississippi, born in 1929, Wharlest Jackson served in the Korean conflict and returned from combat duty to find that nothing had changed for African Americans in the Magnolia State. With George Metcalfe, a coworker at the Armstrong Rubber Company's plant in Natchez, Jackson organized a local chapter of the National Association for the Advancement of Colored People (NAACP) and served as the group's treasurer. That act was perilous in itself, for Mississippi blacks in the early 1960s, but Metcalfe and Jackson raised the ante in August 1965, with a petition demanding that the local school board finally comply with U.S. Supreme Court desegregation orders issued 10 years earlier. Days later, a car bomb left Metcalfe near death. He would survive his wounds but henceforth did not drive, riding with Jackson to work at the Armstrong plant.

Church bombings like this one were among the crimes of the KKK's "Silver Dollar Group," also blamed (but never prosecuted) for the 1967 murder of Wharlest Jackson. (Library of Congress)

Pressure from the NAACP and other civil rights groups forced Armstrong's all-white Natchez management to revise hiring strategies by early 1967. Jackson was offered a promotion to the higher-paying job of chemical mixer, normally reserved for whites. He accepted the post despite threats from the Ku Klux Klan that any blacks promoted to "white men's jobs" would not live to enjoy them. With the extra 17 cents per hour, Jackson told friends in Natchez, "My wife and children should have a chance now." George Metcalf, ever cautious since his own brush with death, warned Jackson to check beneath the hood of his pickup truck before he started it, in case a bomb had been attached to the ignition wires.

Jackson and Metcalfe were scheduled to work different shifts on Monday, February 27, 1967, so Jackson started his third week as chemical mixer by driving alone to the Armstrong plant. It was 8:01 P.M.

when he clocked out and started for home through a pouring rain. He had not checked under the pickup's hood that night, but it made no difference. This time, the bomber's choice of weapons was a time-delay charge, secured to the truck's chassis. It exploded at 8:11 P.M., demolishing Jackson's vehicle and killing him instantly.

The murder enraged Natchez blacks. Charles Evers—whose brother, NAACP leader Medgar Evers, had been killed by a Mississippi Klansman in June 1963—led 2,000 angry marchers to the Armstrong plant on February 28, in a demonstration calculated to "put ourselves before all the Kluxers and say, 'You killed out brother, now kill all of us.'" Addressing the crowd, Evers warned local racists, "Once we learn to hate, they're through. We can kill more people in a day than they've done in 100 years."

The threat of black retaliation galvanized Natchez authorities, where tearful pleas for justice had left them unmoved in the past. The town's board of aldermen offered a $25,000 reward for information leading to the arrest and conviction of Jackson's killers, while Armstrong officials added another $10,000. The mayor and police chief of Natchez, accompanied by Adams County's sheriff, attended a black mass meeting for the first time in history, vowing to solve the case and linking arms with black constituents to sing the civil rights anthem "We Shall Overcome." In Jackson, Governor Paul Johnson deviated from his normal defense of segregation to call Jackson's murder an "act of savagery which stains the honor of our state." Roy Wilkins, NAACP national executive director, was optimistic in the wake of those expressions, telling journalists, "Things have changed throughout the state of Mississippi."

They had not changed enough, however, for authorities to keep their promises and actually solve the case. Even before Jackson's death, FBI agents had blamed the Metcalfe bombing and the 1964 murder of Louisiana victim FRANK MORRIS on a Klan splinter faction known as the Silver Dollar Group (so-called because each member carried a silver dollar minted in the year of his birth). G-men knew the Silver Dollar Klansmen liked to practice with dynamite on weekends, rehearsing demolition of old cars, but reports from covert informants stopped short of providing evidence that would prove a case in court. Natchez police announced a reopening of the Jackson case in April 1998, but no arrests have thus far been made, and no suspects have been publicly identified beyond general references to the KKK.

"JACK the Ripper" Atlanta (1911–12)

In the year between May 1911 and May 1912 black residents of Atlanta, Georgia, were terrorized by the activities of a knife-wielding stalker who preyed exclusively on women of color, leaving them with throats slashed and bodies mutilated after death. Inevitably he was nicknamed "Jack the Ripper" by the local press, and like his namesake in 19th-century London, he was never captured or identified. Unlike his British predecessor, though, Atlanta's Ripper claimed an even 20 victims, four times the original phantom's tally.

The early murders in Atlanta were committed with a shocking regularity, the slayer claiming victims on seven successive Saturday nights, between May 20 and July 1, 1911. White reporters were quick to point out that the victims were all attractive, well-dressed mulattos, with no "out-and-out black women" slain by the killer. In each case there was evidence of the woman being choked unconscious, after which her throat was slit from ear to ear and "the carving of the victim—always in the same area of the body—begins." None of the women had been raped, but from the nature of the mutilations (tactfully unspecified in media reports), it was apparent that the crimes were sexual in nature. As in the case of London's Jack and nearly all his imitators, journalists claimed that the killer "seems to possess some knowledge of anatomy."

Victim number seven was 40-year-old Lena Sharp, slain in the late-night hours of July 1, 1911, with her head nearly severed and her body "horribly mutilated." Concerned when Sharp was late arriving home, her daughter started searching the streets. She was accosted by a well-dressed black man, but his mannerisms frightened her, and he stabbed her in the back as she turned to flee. Escaping with her life, she offered a description of the man, but no arrest resulted from the lead.

The Ripper's first near-miss resulted in a change of schedule, slowing down his pace. He would require 10 months to claim another 13 victims in Atlanta, mutilating his last target—a 19-year-old "comely yellow girl"—on Friday, May 10, 1912. A large reward collected by the black community produced no takers, and the mystery remains unsolved.

It may be sheer coincidence that the years 1911 and 1912 also witnessed 49 unsolved MULATTO AXE MURDERS in Texas and Louisiana.

"JACK the Ripper" London (1888)

Arguably the world's most infamous serial killer, Victorian London's unidentified harlot killer remains an object of study for thousands of armchair detectives today. In an age when random killers rarely attain star status without celebrity victims or a body count in double digits, Jack the Ripper still captivates the public imagination.

Because he got away.

The mystery began on August 31, 1888, with the discovery of a woman's lifeless body on Buck's Row, in the heart of London's Whitechapel slum. The victim was Mary Nichols, Polly to her friends, and she had earned her meager living as a prostitute before her killer turned the final trick. Her throat was slashed, with bruises found beneath the jaw suggesting that she had been choked unconscious before the killer plied his blade. Upon undressing Nichols at the morgue, the medical examiner found deep postmortem slashes on her abdomen and stab wounds to the genitals.

The murder of an East End prostitute was nothing new to Scotland Yard. In fact, detectives had two other unsolved cases on their books for 1888. Emma Smith had been attacked by a gang of four or five assailants on April 2, living long enough to describe her killers. Martha Tabram was found in Whitechapel on August 7, stabbed 39 times with a weapon resembling a bayonet. Neither crime had anything in common with the death of Mary Nichols, and investigators had to wait for further slayings to disclose a pattern.

On September 8, 1888, the police found their link with the discovery of Annie Chapman's corpse, a half mile from Buck's Row. Another prostitute, the victim had first been choked unconscious, after which her throat was cut and she was disemboweled. Her entrails had been torn away and draped across one shoulder; portions of the bladder and vagina, with the uterus and ovaries attached, were missing from the scene. "Obviously," Dr. Bagster Phillips, medical examiner, informed *The Lancet*, "the work was that of an expert—or one, at least, who had such knowledge of anatomical or pathological examinations as to be enabled to secure the pelvic organs with one sweep of the knife."

The first of 217 letters allegedly penned by the killer (this one in red ink) was written on September 25 and mailed three days later, addressed to London's Central News Agency. It read:

Dear Boss,

I keep on hearing that the police have caught me but they won't fix me just yet. I have laughed when they look so clever and talk about being on the right track. That joke about [unnamed suspect] Leather Apron gave me real fits. I am down on whores and shan't quit ripping them till I do get buckled. Grand work the last job was. I gave the lady no time to squeal. How can they catch me now. I love my work and want to start again. You will soon hear of me and my funny little games. I saved some of the proper red stuff in a ginger beer bottle over the last job to write with but it went thick like glue and I can't use it. Red ink is fit enough I hope ha ha. The next job I do I shall clip the lady's ears off and sent to the police officers just for jolly wouldn't you. Keep this letter back till I do a bit more work, then give it out straight. My knife is nice and sharp and I want to get to work right away if I get the chance. Good luck.

Yours truly,
Jack the Ripper

Don't mind me giving the trade name. Wasn't good enough to post this before I got all the red ink off my hands curse it. They say I am a doctor now ha ha.

The Ripper claimed two more victims on September 30, 1888. The first, Elizabeth Stride, was found in a narrow court off Berner Street at 1:00 A.M. Her throat was slashed, but there were no other mutilations, indicating that her killer was disturbed before he could complete his grisly task. Forty-five minutes later, Catherine Eddowes was found by a constable in Mitre Square. According to the officer's report, she had been gutted "like a pig in the market," with her entrails "flung in a heap about her neck." A message had been scrawled in chalk across a nearby wall: "The Juwes are not the men that will be blamed for nothing." Postmortem examination revealed that Eddowes had been slashed across the face, her throat was cut, and she was disemboweled. The killer had removed a kidney, which was missing from the scene. A superficial cut beneath one ear suggested that the killer had attempted to fulfill his promise of a trophy for police.

Later that morning, while police were searching Whitechapel for further evidence or witnesses, another message was mailed to the Central News Agency.

I was not codding dear old Boss when I gave you the tip. You'll hear about Saucy Jack's work tomorrow. Double event this time. Number one squealed a bit. Couldn't finish straight off. Had no time to get ears for police. Thanks for keeping the last letter back till I got to work again.

Jack the Ripper

A third note was mailed on October 16, 1888, this one to George Lusk, head of the newly organized Whitechapel Vigilance Committee. It read:

From hell

Mr. Lusk
Sir I send you half the Kidne I took from one woman prsarved it for you tother piece I fried and ate was very nise I may send you the bloody knif that too it out if you only wait a whil longer
Catch me when you can Mister Lusk

Controversy surrounds the "Lusk kidney." Dr. Thomas Openshaw, pathological curator of the London Hospital Museum, pronounced it "ginny," of the sort expected from an alcoholic. It showed evidence of Bright's disease, as did (allegedly) the kidney left to Catherine Eddowes by her killer. Openshaw also noted that the renal artery is normally three inches long: two inches had remained with Eddowes; one inch was attached to the repulsive trophy mailed to Lusk. Notwithstanding that verdict, another pathologist, Dr. Sedgewick Saunders, reported that Eddowes's remaining kidney was perfectly healthy, with no trace of Bright's disease. Saunders believed the kidney sent to Lusk was a prank played by medical students.

London's panic was fading by Halloween, but the killer was not finished yet. On November 9—Lord Mayor's Day—police were summoned to Miller's Court in Spitalfields to view the remains of prostitute Mary Kelly. Found by her landlord's errand boy, inquiring after tardy rent, she was the only victim killed indoors, and Jack had taken full advantage of the opportunity to sculpt a grisly work of butcher's art.

As usual, the victim had been killed by a slash across the throat, this time so deep that Kelly was nearly decapitated. Jack had skinned her forehead, slicing off her nose and ears. Her left arm was nearly severed at the shoulder, while both legs were flayed from thighs to ankles. Kelly had been disemboweled, one hand inserted in her gaping abdomen, her liver draped across one thigh. Her severed breasts lay on the nightstand with her kidneys, heart, and nose. Police found strips of flesh suspended from the nails of picture frames, and blood was spattered on the walls. Examination showed that Kelly had been three months pregnant, but her killer took the uterus and fetus with him when he fled.

So closed the Ripper's reign of terror. Some students of the case also credit Jack with the murders of prostitutes Alice MacKenzie (in 1889) and Frances Cole (1891), but the private papers of Sir Melville Macnaghten, former chief of Scotland Yard's Criminal Investigation Division confirm a police conviction that the Ripper "had *five* victims and five only." Macnaghten also named three suspects in the case, none of whom was ever charged. They include:

Montague John Druitt (1857–88), a London barrister first on Macnaghten's suspect list, whose body, weighted with stones in an apparent suicide, was dredged from the Thames on December 1, 1888. Macnaghten wrote that "From private information I have little doubt but that his own family suspected this man of being the Whitechapel murderer." An alternative theory, published in 1987 by Martin Howells and Keith Skinner, casts Druitt as both killer and victim, murdered by affluent associates to avert potential scandal from the revelation of his crimes.

PROBLEMS: Macnaghten misidentifies Druitt as a 41-year-old doctor; no evidence links Druitt to the crimes; no incriminating statements from his family have been produced; his apparent suicide note does not mention the murders.

Aaron Kosminski (1864/65–1919), a Polish Jew employed in London as a hairdresser, the second of Macnaghten's suspects was allegedly driven insane by "solitary vices" (masturbation) and confined to a lunatic asylum in 1891.

PROBLEMS: No evident link to the murders; no proven Ripper crimes between November 1888 and February 1891 while Kosminski was still at large.

Michael Ostrog (born ca. 1833), the third official suspect, is described by Macnaghten as "a mad Russian doctor & a convict & unquestionably a homicidal maniac." A known thief and con man, paroled from his last known prison term in 1904, he thereafter vanished from the public record.

PROBLEMS: Ostrog was not a doctor (though he sometimes impersonated one); no evidence connects him to the murders.

Numerous alternative suspects have been collected in the decades since Saucy Jack terrorized London, and the list grows longer all the time. Those presently considered by various researchers include:

"Jill the Ripper," an unknown female suspect, proposed in 1888, allegedly an abortionist concealing her crimes by mutilating patients who died in her care.

PROBLEM: No real-life candidate identified.

William Henry Bury (1859–89), hanged in Scotland five months after the last Ripper slaying, for stabbing his wife to death. The *New York Times* named him as a suspect, based on similarities of wounding, but Bury was forgotten until author Euan Macpherson rediscovered him in 1986.

PROBLEM: London police, including Inspector Abberline, dismissed Bury as a Ripper suspect in 1889.

Dr. Thomas Neill Cream (1850–92), poisoner of four London prostitutes in 1891–92; he supposedly cried out, "I am Jack the——" when he was hanged.

PROBLEM: Cream was imprisoned in Illinois during the Ripper crimes.

Severin Antoniovitch Klosovski (1865–1903), aka "George Chapman," a Polish barber-surgeon and resident of Whitechapel in 1888; poisoned three common-law wives in 1895 and was hanged for the third offense. At his arrest Inspector Frederick Abberline supposedly remarked, "So you've caught Jack the Ripper at last!"

PROBLEMS: Abberline's comment remains undocumented and was probably a posthumous invention; no evidence links Klosovski to the murders; sadistic slashers rarely (if ever) switch to poisoning their victims.

Francis Thompson (1859–1907), British poet and opium addict who lived in London as a homeless "street person" between 1885 and 1888. He allegedly boasted of owning a leather apron (a nickname for the Whitechapel killer) in 1888 and wrote a poem, never published, that described a "lusty young knight" who disembowels women.

PROBLEM: No evident connection to the crimes.

Frederick Bailey Deeming (1842–92), a con man and serial killer who murdered his wife and four children at Liverpool in 1891, then slew a second wife in Sydney, Australia, the following year. Rumors, circulating since the 1920s, claim he confessed the "last two" Ripper crimes to cellmates while awaiting execution in Australia.

PROBLEMS: No evident connection to the murders; Deeming's attorney denied reports of the "confession."

Dr. Alexander Pedachenko (1857?–1908?), a Russian doctor who immigrated to Britain, alleged (in 1928) to have committed the murders in connivance with Czarist secret police "to discredit the Metropolitan Police."

PROBLEMS: Dubious sources; no evident link to the crimes.

Prince Albert Victor Christian Edward (1864–92), the Duke of Clarence and heir presumptive to the throne of England, first named as a Ripper suspect in 1962. Most "Royal Ripper" theories describe the prince as a woman-hating homosexual, driven mad by syphilis, whose deer-hunting experience taught him to gut corpses.

PROBLEMS: No evident links to the murders; no proof of syphilis; official records place him far from London on the dates of all five murders (answered by charges of a royal cover-up); gay serial killers typically seek same-sex victims.

Sir William Gull (1816–90), physician in ordinary to Queen Victoria, who treated Prince Albert Victor for typhus in 1871, first linked to the Ripper case in 1970. Gull is accused of leading a conspiracy to silence those with knowledge of Prince Albert Victor's illegal marriage to a Catholic commoner, mutilating the victims in accordance with secret Masonic ritual.

PROBLEMS: No evident link to the crimes; Gull was partially paralyzed by the first of several strokes in 1887; prevailing law would

have annulled the alleged marriage; subsequent research proved the woman in question was not Catholic.

James Kenneth Stephen (1859–92), a tutor (some say gay lover) of Prince Albert Victor, first publicly named as a Ripper suspect in 1972. Allegedly suspected by Inspector Abberline (based on a diary, possibly forged, that surfaced in 1988), Stephen supposedly hated women in general and prostitutes in particular. Some students of the case regard his handwriting as similar (or identical) to that of several Ripper letters.

PROBLEMS: No evident links to the crimes (or to a homosexual affair with the prince); many "Ripperologists" believe *all* correspondence from the killer was a hoax, authored by newsmen or cranks.

Walter Richard Sickert (1860–1942), a major British artist, described in various theories since 1976 as either the lone Ripper or a participant in Dr. Gull's Masonic conspiracy. A graphologist claimed (in 1993) that the Ripper's "Dear Boss" note was written in Sickert's disguised handwriting. In 2002 best-selling novelist Patricia Cornwell declared herself "100% certain" of Sickert's guilt, vowing that she would "stake [her] reputation" on it.

PROBLEMS: No evident link to the murders; weaknesses of the Gull conspiracy theory as detailed above; failure of Cornwell's forensic experts to find any DNA link between Sickert and the Ripper letters.

James Kelly (d. 1929), a London resident confined to an asylum after killing his wife in 1883; he escaped in January 1888 and remained at large until his voluntary surrender in February 1927. Deceased two years later, he was first named as a Ripper suspect in 1986.

PROBLEMS: No proven link to the murders; no explanation for their brief duration, while Kelly remained at large for another 39 years.

Robert Donston Stephenson (b. 1841), a.k.a. "Dr. Roslyn D'Onston," first named as a Ripper suspect in 1987. Stephenson allegedly committed the murders as part of a black magic ritual.

PROBLEM: No evident link to the crimes.

Prince Albert Victor and *James Stephen*, named as team killers by forensic psychiatrist David Abrahamson, in *Murder and Madness* (1992). Dr. Abrahamson claimed that his book was based on new material obtained from Scotland Yard.

PROBLEMS: Same as above for both suspects; numerous historical errors throughout the text; Scotland Yard denies providing Abrahamson with any information.

James Maybrick (1838–89), a Liverpool cotton broker, allegedly the author of the "Ripper diary" published amid great controversy in 1993.

PROBLEMS: No evidence beside the diary connects him to the crimes; several analysts brand the "Ripper diary" a forgery dating from the 1920s.

Francis Tumblety (1833?–1903), an Irish-American "herb doctor" arrested in London on November 7, 1888, on multiple counts of assault (against four men) dating back to July; released on bail, he fled to the United States before trial. Obituaries named him as a Ripper suspect, but the case against him was first publicized in 1995.

PROBLEMS: No proven link to the crimes; differed greatly in appearance from alleged eyewitness descriptions of the Ripper.

Joseph Barnett (1858–1926), a London fish porter who lived with victim Mary Kelly until two weeks before her murder, first named as a suspect in 1995.

PROBLEMS: Cleared by police in 1888; no proven link to the murders.

Charles Lutwidge Dodgson, a.k.a. "Lewis Carroll" (1832–98), the world-famous author of *Alice in Wonderland,* named as a Ripper suspect in 1996. Richard Wallace names Carroll and Oxford colleague Thomas Vere Bayne as being jointly responsible for the murders, based on supposed anagrams in Carol's published work.

PROBLEMS: No evident link between either suspect and the Ripper crimes; pure supposition in "translation" of the alleged anagrams.

George Hutchinson (?–?), an eyewitness who described a man allegedly seen with Mary Kelly on the night she was murdered, initially proposed as a suspect in 1998 (on the grounds that his description of the presumed killer was "too detailed").

PROBLEMS: No evident link to the crimes; London police did not consider him a suspect.

John George Gibson (?–?), a Canadian-born Baptist preacher who resigned his Scottish parish in 1887 and entered the United States in December 1888, proposed as a Ripper suspect in 1999, by Robert Graysmith. Graysmith blames Gibson not only for the Ripper crimes, but for two California homicides in 1891. (Another suspect was hanged for those crimes.)

PROBLEMS: No evident link to the British crimes; Gibson's whereabouts for most of 1888 are unknown.

David Cohen (1865–89), a Polish Jew named as a suspect by author Martin Fido in 1987. Fido says that the name Cohen was commonly used for Jewish defendants or hospital patients who could not be positively identified, or for those whose names were difficult for authorities to spell. Fido surmises that "Cohen" was Whitechapel boot maker Nathan Kaminsky, a victim of syphilis who vanished around the time Cohen was committed to Colney Hatch asylum, after Mary Kelly's murder. He died at the asylum in October 1889.

PROBLEM: No evidence links Cohen—or Kaminsky—to the murders.

Sir John Williams (1840–1926), a friend of Queen Victoria and obstetrician to her daughter, Princess Beatrice, named as a suspect by authors Tony Williams and Humphrey Price in 2005. Their book claims that all Jack's victims knew Williams, surmising that he killed them during failed experiments to discover a cure for infertility.

PROBLEMS: No evidence links Williams to the crimes; critic Jennifer Pegg proved fraudulent alterations to Williams's notebook, allegedly documenting his contact with victim Nichols.

Carl Ferdinand Feigenbaum (1842–96), named as a Ripper candidate by author Trevor Marriott in 2007. Feigenbaum was jailed for killing a New York widow in 1894 and confessed a hatred of women, including urges to mutilate them. He was executed at Sing Sing prison in April 1896. Feigenbaum's attorney suspected him of the Whitechapel slayings, but produced no proof. Marriott suspects Feigenbaum of other murders in Germany and the United States, during 1891–94, but likewise reveals no proof.

PROBLEM: No evidence ties Feigenbaum to the Whitechapel crimes.

Joseph Silver (d. 1918), alias "Joseph Lis," proposed as a Ripper suspect by South African author Charles van Onselen in 2007. Van Onselen claims that Silver—another Polish Jew, executed in Poland in 1918—ran a string of Whitechapel prostitutes in 1888, but offers no proof. Silver later earned a reputation as a brutal "King of the Pimps" in Johannesburg, before returning to Poland and his execution as a spy during World War I.

PROBLEM: Van Onselen admits that his theory is "intelligent speculation," devoid of any evidence.

"JACK the Ripper" New York City (1915)

At five years old, Lenora Cohn was used to running errands for her mother. She was not required to leave the tenement that housed her family, except on rare occasions, and her chores were never rigorous, but she was learning to rely upon herself. The lesson might have served her well, had she survived.

At 7:30 P.M. on March 19, 1915, Lenora's mother sent her for a pail of milk. It was a simple task—she merely had to run downstairs—and neighbors saw her walking homeward with the brimming pail 10 minutes later. She was nearly home, already climbing toward the third-floor landing of her own apartment, when she passed out of their sight. At 7:45, August Johnson heard what sounded like an infant's cry outside her door, directly opposite the stairwell. Peering out, she saw a small child lying facedown on the floor, apparently the victim of a fall. Concerned, Ms. Johnson rushed to help. The girl was cradled in her arms before she saw the bloodstains soaking through the tiny dress.

Police were summoned to the Third Avenue tenement, but they found little in the way of clues. Lenora's pail of milk was sitting at the bottom of the stairs, where she was found, and not a drop had spilled. Detectives searched the building and found drops of blood on two steps of another staircase, on the far side of the house, but their significance remains obscure. Lenora's left hand clutched a tuft of short gray hair, and bruises on her throat reflected violent contact with a larger-than-average hand. She had apparently been choked unconscious, stabbed and mutilated afterward with something like a leather worker's knife.

As if the nightmare of a murdered child were not enough, Lenora's mother soon became the target of sadistic letters, written by an individual who claimed to be the killer. Picking up on garish headlines in the press, the author signed his letters "Jack the Ripper," after London's gaslight ghoul of 1888. The notes were given to police, who passed them on to United States postal inspectors. On April 29 a 27-year-old Austrian named Edward Richman was arrested in connection with the mailings, but authorities soon cleared him of involvement in the murder.

But Richman's arrest did not stop the letters. On the day after his arrest, another note was posted to Lenora's mother. It read:

> *Dear Mrs. Cohn: Just a line to let you know that the person that is accused of writing letters to you is innocent. I am the fellow that wrote you the letters, and as I said before a man that keeps his ears open and mouth shut will always get along and never get caught. Some day thats if I get the chair I may confess. But as long as I am out they can never get me. Kindly give the enclosed letter to the police and tell them I wrote it. From*
>
> *H.-B. RICHMOND, Jack-the-Ripper*

Enclosed with the letter was a second envelope, marked "Give this to the police." Inside was another letter that read:

> *Why don't you drop the case? You know that man can't get me in 100 years from now so its no youse in sirchen for me. I am a wise guy you know but wise guys never get caught. You may think that I am a fool to write you But I am writing just to show that I ain't afraid. Mr. Richmond [sic] is innocent of the letter which you accuse him of writing to Mrs. Cohn. As I told you in one of my letters that is going to be the biggest murders to be committed in N.Y. that was ever known. Now do you see I am true.*
>
> *H.-B. RICHMOND*
> *JACK-THE-RIPPER*

Police initially suspected Edward Richman of attempting to divert suspicion from himself, and visitors who called on him in jail were shadowed as potential cohorts, but no link between the suspect and the final "Ripper" letters was established.

On May 3, 1915, the threat was realized. Four-year-old Charles Murray did not respond when members of his family called him in from play at 7:30 P.M. A hasty search was organized, uncovering his mutilated body tucked beneath a staircase in the family's First Avenue tenement. Police responding to the call announced that Murray's killer "very likely" was the same man who had slashed Lenora Cohn on March 19. The latest victim's sister, Mamie, offered a description of the killer, but police eventually dismissed it as the product of a child's imagination.

Meanwhile, patrolmen and detectives fanned out through the neighborhood, searching for clues. Five doors up the street, they met the frantic parents of six-year-old Louisa Neidig, who had seemingly escaped the killer's clutches only moments earlier. While playing in the street outside a bakery, waiting for her aunt to get off work, Louisa was approached by a neatly dressed man wearing a black derby hat and sporting a dark mustache. When she refused to speak to him, he grabbed her arm and dragged Louisa through a nearby open doorway, but her screams brought neighbors on the run, and her attacker fled before she suffered any harm.

At 47th Street and Third, Patrolman Curry was approached by several girls who said two men were chasing them with knives. Just then, the suspects came around a corner, stopping short at sight of Curry's badge. When Curry ordered them to halt, they rushed him, drawing blades and slashing him across one hand before he battered one assailant to the ground. The other fled, abandoning a stunned James Daly to his fate, and while a prison cell awaited him for knifing a policeman, no connection was established to the Ripper crimes.

Reports kept pouring in, but all of them were vague, and none contained the crucial information that would crack the case. At Stuyvesant Park, two girls informed police that a stranger with a dark mustache and Vandyke beard had been "annoying" them for several months. Inspector Joseph Faurot told reporters that "the ripper type . . . is one of the shrewdest and most elusive of criminals," an opinion seconded by Coroner Israel Feinberg. More murders were expected, Feinberg said, unless the killer was captured "within 10 days."

The panic spread. On May 8, 1915, a crowd of 50 men and boys attacked a Ripper suspect after two small boys accused him of "suspicious" actions. Rescued by police, the bloodied victim proved to be a Polish shoemaker, visiting friends on the street where he once had his shop.

On Sunday, May 9, two neighborhood housewives found crude penciled notes on their doormats, signed "The Ripper Jack." In each, the author threatened death to children in the target families; they would be killed on Monday afternoon, the letters said, or kidnapped from their homes that night if all else failed. There were no incidents on Monday, though, and on May 12 police secured confessions from two girls who wrote the notes "for fun." That same afternoon, another "Ripper" note was traced to its author, an 18-year-old who had threatened her employer's children out of spite.

Exposure of such childish hoaxes did not ease the local atmosphere of tension. On the evening of May 15, six-year-old Anna Lombardi was lured into a basement by a man who raped her there. A mob went looking for the suspect, but police—who claimed to know his name—denied a link between the rape and murders. Two days later, when patrolmen arrested Stephen Lukovich for beating his wife and child, rumors spread that "a ripper" was in custody, drawing 1,000 outraged vigilantes to the street outside the precinct house.

Nor was the Ripper scare confined to New York City. On June 22, 1915, Inspector Faurot visited Philadelphia, where a man in custody had recently confessed to murdering a child "on 15th Street." Local detectives had no knowledge of the crime, but young Charles Murray had been slain near 16th Street, and so the suspect warranted an interview. Faurot found his man confined to a hospital psychiatric ward, and the interrogation convinced him that the suspect was not New York's Ripper.

In August 1915 Lt. Patrick Gildea was sent to Baltimore, where Ripper suspect Edward Jones had been jailed on charges of defrauding his landlady. Jones's common-law wife, one Grace Elliott, had denounced him as the slayer, and while her own behavior seemed irrational, New York authorities were notified. Investigation revealed that Jones and Elliott had lived in Manhattan when the murders occurred, but there was nothing to connect them with the crimes. Interrogated by Gildea, Elliott withdrew her charges, denying earlier statements that Jones had "confessed" the murders in her presence. Rather, she admitted, he was simply interested in reading articles about the crimes.

The trail grew cold, and panic faded over time. Despite assignment of 100 homicide detectives to the case, interrogation of innumerable "witnesses" and suspects, no solution was forthcoming. As with the New York Ripper's predecessors in London and Atlanta, the crimes remain unsolved today.

"JACK the Stripper" serial murderer (1959–65)

Seventy years after "JACK THE RIPPER" murdered and disemboweled prostitutes in London's East End, a new generation of streetwalkers learned to live with the ever-present fear of a lurking killer. This "Jack" carried no knife and penned no jaunty letters to the press, but he was every bit as lethal (claiming eight victims to the Ripper's five) and possessed of far greater longevity (operating over nearly six years, compared to the Ripper's 10 weeks). At the presumed conclusion of the case, both slayers shared a common attribute: Despite a wealth of theories and assertions, neither Jack was ever captured or conclusively identified.

On June 17, 1959, 21-year-old prostitute Elizabeth Figg was found floating in the Thames, clad only in a slip, her death attributed to strangulation. Four and a half years passed before discovery of the next murder, with the skeleton of 22-year-old Gwynneth Rees unearthed during clearance of a Thames-side rubbish dump on November 8, 1963. The cause of death was difficult to ascertain, and homicide investigators later tried to disconnect both murders from the "Stripper" series, but today the better evidence suggests that these were practice runs, the early crimes committed by a killer who had yet to hit his stride.

Thirty-year-old Hannah Tailford was the next to die, her nude corpse dragged from the Thames by boatmen on February 2, 1964. Her stockings were pulled down around her ankles, panties stuffed inside her mouth, but she had drowned, and the inquest produced an "open" verdict, refusing to rule out suicide, however improbable it seemed.

On April 9, 1964, 20-year-old Irene Lockwood was found nude and dead in the Thames, floating 300 yards from the spot where Tailford was found two months earlier. Another drowning victim, she was four months pregnant when she died. Suspect Kenneth Archibald confessed to the murder later that month, then recanted his statement, blaming depression. He was subsequently cleared at trial.

Helen Barthelemy, age 20, was the first victim found away from the river. On April 24, 1964, her nude corpse was discovered near a sports field in Brentwood; four front teeth were missing, with part of one lodged in her throat. Traces of multicolored spray paint on the body suggested that she had been kept for a while after death in a paint shop, before she was dumped in the field.

On July 14, 1964, 21-year-old Mary Fleming was discarded, nude and lifeless, on a dead-end London street. Witnesses glimpsed a van and its driver near the scene, but none could finally describe the man or his vehicle with any certainty. Missing since July 11, Fleming had apparently been suffocated or choked to death (as opposed to being strangled) and her dentures were missing from the scene.

Margaret McGowan, age 21, had been missing for a month when her nude corpse was found in Kensington, on November 25, 1964. Police noted the similar traces of paint on her skin, and one of her upper incisors had been forced from its socket. The last to die was 27-year-old Bridget O'Hara, last seen alive on January 11, 1965, her body found on February 11, hidden in some shrubbery on the Heron Trading Estate, in Acton. Her front teeth were missing, and pathologists determined that she had died while kneeling. The corpse was partially mummified, as if from prolonged storage in a cool, dry place.

Despite public appeals to prostitutes for information on their "kinky" customers, police were groping in the dark. Inspector John Du Rose suggested that the last six victims had been literally choked to death by oral sex, removal of their teeth in four cases lending vague support to the hypothesis. A list of suspects had supposedly been narrowed down from 20 men to three when one of those committed suicide, gassing himself in his kitchen and leaving a cryptic note: "I cannot go on." It could mean anything or nothing, but the murders ended with the unnamed suspect's death, and so police seem satisfied, although the case remains officially unsolved.

Who *was* the Stripper? Suspects range from a deceased prize fighter to an ex-policeman, but Du Rose favored a private security guard at the Heron Trading Estate, whose rounds included the paint shop where at least some of the victims were apparently stashed after death. The only "evidence" of guilt is the cessation of similar crimes after the suspect's suicide, but other notorious serial killers, from the original Ripper to the "BABYSITTER" and the "ZODIAC" have likewise "retired" without explanation. The best we can say for Scotland Yard's solution is that it is plausible . . . but unconfirmed.

JACOBS, Cecilia See DETROIT MURDERS

JAMIESON, Marie See "HIGHWAY KILLER"

JEFFERS, Perry murder victim (1868)

A former slave with six grown sons, Perry Jeffers worked a plantation located four miles outside Warrenton, Georgia, during the unsettled Reconstruction era, following the Civil War. Like most southern blacks of the period, Jeffers favored the party of Abraham Lincoln in 1868, and he refused to alter his Republican allegiance in the face of threats from members of the Ku Klux Klan. Jeffers made no secret of his plan to vote for Republican candidate Ulysses Grant on Election Day, and his sons likewise. Klansmen and local Democratic Party leaders—essentially the same individuals—therefore decreed that Jeffers and his sons should die.

Forewarned by a friend of the Klan's intention, Jeffers armed his family and waited for the raiders in their stout log home. The terrorists staged their first assault two days before the election, on November 1, 1868. Creeping up to the house after nightfall, they fired through chinks in the walls, but Jeffers and his sons fought back with grim determination. The Klansmen were forced to retreat, bearing one dead comrade—a young man named Geisland, son of a local planter—and at least three more wounded. Geisland was secretly buried, without ceremony or inquest, while the other Klansmen fabricated excuses for their injuries and plotted revenge.

Warren County's sheriff in those days was John Norris, himself a Republican who had survived his share of death threats and murder attempts. Aware that Klansmen meant to massacre the Jeffers family, Norris took Perry Jeffers and five of his sons into protective custody, lodging them in cells at the county jail in Warrenton. The sixth son, a bedridden invalid, was unable to travel and so remained at home, tended by his mother. Frustrated Klansmen kept the jail under surveillance, but their patience was exhausted by November 5, when a second raid was mounted on the Jeffers home.

That night, a band of 50 to 100 night riders surrounded the cabin, all robed in KKK regalia. Invading the house, they dragged out Mrs. Jeffers and her helpless son, hanging the woman from a shade tree in the yard, while the young man was shot 11 times. Next, Klansmen emptied the cabin of its contents, piling furniture and bedding atop the corpse of their latest victim and setting it afire. After they rode away, a white neighbor cut Mrs. Jeffers down from the tree, in time to save her life. At a subsequent inquest armed Klansmen packed the hearing room and ordered the coroner to return a verdict of death at the hands of persons unknown.

Sheriff Norris had by then decided that his jail would not withstand a determined assault by dozens or hundreds of Klansmen. He proposed that Perry Jeffers and his five remaining sons catch a night train to Augusta, then travel by back roads until they reached South Carolina and safety. A house guest of Norris, Freedmen's Bureau agent R. C. Anthony, proposed an alternative plan, suggesting that Jeffers and sons leave Warren County in broad daylight, since "the Ku-Klux would not dare to take him off the cars in day-time."

As it turned out, Anthony was wrong.

The agent escorted Jeffers and sons to Warrenton's railroad depot on the day of their departure, but they did not have the train to themselves. Klansmen also boarded, both at Warrenton and at Camak, several miles north of the county seat. One of those aboard was the father of slain Klansman Geisland, armed with a shotgun and proudly declaring his plan to kill Perry Jeffers. When the train stopped at Dearing, Jeffers's youngest son got off to help a woman load her trunk aboard. He was thus coincidentally saved when Klansmen dragged his father and four brothers from their car. The five prisoners were marched into some nearby woods and riddled with bullets, while the sole survivor escaped overland to Augusta.

Sheriff Norris later told congressional investigators that no effort had been made to apprehend the murderers of Perry Jeffers and his sons. Powerless himself in the face of Klan terror and Democratic silence, Norris filed a report with Governor Rufus Bullock, who in turn requested federal troops from General George Meade, commander of the military district that included Georgia (who ignored the plea). The Freedmen's Bureau sent a private investigator to Dearing, and he there discovered a black witness who testified after being removed to Augusta. The murders were thus confirmed, but no suspects were arrested. Sheriff Norris was gravely wounded in a December 1869 assassination attempt, but he survived his wounds and declined to prosecute the gunmen he had recognized.

JENSEN, Betty Lou   See "ZODIAC"

JEROME, Helene Adele   murder victim (1958)

Two months after the brutal slaying of GENEVA ELLROY, police in Los Angeles County had another unsolved murder on their hands. This time the victim was a bona fide celebrity—or had been, in her prime. Helene Jerome was a New Yorker raised in England, where she studied at the Royal Academy of Dramatic Art. Oscar winners Paul Scofield and Laurence Olivier were Royal Academy alumni, and while Helene Jerome never achieved their status, she had enjoyed a successful stage career in the 1930s, touring the Far East with several British companies. At 50 she was statuesque, full-figured, with a fine aristocratic air, and could have passed for a much younger woman. She was planning on a comeback via motion pictures, which explained her lodging at a small hotel on North Las Palmas Boulevard in Hollywood.

Jerome had been separated from her husband, 65-year-old character actor Edwin Jerome, for "a couple of years, off and on," but they stayed in constant touch. On August 20, 1958, Edwin was concerned about his wife, her recent illness, and the fact that he could not get through to her by telephone. The line was busy every time he called, and mild concern rolled over into worry when the hotel switchboard told him that Helene's phone had been off the hook for hours. Edwin reached the flat around 1:30 P.M. and found the screen door slashed, its latch undone. The front door of Helene's apartment stood ajar. Inside, he found Helene stretched out on the bed, nude and lifeless. The small apartment's air conditioner and an electric fan were both turned on full-blast.

Los Angeles police investigators learned that Edwin had come calling on his wife the night before, as well. She was alive and fully dressed when he left, around 11:00 P.M., but now her robe lay crumpled on the floor, with her pajamas, bra, and panties piled up on a nearby chair. Besides the slashed screen door, detectives found a bathroom window screen torn and pulled from its frame. Bruising on the victim's throat implied death by strangulation, and an autopsy confirmed that impression. According to the coroner's report: "A sex killer committed the crime inflamed by a murderous lust, a sadist who got his sexual kicks from strangling naked women."

Nor was this the only crime of its type recorded by Los Angeles authorities in recent months, according to John Austin in *Hollywood's Unsolved Mysteries* (1970). "Still wide open on the Hollywood police blotter," Austin wrote, "were the unsolved sex stranglings of two lone women in their apartments by a nighttime sex maniac or maniacs." Regrettably, no further details are provided in Austin's account, and a search of local newspapers for the period in question failed to disclose any similar cases. The other unsolved murders, if in fact they ever happened, are another tantalizing mystery.

As for the case at hand, a night clerk told police that he had noticed Jerome's phone off the hook at 4:00 A.M. He walked around the garden path to reach her flat, knocked softly, found the door unlocked, and entered quietly to see if she was ill. Inside the lighted room he saw a man in bed with Ms. Jerome. Both were nude, and the embarrassed clerk retreated unobserved. Approximately half an hour later, he saw a man leaving the flat, apparently in haste. Despite the darkness, he described the visitor as 25 or 30 years old, tall and slim, dark-complexioned, with prominent ears and "a full head of hair." Playfully, the clerk called out to him, "Next time you'd better lock the screen door," but the stranger hurried off without a backward glance.

According to the watchful clerk, a man of similar description had phoned Jerome from the front desk earlier that evening, identifying himself as George. Edwin Jerome had fielded the call, telling the stranger that his wife was asleep. Much later, around 2:00 A.M., a neighbor had seen a man knocking at Helene's door, but she could offer police no description.

Edwin Jerome told authorities that it was not uncommon for his wife to take a "purely motherly interest" in some young actor or writer. One recent visitor, described by Helene as her "protégé," was said to be an electronics technician and part-time actor-producer, but Edwin could never recall the man's name. He had encouraged Helene's pastime,

Edwin told police, in the belief that her involvement with other performers would help "get her out of herself."

Hotel employees told a very different story to Detectives Robert Beck and Jimmy Close. In truth, they said, the matronly Helene had led a very active nightlife. She was out late almost every evening, often after Edwin had come and gone. She patronized a number of saloons on Hollywood Boulevard, frequently bringing younger men back to her flat for one-night stands. "It was a standing joke around here," the night clerk revealed. "Mrs. Jerome evidently thought she was being very discreet, that nobody knew what was going on."

Edwin Jerome confirmed the report of a man named George phoning from the lobby on Tuesday night, but he had never seen the man and could not help police identify him. Homicide detectives traced Helene's "protégé" and swiftly cleared him of any involvement in the murder. He bore no resemblance to the swarthy visitor observed on Wednesday morning, but he did corroborate the tales of Jerome's indiscriminate love life. While he and Jerome were "just good friends," the young man described her as "practically a nymphomaniac when she was drinking"—and that, apparently, was most of the time.

Detectives located several of Jerome's part-time lovers, questioned them, and called for polygraph examinations if their alibis were shaky, but each in turn was finally released. As for "George," he might as well have been a phantom, there and gone. Police never came close to finding him. In October 1958 a coroner's jury returned an open verdict in the case, and Helene Jerome's murder remains unsolved today.

JESSUP, Georgia child deaths (1980–81)

With a period of 16 months, between June 1980 and October 1981, authorities in Jessup, Georgia, logged the sudden deaths of four related children, all of which remain unsolved today. Successive coroner's reports could find no cause of death in any of the cases. As Detective Joel Smith explained to the press, "We have no idea what killed them. It's hard not to think there's some foul play in it, but we have no proof."

The first to die was four-year-old Olympia Reddish, found lifeless in her bed on June 28, 1980, after

playing outside in the yard. A year later, on July 14, 1981, Phyllis Worley was checking another of her children, nine-month-old Tiffany Reddish, when she found the infant stretched out in her crib, not breathing. Three days later, Tiffany was pronounced dead in the intensive care unit of a local hospital. That same morning, July 17, 19-month old April Gaston—a half sister of the Reddish girls—refused to eat her breakfast, returning to bed in midmorning as if she felt ill. Looking in on the child a bit later, Ola May Gaston found her daughter dead. The final casualty, two-year-old Latoia Reddish, displayed similar symptoms on October 13, 1981, refusing breakfast, then complaining of a headache and stomach pains. Sent off to bed by her mother, she was dead within the hour, leaving medical examiners without a clue to help explain her fate.

Authorities in Jessup reported that all four girls had the same father, though he resided with none of them. Paternal visits were infrequent, and the man had not seen any of his children on the days they died. A physical examination of the father and his sole surviving child revealed no traces of hereditary illness to explain the sudden deaths. Detectives hold to their conviction of foul play, but there appears to be no likelihood of a solution in this baffling case.

JOHANNESBURG, South Africa "muti" murders (1997–98)

South African police suspect a serial killer in the deaths of two children and the disappearance of 11 more from Orange Farm township, a shanty town south of Johannesburg. Although they have no suspects and most of the presumed victims are still missing, authorities have theorized that the case may involve "muti"—the Zulu name for a form of traditional religious "medicine" that incorporates human body parts as primary ingredients.

Even the body count is vague in this unsettling case, with the first public announcement of a police investigation aired on January 20, 1998, reporting that 13 children had vanished from Orange Farm "over the past five months." The actual manhunt began two days prior to that announcement, with the discovery of six-year-old Bukeka Nhlonetse's headless body discarded on a rubbish dump at nearby Ennerdale. On January 20 six-year-old Zanele Nongiza's severed limbs (missing the head, torso, and feet) were found near her Orange Farm home. It was unclear whether the skull and rib of an unidentified young girl, found in the same general area, belonged to either victim, but police said the latest find had "been in the area for a considerable length of time."

Thinking back, detectives recalled the case of yet another young girl, whose mutilated corpse was found on the veldt near Finetown in February 1997. Subsequent news reports named two more girls, Nompumelelo Kgamedi and Edith Aron, found "last year" near the site where the latest remains were discovered. Overall, that made at least four murders in the district, and possibly six (depending on the published source), while the *Mail & Guardian* (on February 6, 1998) referred to "16 children who disappeared and were later found dead in Fine Town and Orange Farm in the past few months."

In the wake of the police announcement, local reporters combed missing-persons dockets and produced 26 cases, 13 of them involving subjects below age 18. Investigating officer Mshengu Tshabalala told journalists that most of the children had vanished around Christmastime. The case took an odd turn on January 22, 1998, when two "missing" boys—Bongani Ngubeni and Mpho Lebese—recognized their photos in the newspaper and contacted authorities. Apparently, they had returned home shortly after their parents reported them missing, but no one thought to advise police of the fact.

That left at least seven children unaccounted for around Orange Farm, and while some skeptics waited for the rest to present themselves in good health, no further living runaways have been identified. Police are hampered in their search, meanwhile, by what Capt. Thabang Letlala of the Vaal Rand police describes as negligent and untrained officers around Orange Farm. "We have trouble there," Letlala told the press, "because these people do not have the right skills to do basic police investigative work, but attempts are being made to bring them up to speed." An internal investigation had also been launched, Letlala said, to find out why authorities ignored reports of 13 missing children until bodies were discovered. Zanele Nongiza's mother complained that when she went to report her daughter missing, on January 3, 1998, a policeman slapped her on the buttocks and asked her for sex. Authorities ignored the case, meanwhile, until Zanele's mangled remains were found.

Police downplayed the "muti" angle in their statements to the press, but that did not prevent angry locals from venting their wrath on various suspects. By February 7, 1998, at least four men had been driven from their homes in the Vaal Triangle, as armed mobs scoured the countryside for an elusive killer. Anxiety increased two days later, when an eight-year-old girl was snatched from her home in Portlands by a man who told her she was "never coming back." The child kicked her assailant and managed to escape, but the prowler was long gone before police arrived.

Curiously, by that time police already had a suspect of sorts in custody, arrested on January 30 and vaguely described as "a middle-aged man" who had tried to lure three children away from the Nomini Primary School. According to the principal who spotted him initially, the man showed certain photos to the children "and told them of his club, which he wanted them to join." At sight of the approaching principal the stranger fled, but he was run down by a howling mob and only saved from lynching by the prompt arrival of police. As for his link to the murders and disappearances of children at Orange Farm, police told reporters, "After we have done all the investigations, we will take him to court."

No further reports on that case were forthcoming from South Africa, but the nation is still plagued by ongoing "muti" murders, most of them unsolved. On October 4, 1998, police psychologist Micki Pistorius announced that the September decapitation of three victims at Delmas, Mpumalanga, were the work of mercenary killers who planned to sell the missing body parts at a premium rate. Victims in that case included a 10-year-old child, a "middle aged person," and a third victim undescribed by police. Authorities explained that in such cases "It usually takes about three people to hold down the victim and cut off the parts. Young children are often targeted as it is believed they have an active life force and are uncorrupted. They are symbols of health, like teenage virgins." A fourth mutilated corpse was found at Sundra, Mpumalanga, in April 1999.

South African police occasionally manage to catch "muti" killers, despite the general conspiracy of silence surrounding such crimes. Four months after the last gruesome discovery at Mpumalanga, East Rand police found a dismembered corpse at the home of a known "muti" healer in Ivory Park. The victim was identified as 22-year-old Willem de Lange, reported missing on August 13, 1999. Two years later, in October 2001, authorities at Mount Frere jailed eight persons for the "muti" slaying of 20-year-old Nombovumo Mvinjana, whom they say was dismembered while still alive. Suspects charged in that case included the victim's husband and uncle, accused of killing Mvinjana to secure body parts for a get-rich-quick spell called "ukutwalela ubutyebi," in which fresh human remains are eaten or smeared on the supplicant's body. Another "muti" arrest, this time by West Rand police, was announced on May 16, 2002. The 23-year-old suspect was captured at a slaughterhouse in Krugersdorp, west of Johannesburg, when he tried to sell the head of an unnamed 52-year-old man for 10,000 rand ($980).

Muti murders continue in South Africa. In April 2003, police in the northern province of Limpopo reported that six-year-old Fezeka Maphanga had been abducted from the bedroom he shared with four siblings in a two-room house, then killed and dismembered. When officers found his remains outside Bushbuckbridge, Maphanga's head, arms, and genitals were missing. So far, no suspects in that case have been identified.

Authorities in KwaZulu-Natal were determined to do better, when muti slayers claimed nine victims around Port Edward and Bizana in the early weeks of 2008. Eight of the victims were women, stunned with hammer blows, then raped, with their genitals cut out while they were still alive, according to pathologists. The ninth victim, a man, was bludgeoned, then his skull was opened and his brain removed. Local villagers, who claimed the number of dead was double that acknowledged by police, lynched one muti murder suspect before officers started making arrests.

While the murders from 2008 remain open, officers charged six suspects with the slayings of nine women around Adams Mission, Illovo, Folweni, and Kwa-Makhutha in 2006 and 2007. Those accused included 63-year-old Abigail "MaMpanza" Njapha, 53-year-old Muzikayise Khoza, 43-year-old Clement Ngcobo, 38-year-old Thini Dumakude, 36-year-old ex-policeman Sandile "My Man" Bhengu, and 18-year-old Popo Bhengu. At trial, in June 2008, 19-year-old state witness Xolani Bhengu recanted statements to police that implicated him and the other defendants in six of the murders. A local pathologist, Dr. Ganesen Ramsamy Moodley, also testified that while the nine women were certainly murdered, some of their missing organs may have been eaten by scavengers.

The court acquitted defendants Khoza, Ngcobo, and Njapha on June 30. Nineteen weeks later, on October 10, the court found that "no credible evidence" linked the remaining defendants to any murders. All were acquitted, and the crimes—like so many before them—remain unsolved.

JOHN, JoAnne Betty   See YAKIMA, WASHINGTON, MURDERS

JOHNLY, Karen Louise   See YAKIMA, WASHINGTON, MURDERS

JOHNS, David   See CHASE, RICHARD AND RUSSELL

JOHNSON, A. M. assassination victim (1868)
The 1868 presidential election unleashed a tidal wave of violence in Arkansas, where recently defeated supporters of the Confederate regime (white-supremacist Democrats) waged a brutal guerrilla war against "radical" Republicans and newly enfranchised ex-slaves. Terrorist groups, including the Ku Klux Klan and Knights of the White Camellia, operated in conjunction with the Democratic Party, which alternately praised their efforts and denied their very existence. In the three months preceding Election Day, more than 200 persons were murdered in Arkansas, while local authorities watched in dismay or (in Democratic districts) actively collaborated with the killers.

One victim of the carnage was Dr. A. M. Johnson, a Republican state legislator from Mississippi County, murdered on August 26, 1868, by "a gang of lawless desperados" presumed to be Klansmen. Over the next four weeks, six freedmen were also killed by terrorists, with many others assaulted, wounded, and driven from their homes to find refuge outside Mississippi County. Governor Powell Clayton declared martial law in the district, and while a troop of state militia—mostly war veterans recruited from Missouri, under Colonel William Monks—quelled most of the county's night riding, the murders were never solved.

JOHNSON, Cassandra   See DETROIT MURDERS

JOHNSON, Darlenia Denise   See "FREEWAY PHANTOM"

JOHNSON, Lois   See DETROIT MURDERS

JOLKOWSKI, Jason missing person (2001)
A native of Omaha, Nebraska, born on June 24, 1981, Jason Jolkowski was 20 years old when he disappeared on June 13, 2001. He received an early call to work that day and told his manager that he would have to walk, since his car was in the repair shop. Moments later, Jolkowski's employer called back and agreed to meet him at Benson High School, eight blocks from the home where Jolkowski lived with his parents and younger brother. Jolkowski showered and left home at 10:45 A.M., last seen by a neighbor as he walked toward Benson High, carrying his red uniform shirt. Jason's boss called the Jolkowski home around 11:15 A.M., reporting that Jason had not reached the school.

No trace of Jolkowski has been found since the day he vanished. Investigators note no subsequent activity on Jason's bank account or cell phone. Based on the amount of his last paycheck and his final bank deposit, parents Jim and Kelly Jolkowski estimate that he left home on June 13 with no more than $60 in his pocket. They deny any involvement by their son with drugs or alcohol, describing him on their Internet Web site as "a very shy individual [who] typically did not pursue social activities." Those factors, coupled with tight family bonds and a new job scheduled to begin on June 18, made him a most unlikely runaway.

In October 2003 the Jolkowskis founded Project Jason, a nonprofit organization that assists families of missing persons in tracing their loved ones. In May 2005, Nebraska's state legislature passed "Jason's Law," creating a statewide clearinghouse for information on missing persons. Eighteen months later, Pennsylvania philanthropist Joe Mammana offered rewards exceeding $2 million for solution of Jason's case and 19 others (including that of NATALEE HOLLOWAY), but the bait lured no takers.

JONES, Anton   See NEW YORK CITY TAXI MURDERS

JONES, Cori Louise   See WASHINGTON, D.C., MURDERS (1989)

JONES, Ernest   See BUFFALO, NEW YORK, TAXI MURDERS

JORGENSEN, Martin   See NAHANNI VALLEY MURDERS

JUAN B. Castagnino Museum of Fine Art robbery (1987)
On March 24, 1987, armed bandits invaded the Juan B. Castagnino Museum of Fine Art in Rosario, Argentina, and stole six paintings by European masters while holding the museum staff at gunpoint. One of the paintings, Francisco de Goya's *Dove and Hen*, was later recovered without leading authorities to the thieves. The works still missing include:

> Goya's *"Bandidos Asesinando a Hombres y Mujeres"*
> El Greco's *Evangelist*
> Magnasco's *Landscape*
> Titian's *Portrait of Philip II*
> Veronese's *Restrato de Hombre con Pelliza*

The statute of limitations for criminal prosecution in this case has expired, but Argentine authorities and spokesmen for Interpol stress that the paintings are still considered stolen property, and receipt or possession of purloined items is a separate offense in itself.

JURSA, Lori   See "OCCULT MURDERS"

KAMAHELE, Jeannette   See "Occult Murders"

KASHKA, Sarah   See Fort Worth murders

KELLERMAN, Mary   See Tylenol murders

KELLY, Mary Jane   See "Jack the Ripper" (1888)

KENNEDY, Debra Jean   See "Orange Coast Killer"

KENNEDY, John Fitzgerald assassination victim (1963)
Some historians call it the pivotal event of American history in the 20th century, yet many of the facts surrounding the event remain obscure today. This much is known with certainty: At 12:30 P.M. on November 22, 1963, President John F. Kennedy was shot and fatally wounded while riding in a motorcade through Dallas, Texas. Governor John Connally, riding in the same limousine, was also wounded but survived his injuries. At 1:15 P.M. Dallas police officer J. D. Tippit was shot and killed in suburban Oak Cliff, before multiple witnesses. Authorities captured Tippit's suspected killer, one Lee Harvey Oswald, at a nearby theater; they later accused him of murdering President Kennedy. Two

days later, at 12:21 P.M. on November 24, Oswald was shot and killed by nightclub owner Jack Ruby during a "routine" transfer from one jail to another. Ruby was convicted of Oswald's murder and sentenced to die, but cancer claimed his life before he could be executed.

Hundreds of books and thousands of articles have been written about those seemingly straightforward events, and virtually every detail of the crimes remains a subject of heated debate to the present day. Despite three official investigations, two criminal trials, and 40-odd years of journalistic argument, a definitive verdict in the JFK assassination remains elusive.

The first government investigation of the crime was ordered by President Lyndon Johnson, conducted by a blue-ribbon panel named after its chairman, U.S. Supreme Court Chief Justice Earl Warren. Other members of the Warren Commission included Senators Richard Russell and John Cooper, Representatives Hale Boggs and Gerald Ford, former Central Intelligence Agency (CIA) director Allen Dulles, and former Assistant Secretary of State John McCloy (who presided over the Nuremberg trials). Federal Bureau of Investigation (FBI) Director J. Edgar Hoover was not included, but he guided (some say manipulated) the commission's investigation. In fact, Hoover had delivered his verdict to the media on November 25, 1963, in a press statement that read: "Not one shred of evidence has been developed to link any other person in a conspiracy with Oswald to assassinate

President John Kennedy discusses foreign policy with adviser John McCloy, later a member of the Warren Commission appointed to investigate Kennedy's assassination. (Library of Congress)

President John F. Kennedy." He never wavered from that judgment, and the Warren Commission echoed Hoover's findings when its report was presented to President Johnson on September 27, 1964.

Some investigators believe Kennedy's secret efforts to murder Cuban leader Fidel Castro rebounded to cause his own death in November 1963.

Pronouncement of the lone-assassin theory demanded some curious mental gymnastics, however, as any critical reader of the commission's report soon discovered. Multiple witnesses to Kennedy's assassination had reported gunshots fired from a "grassy knoll" in front of the president's limousine, rather than from the Texas Book Depository building behind Kennedy, where Oswald allegedly lay in wait. Physicians at Parkland Hospital seemed to confirm that testimony with their initial description of an "entrance wound" in Kennedy's throat. FBI marksmen, trying to test the alleged murder weapon, were forced to repair its defective telescopic sight before they could fire the rifle; even then, it was incapable of firing three aimed shots within the narrow time frame dictated by films and audio recordings of the murder.

The Warren Commission's greatest leap of faith—some say the biggest of its various Big Lies—was seen in its pronouncement of the "magic bullet theory." Simply stated, the commission found that lone gunman Oswald fired three shots at Kennedy's limousine. One shot missed the car entirely, while another was the fatal head shot captured in Abraham Zapruder's famous home movie of the assassination. That left one shot to account for all the nonfatal wounds suffered by Kennedy and Connally together—and what a shot it must have been, if one believes the commission's report. Officially, the bullet entered Kennedy's back and exited through his throat, then pierced Connally's back, came out through his chest, shattered his wrist, and buried itself in his thigh. Later, at Parkland Hospital, the slug was found on an abandoned stretcher, having apparently fallen from Connally's leg wound unnoticed.

Numerous problems with that theory were readily apparent. First, Parkland physicians had described the wound in Kennedy's throat as an *entrance* wound, while another relatively shallow wound in his back was probed with a finger and found to be empty. If those early medical reports were accurate, then Kennedy was shot at least three times (including the fatal head shot), while a fourth bullet must have struck Connally—and Oswald could not be the lone shooter. To eradicate that problem, the commission rewrote history and medical reports were altered or "lost." In the final version the shallow back wound disappeared, and Kennedy's posture was contorted to permit a gunshot in the back to exit through his throat. From there, the slug followed an impossible zigzag course to strike Connally at a different angle and inflict his various wounds. Thus it was written: Oswald's first shot wounded Kennedy and Connally, his second missed, and the third shattered Kennedy's skull.

But more problems remained.

First, Governor Connally (and his wife) steadfastly denied that the first shot inflicted his wounds. Connally heard the first shot, he insisted, and turned to look at Kennedy before a second bullet struck him in the back. (All rifle bullets travel faster than the speed of sound, so Connally could not have heard the shot that wounded him before the bullet struck.) To explain that anomaly, the commission fabricated a "delayed reaction" on Connally's part, but the explanation still lacked credibility. Specifically, the bullet in question—Commission Exhibit 399—was "basically intact," according to ballistics experts who examined it. It had not shattered or "mushroomed" on impact; in fact, it was described in several reports as "pristine." And yet, the bullet that struck Connally left fragments in his wrist and thigh—fragments that are not missing from the bullet found at Parkland Hospital.

Having thus "resolved" the central mystery of Kennedy's assassination with an impossible scenario, the Warren Commission had no problem disposing of the other troublesome evidence. It simply ignored the "grassy knoll" witnesses and others who disputed the description of J. D. Tippit's killer, along with the voluminous evidence of "long gunman" Jack Ruby's lifelong connections to organized crime. It reported Oswald's "communist" activities while failing to mention his apparent role as a paid FBI informant, his close working relationship with a retired G-man in New Orleans, and his association with known members of the right-wing paramilitary Minutemen organization. Reports of his appearance with still-unknown companions at critical times and places were dismissed as lies or "mistakes." CIA photographs of an unidentified man who used Oswald's name on visits to the Russian embassy in Mexico City were filed and forgotten. Oswald's 1959 defection to the Soviet Union was highlighted, but the commission had no interest in how he was able to return home so easily in 1962 (after renouncing his U.S. citizenship and marrying the daughter of a reputed KGB officer). Jack Ruby's offer to reveal a conspiracy in return for safe passage to Washington was rejected.

In fairness to the commission, its final verdict was influenced as much by ignorance as by dishonesty. The FBI and CIA withheld critical information for years after Kennedy's murder, only revealed since the 1970s, and more presumably remains unknown today. The Warren Commission did not know, for instance, that both Oswald and Ruby were listed in FBI files as informants. It had no knowledge of the CIA's long campaign to murder Cuban leader Fidel Castro, acting in concert with leaders of the American Mafia. Nor was the commission told that several of those high-ranking mobsters—including Sam Giancana (Chicago), Carlos Marcello (New Orleans), and Santo Trafficante (Miami) had threatened President Kennedy's life—and/or the life of his brother, Attorney General ROBERT KENNEDY—in the year before the assassination. Those threats had been recorded on FBI wiretaps and reported by hired informers, but the White House was not notified. Similar threats were on record from leaders of the Cuban exile community and at least one prominent member of the Ku Klux Klan (which collaborated with the Dixie Mafia on strong-arm work, and with the CIA in training anti-Castro guerrillas).

By 1966 a public opinion poll revealed that a majority of Americans questioned the Warren Commission's lone-assassin verdict. A year later, New Orleans district attorney Jim Garrison announced that he had uncovered a conspiracy in the Crescent City. Oswald had lived in New Orleans for a time, in 1962–63, and Garrison had uncovered links between the alleged assassin and elements of the city's wealthy far-right political fringe. Some of the suspects were already dead, including Mafia pilot and self-styled superpatriot David Ferrie, who "committed suicide" in February 1967, soon after he was interviewed by Garrison. Still, Garrison filed charges against defendant Clay Shaw, a sometime CIA associate with links to Ferrie and cast of characters including Klansmen, foreign agents, flamboyant homosexuals, and a curious sect called the Orthodox Old Catholic Church of North America. Shaw was also a stockholder in the shadowy Permindex company, accused by French president Charles de Gaulle in 1962 of financing right-wing attempts on his (de Gaulle's) life. Jurors acquitted Shaw on March 1, 1969, and he died in New Orleans on August 14, 1974. *Life* magazine, meanwhile, accused Garrison of taking bribes from local mobsters in an exposé (or calculated smear campaign) that failed to prevent his election as appellate judge. Today, students of the JFK assassination remain bitterly divided as to whether Garrison's probe was an honest attempt to solve the case or an elaborate "disinformation" campaign meant to discredit conspiracy researchers.

Either way, the Shaw trial satisfied no one. Calls for a congressional investigation climaxed in September 1976, with creation of the House Select Committee on Assassinations, charged to investigate the murders of President Kennedy and Dr. MARTIN LUTHER KING, JR. The committee's report, published in 1979, concluded that "acoustical evidence establishes a high probability that two gunmen fired at President John F. Kennedy," and therefore Kennedy "was probably assassinated as a result of a conspiracy." Committee investigators assumed Oswald's role as one shooter, but they were "unable to identify the other gunman or the extent of the conspiracy." That said, the panel proceeded to rule out various plotters, including the Russian and Cuban governments, anti-Castro exiles "as groups," and organized crime "as a group." The FBI, CIA, and Secret Service were exonerated of murder, but they were found to have "performed with varying degrees of competency in the fulfillment of their duties." Spe-

cifically, the Secret Service was "deficient" in protecting Kennedy; the FBI "conducted a thorough and efficient" investigation of the crime but "was deficient in its collection and sharing of information with other agencies and departments"; while the CIA "was deficient in its collection and sharing of information both prior to and subsequent to the assassination."

Longtime researcher Robert Groden was one of those who judged the panel's findings harshly. He wrote:

In the end, the Committee consumed millions of dollars and accomplished little. The Select Committee never did the simple things to get to the truth. Reluctantly, the Committee identified the existence of a "conspiracy" in the Kennedy and King assassinations. But the admission of "conspiracy" was a small breakthrough—the public had suspected it for years. The real truth behind the conspiracy was left undisturbed.

Today there are at least ten prominent theories of who killed Kennedy and why. Oswald necessarily figures in all versions, though his role fluctuates from that of prime mover to hapless scapegoat. The major theories and suspects include:

1. *Oswald the lone assassin.* Initially propounded by the FBI and echoed by the Warren Commission, this was the official version from 1963 to 1979 and remains the favorite of those who equate the term "conspiracy theory" with delusional insanity. Defended most recently by author Gerald Posner in Case Closed (1993), the lone-Oswald/lone-Ruby scenario can only be accepted by ignoring mountains of contrary evidence.

2. *Oswald and the Secret Service.* This theory, proposed by Bonar Menninger in *Mortal Error* (1992) keeps Oswald as a would-be lone assassin but calls the fatal Kennedy head shot an accident, triggered by Secret Service agent George Hickey from another car in the president's motorcade. Thus, while the Secret Service did not conspire to kill Kennedy, Menninger finds a plot to hide the truth of the shooting and thus protect the agency's reputation (already tarnished by reports of agents on a late-night drinking spree the night before the shooting). Supporters of the theory note that Menninger was never sued for libel after naming Agent Hickey as the accidental triggerman.

3. *Fidel Castro.* President Kennedy did not plan the 1961 Bay of Pigs invasion, but he allowed it to proceed and subsequently sanctioned various attempts on Castro's life by the CIA, Mafia leaders, and anti-communist Cuban exiles. Gus Russo theorized, in *Live by the Sword* (1998), that Castro finally tired of the murder attempts and retaliated with a more successful attack of his own. Oswald thus emerged as the primary triggerman, implicated with Castro via his Russian exile and later involvement with the leftist Fair Play for Cuba Committee in New Orleans. Acceptance of this theory requires believers to ignore that Oswald's FPCC chapter was a one-man organization sharing office space with retired FBI agent Guy Banister and a host of far-right activists who hated Castro.

4. *The Russians.* Kennedy had humiliated Russian premier Nikita Khrushchev in October 1962, with the Cuban missile crisis, and some theorists believe the Soviet Union struck back a year later in Dallas. Whether the plot was hatched by Khrushchev directly or by rogue elements of the KGB, defector Oswald might have served as the point man. Unfortunately for proponents of this theory, like the Castro plot above, *any* scenario involving Oswald as the primary shooter must first explain how he managed to defeat the laws of physics in Dallas, killing Kennedy and wounding Governor Connally with an obsolete bolt-action rifle and an inoperative telescopic sight.

5. *The CIA.* Kennedy was embarrassed and infuriated by the Bay of Pigs fiasco. In its wake he unleashed FBI raids to shut down guerrilla training camps in the United States, where CIA agents and others prepared anti-Castro Cubans for illegal raids into their homeland. CIA director Allen Dulles (later a member of the Warren Commission) resigned in September 1961, while Kennedy reportedly threatened to fire other leaders or dismantle the agency itself. It therefore seems entirely logical that "rogue" CIA officers, long accustomed to foreign assassinations and other criminal activity, might have staged a preemptive strike against the president to save themselves (and, in their estimation, America). Variations on this theme incorporate conspirators from the Mafia, anti-Castro exile groups, and far-right vigilante movements including the Minutemen and the KKK.

6. *The Mob.* Leaders of organized crime worked hard to elect John Kennedy in 1960, and he betrayed them two months later by appointing brother Robert as attorney general to mount an unprecedented federal campaign against racketeers nationwide. In addition to the aforementioned Mafia leaders (Giancana, Marcello, and Trafficante), Teamster's Union president Jimmy Hoffa and several of his top aides threatened the lives of both Kennedy brothers. The mob had centuries of experience with murder plots and disposal of troublesome witnesses. Jack Ruby's long association with the underworld makes nonsense of his original claim that he shot Oswald in a fit of emotion, to spare Jacqueline Kennedy from testifying at a future murder trial. Variations of the Mafia scenario incorporate CIA elements who employed the mob to kill Fidel Castro, and anti-Castro Cubans who promised resumption of mob-controlled gambling in Cuba should Castro be deposed.

7. *Anti-Castro Cuban exiles.* This angry clique blamed Kennedy for "sabotaging" the Bay of Pigs invasion by withholding military air support, and then for disrupting future plans to kill Castro. The Cuban community's capacity for violence has been demonstrated by a series of unsolved murders and terrorist acts committed by such radical groups as Alpha 66, Omega 7, and a dozen others based in Florida. Cuban links to the CIA, the Mafia, and far-right paramilitary groups offered no shortage of potential assassins in 1963. Exile leader Jose Aleman is known to have discussed assassination plans with Florida mobster Santo Trafficante, and a Miami pamphlet dated April 15, 1963, seemed to call for Kennedy's murder: "Only through one development will you Cuban patriots ever live in your homeland again as freemen.... [I]f an inspired Act of God should place in the White House within weeks a Texan known to be a friend of all Latin Americans."

8. *The FBI.* J. Edgar Hoover hated the Kennedy brothers personally and feared they would dismiss him as FBI director if John was re-elected to the White House in 1964. Oswald and Ruby are both identified in FBI files as bureau informants, a fact Hoover concealed from the Warren Commission while delivering his overnight "lone-assassin" verdict. Hoover was also friendly

with various mobsters on the Kennedy hit list, accepting cash, free vacations, and no-loss guaranteed investment tips over a 30-year period, during which he staunchly denied the existence of organized crime in America. If Hoover did not call the shots in Dallas, he was certainly well placed to aid a cover-up. His primary interest was revealed on November 24, 1963, when he told White House aide Walter Jenkins, "The thing I am most concerned about . . . is having something issued so we can convince the public that Oswald is the real assassin."

9. *The U.S. military-industrial complex.* Pentagon leaders and defense contractors were troubled by President Kennedy's rumored plans to disengage America from the Vietnam conflict in 1963, and his murder came only days after the assassination of South Vietnamese dictator Ngo Dinh Diem (replaced by more pliable leaders in what many observers now consider a coup d'état supported by the U.S. military and the CIA). In this scenario, high-ranking generals and the corporate leeches who grow fat on military cost overruns had billions to gain and nothing to lose by killing a chief executive whom they considered "soft on communism." Lyndon Johnson is often cast as a co-conspirator in variants of this scenario.

10. *The far-right "lunatic fringe."* The day before Kennedy's arrival in Dallas, associates of right-wing oilman H. L. Hunt purchased a full-page advertisement in a local newspaper, announcing that the president was "Wanted for Treason." That attitude prevailed throughout most of Dixie and the right wing nationwide, with groups such as the Minutemen, KKK, John Birch Society, Christian Crusade, and White Citizen's Council blaming Kennedy for a "communist takeover" in Washington. Sore points included the Bay of Pigs failure, Kennedy's civil rights initiatives for African Americans, the president's religion (Catholic), and Kennedy's efforts to close tax loopholes favoring the petroleum industry. Proponents of this theory suggest that Kennedy signed his own death warrant in 1963, when he declared that "no one industry [i.e., oil] should be permitted to obtain an undue tax advantage over all others." Jack Ruby was a known associate of Texas oilmen—and so was Lyndon Johnson.

KENNEDY, Robert Francis assassination victim (1968)

Robert Kennedy ranks among America's most controversial attorneys general. Nepotism was one issue, since newly elected President JOHN KENNEDY named his brother to the sensitive post (reportedly at the insistence of family patriarch Joseph Kennedy) in January 1961. Another problem was the demonstrated gap between Kennedy's liberal ideals and his performance in office—approving illegal FBI wiretaps and bugging not only corrupt union officials and Mafia leaders, but also targeting supposed allies such as Dr. MARTIN LUTHER KING, JR. He was perceived by some as dedicated, by others as ruthless. In either case, it was hard to be neutral about RFK.

Kennedy's term as attorney general is most memorable for his relentless pursuit of organized crime. The campaign carried over from his years as chief counsel for the U.S. Senate's McClellan Committee (investigating labor racketeers), but it was ironic in light of the role played by big-city gangsters in securing John Kennedy's 1960 election to the White House. Teamster's Union president Jimmy Hoffa was a particular target, finally imprisoned for jury tampering, and he threatened RFK's life on several occasions in conversations reported to the FBI. Similar threats against both Kennedy brothers were made by Mafia bosses Sam Giancana (Chicago), Carlos Marcello (New Orleans), and Santo Trafficante (Florida). FBI Director J. Edgar Hoover, who despised the Kennedys and feared they would dismiss him after the 1964 election, filed the threats without reporting them to the White House or the Department of Justice. President Kennedy was murdered in Dallas, Texas, on November 22, 1964, and two days later, his alleged assassin was killed by mobster Jack Ruby in the basement of police headquarters. Moments after that fatal shot was fired, Jimmy Hoffa gloated to a journalist, "Bobby Kennedy is just another lawyer now."

His judgment was correct. JFK's replacement in the Oval Office, Lyndon Johnson, was a close friend of Hoover's who also loathed Robert Kennedy. Johnson retained RFK in office until September 3, 1964, but Mafia prosecutions rapidly dwindled in the wake of President Kennedy's death. (Over the next three years, the Justice Department's organized crime section cut its field investigations by 48 percent, its grand jury presentations declined by 72 percent, and district court briefs were slashed by 83 percent.) Hoover's G-men, meanwhile, openly defied lame-duck Attorney General Kennedy to the point that he told an aide, "Those people don't work for us anymore."

Kennedy soon found another political office to fill, elected as a U.S. Senator from New York in November 1964. His eyes were on the White House, and in 1968 he had an issue, running hard for the Democratic nomination as an opponent of the Vietnam War. By that time, a majority of Americans questioned the government's lone-assassin verdict in President Kennedy's death, and some observers believed RFK would use his presidential powers to find—and punish—his brother's killers. RFK was one step closer to that goal on June 4, 1968, when he won California's Democratic primary election. At midnight he delivered a brief victory speech to some 1,800 supporters at the Ambassador Hotel, in Los Angeles. By 12:15 A.M., surrounded by his entourage, Kennedy was en route through the hotel's basement to a scheduled press conference in the nearby Colonial Room.

He never made it.

In the kitchen a gunman intercepted the procession and emptied his pistol, mortally wounding Kennedy and injuring five others. More than 70 persons were present as Kennedy's bodyguards disarmed the shooter, a Jordanian immigrant named Sirhan Bishara Sirhan. Unlike the chaotic mess in Dallas five years earlier, the Los Angeles murder seemed to be an open-and-shut case. Sirhan was captured at the scene with gun in hand, leaving a journal filled with maniacal scrawls of "RFK must die!" In custody, he claimed to hate Kennedy because the senator supported military aid for Israel. Convicted of first-degree murder at trial, Sirhan was sentenced to die, but that sentence was commuted to life imprisonment in 1972, after the U.S. Supreme Court invalidated current death-penalty statutes.

Open-and-shut . . . but not quite. The second public murder of a Kennedy within five years produced immediate suggestions of conspiracy, and examination of the evidence provided ample fuel for speculation.

Ballistics was an instant problem, as in Dallas. Sirhan's .22-caliber revolver held eight cartridges, but when the wounds and bullet holes were all accounted for, it was apparent that a minimum of 13 shots were fired inside the Ambassador's kitchen. Police resolved that issue with a modified "magic bullet theory"—claiming one slug had somehow drilled two different ceiling panels before striking a bystander in the forehead—and by stripping the

kitchen of bullet-scarred panels and door frames. Photographs remained, however, forcing yet another wriggle as authorities described the pictured bullet marks as "nail holes." The prosecution's ballistic evidence took another hit, years later, when a Los Angeles police technician admitted test-firing the wrong pistol prior to Sirhan's trial. In 1975 ballistics expert DeWayne Wolfer testified under oath that he had matched the murder bullets to a revolver with the serial number H-18602, whereas the serial number on Sirhan's weapon was H-53725. (Wolfer blamed a bystander in his lab, whose name he could not recall, for giving him the "incorrect" serial number. By the time he admitted the error, both pistols had been destroyed.)

Aside from the number of gunshots, there was also a critical problem of range and direction. Kennedy's autopsy revealed that he was shot three times: once behind his right ear (the killing shot) and twice below his right arm, with the wounds 1.5 inches apart. A

Senator Robert Kennedy fell prey to an assassin during his 1968 presidential campaign. (Library of Congress)

fourth shot pierced the right rear shoulder of his jacket without striking flesh. All four shots were fired from behind, at a right-to-left angle. Police reported that the head shot "was fired at a muzzle distance of approximately one inch," marking his flesh with a gunpowder tattoo. Unfortunately for the lone-gunman theory, Sirhan fired from *in front* of Kennedy, and the nearest witnesses insist that he never came closer than "three to six feet" from his primary target. Furthermore, Sirhan was tackled by witness Karl Uecker after firing two shots, and thereafter fired wildly without aiming as others rushed to disarm him.

The likelihood of a conspiracy in RFK's death increased with the statements of witnesses who recalled Sirhan (or a man matching his description) stalking Kennedy in the days before his murder. Several volunteers recalled Sirhan visiting Kennedy's campaign office in May 1968, accompanied by a blond woman and a man who looked enough like Sirhan to pass as his brother. Similar sightings were logged from the Ambassador Hotel, spanning several hours before the assassination. Finally, within seconds of the shooting, multiple witnesses reported a blond woman in a polka-dot dress running from the scene, shouting, "We killed the senator!" The woman was never identified, but witness to her existence was "discredited" by L.A. police in a marathon interview best described as intimidating and coercive.

If Sirhan did not act alone—if, in fact, he was never in position to fire the fatal shots at all—who was the second gunman in RFK's murder? A candidate named in several published accounts is Thane Eugene Cesar, a uniformed security guard working at the Ambassador Hotel on primary night. In a 1969 interview with journalist Ted Charach, Cesar claimed he was standing behind Kennedy and to his right when the shooting started. He also admitted drawing his pistol but denied firing it. That statement was contradicted by CBS News employee Donald Schulman, who stood behind Cesar in the kitchen and gave the following account to radio reporter Jeff Brent moments later:

Schulman: *A Caucasian gentleman [Sirhan] stepped out and fired three times, the security guard hit Kennedy all three times. Mr. Kennedy slumped to the floor. They carried him away. The security guard fired back.*

Brent: *I heard about six or seven shots in succession. Is this the security guard firing back?*

Schulman: *Yes, the man who stepped out fired three times at Kennedy, hit him all three times and the security guard then fired back . . . hitting him.*

Schulman's report was admittedly confused, since Sirhan fired eight times and suffered no wounds from return fire, but he stuck to his story of Cesar returning the would-be assassin's gunfire. Months after the fact he confirmed to Ted Charach that "the guard definitely pulled out his gun and fired."

Thane Cesar's credibility took another hit when he was interviewed by Los Angeles police after the shooting. He claimed the gun he drew (but did not fire) was a standard .38-caliber revolver, yet authorities learned that he also owned a .22-caliber weapon of the same brand as Sirhan's (Harringon & Richardson). Cesar told investigators he had sold the .22 three months before the shooting, but a bill of sale later surfaced bearing a date of September 6, 1968, three months to the day *after* Kennedy died in Los Angeles.

Lies and confusion aside, we know that Cesar was standing close to Kennedy when the senator was shot. Cesar's clip-on necktie was torn loose in the ensuing struggle and is clearly visible in the most famous photo of the Kennedy crime scene, lying beside RFK on the kitchen floor as a stunned busboy cradles the dying victim in his arms.

Who was Thane Cesar? On the night of June 4, 1968, he was assigned to the Ambassador Hotel by Ace Guard Service, which carried him on its books as a temporary employee. Private investigator Alex Bottus later told journalist David Scheim, author of the assassination study *Contract on America* (1989), that prior to the night of Kennedy's murder it had been "months and months" since Cesar had drawn an assignment for Ace. He was reportedly called at the last minute to substitute for a regular full-time employee. Coincidentally or otherwise, Ace Guard also supplied security personnel for the U.S. National Bank in San Diego, which collapsed in 1973 after being looted by members of organized crime. According to Bottus, Cesar had been jailed several times in Tijuana, Mexico, but the charges were "fixed" in each case by California mobster John Alessio—a director of the conglomerate that ran U.S. National Bank. Bottus further told Scheim that Cesar's "whole track record" demonstrated links to organized crime, and that Cesar had "connections like crazy."

In 1987 Cesar sat for an interview with journalist Dan Moldea. Accompanied by an attorney, he omitted any mention of drawing his pistol when Sirhan opened fire. Instead, he claimed that "when the flashes went off, I hit the deck. . . . I went down, went down." Moldea concluded that Sirhan was indeed the lone gunman in Kennedy's murder, while curiously adding that Cesar (whom he believed to be innocent) possessed "motive, means and opportunity" for the slaying. Ted Charach disagreed and devoted years to tracing Cesar's .22-caliber pistol, finally dredging the weapon (serial number Y-13332) from a muddy pond in Arkansas, in 1993. Plans were announced for new ballistics tests, but no results have yet been published.

Conspiracy theories in the RFK assassination focus on most of the "usual suspects" from his brother's 1963 slaying in Dallas. Members of organized crime had every reason to fear another Kennedy presidency, especially if they were involved in JFK's assassination. The Central Intelligence Agency (CIA) has also come under suspicion, with suggestions that Sirhan may have been "programmed" to kill Kennedy. The late Dr. William Joseph Bryan Jr., a hypnotist with CIA connections, is named in multiple published accounts as Sirhan's likely "programmer," although he denied it in a 1974 interview. Proponents of the "Manchurian candidate" theory note the robotic scrawls in Sirhan's journal and his 30-year claims of amnesia surrounding the murder as evidence of mind control in action. Be that as it may, one thing is certain: The last word on RFK's death has yet to be written.

The case is far from closed.

KEY, Frank   See "I-35 MURDERS"

KGAMEDI, Nompumelelo   See JOHANNESBURG "MUTI" MURDERS

KING, Martin Luther, Jr. civil rights martyr (1968)
History remembers Dr. Martin Luther King Jr. as one of the most outstanding Americans in a remarkable American decade. From 1955 to 1968, as leader of the Southern Christian Leadership Conference, he spearheaded the assault on racial segregation in Montgomery, Birmingham, and Selma, Alabama; in Albany, Georgia; in St. Augustine, Florida; and in lily-white Cicero, Illinois. King's tireless pursuit of justice won him the Nobel Peace Prize in 1964, but it also earned him the undying hatred of relentless enemies. Vigilante members of the Ku Klux Klan schemed incessantly to murder King, abetted in some cases by racist police officers. Longtime Federal Bureau of Investigation

(FBI) Director J. Edgar Hoover branded King "the most notorious liar in the country" and unleashed his G-men in a 10-year campaign of harassment that included wiretaps, bugging, break-ins, slander, and a clumsy attempt to make King commit suicide.

King recognized the dangers of his calling and was not dissuaded. By 1967 he had broadened his message to include a call for peace in Vietnam, denouncing America's long Asian war as "politically and morally unjust." (President Lyndon Johnson thereafter complained, "That goddamned nigger preacher may drive me out of the White House.") King also addressed the issue of poverty in the United States, planning the Poor People's March on Washington, D.C., for summer 1968. As a prelude to that campaign, he threw his weight behind striking sanitation workers in Memphis, Tennessee. On the night of April 3, 1968, King regaled a Memphis audience with his now-famous "mountaintop" speech, redolent with intimations of his own mortality. "I just want to do God's will," King proclaimed, "and He has allowed me to go up the mountain. I've seen the Promised Land. I may not get there with you, but I want you to know tonight that we, as a people, will get to the Promised Land. I am happy tonight that I am not worried about anything. I'm not fearing any man. Mine eyes have seen the glory . . . "

At 6:01 P.M. the following day, April 4, King emerged from his second-floor room at the Lorraine Motel. Surrounded by his entourage, he was about to leave for dinner at a local minister's home when a shot rang out across Mulberry Street. A rifle bullet struck King in the face, inflicting massive and irreparable damage. While death was not pronounced until 7:05 P.M., King was for all intents and purposes killed instantly.

Chaos reigned in the next few moments. King's chauffeur, Solomon Jones, reported seeing a masked man leap from the bushes atop an embankment on the far side of the street, running with some long object in his hand. Harold Carter, a tenant of a South Main Street rooming house whose rear windows faced the Lorraine Motel, confirmed Jones's sighting. On South Main, two doors from Carter's rooming house, Guy Canipe saw a stranger pass by his amusement shop and discard a bundle in the recessed doorway. Glancing out, Canipe saw a rifle and a blue bag "like a typewriter" case, as a white Ford Mustang pulled out from the curb. Memphis police were on alert for the white Mustang by 6:25

Martin Luther King, Jr., removes a cross that was burned outside his home in Montgomery, Alabama. (Library of Congress)

P.M., but a series of spurious CB radio broadcasts lured them to the west side of town—while the killer, they would later say, fled southward into Alabama and beyond.

The hunt for Dr. King's killer began on South Main Street, with the Remington rifle and other items discarded moments after the shooting. FBI agents took charge of the evidence at 10:00 P.M. on April 4, 1968, rushing the weapon and sundry other articles to Washington for analysis. G-men would later claim that 26 fingerprints were found on the rifle, on beer cans, and toiletry items, but only three were clear enough for a detailed comparison. It was April 19, more than two weeks later, when FBI clerks identified the owner of those prints as James Earl Ray, a small-time habitual thief who had escaped from Missouri's state prison one year earlier, on April 23, 1967. To prove the point, they found Ray's Missouri inmate number scratched on a transistor radio that had been dumped with the rifle in Memphis.

Hoover's G-men had identified their suspect, but they had no legal recourse in a murder case, so Ray was formally charged with the federal crime of conspiring to violate Dr. King's civil rights. By definition a conspiracy requires at least two persons plotting to break the law, but government spokesmen would later dismiss the charge as a ruse to get FBI agents involved in the manhunt. There was never any evidence, they claim today, of more than one participant in Dr. King's murder.

And yet . . .

For a lifelong bungler who had spent 14 of his 40 years in prison, once falling out of his getaway car as he fled from a robbery scene, James Earl Ray was suddenly graced with amazing luck. Since his escape from prison, though without a source of income, Ray had traveled to Canada and Mexico, studied dancing and bartending in Los Angeles, vacationed in New Orleans, and finally settled in Atlanta, near Dr. King's home. The rifle found in Memphis had been purchased at a Birmingham sporting goods store on March 29, 1968, when agents theorized that Ray had started stalking King. After the slaying, they discovered, he had fled once more to Canada, where he rented rooms in the name of Paul Bridgman (a real-life Canadian who physically resembled Ray) and obtained false passports in the names of Ramon Sneyd and Eric Galt (again, living Canadians who each resembled Ray). On May 6, 1968, he flew from Toronto to London, and on from there to Lisbon, Portugal. Ray returned to London on May 18, 1968, and was planning to leave England again, this time for Belgium, when British police arrested him at London's Heathrow Airport.

Upon his return to Memphis, Ray initially retained attorney Arthur Hanes Sr., a former FBI agent and onetime mayor of Birmingham best known as a defense lawyer for Ku Klux Klansmen charged with the 1965 murder of civil rights worker Viola Liuzzo. Hanes arranged to finance the defense by signing a $40,000 book contract with Alabama author William Bradford Huie. As a prelude to his book (*He Slew the Dreamer*, 1969), Huie wrote three articles about the case for *Look* magazine, published in November 1968 and April 1969. The first two installments spoke of a plot by wealthy right-wing conspirators to kill Dr. King "for maximum bloody effect" during the 1968 presidential campaign, concluding: "Therefore, in this plot, Dr. King was the secondary, not the primary target. The primary target was the United States of America."

Alleged assassin James Earl Ray (left) is shown with the author at Tennessee State Prison in 1982. (Judy Ann Newton/Author's collection)

The third article astounded readers by making a 180-degree reversal of Huie's previous claims, insisting that Ray had killed King on his own, in a quest for "criminal status." Finally, in a strange attempt to resolve his flip-flop, Huie wrote:

Well, there are large conspiracies and little conspiracies. In large conspiracies, rich and/or powerful men are involved. Small conspiracies involve only little men. . . . I believe that one or two men other than James Earl Ray may have had foreknowledge of this murder, and that makes it a little conspiracy. But if there was a conspiracy, I now believe that James Earl Ray was probably its leader, not its tool or dupe.

By the time Huie penned those words, Ray had already pled guilty to King's murder in Memphis and accepted a 99-year prison term. Texas attorney Percy Foreman had replaced Arthur Hanes in the interim, and he secured Ray's agreement for a guilty plea with a peculiar carrot-and-stick approach. On one hand, he loaned money to Ray's relatives, contingent upon a guilty with no "unseemly behavior" on Ray's part; at the same time, he repeatedly threatened Ray that a trial would result in guaranteed conviction and a date with Tennessee's electric chair. Ray filed his guilty plea on March 10, 1969, and instantly regretted it. He spent the rest of his life in prison, filing fruitless motions for a jury trial, telling anyone who would listen that he had been framed for King's assassination by a shadowy cohort he knew only as "Raoul." Ray died on April 23, 1998, still pleading for a day in court.

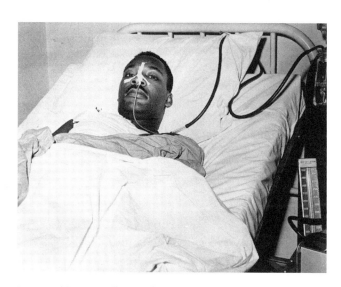

In 1958, King was hospitalized after a deranged woman stabbed him during a public appearance. (Library of Congress)

207

There was evidence of an accomplice in King's murder from the beginning. Between April 1967 and June 1968 Ray spent an estimated $10,000 on travel and living expenses, yet he held only one short-term job at minimum wage. (Spokesmen for the Justice Department speculated that Ray "probably" supported himself by armed robbery, but they identified no specific crimes, and Ray's history of capture after various holdups mitigates against a successful one-man crime wave.) On March 28, 1968, Ray purchased a .243-caliber rifle at a Birmingham sporting goods story, allegedly to go deer hunting with his "brother." He returned to exchange the gun for a larger .30-06 weapon the next day, explaining that his "brother" had told him he bought the wrong weapon. (Ray claimed the instructions and money came from Raoul.) Eyewitnesses at the Memphis Main Street rooming house described a gunman who bore no resemblance to Ray. After King's assassination, while Ray was hiding in Toronto, witnesses saw him with an unidentified man on three occasions. The last time, shortly after a "fat man" visited his apartment, Ray paid cash for an airplane ticket to London. When Ray's car was found in Atlanta, the ashtray overflowed with cigarette butts—but Ray did not smoke.

It was enough, coupled with revelations of the FBI's long vendetta against Dr. King, to prompt demands in Congress for a new investigation of the case. Beginning in September 1976, the Select Committee on Assassinations spent two and a half years (and some $5.4 million) investigating the murders of King and President JOHN KENNEDY. (The equally suspicious death of Senator ROBERT KENNEDY was excluded from review.) The committee's final report, issued in 1979, concluded that "on the basis of the circumstantial evidence available . . . there is a likelihood that James Earl Ray assassinated Dr. Martin Luther King, Jr., as a result of a conspiracy."

Ray's argument, of course, was that he did not murder King at all. Rather, he claimed to be a "patsy," used to buy the rifle that was afterward discarded in Memphis, complete with his fingerprints, to divert attention from the real killer (or killers). That version explained most of the various discrepancies in King's case, but the House committee preferred a "little conspiracy" in the mode of William Bradford Huie, involving only Ray and his two brothers. As outlined in the report:

The committee viewed the likelihood of a financial motive in the assassination as one general indication

of conspiracy. The finding, however, brought the committee no closer to identifying Ray's accomplice(s). Similarly, while several of Ray's activities suggested his preassassination involvement with others, there was no immediate evidence of their identity. The committee's investigation, therefore, necessarily focused on the assassin's known associates, including his brothers, Gerald William Ray and John Larry Ray.

What financial motive was there for the slaying? Committee investigators concluded that a pair of wealthy racists, St. Louis residents John Sutherland and John Kauffmann, had offered a free-floating bounty for Dr. King's murder, and that news of the offer "might have reached James Early Ray" while he was locked up in Missouri's state prison. Neither of the two "serious conspirators" could be questioned by Congress, having died in 1970 and 1974 respectively, but the committee assumed their guilt and went on to draw a tentative (wholly undocumented) link between Sutherland-Kauffmann and the Ray brothers. The House report concluded:

Because of a failure of the evidence, the committee's conclusions must, however, be phrased in terms of alternatives. The committee believed that the St. Louis conspiracy provided an explanation for the involvement of Ray and one or both brothers in the assassination. The manner of their involvement could have taken one of two forms. James Earl Ray may simply have been aware of the offer and acted with a general expectation of payment after the assassination; or he may have acted not only with an awareness of the offer, but also after reaching a specific agreement, either directly or through one or both of his brothers, with Kauffmann or Sutherland. The legal consequences of the alternative possibilities are, of course, different. Without a specific agreement with the Sutherland group, the conspiracy that eventuated in Dr. King's death would extend only to Ray and his brother(s); with a specific agreement, the conspiracy would also encompass Sutherland and his group. In the absence of additional evidence, the committee could not make a more definite statement. The committee believed, nevertheless, that the evidence provided the likely outlines of conspiracy in the assassination of Dr. King.

It is unfortunate that this information was not developed in 1968, when it could have been pursued by law enforcement agencies equipped with tools not available to the committee and at a time when the principals were still alive and witnesses' memories were more precise.

That "unfortunate" result is traceable to one man: King's mortal enemy, FBI Director J. Edgar Hoover. Indeed, there is persuasive evidence that G-men never seriously looked for evidence of a conspiracy in King's death. According to ex-Agent Arthur Murtagh, FBI employees at the Atlanta field office cheered reports of King's murder, and those farther afield were actively discouraged from reporting conspiracy leads. Hoover himself delivered the Bureau's lone-assassin verdict to Attorney General Ramsey Clark in a memo dated June 20, 1968, less than two weeks after Ray was arrested in London.

I said I think Ray is a racist and detested Negroes and Martin Luther King and there is indication that prior to the Memphis situation, he had information about King speaking in other towns and then picked out Memphis.

The Justice Department ultimately rubber-stamped Hoover's conclusion, as it had in the 1963 Kennedy assassination, and department spokesmen deny to this day any suggestion that Ray acted with accomplices, much less that he was framed for a murder he did not commit.

In December 1993, Memphis resident Loyd Jowers—owner of a restaurant near the Lorraine Motel—appeared on the ABC network's *Prime Time Live* program, relating details of an alleged Mafia-government conspiracy to kill Dr. King. Jowers claimed that he had received $100,000 to arrange the murder, dismissed James Earl Ray as a scapegoat, and named the actual triggerman as Memphis policeman Earl Clark. In 1998, soon after Ray died in prison from complications of kidney and liver disease, King's widow and children filed a wrongful-death lawsuit against Jowers and "other unknown co-conspirators." On December 8, 1999, a Memphis jury found Jowers responsible for King's death and declared that his fellow conspirators included unnamed "government agencies." Another Justice Department review of the case, launched in August 1998, concluded in June 2000 that there was "no reason to believe" Jowers's allegations. Jowers died on May 20, 2000.

In April 2002, a Florida minister Rev. Ronald Denton Wilson announced that his late father, Henry Clay Wilson, was King's assassin and "the main guy" in the murder plot. Wilson described his father (who died in 1990) as an active member of the Ku Klux Klan, but insisted that King's slaying "wasn't a racist

thing." Rather, he said, his father "thought Martin Luther King was connected with communism, and he wanted to get him out of the way. He kept saying it was the patriotic thing to do. He said he had to save the country."

Wilson elaborated on his claim, reporting that he had attended meetings between his father and two fellow plotters. "I was invited as a minister," he told the *New York Times.* "My dad wanted me to pray and ask for everything to go right." After the assassination, Wilson said, "I was sworn to never bring it up. I wasn't going to turn Dad in." In fact, he waited for 12 years beyond his father's death, until the other two conspirators also died. "I felt safer now," he explained, "because everybody involved is now dead. Plus, I wanted to cleanse my soul. I've carried this weight for a long time." William Pepper, Ray's last attorney and a lawyer for Atlanta's King Center, told reporters that he first heard from Williams in 1999 or 2000, but had "never seen any hard evidence to justify the allegations now being made."

A spokesman for Jacksonville's FBI office, Agent Ron Grenier, told the *Times* that G-men took Williams's claim seriously, "but that the issue had not risen to the level of a full investigation." Meanwhile, agents assigned to the FBI office in Memphis denied any investigation of the claims. At last report, no effort had been made to recover the alleged murder rifle, which Williams says was dropped into the St. Johns River, southeast of Jacksonville, Florida.

KING, Patricia See "Astrological Murders"

KING, Timothy See "Babysitter"

KINSEY, Charlotte See Oklahoma City state fair murders

KISS, Bela serial killer who eluded capture
A family man and amateur astrologer, Hungarian Bela Kiss began his career as a serial murderer relatively late in life. In February 1912, at 40 years of age, Kiss moved to the village of Czinkota with his wife, Marie, some 15 years his junior. Within a matter of weeks, Marie found herself a lover, one Paul Bikari, and in December 1912, Kiss sadly told his

neighbors that the couple had run off together, leaving him alone. In place of his wife, Kiss hired an elderly housekeeper. She, in turn, learned to ignore the parade of women who came to spend time with Czinkota's newly eligible bachelor.

Around that same time Kiss began collecting large metal drums, informing the curious village constable that they were filled with gasoline, expected to be scarce with the approach of war in Europe. Budapest authorities, meanwhile, were seeking information on the disappearance of two widows, named Schmeidak and Varga, who had suddenly dropped out of contact with their friends and relatives. Both women had been last seen in the company of a man named Hoffmann, residing near the Margaret Bridge in Budapest, but he had also vanished without a trace. Czinkota's constable was generally aware of the investigation, but he saw no reason to connect Herr Hoffmann with the quiet, unassuming Bela Kiss.

In November 1914, Kiss was drafted into military service, leaving for the front as soon as he was sworn into the ranks and issued combat gear. Another 18 months would pass before officials in Czinkota were informed that Kiss had died in battle, one more grim statistic for the casualty rosters in that bloody spring of 1916. Kiss was forgotten by the townsfolk until June, when soldiers visited Czinkota in a search for stockpiled gasoline.

The village constable remembered Kiss's cache of metal drums and led a squad of soldiers to the dead man's home. Inside the house the searchers turned up seven drums, but they contained no gasoline. Instead, each drum held the naked corpse of a woman, strangled and preserved in alcohol. The drawers of Kiss's dresser overflowed with cards and letters from women responding to newspaper advertisements, purchased by Kiss in the name of Hoffmann, a self-described "lonely widower seeking female companionship."

Czinkota's constable recalled that there had been more drums—and many more, at that. A search of the surrounding countryside revealed another 17, each with a pickled corpse inside. Authorities from Budapest identified the missing widows, while Marie Kiss occupied another drum. Her lover, Paul Bikari, was the only male among the 24 recovered victims.

Homicide detectives theorized that Bela Kiss had slain his wife and her clandestine lover in a jealous rage, disposing of the bodies in a manner that—he thought—eliminated any possibility of subsequent discovery. The crime apparently had unleashed some hidden mania, and Kiss spent the next two years pursuing lonely women with a passion, bilking several of their savings prior to strangling them and sealing them inside the makeshift funeral vaults. It was a grisly case, but Kiss had gone to face a higher court.

Or had he?

In the spring of 1919, Kiss was sighted on the Margaret Bridge in Budapest, "Herr Hoffmann's" prewar stomping grounds. Police investigation proved that Kiss has switched his papers with a battlefield fatality, assuming the dead man's identify to make good his escape. That knowledge brought police detectives no closer to their man, however, for Kiss had slipped the net again.

The futile search went on. In 1924, a deserter from the French Foreign Legion told officers of the Sureté about a fellow legionnaire who entertained the troops with tales of his proficiency with a garrote. The soldier's name was Hofman, and he matched descriptions of Bela Kiss, but the lead was another dead end. By the time Hungarian police were informed, Legionnaire "Hofman" had also deserted, vanishing without a trace.

In 1932, a New York homicide detective, Henry Oswald, was convinced that he had sighted Bela Kiss emerging from the Times Square subway station. Nicknamed "Camera Eye" by colleagues, after his uncanny memory for faces, Oswald was unshakable in his belief that Kiss—who would have been approaching 70 by then—was living somewhere in New York. Unfortunately, Times Square crowds prevented Oswald from pursuing Kiss, and he could only watch in helpless rage as his intended quarry disappeared.

In 1936, a rumor spread that Kiss was working as a janitor at a Sixth Avenue apartment building, but again he managed to evade police, and there the trail went cold. Whatever finally became of Bela Kiss (if he was ever in New York at all) remains a mystery, beyond solution with the passage of seven decades. In Hungary he is remembered simply as the one who got away.

KITZMILLER, Nancy   See "I-70/I-35 Murders"

KLINSKY, Mary   See New Jersey murders

KRAVEICHVILI, Jean-Michel   See "Monster of Florence"

L

LABOKRO mass poisoning (2001)

On August 27, 2001, media reports from Abdijan, capital of Côte d'Ivoire (Ivory Coast) announced that 25 persons had died at Labokro, 18 miles away, after eating porridge (or stew; reports vary) laced with an unidentified poison. At least 110 persons consumed the food that afternoon, all of them afterward suffering symptoms that included nausea, diarrhea, and severe abdominal pain. According to the newspaper *Yamoussoukro*, the meal was prepared by a woman whose mother, husband, and two children were numbered among the dead. Eighty other victims of the deadly feast were hospitalized for treatment, but they later recovered. Ivory Coast authorities declared that paramilitary police were assigned to investigate the case, but no further information has yet been released.

"LADY of the Dunes" Provincetown, Massachusetts (1974)

A 13-year-old girl was walking her dog through the Race Point dunes, outside Provincetown, Massachusetts, when she made a gruesome discovery on July 26, 1974. The nude and lifeless body of a Caucasian woman lay stretched out on a beach towel, hands severed "with surgical precision" and missing from the scene. The victim's throat had been slashed to the spine, and the left of her skull was crushed by heavy blows. A pair of jeans lay folded underneath her nearly severed head to serve as a pillow. There were no signs of struggle at the scene, prompting investigators to suspect the victim either knew her killer or had been surprised while sleeping in the dunes.

Missing hands and advanced decomposition frustrated police efforts to identify the woman whom newspapers dubbed the "Lady of the Dunes." Medical examiners reported that she had been 5-feet-6 to 5-feet-8-inches tall, between 20 and 40 years old, with reddish-brown hair and pink-painted toenails. Official estimates on time of death ranged from 10 days to three weeks. The best clue to the victim's identity lay in her mouth, where several thousand dollars worth of gold crowns revealed what police termed "the New York style" of dentistry. Authorities contacted every dentist in the state of Massachusetts, published photos of the crowns in two dentistry journals, and provided others to the FBI and Interpol—all without scoring a hit.

Frustrated by his inability to identify either the victim or her slayer, Provincetown police chief James Meads kept the woman's skull on his desk as a perpetual reminder of the case, vowing not to retire with the case unsolved. (He did nonetheless, in 1992.) For years after the murder, persons unknown commemorated the woman's death by leaving flowers on her grave each July 26, but authorities came no closer to identifying the mourners than they did the victim or her killer. In July 1995 Detective Warren Tobias claimed to know the dead woman's identity—and to have a viable suspect in the case—but no proof was forthcoming to support a murder charge.

As reported by journalist George Liles in the *Provincetown Banner,* Det. Tobias believed the Lady of the Dunes is 25-year-old Rory Gene Kesinger, arrested in a Pembroke, Massachusetts, drug raid in early 1974. Kesinger, who matched the murder victim's general description, escaped from the Plymouth County House of Correction a few weeks after her arrest and then disappeared, shortly before the Lady of the Dunes was found. Tobias also alluded to a police report of the drug raid, citing the presence of a certain car outside the house where Kesinger was arrested. The vehicle was traced to a Provincetown resident, still living in 1995, who admitted ownership of the car but denied any link to the murder. Tobias cited a "gut feeling" that the suspect had lied, but without solid evidence he refused to give a name or even the suspect's gender, referring simply to "that person."

Unfortunately for Tobias, Rory Kesinger remains almost as enigmatic as the Lady of the Dunes herself. Despite her disappearing act in 1974, no one linked Kesinger's name to the murder case until 1990. Today she is remembered as part of a gun-running, drug-smuggling syndicate that eluded federal agents in Alaska, California, Kansas, and Texas, before they were finally jailed at Pembroke. Kesinger tried to shoot a policeman on the night of her arrest and was awaiting trial on charges of assault with intent to kill when she escaped from custody, assisted by a corrupt jailhouse guard. She was never seen again, but one of those arrested with her in 1974 later told police that Kesinger was "pushing up daisies." Det. Tobias believes she was murdered by criminal accomplices who feared she might turn "snitch," her body then discarded in the dunes.

Ex-Chief Meads disagrees with Tobias on how and where the murder was committed. "I'm positive," he told George Liles in 1995. "She wasn't killed elsewhere. Whoever did this to her, she went out there with. She was sharing that towel with someone." In the absence of DNA samples from Kesinger, meanwhile, she can neither be confirmed nor excluded as the Lady of the Dunes.

And there are other prospects, to be sure. A Rhode Island resident told Provincetown police that a female friend had gone walking with her dog near town, in June 1974, and never returned. Years later, in the early 1980s, a local psychic told Chief Meads the victim was a Canadian nurse named Carolyn or Marilyn O'Leary. Another caller reported American nurse Carolyn O'Leary missing since the mid-1970s, but police found her alive and well. In 1987, following an "anniversary" story in the *Boston Globe,* a Canadian caller told authorities that she had watched her father strangle a woman near Provincetown in the early 1970s. The same year, 1987, Chief Meads fielded calls from a Boston resident who claimed the Lady of the Dunes was her sister, missing since 1972.

Meads told George Liles that hundreds of missing-persons files were reviewed in his search for the victim's identity, but those with dental records never matched, while others lacked the photographs or X rays needed for comparison. "There's no doubt in my mind that the name of the victim came across my desk," Mead said, ruefully admitting that "the only way that case is going to be solved is if someone is near their death and wants to get it off their chest."

Drifter Hadden Clark was briefly suspected of the murder in June 1993, the year after Chief Meads retired, but authorities who convicted him of a recent homicide in Maryland could ultimately find no proof that Clark was a long-term serial killer linked to the Provincetown case. Around the same time forensic anthropologist Douglas Ubelaker examined the skull and delivered it to Cell Mark, the Maryland laboratory famous for its DNA analysis in the O. J. Simpson case and others. Cell Mark's experts reported that no viable marrow cells could be recovered from the skull for DNA testing, and despite unconfirmed reports that the Lady of the Dunes was exhumed in 2000 for DNA tests on her headless corpse, no missing person has yet been identified as the Provincetown victim.

LAFERTE, Annie   See NAHANNI VALLEY MURDERS

LAKE Bodom murders (1960)

Lake Bodom lies near Espoo, the second-largest city in Finland, located 14 miles west of Helsinki. The lake is relatively small, less than two miles long and 1,000 yards wide at its broadest point. Lake Bodom's only claim to fame—or infamy—involves a brutal assault on four teenage campers, committed nearly 50 years ago, which remains unsolved today.

On the night of June 4, 1960, two 18-year-old boys, Seppo Antero Boisman and Nils Wilhelm Gustafsson, camped at Lake Bodom with a pair of 15-year-old girls, Maila Irmeli Björklund and Anja Tuulikki Mäki. Sometime between 4:00 and 6:00 A.M., the four suffered a savage attack that left Björklund, Boisman, and Mäki stabbed and bludgeoned to death. Nils Gustafsson survived, with head wounds that included fractured facial bones, a broken jaw, and major bruising to his face. Police were baffled by the crime, and they identified no suspects.

In 1972, on the 12th anniversary of the slaughter, authorities revealed that a man (never publicly identified) had killed himself, leaving a note that claimed he was the murderer. Police confirmed that on the day of the attacks, he worked at a lakeside kiosk and sold lemonade to the victims, subsequently expressing "hard feelings" against the young campers. Nonetheless, the suspect's wife insisted that he was at home, in bed with her, when the murders occurred, and detectives officially verified that alibi.

In 2003, Dr. Jorma Palo published a book about the murders, naming German immigrant Hans Assmann as a suspect. Dr. Palo had worked at a hospital in Espoo during June 1960, and recalled treating Assmann—whom he deemed "suspicious"—for injuries suffered on the night of the slayings. Palo's research convinced him that Assmann was an East German spy in the 1960s, and that Finnish police cleared Assmann as part of a diplomatic cover-up. Veteran officers denied that charge, reporting that Assmann had a valid alibi for the night in question. Claims that Assmann admitted the murders in 1997, making a deathbed confession to a Finnish journalist, remain unverified.

In March 2004, Finnish authorities detained survivor Nils Gustafsson on suspicion of murdering his friends, almost 44 years earlier. Fifteen months later, in June 2005, Finland's National Bureau of Investigation cited newly discovered bloodstain evidence as proof of the theory that Gustafsson had killed his fellow campers in a jealous rage, focused primarily on girlfriend Maila Björklund. His trial began on August 4, 2005, with prosecutors seeking a life prison term, but jurors acquitted Gustaffson of all charges on October 7. The Finnish government subsequently paid Gustaffson €44,900 for mental suffering caused during the months that he spent in jail prior to trial. The Lake Bodom slayings remain officially unsolved.

LAMPLUGH, Susannah missing person (1986)

A British subject, born in 1961, Susannah "Suzy" Lamplugh was a real estate agent with Sturgis Estate Agents in London when she vanished on July 28, 1986. The last clue to her fate was an appointment for 12:45 P.M., with a client known only as "Mr. Kipper." Lamplugh was supposed to show the man a house on Shorrolds Road, in Fulham, West London. The notation "O/S" in her appointment book meant that she was supposed to meet the stranger outside, on the street.

When Lamplugh failed to return after lunch, coworkers contacted London police. Officers found her car parked outside another Fulham house listed for sale, this one on Stevenage Road, a mile and a half from the Shorrolds Road address. Her purse was in the car, but the ignition key was missing. Back on Shorrolds Road, meanwhile, neighbors recalled Lamplugh arguing with a man at the curb, then climbing into an unidentified car. Residents of Stevenage Road described a black BMW sedan, seen on the street around the time Lamplugh vanished, but its owner was never identified.

Detectives learned that an unknown man had delivered a bouquet of roses to Lamplugh's office several days before she disappeared, but he, too, proved untraceable. Speculation that the name "Kipper" might actually be the Dutch name Kuiper sidetracked investigators for a time, but ultimately led them nowhere. Lamplugh was officially declared dead and presumed murdered in 1994. Renewed investigations in 1998 and 2000 failed to locate any further evidence.

Two suspects have been named in Lamplugh's case. The first, John Cannan, stands convicted of murdering 29-year-old Shirley Banks in Bristol, on October 8, 1987. Prior to that crime, Cannan had compiled a long record of crimes against women, including a prison term for rape. A former girlfriend of Cannan's, Gilly Paige, told police in 2000 that Cannan had "suggested" Lamplugh's corpse was buried at Norton Barracks, a former Royal Air Force base in Worcestershire, while an ex-cellmate claimed Cannan buried Lamplugh under the patio at his mother's home in Sutton Coldfield, in the West Midlands. Searches at both sites proved fruitless, and Cannan has denied any role in Lamplugh's disappearance. Some detectives still consider him their prime suspect, and also believe that he killed a woman named Sandra Court, found strangled at Bournemouth on May 3, 1986.

Another "person of interest" in Lamplugh's case, at least briefly, was convicted British serial killer Steven Gerald James Wright. Wright worked as a steward aboard the ocean liner RMS *Queen Elizabeth 2* in 1982, when Lamplugh was employed as the ship's beautician. Subsequently, in 2006, Wright murdered five prostitutes around Ipswich, in Suffolk. Jurors convicted him of those crimes in February 2008, and he received a life prison term. With revelation of his tentative link to Lamplugh, detectives examined Wright as a suspect in her case, but May 2008 brought an official announcement from London police that their investigation "is not a strong line of inquiry."

Meanwhile, in 2006, a Wiltshire estate agent suffered knife wounds inflicted by a still-unidentified male client whom she knew only as "Mr. Herring"—considered a possible link to Lamplugh's case, since both herring and kippers are fish. Police have no suspects in that case, but presently deny any link to Suzy Lamplugh's disappearance.

LANDCRAFT, Elizabeth   See "SOUTHSIDE SLAYER"

LAREY, Mary   See TEXARKANA "PHANTOM GUNMAN"

LASS, Donna   See "ASTROLOGICAL MURDERS"

LAWRENCE, Lillian   See ATLANTA UNSOLVED MURDERS (1980–82)

LECLERCQ, Jacqueline   See "BUTCHER OF MONS"

LEE, George Washington civil rights martyr (1955)
George Lee was a man ahead of his time, in an era and place that despised progress. Born in 1903, the product of a covert union between a white man he never met and an illiterate black field hand, Lee was raised in poverty on a plantation outside Edwards, Mississippi. He was the first in his family to graduate from high school, moving on from there to "see the world" in New Orleans. When he returned to settle at Belzoni, in Humphreys County, Lee was both a Baptist minister and a qualified typesetter. Somehow, he found time to run a print shop while preaching to four scattered congregations each week.

And he dreamed of being equal under the law.

The U.S. Supreme Court's school desegregation ruling of May 1954 brought that goal one step closer, at least in theory. Mississippi's white authorities had no intention of complying with the order, and they proudly joined an all-white Citizens' Council that chose "Never!" as its motto, but Rev. Lee saw a way around the problem. If enough black Mississippians registered to vote, they could topple the Magnolia State's whites-only regime. Humphreys County was a case in point, its population including 7,000 whites and 16,000 blacks. With those odds an election should be no contest.

Lee conceived the idea of a voter-registration campaign at a time, his wife later recalled, when local blacks "weren't even thinking about it." His vehicle was a local chapter of the National Association for the Advancement of Colored People (NAACP), formed in collaboration with 64-year-old grocer Gus Courts and Belzoni mortician T. V. Johnson. Quietly, they urged local blacks to pay the state's poll tax—later ruled illegal—and register to vote before the next election. Lee and Courts proceeded without fanfare, but word of their efforts soon got back to Sheriff Isaac Shelton and the Citizens' Council. A scowling delegation offered suffrage to Lee and his wife, in return for a cessation of Lee's efforts to register others, but the minister declined, unwilling to accept special favors while his people languished in servitude. The white ambassadors left him with dire predictions of catastrophe.

Members of the Citizens' Council—once described by Federal Bureau of Investigation (FBI) Director J. Edgar Hoover in a formal White House presentation as "the leading citizens of the South"—prided themselves on their "peaceable" and "law-abiding" defense of segregation, drawing a line in the sand between themselves and the "low-class" Ku Klux Klan. (In fact, the main difference was an absence of bed sheets at Council meetings, and the two groups often collaborated, in Mississippi and elsewhere.) Initially, the Belzoni Council tried economic pressure against blacks who joined the NAACP and sought to register as voters, cutting off credit at white-owned stores and raising rent on black commercial properties (including Gus Courts's grocery store). When that failed to stem the tide, however, resistance swiftly turned ugly. Cars were vandalized and late-night telephone death threats became routine. A black social club, the Elk's Rest, was ransacked by prowlers who left a note behind: "You niggers think you will vote but it will never happen. This is to show you what will happen if you try."

But try they did, regardless. After 12 months of quiet effort, 92 blacks had registered to vote in Humphreys County, with more on the way. Rev. Lee felt the heat from his white opposition, commenting privately to his wife in words that eerily anticipated Dr. Martin Luther King's Mountaintop speech in Memphis, 13 years later. "Somebody's got to stand up," Lee said. "There may be some bloodshed, and it may be my blood that gets shed. If so, we'll just have to take it. At least we have no children who will suffer."

Lee and Courts met for the last time at 9:00 P.M. on May 7, 1955, the Saturday night before Mother's Day. They talked for nearly two hours at Lee's home, then Lee drove off to retrieve his best suit from a local dry cleaner's shop. He was returning home, a short drive of six or seven blocks through downtown Belzoni, when a second car passed him at speed and a shotgun blast tore into Lee's face. His car swerved, jumped the curb, and crashed into a house. Lee staggered from the wreckage, dazed and bleeding. Two black taxi drivers had witnessed the crash, and they helped Lee into one of the waiting cabs. He died en route to Humphreys County Memorial Hospital.

Within an hour of the shooting, Belzoni's telephone system suffered a curious breakdown, affecting only black customers. Those who tried to place outgoing calls were told to try again later, that all lines were "busy." Several anxious friends of Rev. Lee piled into a car and raced to Mound Bayou, an all-black community nearby, to use the telephones there. In short order calls were placed to Dr. A. H. McCoy (state president of the NAACP), to a friendly congressman, and to the White House. Despite the wall of silence thrown around Belzoni, the ripples had begun to spread.

Mortician T. V. Johnson, with two black physicians in attendance, extracted the lead pellets from Lee's face and skull. Sheriff Shelton, ignorant of modern dentistry (at least), declared the pellets "most likely nothing but fillings from his teeth, jarred loose when the car crashed against the house." Later, when a ballistics report identified the pellets as buckshot, Shelton would change his theory to claim Rev. Lee had been shot by "some jealous nigger," as the result of an illicit love affair.

Even with the White House on alert, it took another 15 days for news of Lee's death to break in the *New York Times*, with a short item reporting that FBI agents

Hundreds attended the 1955 funeral of Rev. George Lee, following his murder by Mississippi terrorists. (Library of Congress)

had been dispatched to investigate a "traffic fatality." By May 27 G-men had found one witness to the murder hiding in St. Louis, where he described the killers' car as a two-toned convertible. Back in Belzoni an all-white coroner's jury finally abandoned the untenable "car crash" scenario and blamed Lee's death on "hemorrhage and probable asphyxiation from a wound, the cause of which is not clear." Sheriff Shelton accepted the report, telling reporters, "This is one of the most puzzling cases I have ever had. If Lee was shot, it was probably by some jealous nigger. He was quite a ladies' man." Strangely, the announcement of that theory did not prompt Shelton to question Lee's wife—or anyone else. Dr. McCoy, addressing a packed house at Lee's funeral on May 22, raised a warning flag for local law enforcement:

Instead of frightening us, this shocking tragedy has served as a stimulus. Sheriff Shelton is sitting outside that door right now, he and his boys. Came back from his fishing just so he could watch this meeting. I say he might better be investigating the murder of the Reverend Lee than watching this meeting, or taking his little tin bucket with some bait in it and going fishing. The sheriff says that the Reverend Lee's death is one of the most puzzling cases he's ever come across. The only puzzling thing is why the sheriff doesn't arrest the men who did it.

But he never would—and with Lee in the ground, Gus Courts was next on the racist hit list. Death threats against the elderly grocer intensified, ignored by Sheriff Shelton and by the Justice Department in Washington. At 8:00 P.M. on Friday, November 25, 1955, Courts was closing his store for the night when a car passed by and gunfire rang out, bullets drilling Courts in the arm and stomach. After futile calls to law enforcement—Sheriff Shelton could not be reached; Belzoni's police chief declined to visit the crime scene—Courts rode with friends to Mound Bayou's Taborean Hospital for treatment that saved his life.

The new investigation was, if possible, even more lackluster than the search for Lee's killers. Sheriff Shelton told reporters, "They took Courts across two counties, though we have the best hospital in the world right here in Belzoni. They didn't even give him first aid here. I'm not going to chase them down. Let the Naps [white slang for NAACP] investigate. They won't believe anything I say anyway." When asked if Courts's civil rights activities prompted the shooting, Shelton replied, "Hell, no. Some nigger had it in for him, that's all." (Presumably the victim's age barred him

from being called "a ladies' man.") A *New York Post* reporter asked Shelton how he knew the gunman was black, leading Shelton to reply that there were "three or four niggers in the store and nobody outside." How, then, did he explain shots fired through Courts's window from the street? Shelton shrugged: "There was bound to be one outside, because that's where he got shot from."

The FBI was little better. Two agents visited Courts in the hospital on November 26, but they showed no real interest in cracking the case. When Dr. J. R. Henry offered the bullets extracted from Courts, the G-men told him to "keep them." They never returned for a follow-up interview and apparently questioned no one in Belzoni, black or white. Courts finally gave up the fight and moved to Chicago, as soon as he was fit for travel. Both shootings, like so many other incidents in Mississippi's long reign of terror, remain unsolved today.

LEECH, Alexander murder victim (1871)

South Carolina suffered more sustained and brutal violence than any other state of the former Confederacy during the chaotic Reconstruction era following the Civil War, and York County was easily the most violent sector of the state. Hundreds of former slaves and white members of the Republican Party were killed, whipped, castrated, or otherwise assaulted in York County by members of the Ku Klux Klan who operated with virtual impunity, protected by leading members of the all-white Democratic Party. Federal troops and state militia did their best to quell the bloodshed, but their forces were spread thin and frequently outnumbered by the terrorists. Matters went from bad to worse when the local militia detachment was disbanded in early 1871, leaving Col. Lewis Merrill and his U.S. Army detachment in Yorkville to fend for themselves.

Alexander Leech, a black former militiaman, was one of those who paid with his life for resisting the York County Klan. A mob of 20 or 30 Klansmen raided his home on the night of March 7, 1871, dragging Leech into the yard and shooting him several times at point-blank range. His corpse was then thrown into nearby Bullock's Creek, where it remained undiscovered for nearly two weeks.

Col. Merrill, called to testify before congressional investigators on July 26, 1871, told his interrogators that a "[r]ecord of coroner's inquest shows that no evidence was produced leading to detection of the murderers. In this case it was stated to me by two different persons—one of them a very intelligent white man who was present at the inquest—that one of the witnesses had first stated that he did not dare testify to what he knew regarding it for fear of the consequences to himself from the Ku Klux, and, receiving no encouragement or assurances of protection, afterward stated that he knew nothing about it. This fact does not appear in the record of the evidence. This witness has since disappeared and is reported to have fled the country." In fact, historian Allen Trelease reports (in *White Terror,* 1971) that armed Klansmen filled the hearing room, joking and laughing with the coroner, glaring at witnesses and jurors until a verdict was returned of murder at the hands of "persons unknown."

LESHEFSKY, Leah   See "WEST SIDE RAPIST"

LEVY, Chandra   murder victim (2001)

A 24-year-old student at the University of Southern California, Chandra Levy was serving as an intern with the Federal Bureau of Prisons when she vanished from her Washington, D.C., apartment on April 30, 2001. The disappearance came shortly before she planned to travel home for graduation, and it seemed to have taken Levy by surprise. Police found her driver's license, credit cards, and packed luggage in her apartment, but no trace of the young woman herself. Examination of Levy's computer revealed that she had logged off for the last time at 1:00 P.M. Modesto congressman Gary Condit, representing Levy's hometown, posted a $10,000 reward for information in the case, thereby boosting the total offered to $42,000. While Condit was admittedly a friend of Levy's, authorities initially dismissed him as a suspect in her disappearance.

That perception changed when one of Levy's relatives told police that Chandra had been engaged in a secret love affair with the 53-year-old politician. Condit aide Mike Lynch denied the charge, and Condit hired an attorney to seek a retraction after the story ran in the *Washington Post,* but another alleged girlfriend soon came forward to describe Condit—a married, conservative Democrat elected with support from the Christian Right—as a compulsive philanderer with "peculiar" sexual fantasies. Police reports disclosed that Levy had telephoned Condit repeatedly on

April 29, but the subject of their conversations remains unknown. Terrance Gainer, Washington's executive assistant police chief, told reporters that "nothing in the review [of Levy's phone records] sheds any light on where she is." He also cautioned the media, "Some would like to make this a lifestyle love story, but we're interested in a missing person. We don't want to get tunnel vision and say, aha! whoever was the boyfriend—and I emphasize whoever—was the suspect."

Any doubts concerning Levy's affair with Condit were soon erased by the congressman's belated confession, but he still denied involvement in her disappearance, and Condit reportedly passed a polygraph test arranged by his personal attorney. The revelations of illicit sex would end his political career, as reports of Condit's "tomcat reputation" soured the born-again voters at home, and a Washington police spokesman dismissed the lie-detector test as "pretty self-serving," but no evidence was found to link Condit with Levy's vanishing act. FBI agents joined city police to search abandoned buildings throughout the nation's capital, without result, and another police official granted that Condit was "more or less cooperating" after detectives scoured his apartment for clues. The detective described Condit as "puckerized by who else is out there in terms of other women. . . . That's got him spooked."

Spooked or not, Condit insisted he was innocent, and top D.C. police officials told the press that he was not a suspect. Rank-and-file investigators dismissed that claim as fatuous. "That's ridiculous," one FBI agent told *U.S. News & World Report* in July 2001. "The first time that he lied he'd be a suspect. And that's when the investigation should have been turned up."

While the media focused on Condit, however, homicide investigators had to admit that Levy's disappearance (and presumed murder) was not a unique event in Washington. Some even feared she might be the latest victim of a serial killer drawn to attractive brunet women. Christine Mirzayan, a 28-year-old graduate of the University of California at San Francisco, had been working as an intern for the National Research Council when bludgeoned and her body discarded near her Georgetown University dormitory on July 29, 1998. Joyce Chang, a 28-year-old attorney with the Immigration and Naturalization Service, disappeared from her Washington neighborhood on January 9, 1999; her corpse was pulled from the Potomac River in Fairfax County, Virginia on April 1, 1999, but the cause of death remains officially undisclosed. A Fox News broadcast on June 11, 2001, referred to five presumed victims of a presumed Washington serial slayer spanning two years, but the others (if they exist) have yet to be identified.

On May 22, 2002, a man walking his dog in Washington's 1,754-acre Rock Creek Park discovered skeletal human remains. Before the day was out, dental records identified Chandra Levy, but the cause of death remained unknown. Police recalled that one of Levy's last known actions, on the day she disappeared, had been a visit to the Web site of Klingle Mansion, located in Rock Creek Park—located four miles from Levy's apartment and a mile north of the point where her bones were found.

Four months after the discovery of Levy's remains, on September 29, 2002, Washington police announced that they were taking a new look at one of their previous suspects, identified as 21-year-old Salvadoran immigrant Ingmar Guandique. Like Gary Condit, Guandique had previously passed a polygraph examination, but authorities now questioned its validity since the test had been administered using a Spanish-speaking interpreter. Detectives referred vaguely to "some kind of discrepancy" in the first polygraph test, while requesting another, but they refused to discuss specifics. Guandique stands convicted of assaulting two female joggers in Rock Creek Park, one on May 14, 2001, and the other on July 1. Both victims told police that he approached them from behind, armed with a knife, while they listened on headphones to portable radios. A similar radio with headphones was found by police among Levy's remains. Washington police chief Charles Ramsey told reporters that Guandique "said nothing to implicate himself with [Levy] but then again we didn't know she was in Rock Creek Park." In February 2009, investigators were finally ready to arrest Ingmar Guandique in Levy's murder, nearly eight years after her death.

LIMACHI Sihuayro, Clemente murder victim (1986)

A 37-year-old resident of Yunguyo, Peru, Clemente Limachi vanished on February 16, 1986, after leaving home to sell a donkey at the village marketplace. His disappearance coincided with the last day of the pre-Lenten festival, a mystic connection confirmed when his mutilated body was found the next morning, at a ritual site on nearby Mount Incahuasi. Limachi's killer (or killers) had removed his ears and tongue, slicing the skin from his face and draping it over his head like a mask, while his corpse reclined in a hollowed-out stone. Limachi's blood was also drained and removed from the scene, presumably for use in future rituals.

A young woman had been sacrificed at the same place in 1982, and while police had no doubt of the murder's religious significance, they disagreed on motives. Yunguyo had been punished by torrential rains before Limachi's death, and human sacrifice was still a favorite peasant method of appeasing the unruly elements, but Limachi's widow placed the blame on local narcotraffickers. Two of Limachi's cousins, Alejandro Lopez and Fausto Quispi, were jailed on suspicion of killing Limachi, but their first visitor—a wealthy merchant named Simon Montoya—pulled strings with the court to secure their release. Leucaria Limachi publicly denounced Montoya as the man behind her husband's murder, but the victim's own father, ranking shaman and suspected drug runner Angelino Limachi, was also suspected. Off the record, police named another self-styled magician, Limachi's uncle Clemente Fargin, as coordinator of the sacrifice, but the case remains officially unsolved today.

LINDBERGH kidnapping miscarriage of justice

Aviator Charles Lindbergh was arguably the most famous American of the 1920s. His solo transatlantic flight of 1927 catapulted the Lone Eagle into global headlines rivaling (if not eclipsing) sports heroes Babe Ruth and Red Grange, bootlegger Al Capone, and a series of lackluster U.S. presidents. Lindbergh's son, Charles Jr., was inevitably dubbed "the eaglet" by journalists, sometimes described in the press as "America's child." His kidnapping and murder at the age of 18 months would be described by newsman H. L. Mencken as "the biggest story since the resurrection."

It began at 10:00 P.M. on March 1, 1932, when a nursemaid found the boy missing from his second-floor nursery in the Lindbergh home, near Hopewell, New Jersey. A semiliterate ransom note demanded $50,000 for the child's safe return. Outside, a crude homemade ladder with a broken step suggested how the kidnapper gained access to the house.

News of the kidnapping provoked a national outcry. President Herbert Hoover vowed to "move Heaven and Earth" to recover Charles Jr., but Washington had no jurisdiction in the case, which was run from start to finish by Col. H. Norman Schwarzkopf of the New Jersey State Police. As usual in such high-profile cases, the Lindbergh family was soon deluged with crank

Charles Lindbergh (center, without hat) arrives at court for the trial of his infant son's alleged murderer. (Library of Congress)

calls and letters, including multiple ransom demands. A stranger to the family, 72-year-old Dr. John F. Condon of the Bronx, volunteered to serve as a go-between in contacting the real kidnappers, and his bumbling services were unaccountably accepted by the Lindbergh family. Using the code name "Jafsie" (after his initials, J.F.C.), Condon placed an ad in the *Bronx Home News* that led to contact with a self-described member of the kidnap gang, known only as "John." A late-night cemetery meeting saw the ransom demand increased to $70,000 since Lindbergh had alerted police and the press, but Condon demanded proof that "John" had the child. Three days later, on March 15, 1932, a package arrived at Condon's home containing a child's sleeping suit, identified by Lindbergh as his son's.

The ransom drop was set for April 2 at St. Raymond's Cemetery in the Bronx. Lindbergh waited in the car while Condon entered the graveyard with two bundles of U.S. gold certificates, one containing $50,000, the other $20,000 (with all the serial numbers recorded). When "John" called out from the shadows, Condon handed over the $50,000 but inexplicably held back the second package. In return, he got a note with direction's to the child's alleged whereabouts, aboard a boat near Elizabeth Island, off the Massachusetts coast. Exhaustive searches by the U.S. Coast Guard and civilian volunteers proved fruitless; the Lindbergh baby nowhere to be found. Meanwhile, one of the ransom bills was identified at a New York bank on April 4, 1932, others surfacing around the city in months to come.

The search for Charles Lindbergh Jr. ended on May 12, 1932, with discovery of a child's badly decomposed corpse in a wooded area four and a half miles from the Lindbergh estate. Police had searched the forest thoroughly in March, but if one accepts the prosecution's story, they had somehow missed the body. The child's skull was fractured; its left arm was missing, as was the left leg below the knee and various internal organs. Decomposition was so advanced, in fact, that medical examiners could not determine the child's gender. Charles Lindbergh and the family's governess identified the pitiful remains, but Charles Jr.'s pediatrician refused to do so, telling reporters that if he were offered $10 million for a positive ID, "I'd have to refuse the money."

There the case rested for two and a half years, while authorities chased reports of ransom bills found across the country. In fact, 97 were recovered between January and August 1934, most spent in or near New York State, with others found in Chicago and Minneapolis. Police got a break on September 15, 1934, when a $10 gold certificate was passed at a Manhattan gas station. Aware that all such bills had been recalled from circulation, the attendant noted his customer's license plate number, thus leading detectives to the Bronx home of Bruno Richard Hauptmann.

A 35-year-old carpenter, Hauptmann had served three years for burglary and armed robbery in his native Germany, before he stowed away on a ship bound for America in 1924. Police found more than $14,000 of the Lindbergh ransom money stashed in his garage, Hauptmann explaining that a friend, Isidor Fisch, had left a shoebox in his care before he (Fisch) returned home for a visit to Germany, later dying there of tuberculosis. Hauptmann said he had forgotten the box, stored in his closet, until a leak demanded his attention and he found it wet. Upon discovering the cash inside, Hauptmann took enough to satisfy the debt Fisch owed him from a failed business venture, then stored the rest for safekeeping in case Fisch's relatives came looking for it.

Authorities were naturally skeptical of Hauptmann's "Fisch story," and New York police went to work in their usual style to extract a confession. Hauptmann later described hours of beatings, with detectives screaming at him, "Where's the money? Where's the baby?" And while the latter question made no sense, a jailhouse physician, Dr. Thurston Dexter, confirmed on September 20, 1934, that Hauptmann "had been subjected recently to a severe beating, all or mostly with blunt instruments."

The third-degree aside, there seemed to be no lack of evidence incriminating Hauptmann. When his trial

opened at Flemington, New Jersey, on January 2, 1935, eight handwriting experts stood ready to swear he had written the Lindbergh ransom note and other correspondence. A neighbor of the Lindbergh's would swear he had seen Hauptmann scouting the estate before the kidnapping. A New York cab driver would identify Hauptmann as the man who hired him to drop a letter at Dr. Condon's home. Detectives would describe finding Condon's address and telephone number, along with the serial numbers of two ransom bills, written inside Hauptmann's closet. Hauptmann would be linked to another ransom bill by the clerk at a Manhattan movie theater. A wood expert was called to testify that the ladder used to kidnap Lindbergh's son included a plank from the floor of Hauptmann's attic. Finally, Dr. Condon and Lindbergh himself would swear under oath that Hauptmann was the "cemetery John" who accepted $50,000 in ransom money on April 2, 1932. Hauptmann was duly convicted of murder on February 13, 1935; his various appeals were denied, and he died in the electric chair on April 3, 1936.

Persuasive evidence now indicates that suspect Bruno Hauptmann did not kill Charles Lindbergh, Jr. (Library of Congress)

But was he guilty?

A review of the prosecution's evidence, coupled with FBI documents declassified in the 1990s, reveals a blatant frame-up in the case. Glaring examples of prosecutorial fraud include:

The witnesses: (1) New York cabbie Joseph Perrone, in 1932, repeatedly told police that he could not recognize the stranger who gave him a note for delivery to Dr. Condon since "I didn't pay attention to anything." At the time, Col. Schwarzkopf labeled Perrone "a totally unreliable witness," but he was trusted at trial to identify Hauptmann as the note-passer. (2) Impoverished Lindbergh neighbor Millard Whited twice told authorities in 1932 that he had seen no strangers in the area before the kidnapping; by 1934, with reward money in hand and promises of more, Whited "positively identified Hauptmann as the man he had twice seen in the vicinity of the Lindbergh estate." (3) Col. Schwarzkopf also lied under oath, stating falsely that Whited had described the lurking stranger on March 2, 1932. (4) Dr. Condon spent two years denying any glimpse of "cemetery John's" face and refused to identify Hauptmann's voice at their first meeting, when an FBI agent described Condon as "in a sort of daze." Later, under threat of prosecution as an accomplice to the murder, Condon reversed himself and made a "positive" ID under oath. (5) Charles Lindbergh heard two words—"Hey, Doc!"—from "cemetery John" in April 1932, and those from 80 yards away. He later told a grand jury, "It would be very difficult for me to sit here and say that I could pick a man by that voice," but he did exactly that at trial, identifying Hauptmann under oath.

The ransom notes: Police ordered Hauptmann to copy the Lindbergh ransom notes verbatim, misspellings included, producing seven copies with three different pens, slanting his handwriting at different angles and so forth. Expert graphologist Albert Osborn reviewed the samples and told Col. Schwarzkopf he was "convinced [Hauptmann] did not write the ransom notes." At trial, though, Osborn joined seven other experts in stating the exact opposite. (He also went on, in 1971, to erroneously certify alleged writings of billionaire Howard Hughes that were forged by celebrity hoaxer Clifford Irving.)

The closet writing: According to coworkers and acquaintances, New York tabloid reporter Tom Cassidy "bragged all over town" that *he* wrote Dr. Condon's address and phone number, with the serial numbers of two ransom bills, inside Hauptmann's closet, in order to report the "discovery" and score himself an exclusive front-page story. Prosecutors accepted the fraudulent writing as evidence, while Cassidy and friends considered it a harmless indiscretion, in the face of Hauptmann's "obvious guilt."

The attic plank: Wood expert Arthur Koehler initially reported, based on nail holes in the kidnap ladder, that its planks had not been previously used for flooring, but he changed his story when a long plank was discovered missing from the floor of Bruno Hauptmann's attic. That "discovery" was made by two state troopers on September 26, 1934, a week after three dozen officers searched every inch of Hauptmann's apartment and saw no gaps in any of the floors. Because the attic plank was two inches wider than any other board used to build the ladder, prosecutors surmised that Hauptmann had planed it down by hand to make it fit. It remains unexplained why a professional carpenter, having purchased all other wood for the ladder from a local lumberyard (as prosecutors insisted), would rip a lone board from his landlord's attic and spend hours (not to mention untold wasted energy) at the laborious task of planing it to match his other boards on hand.

Long after Hauptmann's death, as glaring discrepancies in the state's case began to surface, alternative scenarios for the kidnapping emerged. The suicide of a former Lindbergh maid suggested possible collusion in the crime, an inside job. Underworld involvement was another possibility, based on offers from imprisoned gangster Al Capone and others to retrieve the Lindbergh baby in return for cash or legal favors. Some theorists surmise, based on shaky identifications of the infant's corpse, that Lindbergh's son survived the kidnapping and grew to manhood in another home. (Inevitably, one such man claimed to be the grown-up child himself, but DNA testing disproved his tale in October 2000.) The most unsettling scenario to date, proposed by Noel Behn in 1994, suggests that Lindbergh's jealous sister-in-law murdered Charles Jr. in an act of revenge against her sibling, for winning the Lone

Eagle's affection. In Behn's unverified account, Charles Lindbergh then devised the kidnap story to avoid a scandal and collaborated with the Hauptmann frame-up to spare his family from social stigma. Today, the only certainty about the Lindbergh case is that police and prosecutors conspired to frame Bruno Hauptmann for the crime and send him to his death.

Heated controversy still surrounds the Lindbergh kidnapping. Widow Anna Hauptmann fought for six decades to clear her husband's name, without success. In 1982 she filed a $100 million wrongful-death claim against the State of New Jersey, plus various ex-policemen and reporters. In 1983 she accused the federal trial judge of bias against her, but the U.S. Supreme Court refused Anna's request to disqualify the judge—who dismissed her claims in 1984. A year later, more than 23,000 pages of police documents related to the Lindbergh case surfaced in a garage once owned by late governor Hoffman. Also found at the same time were 30,000 pages of FBI reports never introduced at trial, which prosecution critics feel may have prompted jurors to acquit Hauptmann. Governor Jim Florio refused to meet with Mrs. Hauptmann and discuss the case in 1990. Anna Hauptmann died in Pennsylvania on October 10, 1994—her 69th wedding anniversary.

In 2005, Court TV's *Forensic Files* program enlisted four forensic experts to defend the prosecution's case against Hauptmann. While ignoring the documented evidence of police malfeasance and brutality, those experts focused on two specific aspects of the case. Kelvin Keraga—who, according to Court TV's Web site, spent nine years studying the 1932 kidnap ladder, presented a 35-page report claiming that part of the ladder was made with floorboards ripped from Hauptmann's attic. To reach that conclusion, he relied on police photos and reports from 1935 and never viewed the attic itself (which no longer existed). Keraga failed to explain why Hauptmann, a professional carpenter, should build such a clumsy and unstable ladder, using only one board from his attic for a single rail, when he had other lumber readily available.

Court TV's other three spokesmen were handwriting experts Peter Baier, Gideon Epstein, and Grant Sperry. Working independently, all three deemed Hauptmann guilty of writing various Lindbergh ransom notes, but critics found gaps in their logic. First, none examined the original ransom notes or examples of Hauptmann's known writing: Baier viewed 15 letters in digitized document files, while Epstein and Sperry examined 55 and 62 photocopied documents, respectively.

With that in mind, their conclusions were less than impressive. Baier found that some of the submitted documents were "written by a third person," while in others, the noted "similarities result from successful imitation, some kind of family similarity, similar national or social habits, or fortuitousness"—i.e., blind luck. Epstein declared that Hauptmann made an "obvious attempt to disguise [his] normal handwriting characteristics" in some letters, further announcing that he displayed "a wide range of variation in his handwriting and that he had two distinct levels of handwriting skill." Ignoring the fact that police ordered Hauptmann to misspell certain words as they read the ransom notes to him aloud, Epstein claimed that Hauptmann "unconsciously formed some letters consistent with the German system of writing." This, Epstein concluded, served as "overwhelming proof" that all 55 documents were penned by one person. Finally, Sperry found it "highly probable" that Hauptmann wrote all 62 items examined, but grudgingly admitted that certain "inconsistencies contributed to the slightly less than definitive finding."

Few, if any, skeptics were persuaded by the documentary. The controversy over Hauptmann's conviction and execution endures.

"LISBON Ripper" Portugal (1992–93)

A modern bogeyman in the tradition of 19th-century London's "JACK THE RIPPER," this slayer of drug-addicted prostitutes in Lisbon has inspired police to link him, albeit tentatively, to murders in six nations, on both sides of the Atlantic Ocean. Unfortunately, none of those additional murders (ranging in number from three to 18, depending on the source) has yet been solved, and the killer remains at large.

Lisbon's nightmare began in July 1992, when factory workers found a young woman's body discarded in a shed at their workplace. Her throat was slashed, and she had been disemboweled with a broken bottle, found at the scene. By March 1993 two more victims were found in similar condition—the third within 50 yards of the first murder site—all identified as streetwalkers and addicts in their twenties. Two of the victims were HIV-positive, prompting speculation that the killer might be a "john" infected with AIDS and venting his rage on prostitutes chosen at random.

In March 1993 Lisbon detectives visited NEW BEDFORD, MASSACHUSETTS, where a still-unidentified killer had slaughtered 11 prostitutes between April and September 1988. The technique varied, and several Massachusetts victims had been found as skeletal remains, but New Bedford's large Portuguese population prompted detectives from both countries to speculate that New Bedford's unknown stalker may have gone home to avoid arrest and continue the hunt in a new territory. The theory could never be proved without suspects, however, and Lisbon authorities came away from their visit with little more than official sympathy for their dilemma.

Back in Europe, meanwhile, the same killer or one with a remarkably similar *modus operandi* had apparently taken his game on the road. Between 1993 and 1997, police in Belgium, Denmark, the Czech Republic, and the Netherlands reported one "nearly identical" murder of streetwalkers in each of their countries. Police now speculate that their hypothetical AIDS victim-cum-psycho slasher is also a long-haul truck driver, thus granting him access to victims throughout Europe. Predictably, expansion of the hunting ground did nothing to improve the odds of capture, and the Lisbon Ripper case remains unsolved today.

LIVINGSTON, Sherri   See "Independence Avenue Killer"

LLOYD, Anna   See Cumminsville, Ohio, murders

LO Bianco, Antonio   See "Monster of Florence"

LOCCI, Barbara   See "Monster of Florence"

LOCKWOOD, Irene   See "Jack the Stripper"

LOGANBILL, Patricia   See Salem, Oregon, murders

LOLLAR, Vernell   See Chicago holdup murders (1971–72)

LOMBARDI, Anna   See "Jack the Ripper" (1915)

LONG Island, New York   unsolved murders (1984–85)
Between June 1984 and April 1985 Long Island was the scene of several rapes and murders involving teenage girls, with evidence suggesting that the crimes had been committed by a mobile gang of three or more men. Police have solved one case, with indications that the perpetrators and unknown accomplices may be responsible for other slayings in the area. Independent evidence, secured by journalist Maury Terry, further indicates the possible involvement of a devil-worshiping cult with members still at large.

The first Long Island victim was 15-year-old Kelly Morrissey, who vanished on the short walk home from a popular teenage hangout on June 12, 1984. Five months later, a friend of Morrissey, Theresa Fusco, was forced into a van after leaving a skating rink in Lynbrook, one mile from the spot where Morrissey disappeared. Fusco's body, beaten, strangled, and raped by at least three men, was found on December 5, 1984, realizing the worst fears of family and friends.

John Kogut, a 21-year-old high school dropout and unemployed landscaper, was jailed on charges of burglary and disorderly conduct when authorities began to question him about the Fusco homicide. Cracking under interrogation, Kogut confessed to the crime, naming two accomplices, and was formally charged with the murder on March 26, 1985. Kelly Morrissey was still missing, but her diary contained entries describing at least one date with Kogut prior to her disappearance.

Eight hours after the announcement of Kogut's arrest, 19-year-old Jacqueline Martarella was reported missing from Oceanside, a short four miles from the scene of Theresa Fusco's abduction. Kogut was obviously innocent of the latest crime, but his alleged accomplices were still at liberty, and police were collecting evidence of Kogut's alleged participation in a satanic cult that favored the rape of young virgins as a form of "sacrifice." Kogut's friends informed detectives that he had once burned the mark of an inverted cross on his arm, and acquaintances of Theresa Fusco recalled her discussions of a satanic coven reportedly active in the Long Beach–Oceanside area.

On April 22, 1985, Jacqueline Martarella's raped and strangled corpse was found beside a golf course at Lawrence, Long Island. Visiting the scene, reporter Maury Terry discovered a "cult sign" allegedly linked to Satanists in Queens and Yonkers, whom he suspected of playing a role in the infamous "Son of Sam" murders in 1976–77. Near the site where Martarella was found, searchers discovered an abandoned cellar, its walls festooned with cult symbols and slogans. Outside, some articles of clothing were found, described by Martarella's parents as "very similar" to items she wore on the night she disappeared.

John Kogut steadfastly refused to discuss the cult rumors, while freely admitting his role in the rape and murder of Theresa Fusco. After she was raped, he said, the girl threatened to tell police, whereupon one of Kogut's cronies handed him a rope and told him, "Do what you gotta do." On May 9, 1985, authorities went public with their theory that a gang of 12 associates were linked to three known murders and at least four rapes in which the victims survived. By June 21, 30-year-old Dennis Halstead and 26-year-old John Restivo were in custody on charges of first-degree rape and second-degree murder in the Fusco case. Kogut was convicted and sentenced to life for that crime in May 1986, with Halstead and Restivo joining him in prison before year's end. Prior to Kogut's trial, a teenage friend who had testified to Kogut's Satanism and involvement in commercial pornography—one Bob Fletcher—"committed suicide" in Rosedale, Queens. Police have been unable to explain the disappearance of the gun he used to shoot himself.

LÓPEZ, Jorge Juilo missing kidnap victim (2006)

Double-kidnap victim Jorge López was born in 1929, in Argentina's Buenos Aires Province. He worked as a bricklayer until October 21, 1976, when he was "disappeared" by agents of the country's secret police, one of thousands abducted during military dictator Jorge Rafael Videla Redondo's "dirty war" against alleged "enemies of the state," formally dubbed the "National Reorganization Process." López was held without formal charges or trial, and repeatedly tortured, until his surprise release on June 25, 1979. Videla Redondo ceded power to successor Roberto Eduardo Viola Prevedini in March 1981, but the "dirty war" continued until 1983, when the military junta dissolved.

As a condition of relinquishing their power, junta leaders were protected by the "Law of Due Obedience" and "Full Stop Law," which prohibited investigation of any crimes committed prior to December 12, 1983. Argentina's Supreme Court overturned those statutes in June 2005, paving the way for belated prosecution of "dirty war" felons, while a National Committee on the Disappearance of Persons investigated 9,000 kidnappings committed between 1976 and 1983.

López was scheduled to testify at the trial of Miguel Osvaldo Etchecolatz, former director of investigations for the Buenos Aires Provincial Police, charged with "crimes against humanity in the context of the genocide that took place in Argentina." López was to identify Etchecolatz and 62 other officials involved in his abduction and torture.

López vanished for the second time on September 17, 2006, one day before Etchecolatz received a life prison term for his crimes. Authorities offered a reward of 200,000 pesos ($66,000) for information on his whereabouts, but none was forthcoming. Police initially speculated that López, who suffered from Parkinson's disease at age 77, may have lapsed into posttraumatic shock at the prospect of facing Etchecolatz again, but they now believe that he was kidnapped to prevent him from testifying against the defendant and the 62 others identified in his recorded statements. He remains missing, while Etchecolatz remains defiantly unrepentant. At his sentencing, he told the court, "You are not the judge. The supreme judge awaits us after death."

LORDI, Cheresa See "INDEPENDENCE AVENUE KILLER"

LOS Angeles, California holdup murders (1980)

On November 6, 1980, the Los Angeles Police Department asked for public help in their pursuit of three Hispanic men suspected in a string of robberies, assaults, and fatal stabbings in the San Fernando Valley area. Lt. William Gaida said of the elusive trio, "They seem to derive sadistic pleasure out of stabbing people. Apparently robbery is the primary motive, but the suspects stabbed the victims in almost all cases; stabbed them even if the victim complied with all their demands."

The reign of terror began on May 17, 1980, when three separate victims were killed and a fourth gravely wounded over a period of three hours and 15 minutes. A task force was organized to solve the case on September 29, and police credited the nameless trio with a minimum of seven murders by October 30, when 19-year-old Jesus Solis was knifed to death by assailants matching the suspect descriptions. Two of the elusive suspects were described as Hispanic men between the ages of 25 and 30 years, while no description was available for their companion. The killers reportedly lurked in restrooms of taverns or waited outside, choosing Hispanic males as their primary targets of robbery and murder. To date, no solution in the case has been announced by Los Angeles investigators.

LOS Angeles, California racist drive-by murders (1993)

Gunfire in the streets is not uncommon in Los Angeles, where turf wars between drug-dealing street gangs added the phrase *drive-by shooting* to America's criminal lexicon in the 1980s and high-crime neighborhoods are kept under surveillance by "spotter" microphones mounted on telephone poles, to register gunshots unreported by jaded residents. Hundreds of gang members and innocent bystanders, most of them black or Hispanic, have been killed or wounded in such shootings over the past quarter-century, but there was something radically different about the drive-by murders that terrorized L.A.'s Harbor City district in the early months of 1993.

The gunman in those crimes was white, with red hair, driving a red-and-white Jeep Wrangler as he prowled the streets of Harbor City after nightfall. He seemed fixated on a certain area, all four of his attacks falling within a two-block radius, and his technique never varied. In each case, the unknown shooter singled out a black or Latino pedestrian, as if to ask for help. "He beckons to them," police lieutenant Sergio Robleto told reporters, "and as soon as they come up to the car, he shoots them for no apparent reason. He doesn't miss."

Thirty-two-year-old Howard Campbell was the first known victim, shot dead on January 31, 1993. Two weeks later, 35-year-old Michael Meador was killed at the very same place. Joseph Maxwell, age 26, answered the gunman's call on April 15, 1993, and was killed for his trouble, two blocks away from the first murder scene. On May 22, a 38-year-old African-American male (unnamed in the press) was shot three times, a block away from the first murder site, but he managed to survive his wounds.

Aside from identical descriptions of the gunman and his vehicle, authorities noted that three of the shootings occurred between 8:00 and 9:30 P.M., while the fourth took place at dawn. Los Angeles police, already plagued with serial killers, were reluctant to claim yet another at large in their city, but Lt. Robleto acknowledged the grim possibility. "There are murders in the same location all over the city," he told reporters, "but when you have a third one it starts to look really bad. It certainly looks like the same person."

And yet, despite increased patrols, vigilant neighbors, and a distinctive vehicle, the gunman eluded capture. At the date of this writing, no new murders in the series have been publicized, nor have authorities identified a suspect in the case.

LOS Angeles, California random shootings (1982)

Between August and October 1982, Los Angeles police were mobilized to track a prowling gunman who randomly selected motorists as targets, emulating New York City's "Son of Sam." Before the rampage ended with the gunman still at large, two victims had been killed and three more wounded in a spate of unprovoked attacks.

The first two victims, killed in August, were a local oceanographer and a vacationing student from Princeton University. On September 4, 1982, 51-year-old Jack Listman was wounded by shots fired through a window of his car, while he was waiting for a traffic light to change at a downtown intersection. In the week of October 11–15 two Beverly Hills women were wounded in separate shooting incidents, apparently by the same gunman.

Detective Sherman Oakes offered little hope for a solution in the case when he addressed the media in mid-October 1982. Describing the gunman's technique, Oakes said, "He just walks up, never says a word, and starts shooting. Once the victim is dead, he then goes through the victim's pockets." Moving on or tiring of the game with the October shootings, L.A.'s phantom gunman faded from the scene as mysteriously as he had arrived, still unidentified. Police still have no suspects and no leads.

LOVETT, LaBrian See ATLANTA "LOVER'S LANE" MURDERS

LOWE, Anna See NEW ORLEANS AXEMAN

LOWTHER, Henry castrated by terrorists (1871)

A former slave, born in Newton County, Georgia, and later settled in Wilkinson County, Henry Lowther angered members of the Ku Klux Klan by prospering in business and by voting the Republican ticket during Reconstruction, after the Civil War. He also filed civil lawsuits against several white men who owed him money and refused to pay their debts, but Lowther's ultimate breach of southern decorum involved his part-time labor for a white woman of dubious reputation. Klansmen imagined an interracial love affair in progress and determined that Lowther must be killed or driven from the county.

On their first attempt, the night of August 27, 1871, the raiders missed Lowther. He had seen them coming and fled his house to hide in some nearby woods. Enraged, the Klansmen ransacked Lowther's home and warned his wife that he had five days in which to leave Wilkinson County forever. Friends urged him to stay and mounted armed guards at his home the next night, whereupon Klan leaders tried another tack. A local black man was induced to swear that Lowther and a company of unknown men had tried to murder him a few days earlier. The sheriff jailed Lowther on September 2 and subsequently arrested 24 of his friends, grilling the prisoners about the mythical murder attempt before each was fined $2.70 for "court costs." Lowther alone remained in jail when Eli Cummings, leader of the county's Klan, dropped by for a conversation. Lowther described the substance of their talk for congressional investigators in October 1871.

Captain Cummins sat down and talked with me about an hour, but there was nothing he said that I thought had any substance in it, only when he went to leave he said, "Harry, are you willing to give up your stones to save your life?" I sat there for a moment, and then I told him, "Yes." Said he, "If they come for you will you make a fight?" I said, "No." He said, "No fuss whatever?" I said, "No."

Around 2:00 A.M. the next day, a party of some 180 Klansmen invaded the town and removed Lowther from jail. They conveyed him to a swampy area two miles away, where he was threatened with a noose and pistols, then stripped and castrated. When they were finished, around 3:00 A.M., the raiders told Lowther to visit a doctor and then leave the county as soon as he was fit to travel. The rest of the night was a waking nightmare, Lowther nude and bleeding, wandering from one house to the next, while each white occupant in turn urged him to "go lie down." He finally reached the town doctor's home, and there collapsed unconscious when no one answered his knock. A black woman summoned Lowther's wife and son, who carried him home. When Lowther's son returned to the doctor's house, his first knock was answered—a circumstance that made him suspect the physician had been part of the Klan raiding party.

That charge created no end of controversy in Wilkinson County. A series of white men visited Lowther at home, insisting that he had never reached the doctor's house, but a trail of blood through town, pooled at the doctor's gate, gave the lie to that story. For his part, the doctor—a brother of Klansman Eli Cummins—first claimed he was sleeping, then changed his story to say he was out on a house call when Lowther came knocking. Finally, in seeming desperation, Dr. Cummins changed his tale again: He had been hiding from the Klan himself, he claimed, after they visited his house on the night of the raid. Lowther, for his part, remained convinced that Dr. Cummins was the man who mutilated him.

On the 17th day of Lowther's convalescence, Eli Cummins visited his home for another chat. This time, the Klan leader referred to Lowther's alleged threats "of what you are going to do when you get well." Lowther denied making any such statements, but Cummins assured him that "some of the responsible people in town do believe it." After Lowther apologized, Cummins turned magnanimous, suggesting that the KKK would leave Lowther alone "if this talk dies out." Understandably skeptical, Lowther fled the county on September 22, 1871, and never returned. No suspects were charged in his castration, or in a series of similar incidents throughout Wilkinson County. After his departure Klansmen spread false rumors that Lowther had been emasculated for committing incest with his stepdaughter.

LOZANO, Pete   See SAN ANTONIO TAXI MURDERS

LUBIN, Wilton   See MONTREAL CHILD MURDERS

LYNCH, Dennis   See BELL, CALIFORNIA, MURDERS

MACDIARMID, Sarah missing person (1990)

Sarah MacDiarmid was a native of the Scottish Highlands, born in 1967, who emigrated to Australia with her family at age 20. Three years later she vanished without a trace, and while police assume that she is dead, no proof of her murder has yet been discovered.

After leaving work on July 11, 1990, MacDiarmid played tennis with two friends at Flinders Park, on Batman Avenue in Melbourne. After their game, the trio walked to the Richmond railway station and discovered that they had missed their train to Frankston. They boarded a train to Caulfield instead, with MacDiarmid's friends disembarking at Bonbeach, while she continued on alone toward Kananook Station and her waiting car. Witnesses later recalled MacDiarmid leaving the train and walking into the station's dimly lit parking lot around 10:20 P.M., but she never reached home.

Melbourne police responded to a missing-person report from MacDiarmid's family and found bloodstains on the pavement beside her car, still parked in the lot at Kananook Station. A three-week search, involving 250 officers with air support and boats cruising offshore, failed to uncover MacDiarmid's remains. In September 2004, her case was featured on the first episode of *Sensing Murder,* an Australian television program showcasing psychic detectives. Participants in that episode suggested that MacDiarmid had been murdered, with her body discarded at a garbage dump on the Mornington Peninsula. Dumping at that site had been discontinued during the 14 years since

MacDiarmid's disappearance, but follow-up searches revealed no trace of her body.

Suspicion in MacDiarmid's case initially focused on Paul Charles Denyer, an Australian serial killer born in 1972, whose hatred of women drove him to kill three victims in Frankston, Victoria, during a seven-week crime spree in 1993. At trial, Denyer received a life sentence for those slayings—including victims Debbie Fream (age 22), Natalie Russell (17), and Elizabeth Stevens (18)—but no evidence has surfaced linking him to MacDiarmid's case. An alternate theory, espoused by private researchers and rejected by Melbourne authorities, blames MacDiarmid's presumed slaying on a still-unidentified homeless drug addict.

MACDONALD, Jeffrey wrongly convicted of murder

Shortly after 3:30 A.M. on February 17, 1970, military police at Fort Bragg, North Carolina, were summoned to the on-post residence of a Green Beret captain and licensed physician, Dr. Jeffrey MacDonald. They found the house ransacked, MacDonald bleeding from a stab wound to his chest. The other members of MacDonald's family—26-year-old wife, Colette, five-year-old Kimberly, and two-year-old Kristen—had been stabbed and beaten to death in their bedrooms. Dr. MacDonald told investigators that he had awakened in the predawn hours to find four strangers in his home. Three men—two white, one black—attacked MacDonald and his family, while a "hippie-type" woman with long blond hair watched from the sidelines, holding a candle and chanting, "Acid is groovy. Kill the pigs."

Despite the recent Charles Manson cult murders in Los Angeles and Dr. MacDonald's extensive work with drug addicts in nearby Fayetteville, army investigators quickly dismissed his story and focused on MacDonald as a suspect. Federal Bureau of Investigation (FBI) agents (responsible for any crimes committed by civilians on a military reservation) found themselves excluded from the crime scene, relegated to questioning local drug dealers and users. One who volunteered to "help" with the investigation was part-time police informant Helena Stoeckley, herself an addict with alleged involvement in occult religious practices. (Despite her strong resemblance to the female assailant described by Dr. MacDonald, Stoeckley was never presented to MacDonald as a possible suspect.) The FBI's turf war with military police produced some curious results, but bureau documents were suppressed until 1990, when they were finally released under the Freedom of Information Act.

MacDonald was charged with killing his wife and daughters in July 1970, but a three-month military hearing revealed so many clumsy errors by army investigators that the charges were dismissed on October 27. A memo from FBI director J. Edgar Hoover, dated one day later, declared that he would resist any efforts to involve the bureau in MacDonald's case because "the Army handled the case poorly from its inception."

Dr. MacDonald subsequently left the army and entered private practice in California. In 1974 the FBI reversed Hoover's decision and agreed to examine evidence from the MacDonald case, although that evidence had previously been examined in various army laboratories. (The bureau's Laboratory Division had a standing rule against accepting previously tested evidence, because it might be altered or contaminated; the rule was curiously waived in MacDonald's case.) FBI involvement in the case scarcely improved matters, though. In fact, a review of the FBI's records long after the fact revealed at least 53 items of potentially exculpatory evidence that were either misrepresented or concealed from the defense during MacDonald's 1979 murder trial. The items include:

1. Unidentified candle wax on the living room coffee table.
2. Unidentified wax on a washing machine in the kitchen.
3. Bloodstains on both sides of the washing machine.
4. Fingerprints noted on the washing machine but never collected.
5. Unidentified pink wax on the kitchen floor, near the refrigerator.
6. Blood on the refrigerator door.
7. Three bloody gloves in the kitchen.
8. Blond wig hairs up to 22 inches long found on a chair beside the kitchen telephone.
9. Unidentified wax and an unidentified human hair found on a wall in the hallway.
10. A bloody syringe containing unidentified liquid found in the hall closet.
11. An unidentified hair, covered with a tarlike substance, found in the bathroom sink.
12. Two unmatched blue cotton fibers and a crumpled pink facial tissue in the bathroom sink.
13. An unidentified hair with root intact under one of Kimberly's fingernails.
14. Unidentified candle wax on Kimberly's bedding.
15. An unidentified hair on Kimberly's bed.
16. An unmatched black thread on Kimberly's bottom sheet, near a bloody wood splinter.
17. Unmatched pink and blue nylon fibers on Kimberly's bottom sheet.
18. Unmatched purple and black nylon fibers on Kimberly's quilt.
19. Unidentified candle wax on the arm of a chair in Kimberly's bedroom.
20. Unidentified red and blue wax on Kimberly's window curtain.
21. An unidentified red wool fiber and a speck of type O blood on Dr. MacDonald's reading glasses.
22. Human blood of unknown type from the living room floor near Dr. MacDonald's glasses.
23. An unidentified fingerprint on a drinking glass from the living room end table.
24. An unmatched blue acrylic fiber found in the living room, where Dr. MacDonald claimed to have lain unconscious.
25. Two unmatched black wool fibers found on the murder club.
26. Three hairs that allegedly shook loose from the murder club inside an evidence bag. In 1970 the army called them "human pubic or body hairs"; in 1974 the FBI laboratory identified them as "animal hairs."

27. An unidentified bloody palm print on the footboard of the master bed.
28. An unmatched pink fiber from the bed's footboard.
29. Two unidentified human hairs from the footboard.
30. Two unidentified hairs from the master bedspread.
31. An unidentified hair found on a fragment of rubber glove inside a crumpled blue sheet from the master bedroom.
32. A piece of skin tissue from the same sheet, "lost" after it was cataloged, but reportedly before analysis.
33. An unidentified piece of skin found under one of Colette's fingernails and subsequently "lost."
34. An unmatched blue acrylic fiber found in Colette's right hand.
35. An unidentified hair found in Colette's left hand.
36. An unmatched black wool fiber found near Colette's mouth.
37. An unmatched pink fiber from Colette's mouth.
38. An unmatched purple fiber from Colette's mouth.
39. An unmatched black wool fiber found on Colette's right biceps.
40. Two unidentified body hairs found on the bedroom floor near Colette's left arm, with three bloody wooden splinters.
41. An unidentified hair found beneath Colette's body.
42. An unmatched green cotton fiber found under Colette's body.
43. An unmatched gold nylon fiber stained with blood found under Colette's body.
44. Two pieces of facial tissue found beneath Colette's body.
45. A clump of fibers, all but one unmatched, found stuck to a bloody hair from Colette's scalp.
46. An unmatched clear nylon fiber stuck to a splinter from the murder club found on the bedroom floor near the crumpled blue sheet.
47. An unidentified hair with root intact found under one of Kristen's fingernails.
48. Two unidentified hairs found on Kristen's bed, near her body.
49. An unmatched blue nylon fiber found on Kristen's blanket.
50. Several unmatched clear nylon fibers from the same blanket.
51. A clump of unmatched purple nylon fibers on Kristen's bedspread.
52. Unmatched cotton fibers from Kristen's bedspread.
53. An unmatched yellow nylon fiber stained with blood found on Kristen's bedspread.

In addition to suppressing physical evidence at trial, the FBI also apparently misrepresented statements from critical witnesses during MacDonald's appeals. A forensic pathologist, Dr. Ronald Wright, reported that Colette MacDonald was clubbed by a left-handed assailant standing in front of her, whereas her husband was right-handed. In 1984 FBI Agent James Reed prepared an affidavit falsely stating that Dr. Wright had "retracted" his opinion. Wright contradicted that claim, but MacDonald's attorneys did not learn of the lie under oath until October 1989. G-men also tinkered with the statements of witness Norma Lane, who reported that suspect Greg Mitchell (a left-handed soldier and addict) had confessed the murders in her presence, in 1982. An FBI affidavit claimed that Lane was uncertain whether Mitchell had referred to events at Fort Bragg or in Vietnam, a falsehood Lane flatly denies.

Greg Mitchell was not the only suspect who confessed to the MacDonald murders. Mitchell's friend and fellow addict, Helena Stoeckley, offered multiple confessions to military police, the FBI, and retired G-man Ted Gunderson, both before and after MacDonald's murder trial. She denied involvement on the witness stand, however, and FBI agents buttressed her denial with reports that she "appeared to be under the influence of drugs" when she made an earlier confession (a claim refuted by hospital blood tests performed the same day). Unfortunately for MacDonald's defense, Stoeckley and Mitchell both died from apparent liver disease (in 1981 and 1982, respectively), before their stories could be verified.

Suggestions of official misconduct continue to surface in the MacDonald case. Prosecutor Jim Blackburn, retired to private practice, received a three-year prison term in December 1993, after pleading guilty to various felony counts that included fabricating a lawsuit, forging court documents (including judges' signatures), and embezzling $234,000 from his law firm. In 1997 MacDonald's attorneys discovered that FBI lab technician Michael Malone, accused of offering false testimony in other cases, had misrepresented fiber evidence in MacDonald's case. (Specifically, Malone testified that the FBI's "standard sources" revealed that saran fibers could not be used in human wigs; in fact, two of the leading source books in the bureau's lab stated the exact opposite.) Despite such revelations of suspicious activity on the prosecution's part, all appeals in MacDonald's case have thus far been denied. The effort to secure a new trial for MacDonald continues, despite a November 2008 denial by a U.S. district court.

MACDONALD, Mima   See "Bible John"

MACLEOD, Frank and Willie   See Nahanni Valley murders

MACNIVEN, Donald   See New York City gay murders

MACRAE, Renee and Andrew missing persons (1976)
Scottish native Renee MacRae was born in 1940. At the time of her disappearance, she lived in the Cradelehall district of Inverness with her two sons. On November 12, 1976, she delivered nine-year-old Gordon Jr. to his father's residence, then drove south on the A9 motorway toward Perth, with three-year-old Andrew. Renee planned to visit her sister, but never arrived. Neither she nor Andrew have been seen since that Friday afternoon.

On the evening of November 12, a railroad engineer saw MacRae's BMW sedan engulfed by flames at a highway rest stop. Police answered the call and found the car unoccupied, with bloodstains on its carpet that matched Renee's blood type. (DNA testing had not been invented in 1976.) Two motorists claimed they had seen a man parking a car along the A9 and climbing its embankment, dragging a heavy bundle toward nearby Dalmagarry Quarry, shortly before the car fire. Another pair of passing witnesses reported a man pushing a child's stroller along the highway around the same time.

Detectives assigned to the case found Renee's life complicated by romantic entanglements. They learned that MacRae's married lover, one Bill MacDowell, was both Andrew's biological father *and* employed as Gordon MacRae Sr.'s secretary. MacDowell admitted the affair but denied any involvement in the double disappearance, which police now classify as presumed homicides. Subsequent reports suggest that Renee actually planned to meet MacDowell in Perth, to let him spend time with Andrew.

In July 1977, Detective Sergeant John Cathcart led a search team equipped with a borrowed bulldozer to Dalmagarry Quarry. While excavating the site, Cathcart noted a strong smell of decomposing flesh, but a superior officer terminated the search on grounds that the bulldozer's owner—a building contractor—needed to use the machine. Despite public criticism of that decision, the digging never resumed, and the case was effectively closed in 1978.

A quarter-century later, in 2004, Grampian Television's *Unsolved* program presented the case to a new audience, including many viewers born since the abductions occurred. Since then, £248,000 has been spent in searches around Dalmagarry Quarry, including removal of some 2,000 trees and excavations shifting 30,000 tons of soil. Ground-penetrating radar located three objects which "could be" human remains and Andrew's stroller, buried at a depth of seven feet, but spokesmen for Scotland's Northern Constabulary later declared that "nothing conclusive was found." John Cathcart died in June 2007, with the riddle still unsolved.

MADDEN, Wendy   See Woonsocket, Rhode Island, murders

MADEIROS, Debra   See New Bedford, Massachusetts, murders

MAENZA, Michelle   See "Alphabet Murders"

MAGERS, Patricia   See "I-70/I-35 Murders"

MAGGIO, Joseph   See New Orleans axeman

MAINARDI, Paolo   See "Monster of Florence"

MALCOLM, Pamela See MARYLAND MURDERS (1986–87)

MALCOLM, Roger and Dorothy murder victims (1946)
Race relations are notoriously volatile in the American South, and especially in Georgia—America's all-time leader in unsolved lynchings and national headquarters of the Ku Klux Klan from 1915 to 1961. Some Georgians hoped the situation would improve after World War II, with federal civil rights initiatives and global exposure of Nazi racist atrocities, but the optimists reckoned without hard-line white supremacist Governor Eugene Talmadge and a violent rebirth of the Klan under "Grand Dragon" Samuel Green. Talmadge—a proud "former" Klansman who boasted of flogging blacks—staffed his administration with KKK members and openly encouraged mayhem against "uppity" blacks. On July 17, 1946, after Talmadge's latest election to office, terrorists murdered the only black man who had dared to vote in Newton County. The same day, rioters sacked a newspaper office in Thomaston, dragging the editor through the streets and forcing him to publicly apologize for backing Talmadge adversary Ellis Arnall.

Three days before that chaotic primary election, black sharecropper Roger Malcolm ran afoul of his landlord, white supremacist Talmadge supporter Bob Hester, in rural Monroe. Hester's son, 22-year-old Barney Hester, set out to whip Malcolm on July 14, 1946, allegedly because Malcolm had beaten his [Malcolm's] wife. Another, more likely version of events contends that Hester and Malcolm fought over Hester's sexual advances to Dorothy Malcolm, who was then seven months pregnant. Whatever the source of the quarrel, Malcolm wound up stabbing Barney Hester with a pocketknife, inflicting a wound that required brief hospitalization. Walton County sheriff E. S. Gordon arrested Malcolm for assault, and Dorothy Malcolm left the Hester plantation to work on a spread owned by J. Loy Harrison (who also employed her brother and his wife, George and Mae Dorsey). Harrison initially denied requests that he pay Malcolm's bail, but he finally relented and agreed to post the bond if Malcolm would go to work on his farm.

On July 26, Harrison drove Dorothy Malcolm and the Dorseys into Monroe, where he paid Roger Malcolm's $600 bail at 2:00 P.M. Curiously, jailers kept Malcolm locked up for another three hours, while Harrison "made some purchases" in town and

his three passengers adjourned to an all-black saloon. When Malcolm finally joined them and the group started for home, Harrison claimed that his passengers "were all lit [drunk]." Whether planned or not, the three-hour delay in releasing Malcolm had given a mob of vigilantes time to lay an ambush on the road to Harrison's plantation.

Approaching Moore's Ford, where a wooden bridge spanned the Appalachee River, Harrison found his way blocked by a car parked in the middle of the bridge. As he slowed, a second vehicle suddenly appeared and rammed his car from behind, while a group of 20-odd men swarmed from the woods on either side and surrounded the car. As Harrison later described the event, "I thought to myself: 'Federal men!' One of the men came out, put a shotgun against the back of my head and said, 'All of you put 'em up. We want Roger.' Some of the men in the group then went to the two Negro men slipped ropes around their hands—expert like, pretty like."

As Malcolm and George Dorsey were pulled from Harrison's car, one of the gunmen told Dorsey, "I bet you're one of those niggers who voted the other day." Dorothy Malcolm at once began "cussing like everything," calling out to the gang for her husband's release, apparently shouting the name of a man who seemed to be commanding the group. Harrison described the leader as "tall and dignified looking," resembling "a retired business man. He was about 65, wore a brown suit and had on a big broad brimmed hat. He looked like he had a good healthy Florida tan." Turning back toward the car, the ringleader ordered his gunmen to "get those black bitches, too," and both women were then carried off with their husbands, fighting with such determination that their nails scratched the paint of Harrison's car. Harrison, held at gunpoint by the vehicle, heard three volleys of gunshots. He was released after swearing that he recognized no members of the unmasked gang, and summoned Sheriff Gordon to the scene with coroner W. T. Brown.

Together, the three men found the Malcolms and the Dorseys lying in a nearby grove of trees, riddled with bullets and buckshot. Both women had additionally suffered broken arms and elbows, presumably during their fight to remain in Harrison's car. Dorothy Malcolm's face had been obliterated by a close-range shotgun blast, while her husband—the gang's primary target—had absorbed more lead than any of the other victims. Coroner Brown issued a ruling of "death at the hands of persons unknown," but questions lin-

231

gered surrounding Harrison's role in the slaughter. Rumors flourished—never documented—that he had quarreled with Dorsey over a crop settlement, and Major W. E. Spence from the Georgia Bureau of Investigation remarked, "It looks like it was a rehearsed affair. It looked like it might have been planned since the Negro was first confined to jail."

If so, the planning paid off for the killers. Despite a national outcry over Georgia's first postwar lynching, no suspects were ever identified or prosecuted. Threats from Walton County racists discouraged kinfolk of the victims from attending the funerals, prompting one black mortician to tell journalists, "They ain't home. They ain't nowhere. They hid out." Major Spence, an atypical Georgia lawman of the period, termed the quadruple murder "the worst

thing that ever happened in Georgia," complaining of Monroe that "the best people in town won't talk." Sixty years later, they still aren't talking—and the case remains officially unsolved.

MALCOLM X See X, Malcolm

MALLARD, Robert murder victim (1948)

Between 1882 and 1940, white mobs in Georgia lynched at least 570 African Americans in public displays of savagery that failed to result in a single criminal conviction for the killers. Toombs County, located 175 miles southeast of Atlanta, was less violent than most, but it still held many perils for blacks

The election of Governor Eugene Talmadge (left, seated) sparked racial violence throughout Georgia in 1946, including the murder of Robert Mallard. Here, state attorney general Dan Duke chastises Talmadge for pardoning convicted racist floggers. (Library of Congress)

in the unsettled years after World War II. Governor Eugene Talmadge was elected to his third term in 1946, after a racist campaign that paralleled state-wide revival of the terrorist Ku Klux Klan. Talmadge himself was a proud former Klansman; when he died prior to inauguration, son Herman Talmadge was picked by the state legislature to carry on the family tradition. Running on his own in 1948, Herman Talmadge appeared as a guest speaker at Klan leader Samuel Green's birthday party, telling the audience that George was lucky to have Klansmen "ready to fight for the preservation of our American traditions against the communists, foreign agitators, Negroes, Catholics and Jews." Green returned the favor by endorsing Talmadge as "the man who will put Georgia back in the white man's column."

That political tempest meant little to Robert Mallard, a black resident of Toombs County who had prospered as a salesman, in addition to running a 32-acre farm outside Lyons, the county seat. Mallard focused on earning a living for his family, seemingly unaware that local whites—including Klansmen—believed he had become "too big" in the years since V-J Day. On Sunday morning, November 20, 1948, Mallard was returning from church with his wife and two friends when he found the road blocked by several cars. White men in masks and robes formed a skirmish line across the black-top, one of them firing a shot through Mallard's windshield that killed him in the driver's seat. That done, the Klansmen climbed into their cars and left the scene at a leisurely pace.

The search for Mallard's slayers was predestined to fail. Sheriff R. E. Gray acknowledged that the killers had worn "white stuff," but he refused to blame the Klan. Governor Talmadge ordered a review of the case by the Georgia Bureau of Investigation (an agency led by and riddled with Klansmen), while "Grand Dragon" Green announced that the KKK would make its own investigation of the murder. Sheriff Gray blamed Mallard himself for the shooting, telling reporters, "This Negro was a bad Negro, as I have had dealings with him. I further know that this Negro was hated by all who knew him." GBI agents arrested Mallard's widow at his funeral, on November 27, and charged her with the murder; two other blacks and a white reporter were also jailed as "material witnesses." Lieutenant W. E. McDuffie told journalists, "I think the Ku Klux Klan was wrongfully blamed in this case," but the charges

against Mrs. Mallard were later dismissed for lack of evidence. Five white men were arrested on December 4, 1948, two of them formally indicted for murder six days later, but neither was convicted, and the case remains officially unsolved today.

MANHATTAN axe murders (1985)

On May 25, 1985, 85-year-old Janet Scott was found murdered in her New York City hotel room. An autopsy determined that death was caused by repeated blows to the head with a heavy, sharp instrument similar to an axe or hatchet. Following the murder, pieces of the victim's skull were removed and placed near the body, arranged in a pattern bearing some unknown significance to the killer.

Five days later, friends of 58-year-old Ruth Potdevin became concerned when she failed to appear at a business luncheon held in another downtown Manhattan hotel. One member of the party was sent to check Potdevin's room and found the door ajar. Inside, Potdevin lay dead on the floor, her skull crushed by more than 40 blows with an axelike instrument. Once more, selected fragments of the victim's skull and scalp had been arranged to form a cryptic pattern on the floor beside her corpse.

The day after the second murder, two African-American suspects were arrested for trying to purchase a radio with one of Potdevin's stolen credit cards, but police were unable to link them with the actual slaying. On June 10, 1985, authorities announced that there were sufficient similarities between the Scott and Potdevin murders to treat them as the work of a single killer—and there the matter rests. Thus far, two decades later, there apparently have been no further slayings in the series, and the case remains unsolved.

MARTIN, Effie   See "WEST SIDE RAPIST"

MARTIN, James   murder victim (1870)

Black Republicans were an endangered species in the American South during Reconstruction (1865–77), as white Democrats—lately dubbed "Conservatives"—waged ruthless guerrilla warfare to effectively reverse the political effects of the recent Civil War. Alabama witnessed widespread violence by the Ku Klux Klan during that troubled era, with scores of victims murdered, while hundreds more were whipped, castrated, raped, or otherwise outraged.

One who fell in the struggle to gain equal rights for his people was James Martin, a prominent black Republican in Greene County, Alabama. On the night of March 31, 1870, Martin was shot by unknown gunmen near his home, at Union. A physician tried to remove the bullet from his body, but armed men interrupted the operation and carried Martin off, his final resting place unknown to this day. On the same night he was murdered, Klansmen assassinated Greene County solicitor ALEXANDER BOYD at nearby Eutaw, another crime destined to remain perpetually unsolved.

Governor William Smith was initially hopeful, dispatching a special agent, one John Minnis, to investigate the Greene County crimes. Minnis later served as a U.S. attorney and federal prosecutor of Alabama Klansmen, but he had no luck with his present assignment. Minnis blamed the Klan for both murders, but he concluded the killers had been imported from another county and were thus unlikely to be recognized by locals. A grand jury convened to examine the Boyd assassination ignored Martin's death, presumably because black victims were considered insignificant at the particular time and place.

MARTIN, Michelle See "FRANKFORD SLASHER"

MARTIN, Paul See TEXARKANA "PHANTOM GUNMAN"

MARYLAND gay murders (1996–97)
Between October 1996 and January 1997 five gay African-American men were murdered in Maryland by an unknown home invader who left no signs of forced entry at the crime scenes. Homicide investigators suspected a serial killer at work when they learned that all five victims had visited certain popular gay bars—Bachelor's Mills, the Full House, and "360"—in nearby Washington, D.C. A spokesperson for the Prince Georges County police, Corporal Diane Richardson, told reporters, "At some point they all frequented the same clubs, but we have not established that they knew each other."

The first to die, and the only victim killed alone, was 42-year-old Anthony Barnes, found stabbed to death in his Bladensburg home on October 6, 1996. Ten weeks later, on December 21, 1996, 33-year-old Jimmy McGuire and 27-year-old James Williams were shot execution-style in the home they shared at Clinton, Maryland. The last two victims were 22-year-old Derrick Hilliard, a Washington resident, and 41-year-old John Whittington of Hyattsville, found shot in a ground-floor room at the Motel 6 in Camp Springs, Maryland. To date, no suspects have been named by police in the case, and no more slayings have been added to the list.

MARYLAND unsolved murders (1986–87)
During December 1986 and January 1987 five African-American women from Washington, D.C., were murdered and their bodies dumped near Suitland, Maryland, in Prince Georges County. By September 1987 at least four more women were murdered in Washington, but the conviction of a suspect in one of those cases has brought authorities no closer to solution of the other crimes.

The first victim, 20-year-old Dorothy Miller, was found in the woods near Suitland's Bradbury Recreation Center on December 13, 1986. Killed by an apparent drug overdose, Miller had also been violently sodomized, a fact that linked her death to those of four other victims discovered a month later.

On January 11, 1987, young patrons of the Bradbury Recreation Center noticed women's clothing hanging in a nearby tree. Investigating, they discovered the body of 25-year-old Pamela Malcolm, missing from her Suitland home since October 22, 1986. An autopsy revealed she had been sodomized and stabbed to death. On January 12 a team of 50 police recruits swept through the forest north of the U.S. Census Bureau's headquarters, seeking more clues in the two homicides. Instead of evidence, they found two more bodies, identified as 22-year-old Cynthia Westbury and 26-year-old Juanita Walls. Both had been reported missing from the District of Columbia and both were sodomized, either before or after they were stabbed to death.

Victim number five, 22-year-old Angela Wilkerson, was found near Suitland on January 13, 1987. Soon after that discovery, authorities reported that four of the five victims had lived within a one-mile radius of one another, in southeast Washington. All four of the Washington victims were unemployed, and at least two had frequented the same restaurant on Good Hope Road.

Another "pattern" victim, 20-year-old Janice Morton, was found in a northeast Washington alley on January 15, 1987; she had been stripped, beaten, and strangled to death. That investigation was still in progress on April 5, when a nude "Jane Doe" victim was found near Euclid and 13th Street, Northwest, her body dumped in a secluded driveway. A 31-year-old suspect, Alton Alonzo Best, was indicted for Norton's murder on April 7, and he confessed to the crime two months later. Authorities say Best knew two of the Maryland victims, but his conviction on one murder count did not stop the killing.

On April 10, 1987, with Best in jail, an unknown suspect in a van attempted to kidnap a 25-year-old woman one block from the home of Suitland victim Pamela Malcolm. Police were still checking the facts of that case five days later, when another victim, Donna Nichols, was beaten to death in a Washington alley. On June 24, 1987, 21-year-old Cheryl Henderson was found in a wooded area of southeast Washington, less than two miles from Suitland, with her throat slashed from ear to ear. Another female victim was discovered on September 21, at a southeast Washington apartment complex, but authorities refused to discuss the cause of death or possible connection to their other open cases.

The Maryland-Washington murders remain unsolved today (in August 2003), with the elusive killer (or killers) unidentified. The slayer's preference for African American victims led to speculation that the "FREEWAY PHANTOM" may have resurfaced after 15 years in retirement, but homicide detectives have revealed no evidence of a connection to the earlier unsolved crimes.

MASON, Simpson murder victim (1868)

While the U.S. Civil War ended officially in April 1865, violence continued throughout the late Confederacy during most of the subsequent Reconstruction era (1865–77). White Democrats, allied with such groups as the Ku Klux Klan and Knights of the White Camellia, used any brutal means at their disposal to disenfranchise former slaves and to drive "radical" Republicans from office. Arkansas suffered as much postwar mayhem as any southern state, and troubled Fulton County, on the Missouri border, witnessed more than most regions of the state.

Fulton County Democrats organized a local KKK chapter in September 1868 to terrorize blacks in advance of November's presidential election, but their efforts were not unopposed. Republican sheriff E. W. Spear raised a militia company to patrol the district, registering voters and (at least in theory) guarding them against Klan reprisals. An officer of that militia, Capt. Simpson Mason, was leading a dozen troopers on routine patrol when sniper ambushed his party on September 19, 1868. Mason was killed in the first blaze of gunfire, his soldiers retreating to gather reinforcements for a belated counterattack.

Suspicion in the case immediately fell on N. H. Tracy, a local farmer and reputed leader of the county's Klan. Presuming that Tracy must have knowledge of violent actions undertaken by his Klansmen, Sheriff Spear gathered a 30-man posse and went looking for his suspect. Tracy, forewarned of the threat, fled Fulton County and was never captured. Several lesser Klansmen were arrested, but it proved impossible to charge them in the absence of hard evidence. In such manner was Arkansas (and the South at large) eventually "redeemed" for white supremacy and one-party rule that endured for the best part of another century. The death of Capt. Simpson Mason is officially unsolved.

MASSEY, Rodney   See "I-35 MURDERS"

MAURIOT, Nadine   See "MONSTER OF FLORENCE"

MAXWELL, Joseph   See LOS ANGELES DRIVE-BY MURDERS

MCCANN, Madeleine Beth missing person (2007)

Madeleine McCann was born on May 12, 2003, in Leicester, England. Both of her parents are physicians: Father Gerald is a cardiologist employed at Leicester's Glenfield Hospital, while mother Kate is a general practitioner who worked in Melton until 2007. The family expanded with the birth of twins Amelie and Sean in 2005.

In late April 2007, the McCanns left England for a vacation at the Praia da Luz resort in southern

Portugal's Algarve region. On the evening of May 3, Gerald and Kate left their three children alone in their unlocked suite, while they joined a group of seven friends for dinner at a restaurant 120 yards from their ground-floor apartment. The McCanns later told police that they took turns checking on the children at approximate half-hour intervals. Gerald looked in at 9:05 P.M., followed by dinner companion Dr. Matthew Oldfield at 9:30. When Kate McCann took her turn at 10 P.M. she found Madeleine's bed empty and a nearby window open. Her cries of "Madeleine's gone! They've taken her!" brought resort nanny Charlotte Pennington to the apartment, followed by others.

The McCanns say that police were summoned within 10 minutes of Kate's discovery, but Lieutenant Colonel Costa Cabral, speaking for Portugal's gendarmerie, the National Republican Guard, maintained that officers were not called until 11:50 P.M., with a report that Madeleine had vanished

A police handout shows the sketch of a man believed to have abducted Madeleine McCann from her family's apartment in Praia da Luz in Portugal. (epa/Corbis)

"by 10:40." Cabral said that officers of the Judiciary Police (Portugal's primary criminal investigation force) reached the resort at 12:05 A.M. on May 4 and began their formal investigation within 30 minutes. Resort staff and guests joined in a search of the grounds that continued until 4:50 A.M., while bulletins on the presumed kidnapping were transmitted to officers manning the Portuguese border, plus all airports in Portugal and Spain.

Spokesmen for the Judiciary Police initially regarded Madeleine's disappearance as a kidnapping, but after eight days of local searches that included tracking dogs, they declared that she might have been killed in the family's suite. Other fruitless searches were conducted by the Maritime Police offshore, and by volunteers who scoured sewers, drainage channels, local ruins and abandoned houses, garbage dumps, and open wells. Portuguese newspapers hinted at dual investigations, targeting a black-market adoption network and a supposed international ring of unnamed pedophiles.

The last photo of Madeleine, taken at 2:29 P.M. on May 3, showed her at poolside with her father and younger sister. The McCanns stated that Gerald was playing tennis when Kate fed the children at 5 P.M., but resort restaurant manager Miguel Matias placed the whole family on the beach at that time, reportedly confirmed by closed-circuit TV footage from security cameras. On June 17, Chief Inspector Olegário de Sousa complained that bumbling efforts by amateur searchers had obliterated any scientific evidence from the scene of Madeleine's disappearance. A DNA sample found in Madeleine's bedroom failed to match the child, any member of her family, or any suspect identified so far.

While police pursued their search for a presumed corpse, they were distracted by alleged sightings of Madeleine throughout the country and abroad. Within Portugal, various witnesses claimed sightings of Madeleine at Nelas, Portimão, and Silves while suspected kidnap cars were reported from near Praia da Luz and Pinhal Novo. Farther afield, sightings were also reported from Cartagena, Spain; from Marrakech and Zaio, in Morocco; from Valletta, on Malta; from Liège and Tongeren in Belgium; from Međugorje, Bosnia; from Sydney, Australia; from Dorset, in England; and at a L'Arche service station in southern France. All proved to be false alarms.

On May 17, 2007, police searched a villa owned by British citizen Jennifer Murat, near the resort where Madeleine vanished. Officers questioned Murat's son Robert, age 33, and formally branded him a suspect on May 15, while admitting they had insufficient grounds for an arrest. Three dinner companions of the McCanns claimed they had seen Murat near the crime scene on the night Madeleine vanished, but Murat's mother corroborated his alibi. Police also questioned 22-year-old Russian expatriate Sergey Malinka, without filing charges. Several other suspects remain unidentified, including:

- A Caucasian man approximately five feet seven inches tall, estimated age 35–40 years, allegedly seen near the McCann suite carrying "something which might have resembled a child." This suspect generally matched descriptions of an unidentified felon who previously kidnapped two children in the Canary Islands. Sketches of the suspect failed to produce an identification.

- An unnamed British man who lived aboard his yacht in the local harbor for two years prior to Madeleine's disappearance, then left shortly after.

- Urs Hans Von Aesch, a resident of Spain who vacationed in the area around the time Madeleine vanished. Swiss police suspected Von Aesch in the disappearance and presumed murder of five-year-old Ylenia Lenhard from Appenzell, but he committed suicide without admitting any crimes.

On September 7, 2007, Portuguese police named Gerald and Kate McCann as suspects in their daughter's disappearance, but they still allowed the parents to depart for England two days later. Friends and relatives of the McCanns told reporters that police had offered a plea bargain in exchange for Kate's confession to accidentally killing Madeleine. Kate, in reply, told the press, "The police don't want a murder in Portugal and all the publicity about them not having paedophile laws here, so they're blaming us." On September 10, reporter Martin Brunt claimed that forensic evidence "shows the presence of Madeleine's body in the boot of the family's hire car five weeks after she disappeared," but police spokesman Alípio Ribeiro cautioned that forensic test results from the rental car were inconclusive. On September 13 the McCanns challenged Portuguese authorities to "find the body and prove we killed her."

Madeleine's case produced an all-out media frenzy in Great Britain, with some journalists criticizing Portuguese police, while others pursued the parents as suspects or criticized them for leaving their children unattended. Portuguese attorney Francisco Pagarete, representing Robert Murat, joined that chorus in November 2007, declaring that the McCanns "deserve to be cursed" for leaving their children alone. London's *Daily Express* formally apologized to the McCanns in March 2008, for suggesting their guilt, but that concession brought the case no closer to solution.

At last report, three separate teams of private investigators had been hired to pursue Madeleine's case. One, funded by business mogul Brian Kennedy, pursued slim leads in Morocco, while others searched for evidence in Portugal and Spain. Lawyer Marcos Aragão Correia hired divers to search the Barragem do Arade reservoir, 35 miles from Praia da Luz, where they found a plastic bag filled with bones, which turned out to be from an animal.

Four months after that discovery, on July 21, Portuguese Attorney General Fernando Pinto Monteiro announced the formal closure of his government's investigation, with no further leads or viable suspects in sight. Kate McCann vowed that she would leave "no stone unturned" in the search for her daughter and Madeleine's abductor(s).

MCCONNELL, Deborah   See NEW BEDFORD, MASSACHUSETTS, MURDERS

MCCOWN, Marilyn Renee ("Niqui") missing person (2001)

A resident of Richmond, Virginia, born January 6, 1973, Marilyn "Niqui" McCown vanished while washing her clothes at a local laundromat on July 22, 2001. Witnesses from the laundromat recalled the attractive 28-year-old African American primarily for her clothing: a pink-and-purple bikini top and dark-colored shorts. McCown's car, a 1990 GMC Jimmy, was found abandoned at a Richmond apartment complex on November 3, 2001, its battery and radio missing, the lock on the driver's door punched in.

No trace of McCown has been found thus far, although her family and Richmond police naturally suspect foul play. McCown's case was profiled without result on TV's *Unsolved Mysteries,* and two of McCown's sisters—Michelle Lester and Terri Jett—flew to New York City in September 2002 to tape a session of the Montel Williams talk show featuring psychic Sylvia Browne. Browne's verdict on the case, that McCown had been murdered, was aired on November 5, 2002. Local journalists reported that McCown's mother "was not totally pleased" with the broadcast. "Until I see her body," Barbara McCown declared, "I can't give up."

MCCOWN, Michael   See "I-70/I-35 MURDERS"

MCDONALD, Mary   See CUMMINSVILLE, OHIO, MURDERS

MCELROY, Kenneth Rex   murder victim (1981)

Ken Rex McElroy, a hulking 230-pound bully known for his heavy drinking, explosive temper, and a tendency to settle arguments with lethal weapons, terrorized the small town of Skidmore, Missouri, for most of his life. The illiterate son of a sharecropper, born in 1934, McElroy dropped out of elementary school to make his living as a thief and poacher, once removing the backseat from his car to smuggle hogs stolen under cover of darkness. On another occasion, while rustling cattle, Ken Rex dropped his loaded trailer in the middle of a bridge to escape pursuing lawmen—and then informed police that his trailer had been stolen. In his free time McElroy married three times and sired dozens of children, whom he encouraged to follow in their father's outlaw footsteps.

Theft was one thing, aided and abetted by the farmers who purchased stolen stock and grain from Ken Rex, but McElroy found his true vocation in the role of hometown terrorist. Seldom seen without a pistol in a shoulder holster, rifles and shotguns racked in the window of his pickup truck, McElroy delighted in bullying neighbors, shopkeepers, and anyone else who had the misfortune to cross his path. McElroy loved to boast that he would never spend a day in jail, and his prediction was nearly correct. Arrested after shooting one of his Skidmore neighbors, McElroy produced alibi witnesses at his trial, and a local jury acquitted him of all charges. That victory prompted even more outrageous behav-

ior, leading to the incident that would finally cost McElroy his life.

The trouble began when grocer Bo Bowkamp's wife caught one of McElroy's children shoplifting candy. An angry confrontation with Trena McElroy escalated into a full-blown harassment campaign against the Bowkamps, with threatening telephone calls, items stolen from their yard, their mailbox smashed repeatedly, and Ken Rex parked outside their home on a daily basis, glowering from behind the wheel of his gun-laden pickup. The war of nerves dragged on for a year before McElroy finally snapped, invading Bowkamp's store one afternoon and wounding him with a shotgun blast to the neck.

Bowkamp survived the attack, and McElroy was charged with attempted murder. At trial, he claimed the elderly victim had rushed him with a butcher knife, forcing him to fire his conveniently handy shotgun in self-defense. Jurors settled for a compromise verdict, convicting McElroy of second-degree assault, but he remained free on bond pending appeal of the verdict, still threatening Bowkamp's life. McElroy's lawyer, Richard McFadin, warned him to stay out of Skidmore, where "feelings were running too high," but McElroy replied with typical arrogance. "No one can tell me to stay out," he sneered. "That's my right, to go where I please."

Ken Rex and Trena went to Skidmore on July 10, 1981. They spent the morning in a local bar, McElroy drinking and spewing the usual threats against Bowkamp, while an estimated 60 men gathered for a meeting with the sheriff at a nearby American Legion hall. The sheriff explained that his hands were tied under Missouri law, until McElroy's conviction was affirmed by the appellate court. Discussion continued after the sheriff left—until a new arrival alerted the group to McElroy's presence in town. The crowd adjourned, moving en masse to the bar where McElroy sat drinking. Several men entered, watching Ken Rex, while McElroy returned their silent glares. At last, he purchased a six-pack to go and walked out to his truck, parked in front of the bar. At least 10 shots were fired into the vehicle as Ken Rex sat behind the wheel, with Trena at his side. Ken Rex was killed instantly, struck in the head and neck, while Trena emerged unscathed.

Trena McElroy identified one of the gunmen as Del Clement, co-owner of the tavern where Ken Rex sipped his last beer, but Clement denied it, and a local coroner's jury ignored Trena's sworn testimony, returning a verdict of "death at the hands of persons unknown." Investigators found shell casings from two different weapons at the crime scene—one .22-caliber, the other a .30-30 rifle—but witnesses to the shooting (various estimates place their number between 12 and 60 persons) were unanimous in claiming that they had not seen the shooters. Don Shrubshell, a photographer for the *Maryville Daily Forum,* had arrived in time to hear Skidmore's sheriff shouting, "You didn't have to kill him," but the remarks had been addressed to no particular suspect. No guns were found at the scene, Federal Bureau of Investigation (FBI) agents left town empty-handed, and a grand jury failed to lodge indictments. The case remains unsolved today, its secrets locked behind an enduring wall of silence in Skidmore.

Twenty years after the fact, in July 2001, lawyer McFadin still mourned the passing of his most-hated client. "Someone got away with murder in Skidmore," he told reporters on the slaying's anniversary. "It was a vigilante killing, and it must be weighing on someone after 20 years." If so, the pressure has not led to a confession in the case. Nodaway County prosecutor David Baird, still in office as the murder's 20-year anniversary approached, told reporters, "I can pick up a case and read a case and I can tell, yeah, I'm comfortable that this is who did it. But this case, at least what I've seen, doesn't take me to that level yet." And while outsiders speculated that Skidmore's silent residents were being "eaten up by guilt," Internet author William Anderson penned an essay declaring McElroy's summary execution "vigilante justice—a proper response to government failure." Whatever the feelings in Skidmore itself, there seems to be no prospect for indictments or convictions in McElroy's case.

MCGOWAN, Margaret   See "JACK THE STRIPPER"

MCGUIRE, Jimmy   See MARYLAND GAY MURDERS

MCKENZIE, Dorothy   See NEW JERSEY MURDERS (1965–66)

MCLAUGHLIN, Susan   See "ASTROLOGICAL MURDERS"

MCLEAN, Barbara   See "HIGHWAY KILLER"

MCMILLAN, Colleen   See "HIGHWAY KILLER"

MCQUEEN, Arlette   See DETROIT MURDERS

MCSPADDEN, Earl   See TEXARKANA "PHANTOM GUNMAN"

MEADOR, Michael   See LOS ANGELES DRIVE-BY MURDERS

MEADOWS, William R. murder victim (1868)
Louisiana witnessed more violence than most southern states during the Reconstruction era (1865–77), thanks to the combined efforts of two powerful terrorist groups, the Ku Klux Klan and the Knights of the White Camellia. The most chaotic period of all was during 1868, as leaders of the all-white Democratic Party fought to keep ex-slaves and white Republicans from voting in November's presidential contest. Louisiana authorities recorded 1,800 murders between August and November 1868, while many others were doubtless overlooked, the victims disappearing into swamps, rivers, or shallow graves.

One early victim of the violence, killed three months before the general slaughter began, was William Meadows. A former slave who attended the state constitutional convention as a representative from Claiborne Parish, therefore doubly despised by local terrorists, Meadows was gunned down by "persons unknown" on May 6, 1868. Around the same time, newly-elected Republican congressman W. Jasper Blackburn moved from Claiborne Parish to New Orleans, following threats on his life, and the local Freedmen's Bureau agent was advised to leave the district or die. Masked raiders struck numerous black homes in the dead of night, disarming and flogging their inhabitants, and rioters destroyed the presses of the area's only Republican newspaper, the Homer *Iliad,* in July 1868. Local authorities professed themselves unable to identify the terrorists responsible, and the crime wave continued without arrests or indictments until November, when Democratic votes carried the state by a margin of 88,225 to 34,859.

MEDEIROS, Louise See "Honolulu Strangler"

MENDES, Dawn See New Bedford, Massachusetts, Murders

MERCHANT, Brenda See "Occult Murders"

METCALFE, George terrorist victim (1965)

Natchez, Mississippi, ranked among the most dangerous locations for black activists during the civil rights movement of the 1960s. Segregation was absolute, enforced by heavy-handed police and four competing factions of the vigilante Ku Klux Klan. Unlike most southern communities, where black ministers led the push to register voters and integrate public facilities, the Natchez civil rights movement was led by two employees of the local Armstrong Tire and Rubber plant. George Metcalfe presided over the Natchez chapter of the National Association for the Advancement of Colored People (NAACP), while friend and coworker WHARLEST JACKSON served as the group's treasurer. Together, the men were accustomed to insults and threats from white colleagues and strangers alike.

Their risk increased on August 19, 1965, when Metcalfe presented the Natchez school board with a petition demanding integration of local public schools, in compliance with the United States Supreme Court's desegregation orders of 1954–55. Eight days later, a bomb wired to the ignition of Metcalfe's car exploded when he turned the key, shattering Metcalfe's legs and blinding him in one eye. He would survive the wounds and return to his job at Armstrong, but his driving days were done. Henceforth, Metcalfe would ride with Jackson—until another car bomb killed his friend in February 1967.

Neither crime was ever officially solved, though Federal Bureau of Investigation (FBI) agents blamed both bombings (and the 1964 arson death of Louisiana victim FRANK MORRIS) on members of a Klan faction known as the Silver Dollar Group. Fond of describing themselves as "the toughest Klansmen in Mississippi or Louisiana," the Silver Dollar terrorists rehearsed on weekends with explosive devices, including practice in wiring their bombs up to cars. Klan oaths of secrecy and the pervasive fear of violence in Natchez averted prosecution of the guilty

parties. Aging survivors of the Silver Dollar Group remain at large today.

METIVIER, Sebastien See Montreal Child Murders

METZGER, Vickie Sue See "Redhead Murders"

MEYER, Horst See "Monster of Florence"

MEYER, Mary Pinchot murder victim (1964)

A Maryland native, born in October 1920, Mary Pinchot was the daughter of Amos Pinchot, a wealthy lawyer who helped found the Progressive Party in 1912 and financed the *Masses,* a socialist periodical. Mary's mother Ruth also worked for liberal magazines including the *Nation* and the *New Republic.* With that left-wing political background, it seems ironic that Mary fell in love with Marine Corps lieutenant Cord Meyer in 1944 and married him at the end of World War II, four years before he joined the Central Intelligence Agency under director Allen Dulles. Cord subsequently became a "principal agent" in the CIA's Operation Mockingbird, an effort to influence U.S. journalists, which was legally banned by the agency's charter (forbidding any operations within the continental United States).

Despite that service, witch-hunting senator Joseph McCarthy branded Cord Meyer a communist in 1953, while J. Edgar Hoover's Federal Bureau of Investigation maintained surveillance on the whole family. Hoover's antipathy toward the Pinchots and Meyers increased after 1954, when Cord and Mary became close friends of future president JOHN F. KENNEDY. Mary's friendship—some say romantic involvement—with JFK endured after she divorced Cord in 1958, on grounds of "extreme cruelty, mental in nature, which seriously injured her health, destroyed her happiness, rendered further cohabitation unendurable." CIA phone taps and other evidence suggest that Mary and JFK had "about 30 trysts" between October 1961 and Kennedy's assassination in November 1963.

On October 12, 1964, two weeks after publication of the Warren Report on the Kennedy assassination, Mary Meyer was shot and killed while strolling along the Chesapeake and Ohio Canal in Georgetown, Washington, D.C. Witness Henry Wiggins heard the fatal shots and saw an African American man standing over Meyer's body, then fleeing the scene. Postmortem examination revealed two bullet wounds, one each to the back of Meyer's head and to the heart, which FBI analysts determined had been "fired at close range, possibly point-blank."

Washington police charged suspect Raymond Crump with the slaying, but they found no weapon and produced no motive. Any mention of Meyer's private life was banned from Crump's trial, where jurors acquitted him of all charges on July 29, 1965.

Cord Meyer left the CIA in 1977 and subsequently published a memoir in which he declared, "I was satisfied by the conclusions of the police investigation that Mary had been the victim of a sexually motivated assault by a single individual and that she had been killed in her struggle to escape." That statement notwithstanding, former personal assistant Carol Delaney insisted that "Mr. Meyer didn't for a minute think that Ray Crump had murdered his wife or that it had been an attempted rape. But, being an Agency man, he couldn't very well accuse the CIA of the crime, although the murder had all the markings of an in-house rubout." Six weeks before his own death, in early 2001, Cord Meyer told author C. David Heymann that Mary was killed by "the same sons of bitches that killed John F. Kennedy."

Author Jim Marrs had reached the same conclusion 12 years earlier, when his book *Crossfire* (1989) listed Mary Meyer with other individuals whose strange deaths were theoretically linked to the JFK assassination. Internet author Ben Hayes takes a contrary view, asserting that "[a]fter extensive investigating, we can see that Mary Pinchot Meyer's death had nothing to do with the assassination of President John F. Kennedy. As with so many other mystery deaths, we find that Mary Pinchot Meyer died because of an unlucky set of events. She was brutally murdered by a disturbed young man, as was her lover [Kennedy], as are so many people each and every day."

MEYERS, Debra See RAWLINS, WYOMING, RODEO MURDERS

MICHIGAN prostitute murders (1990–97)

On February 3, 1998, spokesmen for the Michigan State Police announced the formation of a task force to investigate "at least 20" murders of known prostitutes across the state, dating back to 1990. No details were provided on the crimes, as officers from various jurisdictions prepared for the first task force meeting at Livonia. Media reports noted that the team would also "focus on attempted murders and missing person reports throughout southeastern Michigan," suggesting that the final body count may well exceed the initial reference to 20 victims.

Members of the task force noted that their job was complicated by the lifestyle of the women who had fallen prey to one or more unidentified predators over the years. As Macomb County sheriff's lieutenant Cal Eschenburg told reporters, "It's hard enough for a detective to do their job [sic] when they're dealing with people who abide by the legal system. But when you involve someone who may be dealing in [a] criminal enterprise like drugs and prostitution, it really takes the investigator into a whole subculture."

Lt. Brian Krutell, with three unsolved murders on file in Mt. Clemens, told the press, "We have nothing concrete on any of the cases. A task force can't hurt." But neither has it helped, thus far, as all the homicides remain unsolved, the killer (or killers) still at large.

MIDWEST missing students (2002)

Within an 11-day period in fall 2002, four young people in their twenties vanished from college towns in Minnesota and Wisconsin. Three of the four were students currently enrolled in various universities. All disappeared late at night, after drinking in bars or at parties. Thus far, none of the four has been found by authorities, and while police refuse to formally link the cases, area residents have voiced fears that a serial killer may be prowling the upper Midwest.

The first to vanish—and the only nonstudent—was Erika Marie Dalquist, a 21-year-old employee of a Brainerd, Minnesota, telemarketing firm who doubled as a union shop steward at her workplace. Dalquist went out drinking in Brainerd on the night of Tuesday, October 29, 2002. She was last seen sometime after 1:00 A.M. on October 30, when she left a downtown bar—the Tropical Nites—with a group of friends. Brainerd police sergeant David

Holtz told the *New York Times* that Dalquist's party was waiting for a taxi outside the bar, when Dalquist saw a man she recognized. After telling her friends not to wait for her, Dalquist "walked away with this man," whom her friends did not know. No introductions were made, no names mentioned. Witnesses vaguely described Dalquist's last known companion as a Caucasian male of indeterminate age, wearing blue jeans and a blue sweatshirt.

Erika Dalquist had been missing for only 24 hours when a second mystery began in Minneapolis, 127 miles southeast of Brainerd. It was Halloween, and Eden Prairie native Christopher Jenkins wanted to party. Dressed in a stylized American Indian costume, the 21-year-old University of Minnesota senior made his way to a downtown saloon, the Lone Tree Bar & Grill. The management student and lacrosse goalie left around midnight—and disappeared without a trace. Friends posted photos of Jenkins throughout Minneapolis, and searchers scoured the Mississippi River where it cut through the university campus, all in vain. Jenkins had become a statistic, one of an average 180 persons reported missing from Minneapolis each year.

The deepening mystery spread to Wisconsin on November 6, 2002, when 22-year-old Michael Noll disappeared from Eau Claire, Wisconsin. A native of Rochester, Minnesota, enrolled at the University of Wisconsin–Eau Claire, Noll celebrated his 22nd birthday that Wednesday night with a zealous round of bar-hopping. He was visibly intoxicated when he left a Water Street tavern, the Nasty Habit Saloon, sometime between 11:00 and 11:30 P.M. A short time later, he wandered drunkenly into a stranger's unlocked home on Oxford Avenue, near Grace Lutheran Church, but the elderly tenant persuaded him to leave peaceably. In the process, Noll dropped his baseball cap, subsequently delivered to police and identified by Noll's relatives. Deputy Chief Gary Foster of the Eau Clair Police Department saw "no indication foul play was a factor in the disappearance," but authorities who searched the campus and the nearby Chippewa River still found no trace of Noll.

The last to vanish was 20-year-old Josh Guimond, a native of Maple Lake, Minnesota, enrolled as a junior political science major at St. John's University in aptly named Collegeville. Like the others before him, Guimond disappeared after a night of drinking, last seen when he left a campus party on November 9, 2002. Reported missing when he failed to keep a study date on November 10, Guimond disappeared somewhere during the short walk between Metten Court (the party site) and his dorm room in St. Maur House. Authorities dragged nearby Maple Lake, without result, and concern for Guimond's safety deepened after his car was found on campus, parked in its usual place. Sergeant Bruce Bechtold, speaking for the Stearns County Sheriff's Department, formally denied any link between Guimond's case and the other recent disappearances.

In retrospect, however, friends and relatives of the four missing persons believe police may have been too hasty in their pronouncements. Meeting with reporters in St. Paul, relatives of Jenkins, Noll, and Guimond called for the creation of a task force to investigate the missing-persons cases. Speaking of his son's disappearance, Brian Guimond said, "It seems right to me that this stuff's all connected somehow. We might not think or know it right now, but once this all gets taken care of we'll find that this is all connected." Jan Jenkins complained that police had stalled any search for her son for nearly five days, because he was an adult. "While we are trying to deal with the unbelievable, awful horror of not knowing where Chris is," she told the press, "in addition we have to be organized enough and sane enough to do this ourselves."

And still, despite the apparent best efforts of police and civilian searchers alike, the four cases remained unsolved, each one a haunting mystery. Brainerd police chief John Bolduc admitted that kidnapping was a possibility in Erika Dalquist's case, while ruefully declaring that "there's nothing new" in terms of evidence or suspects. Minneapolis police spokesperson Cyndi Barrington, questioned on the Jenkins case, told reporters, "It's been two weeks, and no contact has been made, and he's still not home. We have been working closely with his family, but there are no clear, concrete indicators. We just don't know, and at this point anything we could say would be speculation." Still avoiding any overt suggestion of a link between the cases, some law enforcement officers edged closer to the realm of speculation. As Stearns County sheriff Jim Kostreba told the *New York Times*, "What's unusual about this is that we have four young people missing within a relatively small area. They're all about the same age, and they all disappeared at night."

And they all remain missing today.

A reward of $10,000 was offered for information leading to Erika Dalquist, but its sole result to date has been the propagation of false rumors that she had been found in Crow Wing County. Chief Bolduc hastened to quash those stories even as they spread. "We have not found her or any evidence of her location," Bolduc told journalists. "Those rumors are irresponsible and immature and the public needs to be mindful of where they're getting their information. We're losing patience with those people starting these rumors, and if someone is intentionally impeding the investigation [by spreading false stories], they will be charged with a crime." Days later, on November 26, 2002, Brainerd police declared themselves in possession of unspecified "new evidence" suggesting that Dalquist was murdered. Chief Bolduc called the new revelation "a worst case scenario. We're looking for a body, clothing, evidence of Erika Dalquist. We need to clear some hurdles. We don't want to miss anything."

If Chief Bolduc's audience anticipated a breakthrough, however, they were soon disappointed. To date, no new evidence has been revealed in Dalquist's case or any of the other Midwest disappearances. By January 2003, local reporters were reduced to chronicling the controversy raised by Penny Bell, a 54-year-old bloodhound handler from Milwaukee who volunteered her prize dog—one Hoover Von Vacuum—to search for Chris Jenkins and Josh Guimond. Critics challenged Bell's claim that her hound could pick up scents from the missing men more than two months after they vanished from public locales, and Minneapolis police detective Dave Hoeschen told reporters that he had "no confidence" in Bell's work. In spite of Hoover's reported olfactory skills, he failed in this case.

Police pulled Christopher Jenkins from the Mississippi River in February 2003 and blamed his death on accidental drowning while intoxicated. Michael Noll was Found in Eau Claire's Half Moon Lake on March 25, 2003, and buried with an identical diagnosis. While Josh Guimond remains missing, police found Erika Dalquist's remains on May 16, 2004, buried on property owned by the grandparents of William Gene Myears—suspected in her death since January 2003, when prosecutors filed, then dropped, charges of second-degree manslaughter. Charged with murder after the discovery of Dalquist's body, Myears fled Minnesota but was captured in Michigan on June 25, 2004, after his case was profiled on *America's Most Wanted*. Myears pled guilty in October 2005 and was sentenced to prison.

Meanwhile, the other Midwest deaths were filed away as accidents, until retired NYPD detectives Anthony Duarte and Kevin Gannon began investigating the case and came to some startling conclusions. In April 2008, Duarte and Gannon told reporters that they believed that serial killers were responsible for the alleged accidental drownings of 40 young men nationwide, including 19 from Minnesota and Wisconsin. In at least 12 cases, the officers reported, "smiley faces" had been found at the locations where young men were dropped into rivers or lakes. As described by Duarte and Gannon, the crimes followed a pattern repeated in 25 cities and 11 states.

In May 2008, FBI headquarters issued a dismissive statement that read: "To date, we have not developed any evidence to support links between these tragic deaths or any evidence substantiating the theory that these deaths are the work of a serial killer or killers. The vast majority of these instances appear to be alcohol-related drowning." Kevin Gannon responded by saying, "Unless you've been out there to the scenes to evaluate [them] yourself, if you haven't done that, you're basically Monday-morning quarterbacking. I don't think any of them went out to the field and beat the bushes."

Previously, scrawled happy faces were the trademark of serial killer Keith Hunter Jesperson, a truck driver imprisoned since 1995 for eight murders committed in the early 1990s.

MIGLIORINI, Antonella See "MONSTER OF FLORENCE"

MIHELICH, Kristine See "BABYSITTER"

MILLER, Allana See HOSPITAL FOR SICK CHILDREN MURDERS

MILLER, Christine See WOONSOCKET, RHODE ISLAND, MURDERS

MILLER, Dorothy See MARYLAND MURDERS (1986–87)

MILLICAN, Cathy See "VALLEY KILLER"

MINCEY, S. S. terrorist murder victim (1930)

While violence by the Ku Klux Klan and allied groups effectively suppressed the Republican Party in most of America's Deep South states after 1877, isolated pockets of GOP activity remained. One of those, curiously, was found in Montgomery County, Georgia, where racial dissension within the party mirrored that found throughout much of the South at large. In 1930, Montgomery County's black Republicans were led by 70-year-old S. S. Mincey, described in press reports of the day as "a prominent Negro" (although his given name has still been lost to history). Mincey was not only active in the county GOP, but also made his voice heard at statewide Republican meetings and several times served as a delegate to the party's national conventions, beginning in 1912. In his spare time Mincey served as secretary and treasurer for the Widows and Orphans Department of the Negro Masonic Lodge of Georgia.

Contesting Mincey's role in county politics, ironically, were not the typical Klan-allied Democrats, but rather a self-styled group of "lily white" Republicans, organized in April 1930 with the stated intention of seizing control from established black Republicans. White Democrats had heretofore ignored the GOP in Georgia, since its dominant membership was barred from voting by a combination of poll taxes, "literacy" tests, and other legal impediments to black suffrage. With whites in control, however, Montgomery County—and, by extension, the state—might be forced to acknowledge a two-party system of government. Accordingly, some well-known local whites urged Mincey to resist the "lily white" faction and keep the Republican Party "pure" through the next election. Thus encouraged, Mincey denounced the interlopers in April 1930 as "poor white trash" defectors from the Democratic Party, and three months later he refused to support a "lily white" candidate's bid to become postmaster in Montgomery County. The stage was thereby set for violence in the traditional southern style.

On the night of July 29, 1930, a truck filled with masked white men arrived at Mincey's rural home, one mile north of Ailey. Mincey heard the truck outside and first thought the new arrivals were friends, come to celebrate his recent promotion within the Masonic lodge. Even when they burst into the house with pistols drawn, he thought it was a joke—until one of the raiders struck him viciously across the head. Mincey staggered off to fetch a hidden gun, but he was beaten down before he could defend himself. The nightriders told him that he had been "too active" in politics, and that they meant to run him out of the county. Mincey, in turn, promised to renounce his political activities if they would leave the house.

Unsatisfied, the raiders carried Mincey to their truck and drove him to a wooded region near Uvalda, in neighboring Toombs County. There they proceeded to flog him with leather straps, leaving him at last with "his clothing beaten into shreds and his skin and flesh torn from his back." Mincey afterward crawled to a nearby road, where a Toombs County farmer found him at daybreak. An offer of seven dollars secured Mincey a ride into Ailey, after the farmer first stopped to unload his tobacco at Vidalia. The doctor treated Mincey's visible wounds and sent him home, where he lapsed into a coma. Mincey died at 2:00 P.M. on July 30, apparently from a cerebral hemorrhage caused by the initial beating at his home.

In contrast to the typical silence (or public acclamation) that greeted southern lynchings, S. S. Mincey's murder touched off a storm of criticism in the local press. On July 31, the Montgomery *Monitor*—a Democratic paper—took the lead with a front-page editorial titled "Hail the Conquering Heroes!"

When we learned that the life of a local citizen had been taken by a mob of unknown assailants without the least known provocation we were dumbfounded. We did not believe there to be enough men in this section of such brutal and bloodthirsty temperament as to commit such a horrible crime. But the crime has been committed, right here in our midst. A citizen has been taken from his home in the dead of night and deliberately deprived of his life by a mob of masked people. It is one of the most brutal crimes we have yet heard of among civilized people in this enlightened age and country . . .

It is reported that those who killed Mincey warned him to sever his relations with the Republican party in this county and get out of the county in thirty days. If such be true, these fellows can take delight in the fact that their request has been granted. His relations with the party have been severed and he has left the county.

These fellows can now come forth and claim their spoils. We shall watch and wait for their arrival. The public will observe as they step into the coveted place of their dead adversary, but we doubt there being anyone to congratulate them on their splendid victory. They are the victors, "and to the victors belong the spoils." They laid siege upon the stronghold of S. S. Mincey. They planned the line of battle and were in the thick of the fight. They have won, and to them shall go the laurel wreath of victory. Even now there must be rejoicing in their victorious camp as the jubilant spirit of the Goddess Victory hovers over their forces. The enemy has been conquered. S. S. Mincey is dead. A new leader must be chosen from among the conquering forces. To this fortunate soul will go the heritage of the dead Negro leader. Upon his honored brow will be placed the crown of authority . . .

We do not know who took this Negro's life or how on earth you reasoned that you or anybody else would be helped in any possible manner by such an act of dastardly cowardice. But we do know that you have upon your hands the blood of a human being which will curse you until your dying day and your children's children yet unborn . . .

The majority of citizens of this county do not approve of such things. We speak for the majority when we say that Montgomery County condemns such brutal actions. Yet, we can make no apologies and do not attempt to do so. The minority which indulges in such practices has, so far, gone unpunished, and we can assure no man that he is safe in his liberty or life while in our midst.

A mass meeting was held to denounce mob violence in Montgomery County on August 4, 1930, while newspapers from neighboring districts weighed in with editorials condemning the still-unknown killers. Since Klan raids and lynchings were common throughout the area from the late 1860s onward, with few if any condemned by the press, it is impossible to overlook the Democratic Party's role in the rhetorical attack on Mincey's slayers. That fervent hand-wringing did not translate into action, however, and a grand jury convened to investigate the murder found "no definite clues" to the identity of Mincey's slayers.

Arthur Raper, in his 1933 study of lynching, did somewhat better. After personal investigation on the scene, Raper published the following "definite clues":

1. On the night Mincey was killed, a new International truck was reported missing from a Montgomery County prison farm, between 9:30 P.M. and dawn.

2. Tire tracks found at Mincey's home matched the tires on the county-owned truck.

3. On the night of the flogging, a Uvalda resident saw an International truck filled with hooded men traveling along the road between the prison camp and Mincey's home. Prosecutor M. H. Boyer was informed of the sighting, but did not call the witness to testify before the grand jury.

In summary, Raper described the prime suspects as follows:

Practically all those believed to have taken part in Mincey's death are "lily white" Republicans, and reputed former members of the Ku Klux Klan. Some of them have court records for bootlegging, participation in previous floggings, seduction or other immoral conduct. Nearly all are either landless farmers or roustabouts who earn a living as convict guards, making and selling liquor, and so on.

Still, despite their "white trash" status, the floggers were never publicly identified or punished. Their victim was simply another black man who "forgot his place" and grew "too big" for racist whites to tolerate. White Democrats retained control of Georgia for another three decades, until passage of the 1964 Civil Rights Act drove them to abandon the party of their fathers and vote for ultra-conservative GOP presidential candidate Barry Goldwater—a candidate endorsed, albeit over his own protest, by the KKK.

MISHELOFF, Ilene   See BAY AREA CHILD MURDERS

MODAFFERI, Kristen   missing person (1997)
A college student from North Carolina, born June 1, 1979, Kristen Modafferi completed her freshman year at North Carolina State University's School of Design in May 1997. Prior to returning for her sophomore studies, Modafferi planned a summer of "enriching life experience" in San Francisco, California, where she planned to work and study photography at the University of California in Berkeley. She left for San Francisco on her 18th birthday and soon found full-time work at Spinelli's Coffee Shop in the Bay City's downtown financial district, with a second job on weekends at the San Francisco Museum of Modern

Art. Modafferi was scheduled to begin her Berkeley studies on Tuesday, June 24, 1997, but she never made it to class. One day earlier, at 3:00 P.M. on June 23, she left Spinelli's after work and vanished without a trace.

Police and relatives discount the possibility that Modafferi may have disappeared voluntarily. She was known to have a close relationship with her parents and was said to be "very excited" about continuing her studies in North Carolina. Furthermore, she had already paid $925 for her first class at Berkeley and left a $400 paycheck unclaimed at Spinelli's Coffee Shop. While acknowledging a possibility that Modafferi may have suffered an accidental head injury, "causing amnesia or some other mental trauma that has incapacitated her to the point that she can't remember her past," authorities and family believe she was abducted. Thus far, the best efforts of detectives and a "Kristen Search Team" have failed to reveal any evidence leading to Modafferi's whereabouts or the identity of a suspect. Still, the missing woman's loved ones cling to diminishing hopes that she may be alive.

Kristen Modafferi is described as an attractive Caucasian, five feet eight inches tall and 140 pounds, with brown hair, brown eyes, and "distinctive dimples." Her family has offered a $50,000 reward for information leading to solution of the case. Tips may be reported to the Vanished Children's Alliance at (800) VANISHED.

MOFFITT, Diana See SAN DIEGO MURDERS (1985–88)

MONDRAGON, Rosenda murder victim (1947)

At 3:30 A.M. on Tuesday, July 8, 1947, postal clerk Newton Joshua was walking to work when he found a woman's naked body lying in the gutter of Elmyra Street, below Elysian Park in Los Angeles. A stocking had been tightly wrapped around her neck, and her right breast slashed with a knife. The only items of apparel left to her in death were bits of jewelry, a religious medal, and a ring.

The victim was identified as 21-year-old Rosenda Mondragon. She lived on South Crocker Street, about two miles from the spot where her body was found. A New Mexico native, married in 1943, she had been separated from husband Antonio Mondragon since late April 1947. They kept in touch, however, and her latest visit to Antonio had been at

2:00 A.M. the day she died. Antonio described her as intoxicated, prattling on about a date, and he had watched her drive away in a coupe, not otherwise described. Police did not consider him a suspect in Rosenda's death.

Local newspapers quickly jumped on Mondragon as the "sixth victim in the BLACK DAHLIA murder cycle," a reference to victim Elizabeth Short, found dead in January 1947. Similarities between the homicides included breast mutilation and police suspicions that Mondragon had been murdered elsewhere, then dumped at the curb from an automobile. A coroner's report confirmed death by ligature strangulation, with a notation of "traumatic subarachnoid hemorrhage" indicating one or more heavy blows to the skull. Whether Mondragon and Short were killed by the same man or by different predators, both crimes remain officially unsolved.

MONK, Graham See NEWCASTLE, AUSTRALIA, MURDERS

MONROE, Marilyn possible murder victim (1962)

One of the most famous movie stars of all time, Marilyn Monroe was a Los Angeles native, born Norma Jeane Mortensen on June 1, 1926. After spending two years in an orphanage (1935–37), she moved through a series of foster homes and married for the first time at age 16. She graced her first national magazine cover in April 1944 and signed a contract with 20th Century-Fox studios four months later, officially adopting her world-renowned screen name at the same time.

Monroe was as famous for the details of her personal life as for any work on stage or screen. Biographer Anthony Summers suggests a love affair with rising political star JOHN F. KENNEDY in the early 1950s, and any such liaison would have drawn attention from the Federal Bureau of Investigation (FBI). Ex-agent G. Gordon Liddy told Summers, years later, that "[t]he stuff on the [Kennedy] brothers and Monroe was very, very closely held" in Director J. Edgar Hoover's personal files. Monroe certainly enjoyed a brief affair with Kennedy after the 1960 presidential election, reportedly meeting him more than once at the home of Kennedy brother-in-law Peter Lawford. Hoover, in turn, warned President Kennedy that Lawford's home "had very likely been bugged by the

Mafia," but he neglected to mention that G-men were also bugging the actor's residence. JFK reportedly saw Monroe for the last time on May 19, 1962, in New York City.

The break-up did not signal an end to Monroe's links with the Kennedy clan, however. She soon proclaimed herself in love with the president's brother, Attorney General ROBERT KENNEDY, once claiming that Robert had promised to leave his wife and marry Monroe. Recounting other conversations with the high and mighty, Monroe told friends that the Kennedys wanted to replace Hoover with a new FBI director, but the move had been postponed until after JFK won reelection in 1964. Monroe's housekeeper afterward claimed that Robert Kennedy visited Monroe's home on June 27, 1962. Six weeks later, on August 4, 1962, the actress was found dead from an apparent prescription drug overdose, variously reported as accidental, suicide, or murder.

Monroe's death was rife with suspicious circumstances, detailed in a time line of the star's final 24 hours, compiled from various published accounts of the case. Obvious contradictions among the reported events of August 4–5, 1962 compound the mystery.

Dawn Monroe telephoned friend and self-described "sleeping-pill buddy" Jeanne Carmen, speaking in "a frightened voice and very tired," complaining that she "had not slept the entire night." Monroe's sleep was disturbed by incessant phone calls "with some woman saying, 'You tramp, leave Bobby [Kennedy] alone or you're going to be in deep trouble,'" Monroe asked Carmen to "bring a bag of pills," but Carmen was busy and could not comply.

Midmorning Monroe telephoned Ralph Roberts, her friend and private masseur, to schedule dinner at her home for that evening. Hairdresser Agnes Flanagan found Monroe "terribly, terribly depressed," while Norman Jeffries Jr. (handyman son of Monroe housekeeper Eunice Murray) judged the star "desperately sick," as if "she must have taken a lot of dope or was scared out of her mind."

Early afternoon A neighbor of Monroe's allegedly saw Robert Kennedy enter Monroe's house, accompanied by a man "carrying what resembled a doctor's bag." The neighbor's family later reported weeks of harassment following August 4, by men warning the witness "to keep her mouth shut." (Kennedy *was* in California on August 4, 1962, ostensibly to attend a meeting of the American Bar Association in San Francisco. His sworn deposition, submitted to investigators after Monroe's death, has never been published.)

4:45 P.M. Dr. Greenson, Monroe's psychiatrist and fellow Brentwood resident, was summoned from his nearby home and found his patient in an "anxious" state, apparently "depressed and somewhat drugged." Greenson later estimated that he spent "about two and a half hours" with Monroe before returning home at 7:15 P.M. Greenson asked Eunice Murray to stay with Monroe overnight, but his statement makes subsequent events all the more curious.

5:30–6:30 P.M. Joe DiMaggio Jr., son of Monroe's famous ex-husband, telephoned twice; both times, Eunice Murray informed him that Monroe was not at home. Ralph Roberts got a similar brush-off from Dr. Greenson when he called to confirm his dinner plans with the actress.

7:40 P.M. Monroe "seemed in better spirits" when she phoned Dr. Greenson at home, reporting that she had spoken to Joe DiMaggio Jr.

8:00 P.M. Monroe bid Mrs. Murray good night and retired to her bedroom, taking with her a telephone with an extra-long cord.

11:00 P.M. Monroe press agent Arthur Jacobs was called away from a Henry Mancini concert by a man who entered his box and said, "Arthur, come quickly! Marilyn is dead, or she is at the point of death." Jacobs dropped his wife at home, en route to Monroe's house, and did not return for two days, his wife later explaining that "he had to fudge the press."

11:00 P.M. While Jacobs was leaving the concert, actor and Kennedy in-law Peter Lawford received a call at home from Monroe herself. According to Lawford's ex-wife, Deborah Gould, Monroe told Lawford in a sleepy voice, "Say good-bye to Jack, and say good-bye to yourself, because you're a nice guy." Gould says that Lawford rushed to Monroe's residence, later stating that he had found and destroyed a suicide note.

2:00 A.M. An emergency team from Schaefer Ambulance Service, L.A.'s largest ambulance firm in 1962, was summoned to Monroe's home.

Although the death of actress Marilyn Monroe was officially deemed suicide, many nagging doubts remain. (Library of Congress)

Twenty years after the fact, driver Ken Hunter and attendant Murray Liebowitz confirmed the run, but refused to discuss any details. The company's owner, Walter Schaefer, was more forthcoming. Schaefer claims his employees found Monroe alive and rushed her to Santa Monica Hospital for treatment. By 1982, when the story surfaced, no medical records remained to confirm Schaefer's story.

3:00 A.M. Private detective Fred Otash claimed that Peter Lawford barged into his office "completely disoriented and in a state of shock, saying that Marilyn Monroe was dead, that Bobby Kennedy was there, and that he [Kennedy] was spirited out of town in some airplane, that they [Monroe and Kennedy] had got in a big fight that evening, that he'd like to have someone go out to the house and pick up any and all information regarding any involvement between Marilyn Monroe and the Kennedys." Otash apparently declined the job.

3:30 A.M. A "sixth sense" for trouble allegedly roused Eunice Murray from sleep and sent her to check on Monroe. She was alarmed to find the telephone cord—normally disconnected at night—still protruding beneath Monroe's bedroom door. Afraid to knock and thus wake her employer, Murray claimed she telephoned Dr. Greenson, who ordered her to knock on the door. When Monroe did not respond, Greenson announced that he was on his way, commanding Murray to telephone Monroe's personal physician, Dr. Hyman Engleberg. While waiting for the medics to arrive, Murray walked around outside the house and peered through Monroe's bedroom window, seeing the actress nude and immobile on her bed. (In 1985 Murray changed her story, telling BBC news that she found Monroe dead "around midnight"—which made subsequent events all the more curious.)

3:35 A.M. Dr. Greenson arrived and entered Monroe's bedroom after smashing a window. He found Monroe lifeless, "fiercely" clutching the phone in her right hand.

3:40 A.M. Dr. Engleberg arrived on the scene.

4:00 A.M. One of Monroe's attorneys, Milton Rudin, telephoned Peter Lawford's agent to tell him that Monroe was dead.

4:25 A.M. Police were finally called to Monroe's residence. One of the first officers to respond, Sgt. Jack Clemmons, questioned Drs. Engleberg and Greenson. They showed him a bottle of Nembutal tablets prescribed by Greenson on August 3, arranged with 14 other bottles of medication on Monroe's nightstand. Of 50 tablets from the original prescription, only 10 remained. Sgt. Clemmons noted that there was no glass of water in evidence. He found no suicide note.

Coroner Thomas Noguchi performed Monroe's autopsy. He found 8 mg of chloral hydrate in her blood and 13 mg of pentobarbital (Nembutal) in her liver tissue. Both amounts ranked "well above fatal doses," yet Noguchi found "absolutely no evidence of pills in the stomach or the small intestine." A "painstaking" search revealed no needle marks, but Noguchi did report a "purplish discoloration" of Monroe's colon, which Deputy District Attorney John Miner termed the "most puzzling" aspect of Monroe's postmortem. Miner admitted that such colonic staining "is not characteristic of a barbiturate OD death," but he noted that it "does indicate the possibility that the drugs, or some portion of the drugs, were introduced into the large intestine rather than being swallowed." Thus was born the theory of a toxic enema, forcibly administered by unknown assassins. Another curious aspect, noted by Noguchi, was a fresh bruise spanning Monroe's lower back and hip which "might have indicated violence."

Such oddities notwithstanding, Noguchi concluded that Monroe had committed suicide. Deputy Coroner Lionel Grandison signed the death certificate under protest and later resigned his position, surfacing in

1978 to dispute the suicide diagnosis, claiming his signature was "forced." He also described numerous bruises on Monroe's corpse that were not listed in Noguchi's report, suggesting a violent struggle prior to death. Critics challenged Grandison's credibility when he went still further, claiming that one or more necrophiles employed at the county morgue had violated Monroe's corpse before it was released for burial.

Los Angeles Police Chief William Parker raised eyebrows at headquarters when he removed the case from detectives in the Robbery-Homicide Division and assigned it to the "spooks" in LAPD's Intelligence Division. From that point onward, future chief Tom Reddin recalled, no one outside of Intelligence "knew a bloody thing about what was going on." Mayor Sam Yorty asked to see the police file on Monroe, but was told that it "could not be found." Forty years later, the file is still missing, its fate officially unknown.

If Marilyn Monroe was murdered, what was the motive? An intimate friend, Robert Slatzer, claims that Monroe showed him a diary 10 days before her death, permitting him to scan its pages while they talked. Many of the entries opened with the same phrase—"Bobby told me . . . "—and went on from there to recount details of Kennedy's war against the Mafia, his long pursuit of JAMES HOFFA, and more. One startling entry read: "Bobby told me he was going to have [Fidel] Castro murdered." (In fact, unknown to Slatzer or the rest of America in 1962, the White House and the CIA had been working with members of organized crime to assassinate Cuba's dictator since 1960. The futile, illegal efforts were not publicly revealed until 1975.) Slatzer says Monroe planned to hold a press conference and "blow the lid off this whole damn thing," including her affairs with both Kennedys and the "promises that had been made to her" (including alleged proposals of marriage by one or both Kennedy brothers). The alleged date of her planned news conference was August 6, 1962, two days after her "suicide." Ex-coroner Lionel Grandison confirmed the existence of Monroe's diary and Slatzer's description of its contents, reporting that the book disappeared from the coroner's office soon after Marilyn's autopsy.

Officially, the FBI did not investigate Monroe's death, but Hoover's hatred for both Kennedys made it impossible for G-men to stay on the sidelines. Assistant FBI director Cartha DeLoach once claimed that a Kennedy telephone number was found at Monroe's bedside, then suppressed to spare the president from scandal. Columnist Walter Winchell, a frequent recipient of classified FBI material, penned an article virtually accusing Robert Kennedy of Monroe's murder, while a half brother of Chicago mobster Sam Giancana claimed that Giancana ordered Monroe's death in a bid to embarrass Robert Kennedy. The young attorney general, once committed to dethroning J. Edgar Hoover, told the press on August 7, 1962, "I hope Hoover will continue to serve the country for many, many years to come." Ten days later, two men flashing FBI badges visited the New York offices of Globe Photos, confiscating Globe's thick file on Monroe "for the presidential library."

Rumors persist that covert tapes were made of Monroe and Robert Kennedy, captured in the act of sex by hidden microphones. In 1968, with Kennedy a front-runner for the Democratic presidential nomination, Republican leaders reportedly hired a right-wing journalist, Ralph de Toledano, to find out if such tapes existed and whether they could be purchased for use on behalf of GOP candidate Richard Nixon. De Toledano allegedly learned that the tapes were held by a former Los Angeles cop, who offered them for sale with a curious $59,000 price tag. The GOP strategists supposedly agreed to the price on June 4, 1968, requesting "a couple of days" to raise the money. As luck would have it, Kennedy was murdered in L.A. that very night, and his adversaries suddenly lost interest in the bedroom tapes.

In 1982, with the Schaefer ambulance story and other stories making weekly headlines in Los Angeles, the district attorney's office officially reopened Monroe's case. Skeptics denounced the review as a whitewash, roundly dismissing the official verdict that "no further criminal investigation appears required." In Washington, meanwhile, only 80 heavily censored pages of the FBI's dossier on Marilyn Monroe have yet been released under the Freedom of Information Act.

MONROE, Terry See SALEM, OREGON, MURDERS

"MONSTER of Florence" serial murderer (1968–??)

The countryside surrounding Florence, Italy, has long been favored as a prime vacation spot for campers, hikers, and nature lovers. In the summer months, warm breezes, starry skies, and rolling meadows make the district a perfect trysting spot for lovers, honeymooners, or couples seeking to rekindle a romantic flame in their relationships. In the latter half of the 20th century, however, Florence acquired a different sort of reputation, as the preferred hunting ground of a serial killer who preyed exclusively on couples. Nearly four decades after the commencement of the terror, many details of the case remain in doubt—and there are some who think the killer may be still at large.

The Florence slayer's first appearance was recorded on August 21, 1968, when Barbara Locci and her adulterous lover, one Antonio Lo Bianco, were shot to death as they lay on the front seat of a car parked beside a rural lane. In the backseat, Locci's six-year-old son slept through the double murder undisturbed, suggesting to police that the killer may have used a silencer. Despite a paucity of evidence, the crime appeared routine to local homicide investigators, and Locci's husband was convicted of the murders at trial. Six years elapsed before his innocence was proven, when the killer struck again.

The second set of victims, 19-year-old Pasquale Gentilcore and 18-year-old Stefania Pettini, were slain on September 14, 1974, with the same .22-caliber Beretta automatic pistol used in 1968; once more the gunman used distinctive copper-jacketed Winchester bullets, manufactured in Australia in the 1950s. Unlike the first crime, however, this time the female victim was sexually mutilated after death, a grim addition that would become the Florence slayer's trademark.

Another long hiatus in the murders followed, broken on June 6, 1981, when the unknown gunman killed 30-year-old Giovanni Foggi and 21-year-old Carmela De Nuccio. The young woman was stabbed more than 300 times, with a severed grape vine thrust into one of her wounds. Breaking his pattern, the killer struck again on October 23, 1981, claiming the lives of 26-year-old Stefano Baldi and 24-year-old Susanna Cambi. Again, the female victim was mutilated, Cambi's genitals excised as Stefania Pettini's had been in 1974.

The murders continued with numbing regularity over the next four years. On June 19, 1982, 22-year-old Paolo Mainardi and 20-year-old Antonella Migliorini were shot with the familiar pistol, Migliorini posthumously savaged with a knife. Fifteen months later, on September 9, 1983, the "Monster of Florence" made his first "mistake": instead of killing a man and woman, he shot two male tourists from Germany, Horst Meyer and Uwe Rusch Sens. (Public speculation that the victims might be gay was not substantiated and appeared to have no bearing on the crime.) The lethal balance was restored on July 29, 1984, when another male-female couple was shot, the woman stabbed more than 100 times, her genitals excised. On September 9, 1985, the stalker killed two French tourists, 25-year-old Jean-Michel Kraveichvili and 36-year-old Nadine Mauriot, claiming Mauriot's left breast and genitals as ghastly souvenirs. On the morning the bodies were found, a copper-jacketed Winchester bullet was also discovered, lying on the sidewalk in front of a hospital close to the crime scene. The next day, police received an envelope addressed with letters clipped from a newspaper; inside, they found part of Mauriot's genitalia, a mocking gift from their elusive quarry.

Re-creation of the "monster's" crimes revealed a striking similarity in every case. Each of the double murders occurred on moonless nights, between the hours of 10 o'clock and midnight. In each incident authorities believe the man was murdered first, the woman subsequently shot and mutilated as the killer exorcised his private frenzy. Fingerprint examinations of the murder scenes indicate that the gunman typically wore rubber surgical gloves, and that lead, coupled with the bullet found near the hospital and possible use of a scalpel to mutilate the female victims, led authorities to question hospital staffers. No suspects were identified, and homicide detectives freely admitted they had no leads in the baffling case. As described by Francisco Fleury, the district attorney in charge of the investigation, "The man could be your respectable next-door neighbor, a man above suspicion."

Three movies have been made, so far, about the "monster" and his crimes, ranging from a pornographic feature to a documentary. One film was in production in September 1985, and members of the crew rushed to the latest murder site, shooting new scenes to update their story. Police, meanwhile, were fearful that increased publicity might prompt the killer to become more active or encourage copycats to emulate his crimes. In fact, however, the slayer appeared to have retired from the hunt, with no confirmed kills since 1985.

Italian police questioned more than 100,000 persons and briefly charged six different suspects in the Florence case, before they identified their best suspect yet. Arrested on January 17, 1993, 71-year-old Pietro Pacciani was a semiliterate farmhand and amateur taxidermist, convicted in 1951 of murdering a traveling salesman caught "in an affectionate embrace" with Pacciani's girlfriend. (Following the murder, Pacciani made the woman lie beside the corpse and raped her there.) Paroled after 13 years in prison, Pacciani was later arrested for beating his wife and served four more years in prison (1987–91) for molesting his two daughters. Convicted of seven double murders in November 1994, Pacciani still maintained that he was "as innocent as Christ on the cross," and an appeals court overturned his conviction on February 13, 1996.

Ironically, Pacciani's release from prison came within hours of police arresting his good friend, 70-year-old Mario Vanni, on charges of murdering victims Mauriot and Kraveichvili in 1985. Authorities soon revised their original theory, deciding that the "Monster of Florence" was in fact a gang of killers led by Pacciani, its members including Vanni, 77-year-old Giovanni Faggi, and 54-year-old Giancarlo Lotti. Ten months after Pacciani's release from custody, on December 12, 1996, the Italian Supreme Court reversed the appellate court's decision and ordered a new murder trial for Pacciani. His three alleged accomplices went to trial in Florence on May 21, 1997, charged with five double murders, while their supposed ringleader was confined to his home at Mercatale, watched by police as a "socially dangerous character." Pacciani died of natural causes on February 22, 1998, one day before closing arguments began in the trial of his three alleged confederates. The final verdict, on March 26, 1998, was a mixed bag: Faggi was acquitted on all counts; Lotti was sentence to 30 years for his involvement in the deaths of eight victims; and Vanni drew a life sentence for participating in five of the "Monster's" double slayings. The remaining cases are officially unsolved.

Rumors of the phantom slayer's return circulated through Florence in June 2002, after caretakers at Cappelle del Commiato (a complex of mortuary chapels set in the hills above the city) reported five corpses mutilated by night-prowling vandals over a span of eight days. The first incident, involving an elderly woman's remains, was initially blamed on wild scavengers, but examination of the next two posthumous victims, one day later, revealed "careful removal of skin" in mutilations deemed "similar to those left on the victims of the Monster of Florence." Defense attorneys for defendants Lotti and Vanni cited the latest crimes as proof of their clients' innocence, while police investigated allegations of satanic cult involvement in the case. Most troubling were reports that the final corpse, of yet another woman, had been mutilated while armed guards stood watch outside her tomb.

MONTEIRO, Christine   See NEW BEDFORD, MASSACHUSETTS, MURDERS

MONTEIRO, Linda   See DETROIT MURDERS

MONTES de Oca, Rafel   See NEW YORK CITY TAXI MURDERS

MONTI, Marina   See "OPERATION ENIGMA"

MONTREAL Museum of Fine Art robbery (1972)
On the night of September 4, 1972, thieves invaded the Montreal Museum of Fine Art by way of a skylight, escaping with 17 paintings and various other art objects from the museum's European collection. The prize of the haul was Rembrandt's *Landscape with Cottages,* valued in excess of $1 million at the time of the theft. Other paintings stolen in the raid included:

Elder Brueghel's *Landscape with Buildings and Wagon*
Jean Baptiste Corot's *June Fille Accoude sur le Bras Gauche* and *La Reveuse à la Fontaine*
Gustave Courbet's *Landscape with Rocks and Streams*
Honoré Daumier's *Head*
Ferdinand Delacroix's *Lionne et Lion dans leur Antre*
Thomas Gainsborough's *Brig. Gen. Sir Thomas Fletcher*
Jan de Heem's *Still Life with a Fish* and *Vanities*
Jean Millet's *Portrait de Madame Millet* and *La Baratteuse*
Narcisse Penna's *La Sorcière*
Giovanni Piazetta's *Portrait of a Man*
Peter Paul Rubens's *Head of a Young Man*

François-Andres Vincent's *Portrait d'un Homme* and *Portrait d'une Dame*

None of the stolen art works were recovered, and while the statute of limitations for criminal prosecution has long since expired, Canadian authorities remind the public that possession of stolen property is a separate and distinct offense.

MONTREAL, Quebec child murders (1984–85)
Between November 1984 and June 1985 parents in Montreal were terrorized by the specter of an anonymous child-killer stalking their city, selecting his male victims at random, brutalizing and sexually assaulting them before discarding their bodies. Although police made every normal effort to identify the killer, he remains unidentified today, presumably still at large.

The first to die were 12-year-old Wilton Lubin and his eight-year-old playmate Sebastien Metivier, reported missing on November 1, 1984. Lubin was pulled from the St. Lawrence River a month later, his throat slashed, but Metivier was never found. On December 2, 1984, four-year-old Maurice Viens disappeared from his Montreal home; discovered in a vacant house five days later, he had been sexually abused, then killed by heavy blows to the back of his head. Twelve-year-old Michel Ethier disappeared on Christmas Day 1984 and was retrieved from the St. Lawrence, a reported drowning victim. Denis Roux-Bergevin, age five, had been missing for three days when hikers found his bludgeoned, violated body on the shoulder of a highway 12 miles east of Montreal.

Based on the available forensic evidence, authorities reported a connection only in the Viens and Roux-Bergevin murders, but the frightened residents of Montreal were not so easily convinced. Gary Rosenfelt, who lost a child to sex-slayer Clifford Olson in the 1970s, told reporters, "Everything indicates that there is a serial killer in Montreal, and the police do not seem to even acknowledge it." Speaking for his department, Detective Sgt. Gilles Boyer replied that all 16 members of Montreal's homicide squad were involved in the manhunt. "We are looking all over—in sewers, everywhere," he said. "The kids are not that big. They are easy to get rid of." To date, the long search has identified no suspects.

MONTREAL, Quebec gay murders (1988–93)

Montreal's homosexual community has been plagued for years by rumors of a serial stalker at large, knifing victims to death in their homes after casual meetings in various local gay bars. Police responded to the spreading alarm in 1991 by creating a task force to investigate a dozen murders of gay men in Montreal since 1988. At least eight of the 12 had been stabbed, several with their throats slashed and skulls crushed by heavy blows. Three of the slayings were ultimately solved, and while authorities stopped short of blaming a serial killer for the rest, they did issue a warning in autumn 1991 for gay men to "be careful."

The investigation seemed to help, at least for a time, as no more slayings of the same type were reported during 1992. Then, in January 1993, two more victims were stabbed to death in similar style—one in his Montreal apartment, the other at his home in suburban Chomedey. Still, police spokesmen refused to apply the dreaded "serial" label. As Pierre Sangollo, head of the Montreal Police Department's Major Crimes Division told reporters, "There are still some steps before we can say, 'Yes, a serial killer.'" At the same time, however, Sangollo acknowledged that "there is a certain pattern that links [the murders] together." Whatever that may be, it remains a secret closely guarded at police headquarters, and the killer (or killers) of gay men in Montreal remains at large.

MONZO, Lisa   See ALAMEDA COUNTY, CALIFORNIA, MURDERS

MOORE, Charles Eddie   See DEE, HENRY

MOORE, Harry Tyson civil rights martyr (1951)

A Florida native, born in Suwannee County on November 18, 1905, Harry Moore grew up with a keen sense of the injustice suffered by his fellow African Americans in the Sunshine State. In 1934, he founded Brevard County's first chapter of the National Association for the Advancement of Colored People (NAACP), and a year later he hired private attorneys to investigate the racist murder of a local NAACP member. (No charges were filed.) In 1937, Moore filed a lawsuit to correct the racial disparity in Florida teachers' salaries, but the state supreme court ruled against him two years

later. Moore challenged the governor (unsuccessfully) to investigate a series of lynchings in 1943–45, then organized a Progressive Voters' League to defeat candidates who ignored racial terrorism. More than 48,000 Florida blacks had registered to vote by early 1946, and while intimidation kept 38 percent of those from the polls in May, a record 30,000 blacks cast their ballots that month in Florida's Democratic primary.

The white establishment struck back with a vengeance. Moore and his wife, Harriette, were fired from their teaching jobs in June 1946, but the move backfired, leaving the couple more time for civil rights work. In April 1947, Moore spearheaded the Conference to Help Defend Democracy in Florida, a black-white liberal coalition that defeated legislation aimed at making the state Democratic Party an all-white "private club." The Ku Klux Klan responded as it always has, with an escalating series of murders, bombings,

Harry Moore's civil rights activities placed his life in daily jeopardy during the 1940s and early 1950s. (Florida State Archives)

On Christmas Day 1951, a powerful bomb killed Moore and his wife in their home. (Florida State Archives)

drive-by shootings, and whippings throughout central Florida. Governor Fuller Warren, supported by Moore in 1948 for his promise to curb racial violence, was himself a former Klansman. So was the retired Georgia policeman, J. Jefferson Elliott, whom Warren hired to investigate "special" cases statewide (with a notable lack of success).

On December 25, 1951, 50 Klansmen gathered for a cookout at Lake Jessup, with some of the group's most notorious "head-knockers" in attendance. Fifteen miles away, in Mims, Harry Moore and his wife were busy celebrating Christmas and their 25th wedding anniversary, Moore trying to forget the recent threats against his life, despite the pistol he now habitually carried "to take a few of them with me." It did him no good that night, at 10:20 P.M., when a powerful bomb exploded beneath his bedroom, killing Moore outright and fatally wounding Harriette.

The state investigation was led by "special agent" Elliott, producing little in the way of leads. The Federal Bureau of Investigation (FBI) had somewhat better luck, tapping its spies in various Klan units for information on recent acts of violence. County authorities knew that two white men had stopped at a Mims candy store in July, asking directions to Moore's home; FBI agents identified one as Orange County Klansman Early Brooklyn, strongly suspecting that the other was onetime Orlando "exalted cyclops" Tillman Blevin. Brooklyn, they learned, had displayed a floor plan of Moore's house at an Apopka Klan meeting, asking Kluxers there to help him "do a few jobs." G-men also discovered that Orange County law enforcement was riddled with Klansmen, from Sheriff Dave Starr

to Apopka police chief William Dunnaway and most of his officers. One informant estimated that three-fourths of Apopka's white male population was linked to the KKK "in one way or another." Some of those interviewed confessed to floggings, but others were stubbornly silent. Joseph Cox, secretary of the Orlando chapter, killed himself in March 1952, after his second FBI interview; suspect Blevin died of cancer five months later, and Early Brooklyn also died of natural causes on the first anniversary of Harry Moore's murder. Despite FBI hopes that suspect Klansmen would crack before a federal grand jury, they reported that Orange County residents were "mortally in fear of the Klan . . . analogous to the fear of reprisal fostered by the Mafia and underworld groups."

There the case languished for more than a quarter-century, until ex-Klansman Edward Spivey contacted the Brevard County sheriff's office on January 16, 1978, stating that he was dying and wanted to clear his conscience by revealing details of the Moore assassination. Sheriff Rollin Zimmerman had reopened the case one week earlier, under pressure from the NAACP and journalists pursuing old FBI records via the Freedom of Information Act. Now he had a potential witness—and not just any witness, but a longtime Klansman with a history of violence dating back to 1935. Unfortunately, Spivey was drunk when detectives visited his Winter Park home, and parts of his story were barely coherent. After boasting of his role as chief head-knocker for the Klan's "wrecking crew," Spivey denied any KKK participation in Moore's murder. "We didn't authorize it," he declared. "I was on the wrecking crew and I, by God, didn't authorize it." As for Harry Moore, Spivey maintained, "I never knew who the son of a bitch was." He *did* know the killer, however; deceased Klansman Joe Cox had boasted of accepting a $5,000 murder contract on Moore, Spivey said, but Cox never named his client. More than anything, Spivey seemed concerned that the Klan's "good name" would suffer by association with a hired assassin. "I hate it," he raged, "because it makes the Ku Klux Klan look like a goddamn idiot!"

Six weeks later, on March 1, 1978, another drunken white man accosted Fort Pierce NAACP leader Charlie Matthews on a public street, telling him, "You raise a lot of hell around this town, but if I was active now, I would do you like I did Harry T. Moore." Remaining calm, Matthews invited the stranger home to hear his story, calling police to join them a half hour later. The latest suspect, Raymond Henry Jr., claimed to be

Some investigators claimed Sheriff Willis McCall (shown here with two shooting victims in 1950) played a key role in Harry Moore's murder, but no evidence was ever found. (Florida State Archives)

a former Marine and demolition expert, hired by the KKK in 1951 to plant a "contact bomb" under Harry Moore's bed. After watching the blast, Henry said, he had returned to Fort Pierce with his accomplices, where they all "had a big drink together." Henry named the other members of the hit team as a grocer and policeman from Fort Pierce, plus a lieutenant from the St. Lucie County Sheriff's Department, identified as the bomb's trigger man. The bad news was that Henry thought the murder was committed "just before Easter, 14 years ago"—that is, in 1964. His written statement added further details, claiming he was home on convalescent leave from the Marine Corps when he heard Moore mentioned at a Klan meeting and volunteered to build the fatal bomb. He also expanded the cast of characters to include a second high-ranking sheriff's officer from St. Lucie County, a Broward County deputy who allegedly escorted the killers, and a black man called "Cowboy" who supposedly lured Harry Moore

away from his house while Henry crept in to plant the bomb. FBI agents scheduled a meeting with Henry, but he stood them up.

By November 1979, Ray Henry had an even more elaborate story to tell the *Orlando Sentinel-Star*, now claiming that the assassination was planned by Klansmen from three counties—Brevard, Lake, and St. Lucie—with Lake County sheriff Willis McCall bankrolling the plot. Henry had never received his share of the payoff, an insult he described as "treason beyond trust." FBI agents reported that the tale did not check out, prompting NAACP accusations of a whitewash. Sheriff McCall, addressing journalists from his home on a street that bore his name, dismissed Henry's story as "some of that shit you reporters make up."

May 1982 brought a revival of interest in the Moore case, with publication of an article in the NAACP's *Crisis* magazine. Confessed bomber Raymond Henry had long since disappeared, but after 15 months of research Stetson Kennedy produced the most detailed and sensational report on the murder to date. His article alleged that Henry was in hiding "under the aegis of the FBI's witness protection program," moving on from there to describe the activities of an eight-man death squad aided by the black Judas nicknamed Cowboy. A Brevard County deputy had run interference for the killers, Kennedy claimed, diverting traffic from Old Dixie Highway and the murder scene while the bombers were at work. Sheriff McCall had attended the planning sessions, also renting three cars for the hit team and picking up the tab for their victory celebration in Fort Pierce. McCall would wait another decade to address the *Crisis* article, by which time much of the story had been discredited. Four lawmen named as plotters by Henry and Kennedy had ranged in age from eight to 14 years when Moore was killed; the alleged "trigger man" had not even lived in Florida prior to 1959, and he had only become a sheriff's deputy in 1968.

A case that would not die, Harry Moore's murder resurfaced in 1991, when Stetson Kennedy sent Governor Lawton Chiles a tape-recorded interview with one Dottie Harrington, who described her ex-husband as a boastful Klansman "involved" in the crime. According to the tape, she had approached the Broward County sheriff's office with her information in the 1980s, only to be targeted by vicious Klan harassment in return. Chiles ordered the Florida Department of Law Enforcement (FDLE) to investigate on August 30, 1991, although the probe was not announced until September 29. Another month passed before Frank Harrington was traced to Hollywood, Florida, but he denied any role in the Moore assassination, his statements supported by a polygraph test. By November 13, 1991, Dottie Harrington had recanted her previous story, admitting that Frank was "quite a talker" with the boys, though she would "never believe that he could be involved in any type of violent crime." It was, apparently, another dead end.

Winter of 1991 brought new revelations and confusion to the Moore case. FDLE investigators finally tracked Raymond Henry to Vero Beach, where he changed his story yet again. Still claiming knowledge of the murder, Henry now denied participating and insisted that he had not moved to Florida until 1963. His version of events allegedly derived from overhearing fellow Klansmen (including two Fort Pierce policemen) joke about the bombing. Former sheriff Willis McCall again denied participation in the crime when he was

questioned in January 1992. By February, Henry had recanted the latest of his statements, claiming that he implicated various lawmen out of spite, as revenge for harassment he had suffered at their hands. Tallahassee used the last day of Black History Month to announce "important progress" in the case, but no details were forthcoming, and the file was formally closed—apparently for the last time—on April Fool's Day 1992.

On August 24, 2006, the Florida attorney general's office issued a bulletin announcing that a 20-month investigation had reviewed "extensive circumstantial evidence" that identified four suspects in the Moore bombing. All were deceased Klan members, and their names surprised no one: Tillman Belvin, Earl Brooklyn, Joseph Cox, and Edward Spivey. In the absence of living suspects, no further action is anticipated.

MOORE, Lynda   See "VALLEY KILLER"

MOORE, Martha   See PRINCE GEORGES HOSPITAL MURDERS

MOORE, O'Neal murder victim (1965)
Washington Parish, Louisiana, was a hotbed of racial violence in the early 1960s. The county seat at Bogalusa was renowned for boasting the largest per capita Ku Klux Klan membership of any town in the United States, and unpunished night-riding violence was so frequent that blacks had organized an armed resistance group, the Deacons for Defense and Justice, to protect themselves. On June 3, 1964, in response to pressure from the black community, Sheriff Dorman Crowe appointed O'Neal Moore and Creed Rogers as the first African-American deputies in Washington Parish history.

One year later to the day, on the night of June 3, 1965, partners Moore and Creed had completed their shift and were driving home to Varnado, north of Bogalusa, when a pickup truck overtook their patrol car. Gunshots rang out from the truck, killing Moore instantly with a shot to the head; Rogers was wounded in his shoulder and blinded in one eye by shotgun pellets. The gunmen sped away, leaving Rogers to radio for help, slipping in and out of consciousness while he waited for the ambulance.

An all-points bulletin was broadcast for the suspect pickup truck. One hour after the shooting, Bogalusa resident Ernest Ray McElveen was arrested at Tylertown, Mississippi, 20 miles northeast of Bogalusa. Walthall County's sheriff reported that McElveen's pickup matched the broadcast description, and that he was armed with two pistols, one of them recently fired. McElveen waived extradition on June 4 and returned to Bogalusa, there hiring a lawyer who often represented members of the local Ku Klux Klan. Investigators reported that McElveen belonged to several racist groups, including the White Citizens' Council, the neo-Nazi National States Rights Party, and the United Conservatives (identified as a front group for the Louisiana KKK). A relative of the suspect, D. D. McElveen, was also identified by congressional investigators in 1966 as a member of the Bogalusa Klan's "wrecking crew."

Violence continued following the ambush. On the night of June 6, 1965, unknown gunmen fired shots into the home of Doyle Holliday, a white sheriff's deputy assigned to investigate Moore's murder. Naturally alarmed, the Deacons for Defense mounted armed guards in black communities around the parish (and were thus declared "subversive" by the FBI, which launched an investigation of the group's membership). Louisiana governor John McKeithen offered a $25,000 reward for information leading to arrest and conviction of the killers, but it brought no takers, and Ernest McElveen was soon released by prosecutors for lack of evidence. A quarter-century after the crime, FBI agents announced they were reopening the case, and while details were featured on the television program *Unsolved Mysteries* in 1989, no new leads were reported.

In March 2007, FBI director Robert Mueller announced a "new initiative" in unsolved civil rights assassinations from the 1960s, including Moore's slaying. According to that statement, "It's unclear which cases will be prosecuted first, but the Justice Department says several investigations are already under way." Thus far, no new developments have been reported in Moore's case, and federal legislation proposed in June 2007 to accelerate investigation of various unsolved hate crimes spanning three decades remains stalled in Congress.

MOORE, Polly Ann See Texarkana "Phantom Gunman"

MOORE, Victoria See Grand Rapids, Michigan, murders

MOORE, William L. civil rights martyr (1963)

Born in Mississippi and raised in Binghamton, New York, William Moore grew up believing that his destiny involved some action that would change the world. At age 11, in 1938, he left home for a solo pilgrimage to the Holy Land but returned the same night, rain-soaked and shivering. Fresh out of high school in the midst of World War II, he joined the Marine Corps and served two years on Guam, but came back to the United States a committed pacifist. The G.I. Bill paid his way to England's University of Southampton, but he soon withdrew to tour Europe on a motorcycle. Back in Binghamton at last, Moore earned a bachelor's degree in social sciences and moved on to graduate studies at Johns Hopkins University, in Baltimore. There, he suffered a mental breakdown and spent 18 months in a psychiatric ward, treated for delusional behavior with electroshock therapy and massive doses of insulin. Released in August 1954, Moore returned to Binghamton and joined the city's welfare department as a social worker.

Life seemed to stabilize for a time, as Moore married a divorcée with three children and found new employment as a mail carrier for the U.S. Postal Service. He also wrote and privately published a book about his time in the sanitarium, titled *The Mind in Chains*. Moore's long pursuit of a heroic destiny seemed well behind him until May 1961, when he viewed television coverage of the integrated Freedom Rides in Alabama, sponsored by the Congress of Racial Equality. As Moore watched the coverage—a bus in flames, unarmed demonstrators beaten bloody by Ku Klux Klansmen while police stood by and watched—it struck him that the civil rights movement might be the crusade he had waited for since childhood.

Moore requested a transfer to Baltimore, where he joined the Congress of Racial Equality (CORE) and was soon arrested with 412 other demonstrators while trying to integrate an all-white movie theater. Next, in February 1963, he staged a one-man "march" from Baltimore to Annapolis in protest of Maryland's segregation statutes. A month later, Moore broadened his range, hiking along from Baltimore to Washington, D.C., with a letter for President John Kennedy. (A White House guard told him to drop it in a mailbox.) Those adventures inspired him to try an even more ambitious protest, walking from Chattanooga, Tennessee, to Jackson, Mississippi, with a letter for hard-core racist governor Ross Barnett.

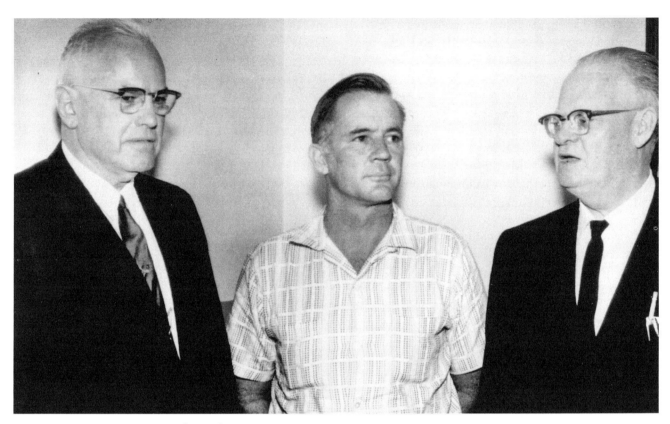

Alabama grocer Floyd Simpson (center) was arrested but never prosecuted for the 1963 murder of civil rights activist William Moore. (Library of Congress)

The new project met with near-unanimous lack of support. CORE refused to back Moore's solitary effort, deeming it unproductive and dangerous. An aunt of Moore's in Birmingham, Alabama, sent him a discouraging letter that read, in part: "Our home will be closed to you on a trip of this nature.... You'll probably find out when you hit this section of the South what you are doing is not a joke after all." She closed the letter "With love, and a prayer to God that he will deliver you from this thing that has taken possession of you."

Possessed or not, Moore was determined to proceed. He bused from Baltimore to Chattanooga on April 20, 1963, and set off from there the next morning, on foot. He wore a large sandwich sign. The message in front read:

END SEGREGATION IN AMERICA
BLACK OR WHITE
EAT AT JOE'S

The back of his sign was emblazoned with the message:

EQUAL RIGHTS FOR ALL
MISSISSIPPI OR BUST

The two-wheeled postal cart that held Moore's meager belongings also bore a third sign guaranteed to raise hackles in the southern Bible Belt.

WANTED
JESUS CHRIST
AGITATOR, CARPENTER BY TRADE,
REVOLUTIONARY, CONSORTER WITH
CRIMINALS AND PROSTITUTES

Moore crossed the northwestern corner of Georgia without incident, but real trouble began when he entered Alabama, where Governor George Wallace and a violent Ku Klux Klan vowed to maintain "segregation forever." Soon after crossing the border, Moore was treated to shouts of "Nigger lover!" from passing motorists, and a group of teenagers pelted him with stones. Blistered feet were another drawback, prompting Moore to remove his shoes and continue the march barefoot.

South of Colbran, Alabama, on April 23, Moore stopped to speak with Floyd Simpson, the owner of a local grocery store. Jack Mendelsohn described the aftermath of that encounter in his book *The Martyrs* (1966): "[W]hen the groceryman got back to his store he was bursting to tell everybody about the Jesus Christ sign. He seemed to have missed entirely its point that if Jesus were alive today, self-proclaimed Christians would hound him as a criminal and a subversive. The civil rights posters may have angered Simpson, but the Jesus placard outraged him." Later that afternoon, Simpson caught up with Moore again, this time accompanied by local mailman Gaddis Killian. Moore described their encounter in his traveling journal.

3:30 Fellow says my walk mentioned in today's Birmingham Post Herald a couple of men who had talked to me before drove up and questioned my religious and political beliefs. "Now I know what you are" and one was sure I'd be killed for them, such as my Jesus poster on my buggy.

He was right. That evening, while Moore rested beside Highway 11 near Reece City, he was shot twice with a .22-caliber rifle. The bullets pierced Moore's head and neck, producing near-instant death. In Washington President Kennedy called the slaying an "outrageous crime," and Governor Wallace offered a $1,000 reward for the arrest of Moore's killer. Floyd Simpson was jailed on suspicion of murder, then formally charged on April 29, 1963, after the Federal Bureau of Investigation (FBI) laboratory matched his rifle to the fatal bullets. With Gaddis Killian on tap as a voluntary witness it appeared to be an open-and-shut case, but nothing is simple in Alabama where race is concerned. The Etowah County grand jury convened to consider Moore's death, and that panel presumably reviewed the ballistic evidence before refusing to indict Floyd Simpson. The crime—like so many other slayings linked to the 1960s civil rights movement in Dixie—remains officially unsolved today.

Moore's pilgrimage was not entirely wasted, though. Soon after his death, 10 young activists from the Student Non-Violent Coordinating Committee stepped in and completed the "William L. Moore Memorial Trek." The lead marcher wore a sandwich sign like Moore's, with the same message:

EQUAL RIGHTS FOR ALL
MISSISSIPPI OR BUST

MOORMAN-FIELD, Sally   See SAN DIEGO MURDERS (1985–88)

MORETTI, Willie gangland murder victim (1951)

A child of Italian immigrants and boyhood friend of future underworld "prime minister" Frank Costello, born in 1894, Willie Moretti was something of a legend in the Mafia. According to persistent rumors, it was Moretti, in 1939, who shoved a pistol into bandleader Tommy Dorsey's mouth and forced Dorsey to release rising superstar Frank Sinatra from a contract that capped his salary at a paltry $125 per week—an incident later fictionalized in Mario Puzo's novel *The Godfather*. Whether or not that story was true, Moretti was a gangland power to be reckoned with for over 20 years, serving as second-in-command to reigning Jersey mobster ABNER "LONGY" ZWILLMAN.

Moretti's dual specialties while working with Zwillman were management of the mob's lavish illicit casinos and summary execution of targets fingered for death by his boss. To that end, Willie maintained a troop of 60 professional killers in New Jersey, operating as an adjunct to ALBERT ANASTASIA's gang of Brooklyn assassins (dubbed "Murder Incorporated" in the late 1930s). Unfortunately for Moretti, an untreated case of syphilis left him mentally unbalanced by 1950, when he put on a rare comic performance for television cameras and members of the U.S. Senate's Kefauver Committee investigating organized crime in interstate commerce. Rambling on the verge of incoherency, Moretti told the senators he couldn't be a member of the Mafia, because no one had ever given him a membership card. Loan-sharking? "They call anybody a mob who makes six percent more on money," Moretti declared. The prominent gangsters he knew were "well-charactered people [who] don't need no introduction." At the conclusion of Moretti's testimony, Sen. Charles Tobey thanked the witness for his "rather refreshing" candor. Moretti answered with a smile, "Thank you very much. Don't forget my house in Deal if you are down on the shore. You are invited."

Moretti's condition deteriorated after his Kefauver appearance. He spoke openly with journalists, and once announced plans to hold a press conference on the subject of illegal gambling in New Jersey. The gathering never occurred, but Moretti's old comrades were worried. New York mobster Vito Genovese, never a friend of Moretti or Costello, argued that Willie should be killed for the good of the syndicate. Anastasia, an ally, reportedly agreed with Genovese that a "mercy killing" was in order, but that it should be conducted with "respect"—i.e., a face-to-face assassination, allowing Moretti to face his killers.

On the evening of October 4, 1951, Moretti dined in a New Jersey restaurant with three or four male companions (reports of eyewitnesses vary). The men were amiably speaking in Italian as the waitress left their table, retreating to the kitchen with their orders. She was barely out of sight when a flurry of gunshots rang out from the dining room. By the time employees mustered the courage to look, Willie Moretti was sprawled in a pool of blood on the floor, his companions long gone. Various suspects were suggested as the triggermen, but as in the case of so many other gangland murders, no charges were ever filed. The case remains officially unsolved today.

MORGAN, Corinne See NEW ORLEANS MURDERS (1987–88)

MORRIS, Frank murder victim (1964)

An African-American resident of Ferriday, Louisiana, born in 1913, Frank Morris was the proprietor of a shoe repair shop that served both black and white customers. On Sunday mornings, he also hosted a radio program featuring gospel music and short sermons by guest clergymen. Morris was not involved in the civil rights movement sweeping Louisiana during the 1960s, but in 1964 rumors spread around Ferriday that he had been "flirting" with certain white women who patronized his shop.

In short order those stories reached the ears of local Ku Klux Klansmen, affiliated with a rogue faction known to its members as the Silver Dollar Group. Most of the offshoot Klan's members resided in Adams County, Mississippi, or neighboring Catahoula Parish, Louisiana; all agreed that larger Klan organizations in their respective states had shown a "lack of guts" in holding the line for white supremacy. The group derived its name from the fact that each member carried a silver dollar minted in the year of his birth, as a means of covert identification. On weekend outings Silver Dollar Klansmen practiced with explosives and incendiary devices, rehearsing for murder while their wives gossiped and served picnic lunches.

Frank Morris became the group's first "project." In the predawn hours of December 10, 1964, he was

awakened by the sound of breaking glass and rushed from his bedroom, at the rear of his shop, to find a white man sloshing gasoline through a newly broken window. A second stranger, brandishing a shotgun, barked, "Get back in there, nigger!" Seconds later, one of the men struck a match and the shoe shop exploded into flames.

A half-block down the street, the attendant at an all-night gas station heard the blast and emerged from his office in time to see a dark-colored sedan speeding eastward out of town, toward Ridgecrest and Vidalia. Moments later, Frank Morris staggered from the flaming ruin of his shop, lurching into the street with his clothing and most of his skin burned away. Morris survived until December 14, his agony dulled by morphine while police and Federal Bureau of Investigation (FBI) agents tried to question him. Even so, his memories were fragmentary and confused.

I don't know what happened and here is what it . . . I was laying there asleep and I heard someone breaking glass out. They broke the glass out . . . they broke the glass out. I come into my shop and . . . it look like one, he beat on the window with a axe handle or something, and then two and another man around there . . . pouring gasoline around the place . . . I said, "What are you doing there?" . . . Told me to get back in there, nigger . . . better off . . . shotgun.

No suspects were identified or charged in Morris's death. FBI agents suspected Silver Dollar Group members in the 1965 car bombing that crippled NAACP activist GEORGE METCALFE and the near-identical blast that killed victim WHARLEST JACKSON in 1967, but those crimes also remain unsolved. One G-man assigned to the case later told author Don Whitehead, "Perhaps the perfect crime is one in which the killers are known, but you can't reach them for lack of substantive evidence."

MORSE, Eva See "VALLEY KILLER"

MORTON, Janice See MARYLAND MURDERS (1986–87)

MOSCOW Murders unsolved serial crimes (2003)

During July 2003, Russian police reported slayings of 11 women in Moscow. While the techniques of murder varied, 10 of the victims were killed on the city's north side, and detectives have said that "at least eight" of the crimes "appear to be linked."

Yulia Bondareva, aged 28, was the first identified victim. She visited Moscow's Botanical Garden at noon on July 1 with a boyfriend, and the couple separated upon leaving. Bondareva walked alone toward the nearest subway stop, but never reached her home. An hour later, strollers in a public park found her body, beaten and strangled, gagged with cloth torn from her shirt. Postmortem tests revealed that she had been raped.

Prior to dawn on July 2, police found 17-year-old Kseniya Medintsevaya dead in a kindergarten courtyard. As with Yulia Bondareva, the second victim was beaten, raped, and strangled, left with her dress torn open. Investigators learned that Medintsevaya had left her apartment around 11 P.M. on July 1 and never returned.

Two days later, on July 4, officers found Irena Gera, a 28-year-old resident of central Moscow, raped and strangled to death with the strap of her purse on the city's north side. Her corpse was nearly nude, and the missing clothes were never found.

On July 8, friends found victim number four—a Ukrainian prostitute identified only as Alexandra— slain in her apartment. The murder weapon was one of Alexandra's own belts, found with one end tied around her neck, the other wrapped around a nearby doorknob. As the murder spree dragged on, Alexandra would remain the only victim slain at home.

Moscow suffered its next shock on July 11, with the discovery of a fifth victim. Elena Tolokonnikova was a 32-year-old teacher, murdered after a night out with friends, her half-naked body dumped near victim Alexandra's home.

On July 15 police hauled the decomposed remains of a still-unidentified woman from a Moscow pond. Medical examiners attributed her death to strangulation, and acknowledged the woman's resemblance to previous victims—all slender, with long hair.

On the night of July 21–22, between dusk and dawn, unknown killers claimed four more female victims in Moscow. The first to die was Tatyana Nikishina, a 17-year-old student strangled with her own brassiere in northwest Moscow, after a failed attempt at rape. Police have not released the names of that bloody night's other three victims, and details of their

slayings are sparse, beyond official statements that one was struck from behind with a blunt instrument, while another's head was slammed into a concrete structure at the crime scene.

The last slaying was reported on July 28, when officers retrieved the body of a 42-year-old woman from a schoolyard in northwest Moscow. The victim, still not publicly identified, had been raped before she was strangled.

Official statements on the murders have exacerbated confusion in Moscow. Alexei Vakhromeyev, a senior officer with the Criminal Investigations Directorate, dismissed three of the slayings on July 21–22 as "coincidences" and denies that any evidence exists to link the murders. Boris Gryzlov, Russia's Minister of the Interior, maintains that all 11 victims were killed by different attackers, though no suspects are identified in any case. Nervous Muscovites, meanwhile, recall official cover-ups in other cases of serial murder and treat such pronouncements with outspoken skepticism. At last report, Gryzlov's ministry was "reconsidering its position" on the existence of one or more serial killers in Moscow.

MOSIE, Maureen See "HIGHWAY KILLER"

MOSLEY, Priscilla See WASHINGTON, D.C., MURDERS (1996–97)

MOZYNSKI, Joseph See "3X" KILLER

"MR. Cruel" unidentified rapist-murderer (1987–91)
"Mr. Cruel" is a nickname applied to a sexual predator who stalked the suburbs of Melbourne, Australia between August 1987 and April 1991. (Some reports of the case also dub him the "Hampton Rapist.") He was a home invader who took significant risks in pursuit of underage female victims, and despite an epic police investigation supported by large cash rewards, he remains unidentified today.

The prowler's first known crime occurred in the community of Lower Plenty. Masked and armed with a pistol and knife, Mr. Cruel entered his target residence by removing a pane of glass from a lounge room window around 4:00 A.M. on August 22, 1987.

He cut telephone lines to the house, bound both parents hand and foot before locking them in a closet, and tied their 7-year-old son to a bed before raping the family's 11-year-old daughter.

Sixteen months later, two days after Christmas 1988, a man identically masked and armed invaded a suburban Ringwood home, at 5:30 A.M. He demanded cash, then bound and gagged both parents before turning on their 10-year-old daughter. Mr. Cruel taped the girl's eyes shut and shoved a rubber ball into her mouth before dragging her out of the house. At another location, he raped her repeatedly before releasing her at Bayswater High School, around 1:30 A.M. on December 28. The victim described being shackled to a "detention bed," with persistent airplane sounds suggesting proximity to an airport.

Mr. Cruel struck for the third time on July 3, 1990, in suburban Canterbury. After entering through a window, at 11:30 P.M., he found a 13-year-old girl alone in the house, blindfolded her with tape and tied her up, then searched the house for valuables and disabled the telephones. After that search, he drove his latest victim to another still-unidentified house, where she suffered 50 hours of sexual abuse before she was released at last, near an electric power station in Kew. The girl's description of the house where she was held matched that of the second victim in all essentials.

The human monster's last known raid occurred in Templestowe, on April 13, 1991. Using a knife to cut a window screen at 9:15 P.M., he confronted 13-year-old Karmein Chan and her two younger sisters. Mr. Cruel put the two smaller girls in a closet and pushed a bed against the door to trap them, then fled the premises with Karmein. Her decomposed remains were found on April 9, 1992, shot three times in the head.

Although no living witness could identify the masked rapist, police surmise from his methods—wiping down fingerprints at crime scenes and bathing his victims before he released them—that one man was responsible for all four attacks. They suspect that Mr. Cruel may have been a public school employee, since the attacks occurred during school holidays. One surviving victim saw a camera tripod in the bedroom where she was held captive, suggesting that Mr. Cruel photographed and/or videotaped his victims to commemorate their suffering. Police suppressed that fact for 15 years, fearing that their

quarry would destroy the photographic evidence of his crimes, but they finally announced it in 2006, as hope of an arrest faded away.

Detectives assigned to Mr. Cruel's case interviewed some 27,000 suspects and searched 30,000 homes for clues, without discovering a useful lead. Based on an FBI profile predicting that Mr. Cruel would collect child pornography, members of Melbourne's 40-member "Spectrum" task force pursued that angle and identified 150 local subscribers to mail-order porn distributors, but none proved to be the killer. Seventy-three defendants were jailed on unrelated charges, most involving sex crimes, but Mr. Cruel slipped through the net. Finally, after 29 months of fruitless investigation costing $4 million, the task force disbanded. An outstanding $A300,000 reward for information leading to the prowler's capture has thus far lured no takers.

Following Karmein Chan's kidnap-murder, unfounded rumors attributed the crime to Asian drug dealers. Another widely circulated story, unsupported by any known evidence, claimed that Mr. Cruel's first crime involved the molestation of two Melbourne sisters, allegedly held hostage in their own home during a holiday weekend in 1985. Televised reenactments of the prowler's crimes created such hysteria in Melbourne that they were finally banned from TV during prime-time viewing hours.

The FBI's profile of Mr. Cruel now gathers dust, a testament to failure. It warns that "The offender has an intense interest in children, especially children in the age group he is assaulting. He will spend a great deal of time with these children in what appears to be selfless dedication to students. This apparent dedication may well have earned him recognition and awards (teacher of the year, coach of the year, exceptional volunteer, etc). He is a functional individual, one with steady employment, is generally regarded as a good neighbor, polite, quiet, somewhat introverted, but may be involved in certain community-minded projects."

Based on statistics suggesting that most sexual predators remain active until they are killed or confined, Melbourne police speculate that Mr. Cruel may have died, been disabled in some way, or might be serving prison time on charges unrelated to his home invasions. They admit, however, that he may have left Melbourne for greener pastures, to continue his raids somewhere else.

MUELLER, Louise See Cumminsville, Ohio, murders

MUENTENER, Mary See Riverdell Hospital murders

MUIR, Ruth See San Diego murders (1931–36)

MULATTO Axe Murders Louisiana and Texas (1911–12)
Between January 1911 and April 1912 an unidentified killer (or killers) slaughtered 49 victims in the states of Louisiana and Texas, leaving police baffled. In each case the dead were mulattos or members of families with mulatto children. The killers were presumed, by blacks and police alike, to be dark-skinned African Americans, selecting victims on the basis of their mixed—or "tainted"—blood.

The first attack took place in early January 1911 at Rayne, Louisiana, where a mother and her three children were hacked to death in their beds. The following month, three members of the Byers family were dispatched in identical fashion at Crowley, 10 miles from Rayne. Two weeks later, the scene shifted to Lafayette, where a family of four was massacred in the predawn hours.

Texas endured the killer's first visit in April 1911, when five members of the Cassaway family were axed to death in their San Antonio home. As in preceding cases, the victims died in their sleep, with no evidence of robbery or any other "rational" motive.

On November 26, 1911, the action shifted back to Lafayette, Louisiana. Six members of the Norbert Randall family were slain in their beds, each killed with a single blow behind the right ear. This time police arrested a black woman, Clementine Bernabet, on suspicion of involvement in the crime. She was held in custody through spring 1912, but her incarceration did not halt the carnage. On January 19, 1912, a woman and her three children were hacked to death as they slept at Crowley, Louisiana. Two days later, at Lake Charles, Felix Broussard, his wife, and three children were killed in their beds, each with a single blow near the right ear. This time the killer left a note behind. It read: "When He Maketh the Inquisition for Blood, He forgetteth not the cry of the humble—human five."

Stirred by the quasi-biblical implications, police made several arrests, including two members of the

minuscule "Sacrifice Church." Rev. King Harris, leader of the sect, had addressed a meeting in Lafayette on the night of the Randall massacre, and informants reported links between the Sacrifice Church and certain voodoo cults in New Orleans. Try as they might, though, police could find no evidence against their several suspects, and all were soon released.

On February 19, 1912, a mulatto woman and her three children were axed to death in their sleep at Beaumont, Texas. Seven weeks later, on March 27, another mulatto mother, her four children, and a male overnight guest were slaughtered at Glidden, Texas.

Police now began to note a geographical pattern in the crimes. Since November 1911, the slayer (or slayers) had been moving westward, striking at stops along the Southern Pacific Railroad line. The next murders, likewise, would occur further west on that line, in San Antonio. Meanwhile, in early April 1912, Clementine Bernabet surprised authorities with a confession to the early murders. While she admitted sitting in on meetings of the Sacrifice Church, Bernabet insisted that the slayings were related to a voodoo charm (or *candja*) she had purchased from a local witch doctor. The charm reportedly assured Bernabet and her friends that "we could do as we pleased and we would never be detected." For no apparent reason, they had chosen to test the magic by committing a random series of murders. Police eventually dismissed the story, and Bernabet was never sent to trial.

On the night of April 11–12, 1912, five members of the William Burton family were hacked to death in their beds at San Antonio. Two nights later, the axe-wielding night stalker claimed three more mulatto victims at Hempstead, Texas, thereafter lapsing into a four-month hiatus. The lull was broken in San Antonio at 4:00 A.M. on August 6, 1912, when the wife of mulatto James Dashiell woke to the pain of an axe shearing through her arm. The killer had missed his mark for the first time, and he took to his heels as screams roused the sleeping family. His shaken victim glimpsed only one prowler, and she could offer police no coherent description.

The bungled raid in San Antonio wrote *finis* to the murder spree and left police without a single solid piece of evidence. Defectors from the Sacrifice Church referred authorities to a verse from the New Testament, Matthew 3:10—"And now also the axe is laid unto the root of the trees: therefore every tree which bringeth not forth good fruit is hewn down, and cast into the fire"—but detectives never managed to identify a valid suspect in the case. It may be sheer coincidence that an unknown killer dubbed "JACK THE RIPPER" by reporters murdered 20 black women in Atlanta, Georgia, during the same period when the South's night-prowling axe murderer was at large.

MULHOLLAND, Joe   See NAHANNI VALLEY MURDERS

MURPHY, Gary   See HOSPITAL FOR SICK CHILDREN MURDERS

MURRAY, Charles   See "JACK THE RIPPER"

MYOJO 56 fire arson-murder (2001)

Kabukichō is the red-light district of Tokyo's Shinjuku neighborhood, known since the late 1940s for its nightclubs, "hostess" bars, and "love hotels" where prostitutes ply their trade without police interference. Locals call Kabukichō "Sleepless Town," for its non-stop action, and tourists visit in hopes of glimpsing Japan's notorious Yakuza mobsters at work or play.

At 1:00 A.M. on September 1, 2001, an explosion rocked the four-story Myojo 56 building in Kabukichō, also known as Meisei 56, and flames swept through the structure's top two floors, engulfing a mah-jongg parlor and a hostess bar. Firefighters recovered the corpses of 32 men and 12 women from the ruins, most of whom died from carbon monoxide poisoning. Three other persons suffered nonfatal injuries while leaping from upstairs windows to escape the fire.

Rumors instantly spread through Kabukichō that the building had been firebombed by some unnamed mobster, to settle some undefined score. Authorities initially announced that they had "tentatively" ruled out arson as a cause of the fire, but failed to state its actual cause. The death toll from the fire—fifth-worst in postwar Japanese history to date—was exacerbated by multiple fire-code violations, including blocked exits and stairwells.

In February 2003, authorities indicted six members of the Myojo Kosan Group with criminal violations of Japan's Fire Services Law. Those charged included President Kazuo Yamada and CEO Shigeo Segawa, with four underlings. Segawa blamed Yamada for the fire code violations, while Yamada told police and reporters, "I am confused and cannot talk." Five of the

six defendants were convicted of negligence in Tokyo District Court on July 2, 2008, while the sixth was acquitted.

One day later, Tokyo police reversed their original judgment on the Myojo 56 fire, declaring its cause to be arson. No arrests have been made, but suspicion centers on an unidentified "injured man," seen near the building on the night of the fire. *Japan Today* describes the Myojo 56 building's mah-jongg parlor as "an illegal gambling den" that grossed 8 million yen ($73,742) daily—in short, an operation that required protection from the Yakuza and from corrupt police.

MYTHICAL unsolved murders

Unsolved murders, and particularly unsolved *serial* murders, simultaneously fascinate and frighten millions of Americans. Such crimes are so attractive, in fact, that some reporters apparently cannot resist fabricating cases of their own. Sometimes the "data diddling" amounts to simple exaggeration of known body counts for well established killers, but in other cases the authors (including some alleged "scholars" writing for an academic audience) go all out, manufacturing slayers and victims out of whole cloth.

One of the earliest, most frequently exaggerated cases involved London's "JACK THE RIPPER," active in the fall of 1888. Police involved in the manhunt generally agreed that the Ripper killed only five victims, but speculation on additional slayings continues to the present day, with speculative body counts ranging from seven to 20 or more. Some of the "extra" victims really were killed in London during the Ripper's heyday (or shortly thereafter), but in circumstances that cast doubt on any link to the original murder series. (See FRANCES COLES.) Others died outside of England, connected to Jack by tenuous theories of a globe-hopping madman, while sundry victims unknown—generally listed only as anonymous statistics—are apparently figments of the individual author's imagination.

The NEW ORLEANS AXEMAN has received similar treatment, beginning soon after his first two murders in 1918. Local reporters suddenly "remembered" a series of similar crimes in 1911, garbling names, dates, and details to create the illusion of a home-invading phantom who struck at seven-year intervals. Others, beginning some three decades after the crimes, fabricated (and killed off) a suspect whose existence and subsequent murder remain entirely undocumented.

More disturbing than the careless inflation of body counts (at least from the viewpoint of serious scholars) are the instances wherein various authors produce books or articles on "unsolved" cases that have been resolved with or, worse yet, appear to be complete fabrications. Once published, such mythical cases take on a life of their own and may appear repeatedly under the bylines of multiple authors. Some examples from the current literature include:

- *"Australian Ripper"* An alleged series of mutilation slayings claiming at least seven victims between 1976 and 1979. While certainly plausible, descriptions of the events match none of Australia's present unsolved cases and authorities profess no knowledge of the crimes. Source: Jay Robert Nash, Crime Chronology (1984).

- *"Chicago Ripper"* Initially presented as an unidentified mutilation-slayer of 20 women, the last killed in January 1906; a later, garbled version claims all 20 murders occurred in 1906. Chicago newspapers reveal that the January 1906 victim was shot, with no reported mutilations, and that her death was speculatively linked to one other homicide. No trace of the elusive Ripper or his 20 female victims is found in contemporary reports. Sources: Nash, *Crime Chronology;* Eric Hickey, *Serial Murderers and Their Victims* (1997).

- *"Dunes case"* A wildly exaggerated account of the Provincetown, Massachusetts, "LADY OF THE DUNES" murder case, wherein readers are told that "police are investigating the serial killer who left the bodies of twelve young women in sand dunes." In fact, there was only one such murder. Source: Joel Norris, *Serial Killers* (1988).

- *"The Executioner"* Described as an unidentified serial killer who murdered "at least nine transients" around Los Angeles in 1986, this "unsolved" case roughly mirrors the crimes of "Skid Row Slayer" Michael Player, who shot nine men (eight of them homeless) before killing himself in October 1986. The case was closed in February 1987, after ballistics tests linked Player's pistol to the murders. Source: Hickey, *Serial Murderers and Their Victims.*

- *Galveston, Texas* A report of alleged serial murders at a local convalescent home, with police "investigating the deaths of twenty-eight geriatric patients" in 1983. This case apparently *does* have some basis in fact, but it was not an example of serial murder. Rather, Galveston journalists report that authorities investigated the "home" in question for chronic neglect of its inmates, resulting in several deaths. Source: Norris, *Serial Killers.*

- *Joliet, Illinois, murders* Erroneously presented as the unsolved 1983 slayings of "fifteen victims" in the city named, this series of crimes actually included 17 deaths in two Illinois counties. Local authorities consider at least 12 of the murders solved with the 1984 arrest of serial killer Milton Johnson. Source: Hickey, *Serial Murderers and Their Victims.*

- *"Los Angeles Slasher"* Vaguely described as the killer of eight victims in 1974, this nonexistent stalker was apparently spawned by a hasty reading of inaccurate reports on the "Skid Row Slasher" case (see below). Source: Hickey, *Serial Murderers and Their Victims.*

- *Mexico City murders* Described as an ongoing series of homicides that have claimed more than 100 female victims, this report is a garbled reference to unsolved serial murders in CIUDAD JUAREZ, some 1,100 miles north of the Mexican capital. Source: Ronald Holmes and Stephen Holmes, *Murder in America* (2001).

- *"Midtown Slasher"* A brief but notorious series of stabbings in Manhattan, solved in July 1981 with the arrest of Charles Sears, but still sometimes erroneously cited as an unsolved case. Source: Norris, *Serial Killers.*

- *Moscow decapitation murders* An alleged series of beheadings in the Russian capital, claiming "several" female victims during 1979. No supporting evidence for this case has been found in the 20 years since its original publication. Source: Nash, *Crime Chronology.*

- *Joseph Mumfre* Named in various accounts as the probable New Orleans "Axeman," Mumfre has been described as a convicted felon, imprisoned for burglary between 1911 and 1918, murdered in Los Angeles two years later by the widow of an Axeman victim. Unfortunately for such theories, there is no evidence that Mumfre ever existed. California death records no person by that name between 1905 and the present day. Sources: Robert Tallant, *Murder in New Orleans*

(1953); Jay Robert Nash, *Bloodletters and Bad-men* (1973).

- *"Skid Row Slasher"* Described as an unsolved case, including erroneous dates and an incorrect tally of victims, in works published long after the arrest and conviction of killer Vaughn Orrin Greenwood. Sources: Jay Robert Nash, *Open Files* (1984); Norris, *Serial Killers.*

- *"SODA POP SLASHER"* The alleged mutilation slayer of 13 victims in New York City's Greenwich Village, still at large although identified and "controlled" by the vigilance of his psychiatrist, who tells the tale. Melodrama and admitted deviations from the truth mark this case as a probable literary hoax. Source: Martin Obler and Thomas Clavin, *Fatal Analysis* (1997).

- *"Sunday Morning Slasher"* The murders of three women in Ann Arbor, Michigan, between April and July 1980, solved with the 1982 confession of suspect Coral Eugene Watts. Six years later, a garbled report described the "unsolved" case, allegedly including murders of "more than forty black women" in Houston, Texas, during 1981. Source: Norris, *Serial Killers.*

- *"Texas Strangler"* Reported as a series of 11 or 12 unsolved murders committed in the late 1960s and early 1970s. Several of the crimes included were solved in 1972, with the conviction of defendant Johnny Meadows. Sources: Nash, *Open Files;* Hickey, *Serial Murderers and Their Victims.*

- *"3X"* The unidentified New York gunman who killed two men in June 1930 is unaccountably portrayed in later accounts as a "mad bomber"

who "terrorized the city in the early 1930s." Sources: Nash, *Open Files* and *Bloodletters and Badmen* (1996).

- *"Trailside Killer"* The case of eight hikers murdered around Port Reyes, California, between August 1979 and March 1981, solved with the 1984 conviction of defendant David Carpenter, erroneously described in 1988 as involving "a cult killer of seven hitchhikers" in 1980, with the slayer "still at large." Source: Norris, *Serial Killers.*

- *"Tulsa bludgeonings"* The murders of four red-haired women between 1942 and 1948, solved with the arrest of suspect Charles Floyd in 1949, still presented as an unsolved case a half-century after the fact. Sources: Jay Robert Nash, *Encyclopedia of World Crime* (1992) and *Terrorism in the 20th Century* (1998).

- *White Plains, New York* An alleged series of unsolved murders claiming four female victims in 1983. Queries to police and journalists in the area have failed to discover evidence of any such crimes. Source: Norris, *Serial Killers.*

- *"ZODIAC"* California's elusive serial slayer of six adult victims between 1966 and 1969, cited in print as a killer who "murdered and sexually assaulted several children" in San Francisco during 1974, and who was "[g]iven his name by the police because he carved the sign of the zodiac into the bodies of his victims." In fact, no such mutilations occurred and none of Zodiac's victims were sexually assaulted; the killer coined his own nickname in letters to the press. Sources: Norris, *Serial Killers.*

NAHANNI Valley, Canada unsolved murders (1910–46)

A mystery of near-supernatural aspect haunts the beautiful but sinister Nahanni Valley, located in the southern part of the Mackenzie mountain range, in Canada's vast Northwest Territories. Published reports differ on the number of victims slain in the valley and the dates of their murders, but all agree that the area is—or once was—stalked by an unknown headhunter who decapitated some of his victims, while others disappeared entirely. A compilation of the Nahanni Valley cases, drawn from several sources, includes:

- Brothers Frank and Willie MacLeod, of Fort Simpson, found dead and beheaded in the valley around 1910. (Jay Robert Nash, in his error-riddled *Encyclopedia of World Crime,* adds an unnamed engineer to the MacLeod expedition, claiming all three victims disappeared in 1904, with their severed skulls found three years later.)

- Martin Jorgensen, found decapitated in a burned-out cabin, in 1917.

- Annie Laferte, missing and presumed dead in the Nahanni Valley, circa 1926.

- Phil Powers, reportedly found burned to death inside his cabin, in 1932.

- Two unnamed prospectors reported missing from the valley in 1936, while a "John Doe" corpse was found, apparently unrelated to the missing men.

- Prospector Ernest Savard, who had previously emerged from the valley with rich ore samples, found dead in his sleeping bag in 1945, his head nearly severed from his body.

- Another prospector, John Patterson, who missed a rendezvous with his partner in 1946, listed as missing and presumed dead.

A 1950 magazine article on the Nahanni Valley named additional victims of the local "curse" as Joe Mulholland, from Minnesota; Bill Espler of Winnipeg; Yukon Fischer; Edwin Hall; Andy Hays; and "one O'Brien," but no details were provided for those cases beyond a vague reference to "Canadian police records."

There are clearly varied reasons why a man or group of men might disappear in the Nahanni Valley—a rugged area sometimes used for survival exercises by elite military forces—but the record of at least six murders, most of them involving partial or complete decapitation, clearly indicates that the Nahanni once played host to a determined killer, one whose identity is obscured, perhaps forever, by the chill mists of the Great White North.

NAPP, Elyse   See FLAT-TIRE MURDERS

NASTASIA, Sherry   See "VALLEY KILLER"

NEEDHAM, Ben missing person (1991)

Ben Needham was a British subject, born at Sheffield, England, on October 29, 1989. At age three, in July 1991, he traveled to Greece with his mother and her boyfriend to visit his expatriate maternal grandparents at their home in the village of Iraklides, on the island of Kos, in the Dodecanese group of the Southern Sporades. Ben's mother, Kerry Needham, described the visit as a prelude to full-time residence in Greece, where she would reside with her parents and two younger brothers. To that end, Kerry found work at a local hotel.

On July 24, Kerry Needham left Ben with her parents at their rural farmhouse while she went to work. He vanished sometime that afternoon, while grandparents Eddie and Christine Needham were eating

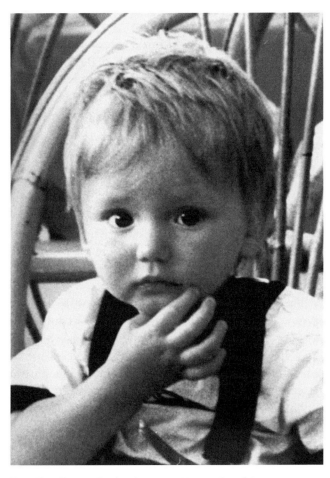

Ben Needham, shown above at 21 months old, went missing as a toddler in Greece in 1991. (Press Association via AP Images)

lunch. Christine later said that she only took her eyes off Ben for a few minutes, while he played near the home's front door, then she noted his absence at 2:30 P.M. Family members searched property, first suspecting that Ben had wandered off, then thinking that 17-year-old Stephen Needham had taken the child for a ride on his moped, but no trace of Ben was discovered. His grandparents then called police, who grilled the grandparents as suspects while delaying any wider search or notification to airports and nearby shipyards.

More than 300 sightings of boys matching Ben Needham's description were logged throughout Greece during 1991–92. The first came on the evening of his disappearance, when a shopkeeper in Iraklides allegedly saw Ben walking with an older boy, but by the time police bestirred themselves to investigate that lead, the trail had gone cold. None of the other sightings proved any more helpful, and while the Needhams believe Ben was snatched for sale to child-traffickers, no proof of that theory has surfaced to date. Likewise, suggestions that Ben wandered to the coast and drowned are unsupported by discovery of any child's remains.

An alternate theory, perhaps influenced by racism, suggests that Ben was kidnapped by wandering Gypsies. Late in 1995, private investigator Stratos Bakirtzis found a blond boy, roughly six years old, living in a Gypsy camp in Salonika. The boy claimed that his biological parents had abandoned him, while his adoptive mother said that she had purchased him from other Gypsies. Whatever the truth of his origins, the boy lacked Ben Needham's telltale strawberry birthmark on the nape of his neck, and police dropped the case.

Stratos Bakirtzis made news again in May 1997, when he targeted a Greek expatriate and his wife, living with two boys in an unnamed German town. According to London's *Sunday Mirror,* British detectives were sent to investigate the German lead, while a Foreign Office spokesman told reporters, "There is a strong possibility that this man is holding Ben." The lead came from a Greek armed robber serving life in prison, whose revelations prompted the arrest of five alleged child-smugglers. The convict told his story in pursuit of a £500,000 reward for Ben Needham's recovery, but despite initial optimism—and a claim from professional psychic Uri Geller that Ben would be found in Germany—neither of the boys was Ben Needham.

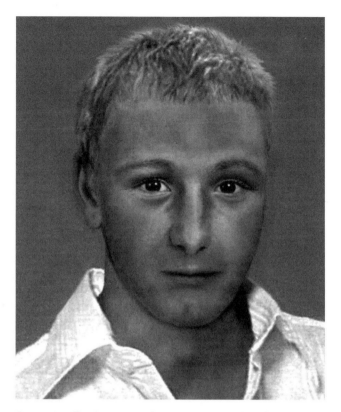

Created in October 2007, this computer-rendered image shows how Ben Needham was expected to look at age 18, 16 years after his disappearance. (Press Association via AP Images)

In 1998, while vacationing on Rhodes, British tourist John Cookson noticed a blond boy around 10 years old playing on the beach. Recalling the Needham case, Cookson questioned local residents and learned that the boy's friends called him "the blond one," to distinguish him from dark-haired Greek playmates. Cookson photographed the child, and procured a sample of his hair, but DNA analysis and presentation of the boy's Greek birth certificate disappointed the Needhams once again.

Kerry Needham left Kos after Ben's disappearance, and separated from her lover of the moment, then reunited with him long enough to have another child, daughter Leighanna, in 1994. In 2003, she hired private investigator Ian Crosby to pursue the case, including fruitless efforts to identify a blond youth photographed by tourists in Turkey during 1999. While Crosby flew off to Kos with Kerry's brother Daniel, seeking leads they never found, Great Britain's South Yorkshire police produced new photos of Ben Needham, "aged" with computers to show a young man in his teens. At last report, Kerry Needham had spent £20,000 pursuing false leads to

her son, but she remains confident that they will be reunited.

NEW Bedford, Massachusetts "highway murders" (1988)

Between April and September 1988, at least nine women from New Bedford, Massachusetts, were abducted and murdered by an unidentified serial killer who dumped their bodies near highways surrounding the city. Two other women reported missing from New Bedford in the same time period are also presumed to be dead. Several of the victims were known prostitutes, while others were described by police as drug-addicted "semi-pros." At least six knew one another in the months before they died, frequenting the same saloons, sometimes walking the same streets in search of "tricks."

The first hint of a killer on the loose around New Bedford came on July 2, 1988, when a motorist stopped to urinate in some bushes near the Freeport exit ramp of Interstate 140. Instead of a quiet rest stop, he found the partially clad skeleton of a woman, identified five months later as 30-year-old Debra Madeiros, last seen alive on May 27, when she left her boyfriend's apartment in the wake of a lover's quarrel.

Four weeks after that discovery, on July 30, more decomposed remains were found near the Reed Road exit ramp of I-195, six miles west of New Bedford. The victim was identified on December 7 as Nancy Paiva, a 36-year-old heroin addict last seen alive on July 11. Despite her addiction and various run-ins with the law over drugs, Paiva's relatives denied she was a prostitute, and her record revealed no arrests for soliciting sex.

A little more than three months passed before the next grim discovery, on November 8, 1988, when a third victim's remains were found near the Reed Road exit on I-195. Two days after Christmas, the body was identified as that of 34-year-old Deborah DeMello, a fugitive from justice who had fled a prison work-release program in June, while serving time for prostitution. Last seen alive on July 11, DeMello was found with some clothing and other personal items identified as belonging to Nancy Paiva.

Eleven days after DeMello was found, on November 19, a road crew clearing brush along I-195 found the nude, decomposed corpse of Dawn Medes, a 25-year-old New Bedford resident missing since September 4. Her remains were identified by fingerprints, which matched her record of arrests for prostitution.

Less than two weeks passed before discovery of the next victim, on December 1, 1988. By that time, police were out searching with dogs and their effort paid off with the recovery of a skeleton near Interstate 140, two miles south of the point where Debra Madeiros was found in July. This time the skeleton was fully clothed, with a sack of extra clothing found nearby. Three full months would pass before the latest victim was identified, on February 28, 1989, as 25-year-old Deborah McConnell, missing from New Bedford since May.

By the time McConnell was identified, police had a sixth victim on their hands, found by hunters on December 10 at an abandoned gravel quarry, half a mile north of the Reed Road exit on I-195. Nine days later, the skeleton was identified as that of 28-year-old Rochelle Clifford, last seen alive on April 27, 1988, in company with an ex-convict known as Nancy Paiva's sometime live-in lover. An automatic suspect in two of the murders, the man was investigated and apparently cleared on both counts, since no charges were filed.

The first victim in 1989 was found on March 28, on the southbound side of I-140, directly opposite the spot where Debra Madeiros was found nine months earlier. The skeleton had a full set of teeth, and identification was made the next day, naming victim number seven as Robin Rhodes, a 28-year-old single mother last seen alive in April 1988. While not a working prostitute, according to her family and friends, Rhodes was acquainted with victims Clifford, Paiva, and Mendes from various New Bedford saloons.

Rhodes was also a friend of the next victim found, 26-year-old Mary Santos, whose skeleton was discovered along Route 88 on March 31, 1989. The dump site placed her miles from the first seven bodies, but the killer otherwise held to his pattern, hiding the corpse in brush some 25 feet from the roadway. Last seen alive in New Bedford on July 15, 1988, Santos was a known heroin addict and friend of victims Clifford, Paiva, and Santos.

The last victim found, on April 24, 1989, was identified as Sandra Botelho, dumped nude beside I-195, eight miles east of New Bedford. A 24-year-old college dropout, addict, and prostitute, Botelho was last seen alive on August 11, 1988, leaving her apartment for a night on the stroll. She never returned, and her fate remained a mystery for eight months, until her skeletal remains were found.

By that point in their search for clues, police had listed two more women has probable victims of New Bedford's elusive "Highway Killer." Nineteen-year-old Christine Monteiro, an addict with arrests for prostitution on her record, had vanished in May 1988, while her next-door neighbor, 34-year-old Marilyn Roberts, disappeared the following month. Both women are still missing today, presumed dead.

By late November 1988 local and state authorities were trying to coordinate their manhunt for the Highway Killer. Sadly short of evidence, they concentrated first on rumors that a knife-wielding rapist had been terrorizing local prostitutes for more than a year. Police had a vague description of the suspect and his white pickup truck, but they made no further progress until December 13, 1988, when one alleged victim spotted the pickup again and recorded its license number. Detectives traced the vehicle to Neil Anderson, a 35-year-old unemployed trucker and fish-cutter who lived with his mother, boasting convictions for assault and battery with a dangerous weapon (1978), attempted breaking and entering (1981), plus various arrests involving drugs and alcohol. Charged with rape on December 15, 1988, Anderson was initially held in lieu of $20,000 bond, subsequently convicted on one count of sexual assault and sentenced to a prison term of three to five years. No evidence was found connecting him to any of the murders in New Bedford.

Another alleged hooker rapist was known to his victims as "Flat Nose," identified in January 1989 as one Anthony DeGrazia. Seventeen prostitutes reportedly named DeGrazia as their rapist before he was detained for questioning on April 19, 1989. He denied any wrongdoing but allegedly admitted to detectives that "everyone" suspected him of murdering the Highway Killer's victims. Formally arrested on May 4, 1989, DeGrazia was held in a mental hospital for testing, while various forensic samples from his body, home, and pickup truck were rushed to the Federal Bureau of Investigation (FBI) lab in Washington. Those test results were a mixed blessing for investigators: DeGrazia was eliminated as a murder suspect in New Bedford, but hairs recovered from his vehicle appeared to match those of several rape victims. Released on $37,500 bond in January 1990, DeGrazia was still awaiting trial a year later, when he was arrested once more on charges of raping another prostitute. He denied that charge as well, but sat in jail until July 1991, when he finally made bond on the latest charge. A few days after his release from custody, DeGrazia committed suicide with an overdose of antidepressant medication.

Long before that time, however, local police and prosecutors had focused on another suspect as their most likely candidate for the Highway Killer title. Kenneth Ponte was a practicing attorney, honorary sheriff's deputy for Bristol County, and a known associate of murder victim Rochelle Clifford. On April 3, 1988, before she disappeared, New Bedford police found Ponte armed with a pistol, accused of threatening a man he claimed had raped Clifford, but Clifford vanished a short time later with the case still unresolved. On June 7 police questioned Ponte again, after they found him sitting in a car with a young woman, on a street notorious for prostitutes. Ponte claimed the woman had "lured" him there, and a quick search led to her arrest for possession of drug paraphernalia. Ponte, for his part, was carrying another gun. His permit was at home, he told the officers, and while he promised to retrieve it for them, Ponte never reappeared. On June 8, 1988, he was charged with possessing an unlicensed weapon, but the charge was dismissed one day later by a New Bedford magistrate.

Seeking a change of scene, Ponte closed his law practice in September 1988 and moved to Florida a month later. Police called the move suspicious, noting that Ponte sold his home at a reported price $100,000 below the fair market value, making just enough on the deal to cover some outstanding debts. Three days after Christmas, when Ponte missed a scheduled interview with New Bedford police concerning the recent murders, one detective allegedly threatened to "screw him in the media." True or not, the first front-page story naming Ponte as a suspect in the Highway Killer case broke nine days later, with police describing their search of the attorney's home and office. According to authorities, a dog trained to sniff out human corpses had scored a "hit" on the carpet in Ponte's former office. A day later, on January 7, 1989, a local drug dealer supposedly approached police, naming Ponte as a regular customer from 1984 through 1987.

Troubles began to multiply for Ponte with the new rash of publicity. On January 18, 1989, he was back in court, charged with assault for the

April 1988 gun-waving incident. Five days later, a New Bedford prostitute regaled police with stories of Ponte's alleged sexual exploits and drug abuse. Before the month was out, however, Ponte scored his first legal victory, winning indefinite postponement of the firearms charge, because a judge found the police collection of blood and hair samples (for use in the Highway Killer investigation) unreasonable in a case of simple assault.

A special grand jury was impaneled to investigate the Highway Killer case, with its first hearing held on March 2, 1989, continuing sporadically through July 1990. Most of the testimony focused on Ponte, resulting in his March 29, 1990, indictment (with three confederates) on charges of conspiring to possess cocaine. Back in Florida, on June 11, 1990, Ponte was jailed for leaving the scene of an accident, after a neighbor claimed he tried to hit her with his car. Riding with Ponte at the time of his arrest was a young woman sought by police for violating probation. In custody, the officers noted bruises on her neck, and she soon accused Ponte of assaulting her on two occasions during the week before his latest arrest. On June 12 Ponte was slapped with brand-new felony charges, including aggravated assault, aggravated battery, false imprisonment, and using a firearm in commission of a felony. Ponte's accuser recanted in court two days later, telling the judge her statement was coerced by police withholding medication until she agreed to press false charges. It should have been a win for Ponte, but on June 15 the judge increased his bond to $205,000, citing the arrival of a Massachusetts police affidavit naming Ponte as a murder suspect.

New Bedford's special grand jury finally got around to indicting Ponte on one count of first-degree murder, for victim Rochelle Clifford, on August 17, 1990. Ponte pled not guilty at his arraignment, and bond was set at $50,000. Authorities seemed confident at first, but it was all for show. In March 1991, special prosecutor Paul Buckley was appointed to investigate the Highway Killer case from scratch. Four months later, he announced that Kenneth Ponte's murder charge would not be tried. "It would get to the judge," Buckley told reporters, "and he would rule as a matter of law that there is no evidence."

Official interest persists in the New Bedford case. District Attorney Paul Walsh, Jr., reexamined the evidence in 2002, but found no grounds for charges. Walsh lost his reelection bid in 2006, and successor

Samuel Sutter announced a reopening of the case in May 2007, when police dug up the driveway of Kenneth Ponte's former home and carted off eight bags of soil. Sutter told the *Boston Globe*, "We're devoting resources to that investigation, considerable resources at the district attorney's office, and we're pursuing every lead. When we do a review of an unsolved homicide, we look at everything, and if there's something that we think should be done that was not done in the past and we have the resources to do it, we're going to do it. That's how you solve unsolved homicides." Such statements encouraged relatives of the dead and missing, but no new charges were filed.

A year later, in May 2008, authorities cast their eyes upon a new suspect. Alex Scesny, a 38-year-old resident of Berlin, Massachusetts, had been charged with raping a woman on Cape Cod in 2002, but that case was dropped when the victim died prior to trial. A second rape charge, involving a girlfriend assaulted in 2007, resulted in Scesny's DNA being tested—and allegedly matched to evidence collected in 1996, from the corpse of Fitchburg prostitute Theresa Stone. The ink was barely dry on that report when authorities named Scesny as a "person of interest" in the slayings of five Worcester prostitutes, during 2003–04. New Bedford prosecutors quickly voiced an interest in Scesny, requesting samples of his DNA for comparison with evidence found in the 1980s. Skeptics note that Scesny would have been 18 and 19 years old during the New Bedford murders, but various serial killers have launched their "careers" at younger ages. At press time for this book, no charges had been filed against Scesny or any other suspect, and the Highway Murders remained officially unsolved.

NEWCASTLE, Australia unsolved murders (1979–94)

On March 22, 1998, police in New South Wales announced the formation of a special task force, dubbed "Strike Force Fenwick," to investigate various deaths and disappearances in the district dating back to 1979. Police Commissioner Peter Ryan told reporters that the team of 25 detectives was initially assigned to probe the cases of four missing persons, but that their investigation had expanded to include an unspecified number of additional cases.

Prior to mid-March 1998, the investigation had focused solely on a short list of victims including 20-year-old Leanne Goodall and 16-year-old Amanda Zolis, missing since 1979; 23-year-old Graham Monk, vanished in 1993; and 16-year-old Gordana Kotevski, reported missing in 1994. The expanded inquiry was occasioned by the March 1998 discovery of an unmarked desert grave and the report of a human jawbone found on a Newcastle beach, near the spot where a 24-year-old woman had been murdered in 1992. Assistant Police Commissioner Clive Small refused to specify how many new cases were under investigation by Strike Force Fenwick, but he told reporters that "quite a substantial list" had been compiled, with police reviewing a list of all persons between the ages of 12 and 40 reported missing in the Newcastle area since the mid-1970s.

Resident Jim Hickie, whose 18-year-old daughter Robin vanished on April 7, 1979, complained that the new search appeared to be covering old ground, and that "their chances of finding something nearly 20 years later seem fairly remote." (Another victim, 14-year-old Amanda Robinson, disappeared from the same area on April 20, 1979, while walking home from her school bus stop.) Hickie also alleged that police had warned him in 1979 that they would cease looking for his daughter if he gave any statements to the media. "They are totally insensitive to the feelings of parents in this matter," he told reporters. "I have to read in the papers what's going on."

Coincidentally or otherwise, the region under study—including scenic Hunter Valley—had also served as the stalking ground for serial killer Ivan Milat, convicted and sentenced to life in July 1997 for killing seven young backpackers between 1989 and 1992. Authorities were quick to deny that they were trying to clear old cases at random by pinning them on Milat, but Newcastle police spokesmen described the imprisoned killer as "a person of interest" in the disappearance of six local victims—including Robin Hickie and Amanda Robinson—since the late 1970s. At last report, no further charges have been filed against Milat, nor have any other suspects been named in the Newcastle crimes.

NEW Castle, Pennsylvania "headless murders" (1925–39)

While homicide detectives in Ohio labored to solve the CLEVELAND TORSO MURDERS in the latter 1930s, they were periodically distracted by reports of unsolved slayings from the area of New Castle and

West Pittsburgh, Pennsylvania. No solid link between the crime sprees was established, but coincidence of timing, the proximity of common railway lines, and the unanimous decapitation of victims in both states have produced some tantalizing theories. No two reports agree on the number of New Castle victims, and several accounts make surprisingly detailed references to crimes never reported by the media. A retrospective in the local newspaper, published in December 1971, refers to 11 victims between 1921 and 1940, but a detailed review of press coverage on the case reveals only five confirmed murders, spanning a period of 14 years.

The first victim, a young man, was found in a marshy area between New Castle and West Pittsburgh—later dubbed the "murder swamp"—on October 6, 1925. Nude on discovery, he had been dead at least three weeks when found, and the discovery of his severed head on October 8 provided no clue to his identity. As with the other Pennsylvania victims, he remains unidentified today.

On October 17, 1925, a headless male skeleton was found in the swamp. The matching skull was unearthed two days later, along with that of a woman killed at least a year earlier. Neither victim was identified by authorities, and no trace of the woman's body was ever found.

The local "headless murders" were a fading memory by July 1, 1936, when a man's decapitated corpse turned up on a slag dump of the Pittsburgh & Lake Erie Railroad, at New Castle Junction. The victim's head was never found, and he remains anonymous. Newspapers spread beneath the body included issues from Pittsburgh and Cleveland, dating from July 1933.

On October 13, 1939, another headless, decomposing male body was fished out of the swamp near West Pittsburgh. Charred newspapers found with the body included month-old copies from Youngstown, Ohio. The victim's head was found nearby in an abandoned boxcar on October 18.

Were the Pennsylvania crimes and Cleveland's murder spree connected? Did Ohio's "Mad Butcher" first try his hand in New Castle, taking a decade off before he resumed killing around Cleveland? Detective Peter Merylo, stalking the Ohio headhunter into retirement, blamed one man for both sets of murders, plus 20 to 30 other slayings nationwide. The final truth has eluded authorities for more than seven decades, and it may well lie buried in the Pennsylvania "murder swamp."

NEW Haven, Connecticut unsolved murders (1975–90)

Over a span of 15 years, at least a dozen young women, all African American, many of them prostitutes, were murdered in or near New Haven, Connecticut. The first victim, strangled and dumped beside Interstate 95 in East Haven, remains unidentified today. Authorities believe at least seven of the victims were slain by a single killer, but despite exhaustive efforts by two separate task forces, no charges have been filed. The posthumous identification of a suspect in 2000, while encouraging to some investigators, still left many questions in the case unanswered.

New Haven's first task force was organized in the late 1970s to investigate a series of murders along I-95 between New York and Massachusetts. Seven of the listed victims, most of them strangled or stabbed, had been dumped around New Haven between 1976 and 1978. The atypical murder of 23-year-old prostitute Terry Williams, found shot to death in a New Haven motel room, sparked the creation of ghetto "soul patrols," with men escorting streetwalkers to their "jobs" and standing by to watch for suspects while they worked, but the effort produced no results. In the early 1990s another investigative team, the Connecticut Homicide Task Force, was created to determine whether various prostitute slayings in New Haven, Hartford, and Waterbury were the work of a serial killer. While it produced few leads, the task force review of one murder raised new questions that remain forever unanswered.

Once again, the slaying was atypical: prostitute Jacqueline Shaw, last victim on the list, had been shot in the head behind New Haven's Wilbur Cross High School in October 1990. While investigating Shaw's final days, detectives received a call from Florida police, concerning suspect Roosevelt Bowden, late of New Haven, sentenced to death for the April 1988 beating death of a man at Tarpon Springs, Florida. Bowden clearly had not murdered Jacqueline Shaw, but his criminal record intrigued New Haven authorities. In 1978, he had stabbed his one-year-old daughter to death in broad daylight, on a New Haven street corner. Murder charges were bargained down to manslaughter, and Bowden was paroled in September 1983, after serving one-third of a 15-year sentence. Five of the New Haven murders occurred before Bowden was jailed for killing his daughter, two more between the date of his parole and his July 1986 departure for Florida. (At least three others, in August and September 1978, took place while he was in custody.) A Florida cellmate told police that Bowden had bragged about committing "several" murders in New Haven, but the task force was too late to question Bowden in person. He died in a prison hospital of AIDS-related complications during April 1994, leaving New Haven's riddle without a solution.

NEW Jersey unsolved murders (1965–66)

Between September 1965 and August 1966, the Jersey Shore of Monmouth and Ocean Counties was the scene of six unsolved murders, marked in each case by similar (if not identical) techniques. Four decades later, homicide investigators are no closer to a suspect in the case than when the crimes occurred.

The slayer's first target was 18-year-old Mary Klinsky, a high school senior in West Keansburg, killed in what police termed an "especially vicious attack." Klinsky left her home at 9:00 P.M. on September 15, 1965, bound for the corner mailbox with a letter for her fiancé. Seven hours later, her nude and battered body was found by motorists near the entrance to Garden State Parkway.

The next victim was Joanne Fantazier, a 17-year-old high school dropout, found on the ice of Yellow Brook in Cold Neck Township on February 11, 1966. Fantazier had been fatally beaten and thrown off a highway bridge, her impact failing to break the ice as her killer plainly intended.

A month later, on March 17, 16-year-old Catherine Baker left her home in Edison Township, walking to a nearby bakery. She had barely a block to travel, but Baker never returned. Her semi-nude body was found on May 14, floating in a branch of the Metedeconk River, in a remote area of Jackson Township. Death was attributed to multiple skull fractures, the result of a vicious beating.

The first male victim, five-year-old Paul Benda, was discovered on June 21, 1966, in the high grass bordering an unpaved road near Raritan Bay. Sexually abused before death, he had also been beaten, tortured with lit cigarettes, and finished off with five strokes of an ice pick. The body was nude on discovery, his clothes piled nearby.

Another male victim, 18-year-old Ronald Sandlin, was abducted from his job at a Lakewood service station on August 7, 1966, beaten to death with a tire iron and dumped in a ditch in Manchester Township. Three days later, 44-year-old Dorothy McKenzie was found shot to death in her car, the vehicle mired in sand near a diner on Route 9. The latest victim was fully clothed, her purse untouched on the seat beside her.

In the absence of a suspect or a clear-cut motive, officers could say only that the McKenzie murder, with its use of firearms, seemed to break the chain—or did it? As with Joanne Fantazier, there had been no sexual assault, and if one slayer was responsible for all five murders, he had already shown diversity in raping boy and girl alike, abstaining when it suited him. It may have been no great challenge to swap his tire iron for a gun, but we can only speculate, because the crimes remain unsolved, the killer (or killers) still at large.

NEW Orleans, Louisiana "Axeman" murders (1918–19)

Often reported, but seldom accurately, this strange case from the Crescent City involved a home invader who murdered victims in their sleep. The killer, while less prolific than either Atlanta's "JACK THE RIPPER" (1911–12) or the axe slayer(s) of 49 mulatto victims in Texas and Louisiana (also 1911–12), managed to capture public attention in a way unrivaled by any serial slayer since London's original Ripper in 1888. Today, nearly a century after the crime spree, many aspects remain controversial and new evidence may still be found.

The story began in the predawn hours of May 23, 1918, when New Orleans grocer Joseph Maggio and his wife were murdered in bed by a prowler who chiseled through their back door, used Joseph's axe to strike each victim once across the skull, then slit their throats with a razor to finish the job. Maggio's brothers discovered the bodies and were briefly held as suspects, but police could find no evidence of their involvement in the crime and both were released.

A few blocks from the murder scene, detectives found a cryptic message chalked on the sidewalk. It read: "Mrs. Maggio is going to sit up tonight just like Mrs. Toney." Police could offer no interpretation, so the press stepped in. The *New Orleans States* reported a "veritable epidemic" of unsolved axe murders in 1911, listing the victims as Italian grocers named Cruti, Rosetti (allegedly killed with his wife), and Tony Schiambra (whose spouse was also reportedly slain). Over nine decades half a dozen authors have accepted the report as factual, relying on the alleged previous crimes to bolster this or that supposed solution to the case, but in fact the 1911 slayings remain shrouded in mystery.

Examination of New Orleans coroner's records and police reports for 1911 reveal no Crutis or Schiambras listed as deceased from any cause, while the death of one Mary Rosetti—identified as a Negro—was blamed on dysentery. Researcher William Kingman, after a further search of official records in New Orleans, reports that a "Mr. Crutti was killed in August 1910," no method stated, while Anthony and Johanna Sciambra (or Schiambra, in some reports) were found *shot* to death in their home during May 1912. Kingman further reports, in undated personal correspondence: "A Mr. and Mrs. Davi were hacked in June of 1911, [but] only Mr. Davi died, and in September of 1910 the Rissetto's [sic] were also attacked."

On June 28, 1918, a baker delivering bread to the grocery of Louis Besumer found a panel cut from the back door. He knocked, and Besumer emerged, blood streaming from a head wound. Inside the apartment, Besumer's "wife"—divorcée Anna Lowe—lay critically wounded by blows from an axe. She lingered on the brink of death for seven weeks, frequently delirious, once denouncing Besumer as a German spy and later recanting. Lowe died on August 5, 1918, after naming Besumer as her attacker, and he was arrested on murder charges. Nine months later, on May 1, 1919, a jury deliberated for all of 10 minutes before acquitting him.

Returning late from work on the night Anna Lowe died, Ed Schneider found his pregnant wife unconscious in their bed, her scalp laid open. She survived to bear a healthy daughter, but her memory of the attack was vague at best. She recalled a hulking shadow at her bedside, the axe descending—and nothing more.

On August 10, 1918, sisters Pauline and Mary Bruno woke to sounds of struggle in the adjacent room occupied by their uncle, Joseph Romano. They rushed next door to find him dying from a head wound, but they caught a glimpse of his fleeing assailant, described in official reports as "dark, tall, heavy-set, wearing a dark suit and a black slouch hat."

The rest of August 1918 was a nightmare for police, with numerous reports of chiseled doors, discarded axes, and lurking strangers. Several of the latter were pursued by vengeful mobs but always managed to escape. At last, with time and the distraction of an armistice in war-torn Europe, the hysteria began to fade.

On March 10, 1919, the scene shifted to Gretna, across the Mississippi River from New Orleans. There a prowler invaded the home of Charles Cortimiglia, helping himself to the grocer's own axe before wounding Charles and his wife, killing their infant daughter. From her hospital bed, Rose Cortimiglia accused two neighbors, Iorlando Jordano and his son Frank, of committing the crime. Despite firm denials from Charles, both suspects were jailed pending trial.

Meanwhile, on March 14, the *Times-Picayune* published a letter signed by "The Axeman." Describing himself as "a fell demon from the hottest hell," the author announced his intention of touring New Orleans on March 19—St. Joseph's Night—and vowed to bypass any home where jazz was playing at the time. "One thing is certain," he declared, "and that is that some of those people who do not jazz it (if there be any) will get the axe!" On the appointed night, already known for raucous celebration, New Orleans was even noisier than usual. The din included numerous performances of "The Axman's Jazz," a tune composed specifically for the occasion, and the evening passed without a new attack.

The Jordano trial opened in Gretna on May 21, 1919. Charles Cortimiglia did his best for the defense, but jurors believed his wife and convicted both defendants of murder on May 26. Frank Jordano was sentenced to hang, while his elderly father received a term of life imprisonment. (Charles Cortimiglia divorced his wife after the trial, and Rose was arrested for prostitution in November 1919. She recanted her testimony on December 7, 1920, explaining to police that spite and jealousy prompted her accusations. The Jordanos were pardoned and released from custody.)

And still the raids continued. Grocer Steve Boca was wounded at home on August 10, 1919, his door chiseled through, the bloody axe discarded in his kitchen. On September 3 the Axeman or an imitator entered Sarah Laumann's bedroom through an open window, wounding her in bed and dropping his weapon on the lawn outside. Eight weeks later, on October 27, grocer Mike Pepitone was murdered at home; his wife glimpsed the killer but offered detectives no helpful description. There the crime spree ended as it had begun, in mystery.

Robert Tallant proposed a solution to the Axeman riddle in his 1953 book *Murder in New Orleans*. According to Tallant, a man named Joseph Mumfre was shot and killed in Los Angeles on December 2, 1920, while walking on a public street. Mumfre's female assailant, veiled and dressed in black, was identified as the widow of Mike Pepitone. At her murder trial, resulting in a 10-year prison sentence, she named Mumfre as her husband's killer—and, by implication, as the Axeman of New Orleans. Tallant reports that New Orleans detectives checked Mumfre's record and found that he was serving time in jail for burglary during the Axeman's hiatus from August 1918 to March 1919.

Other authors have seized upon Tallant's solution, reporting that Joseph Mumfre was imprisoned between 1911 and 1918, thus implying a connection to earlier New Orleans homicides, but Mumfre would still be excluded as a suspect from the 1912 Sciambra attack. Jay Robert Nash "solved" the case in his book *Bloodletters and Badmen* (1973), calling Mumfre a Mafia hit man, allegedly pursuing a long vendetta against "members of the Pepitone family." The explanation fails when we recall that only one of the Axeman's 11 victims—and the last, at that—was a Pepitone. Likewise, speculation on a Mafia extortion plot against Italian grocers ignores the fact that four victims were non-Italian, while several were completely unconnected to the grocery business.

Still, there is a more deadly flaw in the Tallant-Nash solution to the Axeman mystery: the Joseph Mumfre murder in Los Angeles *never happened!*

Three years after the first edition of this book went to press, researcher Sheila Snyder e-mailed the following information, in response to Kingman's report. She wrote:

Being the endlessly curious type and a rabid genealogist, I searched Ancestry.com for info and found an article on Mrs. Esther Albano being tried for the murder of Leon Menfre in the Nevada State Journal *(Reno, Nevada), April 11, 1922, that states she shot him in self-defense after he had entered her home and demanded $500 under threat of death. She testified she believed he was responsible for the disappearance of her husband Angelo Albano. She was acquitted at this trial. There is also a death record from New Orleans showing Esther Pipitone Albano who died in August 1940. Another newspaper mentions Joseph Mumfre being killed [by] Mrs. Albano and it is the* Oakland Tribune *(Oakland, California) from December 15, 1921.*

While Robert Tallant is now deceased, and thus beyond interrogation with respect to Mumfre's case,

it now appears that he somehow confused a Nevada murder case with the New Orleans Axeman's crimes, while garbling the names of all concerned (perhaps as a result of careless reporting by the *Oakland Tribune*). We cannot say if Esther Pipitone Albano was somehow related to Axeman victim Mike Pepitone, although her subsequent death in New Orleans may be suggestive. In any case, she blamed Leon Menfre for the disappearance of her husband, Angelo Albano, who was not an Axeman victim. There—at least, for now—the matter rests as it began, in mystery.

NEW Orleans, Louisiana unsolved murders (1987–88)

In the space of a year, between December 1987 and December 1988, five African-American women in their twenties were strangled or asphyxiated in New Orleans by persons unknown, prompting authorities to speculate—however cautiously—on the possibility of a serial killer at large.

The first victim, 27-year-old Ruth Peart, was found in the Hollygrove neighborhood, her nude body hidden in the crawl space beneath a house. On January 2, 1988, 24-year-old Corinne Morgan was strangled in Hollygrove, six blocks from the Peart murder scene, her corpse found fully clothed. Number three, 24-year-old Carol Bissitt, was found strangled in her home on June 13, 1988, a telephone cord and the sash from a robe still wrapped around her neck. A "Jane Doe" victim, excluded from the series in some published reports, was found in a New Orleans park on November 30, 1988, choked to death by wads of paper shoved down her throat. The last to die, one week later, was Krystal Burroughs, found nude and strangled in a condemned dwelling frequented by homeless squatters.

So far, no suspects in the Crescent City murders have been publicly identified. Authorities insist that the murders are unconnected to another series of 24 slayings that plagued New Orleans between 1991 and 1996.

NEW Orleans, Louisiana unsolved murders (1991–96)

Between 1991 and 1996, a suspected serial killer claimed at least 26 lives in New Orleans, dumping the nude corpses of his victims in swamps surrounding the Crescent City. The victims were a mixed bag: By August 1995 their number included 17 black women, two white women, four black men, and one white man. Police said many of the dead were drug-addicted prostitutes, but six of the 24 were unidentified. Some of the victims were strangled, asphyxiated, or drowned; in several cases, advanced decomposition barred medical examiners from determining the cause of death.

The killer (or killers) seemed to operate on no particular schedule. The murders apparently began on August 4, 1991, and claimed five victims by year's end. All five were linked to the city's Algiers district, separated from New Orleans proper by the Mississippi River. Following his first spate of activity, the slayer took a six-month break, then killed four more victims between June and December 1992—all from Treme, an old residential district adjoining the city's French Quarter. A suspect sketch circulated by police in 1992 depicted a large, muscular black man in his thirties, but its publication brought no useful leads. The slayings lagged in 1993, with only two confirmed victims, then escalated rapidly with six dead in 1994 and seven more in the first five months of 1995.

New Orleans detectives were slow to recognize the signs of a predator at large. A media report dated August 12, 1995, declared that police had suspected a serial killer at large "for about a year," but they kept it to themselves and did not organize an investigative task force until May 1995. By that time, they had focused on a suspect whose identity was guaranteed to embarrass City Hall.

The key event in the murder series, authorities believed, was the April 1995 double murder of 28-year-old Sharon Robinson and a friend, 30-year-old Karen Iverster. The women were found together, floating in a swamp on April 30, and Robinson was soon identified as the girlfriend of Victor Gant, a 15-year veteran of the New Orleans Police Department. Gant denied any wrongdoing and submitted blood samples for DNA testing to assist the investigation. His superiors left Gant on the job, albeit confined to desk work, and in August 1995 they named Gant as a murder suspect, prompting media speculation on his possible role in two dozen slayings. Investigators from NEW BEDFORD, MASSACHUSETTS, expressed interest in Gant, suggesting a possible link to that city's series of unsolved murders in 1988, but Gant possessed iron-clad alibis for all 11 crimes. Back in New Orleans, Gant's attorney demanded that his client either be charged or formally exonerated, whereupon prosecutors grudgingly admitted that they had no case.

There the matter rested for more than two years, until police identified a new suspect. Sheriff Harry Lee of Jefferson Parish announced the breakthrough on November 25, 1997, but refused to name the latest target of investigation. In lieu of formal identification, Lee told reporters that the subject was a former French Quarter resident, a freelance photographer, and part-time taxi driver who was "also a suspect in murders in Florida and the Midwest." In addition to physical proximity, Lee said, the suspect was "heavily into the occult . . . [and] also has a history of sexual deviance, violence, and drug abuse and was frequently seen around black prostitutes." Three months elapsed before authorities identified their new suspect as 47-year-old Russell Ellwood. Initially jailed for traffic violations, Ellwood was booked for two counts of second-degree murder on March 3, 1998, simultaneously named as a suspect in at least eight more slayings.

The case against Ellwood initially hinged on statements from a former cellmate in Florida, recorded by police in October 1997. According to the unnamed prisoner, Ellwood had professed that he "enjoyed the fun of having sex with people who were not in control of their bodies." More specifically, the statement claimed, "He said if they were high on cocaine or heroin, the heroin would put them in a state of mind as if they were paralyzed and he could take advantage." Ellwood was formally charged in the deaths of 30-year-old Cheryl Lewis (found in a Hahnville swamp, west of New Orleans, on February 20, 1993) and 40-year-old Dolores Mack (found the following day, one-fifth of a mile from where Lewis was discovered). Both women were under the influence of cocaine when they died, with Lewis listed as a drowning victim, while Mack was strangled and/or suffocated.

Ellwood, an Ohio native, had previously served time in his home state and in Florida for drug possession and probation violations. He returned to Louisiana voluntarily, in January 1998, "in an effort to clear his name and help solve the case," but was then jailed on outstanding traffic warrants from his days as a New Orleans cabbie. Authorities refused to discuss any physical evidence they might possess, but they told reporters that Ellwood's "many contradictory statements yielded enough information to convince a judge to sign the warrant charging him" with murder. Since January, they added, "a stream of witnesses" had come forward to implicate Ellwood in the local slayings. Critics noted that Ellwood—a middle-aged Caucasian—bore no resemblance to the 1992 suspect sketch, but police dismissed that objection with a claim that they also had "four more suspects in the killings." Sheriff Lee assured reporters, "We never thought, from the beginning, that this was the work of one person."

Ellwood, held in lieu of $1 million bond, maintained his innocence of any wrongdoing, while attorney Ross Scaccia insisted prosecutors had misconstrued Ellwood's jailhouse braggadocio. "If you're in a jail," Scaccia told reporters, "a lot of times you are intimidated, put under pressure. Ellwood in effect was defending himself while he was with other prisoners when altercations occurred. 'You know I killed those people and I can kill you too.' I can say the statements he made did not amount to any sort of a confession. It was just to get the other prisoners away from him." Scaccia further asserted that the state's failure to charge Ellwood with first-degree murder proved the case against his client was weak. "Here's a guy who may have supposedly committed 26 murders," Scaccia challenged, "and he's not going to be prosecuted on the death penalty?"

Police countered those charges with a claim that Ellwood was "being investigated as a suspect in the murder of a prostitute in Florida." His prison boasts were said to "closely match the circumstances" of an unspecified slaying in the Sunshine State, but no charges were ever filed in that case, and the victim remains unidentified. By March 7, 1998, police were calling Ellwood "a suspect in at least 14 other killings" besides those in which he was charged. Photos of Ellwood published in local newspapers allegedly produced "a rush of new leads," and detectives soon felt confident enough to name other presumed Ellwood victims. They included:

Lola Porter 35, reported missing in 1992, whose skeletal remains were found near Waggaman, Louisiana, four years later. Porter had once lived in Algiers "with someone who looked like Ellwood," but police later identified her roommate and cleared him of suspicion in the murder.

Linda Coleman fished out of the Mississippi River in 1996. Authorities said she "had lived at the same address as Porter" and "fit the same description as the serial killer's prey," but they acknowledged that those circumstances were "not enough to qualify her as victim No. 27."

Linda DiBenedetto last seen at a New Orleans motel in December 1993, whose skeleton was found in Tangipahoa Parish 15 months later. Speaking of her murder to reporters, Tangipahoa sheriff's spokesman Chuck Reed said, "We have a strong suspicion it may be the work of [Ellwood]," but he refused to elaborate.

"Jane Doe" a still-unidentified victim whose bones were found in March 1995 beneath a highway overpass in Tangipahoa Parish. Geography aside, no hint was offered as to why police suspected Ellwood of the crime.

Lieutenant Sue Rushing, a member of the New Orleans murder task force, speculated publicly that Ellwood may have eluded capture in so many crimes because "He's like a chameleon, he's able to change his appearance so much. It's incredible." Rushing herself was soon in hot water, however, accused of destroying various receipts that placed Ellwood in Ohio during 1993, when victims Lewis and Mack were killed. Rushing failed a polygraph test in November 1998, when she denied "losing" the receipts; the same test showed that Rushing was "not telling the truth" when she denied coaching a witness who claimed Ellwood showed her the Mack-Lewis corpses in 1993. Those revelations prompted Ellwood's attorneys to file a civil rights lawsuit against Louisiana authorities, while Federal Bureau of Investigation (FBI) agents launched an investigation of Lt. Rushing and the task force. As attorney Maria Chaisson complained, "It's clear they have deprived him of his right to a fair trial."

There was still the troubling matter of Ellwood's alleged confessions, however. When police first approached him in Florida, in 1997, Ellwood allegedly told them he had "dreamed" of the New Orleans serial murders. Later, the discredited Lt. Rushing and other detectives claimed, Ellwood had broken down and said, "I'm willing to confess to two cases and give you all the details when I return to Louisiana." Ellwood, meanwhile, insisted that his "confession" was merely a ruse to make contact with lawyer Scaccia, whom he had known for several years. "My only thought," Ellwood told reporters, "was that if I can get to Mr. Scaccia, everything would be all right." Scaccia apparently believed the explanation, describing Ellwood as "just an unswift, lonely man who's always trying to be a success and has never succeeded at anything." Scaccia blamed the self-incriminating statements on Ellwood's craving of attention from detectives "who told him he could help them solve the case."

Sheriff Lee defended the embattled Lt. Rushing, ignoring the recent polygraph results when he told journalists, "I respect her personally and I respect her professionally. As of now, I know of no reason to discipline her. I think we've got a very good case. If we get a conviction, I will let the world know it's mainly because of Sue Rushing's efforts."

At a special hearing on December 14, 1998, Judge Kirk Granier agreed with Ellwood's attorneys that Lt. Rush had willfully destroyed an Ohio gas station receipt taken from Ellwood's possession, but Granier found that the state's key witness had not been improperly coached and he therefore upheld both murder charges. Two months later, on February 23, 1999, Sheriff Lee grudgingly conceded that Ellwood *was* in Ohio on the day of Dolores Mack's murder, and that charge was dropped on March 1. With that controversy resolved, Ellwood finally went on trial for the Lewis slaying in August 1999. Jurors convicted him on August 17, and Ellwood received a life sentence the following day. So far, no other suspects have been named in the Crescent City's five-year murder spree, and the remaining 25 murders are officially unsolved.

NEWTON, Vivian murder victim (1947)

On Thursday, July 17, 1947, Canadian divorcée Vivian Newton was found raped and strangled on Torrey Pines Mesa, 15 miles due north of San Diego, California. The murder site fell within city police jurisdiction, and Lt. Ed Dieckmann, chief of homicide for the San Diego Police Department, told reporters his detectives were seeking a white "John Doe" suspect who had squired the victim around nearby Tijuana, Mexico, on Wednesday. Police had photographs of Newton and the suspect together, smiling underneath sombreros, sitting in a donkey cart, and Newton evidently did some shopping in the border town. Her body, when discovered, was still clad in the white peasant blouse and black-trimmed dirndl skirt she had purchased in Tijuana.

Newton had arrived in San Diego on Saturday, July 12, and settled in a small downtown hotel. One of her neighbors, Edna Mitchell, told police that Newton's date for the excursion into Baja California was a pilot from Los Angeles. When Newton returned from Tijuana on Wednesday night, she had accompanied Mitchell to a downtown dime-a-dance club in the hope of meeting men. She lingered on at the club, dancing with a new male friend, after Mitchell left at midnight, and no one could remember seeing her alive beyond that time. Investigators identified her Tijuana traveling companion as Sgt. Frank Adams, tracing him to the Fairfield Army Air Base near Solano, California, on July 20, but Adams had not seen Newton since their Wednesday outing. Another man, initially believed to be the victim's final dancing partner, was eliminated from the suspect list when Edna Mitchell failed to make a positive identification. The Newton murder file remains technically open, with no realistic hope of solution today.

NEW York City gay murders (1973)

In January 1973 a series of brutal stabbings cast a pall of fear over New York City's homosexual community, sparking angry demands for police protection in quarters where officers are normally viewed as the enemy. Targeting denizens of the gay "leather" scene, an unknown killer mutilated seven victims in a little over three weeks' time, ending the murder spree as suddenly and mysteriously as it began.

The first slaying was recorded on January 4, 1973, when neighbors found 24-year-old Ronald Cabo knifed to death in his apartment, laid out on a burning sofa. Four days later, on the Lower East Side, 40-year-old Donald MacNiven and his next-door neighbor, 53-year-old John Beardsley, were slaughtered in MacNiven's apartment, discovered by firefighters called out to extinguish an arson blaze at the scene. Police confirmed that all three victims were "leather boys," well known in sadomasochistic circles, but rumors of other mutilation deaths were officially dismissed as "grossly exaggerated."

On January 18, 23-year-old Robben Borrero was pulled from the Hudson River off Greenwich Village, along with the corpse of a young "John Doe" victim. Nine days later, the killer committed his last double murder in Brooklyn Heights, invading the apartment that schoolteacher Nelson Roberts shared with his male lover. Neighbors used a pass key to investigate a blaring radio and stumbled on a scene of carnage. In the living room, hands bound behind his back, Roberts lay covered by a blanket, killed by multiple stab wounds in the back. His roommate was found hog-tied in the bedroom, with a broken neck. The couple's pet, a miniature poodle, had been drowned in the kitchen sink.

The killer's apparent retirement after seven murders left police without a single piece of solid evidence. An undercover officer was fitted out with leather gear to infiltrate the seamy world of S&M bondage, and while his exploits helped inspire the Al Pacino movie *Cruising* (1980), he did not identify the slayer.

NEW York City Hispanic gay murders (1985–86)

On March 21, 1986, Pedro Gonzalez, a 43-year-old restaurant worker, was found tied up and strangled in his Corona, Queens, apartment. Six days later, homicide investigators told the press that his murder bore similarities to two other homicides committed in Queens since July 1985. All three victims had been dark-skinned Hispanic homosexuals, known to frequent the same two bars in Queens and Manhattan. Each victim was beaten to death or asphyxiated in his own apartment, left with the lights on and a radio blaring loud music. Objects stolen by the still-unidentified killer included two videocassette recorders and a portable radio. At last report police had no leads or suspects in the case.

NEW York City infant murders (1915)

On September 29, 1915, Joseph Miller, a night watchman at a pier on South 11th Street, in New York City, noticed two dark objects floating in the Hudson River. Scrambling into a boat, Miller followed the current and fished out the pieces of flotsam, appalled to discover that two baby girls had been thrown in the river to drown.

A coroner's report revealed the victims to be less than two days old. Worse yet, a scan of recent files told homicide detectives that a dozen other infants, three days old or less, had been recovered from the Hudson in the past six weeks. Found floating along the waterfront, most of the tiny victims had been tossed in the water naked to drown; a few were bundled up so tightly that they must have suffocated prior to entering the river, since no water was discovered in their lungs.

Without a single lead to follow, investigators organized a special team to prowl the waterfront by night, but the effort was futile. A spokesman for the New York Police Department told reporters that some unknown person was "systematically engaged in the slaying of new-born babies," but a recognition of the problem offered no solution. The grim parade of tiny corpses ceased after Miller's discovery and the resultant publicity—or perhaps the killer (or killers) simply found a new means of disposal. In any event, the case was never solved.

NEW York City strangulation murders (1982)

Investigators cautiously refuse to speculate on possible connections in the deaths of five women, all strangled in Manhattan and Brooklyn between March and August 1982, but spokesmen for the New York Police Department told reporters that a common link in the series of crimes was "not discounted." Evidence in at least one case reportedly pointed to multiple killers, but authorities declined to state their reasons for believing that at least one death was unrelated to the others.

The series of killings (if series it was) began with the strangulation of 22-year-old Sheryl Guida, found at Coney Island on March 18, 1982. Rita Nixon, a 21-year-old visitor from Portsmouth, Virginia, was strangled and dumped behind a school in Chinatown on July 15. The third victim was Gloria DeLeon, a 31-year-old resident of Bergen County, New Jersey, found murdered in Manhattan. Patricia Shea, a 40-year-old physician's assistant from Queens, was found in Brooklyn's Prospect Park on July 26. The final victim, a "Jane Doe," was found floating in the Narrows off Bay Ridge in Brooklyn, on August 3, 1982. She had been beaten, raped, and strangled with an electric cord (still wrapped around her neck).

To date, no solid leads have been discovered in these crimes, no suspects brought to trial. If any further murders are connected to the original five, police and journalists have kept the public in the dark.

NEW York City taxi murders (1990)

Driving a cab in New York City is dirty, dangerous work. In 1990 alone, 35 New York cabbies were murdered on the job, while police arrested suspects in only 10 of those cases, for a solution rate of 29 percent. As if the threat from junkies, teenage gangs, and random stickup artists was not bad enough, the spring of 1990 also saw at least four drivers—some say seven—gunned down by a serial killer who, in the words of one police spokesman, "is getting into cabs and all he wants to do is shoot the driver."

The first known victim in the murder series, 37-year-old Anton Jones, was found dead in his cab at 6:40 A.M. on March 7, 1990, shot once in the head. Jones had picked up his last fare on Eastchester Road, bound for the junction of 241st Street and White Plains Road, but he never made it. His cab was found at Wilder and Stouen Avenues, in the borough's Wakefield district.

Seven days later, at 5:00 A.M. on March 14, 43-year-old Elliott Whitaker radioed his dispatcher to report that he had just picked up a fare on Boston Road, in the Bronx, and was heading for the train station on White Plains Road. A few minutes later, the same dispatcher received a telephone call, reporting that Whitaker's cab had struck a parked car on East 214th Street. Police responding to the accident call found Whitaker dead in the driver's seat, killed by multiple close-range shots to the head.

The killer struck again on April 10. Paul Burghard was a 25-year-old college student, driving cabs at night to make ends meet. At 2:25 that morning he picked up a passenger outside Montefiore Hospital in the Bronx. Fifteen minutes later, another cabbie reported sighting Burghard's cab on Wilson Avenue, in the Williamsbridge section of the Bronx, its driver slumped over the steering wheel. Patrolmen found him dead, shot twice in the head at close range, with an estimated $60 missing from the cab.

So far, all three victims had been killed with the same .22-caliber pistol. A witness to one shooting described the killer as a black man with a thin mustache, and an artist's sketch was distributed on posters offering a $20,000 reward for information leading to the gunman's arrest. Predictably, the offer brought many calls, but none led homicide investigators to a viable suspect.

The sketch was still in preparation on April 11, 1990, when 41-year-old Jamaican native Dennis Forbes was shot in his taxi at the corner of East 169th Street and Sheridan Avenue, in the Bronx. He clung to life for 24 hours at Lincoln Hospital, then died without regaining consciousness. Eyewitnesses reported two black teenagers fleeing the cab, and a .25-caliber pistol was found on the seat near Forbes's body, prompting authorities to speculate that his murder was unrelated to the trio of killings already under investigation.

Three days later, at 10:30 P.M. on April 14, 38-year-old Rafael Montes de Oca was dispatched to pick up a fare on East 188th Street, in the Bronx. He had been specially requested by a frequent customer, known only as "George," but this time the ride ended in death. It was 11:55 P.M. before another cabbie saw Montes de Oca's taxi parked at the corner of East 188th and Webster Avenue, its driver slumped over the wheel. As in the other series slayings, Montes de Oca had been shot in the head at close range with a .22-caliber pistol.

A special police task force created to solve the taxi murders now had 30 officers engaged in the full-time pursuit of one elusive suspect, but they were no closer to their man than they had been when Anton Jones was killed, in early March. On the afternoon of April 21, 1990, while a 300-car procession rolled across the Triborough Bridge, conveying Rafael Montes de Oca to his final rest, news reports announced the death of taxi driver Bakary Simpara, comatose since he was shot in the Bronx district of Clasons Point, on March 21, 1990. Authorities specifically denied a link between his murder and the random gunman they were tracking, calling common robbery "a good bet" in Simpara's slaying.

There were no such doubts on April 22, when 48-year-old cabbie Muhammad Salim was found dead in his taxi, shot once behind the left ear, in the West Bronx district of Tremont. Death had come suddenly for the latest victim, with food half-chewed in his mouth, his wallet lying empty on the seat beside him. Police acknowledged Salim's murder as "part of the same pattern" that included victims Jones, Whitaker, and Burghard.

Mayor David Dinkins held a press conference in the wake of Salim's murder, announcing expansion of the taxi-murders task force to include another 20 officers. "These killings represent more than a brutal attack on the drivers who have fallen victim," Dinkins told his television audience. "They have also become an assault on the vital link in our transportation system." It was a dramatic step, but all in vain. Nearly 15 years after the mayor's announcement, no suspect has been charged in the brutal series of murders.

NEW York City "trash bag murders" (1989)

Between July and October 1989 four Hispanic men were robbed and beaten to death in New York City's borough of Queens, their bodies discarded in bags. To date, only one of the four battered victims has been identified by police and their killer remains at large.

The first unidentified victim was found on July 31, 1989, left on a vacant lot at 135-40 155th Street in Queens. Hands bound behind his back, he had been clubbed to death with a hammer or other blunt instrument, stripped of his wallet, any jewelry he may have worn, and any documents that would have helped police identify the corpse. Four days later, a second unknown victim was found in identical condition, dumped on another vacant lot, this time at 167-20 120th Avenue. The third to die, and the only victim identified, was 32-year-old Fernando Suarez, a deliveryman from Garfield, New Jersey. Found on August 25 at the corner of 172nd Street and 126th Avenue, swaddled in a green canvas bag, Suarez had been left with a single quarter in his pocket. The last victim was found on Cranston Avenue, on October 4, when a pedestrian noticed his leg protruding from a trash bag left on a vacant lot between 134th and 135th Streets.

New York detectives did their best, presumably, with what they had, but it all came to nothing in the end. And while no more "trash bag" murders of Hispanic men have been reported from the area, neither has the killer been identified or punished for his crimes.

NICHOLS, Donna   See MARYLAND MURDERS

NICHOLS, Mary Ann   See "JACK THE RIPPER"

NIHON Shintaku Ginko robbery (1968)

The largest robbery in Japanese history occurred on December 10, 1968, as four employees from the Kokubunji, Tokyo, branch of the Nihon Shintaku bank transported 294,307,500 yen ($2,689,721) earmarked for employee bonuses at Toshiba's factory in Fuchu. As they approached Tokyo's Fuchu prison, with the money stashed in the trunk of their company car, a young motorcyclist dressed in a police uniform stopped their vehicle and told the bank employees that their manager's home had been bombed, while an anonymous caller warned police of a second bomb planted in the transport car.

Naturally frightened, the employees piled out of their vehicle, while the "policeman" crawled underneath it to perform a spot inspection. Seconds later, smoke and flames erupted from beneath the car, and their would-be savior rolled clear, shouting that the sedan was about to explode. The bank employees

ran for cover in the nearby prison, but glanced back in time to see the phony cop speed off with their car and the cash. To their chagrin, the smoke and fire had been produced by a simple highway flare. The thief abandoned the bank's car nearby, switching cash boxes to a stolen vehicle, which was in turn abandoned to *another* stolen car for the final escape.

Authorities found a wealth of evidence at the crime scene—120 items in all, from the white-painted "police" motorcycle to various smaller items. Unfortunately, all were common objects, and detectives surmised that some had been left specifically to confuse their investigation.

In that, the thief or thieves succeeded.

Suspicion initially focused on the 19-year-old son of a Tokyo policeman, who died from an apparent self-inflicted dose of cyanide on December 15, 1968. Investigators noted that the youth had no alibi for the time of the holdup, and that he possessed extensive knowledge of police procedures, but no solid evidence against him was discovered, and the bank's money remained missing. Suicide is common in Japan—Great Britain's *Guardian* newspaper reported an average 100 per day, nationwide, in 2008—and so the teen's death could hardly count as proof of his involvement in a crime.

Japanese authorities mounted an epic investigation of the Nihon Shintaku Ginkō, fielding 170,000 officers to investigate 110,000 suspects, posting 780,000 sketches of the unknown bandit throughout the country. A friend of the original teenage suspect was arrested on unrelated charges in November 1975, shortly before Japan's seven-year statute of limitations expired, and while police found him in possession of unexplained funds, the subject refused to answer any questions and no charges were filed. Today, the bandit is legally immune both to criminal charges and civil lawsuits (the deadline for which expired in 1988), and while prevailing law permits him to sell his story of the heist for profit, no one has come forward to admit the crime.

NITRIBITT, Rosalie Marie Auguste   murder victim (1957)

A German native, born in Mendig on February 1, 1933, Rosalie Nitribitt was raised in poverty by her unmarried mother, with two younger half-sisters, until she was placed in foster care at age six. Five years later, one of her male "caretakers" raped her, a traumatic incident that seemingly propelled her toward a life of petty crime. Confined to a juvenile home as a teen, Nitribitt staged several escapes and finally settled in Frankfurt am Main, where she supported herself first as a waitress, then as a model and prostitute. She logged her first arrest for prostitution in 1951.

The final years of Nitribitt's career as a call girl coincided with West German's postwar "economic miracle" (*Wirtschaftswunder*) under Chancellor Konrad Adenauer and finance minister Ludwig Erhard. Nitribitt studied French and English to attract wealthier, more cosmopolitan clients, and earned enough money to purchase a new Mercedes Benz 190 SL in 1956. That same year found her ensconced in a luxurious apartment, spending an estimated 80,000 Deutschmarks ($63,300) by year's end.

On November 1, 1957, a friend found Nitribitt dead in her Frankfurt apartment. Postmortem tests revealed that she had been beaten and strangled three days earlier, by an assailant who remains unidentified. Nitribitt was buried in Düsseldorf, but Frankfurt police kept her severed head on display at their Kriminalmuseum until February 2008, when the grisly relic was finally reunited with her corpse.

Nitribitt's murder sparked a scandal that prefigured Great Britain's "Profumo Affair" of 1963, and police were accused of destroying critical evidence during the early days of their investigation, perhaps to protect some of Nitribitt's affluent clients. Nonetheless, her identified acquaintances included Fritz Gunter Sachs (a multimillionaire industrialist whose father was a colleague of Nazi leaders Hermann Göring and Heinrich Himmler during World War II) and Harald von Bohlen und Halbach (another millionaire, whose older brother, Alfried Krupp von Bohlen und Halbach, faced trial at Nuremberg in 1947 for using slave labor at his industrial plants).

The only suspect named in Nitribitt's slaying was businessman Heinz Pohlmann, a friend of the victim who admitted visiting her on October 29, 1957. Immediately after Nitribitt's death, Pohlmann appeared flush with cash, settling various debts and buying himself an expensive new car. Police questioned the source of his money and received contradictory answers. They charged Pohlmann with Nitribitt's slaying, but jurors acquitted him in July 1960, after his attorney argued that police had failed to chart the temperature in Nitribitt's apartment, thus rendering invalid any estimates of when she died.

Pohlmann later served time for embezzling funds from his workplace, then published a book about the Nitribitt case.

Conspiracy theorists suggest that unnamed wealthy culprits were responsible for Nitribitt's murder, or at least for suppressing evidence that might have identified her killer. In January 1966, another high-class prostitute, Helga Matura, was murdered in Frankfurt. Like Rosalie Nitribitt, Matura trolled for clients in a new Mercedes. And, again like Nitribitt, her case remains unsolved.

NIX, Tanya See RICHLAND, GEORGIA, MURDERS

NIXON, Charles See INDIANAPOLIS TAXI MURDERS

NIXON, Rita See NEW YORK CITY STRANGULATION MURDERS

NORMAN, Frank terrorist murder victim (1934)
The struggle of America's labor unions has been a long and bloody one, marked by strife and violence from the mid-19th century to the present day. In the early 1930s President Franklin Roosevelt's New Deal offered a glimmer of hope to labor organizers whose unions had been systematically persecuted for decades. Opponents of such "communistic" concepts as minimum wage and the eight-hour day included corporate management, many law enforcement officers, and private reactionary groups such as the American Legion and the Ku Klux Klan. In Florida, where battle lines had been drawn between wealthy citrus growers and the United Citrus Workers' Union (UCW), Klansmen pursued their endless campaign for "100-percent Americanism" by doubling as strikebreakers.

Frank Norman was an agent for the UCW in Polk County, operating from his home in Lakeland. The job was dangerous, made more so by Norman's outspoken belief that black and white workers should unite to obtain equal pay and fair treatment from the region's agribusiness moguls. Several UCW agents were kidnapped and flogged in Polk County and neighboring Orange County during 1933–34, but Norman persevered, campaigning for the union until his opponents agreed that he should be eliminated.

One night in 1934 three men appeared at Norman's door around dinnertime. One introduced himself as "Sheriff Chase" and named the others as his deputies. Chase told Norman that an unknown black man had been lynched at Haines City—no surprise in an era when Florida led the United States in lynchings per capita—and that a card bearing Norman's name had been found in the victim's pocket. Norman was asked to help identify the body, and he readily agreed. Norman's wife, already suspicious, wanted to accompany him, but Norman dissuaded her. Instead, he agreed to take dinner guest Ben Surrency along on the ride to Haines City, some 25 miles east of Lakeland. Surrency describes what happened next:

Mr. Norman stepped in the car in the rear seat; I followed in the middle. The supposed Mr. Chase got in with us in the back seat. As we drove off a possible one hundred yards from the house, Mr. Norman asked Mr. Chase to show his authority as he did not know whether he was the high sheriff or not. The man answered, "I am not Sheriff Chase, but a deputive [sic] from Highland City. It doesn't matter; the Negro has a card with your name and home address on it, and we want you to identify him so we can take him down for an inquest." Mr. Norman says, "Will you please stop about one hundred yards farther down the road so I can pick up another man, as he might be a help to identify the Negro?" The man says, "Sure," and turned on Ingram Avenue instead of following the Bartow Road according to Mr. Norman's instructions. I judge we drove forty yards when the car came to a sudden stop. The man sitting beside the driver covered Mr. Norman with a gun. Then he asked me my name. As I told him my name was Ben Surrency, he said, "Get out. I don't want you." I got out as I was told. Mr. Norman put up both his hands, asking the man what in the world does this mean. Mr. Norman was saying other words as I was rushed out of the car and I could not understand what he was saying. As I got on the street a gun fired. And an awful thumping noise was heard in the car. The supposed-to-be Sheriff Chase took me by the shoulder and faced me back home and told me not to look. Another car forty or fifty feet back of the car I just got out of and facing me stopped with their bright lights on. Both cars remained still until I had passed the second car some distance. Then they both sped on.

Frank Norman's corpse was never found, and while two grand juries heard evidence linking KKK "kleagle" (recruiter) Fred Bass to the murder, no indictments were returned. Nor was this the only unsolved disappearance of Florida's union-busting era. In May 1936 an anonymous vigilante boasted to the *New York Times* that he had helped conceal the bodies of a dozen union organizers in Florida's swamps and flooded phosphate mines.

O

OAKES, Sir Harry murder victim (1943)

A native of Sangerville, Maine, born to affluent parents on December 23, 1874, Harry Oakes was a daydreaming introvert who craved a life of storybook adventure in pursuit of gold. A graduate of Maine's exclusive Foxcroft Academy, Oakes enrolled as a teenager at Bowdoin College (in Brunswick, Maine) and later attended Syracuse Medical School. His studies could not compete with news of the Klondike gold strike, however, and Oakes left school in 1896 to pursue his lifelong dream.

His life, from that point onward, rivaled the fictional exploits of Alan Quartermain and Indiana Jones. While pursuing the Klondike mother lode, Oakes was shipwrecked on Alaska's coast, then captured and briefly imprisoned by Russians. Upon release, he spent more time prospecting in Alaska, then booked passage for Australia, working as a common deck hand to pay his way. Failing to strike it rich Down Under, Oakes tried his luck in New Zealand, then in California—where he nearly died of heat stroke in Death Valley. News of a strike at Swastika, Ontario, brought Oakes to Canada with only $2.65 in his pocket. There, he joined forces with Roza Brown, a Hungarian immigrant described in contemporary accounts as "strikingly ugly and smelly . . . followed everywhere by snarling dogs." Bankrolled by Brown, Oakes enlisted the four prophetically named Tough brothers and finally struck gold at Kirkland Lake, Ontario, in January 1912.

The partners were soon wealthy, but conflict with the Toughs prompted Oakes to sell out his share of the mine and launch new diggings of his own beneath Kirkland Lake itself. By 1918 Oakes's Lake Shore Mines ranked among the largest gold producers in the Western Hemisphere, banking an estimated $60,000 per day for its owner. Soon the richest man in Canada, Oakes built a mansion and a private golf course overlooking the site of his strike in 1919. Still, wanderlust consumed him, and in 1923 he embarked on a world cruise to seek new adventures. What he found, instead, was comely 24-year-old Eunice MacIntyre, en route to England from her native Australia. Despite great differences in age and temperament, the couple fell in love, became engaged, and married in Sydney, Australia, on June 30, 1923. Settling at Kirkland Lake, in a new mansion Oakes built for his bride, they produced three sons and two daughters.

While living in Canada, Oakes renounced his U.S. citizenship to become a Canadian citizen. Eunice did likewise, but Harry could never stay settled for long. In the 1930s, unhappy with Canada's rising taxes, Oakes moved his family to Nassau and became a Bahamian citizen. The move ushered in an unprecedented economic boom for Nassau, as Oakes bought half the island, building several large homes for himself, plus a hotel and beachfront golf course for tourists, launching a posh country club and creating his own airline as a matter of convenience. Gruff but generous, Oakes also donated thousands of pounds to relieve

Bahamian unemployment and built a new wing on the Nassau children's hospital. He provided transportation for his thousands of employees and furnished free milk to their children. In 1939 his efforts won Oakes a knighthood, bestowed by England's monarch.

By the time he was knighted, Sir Harry's list of Nassau neighbors and acquaintances included a mixed bag of the famous and notorious. The expatriate Duke of Windsor, once King Edward VIII of England, abandoned his throne in 1936 to wed an American commoner, Wallis Simpson. While serving as first Royal Governor and commander-in-chief of the Bahamas, Edward sympathized with Adolf Hitler's Nazi regime (and, some said, schemed with Berlin to replace his successor after World War II erupted in September 1939). Axel Wenner-Gren, a pro-Nazi Swedish industrialist schooled in Germany, reportedly provided Edward with more than $2 million to support the royal couple's extravagant lifestyle. Wenner-Gren's family occupied a Nassau estate dubbed Shangri-La, where he entertained the governor and Sir Harry at lavish parties (while under surveillance by British and U.S. intelligence agents). Harold Christie, Nassau's most prominent real estate broker, was a native Bahamian who made millions selling land to Harry Oakes. Commerce led to friendship, and Christie may have introduced Oakes to some of his other wealthy customers—including New York mobsters Meyer Lansky and Charles ("Lucky") Luciano. The mob saw Nassau's potential as a Caribbean gambling resort, although the plan would not be realized for another two decades.

Another recent arrival, 33-year-old Count Marie Alfred Fouquereaux de Marigny, was a wealthy native of Mauritius who preferred the nickname "Freddie." Yacht racing and romantic affairs were his two specialties, though Marigny also found time to increase his inherited fortune through land speculation and other Bahamian enterprises. While war raged in Europe and Asia, Marigny romanced Oakes's eldest daughter, 17-year-old Nancy. Soon after her 18th birthday, they eloped to New York and were secretly married. Sir Harry and his wife were shocked by the news, but they tried to make the best of their twice-divorced son-in-law. Marigny's womanizing reputation did not help, and Oakes was soon bitterly at odds with the philandering count.

Their quarrel ended abruptly in the predawn hours of July 8, 1943, when Sir Harry was brutally slain in his bedroom at home. Harry Christie had spent the night in an adjoining bedroom, and he discovered the grisly scene at 7:00 A.M. Christie found Sir Harry's bedroom ravaged by fire, with Oakes's bloody, half-charred corpse sprawled on the bed. Feathers from a gutted pillow covered the body, but Christie observed four wounds on the left side of Oakes's head. A lacquered Chinese screen near the bed was partially burned, smeared with blood, and a single bloody handprint marked the wall beside Sir Harry's bed. A sudden rainstorm overnight had stopped the bedroom fire from spreading, though Sir Harry's corpse and bed were doused with gasoline.

Christie telephoned his brother Frank and reported the murder. Frank Christie, in turn, summoned a doctor who pronounced Oakes dead. The Duke of Windsor imposed a press blackout and took personal charge of the case, bypassing the Bahamas Criminal Investigation Department to import a pair of homicide detectives from Miami. Those officers, 40-year-old Capt. James Barker and 50-year-old Capt. Edward Melchen, were widely regarded as two of America's leading fingerprint experts. Melchen had also served a tour of duty as the duke's personal bodyguard, before joining the Miami Police Department. In his summons, the duke reportedly told the Miami detectives he wished to "confirm the details of a suicide," and the resultant investigation went downhill from there.

Barker and Melchen arrived in Nassau on July 8 and examined the death scene, deciding from blood-flow patterns that Oakes had been lying facedown when he suffered the blows to his skull. Clearly, the death was not a suicide. Detectives Barker and Melchen somehow "forgot" their latent-fingerprint camera on leaving Miami, and they admitted various prominent locals to Sir Harry's mansion over the next two days, contaminating the crime scene as visitors handled various pieces evidence without restriction. The officers had only one witness, since Mrs. Oakes was in Maine, awaiting Sir Harry's arrival at another of their homes, while the couple's children were traveling around North America. Harold Christie, for his part, claimed to have heard nothing strange on the stormy night of the murder.

Thirty-six hours into the case, Barker and Melchen announced that a partial fingerprint from the Chinese screen in Oakes's bedroom belonged to Freddie de Marigny. The count was jailed pending trial for his father-in-law's murder, while furious islanders threatened his life. The duke mobilized the Nassau Fire Brigade to ward off potential lynch mobs, but no vigilante action occurred. Nancy de Marigny hired a private investigator, Raymond Schindler, to clear her husband's name, and Schindler recruited Professor Leonard Keeler (inventor of the polygraph) to assist in the case. On arrival at the Oakes estate, Schindler and Keeler found Nassau police scrubbing the walls of Sir Harry's bedroom, obliterating all forensic evidence. The bloody handprint, already gone, would never be identified. Detective Barker had taken photographs of the scene, including the handprint, but the negatives were "accidentally" destroyed by exposure to light at a developer's lab in Miami. Sir Harry's fingerprints were photographed, but there was nothing to compare them with after Bahamian police finished cleaning his bedroom.

Raymond Schindler suspected an official conspiracy behind Sir Harry's death, a theory buttressed by the discovery of a tap on his telephone line in Nassau. Schindler validated his suspicion of the tap by faking a call to arrange a secret meeting with a supposed informant. Hiding out at the faux meeting place, he watched as two carloads of policemen kept the date and scoured the scene in vain. Despite that evidence of powerful forces controlling the case, however, Schindler and Keeler never identified a suspect.

Count de Marigny's murder trial opened on October 18, 1943, before the Bahamian Supreme Court. Lawyer Godfrey Higgs led the defense team, after Windsor hired de Marigny's first choice—Sir Alfred Adderley—to prosecute the case. A 12-man jury, mostly working-class, was selected to pass judgment on the defendant. The proceedings featured a tour of Sir Harry's sanitized home, with testimony from Harold Christie describing the night of the murder. According to Christie, Oakes had entertained several guests, including a niece, on the night of July 7, 1943. Neighbors Charles and Dulcibelle Hubbard also attended the party, leaving around 11:00 P.M. Oakes and Christie had talked for another half hour, then retired to their respective rooms. After a solitary breakfast the next morning, Christie had found his friend murdered in bed.

On cross-examination, lawyer Higgs suggested that Christie might be to blame for the murder. Capt. Edward Sears, superintendent of the Bahamas Police Force, testified that he had seen Christie riding through downtown Nassau at midnight on July 7–8, in a station wagon driven by some unknown person. Sears believed the station wagon had come from the Nassau waterfront, where a night watchman had described a mysterious powerboat off-loading two unknown men on the night of July 7. Jurors never

heard that tale, however, since the witness drowned prior to commencement of de Marigny's trial.

Another missing witness, Lt. Colonel R. A. Erskine-Lindop, had been the Bahamian police commissioner when Oakes was murdered. Erskine-Lindop had refused to charge de Marigny with murder in July, whereupon the duke transferred him to Trinidad and kept him there throughout the trial, unavailable to testify. Eight years later, Erskine-Lindop told journalist Etienne Dupuch that "a suspect in the case broke down under his cross-examination." The officer refused to name the alleged slayer, but told Dupuch that he (or she) continued "to move about in high society" after de Marigny's trial.

Dr. Laurence Fitzmaurice, who performed Sir Harry's autopsy, testified that the victim's skull was cracked by a heavy blunt object with a "well defined edge" which left triangular wounds. A second physician, Dr. Hugh Quackenbush, was called for the defense. He estimated time of death between 2:00 and 5:00 A.M., noting that Sir Harry's mattress was still smoldering when he examined the body on the morning of July 8, 1943. Quackenbush also stated that various blisters he noted on Sir Harry's neck, chest, leg, and foot were probably formed prior to death, by some unknown cause (and not by the fire set to burn Oakes's corpse).

The Crown's key witnesses were Miami detectives Barker and Melchen, but their testimony raised suspicions of incompetence or worse. Barker claimed to have found de Marigny's fingerprint on July 9, but Melchen claimed his partner had not mentioned it until Sir Harry was buried on July 15; that testimony, in turn, contradicted Melchen's sworn statement at a preliminary hearing, when he claimed that he was unaware of the prints match to Count de Marigny before July 19 or 20. Melchen was also confused about de Marigny's first interview. His first claim, that he questioned de Marigny between 3:00 and 4:00 P.M. on July 9, was corroborated by two Bahamian cops—but it contradicted the report of a police lieutenant who swore de Marigny left the interview no later than 2:00 P.M. Melchen later admitted his "mistake" under oath, but could not explain why two local officers had endorsed his false statement.

Capt. Barker caused more trouble for the Crown when he described his method of preserving fingerprints. Instead of dusting the print with powder, photographing it, and then lifting it with cellophane tape—a process that preserves the latent print *in situ*—Barker had used a rubber gum to lift the print (thereby removing any trace of it from the original surface). Attorney Higgs charged that Barker had found no prints in the murder room at all, but that he had lifted de Marigny's fingerprint from a water glass after his police interrogation, then submitted it falsely as evidence from the crime scene. Barker's credibility was further damaged by a false statement under oath that he had fingerprinted all visitors to the death scene. He later confessed the lie in court and was unable to explain Capt. Melchen's memory of the long-delayed fingerprint identification. Jurors finally placed no credence in the prosecution's case. On November 12, 1943, they acquitted Count de Marigny, after deliberating for less than two hours.

So the question remains: If Freddie de Marigny did not kill Sir Harry Oakes, who did? Various theories—none proven by anything resembling hard evidence—have named the killer (or at least the conspiracy's ringleader) as the Duke of Windsor, Axel Wenner-Gren, and Harold Christie. Another scenario, supported by various true-crime writers, suggests a murder carried out by the Lansky-Luciano gambling syndicate. In that version Sir Harry emerges as a principled opponent of legalized gambling, a roadblock to mob construction of lavish casinos in Nassau. His removal is said to have paved the way for the Bahamas' present tourist industry.

And yet . . .

Although no evidence exists to cast Harry Oakes as a foe of big-league gambling, it seems on balance that his opposition (if any) would have been ineffective. Gambling was legally banned in the Bahamas after 1905, by the Lotteries and Gaming Act, but one thriving casino—the Bahamian Club—had operated openly (albeit illegally) since 1920. An amendment to the law in 1939 allowed the duke to exempt various establishments from the Lotteries and Gaming Act at his sole discretion, a loophole that could have legitimized mob casinos throughout the Bahamas. The duke resigned in 1945, before the end of his appointed term, yet no significant effort was made to legalize Bahamian casinos before the early 1960s. In that respect, Sir Harry's murder—if a mob "contract" it was—seems to have been a wasted effort.

OAKLAND, California "Torso" murders (1990–91)

In May 1991 spokesmen for the Oakland Police Department announced the possibility that an unknown serial killer might be responsible for the murders of two female victims in their city over the past seven months. Victim number one, an African American woman, was found on October 17, 1990, floating in the Oakland Estuary off the 4000 block of Seventh Street. The headless, limbless torso had been stuffed inside a burlap bag, together with a gray knit long-sleeved shirt. No "obvious cause" of death was discovered—i.e., no stab or gunshot wounds apparent on the torso—and the mystery was not resolved when one of the victim's legs washed ashore three weeks later. No trace of the woman's head, arms, or missing leg was ever found.

Seven months elapsed before the second "torso" victim, a red-haired Caucasian female, was found by a fisherman on May 15, 1991. The second torso occupied another burlap bag and was hauled from the estuary within 100 yards of the spot where her predecessor had been found in October. A blue-and-red sunburst tattoo on the victim's left shoulder identified her as 43-year-old Leslie Deneveu, variously described in media reports as "a Berkeley transient" and a resident of nearby Richmond, California.

Acknowledged similarities in the two homicides included "cleanly severed" heads and limbs, the placement of both torsos inside burlap sacks, discovery of both victims in close proximity to each other, placement of each body in the water a short time before it was found, and the absence of "definitive" fatal wounds on either corpse. A sharp knife or a fine-toothed saw was suspected as the instrument of dissection in both cases. Authorities further speculated that the Oakland crimes might be related to the discovery of a woman's severed leg in the Sacramento Delta on March 11, 1991, but no positive link has been proved to date. More than a decade after his last known crime, Oakland's predator is theoretically still at large.

O'BANNION, Charles Dion gangland murder victim (1924)

A Chicago native, born in 1892, "Deanie" O'Bannion led a strange double life in childhood, serving as an altar boy at Holy Name Cathedral while running the streets with tough hoodlums by night earning a reputation as a fearsome mugger and gang fighter who was not afraid to kill. O'Bannion served three months for robbery in 1909, and three more in 1911 for carrying a concealed weapon. More arrests followed, but he would never return to prison. As the Prohibition era dawned in 1920, O'Bannion was

Chicago's foremost Irish-American gangster, unofficial boss of the city's North Side.

O'Bannion's dual personality survived into adulthood. He was a loyal husband and father who shunned gangland's nightlife and preferred to stay home with his family—unless there was a liquor shipment to be hijacked or an enemy to be assassinated. His tenor singing voice moved hard men to tears, but Deanie was equally adept with the three pistols he carried in hidden pockets of his specially tailored suits. He shunned pimping on religious grounds but never flinched from theft or murder. Chicago police credited O'Bannion with 25 murders, but mob historian Carl Sifakis pegs the mobster's personal body count at a minimum of 60 killed. One of O'Bannion's favorite "jokes" was to take an intended victim out target shooting and hand the mark a shotgun whose barrels were packed with clay, then stand back and watch the gun explode in his patsy's face.

A lethal combination of greed and racism led O'Bannion and his North Siders into their last gang war, against the rival Italian bootlegging syndicate led by John Torrio and Alphonse (Scarface) Capone. While the Torrio-Capone gang imported contraband liquor and built massive breweries throughout Chicago, O'Bannion was content to steal shipments from his rivals, thus avoiding any capital outlay for trucks and equipment. When the inevitable shooting started, O'Bannion turned another profit from his floral shop, earning thousands of dollars for the elaborate wreaths displayed at underworld funerals—including those of Deanie's own victims.

O'Bannion's last practical joke was a trick he pulled on John Torrio in 1924. Deanie told Torrio that he was quitting the rackets and leaving Chicago, as soon as he could sell off one last batch of contraband for $500,000. Torrio took the bait and forked over the money, whereupon federal Prohibition agents rushed in to charge Torrio with violations of the Volstead Act's ban on alcoholic beverages. Torrio, enraged, withdrew whatever restraint he had previously exercised over homicidal Al Capone—but O'Bannion remained elusive, mocking his enemies at every opportunity.

Capone got his chance for revenge in November 1924, when Sicilian mobster Mike Merlo died unexpectedly of natural causes. O'Bannion's flower shop was swamped with orders for the funeral, and he thought nothing of it when three well-dressed Italian men entered the shop on November 9. One of them greeted Deanie with a handshake—and then held fast

to his gun hand while the other two drew pistols, shooting O'Bannion six times in the face, throat, and chest from point-blank range. Underworld rumors identified the hand-shaker as New York mobster FRANKIE YALE, especially imported by Capone to lead the murder team of triggermen Albert Anselmi and John Scalise, but no one was charged with the crime, and O'Bannion's slaying remains officially unsolved.

Deanie O'Bannion got an extravagant send-off, his casket swamped in flowers from friends and enemies alike, but his death did not resolve Capone's war with the North Side gang. EARL (HYMIE) WEISS was next in charge of the North Siders, and after his murder in 1926 command would pass to George (Bugs) Moran. North Side resistance to Capone lasted three more years, until Moran's top soldiers were finally eliminated in the ST. VALENTINE'S DAY MASSACRE. Gunmen Anselmi and Scalise, suspected of the latter crime as well, were subsequently murdered by Capone when they attempted to betray him. Scarface Al hosted a party in their honor on May 7, 1929, and there beat them to death with an Indian club.

"OCCULT murders" California (1972–75)

In February 1975 California's Department of Justice issued a confidential report stating that 14 unsolved murders in the past three years had been committed by a single man. Six victims had been found near Santa Rosa, in Sonoma County; five were found in San Francisco, with one each in Marysville, Monterey, and Redding. The murders were distinguished from a host of other unsolved homicides by similar disposal of the bodies and the killer's fondness for retaining souvenirs.

The chain of deaths began on February 4, 1972, when two 12-year-olds, Maureen Strong and Yvonne Weber, vanished on their way home from a Santa Rosa skating rink. Their skeletons were found on December 28 on an embankment near a country road in eastern Sonoma County. The killer had removed all clothing and a single gold earring from each victim.

On March 4, 1972, 19-year-old coed Kim Allen disappeared while hitchhiking in Santa Rosa. Her nude body, strangled with clothesline, was found in a nearby creek bed. There were superficial cuts on her chest, rope burns on her wrists and ankles. Once again, the victim's clothing and one gold earring were missing.

Thirteen-year-old Lori Jursa vanished from a Santa Rosa market on November 21, 1972. She was nude upon discovery three weeks later, and the cause of death was listed as a broken neck. Jursa still had wire loops in her earlobes, but her earrings were missing.

The killer shifted to San Francisco with spring, strangling Rosa Vasquez and dumping her nude corpse on May 29, 1973. Fifteen-year-old Yvonne Quilintang received similar treatment on June 9. Angela Thomas was found naked and smothered to death on July 2. Eleven days later, Nancy Gidley was snatched from a local motel and strangled, her nude body dumped in a high school parking lot.

The "occult" angle surfaced that same month, after Caroline Davis was kidnapped on July 15. A runaway from Shasta County, she was last seen thumbing rides on Highway 101 near Santa Rosa. Davis was found on July 31, poisoned with strychnine and dumped at the precise spot where victims Strong and Weber had been discovered seven months earlier. On the bank above her body, searchers found a strange design arranged from twigs, laid out to form two interlocking rectangles. An unnamed source described the crude sculpture as a "witchy" symbol understood to designate "the carrier of spirits."

On July 22, 1973, the nearly nude body of Nancy Feusi was found near Redding, California. Decomposition obscured the cause of death. On November 4 the scene shifted back to San Francisco with discovery of Laura O'Dell's nude, strangled corpse. Theresa Walsh, age 22, was hitching rides from Malibu to Garberville when she met her killer on December 22, 1973. Raped, hog-tied, and strangled, she was dumped near the spot where Kim Allen had been found in April 1972.

According to police, the same man next murdered Brenda Merchant at Marysville, stabbing her to death on February 1, 1974, discarding her semi-nude corpse beside a rural highway. On September 29 14-year-old Donna Braun was found floating in the Salinas River near Monterey, nude and strangled. And so, presumably, the murders ceased. (A 15th victim, inadvertently omitted from the government's report, was 20-year-old Jeannette Kamahele, a coed who disappeared while hitchhiking near Santa Rosa on April 25, 1972. Her skeletal remains were finally unearthed on July 6, 1979, hog-tied in a shallow grave within 100 yards of Lori Jursa's final resting place.

The "occult" theory's chief proponent was Sgt. Erwin Carlstedt of the Sonoma County Sheriff's Department. Impressed by the stick sculpture found with Caroline Davis's body, Carlstedt also found significance in victims being dumped along the east side of various roads. In support of his theory, Carlstedt told associates that seven women killed in Washington state between January and July 1974 had been kidnapped in the waning ("sacrificial") phase of the moon. The 1975 report suggested that the killer was "familiar with witchcraft or the occult, because of a witchcraft symbol found during the Caroline Davis case and the possible occult involvement in the missing females in the states of Oregon and Washington."

Unfortunately for the Carlstedt thesis, all the victims killed in Oregon were ultimately credited to serial killer Ted Bundy, while research in Bundy's movements cleared him of any involvement in the California crimes. Likewise, the reputed "witchcraft symbol" from the Davis crime scene proved to be a piece of childish art, constructed by a small boy on vacation in the likeness of the family's car and trailer.

Serial slayer Harvey Carignan has also been suggested as a suspect in the unsolved murders, based on a speeding ticket he collected in Solano County, east of Santa Rosa, on June 20, 1973. Again, no solid evidence exists linking Carignan to the crimes, and one week later he was claiming victims in faraway Minnesota, leading to his ultimate arrest in September 1974. Carignan was in jail when Donna Braun was murdered, and the other corpses showed no traces of Carignan's favored weapon, a claw hammer.

An intriguing theory published by Robert Graysmith in 1986 credits the elusive "ZODIAC" killer with these and many other unsolved California homicides. The point is moot, until such time as a solution is discovered. In the meantime, we can say only that one or more sadistic killers may be still at large within the Golden State. See also: "ASTROLOGICAL MURDERS"

OCHOA y Plácido, Digna murder victim (2001)

Digna Ochoa was born at Misantla, in the Mexican state of Veracruz, on May 15, 1964. She studied law in Jalapa and joined the Veracruz attorney general's office in 1986, but subsequently abandoned work as a prosecutor to become a leading human rights attorney who opposed the government's oppressive tactics against labor unions and dissenters. The transition cost her dearly, and would ultimately lead to her assassination.

On August 16, 1988, soon after telling relatives that she had found a "blacklist" of political and union activists at the state attorney general's office, Ochoa was kidnapped from Jalapa and held captive for several days. Upon her release, she named her abductors as state police officers and accused them of rape, but Veracruz authorities declined to investigate the charges.

Five years after her first abduction, in 1991, Ochoa took a break from politics and traveled to Texas, where she entered a convent operated by the Sisters of Charity of the Incarnate Word. She remained cloistered until 1999, but left the convent and returned to Mexico without taking vows as a nun. A short time later, in August 1999, Ochoa was kidnapped again, this time from Mexico City. Her abductors held her briefly in a car, then freed her, but a third kidnapping followed in October 1999. On that occasion, she was questioned overnight, then left bound beside an open canister of unidentified gas, which proved to be nonlethal.

Reluctant police finally investigated the October kidnapping, and while they were unable (or unwilling) to identify the thugs responsible, the Inter-American Human Rights Court recommended full-time official protection for Ochoa. Mexican authorities demurred, whereupon Ochoa moved to Washington, D.C., and subsequently received Amnesty International's Enduring Spirit Award, presented by Martin Sheen.

Ochoa returned to Mexico City in August 2001 and worked at a local human rights center, then opened her own legal office on October 16. Three days later, a client found her dead in the office, shot twice with a .22-caliber firearm. An unsigned note beside her body warned staffers at Mexico City's human rights center that they might face a similar fate. Police attempts to brand Ochoa's death a suicide were foiled by the fact that one shot had been fired into the left side of her head (she was right-handed), while another struck one of her legs. Authorities now classify the slaying as a homicide, but it remains officially unsolved.

O'DELL, Laura   See "Occult Murders"

O'HARA, Bridget   See "Jack the Stripper"

O'HARA, Ellen   See Good Samaritan Hospital Murders

OHLIG, Linda   See "Astrological Murders"

OKLAHOMA City dismemberment murders (1976–95)
Authorities in the Sooner State stop short of blaming a single killer for the murder and dismemberment of four women in downtown Oklahoma City, despite striking similarities in each case. Parts of the first "Jane Doe" victim were found near the state capitol building in 1976. Three more victims followed, all retrieved from the Stiles Circle–Lincoln Terrace neighborhood around Oklahoma City's medical center. The fourth victim was found in 1985, during construction of the Centennial Expressway, but none of the women has been identified to date. A possible fifth victim, described as Hispanic or Native American, was unearthed on April 22, 1995—minus head, hands, and feet—from a shallow grave 50 miles west of Oklahoma City. Investigators cite "similarities in the method of dismemberment" as a possible link to the other four murders, all of which remain unsolved today, their victims still unidentified.

OKLAHOMA City state fair murders (1981)
On September 26, 1981, two 13-year-old friends, Charlotte Kinsey and Cinda Pallett, phoned home to tell their parents that they had been offered work unloading stuffed animals for a midway arcade at the Oklahoma City fairgrounds. Neither girl came home that evening, and police assigned to track them down discovered witnesses who saw them with an unknown man that afternoon, before they disappeared. The search was still in progress three days later, when two more girls—16-year-olds Sheryl Vaughn and Susan Thompson—were reported missing. They left home together for the state fair on September 29 and promptly vanished; their car was found on Interstate Highway 40, east of town, keys still in the ignition, but no trace of the girls could be discovered.

On October 9, 1981, police in Greenville, Alabama, arrested a traveling carnival worker, 36-year-old Donald Michael Corey, on charges of kidnapping Charlotte Kinsey and Cinda Pallett. Returned to Oklahoma City on October 13, Corey was cleared of all charges six days later, when authorities verified that he had been in Texas on September 26. Embarrassed by the error, officers would say only that their suspect bore a "striking" resemblance to the innocent Corey.

Authorities later identified their prime suspect in the Kinsey-Pallett case as truck driver Royal Russell Long, named by two witnesses as the man who hired the missing girls to unload toys at the fairgrounds. Police confirmed that Long, a Wyoming resident, had been in Oklahoma City in September 1981, and they discovered that he had a history of sexual violence toward young women. Detectives traced the Pontiac Grand Prix sedan Long had rented while in Oklahoma, and they scoured it for forensic evidence. Human hairs found in the trunk were "consistent" with Cinda Pallett's, but no conclusive match was possible. Likewise, animal hairs from the Pontiac's trunk matched the kind of dogs and cat Pallett kept as pets, but no specific animal could be identified. A lock of hair from Long's Wyoming residence was "similar" to Charlotte Kinsey's, but forensic tests were inconclusive. Charges against Long in the Kinsey-Pallett case were dismissed without trial, and no evidence thus far connects him to the Vaughn-Thompson disappearances. None of the missing girls has been found, and the case remains officially open.

OLZEF, Susan   See "FRANKFORD SLASHER"

"OPERATION Enigma"   unsolved London murders (1987–94)

The probable existence of a new serial killer in London, England, was revealed on May 26, 1996, when British authorities announced the formation of a special task force, code-named "Operation Enigma," to review files on the unsolved murders of 200 women spanning the past decade. Specifically at issue were the deaths of nine victims, nearly all prostitutes, who were strangled or beaten to death between 1987 and 1994, their nude or semi-nude bodies discarded on open ground in or around London. Unspecified "common features" in the nine slayings suggested to police and journalists that the crimes may have been perpetrated by a single individual.

The murders date back to January 1987, when 27-year-old prostitute and drug addict Marina Monti was found strangled and beaten to death near Wormwood Scrubs Prison in west London. The next official victim in the series, from February 1991, was 22-year-old streetwalker Janine Downs, whose choked and battered corpse was found beneath a hedge along the Telford-to-Wolverhampton Road. Seven more murders would follow in similar style over the next three years, still unsolved when Operation Enigma was conceived.

As part of their effort to catch the elusive strangler, British authorities consulted "mindhunters" from the FBI's Behavioral Science Unit at Quantico, Virginia. One member of the team, Agent Richard Ault (now retired), told Scotland Yard that "from the general information, such an individual is likely to be personable and not stand out. He is able to blend in because he can approach and solicit victims." Ault and company pegged the British stalker as an "organized" serial killer, meaning that he planned crimes in advance and cleaned up afterward to eradicate clues, but their insight brought London detectives no closer to an arrest. Nearly a decade after creation of the task force, police have no suspect in hand, and some are reluctant even to link the nine similar murders. James Dickinson, assistant chief constable from Essex and coordinator of Operation Enigma, told reporters that his investigators "do not feel that there were sufficient grounds to link the nine murders." The killer (or killers), meanwhile, remains unidentified.

ORIGINAL Night Stalker   unknown serial killer (1980–86)

This California predator derives his media nickname from "Night Stalker" Richard Ramirez, a self-styled Satanist convicted and sentenced to death in 1989 for a series of 14 murders committed during 1984–85. As indicated by the "original" tag, some of the still-unknown slayer's crimes predated those committed by Ramirez, but the Original Night Stalker emulated—or, perhaps, inspired—Ramirez's technique of nocturnal home invasions.

The killer's first victims, Lyman and Charlene Smith, were found in their Ventura home on March 13, 1980. Both had been bound with cords from the drapes in their house, using distinctive "Chinese knots," then were beaten to death with a log from their fireplace. Charlene was raped before she died.

Five months later, on August 19, a second double murder was discovered at Dana Point, 106 miles from Ventura, in the "secure" gated community of Niguel Shores. Victims Keith and Patrice Harrington, a medical student and a nurse, were bludgeoned like the Smiths (with Patrice raped beforehand), but while they bore marks of binding on their wrists and ankles, their killer had removed the murder weapon and his ligatures. The Harringtons were newlyweds at the time of their slaying, married only three months earlier.

The stalker waited six months before his next crime, striking in Irvine, 94 miles from Ventura, on February 5, 1981. This time he claimed only a single victim: 28-year-old Manuela Witthuhn was married, but her husband was hospitalized at the time of her murder. As in previous crimes, Witthuhn was tied up, raped, and beaten to death, after which her slayer removed both her bonds and the murder weapon. He also stole a lamp and crystal paperweight, prompting investigators to surmise that the Original Night Stalker hoped to make his latest crime look like a bungled burglary. Police noted that Patrice Harrington had worked as a nurse in Irvine before she was slain, but no links between victims was found.

The killer's last known crime occurred in Irvine after a five-year hiatus. Eighteen-year-old Janelle Lisa Cruz was home alone on May 4, 1986, while her parents vacationed in Mexico, and it cost her life. As usual, the cause of death was blunt-force trauma, following rape. Janelle's father subsequently told police that his pipe wrench was missing, prompting speculation that it may have been the murder weapon.

While the Original Night Stalker's tally of victims officially stands at six, authorities announced in 2001 that DNA traces collected from three women slain during 1980–86 matched semen samples collected from living victims of the "East Area Rapist," an unidentified sexual predator blamed for 50 rapes in Sacramento and Contra Costa Counties between June 1976 and July 1979. According to police, the East Area Rapist initially attacked lone victims in middle-class neighborhoods, but later shifted to couples, binding his victims at gunpoint, then dragging the males into separate rooms before raping his female victims.

Some investigators also blame the Original Night Stalker for the GOLETA MURDERS, a series of home-invasion homicides that claimed four lives in Goleta, California, during 1979–81, but no DNA was found in those cases, and the link remains speculative. Sadly, California leads the United States—some say the world—in serial murders, and the case for the Goleta crimes remains unproved.

OTBERG, Lisa See GRAND RAPIDS, MICHIGAN, MURDERS

OUTLAW, Wyatt murder victim (1870)

A former slave in Alamance County, North Carolina, Wyatt Outlaw rose to local prominence after the Civil War, when "radical" Republicans in Congress sought to reform the archaic southern system and ensure basic civil rights for freedmen. As a GOP loyalist, Outlaw founded the county's Union League and served as its president; he was also elected to serve as a town councilman in Graham. Oddly, that situation did not alarm some white Democrats as much as may have been expected. One white councilman in Graham, while opposed to Wyatt's politics, called him "one of the most polite niggers you ever saw in your life. His deportment was quite gentlemanly. He bore a pretty fair character."

Such praise meant nothing to the terrorist Ku Klux Klan, however. On the night of February 26, 1870, an estimated 75 or 80 Klansmen—some reportedly drawn from neighboring Orange County—rode into Graham on horseback, howling and making "ungodly noises." Twenty of the raiders stormed Outlaw's house and dragged him to the town square, where he was hanged from a tree within 30 yards of the courthouse. On their way out of town, the lynchers stopped at Mayor William Albright's home and left a note on the front gate, threatening Albright with similar treatment. Outlaw's body was left hanging in the square until 11:00 A.M. the next day, while racist sheriff Albert Murray made no effort to pursue the killers. Two weeks later, a black witness to the lynching, one William Puryear, was kidnapped from home and murdered, his corpse found weighted with stones in a mill pond in April 1870.

Outlaw's lynching climaxed a year of Ku Klux Klan terrorism in North Carolina, including an estimated 100 nocturnal whippings in Alamance County alone. The arrogance of his slayers created a statewide uproar among Republicans, who demanded federal troops to restore order and punish the terrorists. "It may be sport to you," one local Republican wrote to Governor William Holden on March 14, 1870, "but it is death to us."

In fact, by the time that letter was written, Governor Holden had already acted. He declared a state of insurrection in Alamance County on March 7, 1870, and sent a detachment of 40 U.S. soldiers to keep the peace. It was a futile effort, outnumbered as they were by local white supremacists, frustrated by Sheriff Murray's inaction. Holden himself harbored no

A lynching like this one claimed the life of black Republican activist Wyatt Outlaw during Reconstruction. (Library of Congress)

illusions about the nature of political terrorism rampant in his state. Speaking from the editorial page of his own newspaper, the Raleigh *Daily Standard,* Holden warned Washington: "We tell the [federal] government that unless it means to allow all that was accomplished by the war to be undone, that it must crush out the Ku Klux and those who aid them, or hell will be a place of rest and peace compared with the South." Still, it was May 1870 before Congress passed a new law to punish Klan violence—and that legislation naturally applied only to crimes committed after its enactment.

In Alamance County, meanwhile, the troops established camps at Graham and Company Shops, protecting Republicans inside the town limits while night-riding Klansmen ruled the countryside. The soldiers lacked any law enforcement powers beyond assisting civil authorities in making arrests, and their time was wasted since Sheriff Murray arrested no

one. (Most of Outlaw's slayers had fled the county by then.) Under fire from his own state legislature, Governor Holden finally lifted the Alamance County insurrection decree in November 1870, but it was too late to save himself. Lawmakers impeached Holden that same month, and the state senate convicted him of exceeding his authority, expelling Holden from office on March 22, 1871.

Nine months later, Judge Albion Tourgee finally persuaded an Alamance County grand jury to indict 18 Klansmen on charges related to Wyatt Outlaw's murder. One of those charged was the KKK's county chief, Jacob Long, but the terrorists had no need to worry. None of them was ever brought to trial, and a general amnesty bill dismissed all charges in 1873. The Outlaw lynching is one of thousands throughout the American South, wherein authorities returned a mocking verdict of "death at the hands of persons unknown."

PAIVA, Nancy See New Bedford, Massachusetts, murders

PALLETT, Cinda See Oklahoma City state fair murders

PANKEY, Jamie See "Independence Avenue Killer"

PATENT, Helen See "Frankford Slasher"

PATTERSON, John See Nahanni Valley murders

PEART, Ruth See New Orleans murders

PEIPER, Joachim murder victim (1976)
German native Joachim "Jochen" Peiper was the son of a career army officer, born in Berlin on January 30, 1915. His father served in East Africa during World War I, and Peiper followed in the family's military tradition by joining the SS-Verfügungstruppe (Combat Support Group) in 1933. He was accepted into Heinrich Himmler's "honor guard," the Leibstandarte SS Adolf Hitler Regiment, in 1934, and attended the SS-Junkerschule (officer's training school) the following year. Peiper served as Himmler's personal adjutant from April 1938 to August 1941, except for a brief term of combat service in France during 1940.

Himmler regarded Peiper as a special friend and oversaw his rise through SS ranks. Peiper's combat assignments included duty on the eastern front, where he participated in the battles for Kharkiv and Kursk in 1943, followed by command of Kampfgruppe Peiper of the Leibstandarte division, assigned to General Josef "Sepp" Dietrich's Sixth SS Panzer Army in the Battle of the Bulge. During that campaign, units under Peiper's command perpetrated the Malmédy Massacre of December 17, 1944, machine-gunning 90 unarmed American prisoners of war.

Germany lost the Battle of the Bulge, but Peiper emerged from the campaign as a full colonel at age 29, proud holder of a Knight's Cross with Oak Leaves and Swords personally awarded by Hitler. Notwithstanding his supposed heroism, the Third Reich's collapse left Peiper in a precarious position, facing trial with Dietrich and 73 others in 1946 for the Malmédy Massacre. Seventy-three defendants were convicted, with Peiper and 42 others sentenced to hang, while 22 received life imprisonment, and the other eight drew terms of 10 to 20 years in prison.

A reinvestigation of the case in 1948 substantiated defense claims of physical abuse, including various defendants "kicked in the testicles beyond repair" by their Allied jailers, whereupon the death sentences were commuted to life imprisonment, then to time served, thereby releasing the accused from custody. Peiper was freed in December 1956, but still faced charges for the massacre of 45 civilians at Boves, Italy, in September 1943. That case evaporated in December 1968, when Germany's minister of justice declared that he could find no grounds for prosecution.

Thus absolved of any crimes committed as a warrior for the "master race," Peiper tempted fate by moving to France in 1972. He settled in Traves, Haute-Saône, where he earned a comfortable living by translating English-language military books into German. Frenchmen had not forgotten Hitler's occupation of their homeland, however. On June 14, 1976, unknown assailants firebombed Peiper's home in Traves, and he died in the flames. A communiqué from unnamed "Avengers" claimed credit for Peiper's slaying. No suspects were ever identified, but French authorities assume the bombers were either members of the wartime French Resistance or their relatives.

PEPITONE, Mike   See NEW ORLEANS "AXEMAN" MURDERS

PERM, Russia serial murders (1996)

Russian authorities have released few details in the case of an unidentified serial killer reported active in Perm, a hundred miles west of the Ural Mountains. On August 29, 1996, the city's police chief, Andrei Kamenev, told reporters, "It's true that we are looking for a killer who has already killed seven people. His latest victim was a woman who was raped and stabbed in an elevator." Even more alarming for local residents, that their local predator had run up his seven-victim body count in a mere three months. Unfortunately, tight-lipped officials have said nothing more about the case to Western reporters since the original announcement. Without official declarations that a suspect has been identified, tried, and convicted, the slayer is presumably still at large.

PERRETT, Ruth   See WILTSHIRE, ENGLAND, MURDERS

PERRY, Arlis murder victim (1974)

Saturday nights are often hectic on a college campus, and California's Stanford University is no exception. There are parties in the dorms and all-night keggers on Fraternity Row. For many students, alcohol replaces academics as the top priority on weekends, with a chance to lay the books aside and raise a little hell.

It did not work that way for Bruce and Arlis Perry, though. The 19-year-old newlyweds from Bismarck, North Dakota, marked their eight-week anniversary on Saturday, October 12, 1974, but they were not inclined to squander time on drunken merriment. For one thing, Bruce was barely getting settled in at Stanford's medical school; for another, Arlis was a gung-ho Christian fundamentalist, known to friends and family as a persistent missionary type. Husband and wife were both involved with Stanford's Fellowship of Christian Athletes, and Arlis was also a member of Young Life, a student evangelical society. On weekdays she worked as a receptionist for a Palo Alto law firm, helping to pay Bruce's bills.

At 11:30 that night, Arlis told her husband she was stepping out to mail some letters home. Bruce went along to keep her company, but they began to argue on the way back from the mailbox, bickering about whose fault it was that they had a flat tire on their car. It was a trivial dispute, but tempers flared as they were passing Stanford Memorial Church around 11:40 P.M., and Arlis told Bruce she wanted some time alone. Steaming, he walked the half-mile back to their quarters in Quillen Hall, reserved for married students.

Late-night worshipers remember Arlis entering the chapel around 11:50 A.M., and she was still there when the stragglers left at midnight closing time. Ten minutes later, security guard Steve Crawford checked the sanctuary, warned an empty room that it was time to go, then locked the outer doors behind him as he left. Back at Quillen Hall, Bruce Perry grew nervous. He walked back to the chapel at 12:15 and found it locked, no sign of Arlis on the premises, then went home to wait. So far, it had not occurred to him that Stanford had no mail pickup on Sunday; any urgency that Arlis felt to stretch her legs that night had nothing to do with a note to her parents in Bismarck.

The doubts would surface later.

At 3:00 A.M., Bruce telephoned campus security to report his wife missing. Officers were sent to check the church and found it locked, but they did not go inside. When Steve Crawford made his next scheduled stop at 5:30 A.M., he found the side door forced open from within. Cautiously, he stepped inside the church—and into a nightmare.

Arlis Perry lay beneath one of the pews, her head aimed toward the sanctuary's altar. She was nude from the waist down, her legs spread wide apart, blue jeans draped over her thighs upside-down to create a diamond pattern when viewed from above. Her blouse had been ripped open, and an altar candle was wedged between her breasts, held in place by folded arms. Another candle, 30 inches long, protruded from her genitals. Arlis had been choked and beaten, but the cause of death was an ice pick buried in her skull behind the left ear.

Police initially suspected Bruce of murdering his wife, but they cleared him after he passed a polygraph test. Back at the church, witnesses recalled a sandy-haired young man in his mid-twenties, casually dressed, about to enter the chapel as the late-night worshipers emerged. FBI technicians found a perfect palm print on the candle removed from Perry's vagina, but it matched none of the prints on file. If nothing else, at least it finally exonerated Bruce Perry—and 100 other suspects culled from local sex-offender lists.

Church spokesmen called the murder "ritualistic and satanic," while police clung to a "sex-nut" hypothesis. Meanwhile, Perry's coworkers at the law firm recalled a curious incident on October 11. Around noon that Friday, a young man with sandy-blond hair and "regular looks" turned up at the office, engaging Arlis Perry in a 15-minute conversation described by witnesses as "serious and intense." Employees had assumed the visitor was Perry's husband, but a glimpse of dark-haired Bruce proved otherwise.

Questions began to multiply around the case, while homicide investigators searched in vain for answers. Who was Perry's visitor the day before she died? Could she have planned to meet him and continue their discussion when she left her apartment on Saturday night, perhaps staging a fight to rid herself of Bruce when he tagged along unexpectedly? Was the blond man Perry's killer, or an innocent third party?

Two weeks later, on the eve of Halloween, the mystery moved east. In Bismarck someone stole a temporary marker from Perry's grave, no other trace of theft or vandalism found anywhere in the cemetery. When detectives started asking questions, they heard rumors of devil-worship in nearby Mandan, coupled with reports that Arlis had once visited the Satanists in an effort to save their souls.

There matters rested for almost four years, until convicted serial killer David (Son of Sam) Berkowitz smuggled a book on witchcraft out of his New York prison cell. Police lieutenant Terry Gardner received the book in Minot, North Dakota, on October 23, 1978, as an anonymous package shipped from Manhattan. Thumbing through the pages, Gardner found underlined passages dealing with the Process Church of Final Judgment. A message written in the margin read: "Arliss [sic] Perry, Hunted, Stalked And Slain. Followed to California. Stanford Univ."

Around the same time, police in Santa Clara, California, received an anonymous envelope postmarked from New Orleans, containing newspaper clippings on Berkowitz and the recent death of John Carr, an unindicted suspect in New York's "Son of Sam" murders. If anyone had taken time to check, as newsman Maury Terry later did, he would have found that Arlis Perry died on John Carr's birthday, also the birthday of late magician Aleister Crowley (the self-styled "Great Beast 666") and the anniversary of cult-killer Charles Manson's 1969 arrest in Southern California.

Kismet.

On October 25, 1978, David Berkowitz penned a letter from prison, reading in part:

Look, there are people out there who are animals. There are people who are a fearless lot. They HATE God! I'm not talking about common criminals. You know who I'm talking about.

There are people who will follow a "Chosen Lamb" throughout the ends of the earth. If they feel that this person is the "next one"—well, they have money. They have brains and hate.

They will even kill in a church. Do you think I am joking? Do you think I am just bending your ear? Well, do this—do this quickly (I'm serious):

Call the Santa Clara Sheriff's office (California). This is by Santa Clara University and close to Stanford University. Please ask one of the sheriffs who have been there since late '74 what happened to ARLISS [sic] PERRY. Remember the name: Arliss Perry!

Please don't let them give you the "Psychopathic Homicidal Maniac" line or something similar. They know how she was murdered. They cannot tell you who did it or why. It was NO sex crime, NO random murder.

Ask them where she was killed. Ask them how. Ask them how often she wandered into that building of gold, purple, and scarlet.

Please ask them for the autopsy report. Let the police provide you with everything—every little detail. Make them tell you what she went through. Don't let them skip one single perverted atrocity that was committed on her tiny, slender, little body. Let the Santa Clara police tell you all.

Oh, yeah, lastly (and this is important), make sure you ask them where she lived—I mean where she came from. Doing this will solve the whole case. Back in little, tiny B——. This is where the answer lies. The place (state) with the lowest crime rate of anywhere!

Two days later, another letter issued from Berkowitz's cell, hitting on the same theme. It included the following passage:

You know damn well that these Satanists cover their tracks pretty good. You are aware of their intelligence (businessmen, doctors, military personnel, professors, etc.). Cults, as you know, flourish around college campuses. They also flourish around military bases. Drugs flow all over these two places (universities and bases). Young servicemen and young college students are involved in sexual relations. So mix the two of them up. Put them near each other and what do you have? You've got a pretty wild, dedicated and nasty bunch of young, zealous, anti-establishment devil-worshipers. And what a deadly mix it is. My, my. Didn't Miss Perry wander around the Stanford Campus frequently? Well, start adding, kid. What have we got here?

In truth, police knew, Arlis Perry *was* in the habit of roaming Stanford's grounds, though the fact was never publicized. Neither had Berkowitz gained his accurate knowledge of the Stanford chapel's color scheme or Perry's "tiny, slender, little body" from four-year-old newspaper clippings. As Maury Terry pressed his investigation of the case, Berkowitz described a New York cult meeting in 1976 or 1977, where a satanic contract killer allegedly passed around photos of Perry and delivered "a detailed soliloquy directed at the victim, describing her annihilation." (Berkowitz later identified Perry's alleged killer as one William Mentzer, presently serving life without parole in California for the May 1983 contract murder of millionaire Roy Radin. Mentzer has declined to comment on the case, or on any of the several other homicides in which he is a suspect.)

Terry's search for proof in North Dakota turned up more than 40 witnesses, including undercover policemen, who spoke of a satanic cult operating in Bismarck and Mandan between 1971 and 1974. At one point the black-garbed cultists had rented quarters across the street from Arlis Perry's grandmother, and Perry's friends were "almost certain" that she had attended at least one cult meeting. On the day before Perry's funeral in Bismarck, some early passersby had spooked a black-caped stranger who seemed bent on breaking into the church.

Another aspect of the mystery, apparently confirming that the crime was planned in advance, dates back to late September 1974. On September 27, Arlis wrote to an old friend in Bismarck, trying to explain a recent breakdown in communication with the home front.

I had to laugh about your call to Bruce Perry. Mrs. Perry [Bruce's mother] made the same mistake. But the strange part of it is that his name is not only Bruce Perry but it is Bruce D. Perry, and not only that but it is Bruce Duncan Perry and he attends Stanford University, and he just got married this summer. One thing, his wife's name is not Arlis. Anyway, next time you get the urge to call the number is ——. This time I guarantee you'll get the right Bruce Perry.

In fact, there were *not* two Bruce Duncan Perrys at Stanford, or anywhere else in the state. Santa Clara police dismissed the event as meaningless, but others disagree. In 1980 Minot reporter Jack Graham was told by a local source that Arlis Perry's murder involved "someone registering at Stanford under a false name."

Bruce Perry, widowed, completed his medical studies and also earned his Ph.D. Today he is an internationally recognized authority on childhood trauma and post-traumatic stress disorder (PTSD). He serves as provincial medical director in children's mental health for the Alberta [Canada] Mental Health Board and is also the senior fellow of the Child Trauma Academy, based in Houston, Texas. A Web site of the Christian fundamentalist American Family Foundation also lists Dr. Perry as a member of that group "concerned about cults and psychological manipulation." The murder of his wife remains officially unsolved.

PERRY, Cora   See "WEST SIDE RAPIST"

PERTH, Australia serial murders (1996–97)

Authorities in Perth, Western Australia, describe the elusive serial killer blamed for slaying three local women as a "verbal, intelligent man who has been able to get the trust of his victims." The first to die, 18-year-old Sarah Spiers, vanished in January 1996 while visiting friends at the Continental Hotel and was never seen again. Twenty-three-year-old Jane Rimmer disappeared from the same affluent Claremont suburb six months later; she was found in July 1996, buried in a desert grave 25 miles from Perth. The third victim, 28-year-old Ciara Glennon, was last seen alive when she left the Continental Hotel on March 17, 1997. Her body was found three weeks later, in a shallow grave some 40 miles outside of town.

Police disclosed that all three victims were attractive blondes who attended the same private school. Evidence found at the grave sites led police to speculate that the killer washes his car after planting each corpse, presumably in an effort to remove trace evidence. Detective Paul Ferguson, in charge of the manhunt, suggested to reporters that the killer might be someone in authority, perhaps a policeman or a security guard. "These are not random attacks," Ferguson declared. "The person or persons responsible are very organized. The age and type of woman targeted show these attacks don't just happen anywhere, to anyone." Another theory popular with some investigators pegged the killer as a taxi driver, and while interrogation of Perth's 3,000 licensed cabbies produced no suspects, public announcement of the theory cut Perth's nocturnal taxi trade by some 40 percent in the wake of Ciara Glennon's murder.

In April 1998 authorities announced that they were "near arresting" Perth's elusive killer, noting that a "significant suspect" had recently been questioned and released. Detective Inspector David Caporn, in charge of a task force created to solve the murders, described the unnamed suspect as "a single male public servant," then qualified the optimistic announcement by saying that the man was only "one of a number of people" police had placed under surveillance. "This person remains to be a significant person of interest," Caporn told journalists. "However, he is not the only person being investigated that is currently significant in this inquiry."

In fact, despite the assistance of an unnamed "FBI-trained American police officer," West Australia investigators had still made no arrest by March 2000, when Caporn told reporters "there is no guarantee that the case will one day be solved." Backpedaling from the optimism of April 1998, Caporn speculated that Perth's killer may have claimed victims in other locales before the Spiers disappearance in 1996, but no evidence was produced to support that speculation. "The bottom line," Caporn told the press, "is I can never guarantee a resolution." The homicides in Perth remain unsolved.

PESCE, Linda   See "HONOLULU STRANGLER"

PETERSON, Stacy missing person (2007)

Illinois resident Stacy Cales was born on January 20, 1984. At age 20, she married Drew Walter Peterson, a police sergeant in Bolingbrook who was 30 years her senior. She legally adopted Peterson's two children from a previous union and bore two of her own: son Anthony in 2004 and daughter Lacy in 2005. She disappeared from home sometime on Sunday, October 28, 2007, and was officially reported missing the next day, after missing an appointment with her sister.

When questioned by police, Drew Peterson claimed that Stacy had phoned him at 9 P.M. on October 28, announcing that she had left him for another man and that he could retrieve her car from Bolingbrook's Clow International Airport. Relatives and detectives were skeptical, in light of Peterson's record as a four-time loser in wedlock. First wife, Carol Brown, divorced him for philandering and called Drew "overbearing," while second wife, Vicki, and her daughter claimed habitual domestic abuse during the couple's 10-year marriage. Third wife, Kathleen Savio, filed for divorce in 2002, claiming that Peterson was engaged in a romantic affair with "a young minor"—presumably Stacy Cales, age 18 at that time.

During 2002–04, Savio called police to her home a total of 18 times, accusing Drew Peterson of misdeeds ranging from late return of their children from court-ordered visitations to physical threats. On March 1, 2004—mere days before her divorce from Peterson was finalized—Savio drowned in a bathtub at her home. An inch-long gash on her head suggested a fall, but while Savio's relatives were suspicious, Stacy Peterson provided an alibi for her husband.

Cassandra Cales (center), sister of missing Stacy Peterson, leads a march to the home Stacy shared with her husband, former Bolingbrook, Illinois, police sergeant Drew Peterson in November 2007. (Scott Olson/Getty Images)

Forty-three months later, Stacy's disappearance prompted Savio's kin to reopen the case. On November 18, 2007, Savio's corpse was exhumed and reexamined by Dr. Michael Baden, former chief medical examiner for New York City, at the request of Savio's family and Fox News. Dr. Baden concluded that Savio drowned following a struggle, when her body was placed in the bathtub. While that autopsy's details remain unpublished, Illinois State Attorney James Glasgow told reporters that he considered Savio's death "a homicide staged to look like an accident." On February 21, 2008, Glasgow announced that an unnamed pathologist had formally labeled Savio's death a murder. Days later, the minister from Stacy Peterson's church, Rev. Neil Schori, reported that Stacy herself suspected Drew of killing Savio, adding that she lived in fear of her husband.

Drew Peterson retired from Bolingbrook's police department three days before ex-wife Kathleen's exhumation, on November 15, 2007. Meanwhile, investigation of Stacy's disappearance continued, with police and FBI agents collaborating on the case. Drew's stepbrother, Thomas Morphey, told authorities that he helped Drew transport a heavy blue plastic container which may have contained Stacy's corpse. A friend of Peterson's Rick Mims, acknowledged that he and Peterson had purchased three such containers from a cable company where they worked part-time in 2003, but the container has not been found and Peterson continues to deny any role in Stacy's disappearance.

Investigators ultimately served four separate search warrants on Drew Peterson's property, seizing his car, Stacy's car, and 11 guns. One of the weapons, an AR-15 assault rifle, had a barrel shorter than any permitted by Illinois law for civilian-owned firearms. In May 2008, Peterson was slapped with weapons charges that carried a potential sentence of five years in prison. He posted $75,000 bail and sought dismissal of the case on grounds that he, as a police officer, was legally entitled to own military-style firearms. A local judge rejected that plea on July 30, 2008, but the charges were dropped the following November 20, when prosecutors refused to hand over internal documents related to the case. Meanwhile, no trace of Stacy Peterson has yet been found.

Finally, Drew Peterson was arrested on May 8, 2009, and charged with killing his third wife, Kathleen Savio. Stacy's murder remains unsolved.

PETTINI, Stefania See "Monster of Florence"

PIIRAINEN, Holly Kristen murder victim (1993)
Holly Piirainen was born in Grafton, Massachusetts, on January 19, 1983. On August 5, 1993, while visiting her grandparents in Sturbridge, Holly vanished from a neighbor's home where she and her brother had gone to see some puppies. Searchers found one of her shoes beside the road, but 11 weeks elapsed before hunters found her remains near Brimfield.

Molly Anne Bish, a Massachusetts native seven months Holly's junior, wrote a letter to the Piirainen family before Holly's body was found, expressing hopes for Holly's safe return. Ironically, Bish herself was kidnapped and murdered on June 27, 2000, while working as a lifeguard at Comins Pond in Warren. Three years passed before her skeletal remains were found, five miles from her family's home, on June 9, 2003. That case, like the Piirainen slaying, remains officially unsolved today, although Molly's mother reported a suspicious man in a white van scouting Comins Pond the day before her daughter vanished. In August 2007, Magi Bish claimed that jail inmate Robert Burno Jr., held on unrelated charges, matched her composite sketch of the stalker from June 2000, but no charges have been filed in Molly's case or that of Holly Piirainen.

Some investigators think that the solution to both cases—and more—may lie with a different suspect. Serial slayer Lewis S. Lent Jr. stands convicted of killing two 12-year-old victims, one each in Massachusetts and New York, and is suspected in at least a half-dozen other child murders. Victim Jimmy Bernardo was snatched from Pittsfield, Massachusetts in October 1990 and found a month later, strangled and nude, with duct tape covering his eyes, in a forest near Newfield, New York. Sara Anne Wood vanished from Herkimer, New York in August 1993 and

remains missing today. Lent was captured in January 1994, when 12-year-old Rebecca Savarese escaped from his car in Pittsfield and alerted police.

Lent received a prison term of 17 to 22 years for the bungled Savarese kidnapping, then was sentenced to life without parole for the Bernardo slaying. He confessed to Sara Wood's murder and directed police to her alleged grave site, but that search proved fruitless and Lent subsequently recanted his confession. Lent pled not guilty to Wood's murder in June 1996, then changed his mind again in October, with a final guilty plea. In April 1997, he received a prison term of 25 years to life in New York, then returned to begin serving his life sentence in Massachusetts.

New York authorities also consider Lent their prime suspect in the July 1992 slaying of 15-year-old Sean Googin, killed while working at an inn near Cazenovia Lake, outside Syracuse. A time line of Lent's travels reveal that he lived in Florida (1967–82), New York (1983–86), and Massachusetts (1986–94), but investigation of unsolved child slayings from those jurisdictions have produced neither confessions nor conclusive evidence of Lent's involvement in additional crimes. While he remains a prime suspect in Holly Piirainen's murder, Lent's 1994 arrest negates suggestions that he also murdered Molly Bish.

"POMONA Strangler" California (1993–95)
African-American prostitutes were the chosen prey of an apparent serial killer who struck seven times around Pomona, in eastern Los Angeles County. The first four victims, killed in 1993, were all known streetwalkers who frequented "The Strip"—Holt Avenue—and police assume they met their killer on the job. Three more women were slain in near-identical circumstances during 1994 and 1995, while authorities remained clueless in the case. Federal Bureau of Investigation (FBI) agents visited Pomona in April 1994 to review the evidence and prepare a psychological profile of the elusive killer, but their efforts were wasted. To date, police still have no suspect in the case.

POOLE, Bryan See San Diego gay murders

POPPLETON, Kelly See Alameda County, California, murders

PORTLAND, Oregon serial murders (1983–84)
While the search for Seattle's "Green River Killer" was under way, police were briefly distracted by a series of murders in Portland, Oregon, 170 miles to the south. No link was ever demonstrated between Seattle's killer (later identified) and the Portland murderer who claimed at least four victims—all African-American streetwalkers—between March 1983 and April 1984.

The first to die, on March 23, 1983, was 24-year-old Essie Jackson, strangled to death by an unknown assailant, her nude body dumped on an embankment near Overlook Park. Four months later, on July 9, 20-year-old Tonja Harry was fished out of the Columbia River Slough, the cause of death recorded as asphyxiation. Angela Anderson, strangled to death at age 16, was found three days before Christmas in a vacant house. Nineteen-year-old Vickie Williams, stabbed repeatedly, was found in shrubbery near a Portland shopping mall on April 23, 1984.

Labor organizer Tom Mooney leaves prison after his pardon on charges that he staged the 1916 Preparedness Day bombing. Evidence proved that police framed Mooney. (Library of Congress)

One published source reported 11 victims in the Portland murder series, without identifying the other seven, and feminists were outraged when a local police lieutenant described murder as "an occupational hazard" for prostitutes. Additional reports claim that Portland authorities refused to cooperate with detectives from the Green River task force, stubbornly withholding the names of two murder suspects. Whether from negligence or plain bad luck, Portland police are still without a solid lead to the elusive killer, some two decades after he retired from the hunt—or moved on to find another killing ground.

POST, Edith See RIVERDELL HOSPITAL MURDERS

POTDEVIN, Ruth See MANHATTAN AXE MURDERS

POWERS, Phil See NAHANNI VALLEY MURDERS

PREPAREDNESS Day bombing terrorist attack (1916)
The outbreak of World War I in Europe left citizens of the United States deeply divided. Many chose an isolationist position, declaring that the war was none of America's business and that European "entanglements" would lead the country to ruin. Others, mainly Socialists and other leftists, opposed U.S. involvement on grounds that the war was a capitalist struggle, with the major powers on both sides committed to oppression and exploitation of impoverished workers. President Woodrow Wilson seemed to favor the isolationist stance, campaigning for reelection in 1916 on the slogan "He Kept Us Out of War."

At the same time, however, other Americans called for U.S. intervention in Europe, or at least a heightened level of preparedness for war in case American interests were threatened more directly by the conflict. In San Francisco conservative business elements and the city's Chamber of Commerce organized a massive "patriotic" parade for Saturday, July 22, 1916, which they dubbed Preparedness Day. The announcement raised a predictable clamor from critics, including spokesmen for America's most prominent radical labor union, the Industrial Workers of the World (IWW). Populist presidential candidate William Jennings Bryan named the parade's organizers as profiteers who hoped for a financial killing if America entered the war. Several days before the parade, an unsigned pamphlet warned San Francisco: "We are going to use a little direct action on the 22nd to show that militarism can't be forced on us and our children without a violent protest."

The threat came at a time when San Francisco's conservative leaders were already engaged in near-guerrilla warfare with striking unionists. Between June 9 and July 17, 1916, two strikers were killed in the Bay City and 38 "scab" replacement workers were hospitalized in violent clashes. On June 22 the Chamber of Commerce publicly endorsed the "open shop" rule, which barred unions from organizing local workers. Just over two weeks later, on July 10, more than 2,000 San Francisco businessmen packed the Merchant's Exchange for a meeting that spawned a new Chamber of Commerce Law and Order Committee, funded to the tune of $1 million. Its primary goal: to rid San Francisco of "anarchist elements" by any means available.

The huge parade—52 bands and 51,239 marchers representing 2,134 different organizations—proceeded on schedule, beginning at 1:30 P.M. on the appointed day. It was barely under way, marchers drawing alternate cheers and hisses from spectators, when a powerful bomb exploded on the west side of Steuart Street, just south of Market Street, at 2:06 P.M. Ten persons were killed instantly, with 40 more wounded in what remains the Bay City's worst-ever act of domestic terrorism. The parade went on, lasting three and a half hours, but the search for the bombers—or for scapegoats—began at the instant of the blast.

Eyewitnesses to the event initially described a pair of dark-skinned men, "probably Mexicans," lugging a heavy suitcase near the site where the bomb exploded. The Chamber of Commerce offered a $5,000 reward leading to arrest and conviction of the bombers, with other groups and individuals quickly boosting the total to $17,000. A *New York Times* editorial condemned the reward offer, calling it a "sweepstake for perjurors"—and that description proved to be prophetic.

On the evening of July 22 private investigator Martin Swanson paid a call on District Attorney Charles Fickert. The two men were acquaintances with much in common. Fickert had been elected in 1909, bankrolled with a secret $100,000 donation from United Railroads founder and president Pat-

rick Calhoun. At the time, Calhoun and two of his aides faced bribery charges in a corruption scandal that had already deposed San Francisco's mayor and ruined political boss Abe Ruef. Calhoun's investment was a wise one, though. Within days of Fickert's inauguration as D.A., all charges against the United Railroads leaders were dismissed.

Martin Swanson was cut from similar cloth, an agent of the Public Utilities Protective Bureau who worked as a strikebreaker for firms including Pacific Gas & Electric (PG&E), the Pacific Telephone and Telegraph Company, plus various other utilities and railroads. Earlier in 1916 Swanson had tried to frame labor leader Thomas Mooney (an active Socialist and leader of a strike against PG&E in 1914–15) for a bombing of PG&E power lines on San Bruno Mountain, south of San Francisco. The detective had offered $5,000 to Mooney's associates, seeking perjured testimony that would send Mooney to prison, but the offer was refused. Undaunted, Swanson kept Mooney and chief aide Warren Billings under constant surveillance, harassing them (with police assistance) at every opportunity.

Despite the eyewitness reports of two Mexican bombers, Swanson told Fickert that he believed Mooney and Billings had bombed the parade. Fickert cheerfully swallowed the story and placed Swanson on retainer. The next morning Swanson resigned his post at the Public Utilities Protective Bureau and went to work full-time on what had now become the Mooney-Billings case. San Francisco police cooperated by visiting the crime scene with fire hoses and washing away any evidence that might have pointed to alternative suspects.

As luck would have it, Mooney and wife, Rena, were vacationing at Montesano, Washington, when Swanson cut his deal with D.A. Fickert. Newspapers owned by right-wing mogul William Randolph Hearst put a spin the journey, claiming that Mooney had "fled the city" (neglecting to mention that he had purchased round-trip tickets at the time of his departure). Nevertheless, on learning he was wanted for the bombing, Mooney returned and surrendered to police. Also charged with the bombing, on July 26, were Rena Mooney, Warren Billings, and two more union organizers, Edward Nolan and Israel Weinberg.

Unfettered by illusions of due process, Swanson promptly undertook recruitment of false witnesses to convict the defendants. None of the original crime scene witnesses recognized the accused when Mooney and company stood in police lineups. Still undaunted, Swanson and Fickert found two new witnesses—Oregon cattleman Frank Oxman and unemployed waiter John McDonald—to testify for the state. Both swore that they had seen Mooney and Billings plant the lethal bomb at 1:50 P.M.; Oxman further testified that he'd seen Tom and Rena Mooney huddled in conversation with Billings a few minutes later, before the explosion. Thus fortified, Fickert and Swanson set out to prove their case in a series of sensational trials.

Warren Billings was the first to face a jury, with witnesses Oxman and McDonald ranged against him. Further damaged by his own prior history of statements that suggested a propensity for political violence, Billings was promptly convicted of second-degree murder and sentenced to life imprisonment. Tom Mooney was next, named as the mastermind of the crime, but his attorneys countered with a challenge to the city's system of jury selection. As explained to the press by lawyer Bourke Cockran, "each Superior Court Judge places in the box from which the trial jurors are drawn the names of such persons as he may think proper. In theory he is supposed to choose persons peculiarly well qualified to decide issues of fact. In actual practice he places in the box the names of men who ask to be selected. The practical result is that a jury panel is a collection of the lame, the halt, the blind, and the incapable, with a few exceptions, and these are well known to the District Attorney who is thus enabled to pick a jury of his own choice." In Mooney's case that meant selection of William MacNevin—a close friend of lead prosecutor Edward Cunha—as the jury's foreman. MacNevin's wife later admitted that MacNevin acted in collusion with the state throughout Mooney's trial.

It was rough going for Cunha and company, even so. Key witnesses Oxman and McDonald were exposed as liars when the defense produced a photograph taken on July 22, 1916, proving that Tom and Rena Mooney had been watching the parade more than a mile from the explosion site at 1:58 P.M. A large clock in the photo's background clearly showed the time, while heavy traffic on parade day meant the Mooneys could not have walked from the bomb site to the photograph's location within eight minutes or less. The snapshot should have meant instant acquittal, but with William MacNevin chairing a jury of conservative merchants and retirees, Mooney was

convicted and sentenced to die. (Rena Mooney and Israel Weinberg were subsequently acquitted, while Edward Norman's charges were dismissed without trial.)

In 1917, with American troops dying on French battlefields, petitions of protest sparked a federal interest in the Mooney-Billings case. Secretary of Labor William Bauchop Wilson (no relation to President Wilson) delegated Director of General Employment John Densmore to investigate the case on Washington's behalf. Densmore, in turn, arranged to hide a Dictaphone in Charles Fickert's private office, recording conversations that strongly suggested Mooney and Billings had been framed by the district attorney and Martin Swanson. Release of that recording, and subsequent publication of a transcript in the *San Francisco Call*, produced a national outcry for justice. President Wilson personally called on California governor William Stephens to review the case, and Mooney's death sentence was commuted to life imprisonment two weeks before his scheduled hanging at San Quentin Prison. Reacting to the news, Mooney fired off a letter to Governor Stephens, declaring, "I prefer a glorious death at the hands of my traducers, you included, to a living grave."

In November 1920 Detective Draper Hand of the San Francisco Police Department confessed to Mayor James Rolph that he had aided Fickert and Swanson in framing Tom Mooney. Aside from fabricating evidence, Hand also admitted finding a job for "witness" John McDonald, when McDonald threatened to air the truth of his perjured testimony in local newspapers. Mooney's lawyers found McDonald in January 1921, and he admitted lying under oath to convict their client. He *was* a witness to the bombing, McDonald insisted, but he never had a clear look at the two men who had left the deadly suitcase beside the parade route. Upon reporting the incident to D.A. Fickert, McDonald now claimed, he was urged to identify the faceless bombers as Mooney and Billings. In return for that false testimony, Fickert had promised, "I will see that you get the biggest slice of the reward." Two other witnesses, Earl Hatcher and Edgar Rigall, later testified that Frank Oxman was 200 miles away from San Francisco on the day of the bombing.

Despite publication of that exculpatory evidence, Governor Stephens refused to pardon Mooney and Billings. Protests against their unjust imprisonment soon spread to Europe. Still, vindication remained elusive, as the innocent defendants were stubbornly ignored by a series of Republican governors including Friend Richardson (1923–27), Clement Young (1927–31), James Rolph (1931–34), and Frank Merriam (1934–39). In 1937 a U.S. congressional delegation asked President Franklin Roosevelt to intercede in the case, but Roosevelt declined. The following year Senators James Murray and Jerry O'Connell introduced a resolution calling on Governor Merriam to pardon Mooney and Billings, but it had no effect.

In November 1938 Culbert Olson was elected as California's next governor—and the first Democrat to hold that office in 44 years. Soon after his 1939 inauguration, Olson ordered Mooney and Billings released from prison. Rena Mooney, on greeting her husband at San Quentin's gates, told reporters, "These twenty-two long years have been moth-eaten. Life to me has been something like a cloak. There is little left but the tatters."

The actual parade bombers were never identified. One theory blames the crime on leftist radicals led or influenced by Alexander Berkman and Emma Goldman, prominent anarchists who lived in San Francisco at the time and who published a newspaper titled *The Blast*. Both advocated violent action against capitalistic regimes, and Berkman had previously served 14 years in prison for the attempted murder of Carnegie Steel manager Henry Clay Frick. Three years after the Preparedness Day massacre, suspected of a role in 1919's ANARCHIST BOMBINGS, Berkman and Goldman were deported to the Soviet Union. An alternative theory, raised in light of the flagrant Fickert-Swanson frame-up, suggests that the bombing may have been plotted by right-wing agents provocateur with the express intent of framing leftist leaders.

PREVOT, Loletha See "SOUTHSIDE SLAYER"

PRIEST Murders United States (1982–89)

Francis Leslie Craven was a second-grade student at St. Mary's Catholic School in Lynn, Massachusetts, when he first voiced his desire to be a priest. Ordained two decades later, in 1963, he served first in Kokomo, Indiana, then spent six years as a chaplain in the U.S. Navy. Returning to civilian life in 1974, Father Craven was assigned to Holy Spirits Church in Tus-

caloosa, Alabama. Twelve years later, he transferred to St. William's parish in Guntersville, northeast of Birmingham, where he served as chaplain for the Marshall County Hospice and the Cursillo Ministry, a spiritual retreat serving 29 Alabama counties. By all accounts, Craven was well liked and respected by all who knew him, untainted by the financial and sexual scandals that have tarred so many clerics in recent years. In short, he seemed to be the proverbial man "without an enemy in the world."

On January 2, 1989, Father Craven flew from Birmingham to spend a week with friends in Fort Myers, Florida. He returned on Saturday, January 7, phoning ahead from a stopover in Atlanta to have a friend drop his van at the Birmingham airport. Craven's flight was on time, and he found the van waiting for him, loaded with expensive electronic gear that included a cellular phone, CB radio, and stereo system, along with two cameras. Shortly after 10:00 A.M. he called from the airport to thank his friend for delivering the van, along with a prayer book left in the van as a gift. Craven announced that he was driving back to Guntersville and hoped to arrive in time for Mass, at 11:00 A.M.

He never made it.

At the time he should have been in church, one of his friends in Florida received a call from Craven's mobile telephone. They had arranged a one-ring signal to confirm his safe arrival, and Craven's friend was understandably confused when the caller stayed on the line to chat. In retrospect, she would describe the call as "strange"—a man whose voice she did not recognize, introducing himself with unprecedented formality as "Father Craven," mispronouncing her name as he reported, "I got back to Birmingham without a hitch." Police later speculated that Craven was speaking in code, perhaps alerting his friend to the presence of an armed hitchhiker in the van, but the prospect seemed unlikely, since Craven was known to avoid picking up strangers.

The call to Florida was Craven's last known contact with a living soul. At 4:00 P.M. that Saturday a motorist near Tuscaloosa—60 miles southwest of Birmingham, in the opposite direction from Guntersville—noted a trash dump burning off Highway 69. A closer look revealed a human body on the smoking pyre, and police were summoned to investigate. By that time 30 hours overdue at home, Father Craven had been listed as a missing person, and his body was identified from dental charts on Sunday, January 8. An autopsy revealed brain damage and broken bones consistent with a brutal beating, but the medical examiner could not determine whether Craven was dead or alive when his killer set him on fire.

Investigators found a service station, roughly two miles from the burn site, where a clerk recalled a shaggy-haired white man, age 20 to 30 years, arriving on foot to purchase a gallon of gasoline on Saturday afternoon. The man was in a hurry, walking off without his change in the direction of the dump where Father Craven's corpse was found an hour later. Craven's burned-out van was found a week after the murder at Windam Springs, some 12 miles north of the spot where his body had been burned. Robbery was discounted as a motive in the slaying, after police found Craven's cameras and electrical gear inside the vehicle, all melted by the blaze. Devoid of clues or suspects, homicide detectives ran a check for similar crimes through the Federal Bureau of Investigation's (FBI) computer system in Washington, D.C., and were surprised to learn of three other Catholic priests murdered in similar circumstances since 1982.

Father Reynaldo Riviera, pastor of St. Francis Church in Santa Fe, New Mexico, had received a telephone call on August 7, 1982, asking him to perform last rites for a parishioner in tiny Waldo, near the eastern border of the San Felipe Indian Reservation. The caller, never publicly identified, offered to meet Father Riviera at a rest stop on Highway 301 and guide him from there to the home in question. An intensive search was launched when Riviera failed to return from his mission of mercy, and he was found on August 9, shot to death in the desert three miles from the highway rest stop. His car was subsequently found abandoned four miles from the murder scene, police reporting that they found no evidence of robbery or sexual activity that would explain the crime.

Two years later, a certain Father Carrigan, newly assigned to Sacred Heart Church in Ronan, Montana, vanished soon after arriving in town. After two days on the missing roster, Carrigan was found near Flathead Lake, some 10 miles north of Ronan, strangled with a wire coat hanger. Once again robbery was ruled out as a motive when police found $12,000 untouched in Carrigan's pocket. (The reason for his carrying so much cash presented yet another mystery.) As in the other priestly homicides, the victim's car was dumped nearby, in this

case five miles from the murder scene. Authorities declared that Father Carrigan had not been in Montana long enough to make a mortal enemy, and nothing in his background pointed to a likely suspect.

Another 28 months elapsed before the third slaying, this one in Oklahoma City. Sixty-six-year-old Father Richard Dogan was the founder of a local halfway house for alcoholics, funding the project through sale of his artwork and social events that had earned him a reputation as the "Bingo King" of Oklahoma City. The victim of a savage beating in his own apartment, Dogan had been dead two days before his landlord found the body. His Oldsmobile station wagon was missing, found stripped of tires and wheels beneath a nearby bridge. Police suspect that Dogan's killer left the car intact and that the tires were stolen later, since nothing was taken from Dogan's apartment and theft of well-worn tires made a dubious motive for murder.

Only the death of Father Craven, with its vague description of a suspect, offered any realistic prospect for solution after so much time had passed. As one detective told the press in Tuscaloosa, "What we need to know is where he was and what he was doing in the four hours from when he left the airport in Birmingham and when his body was burned on the trash pile. Someone someplace has the answer to that question. Someday we will learn who it is."

Perhaps, but as the investigation drags on through its second decade, Alabama investigators are no closer to an answer than they were in January 1989. As for the other brutal homicides of Catholic priests, while no official designation of a murder series has been made, authorities have speculated publicly on links between the several crimes. At present all remain unsolved, the killer (or killers) still at large.

PRINCE Georges Hospital Maryland murders (1984–85)
Jane Bolding was employed as a nurse at Prince Georges Hospital, in a Maryland suburb of Washington, D.C., for nine years before authorities became suspicious of her conduct on the job. For much of that time she worked the intensive care unit (ICU), tending patients in the direst extreme. Death is a daily fact of life in ICU, but during 1984 and early 1985 Bolding's patients died in startling numbers, many suffering from cardiac arrest. On March 9, 1985, she was relieved of duty pending an admin-

istrative probe of what officials called "a pattern of unsubstantiated but suspicious information relating to incidents in the intensive care unit."

The investigation yielded grim results. According to statistical analysis performed by the Centers for Disease Control in Atlanta, Bolding had been the attending nurse in 40 percent of all ICU deaths between January 1984 and March 1985. In concrete terms, she had witnessed the deaths of 57 patients; her next closest competitor on staff had lost only five patients during the same period, and none of the hospital's remaining 93 nurses had lost more than four. Additionally, Bolding was the nurse attending 65 percent of all Prince Georges patients who suffered cardiac arrest in ICU during the night shift.

On March 20, 1985, Bolding was charged with first-degree murder in the death of 70-year-old Elinor Dickerson, who died in ICU at 2:05 A.M. on September 29, 1984. According to police, their suspect confessed to injecting Dickerson with potassium, thereby inducing cardiac arrest in the name of "mercy." While Bolding was released on bond to stay with relatives, authorities announced that they were checking into other recent deaths. It was suggested that the final body count might run as high as 17.

Dismissed from her job on March 26, Bolding was encouraged when the prosecution's case appeared to fall apart two days later. The state's attorney for Prince Georges County reprimanded police for arresting Bolding and branded her confession insufficient to support a case at trial. The murder charge was dropped in May 1985, but detectives returned to the search with a vengeance, seizing 200 boxes of hospital records on May 31, scouring the files for information on 22 "suspicious" ICU deaths.

On December 16, 1986, a Maryland grand jury indicted Jane Bolding on three counts of murder and seven counts of assault with intent to kill. Deceased victims included Elinor Dickerson, Isadore Scheiber, and Martha Moore. Scheiber allegedly survived two potassium injections, on October 2 and 11, 1984, before a third injection killed him on October 12. Martha Moore was less hardy, surviving only one attack (on October 27, 1984) before a second injection finished her the next day. Patient Mary Morbeto reportedly survived a single injection in March 1984, while Gary Dodson weathered three consecutive attacks a year later, in the week before Bolding's suspension from duty.

After various delays, Jane Bolding's murder trial began in May 1988, with prosecutors dubbing her a "killing angel." Bolding waived her right to trial by jury, placing her fate in the hands of a judge who promptly declared her confession—obtained by police after 33 hours of grilling without an attorney—inadmissible as evidence. Deprived of the confession and lacking any witnesses, the prosecution had no case. On June 20, 1988, Bolding was acquitted on all counts. The case of the Prince Georges Hospital murders remains officially unsolved.

PRINCETON, New Jersey unsolved murders (1989)

On September 24, 1989, the *New York Times* announced that authorities in Mercer County, New Jersey, were seeking a possible serial killer blamed for the recent murders of two women at Princeton. According to the *Times* report, both unnamed victims died of multiple stab wounds, one killed on the campus of Princeton's Hun School, the other in a public parking lot. A third female victim had survived near-fatal stab wounds, presumably inflicted by the same assailant, with all three attacks occurring "in less than six months." Police had no suspects at the time and have repeatedly declined to answer any correspondence dealing with the case. From all appearances the Princeton homicides remain unsolved today.

"PROSTITUTE Hunter" Portuguese serial killer (1992–93)

While police in the Portuguese capital were stalking the elusive "LISBON RIPPER," yet another murderer of drug-addicted prostitutes appeared to complicate their work. Still unidentified today, Lisbon's second serial killer, dubbed the "Prostitute Hunter," claimed at least two victims between November 1992 and March 1993. Both victims were streetwalkers in their twenties, tortured with cigarette burns before they were beaten and strangled to death, their corpses stuffed contemptuously into garbage cans.

At first authorities believed the killings might have been committed by their local Ripper, trying out a new technique, but they soon decided that the trash-can murders were the work of a distinct and separate predator. As explained by psychiatrist Alves Gomes, consulted in both manhunts, "The methods are different, but both killers enjoy torturing and killing, and feel aggrandized by the terror they see in the eyes of their victims." Sadly, that psychological insight fell short of singling out a suspect, and the brutal crimes remain unsolved.

"PSICÓPATA" Costa Rican serial killer (1987–??)

In 1997 Costa Rican authorities announced that some 31 victims may have been murdered over the course of a decade, by an elusive slayer aptly dubbed *"El Psicópata"*—The Psychopath. Previous estimates had been more modest, pegging the killer's body count at 19 (including several missing persons now presumed dead), but frustrated police have added another dozen names to the list, all young men and women who vanished without a trace during 1996. Despite a plea for FBI assistance in profiling the killer, detectives in the Central American republic are no closer to their subject today, than when the string of grisly crimes began.

El Psicópata hunted, for the most part, in a rural area branded the "Triangle of Death," stretching from the southwestern quarter of Alejela to the eastern part of Cartago, a few miles east of the nation's capital at San José. Taking a cue from Italy's "MONSTER OF FLORENCE," the killer preyed on young lovers, creeping up on couples and shooting them with a large-caliber weapon, afterward mutilating the female victim's breasts and genitals. Occasional diversions from the pattern involved young women murdered alone, those crime scenes including evidence of postmortem sexual assault.

Police have drawn up several profiles of their unknown subject, all in vain. One theory blames the murders on a deranged ex-soldier or policeman, while another brands the killer as a child of wealthy stock, perhaps a politician's son or offspring of a mighty landlord. The crime spree's duration suggests a killer in his thirties or forties, and police believe he "could be" quite intelligent (presumably because they have not caught him yet). Some investigators believe that *El Psicópata* stalks and observes his chosen prey for several days before striking, but theories remain simply that in the absence of a viable suspect. At last report, no new crimes had been added to the list, nor had detectives managed to discover any worthwhile leads.

PURDY, Vicky See "HONOLULU STRANGLER"

PUTTOCK, Helen See "BIBLE JOHN"

Q

QUERIPEL, Stacey murder victim (1993)
Seven-year-old Stacey Queripel was found strangled on January 24, 1993, in a wooded area of South Hill Park, near her home at Bracknell, Berkshire, England. A preliminary examination of her corpse suggested that the child had accidentally choked herself by catching her green plastic necklace on a tree branch, while playing, but autopsy results demonstrated that she was a victim of deliberate ligature strangulation. Stacey's mother, 34-year-old Gilliane Queripel, was arrested for the murder after soil and pollen samples lifted from her shoes linked her to the sector of South Hill Park where Stacey's corpse was discovered.

Mrs. Queripel denied any part in Stacey's death. Speaking to her lawyer, she claimed that she was running a bath on the night of January 23, when she went to check on Stacey and Stacey's half sister Lynette. To her surprise, she found Stacey's bed empty except for her favorite teddy bear. After rousing her lodger and determining that Stacey was not in his room, Mrs. Queripel began a search but could find no trace of the missing child.

At the formal inquest, convened on June 16, 1994, Barry Queripel offered incriminating testimony against his ex-wife, proclaiming that she was unable to cope with two children. "On one occasion," he testified, "Gill told me that she got hold of Stacey by the neck and held her until she turned blue, until she realized what she was doing." Mrs. Queripel's lodger and several visiting friends recalled that on the night of January 23 Mrs. Queripel had told them the children were in bed and she was off to take a bath. Some thirty minutes later, she came to inform them that Stacey was missing—at which time they noted she had changed her clothing and had muddy feet. East Berkshire's coroner, Robert Wilson, ruled that the testimony and forensic evidence gathered so far failed to make a "100 percent tight case" against Gilliane Queripel. He returned a verdict of "unlawful killing" in Stacey's case, but released the only suspect with a statement that new evidence was needed to identify the killer. Thus far, no such evidence has been uncovered and the case remains open.

QUILINTANG, Yvonne See "Occult Murders"

QUINN, Zebb Wayne missing person (2000)
A resident of Asheville, North Carolina, born May 12, 1981, Zebb Quinn left his job at the local Wal-Mart, on Hendersonville Road, at 9:02 P.M. on Sunday, January 2, 2000. The store's external security cameras tracked him into the parking lot, where he met another young man, later identified as Robert Jason Owens. The pair engaged in a brief conversation, then proceeded to a Citgo gas station four blocks away, where another video camera captured their images at 9:14 P.M. Two minutes later, they left the station in separate vehicles, Owens driving

a Ford pickup truck, while Quinn drove his light blue Mazda Protégé, license number KXK-5057. A short time later, as recalled by witnesses, Quinn and Owens apparently stopped their respective vehicles on Long Shoals road. At least one passing motorist had the impression that the Ford and Mazda were involved in a minor traffic accident. Whatever the cause of the stop, it was the last recorded sighting of Zebb Quinn.

Asheville police suspect foul play in Quinn's disappearance, but thus far they have been unable to file charges, due to lack of solid evidence. Quinn's relatives point the finger of suspicion at Robert Owens, and authorities agree that his behavior in the case merits examination. Aside from the obvious fact that he was the last person known to have contact with Quinn, Owens is a target of suspicion on other grounds, as well. At 9:40 A.M. on Monday, January 3, Owens sought medical treatment for head injuries and a broken rib. When questioned by physicians, he claimed the injuries were suffered in a predawn auto accident on Long Shoals Road. One day later, on January 4, Owens telephoned Wal-Mart and told the manager that Zebb Quinn was too ill for work on that day.

Quinn's missing car was found on January 16, 2000, parked outside the Little Pigs Barbecue restaurant in Asheville. Police examined the vehicle but found no clues that lead them to Quinn or help them determine his fate. Quinn's family has posted a $15,000 reward for information leading to his discovery. The missing subject is described as a white male with blue eyes and light brown hair, five feet nine inches tall, weighing 165 pounds. Identifying marks include distinctive scars between the ring and middle fingers on both hands. Several Internet Web sites provide contact points for Quinn's family and the Asheville detectives in charge of his case.

R

RAILROAD Murders Sweden (1948)

An apparent case of serial murder was reported from Sweden during 1948, wherein five victims, seemingly chosen at random, were pushed from speeding trains at different points along the country's southern railroad network. According to police statements aired on November 29, 1948, the attacks occurred on five successive weekends. Four victims died from injuries sustained in their falls, the bodies recovered from trackside hours later; a fifth, prizefighter Carl Nilsson, survived but could recall no details of the incident that left him gravely injured. Police ruled out accidental falls and declared that they were looking for "a sadist," but his (or her) identity may only be surmised, since no suspect was ever identified or charged. The crimes apparently ceased after public announcement of their occurrence.

RAMSEY, JonBenét murder victim (1996)

At 5:52 A.M. on December 26, 1996, police in Boulder, Colorado, received an urgent summons to the home of millionaire software entrepreneur John Ramsey. His wife, Patricia, made the call, to report the abduction of their six-year-old daughter, JonBenét. A note had been found on one of the mansion's two staircases, Patsy Ramsey reported, indicating that the girl had been kidnapped for ransom. It read:

Mr. Ramsey,

Listen carefully! We are a group of individuals that represent a small foreign faction. We respect your bussiness but not the country that it serves. At this time we have your daughter in our posession. She is safe and unharmed and if you want her to see 1997, you must follow our instructions to the letter.

You will withdraw $118,000 from your account. $100,000 will be in $100 bills and the remaining $18,000 in $20 bills. Make sure that you bring an adequate size attache to the bank. When you get home you will put the money in a brown paper bag. I will call you between 8 and 10 am tomorrow to instruct you on delivery. The delivery will be exhausting so I advise you to be rested. If we monitor you getting the money early, we might call you early to arrange an earlier delivery of the money and hence a earlier ~~delivery~~ pick-up of your daughter.

Any deviation of my instructions will result in the immediate execution of your daughter. You will also be denied her remains for proper burial. The two gentlemen watching over your daughter do not particularly like you so I advise you not to provoke them. Speaking to anyone about your situation, such as Police, F.B.I., etc., will result in your daughter being beheaded. If we catch you talking to a stray dog, she dies. If you alert bank authorities, she dies. If the money is in any way marked or tampered with, she dies. You will be scanned for electronic devices and if any are found, she dies. You can try to deceive us but be warned that we are familiar with Law enforcement countermeasures and tactics. You stand a 99% chance of killing your daughter if you try to out smart us. Follow our instructions and you stand a

100% chance of getting her back. You and your family are under constant scrutiny as well as the authorities. Don't try to grow a brain John. You are not the only fat cat around so don't think that killing will be difficult. Don't underestimate us John. Use that good southern common sense of yours. It is up to you now John!

Victory!
S.B.T.C.

It was, as one analyst later remarked, "the *War and Peace* of ransom notes," peculiar for its length, the odd amount of money demanded, and the (perhaps unconscious) jumps from plural pronouns (*we* and *us*) to singular (*I* and *my*) used in reference to the author(s). Curiously, $118,000 was the amount of John Ramsey's corporate bonus for 1996. More peculiar still, it was determined that the note had been written on paper from a pad found in the Ramsey home, labeled with Patsy Ramsey's name, using one of several felt-tipped pens kept in the kitchen.

Soon after calling the police, the Ramseys telephoned two friends, Fleet White and John Fernie, summoning them to the house with their wives. Both couples rushed over, and thus began the nonstop process of contaminating and corrupting the crime scene. The Whites and Fernies were followed by a minister from the Ramseys' church, various patrolmen, detectives, crime scene technicians, and a pair of victim's advocates employed by the city. It was 10:45 A.M., nearly four hours after Patsy's call to police, before detectives sealed JonBenét's bedroom to preserve potential evidence.

In the meantime, around 10:00 A.M.—the kidnapper's deadline, which passed without a phone call—John Ramsey had gone downstairs to the basement, unaccompanied by police. There, he later claimed, he found a broken window standing open and closed it himself, then went upstairs and read some mail, without reporting his find to detectives. Police, for their part, had already scoured the house and would report no sign of forced entry through the various windows and doors. Officers did not object when JonBenét's brother, nine-year-old Burke, was removed from the house and taken to a neighbor's home.

At 1:00 P.M., ostensibly to keep John Ramsey occupied, Detective Linda Arndt asked Fleet White and John Fernie to take Ramsey on another tour of the house, checking for any personal items that might have been stolen. In the basement White noted the broken window and pointed it out to Ramsey, who replied, "Yeah, I broke that last summer." Again, no

mention was made of the window being found open that morning. Moments later, peering into an unfinished "wine room" previously checked by White, John Ramsey found his lifeless daughter lying on the floor, wrapped in a blanket, arms raised above her head, with a cord tied to her right wrist. She had been strangled with a similar piece of cord, left knotted around her neck, with the broken handle of a paintbrush (one of Patsy's) inserted to create a crude garrote.

Apparently stunned and grief-stricken, John Ramsey lifted JonBenét's corpse and carried it upstairs, thus destroying the probable scene of her murder. After placing the body beneath the family's Christmas tree, he told Detective Arndt, "It has to be an inside job."

Strange details were mounting up in the case. The crime was already unique—no other case in history reveals a murder victim *and* a ransom note together at the same crime scene—and police noticed striking peculiarities in the behavior of the grieving parents. First, when patrolmen arrived before dawn, in response to Patsy's panicked call, they found her in full makeup, with her hair immaculately styled. Patsy's story of discovering the ransom note changed from one telling to the next. First, she told police that she had checked on JonBenét at 5:45 A.M. and found the girl missing from bed, then discovered the note on the stairs; later, Patsy claimed to have found the note first on her way to the kitchen for coffee, and only then had she returned to check her daughter's bedroom. Both Ramseys insisted that their son, Burke, had slept through the discovery and phone call to police, but his voice was clearly audible on the 911 recording, asking from the background, "What did you find?" (His father had replied, "We're not talking to you.") A neighbor reported waking at 2:00 A.M. that Thursday to a chilling scream, but the Ramseys professed to hear nothing within their own house.

The autopsy on JonBenét confirmed death by ligature strangulation, but it also revealed a fracture on the right side of her skull and various lesser injuries. A pubic hair was recovered from the blanket swaddling her corpse, and vaginal abrasion suggested sexual assault. The victim's genital area had apparently been wiped, with several dark fibers recovered, and a scan with ultraviolet light revealed "possible" semen traces on her thighs. Unspecified "DNA material" was found beneath her fingernails and on her underwear.

The Ramseys had a lawyer in attendance by the evening of the 26th, and the effort—dubbed Team Ramsey by Boulder police—quickly expanded. On

December 27 Fleet White and his wife were questioned at home by a three-man team of lawyers and private investigators on the Ramsey payroll. In short order John and Patsy would be represented by separate attorneys, while Team Ramsey recruited public relations specialists and a retired FBI agent famous for profiling serial killers at large.

Before the Boulder investigation ground to a standstill, police interviewed 590 persons and cleared more than 100 suspects; they collected 1,058 pieces of physical evidence, submitting more than 500 for testing in various forensic laboratories; hair, blood, handwriting samples, and other bits of "nontestimonial" evidence were collected from 215 persons; detectives ran down leads in 17 states and two foreign countries. The file on JonBenét's case weighs in at some 30,000 pages—and still, a grand jury three years after the murder found insufficient evidence to name or charge her killer.

Part of the reason, some detectives alleged, was a soft-on-crime attitude in the local district attorney's office. Detective Steve Thomas charged that Boulder's D.A. forced police to "ask permission of the Ramseys" before proceeding with crucial steps of their investigation, and a column in the Boulder *Daily Camera* flayed local prosecutors for a "pattern of laziness, obfuscation and near pathological sympathy for suspects" in criminal cases.

At the same time, Boulder police themselves were not blameless in the abortive investigation. Contamination of the crime scene began within moments of Patsy Ramsey's first telephone call to authorities and continued for days afterward. On December 28 Patsy's sister from Georgia was allowed to enter the house to retrieve "funeral clothes" for John, Patsy, and Burke. In fact, she made at least six trips inside the Ramsey home, removing bags, boxes, and suitcases filled with potential evidence, the vaguely inventoried items including jewelry, credit cards and financial records, photo albums, passports, several of JonBenét's dresses, and various stuffed toys. The observation of one patrolman, advising detectives that "way more than funeral clothes" was vanishing before their very eyes, brought no coherent response from officers in charge of the case.

The evidence that remained was inconclusive, at best. A palm print lifted from the door of the room in which JonBenét's body was found has yet to be identified, but as of January 1998 Boulder police had failed to screen all their officers present at the scene, and the Ramseys say that "around two thousand visitors" had

toured their showcase home on various occasions. A footprint in mildew on the floor next to JonBenét's corpse was identified as the imprint of a Hi-Tec sports shoe, but the shoe itself could not be traced. A black flashlight discovered on the kitchen counter was likewise untraceable, though the Ramseys denied ownership. The donor of unspecified "DNA material" found on JonBenét was never identified, but detectives note that since the material was not blood, semen, or skin, it may be unrelated to the crime.

Within days, the Ramsey case became a media circus unsurpassed by anything seen in the LINDBERGH KIDNAPPING of 1932. Tabloid reporters engaged in wild speculation, offering a new (always unverified) "solution" to the case each week, toting up millions of sales with salacious gossip. JonBenét's involvement in preteen beauty pageants fueled speculation on motives ranging from pedophilia and child pornography to maternal jealousy run amok. Team Ramsey, meanwhile, did its share of grandstanding, granting interviews to CNN while stonewalling police, dispatching friends to plead the family's case on daytime television talk shows.

It is known, statistically, that some 92 percent of all children murdered at home are killed by a family member. Confronted with that knowledge and the scarcity of hard evidence to place unknown intruders in the house, Team Ramsey was compelled to offer up a suspect for examination. Fleet White was the first, labeled by Patsy's mother as "a wild man and a lunatic," while Ramsey friend Pam Griffin told *Vanity Fair,* "The man has a dark side." (Police disagreed, terming White a cooperative witness cleared of any suspicion in the case.) Suspect number two, an elderly neighbor who played Santa Claus at a party the Ramseys attended on Christmas Day, was likewise absolved by detectives. Two other innocent suspects filed libel suits after their names were linked to the murder. Finally, on May 11, 1997, Team Ramsey bought a full-page ad in the *Daily Camera,* seeking information on a nameless young man allegedly seen fraternizing with various Boulder children in late 1996.

Without a name or face to give the killer, John and Patsy turned to retired psychological profilers for help. Their first choice, a private firm composed of 18 former Federal Bureau of Investigation (FBI) and Secret Service analysts, refused to take their case. John Douglas, another retired G-man and best-selling author, later joined Team Ramsey and pronounced the parents innocent. "From what I've seen and experienced," Douglas told reporters, "I'd say they were not involved." Ex-agent Robert Ressler, once Douglas's boss in the FBI's Behavioral Science Unit, emphatically disagreed, describing the kidnap scenario as staged, pointing to "someone in the house" as JonBenét's killer. As an afterthought, Ressler also panned Douglas for his efforts, describing his one-time colleague as "a Hollywood kind of guy."

The Ramseys, in their published version of the case, profiled their daughter's slayer as a pedophile and psychopath, aged 25 to 35, either an ex-convict of someone who associates with hardened criminals. The numeral 118 and the letters "SBTC" would have "some significance to him," but it remains unexplained. They state correctly that the conscience of a psychopath "does not operate well, if at all," then seem to contradict themselves on the very next page, stating as fact that the killer "would have seemed agitated and emotionally upset" in the days after JonBenét's murder. (In fact, the exact opposite may well have been true.)

In the Ramsey scenario of JonBenét's death, the unknown killer entered their home while they enjoyed a party at the White residence on Christmas Day. His point of entry is unknown, untraceable. "Somehow," they say, the killer knew they would be gone "for a number of hours"—"Or perhaps he just knew we were gone and would return later." The original plan was a straightforward kidnap for ransom, the intruder "shrewd enough" to come without a ransom note and to prepare the unusually long, detailed message with materials found in the house, written "carefully and casually" before the family came home. After lights-out, he "probably" climbed the stairs to JonBenét's bedroom and "quite probably" shocked her unconscious with an electric stun gun. (No such weapon was found; the corpse bore no burns.) Instead of fleeing, then, the kidnapper was overcome by "an unexpected turn of events" and carried JonBenét to the basement, where he killed her during a sadistic sexual assault, leaving the corpse behind to cancel out his ransom note.

Celebrity pathologist Cyril Wecht suggested an alternative scenario in 1998. After reviewing the complete autopsy report Wecht concluded:

JonBenét had died during a sex game that went fatally wrong.... As the garrote was tightened—intentionally short of complete strangulation—the noose pinched the vagus nerve and shut down her cardio-pulmonary systems.... The perverse sexual pleasure of her abuser—apparently fueled by this sick torture of the victim—had

been the only goal.... Her death was accidental—probably a voluntary manslaughter under most criminal codes.

That accident, Wecht theorized, produced "a cover-up so violent that it was hard to imagine.... In a panic, amid a frantic search for a way to explain the child's unforeseen death, there had been a cold, cruel decision to hide the truth under the violence of a staged kidnapping and murder. To turn fatal sex abuse into failed abduction and a grisly killing, someone had delivered a vicious blow to the little head under those tinted blond locks."

Someone . . . but who?

Wecht and John Ramsey, poles apart in all other respects, both described JonBenét's murder identically as "an inside job." Boulder police have stated for the record that Burke Ramsey is not a suspect in his sister's death. Colorado Governor Bill Owens declined to appoint a special prosecutor for the case in 1999, but at the same time he accused the Ramseys of "hiding behind their attorneys." John and Patsy, meanwhile, staunchly proclaim their innocence. Profits from their memoir, published in 2000, go to the JonBenét Ramsey Children's Foundation, which "hopes to change the way America responds to the murder of a child."

Soon after the Ramseys published their book on the case, on August 4, 2000, one of their private investigators presented Boulder police with a pair of Hi-Tec boots, size 8½, which allegedly matched the mildew footprint found in the Ramseys' basement on December 26, 1996. The discovery was not announced until August 31, 2000, when Boulder police chief Mark Beckner told reporters, "If you look at them, they look pretty close. You really can't tell." But, he admitted, "We've had other boots that looked like they match as well." Beckner sent the boots for analysis by the Colorado Bureau of Investigation, and the rest is silence as of press time for this volume. Private detective Ollie Gray, from Colorado Springs, refused to name the owner of the boots or to describe the circumstances under which they were discovered.

A year later, on September 8, 2001, administrators of America Online in Dulles, Virginia, furnished police with the name of a subscriber whose Web site postings included a claim that he or she had witnessed JonBenét's murder. According to media reports, AOL customer "BnJazzy4ever45" posted a message on August 7, 2001, that read: "I feel so guilty for what I've. Done," the message read. "I was there when the whole thing occurred. I never wanted any part in it, but they said if I didn't help I would be killed as well. I was only 14 when this took place, so I went along with the whole plan." Detectives reportedly identified the author of the message with help from AOL, and while Boulder police spokesperson Jana Peterson declared, "We certainly would be thrilled if this turns out to be the answer to some of our questions," no further information on the lead has been forthcoming so far.

The sensational case took yet another strange twist in early 2003, when U.S. District Judge Julie Carnes of Atlanta dismissed a libel suit filed by a freelance journalist, whom the Ramseys named in their book as a possible murder suspect. In her decision, published on April 9, 2003, Judge Carnes opined that "the weight of the evidence is more consistent with a theory that an intruder murdered JonBenét than it is with a theory that Mrs. Ramsey did it." Boulder's new district attorney, Mary Keenan, seemed to agree with that judgment in a letter she wrote to Ramsey lawyer L. Lin Wood. Encouraged by the surprise turn of events, Wood told reporters, "I think this should be viewed as an exoneration of the Ramseys. It's a clear signal the investigation is not going to focus on John and Patsy Ramsey."

Still, there are no other viable suspects in the case to date, and Denver attorney Scott Robinson spoke for most legal analysts when he told the Associated Press, "With each passing week, let alone each passing month or year, statistically there's less of a chance a case will be solved."

Patsy Ramsey died from ovarian cancer on June 24, 2006, still under a cloud of tabloid suspicion in her daughter's death. That same month, Michael Tracey—a professor of journalism at the University of Colorado—contacted the Boulder District Attorney's office to report suspicious e-mails received from a correspondent whose address was December261996@yahoo.com—the date of JonBenét's death. Federal agents traced the e-mail address to Bangkok, Thailand, but they could not initially identify the sender. Subsequent letters sent to Tracey via regular mail directed authorities to a Bangkok post office box, whose owner was identified in August 2006 as John Mark Karr, a Georgia native born in 1964.

Police placed Karr under surveillance in Thailand, while they researched his background at home. They learned that Karr's mother—19 years his father's junior, divorced from Karr's father in 1973—thought son John was possessed by demons and built a pyre to burn him alive as an infant, resulting in her commitment to a Georgia psychiatric hospital. Karr lived with his grandparents in Alabama from age

12 onward, and graduated near the top of his high school class in 1983. A year later, at 19, he married a 13-year-old girl, but their marriage was annulled in 1985. In 1989, at 24, Karr married again—this time to his pregnant 16-year-old girlfriend. The couple's twins died soon after birth, in September 1989, but they produced three more children in 1990–93.

In March 1996, Karr started an alleged "world wide support organization for kids, teens and college students," declaring that "all my plans revolve around kids." In June 1997, Karr was licensed to operate a day-care center at his Alabama home, but that business failed and he moved his family westward, to California. Between December 2000 and April 2001, Karr also worked as a substitute teacher in Petaluma and surrounding towns. That career—and his second marriage—ended on April 13, when Karr was charged with five misdemeanor counts of possessing child pornography. Karr missed a court date for that case in December 2001, and his judge issued an arrest warrant which was still outstanding in August 2006.

Boulder authorities matched that warrant with one of their own on August 15, 2006, and Thai officials revoked Karr's tourist visa the following day. Jailed in Bangkok pending extradition, Karr staged a press conference and told reporters "I love JonBenét. I was with JonBenét when she died; she died accidentally." When vaguely asked if he was an innocent man, Karr replied, "No." Lieutenant General Suwat Tumrongsiskul of Thailand's Immigration Police expanded on that statement with claims that Karr had confessed attempting to kidnap JonBenét for ransom. Arriving in Los Angeles on August 20, Karr was formally arrested on suspicion of JonBenét's murder, then was transported to Boulder on August 24. Four days later, Colorado prosecutors announced that DNA evidence failed to place Karr at the murder scene, thereby scuttling their case. He was returned to California on September 12 to face trial on the child pornography charges, but police had lost his computer containing the lewd images, and that case was dismissed on October 5, 2006.

In short, despite all of its media furor, the "solution" to JonBenét's death was a bust.

Twenty-three months after John Karr's exoneration in Boulder, District Attorney Mary Lacy told reporters that new DNA tests suggest JonBenét Ramsey was slain by "an unexplained third party." Lacy released copies of a letter she had sent to John Ramsey, reading in part: "To the extent that we may have contributed in any way to the public perception that you might have been involved in this crime, I am deeply sorry." Surviving members of JonBenét's family are now officially absolved of participation in her murder, and the case remains unsolved.

RAWLINS, Wyoming rodeo murders (1974)

The Rawlins, Wyoming, rodeo murders occurred in July and August 1974, claiming four lives within the span of seven weeks. Unsolved despite intensive work by local law enforcement agencies, the crimes were similar enough in execution to suggest a serial killer at work, but three of the victims are still missing, thus precluding verification of a homicidal "signature" in the case.

The first two victims were 19-year-old friends, Carlene Brown of Rawlins and Christy Gross from Bowdle, South Dakota. They vanished together on Independence Day, while visiting the Little Britches Rodeo in Rawlins. Searchers had found no trace of the young women by August 4, 1974, when 15-year-old Debra Meyers was added to the missing-person list. Nineteen days later, on August 23, 10-year-old Jaylene Banker wandered away from friends at the Rawlins fairgrounds, while watching the Carbon County rodeo, and she was never seen again.

Nine years elapsed before the skeleton of Christy Gross was found on October 27, 1983, three miles south of Sinclair, Wyoming. Killed by two heavy blows to the skull, Gross was identified by means of dental charts and a ring found with her remains. Despite one author's attempt to link serial killer Ted Bundy to the case, no solid evidence exists connecting him or any other identifiable suspect to the homicides at Rawlins.

REAL, Patricia   See DETROIT MURDERS

REDDICK, Wanda Faye   See RICHLAND, GEORGIA, MURDERS

REDDISH, Latoia   See JESSUP, GEORGIA

REDDISH, Olympia   See JESSUP, GEORGIA

REDDISH, Tiffany   See JESSUP, GEORGIA

"REDHEAD Murders" presumed serial killings (1984–92?)

On April 24, 1985, Federal Bureau of Investigation (FBI) agents met with local detectives from various jurisdictions at a special conference held in Nashville, Tennessee. Their purpose: to coordinate investigation into homicides of female victims in a five-state area, committed between mid-September 1984 and early April 1985. (One media account referred to victims murdered since October 1983.) Although the victims were reported to have certain traits in common, leading homicide detectives to suspect their deaths may be related, none have been identified so far. In law enforcement parlance they are all "Jane Does." While one account refers to eight established victims, the only published list is limited to six. They range in age from roughly 18 years to 40; their hair color varies from strawberry blond to deep auburn, with every shade of red in between, suggesting a killer fascinated by redheads. All were strangled or suffocated, their bodies discarded near interstate highways forming a corridor of murder between Arkansas in the southwest and Pennsylvania in the northeast.

The first Jane Doe was found near Shereville, Arkansas, on September 16, 1984. Two days before Christmas a second corpse was found at Cumru Township, Pennsylvania. New Year's Day found number three near Jellico, Tennessee. A fourth victim was discovered near Hernando, Mississippi, on January 24, 1985. Two months later, on March 31, Ashland City, Tennessee, was the site of another gruesome find. The last "official" victim cited by the media was found on April 1, 1985, along Interstate Highway 75, near Corbin, Kentucky. Prior to the Nashville conference, a list of potential victims had included 12 Jane Does. With the meeting behind them, police felt secure in dropping the cases of four women killed at FORT WORTH, TEXAS between September 1984 and February 1985; another found beside Interstate 81 near Greenville, Tennessee, on April 14, 1985; and yet another found in Ohio on April 24, 1985.

Authorities were prematurely optimistic in March 1985, pinning their hopes on the testimony of a living victim. Linda Schacke had been choked unconscious with her own torn shirt and left for dead in a culvert beside Interstate Highway 40, near Cleveland, Tennessee. Details of the crime seemed to fit, and Schacke was able to pick her assailant from a police lineup. Truck driver Jerry Lee Johns was arrested on March 6, 1985, charged with felonious assault and aggravated kidnapping in Tennessee's Knox County, but he had airtight alibis for every other date in question from the murder spree.

To date, neither the Jane Doe redhead victims nor any viable suspect have been identified by authorities. A possible seventh victim—and the first one identified: 45-year-old Delia Trauernicht—was found in Giles County, Tennessee, on April 30, 1990, but her addition to the list gave investigators no new leads. Another 26 months passed before Tennessee authorities declared that ex-nun Vickie Sue Metzger, found strangled near Monteagle on June 11, 1992, was being listed as a victim in the redhead series. Police lieutenant Jerry Mayes, coordinator of Nashville's Crime Stoppers program, told reporters that he had compiled a list of 12 related murders in the case, but without suspects or evidence authorities can only speculate on the killer's identity and whereabouts.

REES, Gwynneth See "Jack the Stripper"

REHOREK, Melissa See "Highway Killer(s)" Canada

RELES, Abraham murder victim (1941)
Abe Reles was a son of Jewish immigrants from Eastern Europe, born in the Brownsville district of Brooklyn, New York, in 1906. Raised in poverty despite his hardworking parents' best efforts, he quit school after eighth grade and ran the streets with fellow juvenile delinquents, logging his first arrest (for theft of gum from a vending machine) at age 15. That charge earned him four months' confinement at a state-run "children's village" at Dobbs Ferry, which failed to reform him.

Upon release, Reles went home to Brownsville, where friends such as Martin "Bugsy" Goldstein and Harry "Pep" Strauss (a.k.a. "Pittsburgh Phil") had found employment as errand boys and muscle for older gangsters. The advent of Prohibition in 1920 transformed small-time hoodlums into millionaire bootleggers, and each would-be gang leader needed his own private army to defend saloons and liquor shipments, collect payoffs, and terrorize the competition. In short order, Reles became one of Brownsville's most feared assassins, nicknamed "Kid Twist" after a homicidal predecessor, mobster Max "Kid Twist" Zwerbach (1884–1908). Reles favored

ice picks, jammed into a victim's ear, but he was not averse to killing with guns, knives, garrotes, or bare hands.

Reles and Goldstein hit the big time when they went to work for the three Shapiro brothers, Brooklyn racketeers who specialized in liquor and gambling. Arrested on an errand for the brothers, Reles drew a two-year juvenile sentence and blamed the Shapiros for failing to spring him. Paroled once more, Reles retaliated against his ex-employers by organizing a rival gang with Goldstein and partner George DeFeo, allied with rising mob star Meyer Lansky. The youngsters set up gambling operations, served as loan sharks, and dabbled in labor racketeering until the Shapiros staged an ambush, wounding Reles and Goldstein. Reles enlisted gunmen Frank "Dasher" Abbandando and Harry "Happy" Maione, eventually killing all three Shapiros and taking over their rackets.

By 1929, gang warfare in New York and elsewhere had convinced visionary mobsters such as Lansky and Charles "Lucky" Luciano that the underworld should reorganize along corporate lines. Gangland's first national convention met that spring in Atlantic City, New Jersey, followed by others in Cleveland, New York City, and Chicago over the next three years. The result was a nationwide criminal network, complete with a team of professional killers that reporters nicknamed "Murder Incorporated." Led by labor racketeer Louis "Lepke" Buchalter, the syndicate army fielded expert assassins for "hits" nationwide, with Reles and his childhood cohorts ranked among the most notorious triggermen. Prosecutors subsequently credited the team—including Reles, Goldstein, Strauss, Maione, Abbandando, Louis Capone, Allie Tannenbaum, Seymour "Blue Jaw" Magoon, Charles "The Bug" Workman, Emanuel "Mendy" Weiss, and Vito "Chicken Head" Gurino—with hundreds of murders nationwide.

While most of those slayings remain officially unsolved, New York police linked Reles to one of his crimes in 1940. Fearing the electric chair at Sing Sing prison, Reles turned informant and provided testimony that sent Buchalter, Abbandando, Capone, Goldstein, Strauss, and Weiss to death row in his place. The next in line for prosecution was ALBERT ANASTASIA, Lepke's second in command and a future New York City Mafia boss. Anastasia's trial was scheduled to begin on November 12, 1941, but Reles would not make it to the witness stand.

Early that morning, Reles plunged from the window of his suite at Coney Island's Half Moon Hotel, where he was living under constant guard by six NYPD detectives. A crude rope made from knotted sheets hung from the open window, prompting a suggestion that Reles had tried to escape from custody. When knowledgeable critics scoffed at that claim, authorities offered an alternate version: Reles, they said, was an inveterate practical joker. Perhaps he planned to lower himself to another floor of the hotel, then reappear to surprise his custodians and enjoy a laugh at their expense. Sadly, he must have slipped and fallen to his death.

Twenty years later, speaking from Italian exile on the eve of his own death, Lucky Luciano told a different story to authors Martin Gosch and Richard Hammer. According to the former "Boss of Bosses," mobsters paid police $100,000 to ensure that Reles did not testify, whereupon Kid Twist's own guards pushed him out the window and set the stage to suggest an accident. Unnamed gangland sources also implicated one of Reles's guards—Detective Charles Burns—in the 1930 disappearance of Judge JOSEPH CRATER, but that claim remains unproved. Disappointed by the death of his star witness, which doomed the state's case against Anastasia, prosecutor Burton Turkus labeled Reles "the canary who sang but couldn't fly."

REMBERT, Betty   See DETROIT MURDERS

RHOADS, Dyke and Karen   murder victims (1986)

In the predawn hours of July 6, 1986, fire swept through the home of young newlyweds Dyke and Karen Rhoads, in Paris, Illinois. Firefighters found their corpses in the rubble, and while their deaths were initially presumed to be a tragic accident, forensic evidence soon changed that view. Arson investigators found that fires had been set at two different points in the house, while postmortem tests revealed that Dyke Rhoads had been stabbed 28 times, Karen 26 times. Most of the wounds measured six inches deep.

The vicious double murder stumped police for two months, until Karen's employer offered a $25,000 reward for information leading to solution of the case. A local alcoholic, Darrell Herrington, approached authorities to claim the bounty, saying that he knew the killers. First, he blamed two men

named "Ed" and "Jim," who proved untraceable. When that flimsy lead failed to reap a bonanza, Herrington tried a new tale. According to his second story, he had spent July 5 drinking with two friends, 41-year-old Herb Whitlock and 35-year-old Gordon Steidl, then accompanied them to the Rhoads home after nightfall. Herrington sat in the car, he said, while the others went inside. Hearing strange sounds from the house, Herrington used a credit card to open a locked door and looked inside, glimpsing the slaughtered victims.

Detectives soon learned that Whitlock and Steidl were part-time construction workers. On the side, Whitlock sold drugs, while Steidl had logged several assault convictions. The case seemed solid—until Herrington took a polygraph test and failed miserably.

Five more months elapsed before a replacement "witness," alcoholic drug-abuser Deborah Rienbolt, offered a new version of the Whitlock-Steidl homicide scenario. She told police that Whitlock borrowed a hunting knife from her in early July 1986, while muttering threats against Dyke and Karen Rhoads over a drug deal gone sour. On a whim, Rienbolt allegedly drove past the Rhoads home and saw Whitlock lurking outside. In a second interview, Rienbolt claimed that she had parked outside the house, heard screams, then rushed in to find Whitlock and Steidl standing over the bodies. A *third* statement claimed that Rienbolt witnessed the attacks in progress and assisted the slayers by holding Karen Rhoads down on the floor while they stabbed her. When Whitlock returned her knife, Rienbolt said, she had boiled it and scrubbed it clean of blood.

Despite her ever-changing testimony and the total lack of any physical evidence to support it, Rienbolt seemed to have impressed local police—specifically, with her description of a broken lamp in the victims' burned-out bedroom. They also kept Darrell Herrington as a supporting witness, using his garbled tales and Rienbolt's to indict Steidl and Whitlock for murder. Incredibly, two juries agreed the defendants were guilty, convicting them at separate trials in 1987. Steidl received a death sentence, while Whitlock was ordered to spend the rest of his life in prison.

After the trials, both Herrington and Rienbolt recanted their sworn testimony, then reaffirmed it. Not to be outdone, Rienbolt then recanted *again*, telling reporters that police had fed her the broken-lamp story. In 1996 she told private investigator Bill Clutter, "They would come up with, 'Well, there was a broken vase or broken lamp there.' And then I'd say 'Well, okay. So there was.'" Cutter noted that the inside of the broken lamp shows white in crime-scene photographs. If the lamp had shattered before the fire, as Rienbolt once said, it should have been covered with soot.

One observer who found the case strange was David Protess, a professor of journalism at Northwestern University in Evanston, Illinois. Protess assigned four of his students to investigate the case as a class project, little dreaming that their efforts would result in freedom for both convicted defendants.

The Northwestern students—Diane Haag, Greg Jonsson, Krista Larson, and Kirsten Searer—spent nine months on their project and uncovered four witnesses whom the police had overlooked or chosen to ignore. Darrell Herrington claimed the home invasion had occurred at midnight, but a surgeon-neighbor of the Rhoadses had been sitting outside his home at the time with a friend (a U.S. marshal), and neither had seen or heard anything strange.

Paris police had missed those witnesses, along with a local gas station attendant who worked on the night of the murders, selling 21 gallons of gasoline to a still-unknown man at 3:00 A.M. The stranger drove a car with Florida license plates and put the gas in seven three-gallon cans. One hour later, the Rhoads home was in flames.

Another neighbor of the Rhoadses told the students she had seen two strangers standing opposite the victims' home at 9:00 P.M. on the night of July 4. They caught her eye because both men wore long trench coats, despite the summer heat. "One of them was a big guy with blond hair," she said, "and the other guy was small-framed and looked like he had dark hair. They were just standing there looking toward Dyke and Karen's house." The following night, she saw the same men circling her block in a white car with Florida plates. "It would just go by, turn in front of Dyke and Karen's house, stop," she said. "And I seen them looking, you know? And then take off. They did this about 10 times, just, I mean, continuously. Why would anyone be doing that?"

As for motive, the students dismissed prosecution claims that Dyke and Karen were drug dealers caught in a soured transaction. Their $200 bank account failed to corroborate a gangland lifestyle, and Karen herself supplied another possible motive, having told family and friends that she had "seen something at work that had scared her." Specifically, while stand-

ing in the parking lot of the pet-food plant where she worked, Karen allegedly saw "large amounts of money" and a machine gun placed in a trunk marked for shipment to Chicago. A friend of Karen's told the students that she had been "very worried" in the days before her murder.

Further assistance came from Lieutenant Michael Callahan of the Illinois State Police, who reviewed the Rhoads files shortly before CBS television's *48 Hours* program aired a segment on the case. Callahan called the prosecution's case "by far the worst investigation I've ever seen"—a statement that prompted his transfer in 2003. Callahan filed suit against the ISP, claiming the transfer was a punitive measure designed to foil his investigation of the murders, and won his case in 2005, receiving a $360,000 settlement. Today, he says of the defendants, "It's my opinion that they were framed."

Local prosecutors adamantly disagreed, but the tide had turned against them. Gordon Steidl was released from prison in May 2004, nearly a year after a federal appellate court agreed that his murder conviction was "faulty." Herb Whitlock was belatedly liberated in January 2008. The Rhoads murders are, once again, officially unsolved.

RHODES, Robin   See NEW BEDFORD, MASSACHU-SETTS, MURDERS

RICHLAND, Georgia unsolved murders (1981–82)
On the night of March 28, 1982, 16-year-old Wanda Faye Reddick was dragged screaming from her bed by a kidnapper who had first crept through the family home in Richland, Georgia, removing light bulbs from their sockets in an effort to forestall pursuit. Her lifeless body was recovered six days later, in rural Stewart County. According to press reports at the time, Reddick's abduction and murder marked the third similar incident targeting local teenage girls in less than a year. Fourteen-year-old Tanya Nix and 17-year-old Marie Sellers had been killed in 1981, the slayer (or slayers) of all three girls still unknown at this writing.

RIFENDIFER, Wayne   See CASTRATION MURDERS

RIMMER, Jane   See PERTH, AUSTRALIA, MURDERS

RITTER, Brenda See WASHINGTON, PENNSYLVANIA, MURDERS

RITTER, Rosemarie See SAN DIEGO, CALIFORNIA, MURDERS

RIVERDELL Hospital murders New Jersey (1965–66)

In 1966, Bergen County authorities launched an investigation of nine suspicious deaths at Riverdell Hospital, a small osteopathic facility in Oradell, New Jersey. In each case patients were admitted to the hospital for surgery and died of unrelated causes, either before or after routine procedures. Despite the identification and trial of a suspect on murder charges, this intriguing case remains officially unsolved.

Seventy-three-year-old Carl Rohrbeck was the first to die, admitted for hernia surgery on December 12, 1965, and lost to a diagnosed "coronary occlusion" the next day. Four-year-old Nancy Savino was signed in for an appendectomy on March 19, 1966, her death on March 21 attributed to some "undetermined physiological reaction." Margaret Henderson, age 26, was admitted to Riverdell on April 22, 1966; she died the following day after successful exploratory surgery. On May 15, 62-year-old Edith Post was booked for surgery, lost two days later to undetermined causes. Sixty-four-year-old Ira Holster entered Riverdell for gall bladder surgery on July 12, 1966, dying without apparent cause on July 29. Frank Biggs complained of an ulcer when he was checked in on August 20, 1966; a week later, the 59-year-old patient was dead. Eighty-year-old Mary Muentener died on September 1, seven days after she was admitted for gallbladder surgery. Emma Arzt, age 70, was another gallbladder patient, admitted on September 18 and dead five days later. Thirty-six-year-old Eileen Shaw also lasted five days at Riverdell, dying on October 23 after a successful Cesarean section.

Hospital administrators opened their investigation on November 1, 1966, after a Riverdell surgeon found 18 vials of curare (most nearly empty) in the locker assigned to Dr. Mario Jascalevich. An Argentine immigrant, Jascalevich—dubbed "Dr. X" by the press—moved to the United States in 1955 and set up practice in New Jersey. Confronted with the vials of poison, he explained that he had been engaged in personal experiments on dogs. No motive was ascertained for homicide, and 10 years passed before

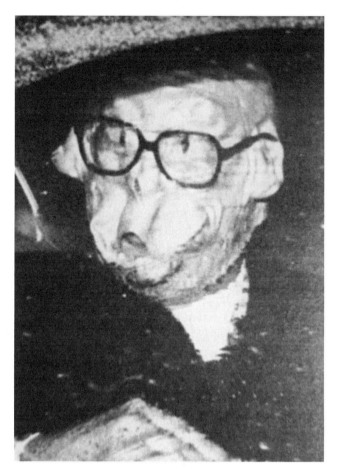

Dr. Mario Jascalevich arrives in disguise for his trial on charges of murdering patients with curare at New Jersey's Riverdell Hospital. Jurors found him not guilty. (Author's collection)

the state charged Dr. Jascalevich with five counts of murder in May 1976. Formally accused of killing patients Rohrbeck, Savino, Henderson, Biggs, and Arzt, the 39-year-old physician surrendered his medical license pending resolution of the case.

At trial in 1978, two of the murder counts were dismissed for lack of evidence. After 34 weeks of testimony, Dr. Jascalevich was acquitted by jurors on October 24 and returned to his native Argentina a short time later. He died there, of a cerebral hemorrhage, in September 1984. The case of the curare deaths at Riverdell Hospital remains officially unsolved today.

ROBERTS, Clarence killer/fugitive/victim (1970–80)

One of Indiana's strangest murder mysteries began on the afternoon of November 18, 1970, when fire swept through the four-car garage of Brown County resident Clarence Roberts, near the small town of Bean Blossom. Volunteer firefighters answered the call at 12:26 P.M. and fought the blaze until 4 A.M., when it was finally extinguished. Geneva Roberts and her son Loren returned from a pizza run to find their home and garage leveled, with no sign of Clarence. At 8:00 P.M., while raking through the ashes, police found a man's charred corpse in the garage. A shotgun lay across the body, while its arms and legs were nearly burned away, the skull shattered. Nearby lay a Masonic ring inscribed with Clarence Roberts's name.

Investigators learned that Roberts—once Brown County's sheriff, then a high-living businessman with numerous projects on tap—had been facing bankruptcy when the fire razed his property. Discovery of a $1 million life insurance police prompted Coroner Earl Bond, a longtime friend of Roberts, to suspect that Roberts may have sought to liquidate his debts through suicide. However, a pathologist from Indianapolis, Dr. James Benz, reported that the corpse found in Beam Blossom had no soot in its trachea or lungs, proof that death occurred before the fire. Dental records, blood typing, and a missing kidney subsequently confirmed that the dead man was not Clarence Roberts.

State police took a closer look at the crime scene, reporting discovery of suspicious holes in the exhaust system of Roberts's truck, found in the burned-out garage. They suspected, but could not prove, that Roberts had gassed some unknown look-alike in an attempt to stage his death for profit. Local witnesses seemed to support that theory, claiming that they had seen someone resembling Roberts "pick up" a drunken stranger at a liquor store in nearby Morgantown or Nashville (published reports differ). Detective Donald Kuster told reporters, "We have no idea of this man's identity, but we have at least 12 witnesses who saw him with Roberts." In 1972, one officer opined that the dead man was former Brown County resident John Kupse, but Kupse surfaced alive and well two years later.

In 1975, a Hoosier tourist reported that he had seen Roberts in Mexico City, but no proof was offered. Other sightings straggled in from time to time, including one from Fulton County, Indiana, where Roberts once had several business investments. Brown County's grand jury indicted Roberts for murder and kidnapping in December 1975, leaving his victim unnamed, but police were unable to serve the resulting arrest warrant. Geneva Roberts, meanwhile, insisted

that her husband was dead. She sued to collect his life insurance but lost that case in May 1979, when Judge James Dixon found no proof of Clarence's demise. At last, nearly penniless, Geneva was reduced to baking pies for a local restaurant, residing in a trailer six miles south of Nashville. Her appeal of Judge Dixon's ruling was rejected in October 1980.

One month later, on November 30, a fiery explosion consumed Geneva's trailer home on Highway 135. Firefighters doused the flames and this time found *two* corpses in the wreckage, both victims of smoke inhalation. Authorities quickly identified the female victim as Geneva Roberts, but her male companion required closer scrutiny. On December 4, 1980, a panel of three forensic pathologists confirmed that the dead man was, in fact, Clarence Roberts. Police classified the fatal fire as arson, set by "an unknown third party using an accelerant." The couple's four sons claimed Geneva's body for burial but refused to accept their father's, whereupon he was consigned to a pauper's grave outside Nashville.

The "second" death of Clarence Roberts remains an unsolved mystery, as does the identity of his 1970 victim. Police have no suspects in the 1980 arson, and have suggested no motive for the crime.

ROBERTS, Leona   See "ASTROLOGICAL MURDERS"

ROBERTS, Marilyn   See NEW BEDFORD, MASSACHUSETTS, MURDERS

ROBERTS, Nelson   See NEW YORK CITY GAY MURDERS

ROBILANT, Alvise de   See ITALY: GAY MURDERS

ROBINSON, Amanda   See NEWCASTLE, AUSTRALIA, MURDERS

ROBINSON, Jill   See "BABYSITTER"

ROCHESTER, New York unsolved murders (1989–92)
Grim memories of imprisoned serial killer Arthur Shawcross were revived around Rochester, New York,

in autumn 1992, when four women with criminal records for drug abuse and prostitution were found murdered in northwestern Monroe County, their bodies discarded within a few miles of one another. A November 1992 report in the *New York Times* claimed that corpses of 10 more women with similar backgrounds had been found "elsewhere" since 1989 (the year Shawcross was arrested), and that police were also searching for two unnamed streetwalkers listed as missing persons. An editorial in the Rochester *Times Union,* dated March 5, 1993, raised the body count to 16 prostitutes, still without providing any names.

Despite the eerie parallels with Shawcross and the apparent geographic link in at least four cases, Rochester police were understandably reluctant to admit the presence of a second serial killer in town. "We know what the public thinks out there," Sheriff Andrew Meloni told reporters, quickly adding that it would be "irresponsible" to speculate on any links between the crimes. Undersheriff Patrick O'Flynn, meanwhile, told the press, "We're definitely not working with one person. There are many similarities, but there are also many dissimilarities." And on that vague note, the story ends. One killer or several, Rochester authorities have seemingly made no progress in their investigation since November 1992. The case (or cases) of Rochester's murdered prostitutes remains unsolved today.

ROHRBECK, Carl   See RIVERDELL HOSPITAL MURDERS

ROMANO, Joseph   See NEW ORLEANS "AXEMAN" MURDERS

ROSANSKY, Patricia   See BATTLE CREEK, MICHIGAN, MURDERS

ROTHSTEIN, Arnold gangland murder victim (1928)
New York City's preeminent "fixer" of the early 20th century, Arnold Rothstein was a son of Jewish immigrants, born in 1882. He prospered in gambling and financial scams, becoming a multimillionaire in his early thirties, going on to become what historian Carl Sifakis has called "the spiritual father of American organized crime." Rothstein was a genius at

Gambler and "fixer" Arnold Rothstein was known to underworld confederates as "the Brain" or "the Big Bankroll." (Library of Congress)

manipulation and conciliation, teaching a new generation of up-and-coming gangsters that bribes were often preferable to bullets.

In 1919, Rothstein was the man behind major league baseball's most embarrassing moment, the World Series "Black Sox" scandal. That event, in turn, immortalized Rothstein in fiction, as Meyer Wolfsheim in *The Great Gatsby* and as Nathan Detroit in *Guys and Dolls.* Around Manhattan, Rothstein was more commonly known to his criminal cohorts as "Mr. Big," "The Brain," or simply "The Man Uptown." His gangland protégés, bankrolled (and often secretly directed) by Rothstein included the notorious likes of Dutch Schultz, Meyer Lansky, Lucky Luciano, Frank Costello, John Torrio, and JOHN ("LEGS") DIAMOND. Those who absorbed The Brain's wisdom inevitably prospered and enjoyed a kind of immunity from the law. In 6,902 liquor violation cases linked to Rothstein during Prohibition, charges were dismissed without trial in a startling 6,474, while the other defendants escaped with minimal punishment.

By the late 1920s, Rothstein and his pupils had branched out from gambling and bootlegging into labor racketeering, diamond smuggling, and narcotics trafficking. Some say the national crime syndicate forged by Lansky, Luciano, and others in the years 1929–32 was another concept hatched by The Brain, but Rothstein would not live to see his grandest scheme become reality.

In September 1928, Rothstein joined in an epic two-day poker game, losing a total of $320,000. It was startling enough for The Brain to lose at cards, but surprise turned to outrage when he welshed on the bet, proclaiming that the game was rigged. Two months later, on November 4, unknown gunmen shot and killed Rothstein at New York's Park Central Hotel. Suspicion focused on the recent game's big winners, California gamblers "Titanic" Thompson and "Nigger Nate" Devine, but neither was charged with the crime. An alternative scenario, aired by Sifakis, suggests that Rothstein may have been killed by one or more of his ambitious apprentices—Lansky, Luciano, et al.—who then went on to found and lead the national mob without him.

ROUX-BERGEVIN, Denis See MONTREAL CHILD MURDERS

RUSH, Susan See WASHINGTON, PENNSYLVANIA, MURDERS

S

ST. LOUIS, Missouri unsolved murders (1993)

On the afternoon of November 18, 1993, nine-year-old Angie Housman vanished on the one-block stroll between her school bus stop and home, in the St. Louis suburb of St. Ann, Missouri. A neighbor told police that she recalled seeing the girl pass by, alone and seemingly untroubled, but the rest was silence until a quail hunter found Housman's body nine days later and some 20 miles away, in a wooded section of the August A. Bush Wildlife Area. The child was nude when found, and while police sealed her autopsy report, official spokesmen granted that her death was "extremely violent."

One day less than two weeks later, on December 1, 1993, 10-year-old Cassidy Senter was reported missing from suburban Hazelwood, four miles north of St. Ann. She had gone to string Christmas lights at a friend's house, again within a block or so of home, but she never arrived. Cassidy's body, swaddled in a quilt and bedspread, was found in a St. Louis alley on December 9, with postmortem examination revealing that she had been beaten to death.

Police decided they were looking for a man— or *men,* although the likelihood of two child killers roaming north St. Louis in such close proximity seemed minimal—but they had nothing in the way of a description to help them in their search. Known pedophiles and sex offenders were interrogated, but the registered molesters all appeared to have firm alibis, leaving investigators at a loss for suspects.

Speaking to the press, Federal Bureau of Investigation (FBI) Agent James Nelson could only say, "We know we have a child killer. The community is very frightened, and they should be." On the basis of "extraordinary similarities" between the two murders and two failed abduction attempts, Nelson confirmed an official belief that the crimes were "the work of one person."

A further element of confusion was introduced with reports that police were seeking links between the two child murders and the beating death of 20-year-old Amy Bohn eight weeks before the Senter homicide. A waitress in Chesterfield, 10 miles west of St. Louis, Bohn had vanished after leaving work at 10:30 P.M. on October 4, 1993. Her half-naked body was found the next day in cornfield north of Hermann, Missouri, her head and hands tightly wrapped with electrician's tape.

The official lone-killer theory collapsed in early 1994, when police arrested 27-year-old Thomas L. Brooks Jr. for murdering Cassidy Senter. A two-time convicted felon who was paroled in August 1993, Brooks occupied a house located between Senter's home and the friend's home she set out to visit on the day she was killed. In custody, Brooks claimed that Cassidy knocked on his door, attempting to find one of his nephews (a story police rejected as false), and that he impulsively tried to rape her, beating the girl to death with a bed slat when she resisted. Convicted on charges of first-degree murder, kidnapping, attempted rape, and armed criminal action in September 1995, Brooks was sentenced to die. (His sister, 29-year-old Cassandra Quinn, received a two-year prison term for lying to detectives during their investigation of the murder.) On July 30, 2000, Brooks died in prison, reportedly from AIDS-related complications. The murders of Angie Housman and Amy Bohn, meanwhile, remain unsolved.

ST. VALENTINE'S Day Massacre (1929)

Prohibition-era Chicago earned (and perversely enjoyed) a reputation on par with such 19th-century Wild West shooting galleries as Tombstone, Arizona, and Dodge City, Kansas. Chicago's crime commission recorded 703 gangland murders within the city limits during Prohibition, while countless other victims disappeared on "one-way rides" or were slain in Chicago's suburbs. Even "Lucky" Luciano, boss of New York's Mafia, described Chicago in the 1920s as "a goddamn crazy place."

The heart of the problem was "Scarface" Al Capone and his endless war to suppress rival bootleggers. Capone killed numerous competitors, but his longest-running campaign involved the North Side gang initially run by Irish mobster DION O'BANNION. Following O'Bannion's murder in 1924, successor EARL (HYMIE) WEISS continued the war for another two years. After *his* ambush slaying, the mantle of North Side authority was inherited by George (Bugs) Moran, and the conflict dragged on. A horse thief in his younger days, Moran followed the O'Bannion-

The St. Valentine's Day Massacre of 1929 remains Chicago's most infamous unsolved crime. (Library of Congress)

Another view of the massacre victims, after police had removed two bodies. (Library of Congress)

Weiss tradition of hijacking Capone's liquor shipments at every opportunity. Finally, Capone took advantage of Moran's larcenous nature to set a trap that would wipe out the North Side gang's leadership once and for all.

The bait, according to most published accounts, was a shipment of Old Log Cabin whiskey, supposedly stolen from Capone en route to Chicago. Federal agents later claimed that an intermediary offered the load to Moran, and Bugs negotiated a mutually agreeable price. Delivery was scheduled for the morning of February 14, 1929—St. Valentine's Day—at Moran's primary warehouse on North Clark Street. Capone allegedly imported two members of Detroit's Purple Gang, unlikely to be recognized by local gangsters, to watch the garage from a nearby

apartment and telephone a waiting strike team when Moran arrived. Unfortunately, so the story goes, the spotters from Detroit had Moran's description but no photograph. Around 10:30 A.M. on D day, they marked the arrival of a man resembling Moran and made the fatal call.

As luck would have it, the visitor was actually Dr. Reinhard Schwimmer, a Chicago optometrist and "gangster groupie" who enjoyed spending time with the North Side crowd whenever possible. Lounging in the mob's garage that morning, Schwimmer found brothers Frank and Pete Gusenberg (Moran's top triggermen), Adam Meyer, James Clark, Al Weinshank, and John May (a mechanic who kept the gang's liquor trucks running). Moran had overslept and was running late to the meeting. As he approached on foot with two bodyguards, shortly before 11:00 A.M., Moran saw a police car stop in front of his garage. Fearing a routine bust, Bugs turned around and left—thus saving his own life.

Inside the garage Dr. Schwimmer and his companions were startled by the sudden appearance of two men dressed in police uniforms. The officers brandished weapons and ordered all present to line up against a brick wall. The North Siders offered no resistance, but they were reportedly negotiating a bribe when two or three other men entered the warehouse, dressed in civilian garb that included heavy overcoats. Before the victims recognized their peril, a storm of fire from .45-caliber Thompson submachine guns cut them down. Two of the dead or dying men were also blasted in the face at close range with a sawed-off shotgun.

A neighbor heard the gunfire, followed by the mournful howling of James May's German shepherd, and asked one of her tenants to investigate. The scout returned moments later to report a grisly scene, and authorities were promptly summoned. Inside the garage officers found six men dead and one clinging to life by a thread. Frank Gusenberg, leaking from a dozen wounds, survived for two hours but upheld the gangland code of silence. "Nobody shot me," he told detectives from his deathbed. "I ain't no copper." Bugs Moran, for his part, was less restrained. Questioned in the wake of the massacre, he told police, "Only Capone kills like that." (Scarface, insulted by the comment, advised reporters, "The only man who kills like that is Bugs Moran.")

An alternative theory was aired by Frederick Silloway, Chicago's Prohibition administrator, who told reporters soon after the slaughter:

> The murderers were not gangsters. They were Chicago policemen. I believe the killing was the aftermath to the hijacking of 500 cases of whiskey belonging to the Moran gang by five policemen six weeks ago on Indianapolis Boulevard. I expect to have the names of these five policemen in a short time. It is my theory that in trying to recover the liquor the Moran gang threatened to expose the policemen and the massacre was to prevent the exposure.

Silloway's "theory" produced a firestorm of official protest, and he changed his tune one day later, claiming he had been misquoted by the press. He was soon transferred out of Chicago and promptly vanished from the public eye. It is a measure of the Chi-

cago Police Department's pervasive corruption that the story of police complicity retains some currency today.

Fred Silloway aside, however, no one seriously questioned Capone's role as the mastermind of the St. Valentine's Day massacre, but making the case in court was a challenge. Capone was on vacation in Miami when the crime occurred; in fact, at the moment the guns went off on North Clark Street, he was "in conference" with Miami's chief prosecutor, an unimpeachable alibi witness. Closer to home, police arrested Capone's chief enforcer, "Machine Gun" Jack McGurn, on suspicion of leading the hit team, but McGurn's girlfriend (later his wife) supplied a bedroom alibi detectives couldn't crack, and McGurn was ultimately freed for lack of evidence.

As planned, the massacre effectively destroyed Moran's North Side gang, but it also backfired on Capone where he least expected it, in the ruling councils of the newly formed national crime syndicate. When the Mob held its first national "convention" in Atlantic City two months later, syndicate leaders from New York and New Jersey to Chicago, Cleveland, and Detroit agreed that Capone's endless warfare was bad for business. Big Al was ordered to adopt a more humble posture, starting with acceptance of a one-year jail sentence in Pennsylvania, on charges of carrying a concealed weapon. At the same time, unknown to Capone, President Herbert Hoover had sickened of the nonstop bloodshed in Chicago and ordered federal agents to find cause for jailing Capone by any means available. J. Edgar Hoover's Federal Bureau of Investigation (FBI) refused to participate, Hoover insisting (as he did for the next 30 years) that America harbored no organized crime, but Treasury agents Elmer Irey and Eliot Ness attacked the Capone syndicate on two fronts. Ness and his "Untouchables" raided Capone's breweries and distilleries, while Irey's accountants built a tax-evasion case that ultimately sent Capone to "The Rock" of Alcatraz. By the time Capone was paroled in 1939, tertiary syphilis had damaged his brain to the point that he spent his last years in gibbering delirium, dying in Florida on January 25, 1947.

Still the question lingers: Who pulled the trigger(s) on St. Valentine's Day 1929? No definitive answer is available, but circumstantial evidence allows us to identify some suspects.

One who boasted of participating in the slaughter was Fred Goetz, alias "Shotgun" George Ziegler, an Illinois native who served as an army pilot during World War I and later studied medicine at the University of Illinois. His scholastic efforts were interrupted in 1925, when Goetz was charged with attempting to rape a seven-year-old girl. As legal fees piled up, Goetz planned to rob a Chicago physician, but he killed his victim in the bungled holdup and fled empty-handed. Thereafter, Goetz lived "on the lam," reportedly serving as a Capone hitman on occasion, alternately robbing banks and kidnapping rich men for ransom as part of the notorious Barker-Karpis gang. In his declining years, brain addled by drugs and alcohol, Goetz often bragged that he had been one of the bogus policemen who lined the Clark Street victims up against the wall. Goetz also spoke freely of his activities with the Barker-Karpis gang, a habit which led to his still-unsolved murder in Cicero, Illinois, on March 21, 1934. (Alvin Karpis, in his self-exonerating memoirs, named the late Fred Barker as Goetz's assassin.)

Another underworld figure linked to the massacre was hitman and bank robber Fred (Killer) Burke. A Kansas native, born Thomas Camp in 1885, Burke grew up in St. Louis as part of the notorious Egan's Rats street gang and later admittedly worked for Al Capone as an occasional contract killer, credited with 20-odd murders. In December 1929, following a traffic altercation in St. Joseph, Michigan, Burke shot and killed Patrolman Charles Skelley. When officers raided Burke's home a short time later, they confiscated two submachine guns, one of which was linked through ballistics testing to the St. Valentine's Day massacre. Burke denied any role in the slaughter, and fellow stickup artist Harvey Bailey (another sometime associate of the Barker-Karpis mob) later claimed that he and Burke were boozing together in Calumet City, Illinois, when the murders occurred. Burke eluded arrest for Officer Skelley's murder until March 26, 1931, when he was captured near Green City, Missouri, (on a farm rented from relatives of Bailey). Burke was extradited to Michigan, where state authorities curiously barred Chicago police from questioning their prisoner. Sentenced to life imprisonment for Skelley's slaying, Burke died in custody on July 10, 1940.

Jack McGurn, presumed architect of the North Clark Street murders on Capone's behalf, was never charged or prosecuted for the crime. Retribution overtook him seven years after the fact, when unknown gunmen mowed him down in a Chicago bowling alley. The killers left a nickel in McGurn's right hand and placed a comic valentine card near his body. It read:

> You've lost your job,
> You've lost your dough,
> Your jewels and handsome houses.
> But things could be worse, you know.
> You haven't lost your trousers.

SAKAMOTO, Regina   See "HONOLULU STRANGLER"

SALAZAR, Luis   See SAN ANTONIO TAXI MURDERS

SALAZAR, Rita   See I-35 MURDERS

SALEM, Oregon unsolved murders (1981–83)

The Pacific Northwest produced a disproportionate number of serial killers in the latter half of the 20th century, and several have managed to escape detection, remaining at large despite the best efforts of state and local law enforcement. One such predator was active in the area of Salem, Oregon, from February 1981 through March 1983, claiming at least six lives in a two-year period.

The first known victim was 21-year-old Terry Monroe, reported missing after she left a Salem tavern to "get some air" on February 13, 1981, and never returned. Her body was discarded in the nearby Willamette River, recovered by searchers more than a month later.

Eighteen-year-old Sherry Eyerly was delivering pizzas in Salem on July 4, 1982, when she vanished en route to a caller's fictitious address. Her delivery van was found abandoned, but Eyerly's corpse has not been recovered. A suspect in the case committed suicide after preliminary interrogation, but police are now uncertain of his guilt.

Four weeks after Eyerly vanished, on July 31, 1982, nine-year-old Danielle Good disappeared from her bedroom with no signs of struggle discovered. Her skeleton was found, along with some of her clothes, by a farmer near Scio, Oregon, on February 14, 1983.

On November 22, 1982, 27-year-old Patricia Loganbill was shot and killed at the Salem veterinary clinic where she worked. An autopsy revealed that Loganbill was pregnant when she died. Some 15 weeks elapsed before the final outrage, on March 8, 1983, when 32-year-old Laurel Wilson and her nine-year-old daughter Erika were shot to death in their beds by an unknown home invader.

Without a suspect, authorities refused to speculate on possible connections in the string of murders, but investigators from Seattle ruled out involvement by Washington's elusive "Green River Killer" (finally identified in 2001), since none of the Salem victims were prostitutes.

Police examined local serial slayer William Smith, convicted of other murders in the same period, as a suspect in the crimes here described, but found no evidence against him. In December 2007, Smith finally confessed to Sherry Eyerly's murder, but the other crimes remain officially unsolved.

SALIM, Muhammad   See NEW YORK CITY TAXI MURDERS

SALZBURG, Austria   missing tourists (1921)

An intriguing case from Salzburg, Austria, involves the disappearance and presumed murder of six tourists, reported by the *New York Times* in July 1921. According to the declaration of authorities, five men and a woman had disappeared within two weeks of the formal announcement on July 28, 1921. Each was hiking alone when he or she vanished, and no trace was found of the tourists thereafter. Police believed the six had been murdered, with robbery suggested as a motive, but in the absence of bodies and suspects no certain verdict could be rendered. The case remains unsolved today.

SAN Antonio, Texas   taxi cab murders (1984–85)

In 1984 and 1985, San Antonio taxi drivers were terrorized by the murder of one Hispanic cabbie and the disappearance of two others over an eight-month period. Driver Pete Lozano was killed in his cab during November 1984, and the unknown assailant was still at large when 68-year-old Julio Villanueva was reported missing on June 17, 1985. His privately owned cab was found in a Brooksville, Florida, parking lot on Independence Day, and searchers acting on a self-styled psychic's tip recovered Villanueva's missing briefcase two days later. Meanwhile, 32-year-old cabbie Luis Salazar had last been seen in San Antonio on the night of July 5, 1985, reported missing by his girlfriend two days later. To date, no trace of the missing taxi drivers has been found and the identity of their assailant(s) remains a mystery.

SANDERS, Lisa   See PERISHO, SHERRY

SAN Diego, California   gay murders (1988)

A sadly underreported case from San Diego involves the shooting deaths of three presumed homosexual victims in November 1988. Authorities report that two of those murdered were transients, and "at least two" were gay, although the press and public have been left to guess at which is which. Thirty-one-year-old David Sino was the first acknowledged victim, found in Balboa Park on November 19, killed by multiple head shots. Six days later, 60-year-old Edward Hope was discovered, gunned down in identical circumstances near the site of Sino's murder. Balboa Park was the scene of a third slaying on November 26, when 36-year-old Bryan Poole was cut down by multiple shots to the head. So far, no charges have been filed in the case and no suspects publicly identified.

SAN Diego, California   unsolved murders (1931–36)

Forty years before another unknown slayer terrorized the city, residents of San Diego were traumatized by a five-year series of murders claiming female victims between the ages of 10 and 22. Details are sparse, given the lapse in time, but newspaper articles from 1947 remarked on a "striking similarity" between San Diego's murders and the slaying of "BLACK DAHLIA" Elizabeth Short (whose nude and mutilated body, neatly severed at the waist, was found in Los Angeles on January 15, 1947). San Diego journalists speculated that Short, who once lived briefly in their city, "could well have been the latest victim of a sadist who has terrorized this city for 15 years," but the claim seems doubly exaggerated, since San Diego's slasher apparently killed no one after 1936, and none of his victim's were dissected in the Black Dahlia style.

The first known victim of the San Diego stalker, in February 1931, was 10-year-old Virginia Brooks, "attacked and murdered" (no details available) after she was lured into a stranger's car. "A few months later," victim Dolly Bibbens—described in press reports as an "attractive and well-to-do widow"—was beaten to death in her own apartment. Two weeks after that crime, 22-year-old Hazel Bradshaw was added to the list, stabbed 17 times by an unknown assailant and left to die in Balboa Park.

The killer (or killers) took a three-year break after Bradshaw, resurfacing in March 1934 to perpetrate a vaguely described "similar crime" against Mrs. Wesley Adams. In April 1934 the nude body of 17-year-old Louise Teuber was found hanging from a tree, police convinced that she was raped and murdered elsewhere. Before that fateful summer ended, 16-year-old Celia Cota was "attacked, tortured and strangled" on her way home from a local movie theater. The final victim, killed by unspecified means in 1936, was Riverside YWCA secretary Ruth Muir, the daughter of a wealthy Arizona banker.

On balance, there seems to be sufficient cause for doubting a lone killer's role in all seven crimes, but San Diego police and reporters were seemingly convinced of a single hand at work. Whether that conclusion amounts to sound detective work or wishful thinking, the end result is still the same. To date, none of the San Diego cases have been solved.

SAN Diego, California unsolved murders (1985–88)

In August 1988, authorities from Washington State and California issued an announcement that at least 10 unsolved murders, logged in San Diego since June 1985, were "definitely" linked with other homicides committed near Seattle and Tacoma by the elusive "Green River Killer." One detective referred to the connection as "common knowledge," and some investigators placed the California body count considerably higher. Lt. Bill Baxter, head of the San Diego County sheriff's homicide department, declared that at least 10—but no more than 12—women had been murdered in the county by a single killer over the past three years. Detective Tom Streed, leading the investigation, was inclined to think the killer's death toll might have reached 18. Whatever their differences of opinion, all concerned agreed upon 10 victims in the case. The alleged Green River connection was later abandoned without fanfare, and no California charges have been filed against Seattle defen-

dant Gary Ridgway, but the San Diego cases still await solution.

The first to die was 22-year-old Donna Gentile, last seen alive on July 25, 1985. Her nude, strangled body was recovered three days later in the neighborhood of Mount Laguna, found with rocks and gravel packed inside her mouth and throat.

The second victim was a young "Jane Doe," her corpse badly decomposed when hikers found it near a rural creek, her head wedged beneath a tree limb, on July 22, 1986. Nearby, authorities found clothing and a wedding ring believed to be the victim's, but the evidence provided no clue to her identity.

Twenty-six-year-old Theresa Brewer was next to face the killer's wrath. Bound in a fetal position and "probably strangled," her corpse was found on August 3, 1986, identified three days later by comparison of dental records.

On April 23, 1987, a group of illegal immigrants discovered the nude, decomposed remains of 29-year-old Rosemarie Ritter. Despite a ruling of death due to methamphetamine poisoning, Ritter was listed by police as one of the San Diego killer's "definite" victims. Two months later, on June 22, 32-year-old Anna Varela was found in Pine Valley by joggers who nearly stumbled over her nude, strangled corpse.

Sally Moorman-Field, a 19-year-old prostitute and drug addict, joined the victims list on September 20, 1987, stripped and strangled prior to her discovery by bicyclists. The cause of death was undetermined for 36-year-old Sara Gedalicia when her decomposed remains were found at Alpine five days later. Likewise, on October 19, 1985, authorities could list no cause of death for 24-year-old Diana Moffitt, but dismemberment of her skeleton placed her on the official victims list.

Another "Jane Doe" victim, found at Rancho Bernardo on April 13, 1988, had been dead roughly one week when her body was discovered; once again, the cause of death was undetermined. Melissa Sandoval, a 21-year-old drug-addicted streetwalker, was last seen alive on May 21, 1988, climbing into the car of an unidentified "trick." Her strangled body was recovered on May 29, within 30 yards of the previous Rancho Bernardo dump site.

Solutions remain as elusive as a definitive body count in the San Diego murders, but there has been no shortage of publicized suspects. One such, 41-year-old ex-convict Ronald Elliott Porter, was arrested in October 1988 for beating and raping a San Diego woman. Porter initially denied the charges, then cut a deal with prosecutors six months later and pled guilty in exchange for a four-year sentence on reduced charges of sexual battery and assault with a deadly weapon. One week before his scheduled parole in September 1991, Porter was indicted for the murders of 26-year-old Carol Gushrowski (slain in June 1986) and 43-year-old Sandra Cwik (found dead in July 1988), plus five counts of attempted murder pertaining to rape victims who survived his attacks. The Gushrowski case was dismissed for lack of evidence when Porter's trial began in August 1992, but he was convicted of second-degree murder (Cwik's), plus two counts of rape with a foreign object and one count of assault resulting in great bodily harm. On October 26, 1992, Porter received a prison term of 27 years to life. Deputy District Attorney Dick Lewis publicly announced that fibers, blood, and other evidence linked Porter to 14 other San Diego murders, but no further charges have been filed to date.

Another suspect, Brian Maurice Jones, was serving 22 years in prison for sexual assault in June 1992, when San Diego authorities charged him with four of their unsolved murders, plus two counts of attempted murder and one count each of rape and sodomy. Convicted on two of the murder charges, Jones was sentenced to die and dispatched to San Quentin prison, where he awaits execution today.

Yet another San Diego killer, tattooed biker Alan Michael Stevens (aka Buzzard), was 46 years old at the time of his December 1988 arrest on charges of murdering 26-year-old Cynthia McVey. McVey was found nude, hog-tied and strangled on the Pala Indian Reservation, on November 29, 1988. Three fingerprints from Stevens were found on masking tape wrapped around McVey's head, and 40-odd prints from the victim were located in a car rented by Stevens. Convicted of first-degree murder in October 1990, Stevens drew a prison term of 25 years to life. Authorities named him as their prime suspect in three more slayings, but no further charges have been filed.

Still another San Diego suspect, 27-year-old Blake Raymond Taylor, was serving a sentence of nine years to life for the attempted murder of a prostitute when authorities named him as a suspect in the deaths of three more streetwalkers. In the now familiar pattern, prosecutors refrained from lodging murder charges against Taylor, despite the public accusations.

A final suspect, Richard Allen Sanders, was linked in media reports to both the San Diego and Green River homicides. No charges were filed, since Sanders was already dead—killed outside Yacolt, Washington, in March 1989 by two close-range shotgun blasts to the back—before he was named as a suspect in the notorious murder sprees. A one-time bouncer and saloon proprietor, Sanders was posthumously named by authorities as a suspected narcotics manufacturer and alleged producer of "snuff" films featuring murders of unnamed prostitutes. The latter information was reportedly provided by police informants. One of them, Joel Hansen, identified Sanders's killer as 30-year-old Clifford Brethour, convicted of the slaying and sentenced to a 15-year jail term in September 1989. (Hansen, convicted as an accomplice, drew a sentence of 11 to 14 years.) Authorities in Washington agreed that Sanders was "once" a low-priority suspect in the Green River killings, but links to those murders are now discounted.

Critics of the San Diego task force, disbanded after spending five years and $1 million on the case, suggest that frustrated authorities have taken the easy way out, claiming "satisfactory resolution of 26 murders" when only four cases resulted in convictions. In fact, those critics say, the self-proclaimed "most successful serial killer task force in U.S. history" blamed 22 of those slayings on four incarcerated suspects without proving a single charge, or even finding evidence enough for an indictment in 20 of the cases. Skeptics may be questioning whether one or more serial slayers remains at large in San Diego.

SANDLIN, Ronald   See NEW JERSEY MURDERS

SANDOVAL, Melissa   See SAN DIEGO MURDERS

SANE, Adnan Abdul Hameed al.   See AL SANE, ADNAN ABDUL HAMEED

SAN Mateo, California unsolved murders (1976)
A "cold" case by police standards, the 1976 stabbing deaths of five young women in San Mateo County, California, is probably unsolvable today, although officers involved in the original investigation still debate the case from time to time. All five victims were attractive brunets who, like most of the women slain by serial killer Ted Bundy, wore

their hair parted in the middle. The presumed killer also left hairs of his own on at least two of the corpses, and authorities took samples from 256 suspects before obtaining a tentative match. (Hairs, unlike fingerprints, cannot be linked to one exclusive source without DNA material from the roots to provide a positive match.)

The owner of the suspect hairs, never publicly identified, was later convicted of raping a teenage girl in a neighboring county, but he was never charged with murder. Federal Bureau of Investigation (FBI) crime lab reports told California authorities that fewer than one person in every 4,000 possessed the same type of hair as their suspect, but in a state with more than 30 *million* residents, that still did not reduce the odds enough to rate indictment or conviction. Imprisoned serial slayer Henry Lee Lucas toured California murder sites in early 1985, confessing to 15 murders committed over the previous decade, but San Mateo detectives dismissed him as a suspect in their string of unsolved stabbings. The *other* suspect, meanwhile, was released on parole and moved to Southern California in 1981, where he presumably remains at large.

SANTOS, Mary See New Bedford, Massachusetts, Murders

SAVARD, Ernest See Nahanni Valley

SAVINO, Nancy See Riverdell Hospital Murders

SAVOY, Frederick See Highway Murders: Canada

SCHIEBER, Isadore See Prince Georges Hospital Murders

SCHILLING, Sharon See I-35 Murders

SCHRIEBER, Barbara See "Flat-Tire Murders"

SCHUSTER, Arnold murder victim (1952)

A 24-year-old clothing salesman in Brooklyn, New York, Arnold Schuster was riding the subway home from work on February 18, 1952, when he recognized a familiar face on the train. Schuster's fellow traveler was William Francis Sutton, a.k.a. Willie the Actor, a notorious bank robber whose name had been added to the Federal Bureau of Investigation's (FBI) Ten Most Wanted List on March 20, 1950. Schuster recognized Sutton from mug shots published in the press and summoned a policeman, watching from the sidelines as Sutton meekly surrendered. On April 1, 1952, Sutton and accomplice Thomas Kling, another Top Ten fugitive, were convicted of a holdup in Queens and received 29-year prison terms for that crime; Sutton also received two consecutive terms of 15 years to life on unrelated weapons charges.

By the time Willie the Actor faced his day in court, however, Arnold Schuster was already dead, the victim of a seemingly motiveless slaying that baffled New York authorities for a decade. On March 9, 1952, less than three weeks after he fingered Sutton for police, Schuster was gunned down on the Brooklyn street where he lived. His unknown killer shot Schuster four times at close range—once in each eye, and twice in the groin.

Schuster's death had all the earmarks of a gangland execution, nothing novel in New York, but police were at a loss to explain the slaying since Willie Sutton had no particular gangland connections. The explanation, if true, was advanced 10 years after the fact by Mafia informer Joseph Valachi, during marathon testimony that exposed the inner workings of the Big Apple crime syndicate.

According to Valachi, mob boss and certified psychopath Albert Anastasia had been watching television reports of Sutton's capture and Schuster's role in the arrest, when he flew into a sudden homicidal rage. Anastasia had never met Sutton, but the bandit's arrest still infuriated him. "I hate squealers!" the Mafioso allegedly told his assembled gunmen. "Hit that guy!"

As explained by Valachi, the murder contract had been issued to Frederick John Tenuto, a 37-year-old hitman ironically known to his fellow mobsters as "The Angel" and "Saint John." Curiously, at the time of the murder, Tenuto was also a federal fugitive and yet another poster boy on the FBI's Ten Most Wanted List, added to the roster on May 24, 1950. His latest known offense was a Pennsylvania prison

WANTED BY THE FBI

BANK ROBBERY

UNLAWFUL FLIGHT TO AVOID CONFINEMENT - ARMED ROBBERY

Photograph taken October 24, 1945   Photograph taken April 3, 1945

WILLIAM FRANCIS SUTTON

with aliases: William Bowles, James Clayton, Richard Courtney, Leo Holland, Julian Loring, "Slick Willie", "Willie the Actor", and others.

DESCRIPTION

Age 48, born June 30, 1901, Brooklyn, New York (not verified); Height, 5'8"; Weight, 155 pounds; Build, medium; Hair, dark brown, possibly graying; Eyes, blue; Complexion, medium dark; Race, white; Nationality, American; Education, eighth grade; Occupations, clerk, driller, florist, gardener, stenographer; Scars and marks, faint ragged vertical scar on fold of left wrist, faint oblique scar on right elbow, end of right little finger scarred and deformed, small red flesh mole on forehead above left eyebrow, scar on back of neck; Remarks, Sutton may have dyed his hair and may be wearing a mustache and eyeglasses in an effort to disguise his features.
FBI Number 241884

Fingerprint Classification: 12 M 1 R 000 13   Ref: 3, 17, 19,
M 4 W 001   4 4 4

CRIMINAL RECORD

Sutton's criminal record includes convictions for the crimes of burglary, grand larceny, armed robbery and escape.

CAUTION

SUTTON IS BELIEVED TO BE ARMED AND IS CONSIDERED EXTREMELY DANGEROUS.

A complaint was filed before a U. S. Commissioner at Philadelphia, Pennsylvania on February 17, 1950, charging this subject with violating Title 18, U. S. Code, Section 1073, in that he fled from the state of Pennsylvania to avoid confinement after conviction for the crime of armed robbery. A complaint was filed before a U. S. Commissioner at Brooklyn, New York on March 10, 1950 charging this subject with violating Title 18, U. S. Code, Section 2113, in that he committed the crime of bank robbery.

If you are in possession of any information regarding the whereabouts of this individual, please communicate with the undersigned, or with the nearest office of the Federal Bureau of Investigation, U. S. Department of Justice, the local address and telephone number of which are set forth on the reverse side of this notice.

JOHN EDGAR HOOVER, DIRECTOR
FEDERAL BUREAU OF INVESTIGATION
UNITED STATES DEPARTMENT OF JUSTICE
WASHINGTON, D. C.
TELEPHONE, NATIONAL 7117

Wanted Flyer No. 61
March 10, 1950

Arnold Schuster's fate was sealed after he fingered fugitive Willie Sutton for New York police officers. (Library of Congress) break, in which one of his three fellow escapees had been Willie Sutton. Schuster's execution—with bullets in the eyes and genitals—was allegedly designed as a warning to future stool pigeons.

By killing a "civilian"—i.e., someone with no mob involvement—Anastasia had committed a serious breach of the Mafia's dubious etiquette. To cover his tracks, Valachi said, Anastasia next ordered Tenuto's execution and made certain that his corpse was never found. (One theory has it that Tenuto got a "double-decker" funeral, his corpse concealed inside a coffin built for two.) In light of Valachi's testimony, Tenuto's name was removed from the FBI's Most Wanted list on March 9, 1964, and the warrants issued in his name were quietly dismissed.

SCIALESE, Mary   See "West Side Rapist"

SCIORTINO, Theresa   See "Frankford Slasher"

SCOTT, Janet   See Manhattan axe murders

SCOTT, Lawanda   See Washington, D.C., murders (1988)

SCOTT, Lieutenant   See Chicago holdup murders (1971–72)

SEDAM, Crystal   See "Truck Stop Killer"

SELLERS, Marie   See Richland, Georgia, murders

SENS, Uwe Rusch   See "Monster of Florence"

"SERVANT Girl Annihilator" serial murderer (1884–85)
Over a 12-month period, between New Year's Eve 1884, and Christmas Eve 1885, an unknown serial slayer claimed eight victims in Austin, Texas. Seven of those slain were female, mostly employed in positions that prompted the killer's nickname.

Initial victim Mollie Smith, a domestic servant, died beside an outhouse near her humble residence, behind the home of William Hall on West Pecan Street (now Sixth Street), on the night of December 31, 1884. Her corpse lay in the snow, with a large hole chopped in her skull.

Five months later, in May 1885, the unknown killer claimed two more victims. Eliza Shelley was found on May 6, at the corner of San Jacinto Boulevard and Cypress Street (now Third Street), three blocks from the old Pearl House hotel. Irene Cross died nearby, on San Jacinto Boulevard, across the street from Scholtz's Beer Garden. Both were stabbed with some unidentified weapon in the form of a spike. On May 10, Austin resident William Sydney Porter—better known as short-story author O. Henry—coined the slayer's nickname in a letter to a friend Dave Hall. Porter wrote: "Town is fearfully dull, except for the frequent raids of the Servant Girl Annihilators, who make things lively in the dull hours of the night."

While Porter spoke in the plural, Austin police suspected they were looking for a single killer. Sadly, that conclusion brought them no closer to an arrest.

August 1885 brought a variation in the killer's pattern, as he claimed Mary (or "Masy") Ramey, a child aged 11 or 12. Ramey lived with her servant mother in humble accommodations behind the home of Valentine Weed, described in contradictory newspaper reports as standing at the corner of Trinity and Cypress or San Jacinto Boulevard and Cedar Street (now Fourth Street). In either case, the crime scene lay within three blocks of victim Eliza Shelley's residence. Postmortem examination revealed that some "long thin object" had been thrust into Mary's brain through one of her ears.

September 1885 brought another double-murder and added a male victim to the slayer's body count. Victim Gracie Vance, an African-American maid, lived with common-law husband Orange Washington in a cabin behind the home of their employer, one Major Dunham, on Guadalupe Street. Two other occupants of the cabin, Sofy Gibson and Lucinda Hoddy, were "knocked senseless with a sandbag" during the attack, which ended with Gracie Vance being dragged through a window, tossed over a fence, then raped and beaten to death in a field. Hoddy identified another black man, Doc Woods, as the attacker, but no record of his trial remains and most published accounts still credit victims Vance and Washington to the Servant Girl Annihilator.

The killer's last known victims, both affluent white women, were found within hours of each other on December 24, 1885. Sue Hancock, age 44, was found in a backyard on the south side of Water Street, a block east of Congress Avenue, stabbed in the ear with a weapon similar (if not identical) to that which killed Mary Ramey. A short time later, passers-by found Eula (or Luly) Philips dead at the corner of Hickory and Lavaca Streets, near her home. Philips was a descendant of the "Old Three Hundred," early Anglo settlers who purchased land from Stephen Austin during 1824–28.

With the double slaying on Christmas Eve, the Servant Girl Annihilator seemingly retired. One suspect, a "Malay cook" known only as "Maurice," was employed during the time span of the murders at the Pearl House, on Congress Avenue. Police briefly placed the man under surveillance, but he eluded them and vanished from Austin in January 1886. A "strong presumption" of Maurice's guilt apparently was based on the occurrence of several slayings near the hotel, without substantiating evidence. Likewise, reports that the killer "typically dragged his victims from their beds and raped them before slashing or axing them to death" are clearly false, since only one case—that of Gracie Vance—fits those criteria.

In 1888, some theorists tried to link Austin's murders to the unsolved crimes of London's "JACK THE RIPPER." Several newspapers, including the *New York World*, the *Atchison* (Kansas) *Daily Globe*, and the *Irish Times* drew connections between London's Whitechapel district and Austin, claiming that Malay Maurice had worked his way to England as a ship's cook and was overheard in London, saying that "he had been robbed by a woman of bad character, and that unless he found the woman and recovered his money he would murder and mutilate every Whitechapel woman he met."

That fanciful solution to the Ripper slayings fails on several points. First, the Malay cook has never been named as a Ripper suspect in British police documents or in the published work of private researchers spanning the past 120 years. Second, Jack's crimes in London—which involved throat slashing and disembowelment—bore no resemblance whatever to the Servant Girl Annihilator's technique. On balance, while we cannot acquit Maurice of the murders in Austin, we must conclude that he did not perform the Whitechapel murders.

SHAFFER, Brian missing person (2006)

Brian Shaffer was born on February 11, 1979. By age 27, a second-year medical student at Ohio State University, he was described by girlfriend Alexis Waggoner as "brilliant, kind, thoughtful, loyal, sweet, funny, talented, and handsome." His one slight nod to eccentricity was a tattoo of the rock band Pearl Jam's logo on his right biceps.

On March 31, 2006, with Alexis absent on a visit to her family, Shaffer joined ex-roommate Clint Florence for a boys' night on the town in Columbus, Ohio. They entered the Ugly Tuna Saloon at 9:15 P.M. and had several drinks before Shaffer called Alexis on his cell phone at 9:56 or 10:30 (published reports differ). Security cameras tracked Shaffer and Florence as they left the Ugly Tuna, at 11:00 P.M., en route to the nearby Short North Tavern. At 1:15 A.M. they returned to the Ugly Tuna, caught on videotape riding the escalators with some girls who were friends of Florence. When the bar closed 45 minutes later, Florence could not find Shaffer on the premises, and a call to his cell phone switched over to voice mail.

Brian Shaffer has not been seen since, and he does not appear on tapes covering the Ugly Tuna's two exits after his return at 1:15 A.M. There *is* another exit from the building that houses the Ugly Tuna, which requires customers to leave the bar and descend to the ground floor via stairs or an elevator, then slip out through a service exit leading to a nearby construction site, but no witness has surfaced to confirm or explain Shaffer's departure by that route. Thus far, his missing cell phone and credit cards have not been activated, and no effort has been made to tap his bank account. A 3:00 A.M. burglary at Shaffer's apartment in May 2006 cannot be linked conclusively to his disappearance the previous month.

Police assigned to Brian's case questioned all known acquaintances, searched the construction site near the Ugly Tuna, and scoured other suspect areas with help from Texas EquuSearch, a mounted search-and-recovery team from the Lone Star State. Thus far, all of those efforts have proved fruitless, and rewards totaling $25,500 for information leading to solution of the mystery have lured no takers.

Alexis Waggoner has continued to call Shaffer's cell phone periodically since his disappearance, in hopes that he might answer, but the line was dead—until September 23, 2006, when Shaffer's phone rang for the first time since March, then switched over to voice mail. An inquiry to Cingular, Shaffer's service provider, elicited two possible explanations—a computer glitch producing a false dial tone, or the possibility that Shaffer's phone was briefly turned on, but unanswered. Regrettably, the phone lacked global positioning satellite capabilities and could not be physically located while it was active.

On July 21, 2008, the A&E network's *Psychic Kids* program featured a segment on Shaffer's case, wherein teenage psychics Travis Sanders and Nicole Slosser visited the scene of Shaffer's disappearance with other investigators. They "felt" that some unknown person had seen Shaffer arrive at the bar, watching from upstairs windows across the street, and that the person harbored some strong animosity or jealousy against Shaffer—but there, the trail ended.

While Shaffer remains missing, some theorists link his disappearance to a series of seven strange deaths around La Crosse, Wisconsin, occurring between July 1997 and October 2005. In each case, the victims were college-aged men who drank heavily at local bars or parties, then turned up dead in various rivers. Victims in those presumed drownings include Richard Hlavaty (July 1997), Chuck Blatz and Tony Skifton (October 1997), Nathan Kampfer (February 1998), Jeff Geesey (April 1999), Jared Dion (April 2004), and Albert Campbell (October 2005). Disturbed by rumors of a serial killer at large, La Crosse police contacted FBI profilers who declared, in September 2007, that no evidence exists to indicate foul play in any of the drownings.

Or does it?

G-men have erred famously in headline cases, including the ATLANTA CHILD MURDERS of 1979–82, the Centennial Olympic Park bombing of 1996, and the ANTHRAX MURDERS of 2001. Their report of September 2007 ignored data published by a criminologist at Minnesota's St. Cloud State University in December 2006, revealing that more than 20 college-aged men had drowned since 1997, after vanishing from bars or parties in Midwestern states ranging from Minnesota to Ohio. Other unsolved disappearances, farther afield, include those of Justin Gaines, 18, last seen in Wild Bill's tavern in Duluth, Georgia, on November 2, 2007, and Kyle Fleischmann, 24, last seen at the Buckhead Saloon in Charlotte, North Carolina, on November 9, 2007.

Those deaths and disappearances may be coincidental, but friends and loved ones of the lost dispute it. Only one thing is certain at the moment: all the cases mentioned here remain officially unsolved.

SHAKUR, Tupac Amaru murder victim (1996)

Rap singer Tupac Shakur was born Parish Lesane Crooks in East Harlem, New York, on June 16, 1971. His mother, an active member of the militant Black Panther Party, gave birth to her son one month after jurors acquitted her (with 20 fellow Panthers) on 150 counts of conspiracy to bomb U.S. government buildings and New York landmarks, including the Statue of Liberty. Fearing that political enemies might seek to harm her son, Shakur's mother changed his name after she married black militant Mutulu Shakur (neé Jeral Wayne Williams).

In October 1981, Mutulu Shakur and several accomplices robbed a Brinks truck in New York, killing one of the guards and two local policemen. While a fugitive, Shakur became the 380th person listed on the FBI's Ten Most Wanted list. Captured in February 1986, Shakur was convicted and sentenced to life imprisonment. He remains incarcerated at this writing.

Another influence on young Tupac Shakur was his godfather, Elmer "Geronimo" Pratt, a member of the Los Angeles Black Panther Party, convicted in 1972 for a 1968 holdup murder. Pratt spent 27 years in prison on that charge, including eight years in solitary confinement, before attorneys proved that he had been framed by Los Angeles police and FBI agents as part of the FBI's often illegal COINTELPRO (counter-intelligence program) operation, one of which was specifically designed to "neutralize Pratt as an effective BPP functionary." Pratt was freed in 1997, but none of the agents responsible for his false imprisonment were ever punished.

That family background, coupled with daily life in the ghetto where he was raised, undoubtedly colored Tupac Shakur's view of American justice and society at large. He sought self-expression through performing arts, joining Harlem's famous 127th Street Ensemble at age 12 and performing in the play *A Raisin in the Sun*. As a high-school junior, Tupac moved with his family to Baltimore and transferred to Baltimore's School for the Arts, where he studied acting, ballet, jazz, and poetry. His friends included young Jada Pinkett (now actress Jada Pinkett Smith), who later told reporters that Shakur "was like a brother. It was beyond friendship for us. The type

Death Row Records Chairman Marion "Suge" Knight (left) and rapper Tupac Shakur are seen in Las Vegas in November 1995. Several months later, Shakur was killed by an unknown gunman on a similar trip with Knight. (AP Photo/Lauren Greenfield)

of relationship we had, you only get that once in a lifetime."

At age 17, Shakur moved west with his family to Marin City, California, where he joined another theater company. An unsettled home life, aggravated by his mother's addiction to crack cocaine, prompted Shakur to quit high school, but he remained a voracious reader and avid performing artist. Formation of his first musical group, Strictly Dope, led to affiliation with the rap singers of Digital Underground, who hired Shakur as a dancer and roadie in 1990.

Shakur soon debuted as a rapper in his own right, releasing the album *2Pacalypse Now* in 1992, followed by *Strictly 4 My N.I.G.G.A.Z.* in 1993, *Thug Life: Vol. 1* in 1994, and *All Eyez on Me* in 1996. Shakur's adoption of the "Thug Life" motto—the name of his final group, tattooed on his stomach—and the lyrics of his songs sparked controversy nationwide. A Texas youth claimed that Tupac's music had prompted him to kill a state trooper, and Vice President Dan Quayle publicly declared in 1992 that Shakur's music had "no place in our society." Tupac responded by explaining that THUG LIFE was an acronym condemning racism, which stood for "The Hate U Give Little Infants Fucks Everybody."

Legal problems followed Shakur throughout his career. In October 1991 he sued police in Oakland, California, claiming that they beat him for jaywalking. The department settled out of court, for $42,000. Two years later, in Atlanta, Shakur shot and wounded two officers whom he said were harassing black motorists. Prosecutors dropped those charges when they learned that the cops in question were drunk and carrying weapons stolen from a police evidence locker. December 1993 found Shakur and several friends charged with gang-raping a woman in his New York hotel room. Shakur denied the charge but was convicted of sexual abuse and received an 18-month jail term. In 1994 he logged a second conviction, for assaulting an ex-employee on the set of a music video. That rap earned him 15 days in custody and a $2,000 fine. In 1995, relatives of six-year-old Qa'id Walker-Teal sued Shakur for wrongful death, after the boy died in a crossfire between Tupac's associates and rival thugs. Shakur settled that lawsuit, paying the family damages variously reported as $300,000 and $500,000. In April 1996 he received a six-month sentence for violating his probation in the sexual assault case.

That judgment was still on appeal in September 1996, when Shakur's life ended in a blaze of gunfire. On September 7, Shakur and music producer Marion "Suge" Knight attended the Mike Tyson-Bruce Seldon fight at the MGM Grand hotel in Las Vegas. Before that event, Shakur and members of his entourage attacked Orlando Anderson, a member of the notorious Crips gang from Los Angeles, in the MGM's lobby, beating him in full view of hotel security cameras. Investigators later learned that Anderson and other Crips had robbed an associate of Suge Knight's Death Row Records several weeks earlier, sparking a personal grudge.

After the boxing match, Shakur and Knight led a caravan of vehicles down the Las Vegas Strip in search of further diversion. Police stopped the motorcade at 11:00 P.M., citing Knight for driving without license plates and violating city noise ordinances with his loud stereo. Fifteen minutes later, unknown gunmen in a white Cadillac pulled up beside Knight's Mercedes-Benz and fired a dozen shots, four of the bullets striking Shakur in his chest, pelvis, right hand, and thigh. Shakur lingered in intensive care at a local hospital until September 13, when he died at 4:03 P.M.

The Vegas shooting was not Shakur's first brush with death. On November 30, 1994—the day before his sexual abuse conviction—Tupac was robbed and shot four or five times (reports differ) by two gunmen dressed in military fatigues, at Manhattan's Quad Recording Studios. Shakur publicly blamed musicians Sean "Puff Daddy" Combs, Andre Harrell, and CHRISTOPHER WALLACE (a.k.a. "Biggie Smalls" or "Notorious B.I.G.") for that shooting, but none were charged. Privately, he also suspected rapper and hip-hop producer Randy "Stretch" Walker of involvement in the attack—a notion that some believe led to Walker's still-unsolved murder in Queens, New York, on the one-year anniversary of Shakur's wounding.

After his release from prison on the rape charge, Shakur launched musical assaults on rival Biggie Smalls and others through his rap lyrics. The animosity between Shakur and Wallace, mirrored in violence between their respective friends in the Crips and Bloods street gangs, sparked an "East Coast–West Coast war" between rappers allied with the headline contenders. Shakur's unsolved murder and the subsequent slaying of Wallace by unknown gunmen on March 9, 1997, apparently ended that conflict.

SHANE, Michael See "ASTROLOGICAL MURDERS"

SHARP, Glenna Sue murder victim (1981)

In November 1980, 36-year-old Glenna Sharp settled in Keddie, California, with her five children: 15-year-old John, 14-year-old Sheila, 13-year-old Tina, nine-year-old Ricky, and five-year-old Greg. Together, they occupied Cabin 28 at the Keddie Resort, an idyllic site built in 1910, with 33 cabins, a renowned lodge and restaurant, forest hiking trails and trout-fishing streams. Life was good until April 11, 1981, when grim disaster struck.

That evening, John Sharp and a friend, 17-year-old Dana Wingate, hitchhiked five miles from Keddie to Quincy, attended a party at Oakland Camp there, then thumbed their way home between 9:30 and 10 P.M. In their absence, Sheila Sharp scheduled a sleepover with the Seabolt family, who lived next door to Cabin 28, while brothers Greg and Ricky invited a male friend identified only as Justin to spend the night with them. Tina Sharp returned to Cabin 28 around 9:30 and went to bed, while her brothers and friend Justin ate popcorn and watched *The Love Boat* on television.

Glenna Sharp had declined an invitation from another Keddie Resort neighbor, Marilyn Smartt, to join her, husband Martin Smartt, and their housemate John "Bo" Boubede at the Backdoor bar in Keddie. According to Marilyn's later statements, Boubede

and Martin Smartt met at veteran's hospital in Reno, Nevada, and became friendly enough for Boubede to move in with the couple. Boubede craved a date on the night of April 11, and Marilyn later claimed that Glenna's refusal to play along angered both men.

Sometime between 10:30 and 11 P.M. on April 11, one or more still unknown killers entered Cabin 28, binding Glenna Sharp, son John, and Dana Wingate with duct tape and wire. Over the next 10 hours, an orgy of torture and mayhem ensued, leaving the victims mutilated almost beyond recognition with knives and a claw hammer. As Plumas County Sheriff's Patrol Commander Rod DeCrona described the scene to reporters, "Whoever did this stabbed the victims so violently they bent one knife totally double from the force. They stabbed and pounded on everything in sight—the walls, the people, the furniture, everything. There was blood sprayed absolutely everywhere. You knew right away we were involved with a psychopath."

Strangely, throughout the long ordeal, the Seabolts and other neighbors heard nothing. Stranger still, Glenna Sharp's younger sons and their guest for the night were unharmed. Early reports claimed that the boys "slept through" the massacre, although that claim was subsequently contradicted.

Sheila Sharp discovered the carnage when she returned home at 7:00 A.M. on April 12. Shocked, she retreated to the Seabolt cabin and secured their help in extricating Greg, Ricky, and Justin through a bedroom window. The Seabolts telephoned the sheriff's office at 7:10 and deputies arrived 10 minutes later to examine the crime scene.

They soon found out that Tina Sharp was missing. Sheila had not seen her sister when she left to sleep with the Seabolts and assumed that Tina had been "playing somewhere outside." Also missing, according to Sheila, was a "shoebox" made by Tina as a school project and normally kept in Cabin 28's kitchen with various tools inside; Tina's red nylon jacket; and a pair of Tina's shoes, with the word "GASS" (for Great American Shoe Store, the slogan of Kinney Shoes) printed on the soles. Detectives found no sign of forced entry, but noted knife marks on various bloodstained walls. The bloodstains were all type O, matching members of the Sharp family and some 41 percent of all Americans.

Other evidence found in Cabin 28 included three murder weapons (a bloody hammer, a butcher's knife, and a bent steak knife); a blue windbreaker with red and white stripes, found near Dana Wingate's body; a still-unidentified fingerprint lifted from a handrail on the outside rear stairs; and a button found on the ground behind the cabin. Officers noted that Cabin 28's telephone was off the hook, all the lights were switched off, and the drapes were pulled shut.

Detectives questioned the Smartts on April 13, searching their home and the Keddie Resort's clubhouse for clues. Marilyn Smartt later told documentary filmmakers that a bloody jacket belonging to Tina Sharp was found in her basement, but if so, no record of the discovery now exists. Martin Smartt told investigators that his claw hammer was missing, but it never surfaced. Sheriff Doug Thomas subsequently claimed that Martin provided "endless clues" in the case, each one designed to "throw the suspicion away from him."

Houseguest Justin X told conflicting stories to police, first claiming that he "dreamed" details of the murders, later saying that he witnessed the crime while awake. According to the latter statement, he was watching TV with Gary and Rick Sharp in their bedroom, when sounds from the living room drew him to investigate. He saw Glenna Sharp with two men, one sporting a moustache and long hair, the other clean-shaven with shorter hair. Both men reportedly wore eyeglasses. John Sharp and Dana Wingate entered the cabin and began to argue with the men, sparking a "fight" that ended in mass murder. During the assaults, Tina Sharp emerged from her bedroom, dragging a blanket and asking, "What's going on?" The intruders then seized her and carried her out the backdoor while she shouted for help. Harlan Embry, a forensic artist with the Reno Police Department, prepared drawings of the killers based on Justin's descriptions. Some who viewed the drawings say that they resemble Martin Smartt and John Boubede, while others deny it. Based on Justin's age and inconsistencies in his statements, some investigators dismiss the sketches as worthless.

Over the next three years, local police spent some 4,000 man-hours investigating the Keddie murders. FBI agents briefly examined Tina Sharp's disappearance as a presumed kidnapping, but were no more successful in solving the case. At last, on April 22, 1984, a man collecting bottles for recycling found human bones near Feather Falls, in Butte County, roughly 100 miles from Keddie. In June, pathologists identified the partial skeleton as that of Tina Sharp. Near the grave site, officers unearthed a child's blan-

ket and blue nylon jacket, a partial pair of Levi's jeans missing one rear pocket, and an empty dispenser for surgical tape. If anything, those discoveries compounded the mystery.

While authorities offered no motive for the Keddie slayings, armchair detectives noted that Dana Wingate was a known marijuana user, suggesting that he may have been caught in a drug deal gone wrong. Family acquaintance Carla McMullen claimed that Wingate and John Sharp stole a quantity of LSD from unnamed dealers, but she offered no proof. Parallel rumors, equally unsubstantiated, suggested that Glenna Sharp sold drugs or was involved in prostitution. Another theory, generally dismissed by police, claims that the slayings were committed by bloodthirsty Satanists.

Long after the murders, Marilyn Smartt told documentary filmmakers that she believed husband Martin and John Boubede committed the Keddie murders. According to her statement, she left Martin and Boubede at the Backdoor bar on April 11, 1980, and went home to sleep, then woke at 2:00 A.M. on April 12 to find them burning "something" in their cabin's woodstove. Martin Smartt died of cancer in Portland, Oregon, in June 2000, and is thus unable to defend himself, but ex-Sheriff Doug Thomas told the film crew, "We gave him a polygraph and he passed it." The whereabouts of John Boubede is presently unknown, but sheriff's officers have made no move to charge him with the crimes.

In 2008, a horror film entitled *The Strangers* depicted an assault by three masked home-invaders on a couple staying in an isolated rural cabin. The film's producers claim that it was "inspired by true events," and Internet bloggers elaborated by linking it to the slaughter in Cabin 28, but the Hollywood version has one striking difference from history—its victims manage to outwit their would-be killers and survive.

SHARP, Lena   See "JACK THE RIPPER": ATLANTA, GEORGIA

SHAW, Eileen   See RIVERDELL HOSPITAL MURDERS

SHEA, Patricia   See NEW YORK CITY STRANGULATION MURDERS

SHEPHERD, Cecilia   See "ZODIAC"

SHERGAR equine kidnap victim (1983)

Sired in 1978 by Great Nephew out of Sharmeen, Shergar was a bay colt with a distinctive white blaze. At age three, in June 1981, he won Great Britain's Derby Stakes at the Epsom Downs Racecourse in Surrey by a record 10 lengths, a feat unrivaled in the race's 226-year history. That triumph merited designation among "100 Most Memorable Sporting Moments of the Twentieth Century" in the *Observer*. After Shergar was named European Horse of the Year, Shergar's owner, Prince Karim Aga Khan IV of Pakistan, retired him from racing in September 1981 and put him out to stud.

At 8:30 P.M. on February 8, 1983, six armed men wearing ski masks and police uniforms invaded the Ballymany stud farm in Ireland's County Kildare, where Shergar shared quarters with 55 mares. The raiders towed a horse trailer behind their Ford sedan and got the drop on groom James Fitzgerald after knocking his son unconscious. At gunpoint, with his family held hostage, Fitzgerald helped the invaders load Shergar into their trailer. The gunmen then forced Fitzgerald into another car and drove him around for three hours before dropping him off seven miles from Ballymany. In parting, they gave Fitzgerald a password for use in future ransom negotiations.

What happened next was a bizarre comedy of errors. Instead of calling the police at once, Fitzgerald first phoned Ballymany's manager, who doubled as Shergar's primary veterinarian. Next, he called a racetrack associate, Sean Berry, who telephoned Irish Minister of Finance Alan Dukes. Incredibly, a full eight hours passed before police were notified of Shergar's abduction.

When Garda officers finally got on the case, they found their efforts hampered by the cleverness of Shergar's abductors. It seems that the theft was timed to coincide with one of Ireland's most prestigious horse auctions, which meant there were hundreds of livestock trailers in transit nationwide. Without a single solid clue to work from, Garda Chief Superintendent Jim Murphy ranged far afield with his investigation, supplementing standard searches of Irish farms and stables with advice from numerous psychics. None of it produced results, and the first phone call from Shergar's kidnappers, received at 1:15 A.M. on February 10, went untraced, as police explained, because "the man who does the tracing goes off duty at midnight."

Later, the thieves called Aga Khan's office in Paris, but were told that Shergar had 34 additional owners who had purchased shares in the champion for £250,000 each. The gang offered to provide proof that Shergar was alive, but a visible police stakeout foiled the drop. The next call threatened death to Shergar and to Aga Khan's negotiators, but a photo was finally sent to police, showing Shergar with a current newspaper. Still the syndicate balked at paying Shergar's £5 million ransom, while continuing negotiations in bad faith. As shareholder Sir Jake Astor later acknowledged, "We were going to negotiate, but we were not going to pay," for fear that every prize horse on Earth would become an extortionist's target.

The kidnappers placed their last angry call on February 12, 1983, and the rest is silence. No trace of Shergar has ever been found.

Shergar's owners issued a public statement blaming members of the Provisional Irish Republican Army for the abduction, presumably carried out to raise money for weapons to continue the PIRA's war against British occupation troops in Northern Ireland. Sean O'Callaghan, a PIRA member turned "supergrass," or police informant, promoted that theory in his book *The Informer* (1998), naming Kevin Mallon as the ringleader and stating that Shergar was shot soon after the abduction. According to O'Callaghan, "One of the gang strongly suggested to me Shergar had been killed within hours. They couldn't cope with him, he went demented in the horsebox, injured his leg and they killed him." Shergar was then buried, O'Callaghan says, in an unmarked mountain grave near Ballinamore, County Leitrim, in the Irish province of Connacht.

Despite O'Callaghan's "inside" account of the crime, no suspects have ever been charged in the case, and Shergar's remains have not been recovered. A large animal's skull with two bullet holes in it was found during 2000, buried in a sack about 100 miles from the Ballymany stud farm, but forensic tests proved it to be a cow's skull.

SHERMAN, Mary Stults murder victim (1964)

Mary Stults was born in Evanston, Illinois, on April 21, 1913. After high school, she studied in Paris, then earned a B.A. from Northwestern University in 1934, followed by a master's degree from the University of Chicago. During 1935–36, she taught classes in Paris, at the University of Illinois' French Institute. At age 30 she earned a medical degree from the University of Chicago, then interned at that school's Bob Roberts Hospital. (Stults had married, meanwhile, but available sources oddly contain no reference to her husband, including his given name.)

Following her internship, Dr. Sherman enjoyed a stellar career. In 1947, she was named assistant professor of orthopedic surgery at the University of Chicago's Billings Hospital. Five years later, she moved to New Orleans as director of the Ochsner Clinic Medical Foundation's bone pathology lab. Specializing in cancer research, she moved on in 1953 to become an associate professor at Tulane Medical School and a senior visiting surgeon at Charity Hospital in New Orleans. Dr. Sherman's other credentials included membership in Phi Beta Kappa and the American Academy of Orthopedic Surgeons.

Sherman's career was tragically cut short at age 51 by a still-unknown prowler who invaded her apartment on St. Charles Avenue in New Orleans. In an apparent frenzy, the assailant stabbed Dr. Sherman with a butcher knife in her heart, stomach, one arm, and one leg, also inflicting random slashes on her torso. Sherman's mattress was then set afire, but local police announced that the smoldering mattress could not account for extensive burns on her corpse. Having thus compounded the enigma, detectives apparently closed the case without suspects, leaving it unsolved to this day.

In the absence of an official solution, however, amateur investigators have had a field day. Conspiracy theorists note that Sherman was killed on the same day that members of the Warren Commission visited New Orleans to hear testimony concerning Lee Harvey Oswald and President John Kennedy's assassination. Building on that possible coincidence, author Edward Haslam published a book in 1995 titled *Mary, Ferrie & the Monkey Virus: The Story of an Underground Medical Laboratory*, suggesting that Sherman was killed because she knew too much about Kennedy's death.

Haslam—who knew Sherman and JFK assassination figure David Ferrie (an acquaintance of Oswald's and acknowledged employee of New Orleans Mafia boss Carlos Marcello)—claims that Dr. Sherman was involved in secret efforts to develop a vaccine against soft-tissue cancers caused by the accidental administration of contaminated polio vaccine to children. Ferrie, a self-proclaimed amateur "cancer researcher" whose

apartment was overrun with white mice when he died from an apparent stroke in 1967 (days after local newspapers named him as a suspect in the JFK conspiracy), allegedly ran one of Sherman's cover labs and may have leaked details concerning the assassination that marked Sherman as a threat to the conspirators. In 2007, Haslam expanded his theory in a second book, *Dr. Mary's Monkey*. That volume explains Sherman's burns as a result of exposure to a linear particle accelerator in her New Orleans lab, which forced her killers to stage a fire to divert police attention from the truth.

Support for that story came, after a fashion, from one Judith Vary Baker during 1999. Baker, an Indiana native born in 1943 and raised in Florida, claimed that she interned with Sherman in 1963 and was thus recruited into plots against the life of Cuban president Fidel Castro, funded by Marcello's crime family and the Central Intelligence Agency. Aside from David Ferrie's controversial role in JFK's slaying, Baker also says that Dr. Sherman's mentor in New Orleans, Dr. Alton Ochsner, was a close friend of former Vice President Richard Nixon, still embittered over his narrow loss to Kennedy in the 1960 presidential race. As frosting on the cake, Baker claims that Oswald was in love with Sherman and hoped to marry her after discarding his Russian wife, Marina. Baker adds that the secret labs run by Sherman, Ochsner, and Ferrie, with occasional help from Oswald, were actually dedicated to producing biological weapons rather than a cancer vaccine. As skeptics are quick to point out, no solid evidence supports the theories propounded by Haslam or Baker.

SHOOK, Marty   See CASTRATION MURDERS

SHORTER, Albert   See CHICAGO HOLDUP MURDERS

SHREEVE, Georgia   See "TRUCK STOP KILLER"

SHROCK, Sheila   See "BABYSITTER"

"SIDNEY Sniper" Virginia serial murderer (1960s)
Nicknamed for the Richmond, Virginia, neighborhood that he terrorized during the early 1960s, the

"Sidney Sniper" killed five persons and wounded seven others in a series of hit-and-run attacks. Never identified, the gunman retired as suddenly and mysteriously as he had launched his campaign, leaving baffled police in his wake. Ironically, the random shootings had a beneficial side-effect on Richmond's high-crime district, with streets deserted and the local crime rate dropping sharply during the sniper's period of peak activity.

SIEGEL, Benjamin (Bugsy) gangland murder victim (1947)

A New York City native, born in 1905, Ben Siegel was an incorrigible delinquent who led his own street gang by age 14. Never a great strategist, he was renowned primarily for his ferocious temper and impulsive violence, including a textbook psychopath's enjoyment of murder. That trait earned him the nickname Bugsy— slang for *crazy*—which Siegel despised but could never shake for the remainder of his life.

Bugsy Siegel might have been a Prohibition casualty like so many other reckless gangland renegades, Vincent (Mad Dog) Coll and JOHN (LEGS) DIAMOND among them, if not for youthful selection of friends. One, a fellow Jew named Meyer Lansky, was almost as violent as Siegel—so much so, in fact, that they were once dubbed "The Two Bugs"—but he learned from older, wiser mobsters like ARNOLD ROTHSTEIN and Cleveland's Moe Dalitz that a corrupt peace was more lucrative than endless war. Another teenage friend, Sicilian Charles (Lucky) Luciano, gave Siegel and Lansky a link to the powerful Mafia and its machinations within Little Italy. Together, that threesome would revolutionize organized crime in New York and beyond, charting the course of a national crime syndicate in the late 1920s and early 1930s.

Prohibition's end coincided with the onset of America's Great Depression, but the Mob suffered no financial headaches. In place of bootleg liquor, newly organized gangsters monopolized prostitution, narcotics, gambling, and a long list of rackets involving "legitimate" business. Faux respectability was a goal for many underworld leaders who longed to rub shoulders with movie stars, Broadway producers, and captains of industry. If only the syndicate's business were legal, mobsters could bank their millions without risking arrest.

A window opened on that dream in 1931, when the state of Nevada legalized casino gambling. It took

Mobster Benjamin "Bugsy" Siegel (center) is remembered as the man who "discovered" Las Vegas, Nevada, and turned it into the heart of a multibillion-dollar skimming operation. (Library of Congress)

another 15 years for eastern mobsters to discover the Silver State's potential mother lode, but in 1946 Ben Siegel—bankrolled by Lansky, Luciano, and others with money from drugs and associated rackets— began construction on the Flamingo hotel-casino on a strip of desert highway outside Las Vegas. Siegel had named the Flamingo on a whim, choosing the nickname of his latest mistress, fiery-tempered Virginia Hill. The volatile redhead had definitely "been around," paired at one time or another with high-ranking mobsters from California to New Jersey and all points in between, but Lansky dubbed the Hill-Siegel union true love after one of his visits to Vegas.

Still, it was a rocky romance, marked by screaming arguments and violence, which frequently distracted Siegel from his supervisory chores at the Flamingo. The hotel-casino was initially funded with 2 million syndicate dollars, but pilferage, bad luck, and Siegel's insistence on high-priced imported fixtures soon tripled the original estimate. Investors from Manhattan and Chicago suspected Siegel of skimming the loot and sending Hill to bank the money in Switzerland, where she made frequent visits for reasons unknown. A disastrous opening night at the Flamingo made matters worse, and mob leaders from around the nation gathered for a summit meeting in December 1946, rallying with exiled Lucky Luciano in Havana. They reportedly passed a death sentence on Siegel, with Lansky's approval, but no action was immediately taken on the "contract." By May 1947 the Flamingo was turning a profit, and Siegel apparently thought he was back in the Mob's good graces.

That proved to be a fatal mistake.

On the night of June 20, 1947, with Virginia Hill absent on yet another European excursion, Siegel lounged with friend Alan Smiley in the living room of Hill's Beverly Hills, California, mansion. He was killing time, chatting with Smiley and perusing the *Los Angeles Times*, when a sniper armed with a .30-caliber carbine fired through a nearby window, striking Siegel in the face. Police summoned to the scene by Hill's brother found Siegel's right eye on the dining room floor, 15 feet from the couch and his corpse. Within moments of Siegel's death in Beverly Hills, a delegation of New York mobsters invaded the Flamingo and announced that they were taking control. No one questioned the move, and play at the tables proceeded without a hitch, pouring millions (some say billions) of dollars in untaxed "skim" into syndicate coffers over the next 50 years.

Who killed Bugsy Siegel?

It was certainly a gangland hit, but speculation concerning the source and the triggerman's identity continue to this day. Some sources claimed that Jack Dragna—a Mafioso dubbed "the Al Capone of Los Angeles," frequently humiliated by Siegel and Bugsy's sidekick Mickey Cohen—fired the fatal shots himself. Years after the fact, Federal Bureau of Investigation (FBI) informer Aladena (Jimmy the Weasel) Fratianno named the shooter as hit man and sometime boxing promoter Frankie Carbo—but Fratianno also credited Carbo with "clipping" Nevada gambler Mert Wertheimer, who in fact died of leukemia.

As for the source of Siegel's death sentence, most authors still assume the contract voted by Lansky, Luciano, et al. in Havana had simply been postponed, giving Bugsy a chance to pay off his debts before he was murdered. In 2001, however, journalist Gus Russo offered a new version of Siegel's murder, based on statements from mob lawyer Sidney Korshak and pseudonymous informer "John DeCarlo." According to Korshak and "DeCarlo," Siegel's cost overruns at the Flamingo *had* been forgiven by his partners, and the traditional tale of his murder was "absolute fiction." In fact, they claimed, Siegel died as the result of a lover's quarrel with Virginia Hill.

According to Russo's report, one of Hill's many gangland paramours was Moe Dalitz, a onetime leader of Detroit's Purple Gang, who later controlled the Prohibition-era syndicate in Cleveland and environs. Dalitz, the informants say, was "very offended" by Siegel's tendency to beat Hill in the heat of verbal battle. As Korshak explained, "He warned Siegel, and Siegel paid no attention, and they whacked him." An FBI file obtained by Russo confirmed the couple's last fight. It reads:

> *Early in June 1947, Siegel had a violent quarrel with Virginia Hill at which time he allegedly beat her so badly that she still had visible bruises several weeks later. Immediately after the beating she took an overdose of narcotics in a suicide threat and was taken unconscious to the hospital. Upon recovery she immediately arranged to leave for an extended trip to Europe.*

According to informer "DeCarlo," Hill displayed her wounds to Dalitz, who became enraged. "When Virginia showed him what Bugsy had done, the contract went out. 'A face for a face,' was what I was told."

Fact or fiction? In 1949, the Dalitz syndicate moved its headquarters to Las Vegas, where Dalitz was soon recognized as the gambling Mecca's "godfather." He reigned in that capacity for the rest of his life, collecting multiple awards for his philanthropy, overseeing construction companies that built much of Nevada's largest city. Dalitz, active in the Mob from 1918 onward, died of natural causes in 1989, without ever serving a day in jail.

SILKWOOD, Karen Gay alleged murder victim (1974)

A native of Longview, Texas, born February 19, 1946, Karen Silkwood studied medical technology at Lamar State College (in Beaumont, Texas) before marrying William Meadows in 1965. The union produced three children, but Silkwood left Meadows in 1972 and moved to Oklahoma, where she soon found work as a metallography lab technician at the Kerr-McGee Nuclear Corporation's Cimarron River plutonium plant. Soon after she was hired, Silkwood joined Local 5-283 Oil, Chemical and Atomic Workers Union (OCAW) and joined in the union's strike against Kerr-McGee. When the strike failed that winter, all but 20 local members deserted the OCAW. Silkwood was one of the few who remained on the union's membership roll.

In 1974, emboldened by the OCAW's decline, Kerr-McGee administrators instigated a decertification campaign to purge the Cimarron plant of union activists. Before the vote was held, in August, Silkwood became the first woman elected to the OCAW's three-person bargaining committee. Her first assignment in that post was a study of the plant's health and safety standards. While pursuing that investigation, Silkwood found evidence of hazardous leaks, spills, and missing plutonium. In September 1974 Silkwood and her fellow committee members traveled to Washington, D.C., for a meeting with the OCAW's legislative director, discussing methods to block Kerr-McGee's decertification campaign. Silkwood's discovery of health hazards at the Cimarron plant figured prominently in the union's last-minute publicity broadsides, and the effort paid off. When the final ballots were counted, Kerr-McGee employees defeated the company's anti-union effort by a vote of 80 to 61.

A short time later, on the evening of November 5, 1974, Silkwood was grinding and polishing plutonium pellets in the plant's laboratory, using a protective glove box, when she decided to test her flesh and clothing with one of the lab's Geiger counters. Alarmingly, the right side of her body registered 20,000 disintegrations per minute (or nine nanocuries), suggesting dangerous exposure to radioactive material. Silkwood rushed to the plant's infirmary, where testing via nasal swabs revealed a "modest positive result" of only 160 disintegrations per minute. Testing of the gloves on Silkwood's glove box revealed plutonium on the "outside"—i.e., the interior surface in contact with the operator's hands—but no leaks were found in the gloves themselves. Likewise, no plutonium was found in the air or on any other surface in the lab where Silkwood was working. After a thorough cleanup, with orders for precautionary urine and feces testing over the next five days, Silkwood returned to her work in the lab and remained on the job until 1:10 A.M. (Although the contaminated gloves had been replaced, she did no further work with the glove box.) On leaving the plant, Silkwood

tested herself once again and found no evidence of radiation.

Silkwood returned to work at 7:30 A.M. on November 6, and tested herself again one hour later, before leaving the Kerr-McGee lab for a union meeting. Although she had not used the glove box that morning, confining herself to paperwork, the Geiger counter registered more radiation on her hands. This time, the plant's medics found significant traces on Silkwood's right forearm and the right side of her neck and face. Another rigorous cleanup ensued, and a plant technician tested Silkwood's locker and car without discovering any radiation. The cause of Silkwood's latest contamination remains unexplained.

A third alarm occurred when Silkwood delivered her urine and stool samples to the plant's Health Physics Office at 7:50 A.M. on November 7, 1974. Infirmary swabs found significant levels of radiation (between 1,000 and 4,000 disintegrations per minute) on Silkwood's hands, arm, chest, neck, and right ear. Furthermore, examination of her bioassay samples registered dangerous radiation levels, with 30,000 to 40,000 dpm in Silkwood's stool. While Silkwood underwent her third successive radiation cleanup, technicians rechecked her locker and vehicle, both of which were radiation-free. Upon examining Silkwood's apartment, which she shared with Kerr-McGee lab analyst Sherri Ellis, searchers found "significant" radiation traces in the bathroom (100,000 dpm on the toilet seat, 40,000 dpm on the bathmat, 20,000 dpm on the floor) and in the kitchen (400,000 dpm on bologna and cheese in the refrigerator, 6,000 dpm on a package of chicken, 25,000 dpm on the stove, 20,000 dpm each on the floor and on top of a cabinet). Lesser traces were found in Silkwood's bedroom, on her sheets and pillowcases. Small traces were also found on Ellis herself, whereupon both women returned to the plant for another personal cleanup.

The radiation levels in Silkwood's apartment were serious enough to mandate further testing of Silkwood, Ellis, and Silkwood's boyfriend at the nuclear lab in Los Alamos, New Mexico. The trio arrived at Los Alamos on November 11, 1974, and all were subjected to intensive examination. Dr. George Voelz, chief of the Los Alamos Laboratory Health Division, reported on November 12 that Ellis and Silkwood's boyfriend, Drew Stephens, bore "small but significant" amounts of plutonium within their bodies. Silkwood, in turn, was found to have six or seven nanocuries of plutonium-239 in her lungs, less than half the "permissible lung burden" of 16 nanocuries decreed for healthy lab workers. Dr. Voelz assured Silkwood that she faced no heightened risk of cancer or radiation poisoning, and that she could bear normal children if she so desired.

Silkwood, Ellis, and Stephens returned to Oklahoma on November 12, and both women duly reported for work the following day. Kerr-McGee barred them from working with radioactive material, but permitted both to complete a full shift. After work, Silkwood attended an OCAW meeting, voicing concerns that quality control of Kerr-McGee's plutonium fuel rods had been compromised. She left the meeting alone at 7:00 P.M., bound for a secret meeting at Crescent, Oklahoma, with a union officer and a reporter from the *New York Times*. Silkwood claimed to have documents that would prove her case against Kerr-McGee, but she never made it to the rendezvous.

At 8:05 P.M. on November 13, 1974, Oklahoma Highway Patrol officers responded to the scene of a single-car accident on Highway 74, seven miles south of Crescent. Karen Silkwood was found in her vehicle where it had run off the road, dead from multiple injuries. No documents were found in the car, and police reported no evidence of collision with another vehicle. Concerned by reports of Silkwood's prior exposure to radiation, Oklahoma's state medical examiner and officials of the Atomic Energy Commission arranged for her autopsy to be performed by surgeons from Los Alamos. The postmortem examination, performed on November 14 in Oklahoma City, included collection of blood and tissue samples for testing. Plutonium traces discovered in Silkwood's bones and internal organs were reportedly consistent with the levels from her latest test at Los Alamos. Blood tests revealed .35 milligrams of methaqualone (Quaalude) per 100 milliliters of Silkwood's blood—nearly twice the recommended dosage for inducing sleep—at the time she died. Another 50 milligrams of undissolved methaqualone was found in her stomach.

Relatives and OCAW spokesmen charged that Silkwood's death was the result of foul play, presumably by someone acting on Kerr-McGee's behalf, but the accusations remain unsubstantiated. The OCAW further charged Kerr-McGee with producing faulty fuel rods, falsifying inspection records, and jeopardizing employee safety. The Cimarron plant was closed in 1975, after National Public Radio reported

that 44 to 66 pounds of plutonium had been "misplaced" at the site.

In the wake of Silkwood's death, her family filed a wrongful-death lawsuit against Kerr-McGee, alleging inadequate health and safety procedures at the Cimarron plant. At trial in 1979, jurors awarded Silkwood's estate $10.5 million for personal injury and punitive damages, but that verdict was subsequently overturned by a federal appellate court in Denver (which limited Kerr-McGee's liability to $5,000 for personal property lost in the 1974 cleanup of Silkwood's apartment). Seven years later, with a new trial pending on the original lawsuit, Silkwood's family accepted an out-of-court settlement from Kerr-McGee in the amount of $1.38 million. Two books on Silkwood's case (both published in 1981) and a 1984 feature film (starring Meryl Streep as Silkwood) made a case for murder and conspiracy, but no suspects have been identified to date.

SINO, David See SAN DIEGO GAY MURDERS

SISMAN, Ronald, and Plotzman, Elizabeth murder victims (1981)

Journalist Maury Terry's investigation of the New York "Son of Sam" murders produced much disturbing evidence of occult crime in America, but none more persuasive than triggerman David Berkowitz's ability to predict ongoing crimes from behind prison walls. In mid-October 1981 Berkowitz informed a jailhouse confidant that his cult had a ritual murder planned for Halloween, described as "an inside, housecleaning thing" that would combine human sacrifice with the elimination of a perceived weak link. As described by the informant, quoting Berkowitz, the murder would take place in or near Greenwich Village. "On October 31, look for a kinky or bizarre assassination," the convict wrote to Terry. "Male(s) and female(s). Their heads shot off. And they'll remove the evidence just like they ransacked Berkowitz's place."

Shortly after midnight, on the morning of October 31, 1981, unknown killers invaded the Manhattan brownstone occupied by Ronald Sisman on West 22nd Street, near Greenwich Village. Before the killers left, Sisman and his companion, 20-year-old Elizabeth Plotzman, were executed by close-range shots to the head. As predicted two weeks in advance, the dwelling was ransacked in an apparent search for concealed valuables.

Police identified Sisman as a 35-year-old photographer from Canada, suspected of pimping and dealing narcotics. The double murder was officially listed as a drug "burn," but Berkowitz provided another motive. In his version Sisman possessed "snuff" tapes taken at the scene of one "Sam" shooting, and he planned to trade them for immunity on pending cocaine charges. Thus, the elimination of a "weak link" in the cult, while his execution provided the desired Halloween bloodletting. Berkowitz also furnished an accurate description of Sisman's apartment, complete with ornate chandelier.

Further investigation by Terry and others revealed that Sisman was a close associate of millionaire movie producer Roy Alexander Radin, himself described by Berkowitz as a "fat cat" or "Mr. Big" in the New York cult. Police questioned Radin about Sisman's death, but he claimed total ignorance. Other questions were pending, about his drug and cult connections, when Radin was murdered in California on May 13, 1983. William Mentzer, named by Berkowitz as an active Satanist, was convicted and sentenced to life for Radin's slaying. The Sisman-Plotzman murders remain unsolved.

SMITH, Patricia   See I-70/I-35 MURDERS

SMITH, Samuel   See INDIANAPOLIS TAXI MURDERS

SMITH, Tammy   See "INDEPENDENCE AVENUE KILLER"

"SODA Pop Slasher" probable literary hoax
Verifiable facts are as elusive as the killer in this case of an unidentified fiend who allegedly killed and mutilated his New York City victims with broken soft-drink bottles. The case was first revealed in *Fatal Analysis* (1997), billed as "a harrowing real-life story of professional privilege and serial murder." Problems arise, however, with a prefatory note explaining that "the authors have changed, added, or altered some events as well as locations, names, and identifying characteristics. The chronology of events has

likewise been altered. The book also makes use of composite secondary characters."

Thus rendered unidentifiable for all intents and purposes, the case has proved impossible to verify. Cover copy on the paperback edition tells us that [t]he New York newspapers dubbed the gruesome killer the 'Soda Pop Slasher,' yet no such nickname appears in any available newspaper index for New York City's dailies. Likewise, with names, dates, locations, and other "identifying characteristics"—including, presumably, the slayer's method of operation—altered to protect all concerned, a random search of murder cases listed in the *New York Times Index* presents researchers with a hopeless task. Still, because the book's publishers list it as nonfiction, it is included here for what it may be worth.

The putative author of *Final Analysis* (assisted, if not ghosted, by veteran *New York Times* reporter Thomas Clavin) is Martin Obler, Ph.D. Like his subject, however, Dr. Obler emerges from the book as a man of mystery, self-described in his own epilogue as "a well-respected psychologist, widely published and a full professor at a leading university." (The book's flyleaf lists Obler as a professor of psychology at Brooklyn College, in New York.) Curiously, a search conducted in 1998 by reference librarians at Indiana University in Bloomington revealed that Dr. Obler was not listed in the *National Faculty Directory*, nor were any academic publications with his by-line readily identified from standard published sources. He *was* listed on the Web site of Brooklyn College, in the Educational Services Division, and a telephone call to that institution (on January 26, 1998) identified Obler as an *associate* professor of psychology. According to the secretary with whom this author spoke, Dr. Obler, while tenured, was not then a full professor. "The difference," she explained, "is the paycheck."

Academic details notwithstanding, the core of Obler's tale, as described in the author's note, is drawn from an alleged experience in private practice, wherein Dr. Obler identified one of his patients—pseudonymous "Devon Cardou"—as the serial mangler of at least 13 victims around Greenwich Village. Obler describes Cardou as a twisted genius (I.Q. 154), referred to him for counseling over problems "of a sexual nature" at an unnamed "major university" in New York. Traumatized in childhood by watching his father sodomize his mother, Cardou allegedly exorcised his private demons with a broken pop bottle, mutilating the rectums of victims male and female, ranging in age from their teens to late thirties. In a climax redolent of Hollywood, New York police Detective Callahan (shades of Clint Eastwood's Dirty Harry!) discovers Obler's link to the killer, but Obler stands fast on professional ethics, refusing to identify the slasher. (This in itself is peculiar, since physicians and therapists in all 50 states are absolved of confidentiality—in fact, they are *required* by law to turn their patients in—when human lives are threatened by ongoing crimes.)

In the film noir finale of *Final Analysis,* Cardou kidnaps Obler's girlfriend "Rachel," but Obler manages to save her in an unarmed confrontation with his patient, using sheer force of will to persuade Cardou that "You want to stop killing." Cardou is free to get on with his life, Obler stipulates, as long as he abstains from random murder in the future. "Remember I'll be checking, listening," Obler warns his patient. "I am the guardian of the gate, Devon, and I'm watching." Obler and Rachel (or "Robyn," in the book's acknowledgments) live happily ever after, while Cardou—not unlike Brett Easton Ellis's fictional character in *American Psycho*—moves on to join a prominent law firm, rubbing shoulders with congressmen at televised press conferences. Through it all, Obler tells his readers, "I *was* still the guardian at the gate. And I had to remain there. My watch was not over."

Fact or fiction? There is no way to be absolutely sure, but some of the events—including Obler's private pursuit of a serial killer, avoiding police even after his lover is kidnapped—are so unusual that doubts arise in any cautious reader's mind, inviting comparison with the near-identical plot lines of such cinematic psycho-thrillers as *Dressed to Kill, Color of Night, Jagged Edge,* and *Final Analysis.* A review of *Fatal Analysis,* posted on the Internet at Amazon.com, adds further confusion to the case. It reads, in part: "I should start by saying that I am the author's son and wrote part of the original text. The original text was completely based in fact with some dramatic license mostly in the dialogue. The murders were real, although some anachronisms were present. However, the book was basically rewritten by the publisher without the consent of the author and greatly fictionalized. Even worse, the publisher did a poor job of this, hence the comments that the kidnapping did not ring true." Barring discovery of details that would make the case susceptible to proof, *Fatal Analysis* must be regarded with the utmost caution, as a probable hoax.

SODDER children missing persons (1945)

West Virginia's most haunting mystery began in the predawn hours of Christmas Day 1945. George Sodder, Sr., and his wife, Jeannie, were the proud parents of 10 children, residing in a new home outside Fayetteville. George, a 50-year-old Italian immigrant, had recently launched a new coal-trucking firm from his home, and it seemed to be prospering. One of the Sodders' sons was in the army, but because World War II had ended four months earlier, he faced no danger. The rest were home with their parents for Christmas. Life was sweet, the future bright.

The Sodder children opened their presents on Christmas Eve, including toys procured by 17-year-old Marian from her job at a Fayetteville dime store. George Sr. went to bed early, followed by children (and coworkers) John (age 23) and George, Jr., (16). Some of the others, including 14-year-old Maurice, 12-year-old Martha, 10-year-old Louis, eight-year-old Jennie, and six-year-old Betty, protested their bedtime but finally retired at 10:00 P.M. Jeannie Sodder took two-year-old Sylvia to bed with her, anticipating a good night's sleep.

But it was not to be.

Jeannie was roused the first time, shortly after midnight, by a ringing telephone in George's office downstairs. She went to answer it and accepted the female caller's apology for dialing a wrong number. A half-hour later Jeannie was wakened again, this time by the sound of some heavy object striking the roof. She waited for the sound to be repeated, then dozed off again when it was not. Some thirty minutes after that she woke a third time, to the smell of smoke.

Leaving her bedroom to investigate, Jeannie found flames spreading quickly through her husband's ground-floor office. She rushed back to the master bedroom, woke George, Sr., and they shouted up the stairs to rouse John and George, Jr., asleep in the attic. George, Sr. also shouted toward the other bedrooms on the second floor, and thought he heard his children answer. John and George, Jr. made it downstairs and out of the house, with their parents, Marian, and little Sylvia, but the other five children never emerged.

Now frantic, George, Sr., reentered the house and found flames engulfing the only staircase, spreading swiftly through the rest of the house. He raced outside, hoping to help his five remaining children exit through bedroom windows, but the ladder he kept propped against the house was missing. (The Sodders later found it 75 feet from the house, thrown down an embankment by persons unknown.) Next, he planned to drive one of his two coal trucks up to the house and stand atop it to reach the windows, but while both trucks had functioned perfectly the day before, neither would start on Christmas morning.

Marian Sodder ran to a neighbor's home to telephone the Fayetteville Fire Department, but the neighbor could not raise an operator to assist her. At 1:00 A.M., another neighbor passing by the scene observed the blaze and drove off to use a nearby tavern's telephone, but again no operator responded. Finally, that neighbor drove on into town and got Chief F. J. Morris on the line, informing him that the Sodder home was burning with children inside.

Even then, firefighters did not arrive on the scene until 8:00 A.M., a lapse explained by wartime depletion of department manpower and the chief's inability to drive Fayetteville's fire truck. Morris had to wait for a qualified driver to surface, but Fayetteville had no fire alarm in 1945, relying instead on a "phone tree" system whereby an operator called one firefighter, who then phoned another, and so on. By the time that sluggish system finally accomplished its objective, the Sodder home had been reduced to a smoking ash-filled basement.

George, Sr., and Jeannie assumed that their five missing children had died in the flames, but the evidence was contradictory. A brief search of the ruins ended at 10:00 A.M. on Christmas Day, with Chief Morris telling the Sodders no trace of the children was found. He suggested that the fire was hot enough to cremate their remains completely and instructed the family to leave the site as it was, pending a more thorough search. George, Sr., waited four days, then obtained a bulldozer and covered the basement with five feet of dirt, explaining that he planned to plant flowers and preserve the site as a memorial. A coroner's inquest deemed the fire accidental and blamed it on faulty wiring, and death certificates for the missing Sodder children were issued on December 30.

But *were* they dead?

Today, we know that the fire—which leveled the Sodder home in roughly half an hour—never reached the temperature required for the obliteration of human remains. (Total cremation takes two to three hours, at 1,400 to 1,800 degrees Fahrenheit.) In fact, various household appliances found in the burned-out basement were still recognizable.

Stranger still, a telephone lineman summoned to the Sodder home site reported that the phone line was not burned through, but rather had been cut 14 feet above the ground and two feet from the nearest utility pole. Neighbors directed police to a man whom they saw at the fire scene, removing an automotive block-and-tackle. He pled guilty to theft but denied any role in the fire, though he *did* admit cutting the phone line, allegedly having mistaken it for a power line. His identity and motives for cutting *any* lines at the scene remain shrouded in mystery.

Nor were they the only unanswered questions.

A late-night bus driver disputed the coroner's verdict of an accidental blaze, reporting that he had seen unknown persons lobbing "balls of fire" onto the Sodders' roof. In March 1946, Sylvia Sodder found a green hard-rubber object near the ruins, believed by some to be part of a firebomb. The Sodders later claimed that their home had burned from the roof downward, rather than from the ground floor up, but no evidence remains to prove the assertion.

Then the sightings began. First, the manager of a motel located midway between Fayetteville and Charleston, West Virginia, claimed he saw the Sodder children there on Christmas Day. A resident of Charleston later said that he saw four of the kids—Martha, Louis, Jennie, and Betty—with four unknown adults, about a week after the fire. The adults spoke Italian and have never been identified. Suspecting that their children had been kidnapped, George and Jeannie hired C. C. Tinsley, a private investigator from nearby Gauley Bridge, to pursue the case. Tinsley discovered that the Sodders has been threatened in October 1945 by a Fayetteville resident who tried to sell them life insurance. When they rejected his spiel, the man warned that their house would "go up in smoke" and their children would be destroyed over "dirty remarks" that George, Sr., allegedly made about Benito Mussolini, Italy's fascist dictator who was lynched in April 1945. The same man, by coincidence or otherwise, had been a member of the coroner's jury that deemed the Sodder blaze accidental.

In 1947 a Fayetteville parson told the Sodders a strange story. While Chief Miller had claimed no remains were found at the fire scene in 1945, he privately claimed to have found "a heart" in the ashes, whereupon he placed it in a dynamite box and buried it at the scene without reporting his discovery. Tinsley and George, Jr., persuaded Miller to show them the "grave." According to author Melody Bragg, "They got together and dug the box up. They took it straight to a funeral home and asked the person in charge there to open the box and examine the interior. When he did open that box, he found what looked like a fresh beef liver." While it could hardly have been fresh after two years underground, other published reports assert that the organ *was* beef liver, untouched by fire.

Later in 1947, George Sr. saw a newspaper photo of several New York schoolchildren, insisting that one of the girls was his daughter Betty. He drove to Manhattan in search of the child, but her parents refused to let him see the girl, and he went home disappointed.

In 1949, Tinsley and the Sodders mounted a new search at the fire scene, discovering four human vertebrae. When state authorities showed no inclination to examine the relic, Tinsley sent it off to the Smithsonian Institution in Washington, D.C. Experts there determined that the vertebrae belonged to a male between the ages of 19 and 22, reporting that they had not been exposed to flame. Published reports state that Tinsley later traced the bones to a cemetery in Mount Hope, West Virginia, but no explanation was forthcoming concerning their theft from an unidentified grave or their placement at the Sodder fire scene.

The Smithsonian report prompted FBI agents to investigate the Sodder case as a possible interstate kidnapping in 1950, but the G-men withdrew from the case two years later without making any progress. Around the same time, West Virginia State Police investigators took a stab at the mystery, with no greater success. In 1965 the Sodders received a photo of a young man in the mail. On its flip side, a handwritten note read: "Louis Sodder. I love brother Frankie. ilil Boys. A90132 or 35." While George, Sr., and Jeannie believed the photo was a likeness of their missing son, they could not interpret the cryptic message or trace the photo's sender.

Still, the family clung to hope. In 1952 they erected a billboard near Ansted, West Virginia, displaying photographs of their missing children with a $5,000 reward for information leading to their recovery. It brought no useful tips. Rumors abounded, including tales of Italian fascists, mafiosi, and child-snatching orphanage wardens. George Sodder, Sr., died in 1969, still hoping for a break in the case. His wife survived until 1989, and the Ansted billboard vanished at her death. The youngest surviving family member, Sylvia Sodder Paxton, keeps the family's haunting story alive with help from her daughter, pursuing leads on Internet mystery Web sites.

So far, all in vain.

SOLIS, Jesus See LOS ANGELES HOLDUP MURDERS

"SOMERTON Man" unknown poison victim (1948)

The unidentified person known as "the Somerton Man" derived his popular nickname from Somerton Beach, in Adelaide, Australia, where his corpse was found in 1948. The mystery began at 7:00 P.M. on November 30, when a man named Lyons and his wife took a walk on the beach before retiring to their home for the night. Passing near the former Crippled Children's Home, they saw a man lying on the sand, fully dressed, with his head against the seawall and feet pointed toward the surf. The reclining figure made an awkward gesture with one hand, as if smoking, and the couple passed on by, believing him to be intoxicated.

A younger couple arrived at 7:30 and sat on a nearby bench for 30-odd minutes, observing the man who had now ceased all visible movement and ignored mosquitoes landing on his face. The boy suggested checking to see if the man was injured or dead, but his girlfriend talked him out of it and they departed, leaving the stranger as they found him.

At 6:30 A.M. on December 1, Mr. Lyons returned to the beach for a morning swim with friends and found the man still lying where he was 12 hours earlier. A closer look convinced him that the man was dead, whereupon Lyons ran home to telephone police. A constable arrived and confirmed that the man was deceased, but found no signs of violence or disturbance of the corpse's stylish clothes: a double-breasted jacket, pullover sweater, white shirt with a red-and-blue tie, and brown slacks—all with the labels removed. A half-smoked cigarette lay on the jacket's right-hand lapel. The man carried no I.D., but his pockets yielded a canceled bus ticket to Glenelg (a nearby Adelaide suburb), an unused train ticket to Henley Beach, sixpence, matches, and an Army Club–brand cigarette pack filled with smokes of a different brand, Kensitas.

Police transported the corpse to the Royal Adelaide Hospital, where an autopsy was performed on December 4. Pathologists described the man as "European" in appearance, 40–45 years old, 5 feet 11 inches tall and in "excellent" condition (aside from being dead). His hands revealed no evidence of manual labor, but his toes were compressed into a wedge shape, like those of a dancer accustomed to tight shoes, and the development of gastrocnemius muscles in his upper calves suggested a preference for shoes with elevated heels. Time of death was pegged around 2:00 A.M. on December 1, but no specific cause could be determined. The man's heart had failed, and his stomach contained a substantial amount of blood, consistent with poisoning, but no recognized poison was found in his system.

Nor could pathologists identify the man. He had no scars, tattoos, or other significant bodily marks, and comparison of his teeth with dental charts of Australian missing persons led nowhere. Circulation of his photograph and fingerprints throughout Australia, New Zealand, Great Britain, and North America failed to produce an I.D.

The mystery deepened in January 1949, when police found an unclaimed suitcase at the Adelaide Railway Station, checked into the depot's baggage room at 11:00 A.M. on November 30. The suitcase manufacturer's label had been excised, along with most labels from the clothing inside, though that apparel (including a coat made in the U.S.) matched the corpse's garb in style and price range. Three pieces of clothing bore laundry marks and the name "T. Keane," but the laundry marks proved untraceable and no "T. Keane" was listed as missing from any English-speaking nation on Earth. Also inside the suitcase were a knife, brush, and scissors commonly used for stenciling cargo labels on merchant ships.

Detectives reconstructed some of the mystery man's final movements, concluding that he arrived in Adelaide aboard an overnight train from Melbourne, Port Augusta, or Sydney and shaved at Adelaide's public bathhouse, then bought a ticket for the 10:50 A.M. train to Henley Beach that went unused. Instead of catching that train, he left his bag at the railroad depot and caught a bus to Glenelg at 11:15 A.M., returning at some unknown hour.

Between January and March 1949, hundreds of persons viewed the stranger's embalmed remains, placed on display in a bid to secure an identification, but none recognized him, and the corpse was finally buried in early April. A coroner's inquest then convened on the case, during which pathologist Sir John Burton reexamined the dead man's clothes and found a clue overlooked by police. Specifically, inside a small watch-pocket of the slacks, Burton discovered a rolled slip of paper bearing the printed words *Taman Shud*—"The End," from the last page of Edward FitzGerald's translation of *Rubáiyát of Omar Khayyám*, originally published in 1859.

Authorities determined that the paper was, in fact, a page torn from a copy of that book. They launched a search for a copy missing its last page, and a Glenelg physician soon came forward, reporting that he had found a copy of the *Rubaiyat* left by persons unknown on the front seat of his unlocked car, parked outside his home on November 30, 1948. Its last page *was* missing, and four cryptic lines of seeming gibberish were penciled inside the back cover. They read:

MRGOABABD
MTBIMPANETP
MLIABOAIAQC
ITTMTSAMSTGAB

That clue, if clue it was, coupled with the facts of the Somerton Man's strange death and the evident pains taken to conceal his identity, sparked rumors that the man had been a spy—perhaps a foreign agent of some hostile cold war power. Cryptographers attacked the "message," but they never cracked it.

Meanwhile, police also found a telephone number inscribed in the book and traced it to female resident of Glenelg. She admitted owning a copy of the *Rubaiyat*, but said that she had given it to a soldier named Alf Boxall, whom she met in Sydney during World War II. Initially believing that the dead man might be Boxall, police saw that theory dashed when they found Boxall alive. Stranger still, he still had the *Rubaiyat* copy his former girlfriend had given him—with its last page intact. How, then, had the woman's phone number found its way into a second copy and into the Glenelg doctor's car? Under questioning, the woman professed amazement and denied any acquaintance with the Somerton Man. Police accepted that denial and declined to reveal the woman's name, for she had married since the war and feared a scandal. Critics of police tactics in the case still regard that decision as a blunder that guaranteed the mystery would never be solved.

Years later, locals noted that persons unknown had begun leaving flowers periodically on the unknown man's grave. Police waylaid a woman at the cemetery after one such offering was made, but she denied any knowledge of the Somerton Man or any role in placing the flowers. Around that same time, a former receptionist from the Strathmore Hotel, near the Adelaide railroad depot, claimed that a "strange man" had occupied Room 21 at the time of the nameless man's death. When he checked out, the receptionist claimed, a maid had found a hypodermic syringe—long since discarded—in his room.

Amateur cryptographers still tackle the *Rubaiyat* codes from time to time, with less than impressive results. One "solution" proposed that the line "ITTMTSAMSTGAB" might be an acronym for the phrase "*It's Time To Move To South Australia Moseley Street*," a street in Glenelg, but that supposition led nowhere. Some theorists suggest that the Somerton man killed himself with an unknown poison, but his motive, method of delivery, and his attachment to the *Rubaiyat* remain obscure—as mysterious as the final verse of that epic poem itself.

> *And when thyself with silver foot shall pass*
> *Among the Guests Star-scatter'd on the grass*
> *And in your joyous Errand reach the Spot*
> *Where I made One—turn down an empty Glass!*

SOUTH Croydon murders England (1928–29)

The unsolved poisoning of three victims at South Croydon, England, during 1928 and 1929 involved two interrelated families, the Sydneys and the Duffs. No motive was ascertained for the crimes, and at to date no suspect has been identified.

First in the series of victims was 59-year-old Edmund Creighton Duff, the son-in-law of elderly Violet Sydney. Returning to his South Croydon home at the conclusion of a fishing holiday, on April 26, 1928, Duff complained of nausea and leg cramps after eating dinner. His condition worsened overnight, and he died on April 27. An autopsy yielded negative results, and his death was attributed to unknown "natural causes."

Ten months later, on February 14, 1929, Vera Sydney—Violet's 40-year-old daughter—remarked on feeling "seedy" after lunch. The cook, her mother, and the family cat all suffered after sharing the meal, but they recovered, whereas Vera Sydney steadily declined. She died on February 16, after hours of cramps and vomiting which her physician blamed on "gastric influenza."

Violet Sydney was the last to go, falling ill after lunch on March 5, 1929. Already under medical care in her bereavement, she died hours later. On her deathbed she blamed the "gritty" tonic prescribed by her doctor. An analysis of the medicine showed nothing out of place, and the cause

of Violet's death was undetermined until surviving relatives demanded an investigation. The two female victims were exhumed on March 22, 1929, autopsies revealing traces of arsenic in both bodies. Edmund Duff was next exhumed (over his widow's protest) on May 15, 1929, and this time arsenic was found, the discrepancy from his first postmortem "explained" by a suggestion that physicians may have analyzed organs from the wrong corpse in April 1928. Inquests on Duff and Vera Sydney attributed their deaths to murder by persons unknown; in the case of Violet Sydney there was insufficient evidence to say if she was murdered or committed suicide. In either case, the mystery remains unsolved today.

"SOUTHSIDE Slayer" Los Angeles, California (1983–87)

Unidentified at this writing, the "Southside Slayer" of Los Angeles is credited with at least 14 homicides between September 1983 and May 1987. At least three other victims are considered possible additions to the list, and three more managed to survive encounters with the stalker, offering police descriptions of a black man in his early thirties, sporting a mustache and baseball cap. The killer's chosen victims have been women, mostly black and mainly prostitutes, tortured with superficial cuts before they were strangled or stabbed to death in a grisly "pattern of overkill," their bodies dumped on residential streets, in alleyways and schoolyards.

Loletha Privot was the killer's first known victim, found dead in Los Angeles on September 4, 1983. Four months passed before the slayer struck again, on New Year's Day, dumping the corpse of Patricia Coleman in Inglewood. Another 10 months slipped away before discovery of a third victim, Sheila Burton (alias Burris) on November 18, 1984.

The elusive killer adopted a regular schedule in 1985, beginning with the murder of Frankie Bell on January 1. Patricia Dennis was the next to die, her mutilated body recovered on 11 February. The first victim for March was Sheily Wilson, murdered in Inglewood on the 20th. Three days later, the stalker claimed Lillian Stoval in Los Angeles proper. Number eight was Patsy Webb, murdered on April 15, with Cathy Gustavson joining the list on July 28.

Thus far the killer had missed only once, leaving one victim comatose after a savage beating. On August 6, 1985, his next intended target managed to escape by leaping from his moving car. She offered homicide detectives a description and assisted in the preparation of a widely publicized sketch, but officers appeared no closer to finding their suspect than they were in 1983.

Rebounding from his recent failure with another kill, the slayer dumped Gail Ficklin's body in Los Angeles on August 15, 1985. A 12-week lull was broken on November 6, with Gayle Rouselle's murder in Gardena, and the killer returned the next day to slaughter Myrtle Collier in Los Angeles. Twenty-three-year-old Nesia McElrath was found murdered on December 19, 1985, and Elizabeth Landcraft's mutilated corpse was discovered three days later. On the day after Christmas, Gidget Castro's body was discarded in the City of Commerce.

The new year was five days old when Tammy Scretchings met her killer in Los Angeles, becoming number 14 on the Southside Slayer's death list. On January 10, 1986, a 27-year-old prostitute was beaten and a male acquaintance stabbed when he attempted to restrain her violent customer. Their descriptions of the suspect tallied with reports from the survivor who escaped the Southside Slayer's grasp in August 1985.

The killer claimed his 16th victim, Lorna Reed, on February 11, 1986, discarding her corpse in San Dimas, 25 miles east of his usual hunting ground. Prostitute Verna Williams was found on May 26, her body slumped in the stairwell of a Los Angeles elementary school, and Trina Chaney joined the list in Watts, on November 3, 1986. Nothing more was heard of the killer until January 1988, when police announced that Carolyn Barney—killed on May 29, 1987—was being added to the Southside victims list.

Three other women have been unofficially connected to the Southside Slayer, though detectives hesitate to draw a positive link. Loretta Jones, a 22-year-old coed with no criminal record, was murdered and dumped in a Los Angeles alley on April 15, 1986. A white "Jane Doe" victim, age 25 to 30, was found strangled in a Dumpster three weeks later. Finally, 22-year-old Canoscha Griffin was stabbed to death on the grounds of a local high school, her body discovered on July 24, 1986.

By early 1988, police were backing off their initial body count, noting that defendant Charles Mosley had been convicted in one of the 1986 murders, while five more cases—involving victims Barney, Burton, Castro, Ficklin, and McElrath—were considered closed with the arrest of two other serial killers, Louis Craine and Daniel Siebert. City police were less fortunate with their hasty arrest of Los Angeles County sheriff's deputy Rickey Ross as a suspect in the Southside case, when ballistics tests on the officer's pistol cleared him of involvement in the crimes. No further pattern victims have been added to the list since January 1988, and the murders of at least eight Southside victims remain officially unsolved today.

SOWLEY, Noel See "3X Killer"

SPANGENBERGER, Robert See Houston Decapitation Murders

SPARKS, Carole Denise See "Freeway Phantom"

SPIERS, Sarah See Perth, Australia, Murders

"SPRING-HEELED Jack" unknown serial marauder (1837–1904)
"Spring-Heeled Jack" is the popular nickname applied to a mysterious—some say legendary—prowler reported first from London, later from Sheffield and Liverpool. Elaboration of the incidents, both in contemporary newspaper reports and in secondary sources published over the past 170 years, have inflated "Jack" to the status of an urban legend imbued with supernatural powers.

The first report, from summer 1837, was filed by a London businessman returning home from work after nightfall, who claimed that a man with "devilish features"—including pointed ears and glowing eyes—had sprung over a cemetery wall to block his progress on the sidewalk. The figure did not attack, but his sudden appearance and equally abrupt leap back into darkness were still frightening.

In October 1837, a servant named Mary Stevens was walking through Clapham Common, after visiting her family in Battersea, when a strange figure ambushed her from an alley near Lavender Hill. The stranger clutched her arms with hands as "cold and clammy as those of a corpse," then

SPRING-HEEL'D JACK:
THE TERROR OF LONDON.

JACK ESCAPES CAPTURE.

along by the side of the hedge of the opposite field, till he came to where it was parted by a ditch, but which at the time was dry, and into this he threw the garments of the men, together with the pistol, then leapt the hedge again into the road.

He could hear, in the still night air, the voices of those whom he had played such a trick far away in the opposite field, and, after listening to them for some few moments, he hurried off in a different direction along the high road.

Suddenly he imagined he heard a heavy footfall; and as he paused to listen, another smote his ear.

"Spring-Heeled Jack" escapes capture by leaping over two bewildered policemen. (Hulton Archive/Getty Images)

ripped at her clothes while trying to kiss her. Stevens screamed, putting her assailant to flight while neighbors rushed to her aid and scoured the nearby alleys in vain. One day later, near Stevens's home, the apparent maniac jumped in front of a passing carriage, causing its driver to crash and injure himself. Bystanders told police the fiend escaped by leaping over a nine-foot wall, while cackling a high-pitched laugh.

Such gymnastics gave Spring-Heeled Jack his famous sobriquet and helped him to elude police as sightings swiftly multiplied. On January 9, 1838, Sir John Cowan, Lord Mayor of London, publicly read a complaint he had received days earlier, signed by "a resident of Peckham." According to that letter:

It appears that some individuals (of, as the writer believes, the highest ranks of life) have laid a wager with a mischievous and foolhardy companion, that he durst not take upon himself the task of visiting many of the villages near London in three different disguises—a ghost, a bear, and a devil; and moreover, that he will not enter a gentleman's gardens for the purpose of alarming the inmates of the house. The wager has, however, been accepted, and the unmanly villain has succeeded in depriving seven ladies of their senses, two of whom are not likely to recover, but to become burdens to their families.

At one house the man rang the bell, and on the servant coming to open door, this worse than brute stood in no less dreadful figure than a spectre clad most perfectly. The consequence was that the poor girl immediately swooned, and has never from that moment been in her senses.

The affair has now been going on for some time, and, strange to say, the papers are still silent on the subject. The writer has reason to believe that they have the whole history at their finger-ends but, through interested motives, are induced to remain silent.

Whether journalists indeed had "the whole history at their finger-ends" or not, one reporter in Cowan's audience spoke up to say that "servant girls about Kensington, Hammersmith and Ealing, tell dreadful stories of this ghost or devil." *The Times* covered Cowan's announcement, followed by other papers in successive days, condemning "wicked pranks" and claiming that several young women in Hammersmith had been spooked into "dangerous fits," with some "severely wounded by a sort of claws the miscreant wore on his hands." Letters pouring in from London and surrounding cities blamed several deaths in Brixton, Camberwell, Stockwell, and Vauxhall on fear sparked by Spring-Heeled Jack. Cowan remained skeptical, citing hoaxers in costume and "the greatest exaggerations" to explain Jack's antics.

On February 20, 1838, 18-year-old Jane Alsop answered a knock at her family's door in London's Bow district, to find an apparent policeman asking for help. The stranger asked Alsop to fetch a lantern, explaining that he and other officers had "caught Spring-Heeled Jack here in the lane." She complied, but once outside the house, the "constable" attacked her, ripping at her hair and clothes until Alsop's cries brought others from the house to help her. Later, she told real police that her assailant "was wearing a kind of helmet, and a tight-fitting white costume like an oilskin. His face was hideous; his eyes were like balls of fire. His hands had claws of some metallic substance, and he vomited blue and white flames."

Days later, on February 25 or 28 (reports differ), 18-year-old Lucy Scales and her sister were passing through Green Dragon Alley, in Limehouse, when a dark figure attacked from the shadows and "breathed fire" into her face. Scales collapsed on the spot and endured several hours of seizures, before her panic subsided. On March 6 both girls described the incident to police in sworn affidavits.

Police had no shortage of odd characters to choose from as suspects in Victorian London. One, Thomas Millbank, even confessed to the Alsop attack, stood trial, and was acquitted by the jury after reluctantly conceding that he could not breathe fire. Reports of Spring-Heeled Jack proliferated over the next two decades, spreading far and wide. In Northamptonshire, during 1843, witnesses described a prowler who personified "the very image of the Devil himself, with horns and eyes of flame." By the time he reached East Anglia, Jack harbored a particular grudge against mail-coach drivers. He was even credited by some for leaving cloven "devil's footprints" across 100 miles of Devon, on the snowy night of February 8, 1855.

A long hiatus then ensued, broken in November 1872, when the *News of the World* announced "a state of commotion owing to what is known as the 'Peckham Ghost,' a mysterious figure, quite alarming in appearance." In the editors' opinion, the "ghost" was identical to "Spring Heeled Jack, who terrified a past generation." During April and May 1873, the *Illustrated Police News* reported sightings of a "Park Ghost" in Sheffield, also compared by witnesses to Spring-Heeled Jack. In August 1877, sentries at the Royal Army's Aldershot barracks met a night-prowling figure who executed impossible leaps and slapped one soldier's face with "a hand as cold as that of a corpse." Gunfire did not faze him, and Jack once again escaped. A mob at Newport Arch, in Lincolnshire, came closer in the autumn of 1877, but Jack—this time wearing a sheep's skin—eluded the would-be lynchers with long-distance jumps.

A different Jack—London's "JACK THE RIPPER"—captured headlines in 1888, but Spring-Heeled Jack refused to be undone. That year found him in Liverpool, frightening student's at Everton's Saint Francis Xavier's Boys' Guild. Sixteen years later, Jack returned to Liverpool, rating mention in the *Liverpool Echo* on September 21, 1904. That story described "a sort of 'spring-heeled Jack'" lobbing stones at homes on William Henry Street, and while police arrested a local youth for that vandalism on September 24, the same day brought new reports from the *News of the World,* in an article titled "Spring Heel Jack—Ghost with a Weakness for Ladies."

With the exception of Liverpool's rock-throwing delinquent, no suspects were ever identified in Jack's 67-year series of incidents. Some skeptics attribute *all* reports of the prowler to mass hysteria, while others point a finger at unidentified copycat pranksters. Some reports claim the "original" Jack was an Irish nobleman, Henry de La Poer Beresford (1811–59), the Third Marquess of Waterford, whose philandering and drunken brawls made him a tabloid headliner during the late 1830s. Still, the *Waterford Chronicle* proved that Beresford was not in London for the Alsop and Scales incidents, and his death in 1859 exonerates him of subsequent cases.

Spring-Heeled Jack remains a staple character of fiction, with the latest version of his saga filmed in 2008, and some paranormal researchers still search for a supernatural explanation to Jack's antics. In 1997, a traveling salesman named Marshall reported that he had seen Spring-Heeled Jack or his twin 11 years earlier, dressed in a black jumpsuit, leaping with incredible bounds along a highway in South Herefordshire. Nor was the phantom simply composed of thin air, as it allegedly paused between bounds to slap Marshall's face.

STARKS, Virgil   See TEXARKANA "PHANTOM GUNMAN"

STEAN, Richard   See CHICAGO HOLDUP MURDERS

STEBBINS, Mark   See "BABYSITTER"

STEINIGEWIG, Alma   See CUMMINSVILLE, OHIO, MURDERS

STEPHENS, Barbara   See "FLAT-TIRE MURDERS"

STINE, Paul See "Zodiac"

"STONEMAN" unknown serial killer (1985–89)
Reports from India suggest that a serial slayer claimed at least 25 lives in two major cities over a four-year period, targeting homeless slum-dwellers who were beaten to death with large stones. While Indian journalists speak of a single "Stoneman," nicknamed for his choice of weapons, some police suggest that 13 of the murders were committed by a copycat offender mimicking the original slayer.

The grisly crime spree began in Mumbai (formerly Bombay), the world's most crowded metropolis, with some 14 million residents inside the city limits. Between 1985 and 1987, a still-unidentified slayer killed 12 victims around Mumbai's King's Circle park (now Maheshwari Udyan) and in the suburb of Sion. In each case, the chosen target was sleeping outdoors when the killer crushed his skull with large stones weighing 50–65 pounds. Six murders had occurred before police noticed the pattern, and most of the indigent victims remain unidentified today. A 13th victim survived his wounds, and while he could not describe his attacker, the crimes ceased thereafter.

The grim action shifted to Kolkata (formerly Calcutta) in June 1989, with the first of 13 nearly identical murders spanning six months. Again, the slayer had plenty of victims to choose from, with 5 million residents inhabiting Kolkata proper and another 10 million jamming its suburbs. The slaughter's pace accelerated, with 13 deaths in half a year versus 12 in 24 months for Mumbai, and while police in Kolkata found no solid evidence to link the murder sprees, journalists insisted that Kolkata's killer must at least be "familiar" with the methodology of Mumbai's Stoneman.

Today, 10 years and counting since the last acknowledged slaying in the series, police can only say that their quarry—based on his habitual employment of large stones or concrete slabs as weapons—must have been a tall, strong man. No motive for the crimes has been suggested, though the poverty of the selected victims rules out robbery. Interrogation of various "suspects" failed to crack the case, which remains officially unsolved today.

STOUT, James See Bell, California, murders

STOVAL, Lillian See "Southside Slayer"

STRIDE, Elizabeth See "Jack the Ripper": London

STRONG, Maureen See "Occult Murders"

SUAREZ, Fernando See New York City "trash bag" murders

SULLENBERGER, Mary See Washington, D.C., murders (1989)

SWARTZ, Amber See Bay Area child murders

SYDNEY, Vera and Violet See South Croydon murders

TAILFORD, Hannah See "Jack the Stripper"

TALLMAN, Daisey Mae See Yakima, Washington, murders

TAPP, James, Jr. murder victim (2003)
New Orleans native James Tapp, Jr., was born on September 9, 1977. He launched a career in rap music at age 17, through association with fellow Crescent City artists Percy "Master P" Miller and his brother, Corey "C-Murder" Miller. (Corey explained his stage name by saying, "They call me C-Murder, cuz I see murder.") Working with Master P's No Limit record label, under the stage name "Soulja Slim," Tapp recorded the albums *Soulja fa Lyfe* (1994), *The Dark Side* (1995), and his platinum-selling *Give It 2 'Em Raw* (1998).

A 1998 armed robbery conviction sent Tapp to prison for three years, but he emerged to cut another gold record, *Streets Made Me*, in 2001. More albums followed his shift to the Cut Throat Committy label, including *Years Later* (2002) and *Years Later... A Few Months After* (2003).

On Thanksgiving Eve—November 26, 2003—Tapp left his mother's home in New Orleans, bound for a local performance. Before he cleared the property, an unknown gunman shot Tapp once in the chest and three times in the face, killing him instantly.

On December 30, police arrested 22-year-old Garelle Smith, a suspected hitman from the city's St. Bernard Projects, but the charges in relation to Tapp's death were dismissed in February 2004. Meanwhile, on Christmas Day 2003, victim Steven Kennedy fell to gunfire in New Orleans. Detectives charged rappers Jerome Hampton and Ivory "B-Stupid" Harris with Kennedy's slaying, publicly calling it retaliation for Tapp's murder.

Once again, the "thug life" shared by many rap or hip-hop artists had cut short a promising career. Two posthumous albums, *Greatest Hitz* and *Uptown Souljas*, briefly revived Soulja Slim's fame in 2005, but his murder remains officially unsolved.

TAYLOR, Barbara Ann Hackman murder victim (1968)
The case of Barbara Taylor rates inclusion here, not only because her apparent murder remains unsolved after four decades, but because the victim herself was an unknown "Jane Doe"—dubbed "Tent Girl" by local reporters—for 30 years after her death.

The mystery began on May 17, 1968, when Wilbur Riddle, a professional well-driller, arrived at his latest job site near Eagle Creek, outside Georgetown, Kentucky. Passing time before his boss arrived with last-minute instructions, Riddle noted telephone linemen replacing old-fashioned glass insulators on utility poles along a nearby rural road. Aware that antiques collectors would pay for the obsolete insulators, Riddle began to collect the discards. He was carrying an armload to his pickup truck when he spied a rolled-up green tarpaulin bound with rope. Pausing to untie it, Riddle was assaulted by the stench of rotting flesh and saw the outline of a human body underneath the tarp's top layer.

Racing off to the nearest gas station, Riddle phoned authorities, then led Sheriff Bobby Vance and Deputy Coroner Kenneth Grant to his find. They finished unwrapping the bundle, revealing a woman's decomposing corpse. Grant performed his postmortem examination at Lexington's St. Joseph's Hospital, reporting that the subject was a white female with short reddish-brown hair, five feet one inch tall and 112 pounds, 16 to 19 years of age. Decomposition stalled recovery of fingerprints until the woman's fingers were severed and rehydrated—but they failed to produce an identification.

A subsequent autopsy, performed by Ohio pathologist Dr. Frank Cleveland, failed to determine the cause of death, but a bruise on the subject's scalp and the clawed posture of her hands suggested that she was clubbed unconscious, then wrapped in the tarp and left to suffocate. In the absence of I.D., a reporter from the *Kentucky Post & Times Star* dubbed the teenager "Tent Girl," after the tarp that served as her shroud.

Harold Musser, a Covington policeman and artist, studied photos of the Tent Girl and prepared a sketch of how she may have looked in life, including an obvious gap between her upper incisors. Publication of that drawing brought letters and phone calls from hundreds of parents across the country whose daughters were missing, and one near-miss sent police in search of suspects for the kidnap-murder of 15-year-old Debbie Krane, last seen alive with brothers Carl and Floyd Colby in Pasadena, California, during March 1968, but Krane's dental records failed to match Tent Girl's.

Another tantalizing lead surfaced in Northampton, Pennsylvania, where 16-year-old Candace Clothier vanished from home on the night of March 9, 1968, and was found dead in a canvas bag, dumped in a nearby creek, on April 13. As in the Tent Girl's case, pathologists could not determine Clothier's cause of death, but prolonged investigation found no link between the crimes.

On August 4, 1968, state police detective Edward Cornett received a phone call from an anonymous man who said, "I know a girl who's the Tent Girl you've been looking for. She's a young kid that disappeared from Covington in late April." That said, the caller hung up, leaving Cornett to search local missing-persons records for a likely victim. The only girl reported missing from Covington in April 1968 was found, alive and well, but Cornett admitted to reporters that "hundreds, perhaps thousands" of missing teenagers nationwide resembled Tent Girl.

The story went national in 1969, thanks to an article in *Master Detective* magazine, with Sheriff Vance pleading: "Any reader in any state who has some idea of who she is, please contact us right away. It is quite possible that she was killed somewhere else and brought here." The report brought scores of tips, but none helped to identify the Tent Girl or produce a suspect in her slaying. She was buried in a Georgetown cemetery under a stone marked "Tent Girl," with a reproduction of the artist's sketch.

Wilbur Riddle retired in 1988 and moved to Tennessee, but he never forgot the Tent Girl. He discussed the case incessantly with friends and family, including future son-in-law Todd Matthews, who in turn became fascinated by the mystery. On his own initiative, Matthews corresponded with authorities and procured an FBI lab report stating that a white cloth found in the tarp with Tent Girl was a diaper, suggesting that she may have had a child. Matthews requested exhumation of the corpse, for a pelvic examine to determine whether Tent Girl was a mother, but he had no legal standing in the case and authorities ignored him. Finally, in 1992, Matthews created an Internet Web site devoted to Tent Girl, broadcasting global pleas for information that might solve the case.

In January 1998, after examining and rejecting some 400 missing-persons reports, Matthews scored a hit. The e-mail came from one Rosemary Westbrook, describing the December 1967 disappearance of her sister, Barbara Taylor, from Lexington, Kentucky. Born in December 1943, Barbara was married to traveling carnival worker George Earl Taylor, who failed to report her missing. When another sister in Florida finally filed a police report in 1968, George Taylor claimed that Barbara had left him for another man, heading for parts unknown.

Kentucky authorities balked at pursuing the lead, but Matthews persevered alone, finally persuading officials to permit exhumation for DNA identification and other tests in March 1998. Dr. Emily Craig, a forensic anthropologist with the Kentucky state medical examiner's office, now determined that Tent Girl had been 20–30 years old when she died, rather than in her late teens. Better yet, DNA from pulp in one of the cadaver's teeth proved a familial relationship to Rosemary Westbrook.

Tent Girl had been identified, and she received a new headstone bearing her proper name, but mystery still surrounds her death. Police remain committed to a presumption of murder, but their only suspect—Taylor's husband—died from cancer in October 1987, and was thus beyond interrogation. *Master Detective* ran an update on the case in December 1998, but it still remains unsolved. Todd Matthews disbelieves George Taylor's story of Barbara's flight with an unnamed lover, but he thinks that her death may have been accidental.

TAYLOR, Gail   See WAYCROSS, GEORGIA, MURDERS

TAYLOR, William Desmond   murder victim (1922)
William Cunningham Deane-Tanner was born at Carlow, Ireland, on April 26, 1872, the third child of a British army officer whose family soon moved to Dublin. At 18, William failed his army entrance exams and was effectively exiled from his family in disgrace, emigrating to New York City. There, he married Ethel Harrison, a stockbroker's daughter, in December 1901. The couple lived in Larchmont, New York, and produced a daughter in 1903. William served as vice president of the English Antique Shop.

Although well-liked by locals and apparently well-settled with his family, Deane-Tanner had a restless spirit. On the afternoon of October 23, 1908, he went out to lunch and never returned. The next day, he telephoned the antique shop for $600 in cash, delivered via messenger—and then he vanished. Adopting the alias "William Desmond Taylor," he reportedly tried his hand at prospecting for gold in Montana, Colorado, and Alaska. In December 1912, soon after Ethel divorced him in absentia, "Taylor" surfaced in the budding motion picture colony of Inceville, California, built by producer-director Thomas Harper Ince near Santa Monica.

Taylor launched his film career as an actor in *The Counterfeiter* (1913). He played roles in 10 more films that year, 15 in 1914, and *An Eye for an Eye* in 1915. When not performing for the cameras, Taylor studied every aspect of the movie business, broadening his repertoire to direct and produce feature films. Between 1913 and 1922, Taylor directed 67 films, three of which he also produced: *Happiness of Three Women* (1917), *Huckleberry Finn* (1920), and *The Soul of Youth* (1920). In the process, Taylor also served three terms as president of the Motion Picture Directors' Association.

Taylor's Hollywood career was interrupted in July 1918, when he joined the Canadian army at age 46 and was shipped off to France in the final weeks of World War I. Stationed at Dunkirk, Taylor missed out on combat but left the service as a lieutenant in January 1919 and returned to Hollywood a hero of sorts. A brief reunion with his former family in 1921 made daughter Ethel Daisy his legal heir, but no long-term reconciliation was forthcoming. In fact, Taylor was running out of time.

At 7:30 A.M. on February 2, 1922, personal servant Henry Peavey found Taylor dead in his bungalow at the Alvarado Court Apartments, in the trendy

William Desmond Taylor is shown in an undated photo, taken sometime around World War I. Taylor was found in his home with a bullet through his heart on February 2, 1922. (AP Photo)

Westlake Park neighborhood of Los Angeles. Before police reached the scene, a crowd gathered outside. One man, a self-proclaimed physician, volunteered to examine the corpse, proclaimed that Taylor had died from a stomach hemorrhage, then left the scene without identifying himself. When police arrived at last, they proved the maybe-doctor wrong, discovering that Taylor had suffered a gunshot wound to the back. Postmortem examination and other investigations pegged the time of death at 7:50 P.M. on February 1.

While medical evidence cannot provide such precise timing, detectives helped out by charting Taylor's known movements. He had returned a phone call from actor Antonio Moreno at the Los Angeles Athletic Club at 7:00 P.M., and actress Mabel Normand had called on Taylor five minutes later, remaining at his bungalow until 7:45 P.M. From that testimony, and the medical evidence, investigators surmised that Taylor was shot within minutes of Normand's departure.

The motive for Taylor's slaying was never determined. Police deemed robbery unlikely, since the killer left $78 in Taylor's pocket and a two-carat diamond ring on his hand, but Taylor had shown a hefty wad of cash to his accountant on February 1, which was not found at the murder scene. While Taylor was laid to rest in a lavish funeral ceremony, rumors of scandal percolated through a Hollywood already reeling from manslaughter charges filed against film star Roscoe "Fatty" Arbuckle in 1921.

Taylor's slayer remains unidentified today, but the suspects scrutinized most closely by police and later published studies of the case include:

- *Edward Sands*, an Ohio-born con man who served as Taylor's valet and chef until August 1921, when he wrecked Taylor's car and forged several checks in Taylor's name while the director was traveling in Europe. After he was fired, Sands returned to burglarize Taylor's apartment, then vanished without a trace following the murder.

- *Henry Peavey*, an illiterate bisexual who replaced Sands as Taylor's manservant. His police record include arrests for vagrancy and public indecency with male minors. Taylor posted bond for Peavey on one such charge, and was scheduled to testify at Peavey's forthcoming trial when a bullet removed him from the witness list. Tertiary syphilis cost Peavey his sanity, and he died in a San Francisco mental institution in 1931.

- *Denis Cunningham Deane-Tanner*, Taylor's younger brother, who mimicked Taylor by deserting his own wife and two children in 1912. A few years later, Denis's wife recognized Taylor on screen and made contact. Taylor initially denied any relationship to his brother, but later relented. Some researchers suggest that Denis Deane-Tanner and Taylor valet Edward Sands were in fact the same person, but proof was not forthcoming. While Sands vanished without a trace sometime in 1922, Denis Deane-Tanner did not pull his final disappearing act until 1930.

- Comic actress *Mabel Normand*, with 218 films to her credit between 1910 and 1921. She was a close friend (some say lover) of Taylor, and the last known person to see him alive. Normand was also a drug addict, whom Taylor had tried to help cure on several occasions. Police dismissed her as a suspect, despite accusations from Henry Peavey—who apparently disliked Normand because she joked about his tendency to wear brightly-colored golf clothing. Still, association with the Taylor mystery and a diagnosis of tuberculosis blighted her career. Normand made only nine more films between 1922 and her death from TB at age 45, in 1930.

- *Mack Sennett*, director of 723 comic features between 1911 and 1949, who was also Mabel Normand's estranged lover. Some theorists surmise that he killed Taylor in a fit of jealous rage over Taylor's relationship with Normand, but L.A. police accepted his alibi for the night of the slaying.

- *Charles Eyton*, general manager of Paramount Pictures, which had Taylor under contract at the time of his death. Several sources allege that Eyton and other Paramount employees entered Taylor's bungalow following the discovery of his corpse and removed unspecified "incriminating items," either before police arrived or with official collusion. Lacking any solid evidence, no motive is apparent for Eyton's supposed slaying of Taylor, but a studio cover-up of potentially scandalous facts would hardly be unique in Hollywood history.

- Actress *Mary Miles Minter,* a Taylor protégé who made 48 films between 1912 and 1921. Minter was eight weeks shy of her 20th birthday when Taylor died, and some researchers claim that "coded" letters from Minter, found in Taylor's home, suggest a sexual relationship with the director beginning when Minter was 17. Paramount dropped Minter after four more films in 1922, and her career ended in 1924, after three final movies from other producers. Questioned by L.A. police on February 7, 1922, Minter claimed that another friend, actor-director Marshall Neilan, had recently described Taylor as "delusional" and "insane."

- *Charlotte Shelby,* Mary Minter's mother, described by various observers as a rabid "stage mother"–type obsessed with profiting from her daughter's talent. Early observers dismissed Shelby's first statement to police as "obviously filled with lies," and pointed to her alleged ownership of a rare pistol similar to the one used on Taylor. Following publication of that report, Shelby reportedly sank the gun in a Louisiana swamp. Shelby's friendship with L.A.'s district attorney spared her from serious investigation in the 1920s, and later, after her daughter openly accused her of the murder, she spent years abroad, avoiding further questions. In 1967, 10 years after Shelby's death, director King Vidor privately accused her of entering Taylor's bungalow while he escorted Mabel Normand to her car, then shooting him from ambush.

- *Margaret Gibson,* née Patricia Palmer, an actress born in 1894 who made 142 films between 1913 and 1929. In two of those, *The Kiss* (1914) and *The Little Madonna* (1914), she shared the screen with Taylor. Gibson's name was not linked to his slaying at the time, but she compiled a minor criminal record including a 1917 arrest for vagrancy (a common euphemism for prostitution in L.A.), and a 1923 bust for extortion. Jurors acquitted Gibson on the first charge, while the second was dismissed without trial. In 1934, by her own accounts, she "fled" America for unknown reasons, then returned to Los Angeles six years later. Gibson converted to Catholicism and married a Mobil Oil employee, whose death benefits supported Gibson in her declining years. On October 21, 1964, she suffered a fatal heart attack at her Hollywood home, where she lived as Pat Lewis. In 1999, the newsletter *Taylorology* claimed that Gibson-Lewis issued a deathbed confession, saying that she "shot and killed a man by the name of William Desmond Taylor."

- *Faith Cole MacLean,* wife of actor-writer-producer Douglas MacLean and Taylor's next-door neighbor. After Taylor was shot, the MacLeans told police they had heard a loud noise around 8:00 P.M. on February 1, 1922, whereupon Faith rushed next door and met a stranger emerging from Taylor's bungalow. The person, she said, was dressed "like my idea of a motion picture burglar" and looked "funny," like a woman made up to resemble a man. At sight of MacLean, the stranger doubled back into Taylor's home, then emerged a second time, smiling, and walked off without speaking. Various armchair detectives suggest that Faith killed Taylor, for some reason still unclear, and then concocted the burglar story with her husband to avert suspicion.

TEUBER, Louise   See SAN DIEGO MURDERS

TEXARKANA "Phantom Gunman" (1946)

America was still recovering from the trauma of World War II and the euphoria of V-J Day when headlines focused national attention on the town of Texarkana, straddling the Texas-Arkansas border. There, between March 23 and May 4, 1946, an unknown slayer claimed at least five victims, surfacing at three-week intervals to murder when the moon was full. His rampage brought hysteria to Texarkana and environs, causing citizens to fortify their homes or flee the town entirely, sparking incidents of violence when a paperboy or salesman was mistaken for a lethal prowler in the night. Despite nearly six decades of investigation and the production of a feature film about the case, it stands officially unsolved today, the "Phantom Gunman" unidentified and unpunished for his crimes.

The killer's first attack, unrecognized at the time, occurred on February 23, 1946. Twenty-four-year-old Jimmy Hollis was parked with his 19-year-old girlfriend, Mary Larey, on a lonely road near Texarkana when a tall masked man approached their car with gun in hand. He ordered Hollis from the vehicle and clubbed him to the ground, next turning on Larey and raping her with the gun barrel, tormenting her to the point that she begged him to kill her. Instead, he slugged her with the gun and turned back toward Hollis, allowing the young woman to escape on foot. Both victims survived their ordeal, but the gunman would not be so lax a second time.

On March 23, 1946, 29-year-old Richard Griffin and 17-year-old Polly Ann Moore were killed on a lonely Texarkana lover's lane. Both victims were shot in the back of the head, Griffin found kneeling underneath the dashboard, while Moore was sprawled in the backseat, but a blood-soaked patch of earth some 20 feet away suggested they had died outside the car. Both bodies were found fully clothed, and recent reports denied any evidence of sexual assault. Contemporary rumors, however, mentioned rape, torture, and mutilation inflicted on Polly Ann Moore.

Precisely three weeks later, on April 13, 1946, 17-year-old Paul Martin and 15-year-old Betty Jo Booker were ambushed in Spring Lake Park, following a dance at the local VFW hall. Martin's lifeless body, shot four times, was found beside a rural highway on the morning of April 14. Booker's corpse was discovered six hours later and a mile away, shot in the face and heart. Again, tales of fiendish torture spread through Texarkana, though a crop of modern journalists reject them as untrue.

The fanfare of publicity, complete with Texas Rangers on patrol and homicide detectives staked out in the guise of teenage lovers, caused the killer to adopt a new technique for what was said to be his last attack. On May 4, 1946, 36-year-old Virgil Starks was shot through the window of his farmhouse, 10 miles from Texarkana, as he read the evening paper after dinner. Emerging from a bedroom at the sound to breaking glass, his wife was wounded twice before she managed to escape and summon help from neighbors. In her absence the intruder prowled from room to room, leaving bloody footprints behind as he fled and dropping an untraceable flashlight in the bushes outside. Tracking dogs were rushed to the scene, but they lost their man at the point where he entered his car and drove away.

Two days after the Starks attack, with Texarkana living in a virtual state of siege, a man's mangled body was found on the railroad tracks north of town. While some reports have suggested that he may have been the killer, capping off his murder spree with suicide, the coroner's report of May 7, 1946, reveals that victim Earl McSpadden had been stabbed to death before his body was placed on the tracks, suffering further mutilation when a train passed over at 5:30 A.M. Today it seems more likely that McSpadden was another victim of the Phantom Gunman, perhaps dispatched in an attempt to end the manhunt with a simulated suicide.

Arkansas lawman Max Tackett claimed to have captured the killer in the summer of 1946, basing his case on disjointed remarks from convicted car thief Youell Swinney and an inadmissible statement from Swinney's wife. At least one Federal Bureau of Investigation (FBI) agent also fingered Swinney (sentenced to life imprisonment as a habitual criminal in 1947) as a prime suspect in the murders, but he was never charged with any of the Texarkana slayings. If Swinney *was* the killer, that fact somehow eluded Capt. M. T. Gonzaullas, officer in charge of the Texas Rangers' investigation at Texarkana. As late as 1973 Gonzaullas listed the "phantom" murders as his most baffling case, vowing that he would never stop hunting the killer as long as he lived. Today, the Ranger captain is no longer with us, and the case remains officially unsolved.

TEXAS tri-county murders (1971–75)

A mystifying case from southeast Texas, still unsolved, involves the deaths and disappearances of girls and young women in a tri-county region on the Gulf of Mexico. Conflicting stories from investigators and the media have so confounded matters that so far the body count has variously ranged from 16 victims to an estimated maximum of 40. After more than 30 years, one thing and one thing only may be said with certainty: the killer is unknown, presumably at large.

On April 5, 1981 a United Press International dispatch quoted Lt. Nat Wingo of the Brazoria County Sheriff's Department as stating that 21 girls had been kidnapped and killed during a four-year span in the early 1970s. Wingo seemed to consider his roster an incomplete list, speculating that as many as 40 victims may have been murdered during the same period. (When pressed for details by this author, Wingo indicated that the press "got that all wrong," but he refused to specify the errors or release a list of victims.) On April 7 the Associated Press announced that bodies of 21 victims had been discovered in Brazoria, Harris, and Galveston Counties since females began disappearing in 1971. At least eight of the deaths in Brazoria County were "similar," but police stopped short of blaming a serial killer. (Lt. Wingo, by contrast, was said to be "certain" of one killer's sole responsibility in "most" of the crimes.)

Based upon available reports, the victims killed or kidnapped in Brazoria and southern Harris Counties ranged in age from 12 to 21, with most aged 14 or 15. All were white and fair, described as slender, with long brown hair parted in the middle. Eight of the dead, recovered over a 10-year period, were reportedly found near bodies of water. At least three Brazoria County victims were shot, while two others were beaten to death.

The only victims publicly identified, 12-year-old Brooks Bracewell and 14-year-old Georgia Greer, vanished from Dickinson, Texas, on September 6, 1974. Their skulls were found by an oil rig worker near Alvin, in 1976, but they were not identified until April 4, 1981, thus reopening a stagnant investigation. Authorities from the affected areas convened that month to share their meager evidence, declaring that a list of 18 victims had been sorted out for special study. Two of the cases had already resulted in convictions, but they were left with the others "for purposes of comparison." All but one of the victims were murdered between 1971 and 1975, with 11 killed in the first year alone. At this writing, September 2002, the case remains open, with no end in sight.

THOMAS, Angela See "OCCULT MURDERS"

THOMAS, William See CHICAGO HOLDUP MURDERS

THOMPSON, Susan See OKLAHOMA CITY STATE FAIR MURDERS

"3X" murders New York City (1930)

Almost half a century before the "Son of Sam" murders, residents of Queens in New York City were familiar with another phantom gunman stalking human targets in their midst. Like "Sam," he kept up running correspondence with the press, explaining his attacks in terms that only he could fully comprehend. Unlike his imitator, though, the original Queens killer managed to escape detection, and his case remains unsolved today.

On June 11, 1930, grocer Joe Mozynski parked with 19-year-old Catherine May along an isolated lover's lane in College Point, a neighborhood of Queens. They wanted privacy, and they were startled by a stranger who approached their car, produced a gun, and shot Mozynski dead without a word of warning. May was ordered from the car and raped by her assailant; afterward, he searched her purse and burned some letters she was carrying. That done, the gunman walked her to the nearest trolley stop and put her on a homebound car, first handing her a note that had been printed with a rubber stamp, in crimson ink. It read:

Joseph Mozynski
3X3-X-097

Suspicious homicide detectives were still holding May as a material witness when the killer's first letter reached a local newspaper on June 13. Despite its brevity, it seemed to make no sense at all.

Kindly print this letter in your paper for Mozynski's friends: "CC-NY ADCM-Y16a-DQR-PA . . . 241 PM6 Queens." By doing this you may save their lives. We do not want any more shooting unless we have to.

A second letter arrived on June 14, branding Mozynski "a dirty rat," declaring that the killer accosted his victim "to get certain documents but unfortunately they were not in his possession at the time." Providing a concise description of the murder gun and ammunition for purposes of verification, the letter closed with a warning that "14 more of Mozynski's friends will join him" if the crucial documents were not delivered.

On June 16, 1930, Noel Sowley and Elizabeth Ring were parked near Creedmore, Queens, when a gunman approached their car and demanded Sowley's driver's license. Turning toward the outer darkness, he appeared to flash a coded signal with his flashlight, finally turning back to Sowley. "You're the one we want, all right," he said. "You're going to get what Joe got."

With that, the gunman executed Sowley, rifling his pockets before he to turned Elizabeth Ring. Avoiding rape with the display of a religious medal, Ring was left with a note similar to the one Catherine May had received five days earlier. Next morning, the killer mailed a new letter with two spent cartridges enclosed. The note described "V-5 Sowley" as "one more of Mozynski's friends," adding that "thirteen more men and one woman will go if they do not make peace with us and stop bleeding us to death."

A massive search of New York City failed to turn up any suspects, even with descriptions from the two eyewitnesses. On June 21 the killer surfaced in Philadelphia, mailing threats to Joe Mozynski's brother in an effort to secure "those papers." While the manhunt briefly shifted to Pennsylvania, New York police received another long and rambling letter from the gunman. Describing himself as an agent of an anticommunist group, "the Red Diamond of Russia," the killer proclaimed: "The last document, N.J. 4-3-44 returned to us the 19 at 9 p.m. My mission is ended. There is no further cause for worry."

True to his word, the "3X" killer disappeared without another note or crime to mark his passing. Six years later, a suspect in New Jersey confessed to the murders, but his story was discredited by homicide detectives, and he was confined to an asylum.

The "3X" legend grew with time and distance, swiftly losing contact with reality. As World War II approached, the homicides were blamed by sundry pamphleteers on Axis spies. Jay Robert Nash, writing of the case in *Open Files* (1984), described "3X" as "a maniac bomber [who] plagued New York City in the early 1930s by planting various homemade bombs throughout Manhattan, particularly at the site of major landmarks." In retrospect, there is no need to make the phantom more or less than what he was. The truth is strange enough.

TINSLEY, April Marie See FORT WAYNE CHILD MURDERS

"TOLEDO Clubber" Ohio serial murderer (1925–26)
A classic American bogeyman, the "Clubber" haunted Toledo, Ohio in 1925 and 1926, assaulting women at random, beating some of them to death and leaving others gravely injured in his wake. Before the madness ran its course, the unknown killer also stood accused of lighting fires and planting bombs in a bizarre campaign of terror that seemed to have no motive or direction.

The war of nerves began in early 1925, when several lumberyards were torched within a period of hours. Guards were posted, and the unknown arsonist (or someone else) then started bombing homes and tenements. Federal agents were called in to investigate when explosives wrecked the mailbox of a Roman Catholic priest, and the bombings suddenly ended, as mysteriously as they had begun.

The madman (or another) was not finished with his game, however. As contemporary reporters put their case, "the alleged fiend then turned to attacks upon women," killing three or four (reports vary) and wounding at least five others in a series of brutal rapes, invariably ending with the victims clubbed insensate and left for dead. Rewards totaling $12,000 were raised for the Toledo Clubber's capture but they brought no takers, and the violence ceased before year's end.

It started up afresh in late October 1926, with two more slayings added to the Clubber's tally in a single day. The first victim was 26-year-old schoolteacher Lily Croy, raped and bludgeoned within sight of her classroom in the early morning hours of October 26. The next to die, 47-year-old Mary Allen, was found murdered at home the same afternoon. Police initially attributed Allen's death to gunshot wounds, but later changed their story to report that Croy and Allen had been killed with the same blunt instrument, postmortem evidence recalling other Clubber homicides.

Around Toledo lapsed rewards were dusted off and boosted by another rash of contributions, while police swept up a crop of local "odd-balls," finding several who had slipped away from mental institutions. A new series of arson fires erupted on November 23, 1926, inflicting $200,000 damage at a single lumberyard, sweeping on from there to damage an ice company ($10,000), two other businesses, the city street department's stable, an apartment building, and a railroad freight car.

Officers made no progress in their search for the Toledo Clubber, but once again, as in 1925, the crime spree ended of its own accord. Was one demented individual guilty of all the rapes and beatings, fires and bombings? Did police create a monster in their bid to "clear the books" on unsolved local crimes? Whatever else he may have been, the Clubber stands reliably accused of half a dozen homicides, together with an equal number of assaults in which his victims lived to tell the tale. He remains unidentified at this writing, another of the ones who got away.

TOWN Hospital murders France (1944–47)

Over a three-year period, beginning in 1944, physicians and police alike were baffled by a string of homicides committed at Town Hospital in Macon, France, north of Lyons. Seventeen patients in the hospital's gynecology ward died mysteriously following successful surgery, with autopsies revealing that each in turn was killed via lethal injection. On June 13, 1947, helpless detectives announced that the killer was growing more cautious, allowing six months to pass between the murders of the last two victims. With public exposure, the killings apparently ceased. No suspect was ever named, and the case remains unsolved today.

TRAIN derailments

Since November 1833, when a train derailed in Hightstown, New Jersey, killing two passengers, railroad accidents have claimed thousands of lives worldwide. Such events are distressingly common—Canada alone suffered 195 train-track derailments in 2005—but the prospect is even more frightening when unknown saboteurs deliberately send trains plunging from their tracks, without regard to the potential cost in human lives. Modern derailments officially blamed on sabotage, and still unsolved today, include:

- *August 12, 1939* The City of San Francisco, a passenger train jointly operated by the Chicago and North Western Railway, the Southern Pacific Railroad, and the Union Pacific Railroad, derailed while crossing a bridge outside Carlin, Nevada, killing 24 passengers and injuring a further 121 en route from Chicago to Oakland. Police blamed the crash on sabotage, but never identified any suspects or motives.

- *August 17, 1949* Unknown saboteurs tampered with tracks on Japan's Tohoku Line, between Kanawagawa and Matsukawa, derailing a passenger train at Matsukawa. Three

crewmen died in the crash, and while police arrested 20 members of the Japanese Communist Party and the "radical" Japan National Railway Union, all were acquitted at trial.

- *July 19, 1981* Authorities blamed sabotage for the derailment of a crowded passenger train en route from Ahmedabad to New Delhi, India. The crash occurred at Gujarat, killing 30 passengers and injuring another 70. Although unsolved, the crash is largely forgotten today and barely stood out during summer 1981, which featured other Indian derailments on June 6 (268 dead, 300 missing), July 17 (39 dead, 43 injured), and July 31 (43 dead, 50 injured).

- *November 6, 1987* New Zealand's Westlander passenger train jumped its tracks at the rural Bindango siding, Hodgson and Muckadilla, causing a fire that killed 10-month-old David Smit. Eight more of the train's 34 passengers were injured in the crash. Examiners found that a saboteur had removed a critical pin from the siding's switch-point equipment, and police surmise the plotter(s) planned to murder some adult Westlander passenger, still unidentified. A $50,000 reward has produced no useful information in the case.

- *October 9, 1995* Amtrak's 12-car Sunset Limited plunged from a 30-foot trestle into a dry river bed near Hyder, Arizona, killing crewman Mitchell Bates and injuring 78 of the train's 248 passengers. Survivors and police found four identical typewritten notes strewn about the crash site, signed "Sons of the Gestapo." The notes denounced local police, as well as federal agents involved in the 1993 Branch Davidian siege at Waco, Texas, which resulted in 86 deaths. Investigators reported that 29 spikes were removed from tracks at the scene of the crash, while an electric cable was used to circumvent emergency alarms. Since the "Sons of the Gestapo" was a name unknown to authorities, FBI agents speculated that the notes were designed to cover a bungled robbery, or perhaps were written by a disgruntled Amtrak employee. In July 1996 agents from the Bureau of Alcohol, Tobacco and Firearms jailed 12 members of Arizona's neo-fascist Viper Militia on weapons and explosives charges, but none were linked to the Amtrak derailment.

- May 13, 2002   Another case of railroad sabotage in India derailed the Shramjivi Express at Jaunpur, in the northern state of Uttar Pradesh, killing 12 passengers and injuring 80. Police announced that the wreck was caused by removal of several fishplates, metal bars that are bolted to the ends of separate rails to create a solid and unified track. While no arrests resulted, Indian authorities note that Uttar Pradesh has a long history of violent conflict between Hindu and Muslim religious extremists, and particular suspicion focused on members of the radical Student's Islamic Movement of India. Unknown terrorists bombed another train at Jaunpur in July 2005, killing 13 persons.

- *September 10, 2002*   Indian terrorists struck again, removing fishplates from the Eastern Railway's track on a 300-foot-tall bridge spanning the Dhave River, near Rafiganj. An estimated 1,000 passengers were aboard the train, bound for New Delhi, when 15 of its 18 cars derailed and plunged into the river. Initial casualty estimates listed 130 dead and 50 missing, with the death toll later climbing past 200. No definitive count was possible, due to the standard overcrowding of Indian trains and the Dhave River's swift current. While early reports blamed poor track maintenance for the crash, police later named sabotage as the cause. Suspicion focused on the Naxalites, a group of Maoist radicals, but no arrests were made.

- *July 31, 2005*   Persons unknown removed vital wiring from a railway signal box near Shenyang, in northeastern China, causing a collision between a freight train and passenger train K127, en route from Changchun to Dalian, to collide with a freight train. The wreck killed six passengers aboard K127 and injured 30 more. China's Ministry of Railways confirmed sabotage as the cause of the wreck, but no arrests have resulted so far.

TRAUERNICHT, Delia   See "Redhead Murders"

TRELSTAD, Laura murder victim (1947)

A 37-year-old mother of three, Laura Trelstad was found dead on May 12, 1947, in a Signal Hill oil field 12 blocks from her Los Angeles home. According to the autopsy report she had been beaten, raped, and strangled with a strip of cotton cloth. There was no mutilation per se, but various reports describe the beating as "savage" and "ferocious" enough to have fractured her skull.

Trelstad's husband, a truck driver three years her junior, told police he had taken his wife to a party on Sunday, May 11, but she left "to go dancing" while he stayed behind to play cards. Detectives tracked down a sailor who was seen leaving a Long Beach café with the victim on Sunday night, but he was later cleared of suspicion in the case. Police believed him when he said he had escorted Trelstad to a bus stop and put her aboard a Huntington Park bus at 11:50 P.M. From there, authorities declared, "she kept a date with another girl," but no details were forthcoming. The crime, speculatively linked in some reports with the January 1947 "Black Dahlia" murder of victim Elizabeth Short, remains unsolved today.

"TRUCK Stop Killer" legendary U.S. serial murderer

A bogeyman tailor-made for America's mobile freeway culture, the "Truck Stop Killer" has bedeviled police from coast to coast for more than 20 years. His crimes smack of sensational fiction: a rootless slayer traveling where his mood takes him, claiming untold numbers of helpless victims in the mold of cinematic thrillers such as *Duel* (1971), *Road Games* (1981), and *Outside Ozona* (1998). Drawn chiefly to hitchhikers, stranded female motorists, and "lot lizards" (prostitutes who work the parking lots of truck stops), the faceless killing machine is said to kidnap his victims, often raping and torturing them prior to death, then dumps their corpses on the shoulder of some highway miles away from the crime scene. Various published reports credit the Truck Stop Killer with body counts ranging from a dozen victims to more than 100, with some authors claiming to trace his murder spree across a quarter-century.

The problem is that he may not exist.

All U.S. states have unsolved homicides on file, and some of them involve women abducted from truck stops, from their stranded cars, or while hitchhiking. Some such victims disappear without a trace, while others are discarded like trash on the roadside, their corpses found days, weeks—even years—after they are reported missing. In some cases frequently involving prostitutes who travel under several different names, there may be no police reports to mark their disappearance. Some of those slayings resemble one another: cause of death, descriptions of the victims or the unknown suspect and his truck. In others, when remains are found at all, advanced decomposition masks the cause of death and even the victim's identity.

Public discussion of the Truck Stop Killer began in the mid-1980s, around the time the Federal Bureau of Investigation (FBI) computerized its files on unsolved murders, and it continues to the present day. No investigator believes that *every* unsolved murder in this category was committed by a single transient predator, but they often speak in terms of certain similarities or bits of evidence (unspecified, to weed out false confessions) that seem to link a string of deaths, particularly in the eastern half of the United States.

Two police statements from January 1992 suggest the scope of the problem. On January 23 authorities in Muncie, Indiana, announced that the recent murder of 23-year-old prostitute Crystal Sedam, found on January 4 along Interstate 69, was "similar" to several other homicides reported since 1989. Detective Robert Pyle compared the case to that of 37-year-old Georgia Shreeve, found in August 1991 along I-74 in Montgomery County, and told reporters, "We are looking into the possibility that this murder is connected to other murders in Indiana and other parts of the country." Three days later, Pennsylvania state police told the press that a serial killer might be responsible for "several" of 17 unsolved slayings committed along Keystone State highways since 1976. The similarities: Many of the victims were prostitutes known to work truck stops, and the killer (or killers) apparently took items of personal identification as souvenirs of the hunt.

A classic Truck Stop Killer case, and the only one to date with a description of the slayer and his vehicle, is the August 1992 murder of 21-year-old Tammy Zywicki. Zywicki was en route to Grinnell College in Iowa after dropping her brother off at Northwestern University in Evanston, Illinois, when she vanished on August 23. By the time a missing-person report was filed, Tammy's car had been found by Illinois state police, parked on the shoulder of Interstate 80 two miles west of Utica, hood raised as if to signal engine trouble. No trace of the young blond driver remained, but reports of her disappearance brought telephone calls from several witnesses. Two had seen Zywicki's car around

3:25 P.M. on the day she vanished, parked behind an 18-wheeler that was painted white with a brown diagonal stripe on the side of its trailer. The apparent driver of the rig had been a white man with shoulder-length hair. He and his truck were gone when another witness passed the site at 4:00 P.M. and saw Zywicki's car parked with the hood up. A highway patrolman arrived on the scene at 5:15 P.M. and logged his discovery of an abandoned car with headquarters.

Ten days later, on September 2, 1992, a truck driver in Lawrence County, Missouri, stopped to investigate something wrapped in a red blanket, lying in a ditch beside Interstate Highway 44. He found a woman's decomposing body swaddled in the blanket and used his CB radio to call police. Dental records confirmed Tammy Zywicki's identity, an autopsy counting 75 knife wounds on her hands, arms, and torso. She had been murdered elsewhere, perhaps in the killer's truck, and then transported 160 miles from the point where her abandoned car was found. Thus far, despite the offer of a $100,000 reward for information leading to the killer's arrest, the case remains unsolved.

Zywicki's murder was one of the first discussed in June 1993, when FBI agents and 100 police officers from seven states gathered in Springfield, Missouri, for a conference dubbed SHARE (Solving Homicides and Retrieving Evidence). Each participant brought at least one unsolved case to discuss, but the main focus narrowed down to 27 murders dating back to 1969, including female victims found in Arkansas, Illinois, Kansas, Louisiana, Missouri, and Nebraska. They were not all truck stop victims—one had been murdered at home, drowned in her own bathtub—but at least five of the victims were transported some distance before their bodies were dumped, and 10 of the 27 were still missing.

Perhaps the most disturbing aspect of the Truck Stop Killer case has been the revelation of how many long-haul truckers seem to get their kicks from raping, torturing, and killing helpless victims as they cruise the nation's highways. Indeed, it now appears that there was never any single killer in the Truck Stop case, but rather a ghoulish subculture of truckers who kill as they travel, discarding victims like litter on the roadside. An incomplete list from recent years includes the following predators, all of whom may be considered suspects in some of the Truck Stop Killer's crimes.

Oscar Ray Bolin Jr. An Indiana native, this long-haul driver was sentenced to death in 1991 for three Florida murders committed five years earlier. That judgment was overturned on appeal, but retrial in 1999 resulted in new convictions and another death sentence. Additional murder and rape charges were filed against Bolin in Texas, while media reports call him "a suspect in dozens of other slayings across the country."

Benjamin Herbert Boyle Suspected of a 1979 Colorado rape and a 1985 California slaying, this trucker was convicted and sentenced to death in October 1986 for the murder of a 20-year-old Texas woman. Boyle was executed for that crime in 1997.

Scotty William Cox Committed to mental institutions on 115 occasions since 1975, this trucker was arrested by Washington State authorities in 1991 on charges of forging IDs. By year's end Cox was publicly identified as a prime suspect in "at least 20 killings" committed in Washington, Oregon, and British Columbia.

James Cruz A trucker since 1984, Cruz was arrested in September 1993 for the murder of 17-year-old hitchhiker Dawn Birnbaum, found beside I-80 in Pennsylvania six months earlier. Convicted of that crime in 1994 and sentenced to life imprisonment without parole, Cruz was also examined as a suspect in five Missouri slayings, but he reportedly was cleared on the basis of fuel receipts and travel logs.

John Joseph Fautenberry A long-haul trucker from 1982 through early 1991, Fautenberry apparently committed his first murder in Oregon during 1984. Charged with five slayings that spanned the continent from Alaska to New Jersey (with four of the victims still unidentified), Fautenberry broke the normal pattern by killing more men than women, typically shooting his victims for their money. A guilty plea to aggravated murder in Ohio earned him a death sentence in September 1992. Fautenberry's appeals continue, with an indefinite stay of execution granted in 2000.

Wayne Adam Ford A 36-year-old trucker, Ford surrendered to the Humboldt County sheriff in Eureka, California, in November 1998. Presenting deputies with a woman's severed breast inside a plastic Ziploc bag, Ford confessed to four California murders spanning the previous 12 months. Indicted on four counts of murder in September 2000, Ford has yet to face trial for his admitted crimes.

Sean Goble A trucker since 1992, arrested in April 1995 for a February murder in North Carolina, this bearded hulk soon pled guilty to that crime and two other slayings of victims discarded in Tennessee and Virginia. Police from 10 other states reportedly questioned the talkative killer, but no further charges have been filed to date.

Keith Hunter Jesperson The Pacific Northwest's "Happy Face Killer," so called for the mocking signature on his notes to police, Jesperson once allegedly confessed to 160 murders, then recanted most of his statements. He stands convicted of three Oregon slayings and one in Wyoming, strongly suspected in at least four more murders (one of them in distant Florida).

Robert Ben Rhoades A sexual sadist who traveled with his own custom-designed torture kit, Rhoades was sentenced to life in September 1992 for the Ohio murder of a 14-year-old girl he kidnapped from Texas. Photographs seized from his apartment document the girl's sexual abuse and torture spanning several days of captivity. Suspected in additional murders, Rhoades has not been charged in any other cases.

Alvin Wilson Convicted in 1984 for trying to rape a Virginia woman whose car he rammed with his truck, Wilson received a six-year prison term and was paroled in June 1986. Next accused of trying to strangle a woman in Ohio, he was "cleared" by his travel log, although the victim had accurately memorized the number of his truck's North Carolina license plate. Jailed by Florida police in 1991 on charges of rape and attempted murder, Wilson was publicly named as a suspect in 11 slayings from Ohio to Alabama and the Carolinas. In June 1991 Ohio authorities officially cleared Wilson of suspicion in six of the Buckeye State's 12 truck stop cases, without commenting on the other six. Four months later, he was convicted in Florida on three counts of sexual battery, burglary, and kidnapping.

Another suspect made the list on July 12, 2007, when police in Nashville, Tennessee, arrested 56-year-old Bruce Mendenhall at a local truck stop. The long-haul driver's rig matched one caught on videotape by security cameras at another Nashville truck stop, where 25-year-old Sara Hulbert was found shot to death on June 26. A search of Mendenhall's truck revealed bloody clothing in a garbage bag, together with a rifle and ammunition, several knives, handcuffs, latex gloves, black tape, a nightstick, and various sex toys. Analysis of the clothing revealed DNA from five different women.

While officers investigated Mendenhall's background and travels, the trucker reportedly confessed to Hulbert's slaying and the murder of Symantha Winters, a prostitute whose body was found in a trash dumpster at a truck stop in Lebanon, Tennessee, on June 6, 2007. A third victim, whom he admitted to killing on July 11, at a truck stop near Indianapolis, has yet to be found. Tennessee authorities indicted Mendenhall for the Winters slaying, while authorities in Birmingham, Alabama, charged him in the death of victim Lucille Carter, found shot on July 1.

Police also suspect Mendenhall of at least seven other slayings, most involving truck stop prostitutes. Victims identified in press releases include student Tammy Zywicki, kidnapped near LaSalle, Illinois, and found dead on September 2, 1992; hitchhiker Belinda Cartwright, run down at a Georgia truck stop in 2001; Deborah Glover of Atlanta, found in Suwannee, Georgia, on January 29, 2007; Jennifer Smith, a prostitute dumped at a Bucksnort, Tennessee, truck stop in April 2005; Sherry Drinkard, a Gary, Indiana, prostitute, found shot in a snow bank outside town on February 22, 2007; Robin Bishop, a prostitute run over at a Fairview, Tennessee, truck stop on July 1, 2007; and Carma Purpura, 31-year-old mother of two, missing from an Indianapolis truck stop since July 11, 2007. Purpura remains missing, but police found her blood, clothing, cell phone, and ATM card in Mendenhall's truck, prompting an April 2008 murder indictment. Authorities in New Mexico, Oklahoma, and Texas say they are also investigating Mendenhall's possible involvement in other, unspecified slayings of women.

TÜTENGIL, Cavit Orhan murder victim (1979)

Tütengil was born in 1921, in the village of Sebil, in southern Turkey's İnçel Province (now Mersin). He graduated from Istanbul's Haydarpa a High School at age 19, then obtained a degree in philosophy from Istanbul University in 1944. For the next nine years, he worked as a high school teacher in the southwestern provinces of Antalya and Diyarbakır. In 1953 Tütengil joined Instanbul University's economics department as a teaching assistant while completing his doctoral studies. Completion of his thesis ("Political and Economic Opinions of Montesquieu") earned him the Turkish Language Association's Science Award for 1957. From 1960 to 1970, Tütengil taught as an associate professor at the university, with a two-year interruption (1962–64) when Turkey's Ministry of National Education dispatched him to Great Britain. He attained full professor's status in 1970, and continued teaching for the remainder of his life.

Outside of Istanbul University, Tütengil's published writings marked him as Turkey's premier sociologist. His regular columns in the leftist newspaper *Cumhuriyet* espoused Kemalism—the belief that Turkey should be guided by the spirit of reforms pursued by Mustafa Kemal Atatürk, Turkey's president from 1921 to 1938. Some critics strongly disagreed, and struck out violently against him on December 7, 1979. Early that morning, while Tütengil waited for a city bus in Istanbul's Levent district, four assassins killed him with close-range gunfire. A note left at the murder scene claimed credit for the Anti Terör Birliği (Anti-Terror Unit). Police made no arrests and the crime remains officially unsolved.

"TYLENOL Murders" (1982)

The unsolved "Tylenol Murders" are unique among serial killings, in that the slayer never actually saw his (or her) victims and had no idea of their identity or number until he (or she) was advised of their deaths by media reports. Perhaps predictably, by its very nature, the case also had a greater impact on global civilization than any other case of serial murder in history.

The terror began on September 29, 1982, when 12-year-old Mary Kellerman, a resident of suburban Elks Grove Village near Chicago, complained to her parents of a scratchy throat and sniffles. Treated with an Extra-Strength Tylenol capsule, Mary was found unconscious on the bathroom floor at 7:00 o'clock the next morning. She died three hours later, at a local hospital. Postmortem tests determined that the capsule Kellerman ingested had contained a lethal mix of Tylenol and cyanide.

Those results had yet to be reported on the afternoon of September 29, when three members of the Janus family, residing in another Chicago suburb, swallowed Extra-Strength Tylenol capsules and afterward collapsed. None of the three was saved, despite the best efforts of physicians working on their case around the clock.

With the body count at four and holding for the moment, a local firefighter, Lt. Phillip Cappitelli, began putting two and two together. He was aware of Mary Kellerman's death from conversations with a relative; now, with reports of the Janus triple poisoning on his police scanner, he huddled with coworkers and soon made the link between Extra-Strength Tylenol and four victims to date. Warnings were issued throughout greater Chicago on September 30, but three more victims had already been poisoned in the meantime, none of whom would manage to survive.

On October 1, 1982, the manufacturers of Extra-Strength Tylenol recalled some 264,000 bottles of their product from stores in Chicago and environs, while the U.S. Food and Drug Administration broadcast warnings for consumers to avoid the drug until such time as an investigation was completed. The recall went nationwide four days later, after police in Oroville, California, blamed Tylenol laced with strychnine for the near-fatal convulsions suffered by victim Greg Blagg. By October 6 authorities in Canada, Great Britain, Norway, Italy, the Philippines, and South Korea were also taking steps to clear the suspect bottles from their shelves. The following day, authorities in Philadelphia retracted their suicide verdict in the April 3, 1982, death of student William Pascual, deciding the incident "might have been connected" to poisoned Tylenol capsules. A fresh examination of Extra-Strength Tylenol capsules from Pascual's apartment found them contaminated with cyanide.

Back in Chicago, meanwhile, investigators traced the deadly capsules to the stores where they were purchased. On October 4 it was announced that one additional tainted bottle of Extra-Strength Tylenol had been found at each of five stores examined.

Because of the small number found citywide, police concluded that the Tylenol was being bought or stolen, "spiked" with poison by a lurking killer, then surreptitiously returned to store shelves. That judgment was buttressed on October 5 after medical examiners toured the Tylenol plant at Fort Washington, Pennsylvania. Cyanide *was* used at the plant, but security measures were tight, and the odds against in-house contamination were pegged at "a million to one."

The immediate result of the scare was a call for new and stricter safety features in packaging of patent medicines. In Illinois, Cook County's board of supervisors passed an ordinance on October 4, 1982, requiring that all such containers sold within the county must have "tamper-proof" seals. The following day a federal task force convened to address the problem on a national basis. By October 6 Richard Schweiker, secretary of health and human services, had issued executive orders requiring tamper-resistant seals on all patent medicines and similar items designed for human consumption. Another step toward safety from random poisoning followed with invention of the "caplet"—i.e., capsule-shaped (but solid) tablets that cannot be opened and contaminated.

Still, prevention was easier than punishment in this troubling case, where the lurking killer (or killers) left no clues behind. It is a testament to human nature that with the Tylenol scare at its peak, certain opportunistic felons tried to jump aboard the bandwagon, demanding cash to avert future poisonings, and while they went to prison on extortion charges, none was ever linked to the actual murders. There was also a brief rash of copycat crimes, with victims in Colorado and Florida injured, respectively, by acid-tainted eye drops and mouthwash. In the final analysis homicide investigators in Illinois, California, and Pennsylvania could never decide if their poisoning cases were linked. Officially, the unknown "Tylenol killer" faces seven counts of murder for the crimes around Chicago, if and when police are able to identify a suspect. After nearly three decades, however, it seems unlikely that the case will ever be solved.

ÜÇOK, Bahriye murder victim (1990)

A native of Trabzon, on northeastern Turkey's Black Sea coast, Bahriye Üçok was born in 1919. She graduated from Istanbul's Kandilli High School for Girls, then studied Medieval Islamic and Turkish history at Ankara University's Faculty of Philology, History and Geography while simultaneously completing opera studies at a state conservatory. Upon graduation in 1940, she taught high school in Ankara and Samsun, then joined the staff of Ankara University in 1953 while completing her doctoral studies, securing her Ph.D. in 1957 with a thesis on "Female Rulers in Islamic Countries."

Üçok's employment as an associate professor, then full professor, at Ankara University prompted escalating threats from Muslim extremists who opposed advancement of a woman into any position of authority. Resigning from the university's staff in 1970, Dr. Üçok shifted her focus from academia to politics the following year, winning election as a legislator from the center-left Republican People's Party. Following a military coup in 1980, Üçok cofounded the Halkçı Parti (Populist Party), and was elected to parliament from Ordu Province in 1983. Three years later, she shifted farther to the left, joining the Social Democratic People's Party and writing columns for the "radical" Cumhuriyet newspaper.

Fundamentalist threats against Üçok escalated following a television appearance in which she declared that hijab—"modest dress for women," often including veils—was not obligatory for Muslim females. Many of the threats came from Turkey's İslami Hareket (Islamic Movement), whose purported members imposed a kangaroo-court death sentence upon Üçok. On October 6, 1990, persons unknown left a parcel on Üçok's doorstep. Expecting a shipment of books, she opened the package and died in the blast of a homemade explosive device. While members of the İslami Hareket are the primary suspects, none were ever arrested.

UPCHURCH, Norma murder victim (1931)

A 20-year-old London prostitute, Norma Upchurch (a.k.a. Norma Laverick) was found murdered on October 2, 1931, in an abandoned shop on New Compton Street. Her corpse was discovered when a contractor, one Douglas Bartrum, entered the premises with employee Frederick Field to remove some advertising signs owned by Bartrum's company. Upchurch had apparently been strangled, left with her clothing disarranged and her purse missing from the scene.

Police had several suspects in the case. One was the victim's current lover and self-styled fiancé, a seaman in the Royal Navy who was later exonerated by police. Another was a one-time British cricket star who hired Upchurch for sex on the night of September 28, thus becoming the last known person to see her alive. He, too, was cleared after interrogation by authorities. A third suspect, identified by Frederick Field, was Peter Webb. Field told police that Webb had borrowed Field's keys to the abandoned shop and had never returned them—an accusation Webb staunchly denied, supported by an iron-clad alibi for the night of the slaying.

The fourth suspect, favored by detectives in the case, was Fred Field himself. Honorably discharged from the Royal Air Force after six years of service, Field was married and lived with his wife in Sutton. Police focused on Field after determining that his accusation against Webb was untrue. Despite suspicion at Scotland Yard, however, no evidence was produced linking Field to the murder. Coroner Ingleby Oddie later summarized Field's charge against Webb for a panel of jurors at the Upchurch inquest, saying:

Does it sound a truthful story? Look at the identification of the man . . . Webb. Does that ring true? You have to ask yourself seriously whether the chain of circumstantial evidence is as complete against Webb as it is against Field. . . . Although the matter is one for you, you will allow me to suggest that the chain of evidence is not sufficiently strong and complete and secure. You may disbelieve Field's story altogether, but that does not prove that he is a murderer.

Accordingly, the coroner's jury returned a finding of murder by persons unknown. No further action was taken in Upchurch's case until July 1933, when Field confessed the crime to a London newspaper. (The paper had initially offered to finance Field's legal defense in 1931 if he was indicted, in return for his exclusive story and a final death row statement.) In his 1933 confession, Field claimed he had bargained for sex with Upchurch and took her to the abandoned shop, where she agreed to perform fellatio but refused to have intercourse. After strangling Upchurch in a rage, Field said, he had left with her purse (discarded in a drainage ditch near Sutton) and took the subway home to his wife. The motive for his belated confession was twofold: First, Field wanted money for his wife to visit her parents in Wales, and he was angry that coworkers mocked his stories of committing a "perfect" murder. Reporters searched the Sutton ditch for Upchurch's purse but found no trace of it.

At trial, Field recanted his murder confession and expressed a desire to clear his name, complaining to the court that he had lost a lucrative job offer from Ceylon (now Sri Lanka) when his involvement in the case was revealed to his prospective employer. The presiding judge was so impressed with Field's testimony that he advised jurors to acquit Field, and they duly complied with the court's direction.

Following his acquittal, Field rejoined the Royal Air Force, but deserted in 1936. Still sought by military police, he was arrested on a charge of larceny in London and confessed to the slaying of another prostitute, one Beatrice Sutton, at her home in Clapham. At trial for Sutton's murder, Field recanted once again, but detectives had obtained from him a detailed description of the victim's injuries and her apartment, thus demonstrating his presence at the crime scene. This time jurors found him guilty, and Field was sentenced to hang. He mounted the gallows on June 30, 1936. Reporters and police are still divided in their opinions of Field's guilt or innocence in the Upchurch murder.

"VALLEY Killer" New Hampshire/Vermont (1978–88)

The scenic Connecticut River Valley forms a natural border between the states of New Hampshire and Vermont, a generally quiet and peaceful place to live. And yet, since 1978, the region has been terrorized by two vicious serial killers. One was captured and imprisoned for his crimes in 1983; the other, and more lethal of the two, remains at large today.

The first known victim of the faceless stalker known to locals as the "Valley Killer" was 26-year-old Cathy Millican. An enthusiastic birdwatcher, Millican was last seen alive on September 24, 1978, when she drove to a wetlands preserve at New London, New Hampshire, to practice her hobby. She failed to return home that night, and her body was found the next day, sprawled near a path through the wetlands, her clothing disarranged and her belongings scattered along the trail, as if she had been dragged for a considerable distance. Millican had died from stab wounds to the throat, after which the killer repeatedly stabbed her lower body in a frenzied sexual attack.

Police were still baffled by that crime a year later, when 13-year-old Sherry Nastasia was reported missing from Springfield, Vermont. Her skeletal remains, found on December 13, 1979, revealed a broken leg and fractured ribs, but Nastasia's death was tentatively blamed on strangulation. Twelve-year-old Theresa Fenton was kidnapped while riding her bicycle in Springfield, on August 29, 1981; found alive the next morning, hopelessly injured by a savage beating, she died on August 31. The next victim, 11-year-old

Caty Richards, was abducted on April 9, 1983, and found beaten to death the next day, but this time a witness was able to describe the killer and his car. Suspect Gary Schaefer was quickly arrested and later confessed to the murders of Fenton and Richards, plus the abduction of a female hitchhiker who managed to escape his clutches in November 1982. In December 1983 Schaefer pled guilty to one murder count (Caty Richards) and one charge of kidnapping (the survivor). He denied involvement in Sherry Nastasia's death, but some investigators think he was responsible for that crime as well.

The Valley Killer, meanwhile, seemed to have gone on hiatus while Schaefer was playing his cat-and-mouse game with police around Springfield. The slayer's next presumed victim was 17-year-old Bernice Courtemanche, last seen alive on May 20, 1984, when she left her job as a nurse's aide at the Sullivan County Nursing Home in Beauregard Village, New Hampshire. A coworker drove Courtemanche to nearby Claremont, where she announced her intention of hitchhiking to Newport for a visit with her boyfriend. Courtemanche never arrived, authorities fearing that she may have drowned in the flood tide of a nearby river. Their hopes for a "natural" solution to the mystery were dashed on April 19, 1986, when skeletal remains were found by two fishermen near Kellyville, New Hampshire. Courtemanche was identified from dental records three days later, knife marks on her cervical vertebrae indicating that she was stabbed to death.

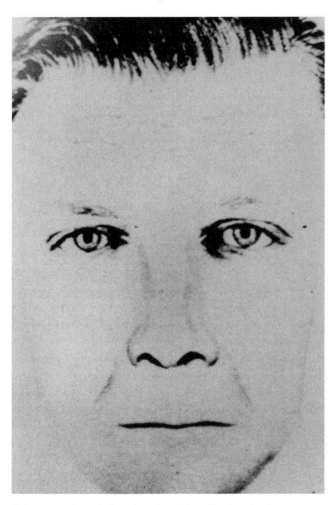

Police circulated this sketch of New England's elusive "Valley Killer," still at large today. (Author's collection)

In the two years between Courtemanche's disappearance and the discovery of her remains, the Valley Killer had claimed three more victims. Ellen Fried, a 26-year-old nurse, was last seen alive on the night of July 10, 1984, reported missing after she missed two days of work at Claremont's Valley Regional Hospital. Her car was found soon afterward, parked on a narrow forest lane nearby, but it was September 19, 1985, before her skeleton was recovered at Newport, New Hampshire. Fried was identified on October 1, and while the first autopsy failed to note a cause of death, subsequent examination found apparent knife wounds, listing her death as a homicide by stabbing.

Eva Morse, a single mother of one 10-year-old daughter, arrived at her regular job in Charlestown, New Hampshire, at 7:00 A.M. on July 10, 1985, but she never punched in. Instead, she lingered barely long enough to make a telephone call, then told her supervisor that she was going home sick. A coworker who spoke to her before she left later told police that Morse was bound for Claremont, hitchhiking to visit her onetime lesbian lover. As word of her disappearance spread, a motorist reported giving Morse a lift to the Charlestown-Claremont line, and there she vanished, until loggers found her skeleton on April 25, 1986, the skull nearly severed by stab wounds.

Lynda Moore was the next to die, found stabbed to death in the kitchen of her home in Saxtons River, Vermont, (south of Springfield) when her husband came home from work on April 26, 1986. The medical examiner counted more than two dozen stab wounds to her throat and abdomen, plus defensive cuts on both hands and arms. Moore's husband was initially suspected by police, as every spouse is suspect in such cases, but investigation swiftly cleared him of involvement in the crime.

The Valley Killer's apparent medical fetish resurfaced in January 1987, when he chose another nurse as his next victim. Thirty-six-year-old Barbara Agnew lived in Norwich, Vermont, and worked part-time at Mary Hitchcock Memorial Hospital, across the river in Hanover, New Hampshire. She was last seen alive on January 10, 1987, after a day of skiing with a friend near Winhall, Vermont. Three days later, her wallet and a woman's bloodstained clothing were found in the Dumpster at a gas station south of White River Junction, Vermont, and a call to the hospital confirmed that she was missing. Agnew's car was found abandoned on January 14 at a highway rest stop in Hartford, Vermont; police noted that her skis were missing, although her poles and boots were left behind. Agnew's remains, preserved by frigid weather, were found by hikers near Hartland, Vermont, on March 28, 1987. An autopsy revealed multiple stab wounds to the neck, apparently inflicted from behind, plus gashes to the lower abdomen that had become the Valley Killer's signature.

By that time, homicide investigators were reviewing two more unsolved murders from the same area, one dating back to June 11, 1968, when 15-year-old Jo Anne Dunham vanished from Claremont, New Hampshire. Found strangled the next day, her death bore no resemblance to the unknown slasher's crimes, but police noted that her corpse was discarded within a mile of the spot where Eva Morse had been last seen alive.

Another victim, 25-year-old Elizabeth Critchley, vanished while hitchhiking from Massachusetts to her home in Vermont, on July 25, 1981. Found two weeks later at Unity, New Hampshire, she had not been stabbed, but neither could the coroner determine any other cause of death. Critchley's body was found three miles from Gary Schaefer's home, and while authorities had questioned him about the case, he was never positively linked to Critchley's murder. In fact, police belatedly noted, her body was found within a mile of the sites where Eva Morse and Jo Anne Dunham had been slain.

To this day authorities cannot agree whether victims Dunham and Critchley belong on the Valley Killer's hit list. They feel more confidence regarding Jane Boroski, a pregnant 22-year-old who was attacked at a country store on Route 9, south of Keene, New Hampshire, on the night of August 6, 1988. An unknown man approached Boroski in the parking lot, dragging her out of her car, and pulled a knife when she fought back. At one point in the struggle, when Boroski asked why the man had chosen her, he replied, "You beat up my girlfriend." Boroski denied it, and the man appeared confused. "Isn't this a Massachusetts car?" he asked. Boroski pointed out her New Hampshire license plates, and the stranger hesitated, began to turn away, then rushed her with the knife again. Boroski was stabbed before approaching headlights caused her attacker to flee, but she survived the wounds and gave birth to a healthy daughter two months later.

Boroski described her assailant for police, assisting in the preparation of a sketch that was widely published throughout the Connecticut River Valley. In 1991 the crime was reenacted and the sketch was displayed for a national audience on television's *Unsolved Mysteries,* hosted by Robert Stack. The program has a history of clearing unsolved crimes, but no useful leads were generated in Boroski's case. The Valley Killer, though apparently "retired" since August 1988, is unidentified and still at large today.

"VAMPIRE" murders Colombia (1963–64)

Between October 1963 and February 1964 at least 10 boys aged 10 to 18 years were found dead in the city of Cali, Colombia, their bodies discarded in vacant lots around town. Medical examiners blamed the deaths on deliberate extraction of blood, and police declared that they were searching for a black market "blood ring," members of which were believed to be slaughtering children and selling their blood for $25 per quart. Commercial vampires had been suspect in the slayings since December 1963, when 12-year-old twins

mysteriously vanished, then turned up four days later, alive but in weakened condition. The boys told police they had been kidnapped, taken to a house where other boys were also being held, and given injections to make them sleep. From that point onward speculation took charge, with officers assuming blood had been extracted and presumably put up for sale. In truth, Cali's modern hospital attracted sufferers from all around the country, thus creating a brisk market in blood required for surgery, transfusions, and the like. Despite police suspicions, though, the Cali "vampire" slayings have remained unsolved, without a shred of solid evidence to build a case in court. An alternative theory, equally plausible in light of Colombia's religious history, suggests that the bloodletting may have occurred during ritual human sacrifice.

VARELA, Anna   See SAN DIEGO, CALIFORNIA, MURDERS (1985–88)

VASQUEZ, Jacqueline kidnap victim (2001)

Fleeting moments sometimes mark a life forever. So it was for 19-year-old Olivia Castaneda on May 6, 2001. Although a teenager herself, Castaneda already had two daughters, two-year-old Nayeli and three-month-old Jacqueline. On that Sunday afternoon she took the girls with her to a swap meet in Avondale, Arizona, west of Phoenix. Midway through their shopping, Nayeli needed to use the restroom and Olivia found a portable facility nearby. Nayeli needed help, and since the cubicle had no room for three people, Olivia left Jacqueline outside the privy, strapped in her portable car seat. When mother and daughter emerged moments later, the baby was gone.

Avondale police arrived promptly and sealed off the swap meet, conducting a thorough search, but no trace of the baby or car seat was found. During the search one vendor remarked on the suspicious behavior of a female customer who had caressed the vendor's own baby and remarked on the child's beauty. Unfortunately, no one still inside the swap meet when police arrived was found to match the woman's description, and her identity remains unknown.

Eleven months after the kidnapping, on April 19, 2002, a tip sent detectives to suburban Glendale, Arizona, seeking a child who resembled Jacqueline Vasquez, but it proved to be a false alarm. Authorities remain cautiously hopeful, since no evidence of murder has so far been found, and Olivia Castaneda refused to believe that her daughter may be dead. "I have faith," she told reporter Judi Villa in May 2002. "I know one day I'll have her back. I just don't know when. I know she's alive. Nothing can happen to her. I don't want to think that way."

VASQUEZ, Rosa   See "Occult" murders

VAUGHN, Marge   See "Frankford Slasher"

VAUGHN, Sheryl   See Oklahoma City state fair murders

VERILE, Pamela   See Grand Rapids, Michigan, murders

VESS, Amy   See "I-70/I-35" murders

VIDOCQ Society amateur sleuths pursuing "cold" cases
Named in honor of Eugène François Vidocq (1775–1857), a French fugitive-turned-policeman who founded the Sûreté in 1811 and recruited a unique team of ex-criminals as his detective force, the Vidocq Society was founded in 1990 as a private organization to investigate (and they hope solve) "cold" cases. The original founders included three experts in forensic science: sculptor and forensic reconstructionist Frank Bender; Richard Walter, a psychologist with the Michigan prison system and an expert in psychological profiling; and Bill Fleisher, a retired Federal Bureau of Investigation (FBI) agent and U.S. Customs inspector. The society was founded in Philadelphia, Pennsylvania, and maintains headquarters there today, across the street from Independence Hall.

With its home base in Philadelphia, the Vidocq Society has naturally evinced an abiding interest in that city's mysterious "Boy in the Box" case from 1957, but the cases accepted for investigation need not necessarily involve an unsolved homicide. At the May 2001 meeting, for example, retired FBI agent Thomas Kimmel presented a lecture exonerating his ancestor (U.S. Navy admiral Husband Kimmel) of negligent responsibility for the Japanese raid on Pearl Harbor in December 1941.

Defending sullied reputations is a prime consideration for the Vidocq Society, since its namesake delighted in liberating wrongfully imprisoned inmates and thereby served as the real-life model for two separate fictional characters, Jean Valjean and Inspector Javert, in Victor Hugo's *Les Miserables*. Thus far, however, the society that bears his name has not successfully emulated Vidocq by freeing any innocent convicts from prison.

Membership in the Vidocq Society was originally limited to 82 individuals at any given time, in honor of Eugène Vidocq's 82-year life span, but now boasts more than 150 members. New members are sponsored by existing members as vacancies occur, selected on the basis of their investigative credentials and without regard to nationality: Active members in 2008 included residents of 17 American states and 11 foreign countries—Canada, Egypt, England, Ethiopia, France, India, Italy, the Netherlands, Saudi Arabia, Thailand, and Uruguay. Officers and prominent members of the Vidocq Society (in 2008) include:

- Frank Bender, forensic sculptor specializing in reconstruction of human skeletal remains.
- Dr. Jolie Bookspan, Vidocq science officer, a military specialist in human survival in extremes of heat, cold, altitude, hypoxia, hyperoxia, G-forces, immersion, and injury states.
- Frederick A. Bornhofen, the society's chairman and case management director, head of the private investigative firm Frederick A. Bornhofen Associates.
- Gregory Caldwell—head of the Caldwell Group, a Colorado-based firm specializing in corporate investigations and security.
- William Fleisher, a former Philadelphia police officer, FBI agent, and assistant special agent in charge of the U.S. Customs Service in Philadelphia.
- Edward Gaughan, a former Philadelphia police department detective.
- Robert Goldberg—a physician-attorney from Marietta, Georgia, frequently retained to testify as an expert witness in criminal cases.
- Nathan Gordon, a society director and head of the Academy for Scientific Investigative Training, a school that trains polygraph operators.

- Wayne Hill Sr.—an expert in firearms and homicide events reconstruction, with 14 years in law enforcement.
- Richard Lavinthal, a legal public relations consultant and former journalist who once handled PR duties for the U.S. attorney's office in New Jersey and the New Jersey Division of Criminal Justice.
- Robert J. Phillips, a forensic document examiner with offices in New Jersey, Nevada, and Massachusetts.
- Norman Reeves, a specialist in bloodstain pattern analysis, crime scene reconstruction, computer imaging, and enhancement at BPA Consulting.
- Robert Ressler, a former FBI agent who spent 16 years profiling unknown subjects for the bureau's Behavioral Science Unit, often (incorrectly) credited with coining the term *serial killer*.
- Mark Safarik, a 12-year veteran of FBI profiling and Ressler's current partner in Forensic Behavioral Services International, a private consulting firm.
- Charles Sulzbach, Jr., a specialist in accident investigation and reconstruction with K & S Investigations of Jamison, Pennsylvania, and Sea Isle City, New Jersey.
- Richard Walter, a former forensic psychologist and crime-scene analyst for the Michigan Department of Corrections, now in private practice.
- David Ziegler, a specialist in forensic hypnosis, fire, arson, and bomb investigations, formerly employed as an agent of the U.S. Bureau of Alcohol, Tobacco, Firearms and Explosives.

VIENS, Maurice See MONTREAL CHILD MURDERS

VILLANUEVA, Julio See SAN ANTONIO TAXI MURDERS

VOGEL, Sylvia See "WEST SIDE RAPIST"

VON Bülow, Sunny victim of attempted murder (1980)
Martha Sharp Crawford was born in Manassas, Virginia, on September 1, 1932. The only child of utilities baron George Crawford, Martha inherited a fortune at age four after her father's death. In July 1957, she married an Austrian nobleman, Prince Alfred von Auersperg, and bore two children from that union. When they divorced in 1965, Martha—more commonly known by the nickname "Sunny"—had a net worth estimated in excess of $75 million.

Nine years after her divorce, Sunny married again, this time to Claus von Bülow, a British subject six years her junior, born in Copenhagen, Denmark. Von Bülow also hailed from an aristocratic line, related by marriage to composer Richard Wagner (1813–83); his maternal grandfather was Fritz Bülow, Denmark's minister of justice (1910–1913) and later Speaker of the upper house of the Danish parliament. Claus completed his university studies in England, practiced law in London, and served as a personal aide to oil magnate J. Paul Getty prior to marrying Sunny. One year after their marriage, Sunny bore a third child, daughter Cosima Iona von Bülow.

By 1980 the von Bülow marriage seemed to be in trouble, fueled at least in part by Sunny's erratic behavior. That April, Sunny was examined at a hospital where doctors diagnosed her as suffering from reactive hypoglycemia, produced by consumption of excessive carbohydrates, which accelerate natural insulin production. She recovered from that episode and spent the next few months managing her symptoms with a special diet.

Then, while celebrating Christmas with her family at the couple's mansion in Newport, Rhode Island, on December 21, 1980, Sunny suffered a relapse. Relatives thought she was merely intoxicated that night, but they could not wake her the following morning. Hospital staffers ran a battery of tests, announcing that Sunny had suffered brain damage that plunged her into a "persistent vegetative state." Claus prevailed against Sunny's children in a debate over long-term artificial life support, but when physicians disconnected her respirator, she continued to breathe on her own.

The combination of marital discord and a large potential inheritance prompted Sunny's children to suspect foul play. They noted that a prenuptial agreement barred Claus from receiving a cent if the couple divorced, but as a widower he stood to inherit $14 million. Sunny's children from her first marriage convinced a former New York County district attorney, Richard Kuh, to investigate the case as an attempted homicide. Kuh found enough evidence to convince Rhode Island prosecutors that Claus had injected Sunny with insulin in an attempt to kill her. In July

Claus von Bülow, the Danish-born socialite, listens to medical testimony at his retrial for the murder of his wife, Martha "Sunny" von Bülow. (AP Photo/pool/ Norm Sylvia)

1981, authorities charged Claus von Bülow with two counts of attempted murder.

At trial, beginning in February 1982, prosecutors coupled circumstantial evidence, including drugs and a used syringe found in the von Bülow mansion, with testimony from various employees and acquaintances who described a tempestuous marriage, topped off by a presumed financial motive for murder. Dr. George Cahill, an endocrinologist from Harvard University, opined that Sunny had lapsed into a coma following malicious insulin injections. The defense countered with evidence of Sunny's illness, plus her excessive use of alcohol and various drugs. Persuaded of Von Bülow's guilt, Newport jurors convicted him on March 16 and he received a 30-year prison term.

For his appeal, von Bülow retained attorney Alan Dershowitz, whose legal team produced further evidence of Sunny's drug abuse. New witnesses on that subject included celebrity author Truman Capote and the second wife of TV talk-show magnate Johnny Carson. At the same time, Dershowitz won a court ruling excluding certain physical evidence and "hypothetical" expert testimony from the original trial. New expert testimony, procured by Von Bülow's latest battery of lawyers, cast doubt on early findings that the syringe found in his home contained traces of insulin. In 1984, after seven months on the job, Dershowitz and company obtained an appellate court's ruling reversing Von Bülow's conviction. At his retrial for attempted murder in 1985, jurors acquitted him of all charges.

Sunny Von Bülow died on December 6, 2008, two weeks shy of 28 years since she lapsed into coma. Her family remains convinced that Claus is guilty of attempted murder. Claus formally renounced his share of Sunny's estate following his acquittal, leaving her entire fortune to her three children. According to published reports, Sunny's son and daughter by Prince Alfred of Auersperg split $45 million, while daughter Cosima von Bülow received $30 million. Under terms of Claus's legal agreement to forego any inheritance, Cosima stands as heir to the fortune of Sunny's mother.

Claus von Bülow lives in London, where he writes art and theater reviews. Alan Dershowitz published a book on the case in 1985, titled *Reversal of Fortune,* which was filmed five years later with Jeremy Irons portraying Claus and Glenn Close cast as Sunny. At Sunny's death, Claus expressed sadness, from London, through the former attorney Dershowitz.

WALES, Thomas Crane murder victim (2001)

Thomas Wales was an affluent native of Boston, born in 1952. He attended the private and prestigious Milton Academy, where he shared a dormitory room with Joseph Kennedy II, son of murdered U.S. senator ROBERT KENNEDY. After graduating from Milton, Wales attended Harvard University, then moved on to Hofstra University's School of Law on Long Island, New York. There, he served as editor in chief of the *Hofstra Law Review*, graduating with distinction in 1979.

Wales's education and connections won him employment with the Department of Justice, as an assistant U.S. attorney in Seattle, Washington. He specialized in the prosecution of banking and business fraud, while serving in his free time as a trustee for the Federal Bar Association.

A 1995 shooting at his son's high school sparked Wales's involvement in gun-control activism. He joined a local group, Washington CeaseFire, and later served as its president, sponsoring a 1997 referendum that would have required Washington gun owners to buy and use trigger locks. That measure failed to pass, but Wales remained active in Washington CeaseFire and other community groups.

At 10:40 P.M. on October 11, 2001, while Wales worked on a computer in the basement of his Seattle home, an unknown gunman entered his backyard, somehow avoided outdoor security lights, and fired several gunshots through a window, killing Wales where he sat. Neighbors heard the fatal shots and may have glimpsed the shooter, but circulation of an FBI

sketch depicting a "person of interest" has failed to identify the gunman. Likewise, a Justice Department reward of $1 million leading to solution of the case has lured no takers.

G-men *do* have a suspect in the murder, but he remains unidentified today since agents possess insufficient evidence to file charges. Described as a commercial airline pilot residing in Bellevue, Washington, the man in question was one of several defendants prosecuted by Wales on fraud charges related to a business venture. The corporation pleaded guilty to fraud in that case. Charges against the individual owners were dismissed, but the alleged suspect was left with legal fees exceeding $125,000, and his civil lawsuit for wrongful prosecution was dismissed. Agents say the pilot was "openly disdainful of Wales in particular," and they surmise he killed Wales in revenge. They further cite a TV appearance by Wales, two weeks before he was shot, in which he opposed suggestions that airline pilots be armed against hijackers.

G-men maintain that they have "plenty of circumstantial evidence" against their man, starting with his refusal to sit for FBI interviews. They claim that a "continuum" of incidents drove the pilot to slay Wales, but searches of his home, court-ordered submission of DNA samples, and repeated grilling of him and his relatives by federal grand juries have failed to produce any substantive admissible evidence. Friends of the suspect claim the feds bungled their manhunt from the start and now target an innocent man to conceal their shortcomings. Federal spokesmen have acknowledged that the timing of Wales's murder, coming exactly one month after the disastrous 9/11 terrorist attacks, resulted in "awkward handling" of the investigation.

One thing is certain: Ballistics tests and cartridge casings from Wales's yard show that the murder weapon was a Makarov semiautomatic pistol, manufactured in Russia and fitted with a replacement barrel sometime after its original production. Early in 2005, G-men claimed that Albert Kwan—a Bellevue resident, sergeant in the U.S. Army, and an avid gun collector—had purchased two replacement barrels for a Makarov. Kwan denied it, insisting that he owned only one. Agents jailed him for three weeks as a material witness, claiming that he failed a polygraph test on questions concerning sale of a Makarov barrel to Wales's suspected killer, but they were finally forced to release him. At the same time, a federal grand jury demanded that Kwan surrender "documents detailing everyone he had come in contact with in the previous 11 years." That fishing expedition produced no useful leads, but colleagues of Wales in the Seattle U.S. attorney's office still refuse to surrender Kwan's personal documents.

WALKOWICZ, Wanda   See "ALPHABET MURDERS"

WALLACE, Christopher George Latore murder victim (1997)

Brooklyn native Christopher Wallace was born on May 21, 1972, the only child of a Jamaican immigrant parents. His father deserted the family in 1974, leaving wife Voletta to support herself as a teacher and raise their son alone in the Bedford-Stuyvesant ghetto, surrounded by gang violence and crack-cocaine addicts. Christopher began his education as a star student at Queen of All Saints Middle School, but childhood obesity tagged him with the nickname "Big" and made him subject to harassment. His grades suffered accordingly, and by age 12 he was selling drugs. A transfer to George Westinghouse Information Technology High School placed him in classes with future rap stars Shawn "Jay-Z" Carter and Trevor "Busta Rhymes" Smith, where he cultivated what his mother called a "smart-ass" attitude.

Wallace quit school for good in 1989, shortly before his Brooklyn arrest on weapons charges. He received five years' probation in that case, but was jailed again in 1990 for violating the terms of the agreement. In 1991, he spent nine months in custody on a North Carolina charge of selling crack cocaine, then posted bond and returned to New York.

At that point, Wallace seemed to turn his life toward hip-hop music. Since high school, he had rapped with Brooklyn groups including the Old Gold Brothers and the Techniques, using the stage name "Biggie Smalls," lifted from a movie gangster in the film *Let's Do It Again* (1975). That pseudonym and others—Big Poppa and the Notorious B.I.G.—referred to his stature and ever-increasing girth, which typically ranged from 300 to 380 pounds. In March 1992 a hip-hop magazine, *The Source,* featured Wallace in an article on aspiring artists, and Uptown Records producer Sean "Puffy" Combs invited Wallace to submit a demo tape. From that audition, he was signed to perform with Heavy D & the Boyz, cutting their first song under the title "A Buncha Niggas."

Wallace issued his first album, *Ready to Die,* in 1994, with single cut "Flava in Ya Ear" reaching number nine on *Billboard* magazine's Hot 100. By that time, Puffy Combs had parted company with Uptown and had launched his own Bad Boy Records. Blossoming success in rap music, coupled with the birth of Wallace's first child, finally persuaded him to drop his sideline trafficking in drugs. *Ready to Die* was soon certified as quadruple platinum, with 4 million copies sold. In 1995 Wallace created a protégé group, the Junior M.A.F.I.A. ("*Masters At Finding Intelligent Attitudes*"), promoting music from childhood friends such as Kimberly "Lil' Kim" Jones who progressed to successful solo careers.

Wallace's rise to hip-hop prominence coincided with a highly publicized feud between rap artists on the East and West Coasts, focused primarily on personal strife between Wallace and former friend TUPAC SHAKUR. Speaking to *Vibe* magazine from prison in April 1995, Shakur accused Wallace and Puffy Combs of advance knowledge concerning a Manhattan shooting that left Shakur wounded in November 1994. Wallace, who *was* present with his entourage in the same recording studio when Shakur was shot and robbed of expensive jewelry, denied any involvement in the crime.

Tension escalated between Wallace and Shakur after Shakur's parole, when he signed with Bad Boy's main rival, Marion "Suge" Knight's Death Row Records. The rap stars insulted each other in song lyrics and public comments to the media, while persistent legal woes disrupted progress on Wallace's second album. New York police jailed Wallace in March 1996, after he assaulted two autograph-seekers and smashed the windows of their taxi. A guilty plea to reduced charges of second-degree harassment earned Wallace 100 hours of court-ordered community service, but it did not keep him out of trouble. Before year's end, he was arrested once more in Teaneck, New Jersey, for possession of illegal drugs and weapons.

Tupac Shakur was fatally wounded by drive-by shooters in Las Vegas, Nevada, on September 7, 1996. Some theorists, including reporter Chuck Philips at the *Los Angeles Times*, suggested that Wallace or members of his clique might be responsible for the still-unsolved slaying. Wallace denied it, noting that he was in New York when Shakur was ambushed, but that alibi failed to satisfy critics who suspected him of arranging the murder through street-gang allies. Further criticism dogged Wallace when he failed to attend a rap "summit meeting" condemning violence, held in the wake of Shakur's funeral.

January 1997 found Wallace back in court, on the losing end of a civil lawsuit filed by a man who claimed Wallace and his entourage beat and robbed him in May 1995. Robbery charges were dropped in that case, but counts of assault were still pending when jurors in the civil trial ordered Wallace to pay the victim $41,000 in damages. Wallace left the courtroom announcing his new quest for "peace of mind," but it would elude him.

Wallace's second album, ironically titled *Life after Death,* was scheduled for release on March 25, 1997. On March 8 he attended the 11th Annual Soul Train Music Awards in Los Angeles, where some Shakur loyalists in the audience jeered him as he presented an award to singer Toni Braxton. Following that ceremony, Wallace attended a party hosted by Qwest Records and *Vibe* at L.A.'s Peterson Automotive Museum, also attended by various rap stars and members of two bitterly hostile gangs, the Crips and Bloods. Wallace and his hangers-on left the party in three vehicles, at 12:30 A.M. on March 9. Fifteen minutes later, while waiting for a traffic light to change at a nearby intersection, Wallace was shot four times by a gunman in a passing car. He died at Cedars-Sinai Medical Center at 1:15 A.M.

Witnesses described the gunman as an African American dressed in a blue suit and bow tie, driving a black Chevrolet Impala. A composite sketch of the killer was published on March 10, curiously followed by a second, different sketch released by the Los Angeles Police Department two weeks later. Members of Wallace's entourage rejected the LAPD sketch as inaccurate, and neither led police to a viable suspect. Various observers advance different theories for Wallace's murder, some calling it retaliation for Tupac Shakur's death. Others claim Wallace was shot by members

of the Southside Compton Crips, angered when Bad Boy Records failed to pay them for "security services" provided during Wallace's California publicity tour. Neither claim has yet been proved.

Wallace's *Life after Death* album—named after a car crash that forced him to walk with a cane—was released on schedule, on March 25. By midsummer it ranked first on *Billboard*'s Top 200 albums list, while the single "Hypnotize" was number one on *Billboard*'s Hot 100, Hot R&B/Hip-Hop Songs, and Hot Rap Tracks. The album was certified diamond, with 10 million sales, in 2000.

In 2002 author Randall Sullivan published his book *Labyrinth,* comprising information on the Wallace and Shakur slayings collected by Russell Poole, a former LAPD detective. Sullivan named Wallace's slayer as one Harry Billups, a.k.a. Amir Muhammad, an alleged associate of LAPD officer and supposed Death Row security officer David Mack, who in turn—according to Sullivan—undertook the murder contract on behalf of Suge Knight. Part of that conspiracy theory, at least, was subsequently dashed when Sullivan's identification of Billups was discredited, chalked up to an erroneous comparison with one of the composite suspect sketches from 1997.

In March 2005, relatives of Wallace sued the LAPD, David Mack, and Harry Billups for wrongful death, based on Poole's revelations as outlined by Sullivan. Mack and Billups were subsequently dropped as defendants, and the case ended with a mistrial in July 2005, when the judge voiced his belief that LAPD was withholding crucial evidence. Five months later, Sullivan wrote an article for *Rolling Stone* magazine, accusing the LAPD of negligence in the murder investigation. The assistant managing editor of the *Los Angeles Times* denounced Sullivan's article as a product of "shoddy tactics," whereupon Sullivan quoted an attorney for Wallace's estate who described the *Times* as "a co-conspirator in the cover-up."

Police formally reopened the case in July 2006, but they failed once again to locate a suspect. Wallace's family filed a second wrongful-death claim in April 2007, this time against the city of Los Angeles and two LAPD officers, Nino Durden and Rafael Perez, identified as key figures in the department's unfolding Rampart Division corruption scandal. The new lawsuit claimed that Perez—named as another alleged Death Row associate—had confessed to his superiors that he and David Mack "conspired to murder, and participated in the murder of Christopher Wallace." Strangely, Mack was not named as a defendant in that case, but the plaintiffs allege that the LAPD's leaders "consciously concealed Rafael Perez's involvement" in Wallace's death.

On another front, L.A. television channel KTTV joined *XXL* magazine in naming a friend of Tupac Shakur, rapper Tyrus "Big Syke" Himes, as a suspect in Wallace's slaying. Himes sued KTTV and *XXL* for libel in July 2006, but a judge dismissed his case in January 2007. The second lawsuit filed by Wallace's kin was dismissed in December 2007.

WALLACE, Julia murder victim (1931)

William Herbert Wallace, a 52-year-old agent of the Prudential Assurance Company, lived with his wife Julia in the Anfield neighborhood of Liverpool, England. On the night of January 19, 1931, he attended a café meeting of the Liverpool Chess Club, where an employee passed him a note outlining a telephone message received a half-hour before his arrival. According to that note, the caller—who identified himself as R. M. Qualtrough—wished to purchase an insurance policy. Qualtrough asked Wallace to visit his (Qualtrough's) home the next night to complete the transaction.

In response to that summons, Wallace boarded a streetcar on the evening of January 20, bound for Qualtrough's home at 25 Menlove Gardens East. Upon reaching Liverpool's south side, however, he discovered that while there were three streets named Menlove Gardens—North, South and West—Menlove Gardens *East* did not exist. Supposing that the café employee had garbled the address, Wallace questioned a passing policeman and a neighborhood newspaper vendor, but neither could direct him to the Qualtrough residence. After 45 minutes of aimless searching, he gave up and went home.

On arrival at his house, Wallace later claimed, he found the doors locked. His next-door neighbors, the Johnstons, were on their way out for the evening when they heard Wallace knocking at his own backdoor. Wallace explained his predicament, then tried the doorknob in their presence—and the door opened. Trailed by the Johnstons, Wallace entered his home to find his wife Julia sprawled lifeless on the parlor floor, bleeding profusely from her battered head.

Postmortem examination revealed that 52-year-old Julia had been slain with a blunt instrument, which crushed her skull with 11 powerful blows. Police immediately focused on Herbert as their sole suspect and swiftly built a case against him, climaxed with his arrest two weeks after the murder. Specifically, they

determined that the phone call from mythical "R. M. Qualtrough" was placed from a public call box located within 400 yards of the Wallace home. A reconstruction of the crime persuaded prosecutors that Wallace could have beaten Julia to death, then rushed to catch his trolley to keep his appointment with R. M. Qualtrough. Wallace denied the crime in court, but jurors disbelieved him, deliberating for only an hour before they pronounced him guilty. The court imposed a sentence of death.

On appeal, Wallace's lawyers attacked the Crown's case piece by piece. First, they noted that the café worker who received the "Qualtrough" call on January 19 insisted that the caller was not Herbert Wallace. Next, they noted that Julia's killer should have been covered with blood from her wounds, yet the suit Wallace wore on January 20 bore no bloodstains and the prosecution's timetable allowed him no time to change clothes, much less dispose of incriminating evidence. Likewise, a milk delivery boy had spoken to Julia Wallace, alive and well, moments before Herbert must have boarded his trolley to Liverpool's south side. Finally, defenders observed that police reconstructions of the murder utilized a strapping young constable as Wallace's stand-in, requiring him to sprint for blocks to catch his trolley, while Wallace suffered from debilitating ailments in middle age. Before year's end, the Court of Criminal Appeal overturned Wallace's conviction on grounds that it was "not supported by the weight of the evidence"—the first legal reversal of a murder conviction in British history.

Liberated from custody, Wallace returned to his job as an insurance salesman, but declining health forced his resignation and a move to Wirral, across the River Dee from Liverpool, where he died at Wirral University's Clatterbridge Hospital in 1933. No other suspect was ever named in Julia's slaying, and the case remains a point of controversy to the present day, with amateur theorists divided on the subject of Herbert's guilt or innocence. As author John Rowland noted in *The Wallace Case* (1949), "Almost every fact in the evidence was accepted by both prosecution and defence; but every fact could be interpreted in two ways."

Jonathan Goodman, in *The Killing of Julia Wallace* (1969), identifies the likely killer as a former Prudential coworker of Herbert's who knew Julia well. The suspect—never publicly identified—was fired for embezzlement and had a record of prior arrests for similar offenses. Fifteen years later, journalist Roger Wilkes named Goodman's suspect as Richard Gordon Parry, aged 22 in January 1931.

According to Wilkes, in *Wallace: The Final Verdict,* Parry was cleared in 1931, after telling police that he spent the evening with his fiancée. Later, when he broke off their engagement, the woman told Wallace's lawyers that her alibi for Parry was false. Wilkes also claimed to have evidence that Parry visited a commercial garage on the night of January 20, wearing bloody gloves while he cleaned his car with a mechanic's high-pressure hose. Wilkes suggests that Parry called on Julia Wallace at home, killed her, then stole money from Herbert's cash box—a theft never reported to police. Parry died at age 71 in Llangernyw, North Wales, on April 14, 1980—four years before Wilkes named him as a suspect in the Wallace case.

WALLACE-BAS, Connie See "Independence Avenue Killer"

WALLS, Juanita See Maryland murders

WALL Street bombing U.S. terrorist attack (1920)
At 12:01 P.M. on September 16, 1920, a horse-drawn wagon filled with dynamite and iron sash weights stopped at the intersection of Wall and Broad Streets in downtown Manhattan. The driver slipped away, leaving his wagon parked outside the U.S. Assay Office and directly opposite the J. P. Morgan building. Moments later, the massive bomb exploded with a thunderous roar. Its detonation, timed to coincide with a lunchtime exodus of workers from buildings in the financial district, instantly killed 30 victims and injured at least 300 (of whom 10 more would die from shrapnel wounds). Hundreds of windows were shattered, some as far as a quarter-mile from ground zero. Witness Charles Dougherty, head of the New York Stock Exchange's messengers, told a reporter from the *Sun,* "I saw the explosion, a column of smoke shoot up into the air and then saw people dropping all around me, some of them with their clothing afire." Other witnesses described a 100-foot mushroom cloud, greenish yellow in color, that rose towering over the wreckage.

William Flynn, chief of the U.S. Secret Service (and soon to be director of the Federal Bureau of Investigation (FBI), denied that the bombing was an attempt to murder financier J. P. Morgan, even then vacationing in Europe. "This bomb was not directed at Mr. Morgan or any individual," Flynn declared.

Witnesses survey the shrouded bodies of victims from New York's 1920 Wall Street bombing. (Library of Congress)

Metal sash weights were packed around the Wall Street explosive charge to serve as deadly shrapnel. (Library of Congress)

"In my opinion it was planted in the financial heart of America as a defiance of the American people. I'm convinced a nationwide dynamiting conspiracy exists to wreck the American government and society." As for the authors of that conspiracy, veteran Red-hunter Flynn had no doubts: They were the same leftist radicals blamed for San Francisco's PREPAREDNESS DAY BOMBING of July 1916 and the still-unsolved ANARCHIST BOMBINGS of 1919.

Proving that case would be problematic, however. Evidence was scarce after the powerful explosion, and forensic testing methods were still in their infancy. Police recovered two charred horse's hooves near Trinity Church and showed their blackened horseshoes to 4,000 Atlantic seaboard blacksmiths

as the investigation proceeded, with no worthwhile result. Dominick De Grazia, a smith on Elizabeth Street in New York, recalled changing horseshoes for a nameless driver with a "Sicilian" accent, but the slim lead went nowhere. New York police collected 10 tons of rubble, storing it for two years while they mined the pile for clues, but all in vain. The FBI did no better, although young Assistant Director J. Edgar Hoover declared he was taking personal charge of the case and would not rest until it was solved.

Theories abounded in the deadly bombing. On September 17 the *New York Times* declared, "Authorities were agreed that the devastating blast signaled the long-threatened Red outrages." Hoover himself had predicted a nationwide Bolshevik uprising in May

1919, but the revolution never transpired, and there was no sign of it happening in 1920 either. Attorney General A. Mitchell Palmer arrested William ("Big Bill") Haywood, boss of the radical Industrial Workers of the World, "as a precaution,"   but no evidence was found linking Haywood or his "Wobblies" to the crime. An alternative scenario claimed the blast had been an accident involving a TNT delivery wagon, but Fire Department officials traced all such wagons in the city and found them intact.

A solution of sorts to the case was advanced when U.S. postal workers turned up a batch of pamphlets mailed a block from the bomb site, sometime between 11:30 and 11:58 A.M. on September 16, 1920. Signed by the "American Anarchist Fighters"—a name similar to the signature on flyers that accompanied some of the bombs found in 1919—the latest message read:

> *Remember*
> *We will not tolerate*
> *any longer*
> *Free the political*
> *prisoners or it will be*
> *sure death for all of you*

Authorities believed the flyers (and perhaps the bombing) were a response to the September 11 indictment of Boston anarchists Nicola Sacco and Bartolomeo Vanzetti for a holdup-murder in Massachusetts.

A strange sideshow to the main event, also reported in the *Times* on September 17, concerned "two cards of warning" mailed by Edwin Fischer, a former professional tennis player, which vaguely predicted the bombing to friends. Fischer's notes had singled out September 15 and 16 as likely dates for the attack; he had also made verbal predictions to a tennis club employee, a Toronto bellboy and a stranger on a train that "some millionaires" would soon "get what they had coming." Fischer's brother-in-law traced him to Canada, where Fischer's public display of "psychic powers" had twice resulted in commitment to mental institutions. A spokesman for the American Institute of Psychic Research, Dr. Walter Prince, told reporters that Fischer may indeed have received a "psychic tip" in advance of the bombing, which Prince compared to "picking up a wireless message." New York authorities soon learned that Fischer had been predicting Wall Street disasters for years. He also claimed to be an alchemist and sparring partner for boxer Jack Dempsey, a flight of fancy that got him committed to Bellevue Hospital for psychiatric testing. After several days of observa-

tion, Bellevue's doctors diagnosed Fischer as insane, discounting any link between the tennis player and the Wall Street bombing.

Fifty years after the fact John Brooks advanced a new theory of the Wall Street bombing in his book *Once in Golconda* (1969). On the day of the bombing, some $900 million in gold was scheduled for transfer out of the U.S. Sub-Treasury Building, next door to the Assay Office, where the wagon-bomb was parked. Brooks theorized that the blast was part of a robbery gone wrong, noting that Treasury workers had closed their doors for a lunch break moments before the explosion, and thus were spared (along with the gold). The theory is enticing, but if true, it still leaves the case unsolved, since no potential robbers were ever identified.

WALSH, Therese   See "OCCULT MURDERS"

WANDERWELL, Walter murder victim (1932)

Born Valerian Johannes Pieczynski in 1893 or 1897 (reports differ), at Thurn, Poland, "Walter Wanderwell" lived up to his adopted name as an international traveler, soldier of fortune, and man of mystery. His father was German, his mother Polish, and he pursued life aggressively as a rootless citizen of the world at large. A global seafarer and hiker, Pieczynski explored Siberia and the Amazon jungle, trekked across the Arabian Desert and the Sahara, then wound up in the United States, changing his birth name to one that Americans could pronounce.

That nod toward accommodation failed to help Wanderwell during World War I, when U.S. authorities confined him to Atlanta's federal prison as a suspected (but unproven) German spy. Some published accounts also refer to Wanderwell's alleged impersonation of a military officer, although he never served in any nation's army. Released in 1918, he met Nell Miller, a Broadway chorus girl born in Seattle, Washington. They married in Alabama and founded the Work around the World Educational Club for International Police—WAWEC, for short—ostensibly created to support the new League of Nations through imposition of "law, not war." Nervous FBI agents, always alert for new threats, noted WAWEC's strict disciplinary code and branded it a private army with subversive potential.

In 1922, bankrolled by investors said to include Henry Ford and the Vacuum Oil Company (later

Mobil Oil), the Wanderwells launched a headline-grabbing race around the world involving two four-member teams. Traveling in armored Ford vehicles, the contestants simply wished to see which team could log the most miles—or so Walter said. Ford and Vacuum Oil seized upon the adventure's built-in publicity, while then-deputy FBI chief J. Edgar Hoover spun fantasies of global espionage. Wanderwell's team reached Egypt in time to witness the opening of King Tutankhamun's tomb in November 1922, rolling on from there in pursuit of endless adventure.

In 1924, while resting up in Paris, Walter met Idris Hall, a blond Canadian who stood six inches taller than his own five-foot-six. Hall's story was nearly as odd as Wanderwell's: Born at Winnipeg in 1906, the daughter of a British Army reservist turned prosperous rancher who joined the Canadian Expeditionary Force at the outbreak of war in 1914 and was commissioned a lieutenant of the Durham Light Infantry on arrival in England. Despite hostilities in Europe, Idris and her younger sister toured England, Belgium, and France with their mother, settling behind Allied lines until father Herbert died in combat at Ypres in June 1917. Grieving and troubled by her eldest daughter's "tomboy" ways, Margaret Hall placed Idris in a series of Belgian and French boarding schools.

Idris fled to Paris in time for Wanderwell's arrival, joining WAWEC as a secretary and driver for the ongoing world tour. "Captain" Walter soon began calling Idris "Aloha Wanderwell," introducing her to strangers as his "adopted sister." Still, there was more than sibling love at work. Walter soon divorced Nell, then married "Aloha" in Los Angeles on April 7, 1925. FBI agents had considered filing Mann Act charges—transportation of women across state lines for "immoral" purposes—but the wedding license foiled their scheme.

Soon, legends surrounded Aloha, as well as her husband. Comic book artist Benjamin "Stookie" Allen claimed that Aloha cropped her hair to join the French Foreign Legion and fought beside men in the Moroccan Riff campaign of May 1925, though no proof exists to support that story. Another tale claims she was captured by Chinese bandits and held for ransom, then released after she taught them to fire machine guns. British social reformer Dame Rachel Crowdy (1884–1964) also reported seeing Aloha, dressed as a cowgirl and driving an armored car through the streets of Geneva, Switzerland. Wherever they went, the Wanderwells and their WAWEC entourage shot movies and fraternized with local celebrities, ranging from British expatriate soldier-of-fortune Frank "One-Arm" Sutton

in China to Douglas Fairbanks and Mary Pickford in Hollywood.

It was an odd life, to say the least. Aloha bore Walter two children, Nile and Valerie, respectively born in Cape Town, South Africa, and Miami, Florida (selected as WAWEC international headquarters). Meanwhile, Walter's roving eye produced adulterous scandals wherever they went, coupled with allegations of "communist subversive" activity against Third World missionaries and petty criminal charges stemming from Walter's habit of posing as a soldier in full uniform.

In 1932, the Wanderwells gave up their armored Fords in favor of the *Carma*, a 20-year-old two-masted schooner seized by U.S. Prohibition agents with 300 cases of outlawed whiskey aboard. Walter paid $2,500 for the *Carma* and announced plans to cruise the South Seas, making movies while he sought "adventure and riches." Newspaper reports described the *Carma* as "about as seaworthy as a cardboard raft." Walter charged would-be passengers $200 per head, enlisting seven men and five women for the voyage, then listed them as crew members to pacify the U.S. Coast Guard. The voyage would be self-supporting, Wanderwell proclaimed, through sale of movie rights and artwork created in transit from one port to the next.

In preparation for departure, Wanderwell moored the *Carma* at the Pacific & Orient docks in Long Beach, California. Several days before he planned to set sail, Wanderwell's revolver vanished and could not be found despite a stem-to-stern search of the *Carma*. Walter shrugged it off and focused on stocking the schooner, while his better half pursued movie negotiations with various Hollywood studios.

Aloha, her children, and seven "crew" members went ashore on the evening of December 5, 1932. Walter was alone in the family's cabin, while five others from the party lounged in the *Carma*'s galley, discussing plans for the trip. Their talk was interrupted when a stranger wearing a cap and gray coat with the collar raised, partially hiding his face, peered through an open porthole and asked for Walter Wanderwell. They directed the man to Walter's cabin, heard Walter greet him in a surprised tone, then heard the crack of a single gunshot. The stranger was gone when they reached Walter's body, sprawled on the deck with a single bullet wound in the back, penetrating his heart.

Detectives searched Wanderwell's corpse and found $600 in his pocket, thus ruling out robbery as a motive. Some investigators thought that Walter's womanizing might have prompted a jealous husband or boyfriend to kill him; others considered Walter's alleged espionage activities, speculating that an agent of some foreign power might have executed him in retaliation for spying, or to stunt WAWEC's international growth. Finally, though, police focused their suspicions on former *Carma* crewman William James Guy, a 24-year-old Welsh soldier-of-fortune whose exploits rivaled Wanderwell's.

The case against Guy seemed solid at first. Two *Carma* passengers, Ralph Dunhip and Marian Smith, identified Guy as the man who asked for Walter moments before the fatal shot. They knew him from a recent voyage to Buenos Aires, where Guy had tried to foment mutiny aboard the schooner and was clapped in irons on Wanderwell's order, and put ashore with his wife in Panama. Later, back in the United States, Guy had reportedly confronted Wanderwell, demanded return of his round-trip payment, and threatened Wanderwell when he refused to pay up.

At trial, in February 1933, witnesses Dunhip and Smith seemed to hedge on their identification of Guy, while the defendant produced six witnesses who placed him at a dinner party miles away from the Long Beach docks at the time of the slaying. Some observers opined that Aloha Wanderwell seemed "too friendly" toward her husband's alleged killer in court, but jurors ignored the indiscretion (if there was one) and acquitted Guy. Soon afterward, he was deported to Great Britain, but that embarrassment—and an arrest while trying to reenter the United States from Mexico—did not intimidate him. He subsequently flew warplanes for Ethiopia against Italian invaders in 1935; joined Loyalists to oppose Francisco Franco's fascists in the Spanish Civil War of 1936; led Chinese partisans against Japanese invaders in 1937; flew Canadian prime minister William Lyon MacKenzie King to a meeting with Winston Churchill in 1940; then ferried military planes across the Atlantic to Great Britain, reportedly logging more trips than any other pilot before he died in a crash during 1941.

Another fleeting suspect in the case, detained for questioning by L.A. police but never charged, was Edward Eugene Fernando Montagu, second son of Great Britain's duke of Manchester and a reputed descendant of William the Conqueror, London-born in 1906. A certified eccentric despite (or, perhaps, because of) his royal lineage, Montagu was another world traveler who gravitated to America and lived at various times as a taxi driver, hot-dog vendor, private in the U.S. Army, a hobo drifter, and a seagoing deckhand. Married five times between 1929 and 1953, Montagu

nonetheless died childless, in Mexico, during 1954 or 1956 (reports vary).

After William Guy's murder trial, Aloha Wanderwell learned to fly a seaplane and participated in a futile search for vanished explorer Percy Fawcett, lost without a trace in the Mato Grosso rainforest in 1925. During that adventure, her plane crashed on the Rio des Mortes (River of Death) and Aloha spent several months with native tribesmen before she was rescued. On the day after Christmas 1933 she married Walter Baker, a former WAWEC cameraman eight years her junior, in Louisiana. The newlyweds embarked on a journey to Indochina, then settled in Cincinnati, where Aloha worked in print and broadcast media. Her final stop was an exclusive gated community at Newport Beach, California, where Aloha died on June 4, 1996.

WARSAW, Poland unsolved murders (1922)

On March 4, 1922, police in Warsaw publicly announced the discovery of 11 murdered women's corpses in a wooded region outside the Polish capital. At the time their report was filed and reported in the *New York Times*, no trace had been found of the slayer who left his young victims with fractured skulls, hair torn from their scalps, and "similar terrible wounds" to their torsos. No solution to the mystery was ever made public, and the crimes apparently remain unsolved today.

WASHINGTON, D.C. gay murders (1971)

On March 3, 1972, police in the District of Columbia announced that 10 of 1971's 38 unsolved murders in their city were "homosexually motivated or related." Though hesitant to speculate about connections between the crimes, investigators did report that they were searching for a single suspect, pictured in a photograph with 55-year-old victim James Williams, found stabbed to death in his Northwest apartment on April 13, 1971. The snapshot was taken by a photographer known only as "Bill," who ignored official pleas for help in solving the case. At last report the suspect remained unidentified, the 10 murders still unsolved.

WASHINGTON, D.C. unsolved murders (1988)

Over a three-month period between mid-August and October 1988, three women were killed and a fourth gravely injured in Washington, D.C., by an unknown assailant who savagely beat and strangled them. Twenty-one-year-old Lawanda Scott was the first victim, found beaten to death on August 12, 1988.

The second victim, a "Jane Doe" in her twenties, was found dead and apparently raped on September 6; autopsy reports attributed her death to a combination of blunt-force trauma and strangulation. Another three weeks passed before a third woman (left anonymous in media reports) was beaten and shot several times by an unidentified attacker. She survived her wounds, but the same could not be said for 21-year-old Gloria Carter, beaten and strangled to death in October.

Despite admitted similarities in at least three of the cases—attacks by violent manual assault, occurring at rough three-week intervals—Washington police hesitated to suggest that they had a serial killer on the prowl. Investigators granted they were "looking into" possible links between the crimes, but they professed to find no evidence "conclusively linking" the cases. That, in turn, led police spokesmen to call the attacks "unrelated," citing any reference to a possible serial killer as "inappropriate." However many perpetrators were at large in Washington that year, the crimes are still unsolved after nearly two decades and seem likely to remain so.

WASHINGTON, D.C. unsolved murders (1989)

In August 1989, police in Washington, D.C., grudgingly admitted there was "some resemblance" between the murder of 20-year-old prostitute Mary Ellen Sullenberger (found naked and shot in the chest on April 2) and the August 12 slaying of another local streetwalker, 29-year-old Cori Louise Jones. According to detectives, Jones had been abducted by her killer within a block of the Sullenberger death scene, after which she was shot several times in the chest, then dumped from the killer's automobile. Further possible evidence of a pattern in the slayings came from the appearance of the victims themselves, both described by police as "overweight" Caucasians. Robbery was suggested as a motive for the crimes, but authorities still have no suspects in the case and no murder weapon to compare with bullets taken from the bodies during postmortem examination.

WASHINGTON, D.C. unsolved murders (1996–97)

Residents of the U.S. capital are no strangers to violent death, or to unsolved serial murders. A case in point involves the slayings of six women in the Petworth and Park View neighborhoods of Washington, D.C. Police apparently solved two of the crimes, with the arrest of a suspect in January 1998. And yet . . .

No cause of death was ever determined for the first four Petworth victims, a circumstance that undoubtedly hampered the filing of criminal charges. The first to die, Priscilla Mosley, was found dead on Newton Place, on November 17, 1996. The next victim, Lateashia Blocker, was discovered on May 8, 1997, hauled up from beneath the floorboards of an abandoned house on Princeton Place, barely three miles from Capitol Hill. Emile Davis was another crawl space victim, found beneath a Princeton Place dwelling on August 9, 1997. Two months later, on October 13, an unidentified woman's torso was discovered in the 1400 block of Meridian Place.

The geographic pattern was readily apparent, with one victim known as a Princeton Place resident, while two others were dumped there, in close proximity to each other. That pattern continued on November 18, 1997, when 39-year-old Jacqueline Birch was found strangled to death inside another Princeton Place building. Nearly two weeks later, on December 1, another strangulation victim was dumped behind a fast-food restaurant, a mile and a half from the Capitol dome. Police identified her as 34-year-old Dana Hill, a Princeton Place native still frequently seen in the district prior to her death.

Petworth residents had lived in fear for 12 months before the *Washington Post* called attention to the crimes in November 1997 and a Princeton Place Task Force was created to investigate. Even then, authorities refused to speculate on the possibility of a serial killer at large, pursuing what the *Post* called "great lengths" to find alternative scenarios. Dana Hill's case, despite her lifelong links to Princeton Place, was initially eliminated from the rest by task force investigators, later reconsidered only when they had a suspect in their sights.

That suspect, arrested on January 29, 1998, was 34-year-old Darryl Donnell Turner, an unemployed Princeton Place resident who lived on the same block once occupied by Dana Hill and next door to the building where Jacqueline Birch was found strangled. Police charged Turner with two counts of first-degree murder in those cases, and while they "have not ruled out" a connection to the other four deaths, Homicide Commander Alfred Broadbent told reporters, "He is not the only target of our investigation."

Indeed, while neighbors lined up to describe Turner as a "quiet gentleman" who never "ran his mouth," court records unearthed by the *Post* revealed at least one other suspect in the Petworth slayings, questioned three times by the task force and jailed in early 1998 on unrelated charges. Acting Police Chief Sonya Procter told the press, "We do expect to make more arrests. The only thing I can say definitely is that we believe we have a strong case in these two murders. There will be other developments." Turner was convicted of the Hill and Birch murders in October 2001, and he received a prison term of life without parole on January 12, 2002. Media reports subsequently claimed that Turner had been charged with killing Mary Ferguson in 1994 and Toni-Anne Burdine in 1995, but no trial was held in those cases. In December 2008 police announced that Turner had belatedly confessed to the 1998 slaying of Jessica Cole. Inspector Rodney Parks, with the D.C. Violent Crimes Unit, seemed to regard the entire case as closed, attributing all of the murders to Turner, whom he described as "a convicted serial sexual murderer."

WASHINGTON, Pennsylvania unsolved murders (1976–77)

Over a span of seven months, between November 1976 and June 1977, five young women were raped and murdered within a 25-mile radius of Washington, Pennsylvania, their killer striking with impunity and leaving homicide investigators at a loss for clues. Despite a fair description of the suspect, published in the form of artist's sketches, there were no arrests, and none are now anticipated in a case that terrorized the peaceful region, holding local women prisoners of fear inside their homes.

The stalker's first victim was 21-year-old Susan Rush, a native of Washington County, found strangled and locked in the trunk of her car on November 25, 1976. Detectives noted that her body had been "hastily clothed," her bra and panties left on the car's front seat, and a postmortem examination confirmed that Rush was raped prior to death.

On February 13, 1977, 16-year-old Mary Gency was reported missing from her home in North Charleroi. She had failed to return from a walk after dinner, and her body was recovered three days later from the woods at Fallowfield Township. Gency had been beaten to death with a blunt instrument and raped before death by an assailant whom the county coroner described as "a mad animal."

Seventeen-year-old Debra Capiola was last seen alive on March 17, 1977, walking to meet her school bus at nearby Imperial, in Allegheny County. She never reached school, and searchers found her body in a wooded section of southwestern Washington County on March 22. Capiola had been raped before she was strangled with her own blue jeans, the pants left wrapped around her neck.

Two months later, on the afternoon of May 19, 1977, 18-year-old Brenda Ritter was found dead in South Strabane Township, in Washington County. Nude but for shoes and stockings, she had been raped and then strangled with a piece of her own clothing, tightened around her neck with a stick in the form of a crude garrote.

The killer strayed from Pennsylvania in June 1977, but he did not travel far. His last known victim was 26-year-old Roberta Elam, a novice at Mount St. Joseph Mother House in Oglebay Park, West Virginia (near Wheeling). Elam was preparing to take her vows as a nun, but her religious career was cut short by the predator who raped and strangled her on June 13, dumping her corpse within 75 yards of the convent.

Authorities released a sketch of their presumed suspect on June 15, 1977, but none of the resultant tips proved helpful in their search. When the murder series ended, as mysteriously as it had begun, police could only speculate about the strangler's identity and whereabouts. Unless deceased or jailed on unrelated charges, he is still at large today.

WAYNE, H. F. See COLORADO MURDERS

WEBER, Yvonne See "OCCULT MURDERS"

WEISS, Earl ("Hymie") gangland murder victim (1926)

A Polish immigrant, born Earl Wajciechowski in 1898, the future Hymie Weiss saw his surname Americanized while his family was still en route to the United States. As a teenager in Chicago, he joined the North Side gang led by Irishman DION O'BANNION, specializing in burglary, auto theft, and sundry crimes of violence in the labor rackets. Weiss was also an accomplished safecracker, so skilled with nitroglycerine ("soup," in gangland jargon) that O'Bannion once called him "the best soup artist in Chicago." By the dawn of Prohibition in 1920, Weiss was O'Bannion's chief lieutenant and top enforcer. A year later, he made gangland history by inventing the "one-way ride."

The occasion for that coup was the capture of Steve Wisniewski, a renegade gangster who hijacked

O'Bannion's beer trucks on occasion. Weiss received the murder contract on Wisniewski and subsequently took his victim on a drive beside Lake Michigan. Returning without his ill-fated passenger, Weiss told his fellow mobsters, "We took Stevie for a ride—a one-way ride."

Grief-stricken and enraged by O'Bannion's murder in November 1924, Weiss wasted no time in plotting revenge against rivals Johnny Torrio and Al Capone. His first attempt, accompanied by George (Bugs) Moran and Vincent (Schemer) Drucci on January 12, 1925, fell flat when the shooters wounded Capone's chauffeur but missed Big Al and his two bodyguards. Twelve days later, Weiss and Moran trailed Torrio home from a shopping trip to the Loop, wounding Capone's mentor with pistol and shotgun fire in his own driveway. Torrio survived his injuries and fled Chicago after spending two weeks in the hospital, leaving Chicago—and the North Side war—to his homicidal protégé.

Still Weiss tried to even the score for O'Bannion. On September 20, 1926, he led a caravan of gunmen to Capone's headquarters, the Hawthorne Inn in Cicero. Cruising slowly past the target, Weiss and his soldiers unloaded more than 1,000 rounds from submachine guns, pistols, and shotguns—once again without hitting Capone. This time a bodyguard was wounded, along with a female bystander, and Capone resolved to eliminate his determined rival.

On October 11, 1926, Weiss arrived at North Side headquarters, still housed above O'Bannion's flower shop on North State Street, directly opposite Holy Name Cathedral. As Hymie crossed the street with four associates, two machine-gunners opened fire from a second-floor window nearby. Weiss and bodyguard Paddy Murphy were killed instantly, their three companions badly wounded. Holy Name also took a beating, its ornate cornerstone flayed by .45-caliber bullets. Before the shooting, the cornerstone's inscription read: "A.D. 1874—AT THE NAME OF JESUS EVERY KNEE SHOULD BOW—THOSE THAT ARE IN HEAVEN AND THOSE ON EARTH." When the smoke cleared, all that remained was

> EVERY KNEE SHOULD
> HEAVEN AND
> ON EARTH

Police found $5,200 in Weiss's pocket, along with a list of jurors selected to serve in an upcoming syndicate murder trial. Raiding the nearby snipers' nest, they found spent cartridges, and a gray fedora purchased from a Cicero clothier. Investigation proved the apartment—and another nearby, where detectives found a loaded shotgun—had been rented under false names on September 21, the day after Weiss's fireworks show in Cicero. The killers, in flight, had tossed one of their tommy guns over a fence, where it landed atop a doghouse and was later recovered.

Hymie Weiss left an estate reported in excess of $1.3 million. His widow complained to Bugs Moran that Hymie's funeral featured only 18 carloads of flowers, while the processions thrown for O'Bannion and North Side mobster Samuel (Nails) Morton had boasted 26 and 20 carloads, respectively. Moran reportedly apologized, explaining that the violent deaths of 30 gang members since 1924 had whittled the number of grieving mourners available to make donations. Less than three years later, Moran himself was forced into hiding after his top guns were silenced forever in the 1929 ST. VALENTINE'S DAY MASSACRE.

WESTBURY, Cynthia See MARYLAND MURDERS (1986–87)

"WEST Memphis Three" miscarriage of justice (1993)
On the evening of Wednesday, May 5, 1993, three eight-year-old boys disappeared from their homes in West Memphis, Arkansas. Authorities later determined that Steven Branch, Christopher Byers, and James Michael Moore had left Weaver Elementary School when classes adjourned for the day at 3:00 P.M. The boys dispersed to their respective homes, but did not linger. Branch left home soon after dropping off his books, and his mother (Pam Hobbs) telephoned police to report him missing at 3:30 P.M. The officers, while not entirely dismissive, saw no cause for alarm at the time. At 5:20 P.M. John Mark Byers found stepson Christopher riding a skateboard some distance from home and ordered him back to the house, where John administered "two or three licks" with a belt and ordered Chris to clean out the carport. Diana Moore saw her son at 6:00 P.M., riding double with Steven Branch on Branch's bicycle, accompanied by Chris Byers on a second bike. She tried to stop the boys, but they sped off without heeding her call.

It was the last time any of the children would be seen alive.

John Byers later told police that he returned home from an errand at 6:30 P.M. and found Chris missing from home, his work in the carport unfinished. With his wife, Melissa, Byers began to drive around the neighborhood, searching for Chris. During the course of that search, Byers allegedly met a policeman on patrol and explained his problem, whereupon the officer supposedly advised him to hold off on filing a missing-person report until 8:00 P.M. (That story was never confirmed.) When Byers telephoned police at eight o'clock, an officer was dispatched to his home. Fifteen minutes later, Byers spoke to Diana Moore and heard her story of the three boys riding bicycles. By 8:30, Byers and Moore were engaged in a search of Robin Hood Hills, a nearby wooded area. Police joined the search at 10:20 P.M., continuing without result into the early hours of Thursday morning.

Searching resumed in the Robin Hood Hills with sunrise on May 6. The effort finally paid off at 1:45 P.M., when police sergeant Mike Allen found the first small corpse submerged in a creek or drainage ditch (reports differ). It was removed from the water at 2:45, and the next grim discovery came 11 minutes later, when Detective Bryn Ridge found a second body 25 feet from the first. Three minutes later, at 2:59 P.M., officers found the last corpse in the creek, five feet south of the second body. The boys were nude, each bound with shoelaces that secured wrists to ankles. Crittenden County Coroner Kent Hale was summoned at 3:20 P.M. and pronounced the victims dead at 4:02 P.M. The boys' clothing and their two bicycles were also retrieved from the creek. Two sticks, apparently used to weight down the clothes, were not collected by detectives at the time, forcing them to return on a later date and bag sticks which they "thought" were the ones from the creek. No blood or murder weapons were observed at the scene, but officers preserved one clear print from a tennis shoe.

Autopsy reports disclosed that James Moore and Steven Branch had drowned after suffering multiple traumatic injuries to their heads, torsos, and extremities. Branch's wounds were more extensive, including a three-inch fracture at the base of his skull, plus numerous scratches and bruises not found on Moore. From that evidence police theorized that Moore had been rendered unconscious early in the attack, while Branch struggled to defend himself. Chris Byers suffered the worst injuries of all, including severance of his genitalia (which were never found), with multiple stab wounds to the groin and three sets of bite marks on his

buttocks. Nontherapeutic levels of Carbamazepine (an anticonvulsant drug used to treat epilepsy) were found in Byers's blood. Contrary to initial supposition by police, none of the boys had been sodomized.

On Friday morning, May 7, 1993, West Memphis police lieutenant James Sudbury called Crittenden County juvenile officer Steve Jones to discuss the murders. (Some accounts claim that Jones was present, for no apparent reason, when the bodies were examined on May 6.) Both officers agreed that the crime had "cult" overtones, suggesting human sacrifice by Satanists or witches. Jones volunteered the opinion that 18-year-old Damien Echols (né Michael Wayne Hutcheson) was an occultist whom Jones deemed "capable" of murdering children. At noon Jones and Sudbury drove to the West Memphis trailer park where Echols lived with his parents, receiving permission from Jack and Pamela Echols to question their son. During that initial conversation, Lt. Sudbury photographed Damien's tattoos, including a pentagram inked on his chest.

At first glance Echols seemed a fair target for witch-hunting police. An alienated child of divorce who habitually dressed in black, he had abandoned the Catholicism of his parents to adopt the nature worship of Britain's ancient Druids. Echols called himself "Damien" after a 19th-century priest who treated lepers in Hawaii, but the sobriquet was easily (and perhaps deliberately) confused with the Antichrist figure portrayed by various actors in the *Omen* series of popular horror films, produced between 1976 and 1992. Arrested at age 17 after running away from home with his girlfriend, Echols was diagnosed as manic-depressive and subjected to hospital treatment, including a prescription for the antidepressant Tofranil. From that point onward Crittenden County juvenile authorities made a habit of questioning Damien about various unsolved crimes, but none led to prosecution. Echols had attempted suicide three times during 1991–93, by methods that included hanging, a drug overdose, and drowning.

Echols submitted to a formal police interview on May 9, 1993. In that conversation detectives asked Echols whether one of the three murder victims suffered more serious injuries than the other two. Damien replied that one boy indeed was more grievously injured, with genital wounds. Police took that statement as evidence of "guilty knowledge"—though in fact most residents of West Memphis had learned as much by then, from media accounts and word of mouth. Despite their seeming certainty of Echols's guilt, authorities released him that day without filing charges—but they were not finished with him yet.

One vehicle of the pursuit was Vicki Hutcheson, a local resident with a history of check fraud. On May 6, 1993, Hutcheson had driven her son Aaron to the Marion County Police Department, where he told Officer Don Bray that he (Aaron) had seen the three murdered boys at a place he called "the playhouse," near the creek where their bodies were found. As his story evolved over time, Aaron Hutcheson claimed to have witnessed the murders, then spun a weird tale of Spanish-speaking motorcyclists who held him captive until he kicked their shins and fled. Another permutation of his tale cast Echols as the killer, illustrated with childish drawings of Damien clad in armor, brandishing a sword. Police soon dismissed Aaron as a witness, but his mother kept track of the case, perhaps attracted by a $30,000 reward posted for information leading to arrest and conviction of the slayer (or slayers).

When her son's strange statements failed to clinch the deal, Vicki Hutcheson turned to 17-year-old Jessie Misskelley, a mentally retarded friend of Damien Echols who often baby-sat for Aaron. Hutcheson asked Misskelley to arrange for Echols to visit her home, in hopes of extracting some incriminating statements. Echols kept the date, but Hutcheson's efforts to secretly record their conversation produced an inaudible tape that police discarded as useless. One day after that bungled attempt, Hutcheson approached police with yet another statement. This time, despite prior denials of ever meeting Echols, Hutcheson claimed she had gone to a satanic gathering with Damien and Misskelley at Turrell, Arkansas, two weeks *before* the murders. Echols had driven to the ritual site in a red Ford Fiesta, Hutcheson said, though investigation proved Damien had no access to such a vehicle, and in fact did not possess a driver's license. (Another "witness," William Winfred Jones, told detectives that Damien bragged of the murders while intoxicated, but Jones later recanted, admitting that his false statement was merely an echo of local rumors.)

Vicki Hutcheson next persuaded Misskelley to visit police with a claim that *he* had seen Echols murder the three eight-year-olds. Whatever the original intent of that statement, Misskelley spent 12 hours with detectives on June 3, 1993, and somehow wound up confessing an active role in the murders. The sequence of events is unclear, since police recorded only a brief portion of Misskelley's interrogation, but the transcript that survives reveals Misskelley's total unfamiliarity

with the crime, fumbling various details while officers "correct" him from the sidelines. In addition to Echols, Misskelley also named another slayer, 16-year-old Jason Baldwin. During the course of his marathon interrogation, Misskelley supposedly "passed" a polygraph examination, thus verifying his statements. (Police photos of the room where the polygraph test was given show a baseball bat standing in a corner near Misskelley's chair, its presence never questioned or explained at trial. Detectives also failed to obtain a waiver of Misskelley's constitutional rights signed by his parents, a lapse that should have invalidated his confession under Arkansas criminal statutes.)

In the course of his rambling statement, Misskelley claimed that he had accompanied Echols and Baldwin to Robin Hood Hills around 9:00 A.M. on May 5—or at noon; he couldn't be sure. (Jessie later changed the time to 5:00 or 6:00 P.M., then pushed it back again to sometime between 7:00 and 8:00 P.M., with a search for the missing boys already in progress.) The three friends were lounging in or near the creek, he said, when victims Branch, Byers, and Moore approached on bicycles. While Misskelley watched, Echols and Baldwin allegedly raped Branch and Byers (contrary to forensic evidence), then made them perform oral sex. James Moore escaped during the sexual assault, but Misskelley caught him and dragged him back to the creek. Baldwin then used a knife to slash the boys' faces and castrate Chris Byers, while Echols beat one victim with a stick and strangled him. Only in death, Misskelley claimed, were the victims undressed and pointlessly bound with shoelaces. Subsequent embellishments included Misskelley's description of cult rituals attended with Echols and Baldwin (where they supposedly killed and ate dogs), and a phone call from Baldwin on May 4, 1993, expressing an intent to snatch and "hurt" unnamed boys on the following day.

Misskelley began his recitation at 2:44 P.M. on June 3, 1993. Nearly nine hours later, at 11:35 P.M., arrest warrants were issued for Damien Echols and Jason Baldwin. Both were held on charges of capital murder, with Baldwin slated for trial as an adult. In their search of Baldwin's home, police seized 16 T-shirts (15 of them black) and a red robe (belonging to Baldwin's mother). From Echols they confiscated a T-shirt, blue jeans, boots, a necklace, and two notebooks filled with "satanic" scribbling. Fibers recovered from clothing owned by Baldwin and Echols (but not Misskelley) were deemed "microscopically similar" to those from clothes worn by the victims. Later, on November 17, 1993, a team of divers found a knife with a serrated blade in the lake behind Baldwin's house, identified by police as "consistent" with Chris Byers's wounds. Ex-girlfriend Deeana Holcomb claimed Echols had owned a "similar" knife—albeit of a different color, with a compass in the handle (which the lake knife did not have). Tiny blood specks on Damien's necklace were analyzed: One of them matched Echols's own blood; the other matched a type shared by 11 percent of the world's population, including victims Branch and Byers. The samples were too small to permit DNA testing for a more specific identification.

On August 15, 1993, Jessie Misskelley joined Echols and Baldwin in pleading not guilty to all charges filed. The trials proceeded in a witch-hunt atmosphere, with Misskelley the first to face a jury, on January 19, 1994. Motions to suppress Misskelley's illegally obtained confession were denied, and the statement was duly used against him. On February 4 jurors convicted Misskelley on two counts of second-degree capital murder, resulting in an automatic sentence of life imprisonment without parole.

Echols and Baldwin went on trial for their lives 18 days after Misskelley was convicted. In the interim between trials John Byers had spread false reports that his stepson's genitals were found in a jar of alcohol under Damien's bed. When the tale was exposed as a lie, Byers claimed he first heard it broadcast over a police radio. Vicki Hutcheson testified for the state, "corroborating" the defendants' participation in satanic rituals. (She later recanted her statement, admitting she lied, but was never charged with perjury.) Song lyrics, heavy-metal T-shirts, and novels by best-selling author Stephen King were introduced to "prove" Echols and Baldwin harbored occult fantasies. A jailhouse snitch, Michael Carson, testified that Baldwin had confessed the murders while they briefly occupied the same cellblock. According to Carson, Baldwin had claimed "he dismembered the kids" and that he "sucked the blood from [Byers's] penis and scrotum and put the balls in his mouth." Two more witnesses, both minors, claimed Echols had boasted of the murders at a girls' softball game. "I killed the three little boys," he allegedly bragged, "and before I turn myself in, I'm going to kill two more, and I already have one of them picked out." Probation officer Jerry Driver (who later resigned in the face of embezzlement charges) testified that he had once seen Echols, Baldwin, and Misskelley walking along the street in black robes, each carrying a wooden

staff. Melissa Byers told the court that six weeks before the murders, an unknown man dressed in black had taken Christopher's photograph.

On March 18, 1994, jurors convicted both defendants on three counts of capital murder. One day later, Judge David Burnett sentenced Echols to death by lethal injection, while Baldwin received a prison term of life plus 40 years without parole. The Arkansas Supreme Court rejected Jessie Misskelley's motion for a new trial on February 19, 1996. The same court denied appeals from Echols and Baldwin on December 23, 1996. In May 1998 Echols won a hearing on charges that his defense counsel had been ineffective or incompetent, but Judge Burnett ruled against him in June 1999. Appeals continue in the troubling case, but with no progress to date.

In their pursuit of Damien Echols, West Memphis police ignored some alternative suspects. One, never identified, was a disheveled black man who stumbled into Bojangles Restaurant at 8:42 on the night of the murders, wearing bloodstained clothes. Restaurant manager Marty King called police and collected a bagful of personal items from the stranger before the suspect disappeared. Detectives assigned to the case responded 24 hours after the fact and reportedly took blood scrapings from the restaurant men's room, but Detective Bryn Ridge later admitted "losing" the evidence. Officers professed no interest in the other items, and apparently left them with King, who threw them away.

Another suspect was John Byers himself. During production of a documentary film on the case, in November 1993, Byers gave a knife with a serrated blade to one of the filmmakers as a gift. The recipient noted apparent bloodstains on the knife and surrendered it to West Memphis police—who tested the stains for blood type and confirmed a match to Chris Byers, but thereby destroyed the blood sample for DNA testing. Questioned by detectives afterward, Byers claimed his wife had given him the knife as a Christmas present. It was never used, he claimed, and Byers insisted that his children never had access to it. Under further questioning, Byers changed his story and "recalled" butchering a deer with the knife. He was unable to explain how human blood of his stepson's type found its way onto the blade. Researchers also note that while forensic experts were examining the human bite marks found on Christopher Byers, stepfather John had all his teeth pulled and replaced with dentures, thereby rendering comparison impossible.

Authorities stand by their evidence and methods in prosecuting the "West Memphis Three," while critics in ever-growing numbers describe the case as a miscarriage of justice. In April 2008, attorneys for Damien Echols sought a new trial on grounds that no DNA from the defendants was recovered from the crime scene or the bodies of the victims. That petition further stated that "a hair containing mitochondrial DNA consistent with that of Terry Hobbs, a stepfather of one of the victims (Steve Branch), was found on the ligature used to bind another of the victims (Michael Moore). Another hair found on a tree root at the scene where the bodies were discovered contains mitochondrial DNA consistent with that of David Jacoby." Counsel alleged that Jacoby, a friend of Terry Hobbs, was in his company during the hours preceding and following the murders.

County prosecutors and Arkansas Assistant Attorney General Kent Holt rejected that evidence as worthless, replying in their brief that "Those unremarkable results do not (and cannot) demonstrate [Echols's] actual innocence." Nor were authorities impressed by the published opinion of former FBI psychological profiler John Douglas, hired by the defense to suggest a new theory of how the crimes occurred. Douglas opined that Terry Hobbs, angry at his stepson over some domestic incident, "wanted to punish and humiliate him, but went further than he intended." (Hobbs denied participation in the crime, in two interviews with Little Rock's *Arkansas Democrat-Gazette*.) Neither did prosecutors accept the judgment of defense forensic experts that various postmortem mutilations suffered by the three victims were inflicted by nonhuman scavengers rather than knives. According to Holt, "The point is that Echols's postmortem animal-predation theory cannot explain the homicides—the crimes for which he must demonstrate actual innocence. Moreover, the state is fully prepared to present at length its own expert evidence clearly refuting Echols's incredible theory of postmortem animal predation."

On June 26, 2008, the Arkansas Supreme Court rejected without comment a defense motion seeking to expand what a circuit judge can consider in reviewing new-trial motions from Jason Baldwin and Jessie Misskelley. Specifically, trial judge David Burnett planned an autumn review of claims alleging new scientific evidence, but Baldwin's lawyers sought to present jailhouse testimony refuting some alleged incriminating statements by their client. Misskelley's petition asked

Judge Burnett to consider the fact that the sole witness linking him to cult activity now says she fabricated her testimony under duress. Based on the supreme court's ruling, Barnett would consider none of that verbal testimony.

"WEST Side Rapist" Los Angeles (1974–75)

Between November 1974 and October 1975, a vicious prowler terrorized the west side of Los Angeles, raping 33 women and killing at least 10. While all of his victims were elderly, ranging in age from 63 to 92 years, the incessant attacks spread an aura of fear city-wide, boosting gun sales and turning neighbor against neighbor as dark suspicions flourished. In the end the killer slipped away without a trace and left police to search in vain for clues to his identity.

The first to die, on November 7, 1974, was 72-year-old Mary Scialese, followed the next day by 92-year-old Lucy Grant. On November 14 the slayer claimed 67-year-old Lillian Kramer, rebounding on the night of December 4 to kill 74-year-old Ramona Gartner. A new year brought no respite from the violence, with 71-year-old Sylvia Vogal murdered on March 22, 1975. Una Cartwright, age 78, was raped and killed on April 8, while 75-year-old Olga Harper was murdered two weeks later. Eighty-six-year-old Effie Martin, slain on May 22, 1975, was identified by police as the eighth fatality in 23 attacks. Her death was followed on September 26 by the murder of 79-year-old Cora Perry. Sixty-three-year-old Leah Leshefsky was the killer's last known victim, murdered on October 28, 1975.

By New Year's Day 1976, two months had passed without a new assault, and residents of West Los Angeles began to breathe a bit more easily. They would forget their fear in time, but homicide detectives still continued searching for their man, covering the same ground endlessly, without result. A possible solution to the case has been raised in the person of serial rapist Brandon Tholmer, confined to a state mental ward for three years after raping a 79-year-old woman in October 1975. Eleven years later, Tholmer was sentenced to life imprisonment for the rape-slayings of four elderly women between 1981 and 1985. Still, no evidence has been produced connecting Tholmer to the earlier series of murders. In 2009, an insurance claims adjuster John Floyd Thomas was arrested and charged with murdering Ethel Sokoloff, 68, in 1972 and Elizabeth McKeown,

67, in 1976. Authorities believed he might also be responsible for many other murders in the same time period, including some or all of those attributed to the West Side Rapist. At the time of this writing, however, no further charges had been made, leaving the West Side Rapist murders still officially unsolved.

WEST Virginia Sniper unknown serial killer (2003)

Over a five-day span in August 2003, a still-unidentified sniper claimed three lives in Kanawha County, West Virginia. Each victim was killed by a single long-range rifle shot, while stopping at gas stations or convenience stores. Some published reports claim that all three victims were slain with the same weapon, while others merely state that bullets recovered from the bodies share "the same characteristics."

Gary Carrier Jr. was the first to die. The 44-year-old professional mechanic and divorced father of four had stopped to use a public telephone at a GoMart convenience store on Charleston's west side, when a bullet cut him down at 11:00 P.M. on August 10. The slug was not recovered, and police found no cartridge casing. Carrier's slaying seemed to be an isolated incident until August 14, when the sniper struck twice more, killing victims 10 miles and 90 minutes apart.

Jeanie Patton, age 31, had filled her car's fuel tank at a Speedway station on Campbell Creek Road, south of Charleston, and was about to pay her bill when a bullet struck her in the back of the head at 10:30 P.M. The single mother of one died instantly, and this time pathologists retrieved a .22-caliber bullet.

About 20 minutes after that shooting, employees at a Go-Mart on U.S. Highway 60, east of Charleston, noticed a black or maroon Ford F-150 pickup truck with an extended cab and gold trim idling outside the convenience store. Its driver was an overweight white male. The truck was still there at 11:15 P.M., when 26-year-old Okey Meadows Jr. came shopping for milk. As in the previous attacks, a single shot rang out and struck Okey in the head as he prepared to pay for his purchase. The pickup sped away immediately afterward, tires screeching on the pavement. As in Jeanie Patton's case, a .22-caliber slug was recovered.

Investigators found no link between the three victims—no similarities even, besides the fact that all three were single or divorced parents. Carrier was a middle-aged NASCAR fan, while Patton worked as a part-time cook and custodian with the Kanawha County School District. Meadows was described by

friends as a "fitness fanatic," who planned to study criminal justice or electronics in college. Some media reports vaguely allude to "drug connections" involving the last two victims, while stating that none were found for Carrier. In any case, suspicion of a drug link in the slayings brought police no closer to the sniper.

Federal agents joined the manhunt, without clear jurisdiction, but their efforts made no difference. Kanawha County Sheriff Dave Tucker announced that his department had questioned 100 suspects—including a man who "resembled" the Ford pickup's driver, and who allegedly made comments "implying" that he was the sniper—but all were released without charges. Convenience store owners were canvassed in search of disgruntled former employees, but none fit the bill. In October 2003 a joint task force created to investigate the slayings offered $50,000 for information leading to the sniper's arrest, but it remains unclaimed. Appearing on CNN's *American Morning* program, Tucker could only state the obvious about the crimes: "They're connected by the site, that they were shot at a convenience store, shot in one single hit shot, the fact they were shot at a distance, and I think the most important

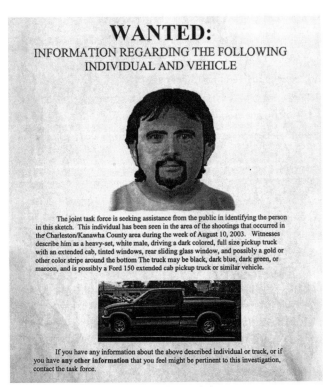

WANTED:
INFORMATION REGARDING THE FOLLOWING INDIVIDUAL AND VEHICLE

The joint task force is seeking assistance from the public in identifying the person in this sketch. This individual has been seen in the area of the shootings that occurred in the Charleston/Kanawha County area during the week of August 10, 2003. Witnesses describe him as a heavy-set, white male, driving a dark colored, full size pickup truck with an extended cab, tinted windows, rear sliding glass window, and possibly a gold or other color stripe around the bottom. The truck may be black, dark blue, dark green, or maroon, and is possibly a Ford 150 extended cab pickup truck or similar vehicle.

If you have any information about the above described individual or truck, or if you have any other information that you feel might be pertinent to this investigation, contact the task force.

Law enforcement officials released this composite drawing of a person they want to interview regarding the three sniper-style shootings in the Charleston, West Virginia, area in August 2003. (Getty Images)

thing, that the bullets that we recover, they have similar characteristics."

Despite the paucity of evidence, local authorities seemed confident that they would solve the case. Charleston Mayor Danny Jones, himself a former lawman, told reporters, "I believe this person will slip up. Maybe they'll talk to somebody. I think it will be solved by a lot of police work." Sheriff Tucker kept it short and sweet: "It's a matter of time. We'll get this guy."

Five years later, Jones was still mayor, 26-year veteran Jonathan Rutherford had replaced Tucker as sheriff… and the sniper was still at large. The case remains unsolved today.

WETTERLING, Jacob Erwin missing person (1989)

Jacob Wetterling was born in St. Joseph, Minnesota, on February 17, 1978. Two siblings followed: brother Trevor in 1979 and sister Carman in 1981. Parents Jerry and Patty Wetterling had achieved their American dream, but they were cautious, well aware that dreams can morph into nightmares without warning.

On the evening of October 11, 1989, Jerry and Patty left Jacob to mind his brother and sister, while they attended a dinner party nearby. A friend of Jacob's, 11-year-old Aaron Larsen, came over to watch TV, but nothing on the air caught their fancy. Trevor phoned his parents, asking permission to rent a video from a Tom Thumb convenience store near their house, but Patty rejected the notion, fearing that drivers might not see children, on the dark country road.

Jacob called back moments later and pitched a new plan to his father. He would wear Jerry's orange reflective vest on the 10-minute journey, while Trevor carried a flashlight and Aaron wore a white sweatshirt. A 14-year-old neighbor would watch over Carmen in their absence. Mindful of Jacob's disappointing performance at hockey tryouts earlier that day, Jerry relented and gave permission for his sons to make their first nocturnal foray. They left the Wetterling home at 9:15 P.M., Jacob and Aaron on bicycles, while Trevor rode a push-scooter. They reached the store without incident, renting a copy of *The Naked Gun*.

Disaster struck on the return trip.

When they were nearly home, a man wearing a stocking mask emerged from a driveway, brandishing a pistol, rasping a command for the boys to stop. He told Trevor to douse the flashlight, then ordered all three off their vehicles and into a roadside ditch, where they lay on the ground. The gunman then peered into Trevor's face and asked his age, then told him to run away without looking back, under threat of death. He repeated the same routine with Aaron Larsen, but Aaron looked back in time to see the stranger walking away with Jacob, clutching his captive's arm. By the time Larsen reached the Wetterling driveway and looked back again, man and boy had vanished. Neither Aaron nor Trevor heard any sounds from a getaway car.

Stearns County Sheriff Charles Grafft got a call shortly before 10:00 P.M. and drove four miles from his home to the crime scene. Two bikes and Trevor's scooter lay where they had been discarded, but there was no trace of Jacob Wetterling. The other boys told their story to detectives, and later to FBI agents, but all in vain. Searchers, including National Guardsmen, trackers with bloodhounds, and airborne spotters in helicopters, scoured 36 square miles of farmland, forest, and stone quarries without uncovering any useful clues. Witnesses at the Tom Thumb store reported seeing a red Chevrolet Chevette moments before the kidnapping, but police traced the car and exonerated its owner. A teenager's subsequent claim that he saw an armed man force a boy into a white car proved to be false.

As news of Jacob's abduction spread, more witnesses came forward, describing a 50-something stranger seen loitering around Tom Thumb and another local convenience store on October 11. The man was roughly six feet tall and heavyset, with receding white hair, and he glowered at store employees without making a purchase. Police circulated sketches of the presumed suspect, but none produced a lead.

Two months after Jacob's disappearance, authorities thought they were close to breaking the case. They revealed that in December 1988, a 12-year-old boy had been snatched from the street on his way home from ice-skating with friends. The male kidnapper had sexually abused him, then dropped him off within 10 miles of where Jacob was kidnapped, telling the victim to run or he would be shot. That man had been unmasked, but yet another sketch—one of five finally published in Wetterling's case—failed to identify the molester.

In 1990, the Wetterlings received a tip that a boy resembling Jacob had been seen with an unknown man at Schiphol Airport, in Amsterdam. They hired a private investigator to visit the Netherlands, but the effort proved to be an expensive disappointment. Before year's end, Sheriff Grafft announced his retirement

Fans at a 1989 Vikings-Rams football game hold a vigil for Jacob Wetterling, who was kidnapped that October. (Gerald R. Brimacombe/Time & Life Pictures/Getty Images)

from law enforcement, conceding that Jacob's abduction had influenced his decision not to seek another term in office. He died in February 2003, at age 75, with the case still unsolved.

In the absence of facts, theories proliferate. Agent Paul McCabe told reporters that Wetterling's case was unique in FBI annals, because "we never had a kidnapping where there were witnesses and someone at gunpoint took the child in front of other children." Use of a mask suggests that the kidnapper may have been known to his victims or other locals, but neither Trevor Wetterling nor Aaron Larsen recognized his voice. In 2004, Patty Wetterling announced that police had changed their minds about Jacob being carried off in a car. She called the new theory "significant," suggesting that detectives "have reason to apply pressure, but not too much pressure" on a neighbor interviewed in 1989.

And again, the "lead" went nowhere.

Most child abductions in America are committed by family members, often during custody disputes, but the Wetterlings suffered from no domestic strife and they had an iron-clad alibi for the time of Jacob's kidnapping. Still, rumor-mongers whispered that Jerry—a practitioner of the unfamiliar Baha'i Faith, which emphasizes the equality of human beings and abolition of racial prejudice—may have killed his own son.

Police dismissed that notion, but *did* consider that Jerry's views on race, coupled with his role as president of St. Joseph's small NAACP chapter, might have prompted a racist to target his family from spite. Minnesota has harbored chapters of the Ku Klux Klan since the 1920s, augmented in more recent years by

small neo-Nazi groups, but no evidence ever surfaced to mark Jacob's abduction as a hate crime.

A more logical theory, reinforced by the December 1988 incident, involved kidnapping by a pedophile. Clearly, St. Joseph and surrounding Stearns County harbored at least one sexual predator who favored boys in the 11-to-12-year-old range, and that still-unknown prowler may have regretted allowing his previous victim to live. James Rothstein, a retired member of the New York City Police Department who tackled Jacob's case in the early 21st century, suggests that Wetterling may have been snatched by a pedophile ring that trades victims worldwide—but again, no evidence exists to support that hypothesis. Meanwhile, interrogation of known Minnesota child molesters has failed to uncover a likely suspect.

Leaving motive aside, some theorists believe that Jacob's kidnapper chose and stalked his victim in advance. On the afternoon before he vanished, Jacob visited a local ice rink with his father and younger brother for a hockey tryout. Jerry later recalled that 20-odd spectators were present at the rink, and that he briefly lost track of Jacob. "It was very strange but very real," Jerry told an interviewer, years after the fact. "I had this sense of danger for Jacob. I can almost point to the spot on the ice where it happened to this day." Jerry found Jacob, and the ominous feeling soon passed, but in retrospect, he said, "It prompted me to wonder if possibly the abductor had been in the ice arena at that time, in a sense looking at Jacob or stalking him." Witness descriptions of the white-haired man loitering around the Tom Thumb store may corroborate that theory—or they may be meaningless.

In February 1990, Jacob's parents created the Jacob Wetterling Foundation, a nonprofit organization based in St. Paul, Minnesota, which offers education on the threat of child-abduction and provides assistance to parents of missing children. In 1994, Congress passed the Jacob Wetterling Crimes against Children and Sexually Violent Offender Registration Act as part of the Federal Violence Crime Control and Law Enforcement Act, requiring all 50 states to maintain registries of child-molesters and violent sex offenders, tracking their movements for at least 10 years after release from prison.

In literal concrete terms, Jacob Wetterling is memorialized by the Bridge of Hope, spanning the Mississippi River between Sartell and Saulk Rapids, Minnesota. The Wetterlings still occupy the same house in St. Joseph, refusing to leave despite its painful memories, on the off-chance that Jacob may someday return or phone home. Lieutenant Dave Nohner, still employed with the Stearns County Sheriff's Department when he spoke to reporters in 2006, also clung to hope. "It's been quite a while," he said, "but there is always the possibility that someone will have a dose of conscience and may talk before their death. There was a huge amount of emotion that ran with this case and whoever did this has to be carrying huge amounts of baggage."

So far, that hope remains unfulfilled.

WEYS, Gale   See "HIGHWAY KILLER(S)"

WHITTAKER, Elliott   See NEW YORK CITY TAXI MURDERS

WHITTINGTON, John   See MARYLAND GAY MURDERS

WILKERSON, Angela   See MARYLAND MURDERS

WILLIAMS, Christina Marie murder victim (1998)

Christina Williams was six weeks past her 13th birthday on June 12, 1998, when she took her dog—a birthday present—for a walk on the grounds of the former Fort Ord Army Base at Seaside, California. She left her family's home at 7:30 P.M., and while the dog came home trailing his leash at 8:20, Christina was nowhere to be found. Relatives conducted a brief search, then summoned local police, who scoured the landscape in vain. FBI agents took over the case on June 13; Fort Ord is still federal property, housing several California Army National Guard units, facilities supervised by the Presidio of Monterey, and an active commissary catering to military retirees.

Early rumors suggested that Christina may have slipped away from home to attend a late-night party. That was swiftly contradicted by her closest friends from school, and two young boys reported seeing Christina with her dog but otherwise alone around 8:00 P.M. Then, a jogger told investigators she had been accosted at Fort Ord on June 12 by two men in a blue or primer-gray car, perhaps a Ford Granada or Mercury Monarch. A police sketch artist prepared drawings of the the car and one passenger, while the jogger submitted to hypnosis in a fruitless bid to recall

the license plate number. Agent George Grotz from the FBI's San Francisco field office told reporters, "We believe that this vehicle and the occupants of the vehicle are significant aspects of this investigation." Asked if the presumed kidnappers might have fled town, Grotz replied, "That scenario would tend to gain credibility the longer time goes by. But we're still confident that someone will recognize the vehicle and witnesses will call it in."

He was mistaken, and FBI pleas for the two men to surrender voluntarily for questioning fell on deaf ears. Christina's father, Navy meteorologist Michael Williams, issued a plea of his own on June 18, addressing the unknown abductors directly. "Just let her go, please," he implored. "This is ripping us apart." Meanwhile, ongoing searches by 100 G-men, military personnel, and sheriff's deputies, coupled with a $20,000 FBI reward for information leading to arrest and conviction of the kidnappers, produced no results. Another rumor, claiming that Christina was involved in an Internet romance with an adult male from Gilroy, California, went up in smoke when agents could find no suggestive e-mails.

On June 19 a new witness surfaced, to report a sighting of a frightened-looking girl resembling Christina, seen in a car with two men around 7:45 P.M. on June 12. While agents pondered that contradiction of prior statements depicting Christina alone with her dog 15 minutes later, Seaside residents and storekeepers phoned in reports of a stranger seen around town who resembled the jogger's suspect. One witness, owner of a Seaside auto body shop, claimed that he often saw the man depicted in the sketch—an Asian or Pacific Islander with a mustache—cruising Broadway Avenue with a second man in a Ford or Mercury sedan. "It's a local car, and I've seen this guy around here for a month," he declared. "They've just been cruising my neighborhood, looking like they were looking for trouble or something to steal." As for the car, "It has gray primer paint pretty much all over the car, and it has a hissing muffler. This is my business. I know cars. This is the one. You couldn't miss it, it was so ugly."

But G-men could not find it, and they had no better luck with security videotapes procured from local 7-Eleven stores where employees allegedly saw the same man. Clerk Derek Bradford—at a store in Marina, on Fort Ord's northern boundary—claimed that the suspect bought a map and coil of clothesline on the night Christina vanished, further stating that he saw Christina with a man and two women around 11:00

P.M. on June 12. Unfortunately, the crucial tape from Bradford's store had been erased. Chief Alexander Kerekes, of the Presidio of Monterey Police Department, told the *San Francisco Chronicle,* "We're not discounting this fellow, but part of his information was inconsistent with what we know about Christina."

Another possible lead came from Chuck Baker, owner of the Gateway Lodge Motel on Fremont Boulevard in Seaside. Baker viewed the suspect sketch and said, "That face was in my place last week. I am sure of it." But again, the lead turned into a dead end. On June 24, hikers found a young woman's corpse in rural San Benito County, some 30 miles from Fort Ord. Christina's parents waited breathlessly until comparison of dental records identified the subject as a missing resident of San Jose.

July brought a touch of celebrity to the search for Christina and her abductors. Singer Mariah Carey filmed a public service announcement on July 15, urging any reluctant witnesses to share their information with authorities, joined in that plea by Baseball Hall of Famer Reggie Jackson and running back Napoleon Kaufman of the Oakland Raiders. G-men increased their reward for useful information to $100,000 on July 23, again without effect. Three days later, *America's Most Wanted* ran the first of five episodes profiling Christina's case. That program brought word from Greensboro, North Carolina, on July 31, that witnesses had seen a girl resembling Christina with an unknown man at a local Sam's Club store, but the lead proved worthless.

By November 1998, Michael Williams admitted the probability that his daughter was dead, but he refused to surrender all hope. "There is no sense in me speculating about it," he told the *Chronicle.* "How can a parent ever give up on his child? Until someone shows me a body, we're going to think she's alive." That grim word came on January 12, 1999, seven months to the day after Christina's disappearance, when a botany researcher found her remains three miles from home, on land owned by the University of California Natural Reserve System. Dental records confirmed the identification, but the find remained mysterious. As local resident Roger Peron told the *Chronicle,* "All kinds of people came through here seven months ago and they went over it with a fine tooth comb." A neighbor, Dan Alvarado, said, "I've been down there a lot of times and I never saw anything."

Advanced decomposition ruled out any verdict on a cause of death, but FBI agents and local police pressed forward with their homicide investigation, vowing to pursue the case to a solution. Persons living near the site where Christina was found told *Chronicle* reporters they had seen a man and vehicle matching law enforcement sketches around the time Christina disappeared, but those belated admissions did nothing to advance the manhunt. Agent Grotz declared that the two unknown suspects from June 1998 "are still a focus of this investigation," but he offered no realistic hopes for their arrest.

Meanwhile, police had indications that the nameless pair might still be trolling the district for victims. In Petaluma, 120 miles south of Seaside in Sonoma County, two men snatched 17-year-old jogger Noelani Burleson from the street on November 23, 1998, then drove her to a remote location with the apparent intent of raping her. Burleson escaped by kicking her abductors and fleeing on foot, then coached the same sketch artist who had drawn Christina's presumed kidnappers in preparation of new suspect portraits. Agent Grotz acknowledged a similarity between the two sets of sketches, but Burleson's mother was more emphatic, telling the *Chronicle,* "They look so much alike it's scary."

And they remained equally elusive. More than a decade after Christina's murder, the case remains unsolved, her killers unidentified.

WILLIAMS, Connie See "INDEPENDENCE AVENUE KILLER"

WILLIAMS, Diane See "FREEWAY PHANTOM"

WILLIAMS, James See MARYLAND GAY MURDERS (1996–97)

WILLIAMS, James See WASHINGTON, D.C., GAY MURDERS

WILLIAMS, Verna See "SOUTHSIDE SLAYER"

WILLIAMS, Vickie See PORTLAND, OREGON, MURDERS

WILLIS, Delores See DETROIT, MICHIGAN, MURDERS

WILSON, Erika See SALEM, OREGON, MURDERS

WILSON, Laurel See SALEM, OREGON, MURDERS

WILSON, Lee See CHICAGO HOLDUP MURDERS (1971–72)

WILSON, Sheily See "SOUTHSIDE SLAYER"

WILTSHIRE, England unsolved murders (1986)

On December 21, 1986, detectives in Wiltshire, England, announced their search for links between the recent slayings of two women killed within hours of each other at Salisbury. In the early morning hours of December 19, 25-year-old Ruth Perrett's nude corpse was found in her room at a halfway hostel for recovering mental patients. Last seen alive the previous evening, Perrett had been raped and strangled by an unknown assailant. The following day, police at Ringwood, near Southampton, found 45-year-old Beryl Deacon dead in her automobile, another victim of sexual assault and strangulation.

A third fatality was added to the list when homicide investigators voiced concerns about a possible link between the two Wiltshire murders and that of 24-year-old Linda Cooke, a former barmaid raped and murdered at Portsmouth on December 10, 1986. Cooke's death was seen as possibly related to a string of unsolved rapes spanning the past year, mostly targeting nurses and female doctors at area hospitals. Police questioned several suspects in the case, but none was ultimately prosecuted. The most recent suspect, described in media reports as a sailor, was released for lack of evidence in January 1987.

Mental patient Daniel Mudd, released from Britain's Broadmoor asylum in May 1983, was convicted of Ruth Perrett's slaying in 1987. More than two decades later, the Deacon and Cooke homicides remain unsolved.

WINDHAM, Evelyn May murder victim (1947)

On March 11, 1947, Los Angeles homicide investigators were called to the scene of the fifth brutal murder involving a female victim in eight weeks. The first victim, on January 15, had been "BLACK DAHLIA" Elizabeth Short. The latest, found at 1:45 A.M. in the gashouse district where Ducommun Street crossed the Santa Fe railroad, was 49-year-old Evelyn Windham, née Winter. She had been clubbed to death by an unknown assailant, the cause of death listed as "subarachnoid hemorrhage and edema of the brain, due to concussion of the brain." In fact, severe blows to the left side of her head—as if delivered by a right-handed man—left portions of her fractured skull exposed. Windham was found with her slip, brown dress, and checkered jacket "pulled nearly off" her body. The victim's underwear and shoes were found a block away, at the corner of Commercial and Center Streets.

A musician and Vassar graduate, once described as a brilliant scholar, Evelyn Windham had been married to Sydney Justin, head of Paramount Studios' legal department, from 1936 to 1941. She, too, had worked at Paramount, as a music copywriter. In 1942 she had married a soldier named Windham, but they divorced two years later. Lately she had fallen on hard times, including a series of arrests for intoxication, drunk driving, and "resorting." At the time she died, her blood alcohol level was .28, nearly three times the legal limit of intoxication.

Two days before her corpse was found, on March 9, Windham had spoken to her mother in the lobby of the Clarke Hotel. She had borrowed five dollars "for expenses" but refused to say where she was living, remarking that "It's too terrible a place. I don't want to tell you." Her mother reported that Windham had once resided at 1850 North Cherokee, a few doors away from January victim Elizabeth Short.

Police detained George Wickliffe, the 28-year-old railroad section hand who had discovered Windham's body, after they found a woman's coin purse in his possession and noted lipstick smudges on his mouth. No stranger to jail, having been arrested for vagrancy in February 1947, Wickliffe had a simple explanation for the lipstick: He admitted kissing Windham when he found her sprawled beside the railroad tracks, allegedly before he realized that she was dead. He was subsequently cleared of involvement in the crime, and police never identified another suspect. Windham's murder remains unsolved today.

WINN, Margie Lee murder victim (1948)

Margie Winn was a resident of Redlands, California, born in 1930. She was in her senior year at Redlands High School, pondering the options of college or marriage, when violence cut her life short and left authorities with one more enduring mystery.

On February 7, 1948—a Saturday—Winn accompanied 18-year-old James Sloan to a rodeo in Palm Springs, 38 miles west of Redlands. They enjoyed themselves, as usual, and it was 2:45 A.M. on February 8 when they stopped beside Highway 99, as Sloan later said, "to set their wristwatches by the dashboard clock." They were engrossed in that activity when a male stranger yanked open Winn's door, brandished a sawed-off .410-gauge shotgun, and demanded money.

Sloan had left his car's motor running, perhaps to power the roadster's heater, and he floored the accelerator as Margie shouted, "Go!" The gunman fired a single shot at point-blank range, scorching the sleeve of Winn's coat as birdshot pellets ripped into her body, piercing her heart. Already dying, she gasped out to Sloan, "I'm shot! Get me to the nearest place!"

That happened to be a farm owned by Adolph Ellis, a mile farther east on Highway 99. When Sloan reached the farm, shortly after 3:00 A.M., he found Ellis at the roadside, peering into a green Packard automobile. Sloan and detectives subsequently learned that a prowler had invaded the Ellis home around two o'clock, startling Adolph's wife awake with a sweeping flashlight beam. When she challenged the intruder, he replied, "Don't move. I've got a gun on you." That woke Adolph, who scrambled for his own shotgun and chased the stranger from his home without any shots being fired.

Prior to Sloan's arrival on the scene with Winn, Adolph had awakened a neighbor, driven the four miles to Beaumont, informed police of the break-in, and returned home. Officers arrived too late to help Margie Winn, who was already dead from damage to her heart and internal bleeding. Deputy Coroner A. M. Depew examined her corpse at a Beaumont mortuary and certified the cause of death as homicide at the hands of persons unknown.

So it remains today.

Police were initially hopeful of solving the case. They traced the green Packard to its registered owner, Riverside resident Albert Strickland, who had discovered it missing from his home around midnight. He warned police that he kept a sawed-off .410 in the car, which they presumed to be the murder weapon, but investigators cleared him as a suspect and could file no charges for the missing weapon without measuring its cut-down barrel. (Both the state of California and the federal government restrict civilian ownership of shotguns with barrels shorter than 18 inches.)

While officers were tracing and interrogating Strickland, others established roadblocks in Beaumont, Indio, Palm Springs Junction, Redlands, and Riverside, seeking a "narrow-faced" white man, age 30 to 40, approximately five feet eight inches tall and 150 pounds, wearing a gray hat with a black band and a black leather jacket. Passing motorists and hitchhikers were questioned, but deputies made only one arrest. Tobe Beams, a 34-year-old former ship's cook from Kentucky, was jailed after officers removed him from a freight train in Beaumont. His gray hat and navy-blue sailor's coat generally matched James Sloan's description of the gunman, but his footprints did not fit those of the prowler, found in soft earth at the Ellis home. Beams was released without charges, to make his way home as best he could.

Meanwhile, searchers scoured the scrublands of Riverside County for Margie Winn's slayer, fielding mounted posses and three airplanes from Hemet's California Aerial Squad. Transients resembling the suspect were detained, interrogated, and released upon producing alibis. Search as they might, police found no trace of the killer or his stolen murder weapon.

In the midst of the manhunt, Redlands police chief A. O. Peterson received a strange letter postmarked from Rodeo, California, 395 miles to the north, in Contra Costa County. The unsigned note confessed Winn's murder and mentioned the name of a railroad ticket agent in Contra Costa County, who in turn identified its author as 20-year-old Richard Olsen, a Rodeo resident and World War II veteran turned drifter. Police found Olsen in Martinez, California, on February 20 and detained him for questioning. He admitted penning the confession, but now regretted it and denied any part in the crime. Driven back to Riverside, he was viewed in a lineup by James Sloan and other witnesses to the events of February 8, none of whom recognized him. Olsen's confession proved to be a symptom of some psychic aberration, akin to the dozens of confessions received in the "BLACK DAHLIA" case.

Around the same time Olsen was arrested, sheriff's deputies found a pair of rubber-soled shoes on a vacant lot in East Los Angeles. Abandoned footwear is far from unique in L.A., but something made the officers collect these shoes and deliver them to renowned forensic chemist Ray Pinker for examination. Pinker announced that the shoes matched four specific points from plaster casts made of the Ellis homestead prowler, but there the trail ended.

Detectives could trace the shoes no farther, and their owner remains unidentified today.

WINTERS, Joan murder victim (1933)

A child of German immigrants, born in Seattle on December 8, 1909, Carol von Niedergesaess saw her family surname Anglicized to "Godfrey" during World War I to circumvent prejudice against German-Americans. She left home at age 19, and apparently swapped "Carol Godfrey" for "Joan Winters" sometime before she won a dancing role in *Bad Girl*, on Broadway, in 1930.

Winters left New York for Europe on April 13, 1932. Her itinerary and the reason for her journey are unclear, but prior to departure she announced plans to return in time for her 24th birthday, in December 1933. Two months before that self-imposed deadline, Joan wrote to her parents—now living in Brooklyn, where her marine-engineer father ran the Godfrey Propeller Adjusting Corporation—informing them that she had fallen in love with a Serbian entrepreneur who did not return her affection. That letter came from Bucharest, Romania, prompting Bert Godfrey to contact the U.S. State Department, but his queries concerning Joan's welfare went unanswered.

Joan's next letter, received in late October 1933, announced that she had been detained as a suspected spy in Istanbul. Police had searched and questioned her, confiscating several letters she carried, then released her hours later without filing any charges. Two weeks after that letter arrived, Winters was found shot to death in Jerusalem's fabled Garden of Gethsemane, sprawled beside the corpse of Mohammad Karamini, an Indian civil service employee from Madras. Greek authorities reported that Winters met Karamini in Athens and employed him as a guide, arriving at Haifa on October 29, and moved on from there to Jerusalem. Investigators blamed the double-slaying on Arab rioters, protesting the creation of Israel's Jewish state five months earlier, and while they briefly detained an East Indian Muslim suspect, one Mohamed Ikram, he was freed without charges.

Joan's mother subsequently told reporters that her daughter had been working on a book about Palestine, but no manuscript ever surfaced. That claim, and Joan's detention in Romania, prompt some theorists to wonder if she was dispatched to Europe and the Middle East on a covert mission of espionage. No evidence exists to support that hypothesis, but stranger things have happened. The Central Intelligence Agency, created in July 1947, makes extensive use of civilian "assets" and "contractors" to spy in foreign countries and at home, which makes the theory feasible, although unproven.

WOOD, Wilma See ZEPHYRHILLS, FLORIDA, MURDERS

WOODS, Jeanette See DETROIT, MICHIGAN, MURDERS

WOODSTOCK, Laura See HOSPITAL FOR SICK CHILDREN MURDERS

WOODWARD, Brenda Denise See "FREEWAY PHANTOM"

WOODWARD, Paulette See DETROIT, MICHIGAN, MURDERS

WOONSOCKET, Rhode Island unsolved murders (1990–91)

Suspects remain elusive in the case of three Woonsocket women found strangled to death between November 1990 and March 1991. Local police report that 32-year-old Dianne Goulet, 18-year-old Christine Miller, and 23-year-old Wendy Madden all died in similar fashion, all with records of arrests on drug and prostitution charges. A report issued on March 22, 1991, declared that authorities were examining certain unspecified links in the series of murders, but no further news was forthcoming until October 16, 1995, when Marc Dumas entered the Woonsocket police station, claiming knowledge of Dianne Goulet's murder. During a 12-hour interrogation, Dumas claimed that he and companion Mike Jellison engaged in sex with Goulet on November 9, 1990, after which Jellison strangled her despite Dumas's efforts to stop the attack. Police charged Dumas with the crime, and he was twice convicted of second-degree murder (the second trial occurring after the first verdict was overturned on appeal). The Miller and Madden slayings remain officially unsolved.

X, Malcolm assassination victim (1965)

An Omaha, Nebraska, native, born May 19, 1925, Malcolm Little was the son of an outspoken black separatist. His father was active in Marcus Garvey's Universal Negro Improvement Association and later led the UNIA's East Chicago, Indiana, chapter. The family settled in East Lansing, Michigan, in January 1928, where they endured successive tragedies: Their house burned on November 7, 1929, and Malcolm's father was killed by a streetcar on September 28, 1931. Malcolm heard rumors that the "accident" was really murder, planned by the Black Legion, an offshoot of the Ku Klux Klan.

Discouraged in school and consigned to a juvenile home in August 1939, Malcolm drifted through odd jobs and a life of petty crime. The army spurned him in October 1943 with the notation "psychopathic personality inadequate, sexual perversion, psychiatric rejection." Convicted of larceny and other charges in January 1946, he converted to the teachings of Elijah Muhammad while serving time in a New York prison. Upon his release in August 1952, Malcolm traveled to Chicago and joined the Nation of Islam (NOI), adopting the name "Malcolm X." Three weeks after his recruitment, on September 23, 1952, an informant gave the Federal Bureau of Investigation (FBI) three letters written by Malcolm at various times. In one of them, penned from prison in June 1950, he declared, "I have always been a Communist."

The FBI kept Malcolm under surveillance from that day forward, charting his rise to assistant minister in Detroit and "first minister" in Boston (1953), then Philadelphia and New York (1954). G-men followed him to temples throughout the United States and eavesdropped on his conversations with illegal wiretaps. On June 8, 1964, FBI headquarters added his name to the Bureau's "COMSAB" (*Com*munist *Sab*otage) and "DETCOM" (*Det*ention of *Com*munists) lists, slating him for potential arrest under terms of the McCarran Internal Security Act. Seven months later, on January 10, 1955, two agents approached Malcolm at home, requesting a list of all NOI temples, officers, and members. Malcolm told them to "go back to Hell"; the memo of that interview describes him as "uncooperative."

As Malcolm X became more prominent, he kept FBI agents busy. On January 28, 1961, he met with Georgia Klan leaders, seeking aid in the purchase of land for an all-black community. He also subscribed to a newsletter published by the Fair Play for Cuba Committee (later made famous by Lee Harvey Oswald). G-men, reading Malcolm's mail, mistook the newsletter's subscription renewal date for a "membership number" and reported him to Washington as a dues-paying member of the FPCC. Elijah Muhammad suspended Malcolm in December 1963, after Malcolm publicly described the assassination of President JOHN KENNEDY as a case of "chickens coming home to roost." A month later, on January

Malcolm X personified the Black Muslim call for separation of the races in America until 1964, when he espoused a new message of brotherhood and cooperation. (Library of Congress)

6, 1964, Malcolm was formally "isolated" from the sect, with an order from Muhammad that barred any NOI members from contact with Malcolm. The rift became irreparable in February 1964, when a former aide in New York warned Malcolm of an NOI plot to bomb his car.

On March 9, 1964, Malcolm announced the foundation of a new religious order, the Muslim Mosque, Incorporated. The next day, he told *Ebony* magazine that Muhammad's Black Muslims have "got to kill me. They can't afford to let me live. . . . I know where the bodies are buried, and if they press me, I'll exhume some." Three weeks later, on March 31, FBI Director J. Edgar Hoover asked Assistant Director William Sullivan for recommendations in the "high-priority" case of Malcolm X. Sullivan responded with a suggestion that Attorney General ROBERT KENNEDY be asked to authorize wiretaps on Malcolm (already maintained illegally for the past decade). Hoover sent the request to Kennedy on April 1, claiming that he sought "information concerning the contacts and activity of Little, and activity and growth of the Muslim Mosque, Incorporated." Kennedy approved the tap request after reading Hoover's report that Malcolm encouraged "the possession of firearms by members of his new organization for their self-protection." On the same day, Justice aide Burke Mar-

shall asked the Central Intelligence Agency for a report on Malcolm. CIA headquarters replied that it "had nothing which would shed light on Subject's recent breakaway from the Black Muslims nor anything reflecting on where he might be getting financial support."

Shadowed by the FBI and CIA, Malcolm traveled widely through Africa and the Middle East in April and May 1964. Back in New York, on June 28, 1964, he announced the creation of the Organization of Afro-American Unity. Death threats were by now routine, but they struck close to home when Malcolm's home was firebombed at 2:46 A.M. on February 14, 1965. One week later, on February 21, Malcolm was shot and killed while addressing a crowd at New York's Audubon Ballroom. Early reports in the *New York Times* declared that three gunmen had been captured at the murder scene, but police later claimed only two were arrested, with a third jailed two days later. All three suspects were linked to the Nation of Islam. On the night of Malcolm's death, an FBI informant gave G-men one of the pistols used in his murder.

The judicial resolution of Malcolm's slaying ultimately solved nothing. Suspects Talmadge Thayer, Norman 3X Butler, and Thomas 15X Johnson were indicted for murder on March 10, 1965. At trial in March 1966, Hayer testified that he and three others were hired to kill Malcolm, while insisting that But-

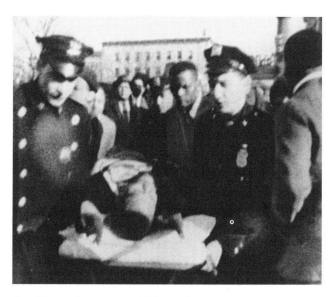

New York police remove Malcolm's body from the Audubon Ballroom following his February 1965 assassination. (Library of Congress)

In the wake of Malcolm's death, Muslims across the United States clashed with one another and with police. These suspects were arrested after an August 1965 gun battle at their Los Angeles mosque. (Library of Congress)

ler and Johnson were innocent. Johnson's wife also swore he was not present at the shooting, but jurors convicted all three defendants on March 11, 1966. A month later, on April 14, all three were sentenced to life imprisonment. Conspiracy theories later surfaced, suggesting that Malcolm was slain by some combination of the FBI, CIA, and/or New York mobsters who resented his June 1964 call for "an all-out war against organized crime" in black communities. On May 29, 1980, New Jersey congressman William Hughes asked FBI Director William Webster to review Malcolm's assassination, but the plea was ignored.

YAKIMA, Washington unsolved murders (1980–92)
Authorities remain divided in their opinions as to whether a serial killer is responsible for the murders of at least 13 women killed since 1980 on the 1.3 million-acre Yakima Indian Reservation, in Washington state. Eleven of the 13 victims were Native American, most of them born and raised on the reservation, many with personal histories of alcohol abuse. A majority of those killed were in their twenties; at least eight left children behind. Some were stabbed to death, while others were beaten, shot, or strangled; two were apparently drowned, and one was run down by car. The corpses have generally been dumped in remote wooded areas, where scavengers, decomposition, and exposure to the elements erase evidence, leaving the cause of death unknown in several cases. At least two other Indian women— Karen Louise Johnly and Daisey May Tallman, both in their twenties—were reported missing between 1987 and 1992, but their names have not been added to the official Yakima victims list.

One lawman who believes a serial killer *is* responsible for the murders, Melford Hall, retired in 1989 after 22 years as a criminal investigator for the Bureau of Indian Affairs, citing the homicides as one of his reasons for quitting. In January 1993 Hall told reporters, "They'll probably say, 'He doesn't know what he's talking about.' But then you look at all these names." Hall linked the slayings to rampant alcoholism, a major problem at Yakima and on other reservations. "My own opinion," he explained, "is

this guy sits at a tavern someplace and waits for an intoxicated woman and grabs her."

Yakima's Tribal Police Department declines all requests for interviews on the murders, but agents from the Federal Bureau of Investigation's (FBI) Seattle field office fulfilled Hall's prediction, deeming it "extremely unlikely" that one killer was responsible for all 13 of the Yakima murders. Bureau spokesman William Gore referred to unspecified "significant evidence" and "logical suspects" in three of the cases, but no charges have yet been filed. On January 27, 1993, the FBI declared that 12 of the Yakima murders "are closed, though they could be reopened if new information surfaced."

But the question remains: Is anyone looking? Melford Hall, for one, was bitter toward the FBI. "A lot of times we would call them," he told reporters, "and they'd say, 'Just send over a report.' They spent millions of dollars over there [on Seattle's "Green River" murders], and wouldn't spend anything here." It was a further point of irony, Hall noted, that the FBI has primary responsibility for all murders committed on U.S. Indian reservations, but none in local murders like the Green River case. The implication, flatly rejected by bureau spokesmen, is that white victims (even prostitutes and drifters) "count" more than Native Americans.

Another lawman who compared the two cases was Yakima County sheriff's deputy Dave Johnson, who complained that murder investigations are hampered by the tendency of some tribal members to leave the reservation without informing friends or relatives. "It's kind of like the Green River victims, many of whom were prostitutes," Johnson said. "You have individuals with no permanent address."

One who resented that comparison was Johnnie Wyman, whose sister—44-year-old JoAnne Betty Wyman John—was found dead on the reservation in 1991, three years after she was reported missing. "The authorities take the attitude that it's just a bunch of drunken Indian women," Wyman told the press. "It's just another slap in the face. I can't candy-coat it for anybody. She was my sister, and she meant something to me."

The most recent Yakima slaying, and that which finally brought national publicity to the murders, was that of Shari Dee Sampson Ewell, found strangled and sexually mutilated on December 30, 1992, in a section of the reservation closed to non-Indians. Sufficient media attention was generated by Ewell's death that the Yakima Indian Nation offered a $1,000 reward for information leading to the killer's arrest, and the FBI added a further $5,000 on May 14, 1993. Thus far, the offer has not helped. The murders on the Yakima reservation remain unsolved.

YALE, Frankie gangland murder victim (1928)

A child of Sicilian immigrants, born Frank Uale in New York, in 1885, the mobster later known as Frankie Yale fought his way up from the mean streets of Little Italy with the infamous Five Points Gang. One of his allies in those days was John Torrio, who later moved to Chicago and established a Prohibition-era bootlegging empire with protégé Al Capone. Yale remained in New York, and in 1918 became president of the Unione Siciliane, a fraternal organization transformed by its previous leader—one Lupo (The Wolf) Saietta—into a virtual front for the Mafia. Operating from the Harvard Inn (where Al Capone served as a bouncer before he moved west), Yale billed himself as a mortician while pocketing millions from illicit liquor sales, gambling, and various extortion rackets. In 1924, he allegedly visited Chicago to help Torrio and Capone assassinate Irish rival DION O'BANNION. On the side Yale manufactured cigars so distasteful and so overpriced that the phrase "a Frankie Yale" became slang for any sort of shoddy merchandise.

Chicago mobster Al Capone remains the prime suspect in the unsolved murder of New York Mafia kingpin Frankie Yale. (Library of Congress)

By early 1928, Yale's once friendly relationship with Al Capone had turned ugly. Capone, no longer restrained by the "retired" Johnny Torrio, resented Yale's efforts to seize control of the Unione Siciliane's Windy City chapter. At the same time, Capone suspected Yale of hijacking and selling shipments of imported liquor, which he—Yale—had already sold to Capone. Big Al dispatched a spy to Brooklyn, but his man was gunned down on the street, thus confirming Capone's dark suspicions.

On July 1, 1928, a telephone call summoned Yale to a Brooklyn speakeasy on some unknown business. Shunning protection, Yale drove his own roadster along Forty-fourth Street in Brooklyn and paid for his overconfidence when a black sedan bristling with guns overtook his vehicle. Before Yale recognized the danger, a fusillade of .45-caliber bullets ripped through his car, killing Yale at the wheel as his roadster swerved, jumped the curb, and crashed into a house. Police found the murder car abandoned nearby and traced it to a dealership in Knoxville, Tennessee, where it had been purchased by persons unknown on June 28. Inside the car lay two revolvers and a Thompson submachine gun, the latter traced to Chicago gun dealer Peter von Frantizius, unofficial armorer for the Capone gang.

No suspects were publicly identified in Yale's slaying, which marked the first use of a tommy gun—or

"Chicago typewriter"—in New York gang warfare. Yale's funeral was an underworld extravaganza, including a $15,000 coffin and 38 carloads of flowers. Flags throughout Brooklyn were flown at half-staff while a 250-car funeral procession wound its way through the streets, with 10,000 spectators crowding Holy Cross Cemetery for Yale's interment.

The *New York Daily News* declared, presumably with no attempt at irony, that Yale's send-off "was a better one than that given Dion O'Bannion by Chicago racketeers in 1924."

YATES, Nenomoshia   See "Freeway Phantom"

Z

ZAPATA Miranda, Laura Guadalupe kidnap victim (2002)

Mexican television actress Laura Zapata was born on July 31, 1956, the daughter of professional boxer Guillermo Zapata. Laura's parents later divorced, and her mother remarried, bearing two more daughters. Laura's half-sisters, Thalia and Ernestina Sodi, are also famous in Mexico as a singer and an author respectively. Laura, for her part, broke into show business as a child star for Televisa, the largest multimedia firm in the Spanish-speaking world. By early adulthood, she was established as a star of Mexican telenovelas, serial productions described as follows by Telemundo production chief Patricio Wills: "The plot is always the same. In the first three minutes of the first episode the viewer already knows the novela will end with that same couple kissing each other. A telenovela is all about a couple who wants to kiss and a scriptwriter who stands in their way for 150 episodes."

During her rise to stardom, Zapata married a nephew of her mother's second husband, who was also half-sister Thalia's cousin, with the result that she (Laura) was also known in Mexico as Laura Zapata de Sodi. Zapata's fame increased from one telenovela to the next, including the popular serials *Maria Mercedes*, *Rosalinda*, *Pobre Niña Rica*, *Esmeralda*, and *Rosa Salvaje*. Fans admired her ability to play heroines and villains with equal enthusiasm.

In September 2002, Laura and sister Ernestina were snatched by still-unidentified kidnappers and transported to an unknown location. Journalists speculated that they were being held for ransom, since Laura was wealthy in her own right and sister Thalia was married to billionaire American music executive Thomas Mottola. Whether true or not, Laura was released after 10 days in captivity, and Ernestina five days later. If ransom was paid, the fact has not been confirmed and no amount was ever disclosed.

The crime remains officially unsolved, but the August 22, 2005, issue of *Mira!* magazine, published in the United States and Canada, claimed that an imprisoned Mexican drug dealer planned the double-abduction from his cell in Lima, Peru, directing his agents by telephone and demanding a ransom of $5 million. Members of the Zapata-Sodi clan have not confirmed those allegations. The magazine report coincided with Laura's announcement of a forthcoming play based on her abduction. That plan had sparked public disputes between Laura and sister Thalia in January 2004, with Thalia threatening lawsuits if the production proceeded. Ernestina raised no objections. In 2008 Laura Zapata announced her return to telenovelas in the series *Cuidado con el Angel*.

ZEPHYRHILLS, Florida unsolved murders (1973–77)

Despite the relative antiquity of this case, authorities and journalists in Zephyrhills, Florida, (the seat of Pasco County, northeast of Tampa) still refuse to answer requests for information on a series of local murders spanning the years from 1973 to 1977. Vague media reports allude to eight female victims, mostly nude dancers or streetwalkers, all described as having long blond or light brown hair. Skeletal remains of the eighth presumed victim, apparently unidentified, were found in December 1977, some 500 yards from the spot where 49-year-old Wilma Wood was discovered in 1973, and barely 100 yards from the site where 38-year-old Emily Grieve was found murdered on October 21, 1977. The rest is shrouded in mystery, along with the identity of the human predator (or predators) who murdered eight women and dumped them around Zephyrhills. It *can* be said with certainty that the last known murder in the series occurred at least a week before serial killer Ted Bundy made his way to Florida in 1977, and roughly seven years before Bobby Joe Long began stalking topless dancers in Tampa, committing 10 known homicides and 50-odd rapes. As for the rest, the case remains unsolved, the Pasco County stalker unidentified.

ZETEROWER, Belinda See "Flat-Tire" murders

"ZODIAC" unidentified serial murderer (1966–??)

California's most elusive serial killer claimed his first known victim at Riverside, on October 30, 1966. That evening, Cheri Jo Bates, an 18-year-old freshman at Riverside City College, emerged from the campus library to find her car disabled, the distributor coil disconnected. Police theorize that her killer approached with an offer of help, then dragged Bates behind some nearby shrubbery, where a furious struggle ended with Bates stabbed in the chest and back, her throat slashed so deeply that she was nearly decapitated.

In November 1966, a letter to the local press declared that Bates "is not the first and she will not be the last." On April 30, 1967, following publication of an article on the case, identical letters were posted to the newspaper, to police, and to Bates's father. They read: "Bates had to die. There will be more."

On December 20, 1968, 17-year-old David Faraday was parked with his date, 16-year-old Betty Lou Jensen, on a rural road east of the Vallejo, California, city limits. A night-stalking gunman found them there and killed both teenagers, shooting Fara-

day in the head as he sat in the driver's seat of his car. Betty Jensen ran 30 feet before she was cut down by a tight series of five shots to the back, fired from a .22-caliber semiautomatic pistol.

On July 4, 1969, 19-year-old Michael Mageau picked up his date, 22-year-old Darlene Ferrin, for a night on the town in Vallejo. At one point Mageau thought they were being followed, but Ferrin seemed to recognize the other motorist, telling Mageau, "Don't worry about it." By midnight they were parked at Blue Rock Springs Park, when a second vehicle pulled alongside and its driver flashed a bright light in their eyes, then opened fire with a 9-millimeter pistol. Hit four times, Mageau survived; Ferrin, with nine bullet wounds, was dead on arrival at a local hospital. Forty minutes after the shooting, Vallejo police received an anonymous telephone call, directing officers to the shooting crime scene. Before hanging up, the male caller declared, "I also killed those kids last year."

In retrospect, friends and relatives recalled that Darlene Ferrin had been suffering harassment through anonymous phone calls and intimidating visits from a heavyset stranger in the weeks before her murder. She called the man "Paul," and told a girlfriend that he wished to silence her because she had seen him commit a murder. Police searched for "Paul" in the wake of Ferrin's slaying, but he was never located or identified.

On July 31, 1969, the killer mailed letters to three Bay Area newspapers, each containing one-third of a cryptic cipher. Ultimately broken by a local high school teacher, the message began: "I like killing people because it is so much fun." The author explained that he was killing in an effort to "collect slaves" who would serve him in the afterlife. Another letter, mailed on August 7, 1969, introduced the Zodiac trade name and provided details of the latest killing, leaving police in no doubt that its author was the murderer. Police reported that at least five "fingerprints of value" were recovered from the killer's July-August correspondence, but they matched no prints found in existing criminal files.

On September 27, 1969, 20-year-old Bryan Hartnell and 22-year-old Cecilia Shepherd were enjoying a picnic at Lake Berryessa, near Vallejo, when they were accosted by a hooded gunman. Brandishing a pistol, the man described himself as an escaped convict who needed their car "to go to Mexico." Producing a coil of clothesline, he bound both victims before drawing a long knife, stabbing Hartnell five times in

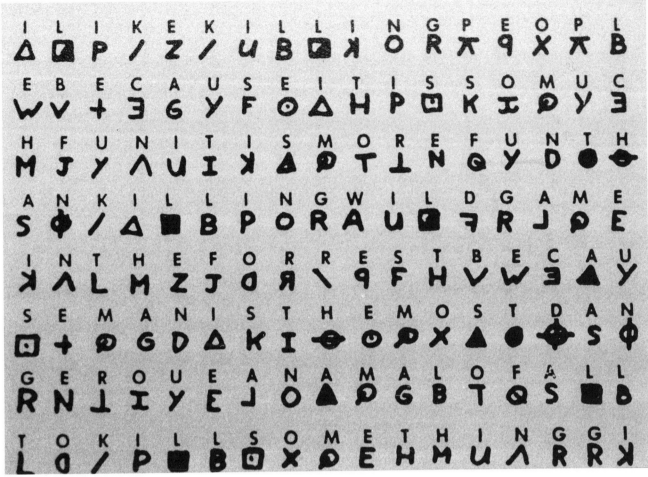

Coded letters like this one explained the Zodiac killer's plan to "collect slaves" for the afterlife. (Author's collection)

the back. Shepherd was stabbed 14 times, including four wounds in the chest as she twisted away from the plunging blade. Departing from the scene, their assailant paused at Hartnell's car to scribble on the door with a felt-tipped pen. He wrote:

Vallejo
12-20-68
7-4-69
Sept 27-69-6:30
by knife

A phone call to police reported the crime, but by that time a fisherman had already found the victims. Brian Hartnell would survive his wounds, but Cecilia Shepherd was doomed, another victim of the man who called himself the Zodiac. Officers located the telephone booth from which the call originated, isolating four "fingerprints of note" that remain unidentified today. A "clear palm-print" was also found on the telephone receiver, found dangling off the hook, but technicians smudged it and thereby rendered it useless.

On October 11, 1969, San Francisco cab driver Paul Stine was shot in the head and killed with a 9-millimeter semiautomatic pistol. Witnesses saw the gunman escape on foot toward the Presidio, as police descended on the area in force. At one point in the search two patrolmen stopped a heavyset pedestrian and were directed onward in pursuit of their elusive prey, not realizing that the tip had been provided by the very man they sought. Back at the crime scene, technicians lifted several fingerprints from Stine's cab that "show traces of blood [and] are believed to be prints from the suspect." Once again, they matched no prints currently on file with California authorities or the Federal Bureau of Investigation (FBI).

In the wake of Stine's murder, the Zodiac launched a new barrage of letters, some containing swatches of the cabbie's bloodstained shirt. Successive messages claimed seven victims instead of the established five, while the killer threatened to "wipe out a school bus some morning." He also vowed to change his method of "collecting souls": "They shall look like routine robberies, killings of anger, & a few fake suicides, etc." (At least one letter, mailed on October 13, 1969, included several latent fingerprints believed to be the killer's.) Five days before Christmas he wrote to prominent attorney Melvin Belli, pleading for help with the chilling remark that "I cannot remain in control for much longer."

On March 22, 1970, Kathleen Johns was driving with her infant daughter near Modesto, California, when another motorist pulled her over, flashing his lights and beeping his horn. The man informed Johns that a rear tire on her car seemed dangerously loose; he worked on it briefly with a lug wrench, but when she tried to drive away the wheel fell off. Her benefactor offered a lift to the nearest garage, then took Johns on an aimless drive through the countryside, threatening her life and that of her child before she managed to leap from the car, hiding in a roadside drainage ditch. While reporting the abduction at a local police station, Johns noticed a wanted poster bearing sketches of the Zodiac, and she identified the man as her attacker.

Nine more letters were received from Zodiac between April 1970 and March 1971, but police were unable to trace further crimes in the series. (A San Francisco detective reported that fingerprints found on a Zodiac note, mailed on April 28, 1970, "were not made by persons handling the card after its receipt.") On January 30, 1974, a San Francisco newspaper received the first authenticated Zodiac letter in nearly three years, signing off with the notation: "Me-37; SFPD-0."

One officer who took the estimated body count seriously was Sheriff Don Striepke of Sonoma County. In a 1975 report Striepke referred to a series of 40 unsolved murders in four western states, which seemed to form a giant Z when plotted on the map. While tantalizing, Striepke's theory seemed to fall apart when serial killer Ted Bundy was identified as a prime suspect in several of the homicides.

The Zodiac mailed his 21st confirmed letter on April 24, 1978, chilling Bay Area residents with the announcement that "I am back with you." No traceable crimes were committed, however, and Homicide Inspector Dave Toschi was later removed from the Zodiac detail on suspicion of writing the letter him-

self. In fact, while Toschi confessed to writing several anonymous letters to the press, praising his own performance on the case, expert handwriting analysts agree that the April note was written by the killer.

Theories abound in the Zodiac case. One was aired by author George Oakes (a pseudonym) in the November 1981 issue of *California* magazine, based on a presumption of the killer's obsession with water, clocks, binary mathematics, and the writings of Lewis Carroll (also named as a suspect in London's "JACK THE RIPPER" homicides of 1888). "Oakes" claimed to know the Zodiac's identity and said the killer had telephoned him several times. He blamed the Zodiac for an arson fire that ravaged 25,000 acres near Lake Berryessa in June 1981, but *California* editors acknowledged that FBI agents "weren't very impressed" with the theory. Spokesmen for the California State Attorney General's office went further, describing the tale as "a lot of bull."

Despite collection of 30 or 40 fingerprints allegedly belonging to the Zodiac (reports vary on the total number), the killer remains unidentified today. Hundreds of suspects were questioned, their fingerprints compared to those on file, but all in vain. Zodiac suspects publicly identified to date include:

Bruce Davis A onetime member of the Charles Manson "family," presently serving a life sentence for two counts of first-degree murder in California, Davis lived in San Francisco prior to joining Manson's tribe and moving south. Although a proven killer with a fascination for occult symbolism, Davis did not fit descriptions of the crew-cut Zodiac, and no evidence exists to link him with the slayer's crimes. His fingerprints do not match those alleged to be the Zodiac's, and Davis was in custody by mid-1970, thus ruled out as a source of Zodiac letters mailed after that time. Finally, researcher Tom Voigt cites a 1970 report from the California Bureau of Criminal Identification and Investigation, noting that "All male members of the Manson family have been investigated and eliminated as Zodiac suspects."

Theodore Kaczynski The elusive "Unabomber," presently serving life without parole in federal prison on three counts of first-degree murder, Kaczynski was named as a Zodiac suspect after FBI agents arrested him in 1998. The "evidence" normally cited in support of his candidacy includes Kaczynski's residency in the San Francisco area during the late 1960s, his penchant for writing to the press after various criminal acts, and his demonstrated expertise at building bombs. (The Zodiac never used explosives, but one of his letters included a crude diagram of a bomb.) Unfortunately for proponents of this theory, Kaczynski has been cleared of involvement in the Zodiac murders by both the FBI and the San Francisco Police Department. According to official reports, Kaczynski was exonerated of the murders by fingerprint and handwriting comparison, and by proof of his absence from California on five specific dates of known Zodiac activity.

Lawrence Kane Profiled as a Zodiac suspect by *America's Most Wanted* on November 14, 1998, Kane was 38 years old in 1962, when he suffered brain damage in an automobile accident. Three years later, a psychologist declared that Kane was "losing the ability to control self-gratification." Darlene Ferrin's sister reportedly named Kane as the man who followed and harassed Ferrin over several weeks before her murder, and Kane disposed of his car five days after the Mageau-Ferrin shooting in July 1969. Kathleen Johns also reportedly identified Kane as the man who abducted her in March 1970. Researcher Tom Voigt claims that Kane's surname "can be easily seen" in a Zodiac cipher mailed to police on April 20, 1970, though other students of the correspondence disagree. Voigt also reports that Kane was living in Nevada "as of early 1999," a fact apparently unknown to producers of *America's Most Wanted* when they broadcast pleas for viewers to locate him three months earlier. Kane's present whereabouts are unknown, but since no charges have been filed against him, he is free to travel where he will.

Rick Marshall A Texas native, 38 years old at the time of the Zodiac's first known murder in 1966, Marshall seems to be linked with the crimes more by geographic coincidence than anything resembling solid evidence. Tom Voigt reports that Marshall "is still considered a strong Zodiac suspect by several investigators," but his fingerprints match none of those collected from the Zodiac's crime scenes or letters. In place of evidence, we are told that Mar-

shall lived in Riverside "at the approximate time" of the Bates murder, later residing in San Francisco from 1969 to 1989. His apartment stood "within a few miles" of the Stine murder scene, and the call letters of a radio station where Marshall worked in the early 1970s (KTIM) allegedly "resemble" cryptic symbols from one of the Zodiac's letters. On balance, it is something less than a compelling case.

Michael O'Hare Initially named as a Zodiac suspect by Gareth Penn in his book *Times 17* (1987), later featured as one of several Zodiac prospects on the Learning Channel's review of the case, O'Hare is linked to the crimes only by an ephemeral web of conjecture involving Morse code and binary mathematics. Penn also flies in the face of established evidence, blaming the Zodiac for homicides committed in Massachusetts as late as 1981. Most students of the case dismiss his theory as implausible; a notation on Tom Voigt's Zodiac Web site goes further, asserting that "it is the opinion of more than one researcher that Penn himself makes a much better candidate to be the Zodiac than does O'Hare."

Charles Clifton Collins Named publicly as a suspect for the first time in October 2002, Collins was fingered by his son, New York journalism student William Collins, in a report aired by television's *Primetime Live*. As the younger Collins explained, he was reading a book on the Zodiac murders sometime in the 1990s, when he saw photocopies of the killer's letters and thought, "Oh my God, that's my dad's handwriting." Further research persuaded Collins that his father (deceased in 1993) resembled suspect sketches of the Zodiac, that his shoe size matched the killer's, and that he lived in San Francisco when the murders were committed. The suspect's initials—"CCC"—were also penned on one of the cards Zodiac sent police in his heyday. William Collins appealed to the producers for help, saying, "I need to know if Charles Clifton Collins, my father, the guy who held me when I was a baby—was a serial killer. I have to know. I have to know." Subsequent DNA testing on an envelope licked by Collins's father formally excluded him as a suspect.

Arthur Leigh Allen The most widely-known Zodiac suspect, named during his lifetime by several California investigators and after his death by Robert Graysmith (among others) in his book *Zodiac Unmasked* (2002). Allen was investigated by various law enforcement agencies from October 1969 until the week after his death in August 1992, and while he pled guilty to child molestation in March 1975, serving 29 months in a California state hospital, no charges were ever filed against him in connection with the Zodiac case. Arguments for and against Allen's guilt in the Zodiac murders include the following points:

1. While employed as a schoolteacher in Calaveras County, California, Allen missed work on Tuesday, November 1, 1966, first claiming the time off as "school business," later changing his story to make it a sick day. Accusers suggest that he took the day off to recuperate from hypothetical "facial wounds" inflicted by Riverside murder victim Cherry Bates on October 30. However, Bates was killed on Sunday night, some 350 miles south of Calaveras County, and Allen taught classes the following day without incident.

2. A Royal typewriter with Elite type, the same kind used to write the anonymous letters following Cherry Bates's murder, was seized in a search of Allen's home on February 14, 1991. Although police specifically listed the typewriter on their search warrant, Zodiac researcher Jake Wark reports that no effort has yet been made (as of 2002) to match the machine with the Bates correspondence. Until a match is made, Allen's possession of the typewriter proves nothing.

3. Sometime in late 1968 or early 1969 (reported dates vary), Allen allegedly told acquaintance Don Cheney that he planned to commit a series of random murders, shooting couples in lover's lanes and taunting police with letters signed "Zodiac." Allen's off-hand discussion of the crimes-to-be supposedly included specific descriptions of his intended weapons and plans to attack a school bus (threatened in one of the Zodiac's subsequent letters). Cheney's credibility suffers because he first revealed the alleged conversation in July 1971, nearly two years after the last known Zodiac murder made international headlines. Even then, he told an employer rather than contacting police directly, and important details of his story changed over time. Critics note that Cheney once complained of Allen's attempting to molest his (Cheney's) daughter on a camping trip, and Vallejo detectives acknowledged that "This might be a motive why Cheney would make such an accusation against Arthur Allen."

4. On October 6, 1969, Allen was questioned by Vallejo police concerning the Lake Berryessa attack. In that interview he reportedly told authorities that he "was going to go to Berryessa" on the day of the crime, but changed his mind and "went up the coast instead." Allen cited a couple from Treasure Island as alibi witnesses but never supplied police with their names, address, or telephone number. Accusers note that Allen's shoe size was identical to that of footprints left by the Lake Berryessa killer (though the prints were never matched to shoes owned by Allen). Survivor Bryan Hartnell allegedly viewed Allen at work, sometime in the mid-1970s, reportedly telling police that Allen's "physical appearance and voice were the same as Zodiac's." While the date of the viewing is uncertain, we must recall that several years (at least) had passed since the attack, and furthermore that Hartnell never saw the killer's face. A foot-long knife was seized at Allen's home during the police search of February 14, 1991, but again researcher Jake Wark reports that no efforts have yet been made (as of September 2002) to match the knife with wounds suffered by the Lake Berryessa victims.

5. Four days after the Vallejo police interview, on October 10, 1969, Allen allegedly told acquaintance Ralph Spinelli that he was "going to San Francisco to kill a cabbie." The Paul Stine murder occurred one day later, reported throughout the United States and around the world. Nonetheless, Spinelli made no report of the conversation until December 1990, when he (Spinelli) was charged with armed robbery in Nevada, facing a 30-year-prison term. As in the case of Don Cheney, Spinelli also had a prior history of conflict with Allen: Allen had been arrested in Vallejo on June 15, 1958, after a fistfight with Spinelli, and the charges were dismissed three weeks later.

6. In July 1992 Zodiac survivor Michael Mageau allegedly picked Allen's mug shot from a police photo lineup, telling detectives, "That's him! He's the man who shot me!" True or not, no charges were filed against Allen prior to his death from natural causes on August 26, 1992.

Despite the allegations against Arthur Leigh Allen, certain facts remain undisputed. A report to Vallejo police from the California Department of Justice, dated July 29, 1971, states clearly that Allen's handwriting had been compared to that of all Zodiac letters received thus far, and none were found to match. A year later, Vallejo police sought a second opinion from FBI handwriting experts, whereupon Allen was "dismissed as a suspect" in the Zodiac correspondence. A search of Allen's home on September 14, 1972, "found nothing that would incriminate Allen in the Zodiac crimes," and he subsequently passed a 10-hour polygraph examination. His fingerprints were also compared with all those collected in the Zodiac case and produced no matches. On balance, Jake Wark is probably correct in his judgment that Allen "was simply one of dozens of Vallejo locals who had been fingered by a friend, an enemy, an acquaintance, or a relative based on little more than a hunch."

Police took what may be their last stab at solving the case in October 2002, when they submitted envelopes from various Zodiac correspondence for DNA testing. Their hope: If the killer licked a stamp or envelope flap, saliva traces might contain enough genetic material to identify the killer once and for all. In fact, Dr. Cydne Holt, supervisor of the San Francisco Police Department's DNA laboratory, did recover DNA samples from one stamp on a Zodiac card, mailed on November 8, 1969, but the test results were disappointing to many investigators. When compared to brain tissue preserved from Arthur Allen's 1992 autopsy, the DNA conclusively eliminated Allen as the man who licked the stamp. The same test also excluded suspect Charles Clifton Collins and an unnamed "prominent San Francisco lawyer who is still living."

But does DNA in fact clear Allen as the killer? Dr. Holt equivocated, noting that the stamp sample contained only four of a possible nine DNA markers, plus gender indicators proving that the subject was male. "It's not enough to positively identify anyone as Zodiac," Holt told reporters, "but it is enough to narrow suspicions, or perhaps even eliminate suspects." Journalist Robert Graysmith, author of two books touting Arthur Allen as the slayer, hedged his bets in an interview with the *San Francisco Chronicle*. "I've always wondered if there wasn't more than one person involved," Graysmith said. "Someone running interference for Allen. It's what makes it one of the great mysteries of all times."

A new twist on the Zodiac case emerged in late August 2008, when the FBI's Sacramento field office announced that it was running scientific tests on various items once owned by a new suspect. The supposed evidence came from 41-year-old Dennis Kaufman, who claimed that his late stepfather, one Jack Tarrance, was the Zodiac. The evidence Kaufman delivered to G-men included handwriting samples from Tarrance, dentures and a come presumably containing DNA traces, a knife stained with what "could possibly be dried blood," and a homemade hood which Kaufman believes was worn by the Zodiac during the murders at Lake Berryessa in 1969.

Kaufman told G-men and reporters, "I've worked to prove this for eight years." His quest began in 2000, when he watched a TV documentary on the Zodiac case and noted a resemblance between his stepfather and composite sketches of the killer. Kaufman subsequently found a stained and broken knife which Tarrance had in storage and claims that measurements of its blade match the wounds inflicted on Cheri Jo Bates in 1966. Finally, after Tarrance's death and cremation in August 2006, Kaufman says he found the presumed Zodiac disguise from 1969 concealed inside an old ham radio owned by Tarrance.

Half brother Charles Tarrance, the new suspect's biological son, seemed to agree with Kaufman's assessment. While describing Jack Tarrance as "a good dad," Charles recalled an incident that occurred in a hospital where his father spent time as a patient. "I was wheeling him down a hallway," Charles said, "[and] he was acting like he was shooting people... He was laughing, saying, 'Ha, ha, Zodiac.'"

Others had radically different memories of "good dad" Jack Tarrance. Tarrance's daughter, Mary Larsen, described him as "verbally, physically, mentally and sexually abusive" during her childhood, a brutal alcoholic whose behavior prompted her and her siblings to leave home by age 14. Larsen's husband also remembered Tarrance telling him, "If you knew who I was, you wouldn't like me very much."

An unnamed relative told reporters that Tarrance once said, "I've been drunk and in fights. I've stabbed so many people I lost count." A neighbor from 1979, identified in press releases only as "Roberta," recalled the suspect telling her, "You ain't been hunting until you hunt people."

Despite that testimony, critics still suggest that Kaufman was conned by his stepfather—or that he may be promoting the story for profit. Kaufman denies that charge, while peddling a one-hour video-tape of his private investigation for $24.95 per copy. Zodiac researcher Tom Voight told reporters, "The reason why Dennis Kaufman is involved with the FBI is he's gone through more investigative agencies than you can count, and they've all found no evidence that Jack Tarrance was the Zodiac. Kaufman's claims have been investigated by numerous law enforcement agencies." Those agencies included the San Francisco, Santa Rosa, and South Lake Tahoe Police Departments—which held Tarrance's knife from 2002 to 2007, but could not tell journalists whether any tests were performed on it.

The final answer may lie with DNA evidence. While Tarrance was cremated in 2006, G-men have collected DNA samples from surviving relatives, as well as from the relics furnished by Kaufman and Charles Tarrance. They plan comparison of those samples with unspecified genetic material recovered from the Bates crime scene in 1966, and in August 2008 they told reporters that "they could get those results back any day." At this writing, in January 2009, no results have been published and the case remains officially unsolved.

ZOLIS, Amanda See NEWCASTLE, AUSTRALIA, MURDERS

ZWILLMAN, Abner ("Longy") gangland murder victim (1959)

A child of Jewish immigrants, born in 1899, Abner Zwillman fought his way up through the ranks of a Newark street gang—the Ramblers—to win renown in Prohibition as "the Al Capone of New Jersey." In fact, he was more successful than Capone, avoiding prison and forging a network of criminal contacts that included Meyer Lansky, Charles (Lucky) Luciano, BENJAMIN (BUGSY) SIEGEL, Cleveland's Moe Dalitz, and Chicago's Tony Accardo. Zwillman par-

ticipated in the various underworld "conventions" that founded America's national crime syndicate between 1929 and 1932, emerging as the undisputed ruler of New Jersey. Local Mafia boss WILLIE MORETTI served as Zwillman's chief lieutenant in the Garden State, executing most of the Jersey mob's murder contracts on Zwillman's orders.

The origin of Zwillman's nickname is unknown, but his influence in the syndicate was never doubted. His mob had outposts as far west as Hollywood, where Zwillman reportedly enjoyed a love affair with movie star Jean Harlow, described in some accounts as a suspect in the curious "suicide" of Harlow's husband. Closer to home, Zwillman operated lavish gambling casinos, corrupted labor unions, and bought politicians. Republican gubernatorial candidate Harold Hoffman solicited Zwillman's support in 1946 and won the election. Four years later, Democratic candidate Elmer Wene rejected Zwillman's offer of a $300,000 campaign contribution and found himself defeated on election day. By the 1950s Longy was well established in "legitimate" business and posed as

Mobster Meyer Lansky (in hat) denied any role in the suspicious "suicide" of longtime ally Abner Zwillman. (Library of Congress)

418

a philanthropist, once donating $250,000 to a Newark slum-clearance campaign.

Still, organized crime was his primary world, and conflicts with other bosses seemed unavoidable. New York mobster Vito Genovese harbored a grudge against Zwillman after Longy opposed his 1957 effort to depose Mafia "prime minister" Frank Costello. Zwillman backed rival warlord ALBERT ANASTASIA against Genovese, but Anastasia's barbershop assassination left Zwillman vulnerable. Longtime enforcer Willie Moretti was gone, murdered by persons unknown in 1951, and Zwillman was abandoned by former allies Dalitz and Lansky, preoccupied with their own gambling empires in Cuba and Las Vegas. In early 1959 the feds added insult to injury, slapping Zwillman with a subpoena to testify before Senator John McClellan's committee investigating mob infiltration of U.S. labor unions. Committee member JOHN KENNEDY (already running for the White House) and chief counsel ROBERT KENNEDY looked forward to grilling New Jersey's premier mobster in front of television cameras.

But they would never get the chance.

On February 27, 1959, Zwillman was found hanged with plastic rope in the basement of his mansion in West Orange, New Jersey. Authorities ruled his death a suicide, although Zwillman's ankles were bound and his hands were tied behind his back with loops of wire. Lucky Luciano, exiled to Italy, blamed the slaying on New York mobster Carlo Gambino and chastised Meyer Lansky for failing to help their old comrade. Lansky, years later, told Israeli journalists that Zwillman had been slain on orders from Genovese, then serving prison time on narcotics charges. Lansky denied any advance knowledge of the crime, but it seems doubtful that a boss of Zwillman's stature would be executed without a unanimous vote from the syndicate's ruling council.

ZYWICKI, Tammy   See "TRUCK STOP KILLER"

Bibliography

Ackroyd, Peter. *Jack the Ripper and the East End.* London: Chatto & Windus, 2008.

Aiuto, Russell. "Lizzie Borden." Crime Library. Available online. URL: www.crimelibrary.com. Accessed November 10, 2003.

Albarelli, H. P., Jr. "Who Killed Gerald Victor Bull?" WorldNetDaily. Available online. URL: worldnetdaily.com. Accessed October 27, 2002.

Altimari, Dave, and Colin Poitras. "A Trail Ends on Death Row." *Hartford Courant* July 23, 2000.

APBNews. "A Desolate Dumping Ground for Killers." Available online. URL: APBNews.com. Accessed September 7, 1999.

Associated Press. "Attempted Abduction in Woodville Could Be Linked to Serial Killer." FoxNews.com. Available online. URL: www.foxnews.com/story/0,2933,6445,00.html. Accessed August 23, 2002.

———. "Authorities Clear Muhammad, Malvo in Baton Rouge Serial Killings." Yahoo! Groups. Available online. URL: http://groups.yahoo.com/group/hlf/message/4962. Accessed November 27, 2002.

———. "Inmate Gets 2nd Look in Levy Probe." Radicus Internet. Available online. URL: www.radicus.net/news/listall/news.law_enforce.asp. Accessed September 27, 2002.

———. "JonBenet Ramsey Case Takes Major Twist." *USA Today.* Available online. URL: www.usatoday.com/news/nation/2003-04-09-ramsey_x.html. Accessed April 9, 2003.

———. "Merchants Say Cross in Memory of Slain Ciudad Juarez Women Bad for Image." Yahoo! Groups. Available online. URL: http://groups.yahoo.com/group/hlf/message/4432. Accessed September 23, 2002.

———. "Mexico's First Lady Calls for End to Slayings of Women in Ciudad Juarez." Yahoo! Groups. Available online. URL: http://groups.yahoo.com/group/hlf/message/4958. Accessed November 25, 2002.

———. "On Guard for a Serial Killer." Yahoo! Groups. Available online. URL: http://groups.yahoo.com/group/hlf/message/4222. Accessed August 19, 2002.

———. "Poison Kills 25 in Ivory Coast." Yahoo! Groups. Available online. URL: http://groups.yahoo.com/group/vampirekiller/message/15483. Accessed August 27, 2001.

———. "Unspecified Evidence Suggests Dalquist, 21, of Brainerd Has Been Killed." Yahoo! Groups. Available online. URL: http://groups.yahoo.com/group/hlf/message/4951. Accessed November 26, 2002.

"Attorney: Suspect Cleared." *Bloomington Herald-Times* August 24, 2001.

Austin, John. *Hollywood's Unsolved Mysteries.* New York: Ace Books, 1970.

Baldwin, James. "Atlanta: the Evidence of Things Not Seen." *Playboy* (December 1981).

Beaubien, Roxanne. "Tips Sought in Unsolved Killings." *Toronto Free Press* February 5, 1998.

Beaufait, Howard. "Kingsbury Run Murders." *Homespun* (November 1955).

Beaupre, Beck. "Key Evidence in 4 Miss. Slayings Untested after Year." *USA Today* August 20 1996.

Belcamino, Kristi. "Police Search Ex-priest's Property for Remains of Amber Swartz." *Contra Costa Times* June 6, 2002.

Bell, Rhonda. "Ellwood Bond Set at Million Dollars." New Orleans *Times-Picayune* March 5, 1998.

Bleksley, Peter. *Ten Most Wanted: Britain's Top Undercover Cop Reinvestigates Ten of the UK's Worst Unsolved Murders.* London: John Blake, 2007.

Boardman, Krist. "Is the Northeast Stalker Still on the Prowl?" *Detective Files* (July 1991).

Bocca, Geoffrey. *The Life and Death of Sir Harry Oakes.* London: Weidenfeld and Nicolson, 1959.

Bragg, Melody. *West Virginia Unsolved Murders.* Beaver, W.V.: GEM Publications, 1992.

Broome, Fiona. *The Ghosts of Austin.* Atglen, Pa.: Schiffer Publishing, 2007.

Brown, A. R. *Lizzie Borden: The Legend, the Truth, the Final Chapter.* New York: Dell, 1992.

Browne, Andrew. "A Serial Killer Stalks a Chinese City." Reuters May 21, 1992.

Busch, Alva. *Roadside Prey.* New York: Pinnacle Books, 1996.

Cameron, Jackie. "Serial Killing of Young Girls Feared." *Independent* February 4, 1998.

Carr, John Dickson. *The Murder of Sir Edmund Godfrey.* New York: Harper/Hamilton, 1936.

Castleden, Rodney. *Great Unsolved Crimes.* Elmsford, N.Y.: Futura, 2007.

Charton, Scott. "Killing of Skidmore Bully Still an Unsolved Mystery." *Jefferson City* (Mo.) *News Tribune* July 9, 2001.

Claire, Christopher. "Why the Mafia Had to Murder Marilyn Monroe." *Scotsman* July 28, 2002.

Clendenning, Alan. "Case Against Accused Serial Killer May Be Falling Apart." Associated Press December 6, 1998.

———. "La. Judge Upholds Murder Charges." Associated Press December 14, 1998.

Codrescu, Andrei. "Terror Stalks the Big Easy." *Playboy* (March 1996).

Cooper, Pam. "No Cover-up at VA." *Missourian* October 1, 1995.

"Cop Suspect in Serial Killings." *Los Angeles Times* September 8, 1995.

Cornwell, Rupert. *God's Banker: The Life and Death of Roberto Calvi.* London: Victor Gollancz Ltd., 1983.

Corsaletti, Louis. "More Than One Body Found at Bothell Site." *Seattle Times* February 13, 1998.

Cox, Bill. "The Texas Child Killers." *Detective Cases* (June 1994).

D'Ambro, Gia. "8 Women Butchered in the Shocking Case of the Philadelphia Slasher." *Headquarters Detective* (September 1993).

Davidson, Bill. "The Town That Lives in Terror." *Good Housekeeping* (September 1977).

Deslatte, Melinda. "Baton Rouge Murders: Was the Killer in Uniform?" Associated Press. Available online. URL: http://groups.yahoo.com/group/hlf/message/4120. Accessed August 5, 2002.

———. "Body of Missing Louisiana State Student Found in Area of Recent Serial Killings." Associated Press March 14, 2003.

Dettlinger, Chet, and Jeff Prugh. *The List.* Atlanta: Philmay, 1983.

Diebel, Linda. *Betrayed: The Assassination of Digna Ochoa.* New York: Carroll & Graf Publishers, 2006.

"Divers Fail to Find St. John's Student in Lake Search." *Minneapolis Star Tribune* November 12, 2002.

"Divers Search Creek Following Tip about Missing Jill Behrman." *Bloomington Herald-Times* April 3, 2002.

Doyle, Stephanie. *Florida Unsolved Mysteries.* Birmingham, Ala.: Cliff Road Books, 2007.

Dray, Philip. *At the Hands of Persons Unknown: The Lynching of Black America.* New York: Random House, 2002.

Drey, Patricia. "Families Ask for Change in Search Cases." *St. Paul* (Minn.) *Pioneer Press* November 15, 2002.

East, Wendy. *The Green Bicycle Murder.* London: Sutton Publications, 1993.

"Ellwood Down to Single Murder Charge." Associated Press February 23, 1999.

Engstrom, Elizabeth. *Lizzie Borden.* New York: St. Martin's Press, 1997.

Erickson, Matt. "Contrary to Rumors, Erika Not Found." *Brainerd* (Minn.) *Dispatch* November 24, 2002.

———. "Police: Cases Not Connected." *Brainerd* (Minn.) *Dispatch* November 21, 2002.

Evans, Steward, and Donald Rumbelow. *Jack the Ripper: Scotland Yard Investigates.* Charleston: S.C.: The History Press, 2006.

Fasnacht, Don. "Psychic Claims Niqui McCown Is Dead." *Richmond* (Va.) *Palladium-Item* November 6, 2002.

FBI press release. "INS Attorney Missing for Six Days." The Mail Archive. Available online. URL: http://www.mail-archive.com/ctrl@listserv.com/msg73735.html. Accessed November 14, 2003.

Fimrite, Peter. "Police Identify Oakland Torso." *San Francisco Chronicle* May 17, 1991.

Flynn, Robert. *The Borden Murders: An Annotated Bibliography.* Portland, Maine: King Philip Publications, 1992.

———. *Lizzie Borden & the Mysterious Axe.* Portland, Maine: King Philip Publications, 1992.

Fonseca, Teresa. "Can You Help Solve the Blue Light Murders?" *True Police* (April 1996).

"Four College-Age Students Are Missing in Minnesota, Wisconsin." Associated Press November 12, 2002.

Franklin, Erica. "Wounded Taxi Driver Makes It to Fire Station Before Dying." *Indianapolis Star* July 13, 1993.

Freund, Paula. "Suspect Named in Behrman Case." *Bloomington Herald-Times* April 11, 2002.

Furillo, Andy. "Police Fear Serial Killer in Oakland." *San Francisco Examiner* May 17, 1991.

———. "Torsos in Bay Suggest a Serial Killer." *San Francisco Examiner* May 16, 1991.

Furst, Randy. "Bloodhound Handler's Credentials Questioned in Search for Missing Men." *Minneapolis Star Tribune* January 5, 2003.

Gates, David. "A New Whack at the Borden Case." *Newsweek* June 4, 1984.

Gentry, Curt. *Frame-up.* New York: W.W. Norton, 1967.

Gibson, Arrell. *Life and Death of Colonel Albert Jennings Fountain.* Norman: University of Oklahoma Press, 1975.

Ginsburg, Philip. *The Shadow of Death.* New York: Jove Books, 1993.

Godwin, John. *Murder USA.* New York: Ballantine, 1978.

Goodman, John. *The Killing of Julia Wallace.* London: Harrap, 1969.

Gordon, Nick. *Murders in the Mist: Who Killed Dian Fossey?* London: Hodder, 1994.

Gosch, Noreen. *Why Johnny Can't Come Home.* Des Moines: Johnny Gosch Foundation, 2000.

Gott, Natalie. "Suspected Serial Killer Sentenced." Associated Press August 18, 1999.

Goudelocke, Ryan. "Yoder's Death Linked to Serial Killer." *Baton Rouge Advocate* March 18, 2003.

Grace, Stephanie, and Rhonda Bell. "Ellwood Photos Prompt Calls; Police Sifting Through Leads." New Orleans *Times-Picayune* March 7, 1998.

Graysmith, Robert. *The Murder of Bob Crane,* New York: Berkley Books, 1994.

———. *Zodiac.* New York: St. Martin's Press, 1986.

———. *Zodiac Unmasked: The Identity of America's Most Elusive Serial Killer Revealed.* New York: Berkley, 2002.

Haining, Peter. *The Legend and Bizarre Crimes of Spring Heeled Jack.* London: Muller, 1977.

Hamilton, Steve. "12-month Manhunt for Kansas City's Gilham Park Strangler." *True Detective* (January 1993).

Haslam, Edward. *Dr. Mary's Monkey.* Walterville, Oreg.: Trine Day Press, 2007.

———. *Mary, Ferrie, and the Monkey Virus.* Cincinnati: Wordsworth, 1995.

Hayes, Harold. *The Dark Romance of Dian Fossey.* New York: Touchstone Books, 1991.

Heise, Jack. "Mystery Slayer of the Okefenokee Swamp." *Detective Files* (May 1994).

———. "Who's Killing the Roman Catholic Priests?" *Headquarters Detective* (November 1989).

Himmelsbach, Ralph, and Thomas Worcester. *Norjak:The Investigation of D. B. Cooper.* West Linn, Oreg.: Norjak Project, 1986.

Hodel, Steve. *Black Dahlia Avenger: A Genius for Murder.* New York: Arcade Publishing, 2003.

Hoffman, Jim. *The Boy in the Box: America's Unknown Child.* San Francisco: Rooftop, 2007.

Holloway, Dave, Stephanie Good, and Larry Garrison. *Aruba: The Tragic Untold Story of Natalee Holloway and Corruption in Paradise.* Nashville, Tenn.: Thomas Nelson, 2006.

Hornbeck, Mark. "Police Suspect Serial Killer Is Loose: Grand Rapids Killings May Be Work of One Person." *Detroit News* October 16, 1996.

Howard, Clark. *Zebra.* New York: Berkley, 1980.

Irving, Robert. "They Rip Horses Don't They?" *Fortean Times* 94 (January 1997): 22–28.

"Jefferson Parish Sheriff Supports Embattled Task Force Leader." Associated Press December 6, 1998.

Jones, Richard. *Jack the Ripper: The Casebook*. London: Andre Deutsch Ltd., 2008.

———, and Sean East. *Uncovering Jack the Ripper's London*. London: New Holland Publishers, 2007.

Jones, Tim. "4 Adults in 20s Missing in Midwest Mystery." *Minneapolis Tribune* November 15, 2002.

Kanhema, Newton. "South African Police Fear Ritual Killings of Children." Pan African News Agency January 20, 1998.

Kelly, Bill. "The Mystery of Laura Bradbury." *Headquarters Detective* (July 1991).

Kelly, Charles. "Fed Clues in 3 Boys' Deaths." *Arizona Republic* May 20, 2002.

———. "Girl Has Never Returned from Trip for Ice Cream." *Arizona Republic* May 24, 2002.

Kern, Emily. "Death of Woman Found in Home Probed." *Baton Rouge Advocate* September 25, 2002.

Kitchen, Martin. *Kaspar Hauser: Europe's Child*. New York: Palgrave Macmillan, 2001.

Knowlton, Janice, and Michael Newton. *Daddy Was the Black Dahlia Killer*. New York: Pocket Books, 1995.

Koenig, Joseph. "Atlanta's Phantom Lovers' Lane Slayer." *Front Page Detective* (August 1979).

Kohn, Howard. *Who Killed Karen Silkwood?* New York: Summit, 1981.

Kohut, John. "Canton Ripper's Grisly Record Remains a Secret." *Times* June 14, 1992.

Koryta, Michael. "Divers Uncover Possible Evidence in Behrman Case." *Bloomington Herald-Times* August 1, 2002.

———, and Laura Lane. "Prosecutor Gets Behrman Report." *Bloomington Herald-Times* November 22, 2002.

———. "No Regrets about Salt Creek." *Bloomington Herald-Times* March 14, 2003.

———. "Police Seek Help in Behrman Case." *Bloomington Herald-Times* August 31, 2002.

Kunstler, William. *The Minister and the Choir Singer*. Piscataway, N.J.: Rutgers University Press, 1964.

"La. Authorities Exploring Possible Link Between Kidnap Attempt and Serial Killings." Associated Press August 8, 2002.

"La. Death Linked to Serial Killings." Associated Press March 18, 2003.

Labalme, Jenny, "4 Men Identified from Hamilton County Bones." *Indianapolis Star* September 13, 1996.

———. "Handcuffs, More Bones Found in Woods." *Indianapolis Star* July 3, 1996.

Lamb, Michael. "Torso Murders: 40 Years Unsolved." *Sunday Plain Dealer* magazine October 12, 1975.

Lane, Briane, and Wilfred Gregg. *The Encyclopedia of Serial Killers*. New York: Diamond Books, 1992.

Lane, Laura. "'Most Wanted' Now Filming Behrman Case." *Bloomington Herald-Times* August 22, 2002.

Latner, Ken. "Houston's House of Horror." *True Police* (February 1997).

Leasor, James. *Who Killed Sir Harry Oakes?* London: Sphere Books, 1985.

Leavy, Walter. "The Mystery of the Disappearing Blacks." *Ebony* (December 1980).

Lengel, Allen. "Levy's Parents Testify Before Grand Jury." *Washington Post* December 12, 2002.

Liles, George. "Is There a Killer Among Us? Investigation Continues in the Case of the Woman in the Dunes." *Provincetown Banner* July 26, 1995.

Lincoln, Victoria. *A Private Disgrace: Lizzie Borden by Daylight*. New York: G. P. Putnam's Sons, 1967.

———. "The Monster of Florence." *Crime Library*. Available online. URL: www.crimelibrary.com. Downloaded November 10, 2003.

Lopez, Robert. "Police Baffled by Woman's Savage Murder." *Oakland Tribune* May 18, 1991.

Lowther, William. *Arms and the Man: Dr. Gerald Bull, Iraq, and the Supergun*. Novato, Calif.: Presidio Press, 1991.

Marriott, Trevor. *Jack the Ripper: The 21st Century Investigation: A Top Murder Squad Detective Reveals the Ripper's Identity at Last!* London: John Blake, 2007.

Martin, John. *Butcher's Dozen*. New York: Harper & Brothers, 1950.

"Mass. Interested in New Orleans Serial Killings." New Bedford (Mass.) *Standard-Times* August 12, 1995.

Masson, Jeffrey. *Lost Prince: The Unsolved Mystery of Kaspar Hauser*. New York: Free Press, 1996.

Mauder, Jack. "The 3X murders." *American Mercury* (June 1940).

Mauro, Larry. "Long-Haul Serial Killer." *True Police* (June 1993).

———. "Missouri Sex Strangler Claims 72nd Victim." *Headquarters Detective* (January 1994).

McConaughey, Janet. "Arrested in Two Deaths, a Suspect in Eight More." *Associated Press* March 3, 1998.

———. "Former Cabbie Arrested in String of New Orleans Slayings." *Associated Press* March 4, 1998.

McConnell, Brian. *Found Naked and Dead.* London: New English Library, 1974.

McDowell, Rider. "On the Trail of the Zodiac." *This World* (May 8 and May 15, 1994).

McMillan, John. "Sheriff: Kidnapping Attempt a 'Red Alert.'" *Baton Rouge Advocate* August 8, 2002.

McNeill, Robert. "Stop 'Bible John' Before He Kills Again!" *Detective Files* (January 1997).

Melvern, Linda. *Conspiracy to Murder: The Rwandan Genocide.* London: Verso, 2006.

"Memorial Service for Christine Mirzayan." *UCSF Today* August 26, 1998.

Michaud, Stephen, and Hugh Aynesworth. *Murderers Among Us.* New York: Signet, 1991.

Milhollon, Michelle, and Amy Wold. "Weapons Caution Urged." *Baton Rouge Advocate* August 8, 2002.

"Mirzayan Remembered as Brilliant, Passionate, Generous." *UCSF Today* August 5, 1998.

Mitchell, Jerry. "Klan Fear Hampered Justice in Slayings." *Jackson Clarion-Ledger* February 13, 2000.

Moon, Roger. "FBI Says Behrman Search Far from Over." *Bloomington Herald-Times* August 2, 2002.

Moore, Melissa. "Investigators: Errors Key to Unmasking Killer." *Baton Rouge Advocate* August 8, 2002.

———. "No La. Database Exists for DNA Comparisons in Slaying Investigations." *Baton Rouge Advocate* August 8, 2002.

———. "Official: FBI Providing Full Aid in Hunt." *Baton Rouge Advocate* August 23, 2002.

———. "Official: Inquiry 'Massive.'" *Baton Rouge Advocate* August 4, 2002.

———. "Women's Killings Unsolved." *Baton Rouge Advocate* August 7, 2002.

Moore, Melissa, and Marlene Naanes. "Serial Killings Confirmed." *Baton Rouge Advocate* July 30, 2002.

Morrison, Blake. "Children Offered Details on Suspect in 3 Killings." *St. Paul Pioneer Press* July 23, 1996.

Morton, James. *Gangland: London's Underworld.* London: Warner Books, 1992.

———. *Gangland Volume 2: The Underworld in Britain and Ireland.* London: Warner Books, 1994.

Mowat, Farley. *Woman in the Mists: The Story of Dian Fossey and the Mountain Gorillas of Africa.* New York: Warner Books, 1987.

Murphy, Brian. "Italians Pack Courtroom to See 'Monster of Florence.'" *Seattle World* May 8, 1994.

Murphy, Katy. "After Long Search for Missing Student Jill Behrman, Remains Identified." *Bloomington Herald-Times* March 14, 2003.

———. "Retraction Not the End, Lawyer Says." *Bloomington Herald-Times* March 27, 2003.

Myers, Laura. "Authorities Discount Idea of Serial Killer Preying on Women." *Associated Press* November 28, 1990.

Nasser, Haya El. "Fear Stalks L.A. Streets." *USA Today* June 3, 1993.

Newton, Michael. *The Encyclopedia of Kidnappings.* New York: Facts On File, 2002.

———. *The Encyclopedia of Serial Killers.* New York: Facts On File, 2000.

———. *Hunting Humans.* Port Townsend, Wash.: Loompanics, 1990.

———. *Raising Hell.* New York: Avon, 1993.

———. *Still at Large.* Port Townsend, Wash.: Loompanics, 1999.

Ni, Perla. "Body that of INS Lawyer." *Asian Week* April 22, 1999.

Nickel, Steven. *Torso.* Winston-Salem, N.C.: J. F. Blair, 1989.

Niekirk, Philip von. "A Time to Kill." *Maxim* (Summer 1997).

Nienaber, Georgianne. *Gorilla Dreams: The Legacy of Dian Fossey.* Bloomington, Ind.: iUniverse, 2006.

Noel, Josh. "Neighbor Says He Broke into Crime Scene." *Baton Rouge Advocate* August 8, 2002.

———. "Police Say Killer May Not Be White." *Baton Rouge Advocate* March 22, 2003.

Oakes, George. "Portrait of the Artist as a Mass Murderer." *California* (November 1981).

Oates, Jonathan. *Unsolved Murders in Victorian and Edwardian London.* London: Wharncliffe Books, 2007.

O'Brien, Christena. "Hat Identified as Noll's Was Dropped, Woman Says." *Eau Claire* (Wisc.) *Leader-Telegram* November 13, 2002.

Oke, Isaiah. *Blood Secrets.* Buffalo, N.Y.: Prometheus Books, 1989.

Oswell, Douglas. *The Unabomber and the Zodiac.* Douglas Oswell, 2007.

Owen, Gordon. *The Two Alberts: Fountain and Fall.* Las Cruces, N.Mex.: Yucca Tree Press, 1996.

Paine, Christopher. "FBI Releases New Information." *Bloomington Herald-Times* June 1, 2002.

Pardo, Steve. "Police Team to Solve Prostitute Killings." *Detroit News* February 4, 1998.

Pearson, Edmund. *The Trial Book of Lizzie Borden.* New York: Doubleday, 1937.

Penn, Gareth. *Times 17: The Amazing Story of the Zodiac Murders in California and Massachusetts, 1966–81.* San Rafael, Calif.: Foxglove Press, 1987.

Philpin, John. *Stalemate.* New York: Bantam, 1997.

Piña, Phillip. "Still No Clues in 4 Searches." *St. Paul* (Minn.) *Pioneer Press* November 15, 2002.

"Police in Levy Case Renew Interest in Park 'Predator.'" *USA Today* September 29, 2002.

"Police Say 1st Description of Serial Killer May Be Off." *Chicago Tribune* March 22, 2003.

"Police Say Three Not Serial-Killer Suspects." *Baton Rouge Advocate* November 28, 002.

"Police Won't ID Found 'Evidence' in Behrman Case." *Bloomington Herald-Times* August 1, 2002.

Porter, Brian. *A Study in Red: The Secret Journal of Jack the Ripper.* Markham, Ontario: Double Dragon Publishing, 2008.

Porter, Edwin. *The Fall River Tragedy: A History of the Borden Murders.* Fall River, Mass.: Press of J. D. Munroe, 1893.

Posner, Gerald. "A Murder in Alabama." *Talk* (August 2000).

Preston, Douglas, and Mario Spezi. *The Monster of Florence.* New York: Grand Central, 2008.

Pron, Nick. "Science Could Solve Murders." *Toronto Star* February 5, 1998.

Radin, Edward. *Lizzie Borden, the Untold Story.* New York: Simon & Schuster, 1961.

Radner, Henry. "'Child Cannibal' Loose in St. Louis." *Detective Dragnet* (October 1994).

Raper, Arthur. *The Tragedy of Lynching.* Chapel Hill: University of North Carolina Press, 1933.

Rashke, Richard. *The Killing of Karen Silkwood.* Boston: Houghton Mifflin, 1981.

Reppion, John. "Spring-Heeled Jack in Liverpool." *Fortean Times* 238 (August 2008): 42–46.

Reynolds, Michael. *The Devil's Adjutant: Jochen Peiper, Panzer Leader.* Drexel Hill, Pa.: Casemate, 2004.

Rowland, John. *The Wallace Case.* London: Carroll & Nicholson, 1949.

Russell, Dick. *On the Trail of the JFK Assassins: A Revealing Look at America's Most Infamous Unsolved Crime.* New York: Skyhorse, 2008.

Salter, Jim. "Police Think Serial Killer Nabbed Girls." *Oregonian* December 11, 1993.

———. "Search for Girl in Pink Results in Tragedy." *Indianapolis Star* December 10, 1993.

Sanchez, Sandra. "In St. Louis, Child Killer Stalks by Day." *USA Today* December 10, 1993.

Schaffer, Michael. "All Chandra, All the Time." *U.S. News & World Report* August 6, 2001.

———. "Chasing Chandra." *U.S News & World Report* July 23, 2001.

———. "The Intern Vanishes." *U.S. News & World Report* June 18, 2001.

Shaffer, Tamara. *Murder Gone Cold.* Chicago: Ghost Research Society, 2006.

Sharp, Deborah. "3 Dead, Rest of City Living in Fear." *USA Today* August 12, 2002.

Shay, Frank. *Judge Lynch: His First Hundred Years.* New York: Ives Washburn, 1938.

Shelden, Neal. *The Victims of Jack the Ripper.* Knoxville, Tenn.: Inklings Press, 2007.

Sherman, Mark, and Brian Melley. "Tests Show Remains in Park Are Chandra Levy." Associated Press May 22, 2002.

Shur, Edward. "Police Use Radar to Search Ex-Priest's Truckee Home." *Reno Gazette-Journal* June 21, 2002.

Sifakis, Carl. *The Encyclopedia of American Crime.* New York: Facts On File, 1982.

———. *The Mafia Encyclopedia.* New York: Checkmark Books, 1999.

Smith, Bruce, and Tammy Webber. "Searches of Creek Were Way Off Base." *Indianapolis Star* March 13, 2003.

Smith, Carlton. *Killing Season.* New York: Onyx, 1994.

Smith, Vern. "Unsolved Murders." *Emerge* (April 1996).

Spiering, Frank. *Lizzie.* New York: Random House, 1984.

Spinks, Sarah. *Cardiac Arrest: A True Account of Stolen Lives.* Toronto: Doubleday, 1985.

Squitieri, Tom. "Slayings of Prostitutes Linked." *USA Today* March 15, 1990.

Stoddart, Charles. *Bible John.* Edinburgh: Paul Harris, 1980.

Sullivan, Robert. *Goodbye Lizzie Borden*. Brattleboro, Vt.: Stephen Greene Press, 1974.

"Suspect Located in Serial Murders." United Press International November 26, 1997.

Swerczek, Mary. "Attorney: Ellwood Case Is Weaker." New Orleans *Times-Picayune* February 23, 1999.

Terry, Maury. *The Ultimate Evil*. New York: Doubleday, 1987.

Thomas, Jamison. "Manhunt for the Serial Rape Strangler." *Startling Detective* (July 1991).

Thomas, Jo, and Jodi Wilgoren. "Young People Are Missing; Authorities Are Baffled." *New York Times* November 16, 2002.

Tierney, Patrick. *The Highest Altar*. New York: Viking, 1989.

Tobias, Ronald. *They Shoot to Kill: A Psycho-Survey of Criminal Sniping*. Boulder, Colo.: Paladin Press, 1981.

Tosaw, Richard. *D. B. Cooper: Dead or Alive?*. Ceres, Calif.: Tosaw Publishing, 1984.

"Tracking the Zodiac: Will DNA solve the 1969 Killings?" ABC News. Available online. URL: http://abclocal.go.com/kgo/news/assignment7/072403_assign7_zodiac.html. Accessed July 24, 2003.

"Truck Sought in Louisiana Slayings." CNN.com. Available online. URL: www.cnn.com/2002/us/south/12/24/batonrouge.killings/index.html. Accessed December 24, 2002.

Tully, Matthew, and R. Joseph Gelarden. "Bones May Propel Behrman Case Ahead—or Rewind It." *Indianapolis Star* March 15, 2003.

"Two Temporary Dams to Be Built to Aid in Behrman Search." *Bloomington Herald-Times* September 9, 002.

Unatin, Don. "Can You Help NYPD Catch the Cruqising Cabbie Killer?" *Official Detective* (July 1991).

———. "The Shocking Rise in Ritual Murders." *True Detective* (May 1987).

Valdez, Diana. "Another Woman's Body Found on Juárez Border." *El Paso Times* October 9, 2002.

———. "DNA Tests Identify 1 of 8 Bodies Found in Juárez Lot." *El Paso Times* November 5, 2002.

———. "Families, Officials Claim Cover-ups Keep Killings from Being Solved." *El Paso Times* July 21, 2002.

———. "FBI Aid Asked in Juárez Killings." *El Paso Times* September 6, 2002.

———. "FBI Seeks Binational Task Force in Juárez Slayings." *El Paso Times* July 18, 2002.

———. "Hopeful Young Women Perish in City of Broken Dreams." *El Paso Times* July 21, 2002.

———. "Latest Discovery of Bodies Fuels Fears Anew in Juárez." *El Paso Times* July 21, 2002.

Van Onselen, Charles. *The Fox and the Flies: The World of Joseph Silver, Racketeer and Psychopath*. London: Jonathan Cape, 2007.

Villa, Judi. "Gruesome Murder Unsolved." *Arizona Republic* May 19, 2002.

———. "Mom Remains Hopeful Daughter Will Be Found." *Arizona Republic* May 21, 2002.

———. "Saboteurs Cut Train Ride Short." *Arizona Republic* May 24, 2002.

Wakefield, H. R. *The Green Bicycle Case*. London: Philip Allan, 1930.

Wark, Jake. "The Zodiac Killer." Crime Library. Available online. URL: www.crimelibrary.com. Accessed November 10, 2003.

Weiss, Mike. "DNA Seems to Clear Only Zodiac Suspect." *San Francisco Chronicle* October 15, 2002.

White, Ed. "'It Eats at You' Says Mom Who Misses Slain Daughter." *Detroit News* November 2, 1996.

———. "Murders Scare Prostitutes into Different Walk of Life." *Detroit News* November 3, 1996.

———."Task Force Hunts Possible Serial Killer of 11 Women." *Los Angeles Times* November 10, 1996.

Wilcox, Robert. *The Mysterious Deaths at Ann Arbor*. New York: Popular Library, 1977.

Wildavsky, Ben. "Questions, No Answers; Chandra Levy's Saga." *U.S. News & World Report* July 2, 2001.

Wiley, John. "Four Slayings in Last Weeks of '97 Heighten Concerns About Serial Killer." Associated Press February 1, 1998.

Wilkes, Roger. *Wallace: The Final Verdict*. London: Grafton, 1984.

Willan, Philip. *The Last Supper: The Mafia, the Masons and the Killing of Roberto Calvi*. London: Constable & Robinson, 2007

Williams, Tony, and Humphrey Price. *Uncle Jack*. London: Orion, 2005.

Williamson, Hugh. *Historical Whodunits*. New York: Macmillan, 1956.

Wilson, Kirk. *Unsolved Crimes: The Top Ten Unsolved Murders of the 20th Century*. New York: Carroll & Graf, 2002.

Wolfe, Donald. *The Black Dahlia Files: The Mob, the Mogul, and the Murder that Transfixed Los Angeles*. New York: Regan Books, 2005.

Wright, Mike. "National Guard to Join in Search for Behrman." *Bloomington Herald-Times* September 18, 2002.

Yallop, David. *In God's Name: An Investigation into the Murder of Pope John Paul I*. London: Corgi, 1985.

Index

Boldface page numbers denote main entries.
Italic page numbers indicate illustrations.

A

Abdullah, Ahmet **1**
Abel, Robert William 176
Adams, Ellis 2
Adams, Wesley 331
Adhahn, Terapon 153
Adkins, Francis Roy **1–2**
Adkins, Joseph **2**, 26
Agnew, Barbara 374
Ahorter, Albert 77
aircraft crashes **2–4**
Alameda County, California 5
Allan, Jane 27
Allen, Kim 289
Allen, Louis **5–6**
Allen, Mary 364
"Alphabet Murders" 7
Al Sane, Adnan Abdul Hameed 7
"Amber Alerts" 153
Amtrak derailment (Arizona) **7–8**
anarchist bombings *8*, **8–9**, 384
Anastasia, Albert **9–10**, *10*
    Carfano, Anthony 69
    Gallo, Joseph 134
    Moretti, Willie 259
    Reles, Abraham 317
    Schuster, Arnold 333
    Zwillman, Abner 418
Anderson, Angela 302
Andrassy, Edward 84
Andrews, Jack 70
Anstey, Marie 17
anthrax murders **11–13**, *12*, 337
Apulia, Italy **13–14**
Aquash, Anna Mae Pictou **14**
Arambatzis, Freddy 170
Arbuckle, Roscoe 360
Arlosoroff, Vitaly **14–15**
Armstrong, Emily **15**
Arne, Peter **15**
Arnold, Maxine, and Gooderham, Terry 16
Aron, Edith 194
Arzt, Emma 320
Ashburn, George W. **16–17**
Ashmolean Museum **17**
"Astrological Murders" **17–18**
Atherston, Thomas Weldon 18
Atlanta, Georgia
    "child murders" **18–23**, 24, 337
    "Jack the Ripper" **183**, 264, 274
    "Lover's Lane" murders 24
    serial murders of women 24
"Atlas Vampire" **24–25**
"Atteridgeville Mutilator" 25
Austin, Annie 25
Australia 81–83, 261–262, 350–352
"Australian Ripper" 265
Avila, Robert, and Davis, Raymond **25–26**

Ayer, Dr. Benjamin **26**
Azzam, Abdullah Yusuf **26**

B

"Babysitter" **27–28**
Bacon, David **28–29**
Bacon, Francis **29**
Bagnols sur Ceze, France art theft **29**
Bahamas 286
Bailes, Marie **29–30**
Baker, Catherine 274
Balchin, Olive **30**
Baldi, Stefano 250
Baldwin, Jason 392
Banker, Jaylene 316
Barcomb, Jill, and Robinson, Kathleen **30–31**
Barham, Harry **31**
Barmore, Seymour **31–32**
Barnes, Angela Denise 130
Barnes, Anthony 234
Barney, Carolyn 353
Barrett, William 20
Barthelemy, Helen 190
Bates, Cheri Jo 412
Bates, Mitchell 365
Bauerdorf, Georgette Elise **32–34**
Baumgartner, Maria 164
Bay Area child murders **34–37**
Beams, Tobe 401
Beardsley, John 279
Becker, Michelle 142
Belgium 64
Bell, California **37**
Bell, Frankie 352
Bell, Joseph 19
Benda, Paul 274
Bender family **37–38**
Bennallack, Nancy 17
Beresford, Henry de La Poer 355
Berkowitz, David 297, 346
Berlin 162
Bermúdez Varela, Enrique **38–39**, *39*
Bernabet, Clementine 263
Bernas, Melanie 60
Besumer, Louis 275
Bhutto, Benazir **39–41**, *40*
Bianchi, Kenneth 7, 31
Bianco, Antonio Lo 250
Bibbens, Dolly 331
"Bible John" **41–42**
Biggs, Frank 320
Biggs, Mikelle 42
Billups, Harry 381
Binder, Timothy James 34
Bingham family murders **42–43**
Bioff, Willie Morris *43*, **43–44**
Birch, Jacqueline 388
Bishop, Robin 369
Bissette, Patricia 52
Bissitt, Carol 276
Björklund, Maila Irmeli 212–213

Black, Helen 52
"Black Dahlia" Murder **44–48**, *45, 46*
    Bauerdorf, Georgette Elise 34
    Ellroy, Geneva 117
    French, Jeanne Thomas 131
    Mondragon, Rosenda 246
    San Diego, California, unsolved murders
      (1931-36) 330
    Trelstad, Laura 366
    Windham, Evelyn May 400
    Winn, Margie Lee 401
Blau, Eva 17
Blessing, Sarah 177
Blevin, Tillman 254, 256
Blocker, Lateashia 388
Boganda, Barthélemy 3
Boggs, Thomas Hale 3
Bohn, Amy 325
Bohn, Martine 64
Boisman, Seppo Antero 212
Bolin, Oscar Ray, Jr. 368
Bompensiero, Frank **49**
Bondareva, Yulia 261
Booker, Betty Jo 362
Borden, Andrew and Abby **49–52**, *50*
Boroski, Jane 375
Borrero, Robben 279
Boston, Massachusetts 179–180
"Boston strangler" **52–54**
Botelho, Sandra 270
Bothell, Washington 54
Boubede, John 340
Boulder, Colorado 311–316
Bowden, Roosevelt 273
Bowker, Sarah Jean 123
Boyd, Alexander **54–55**, *55*, 234
"Boy in the Box" **55–57**, 376
Boyle, Benjamin Herbert 368
Bracewell, Brooks 363
Bradshaw, Hazel 331
Branch, Steven 390
Braun, Donna 290
Brazeau, Pauline 161
Brazell, Rashawn 57
Bresciano, Adolfo **58**
Brest, Belarus 58
Brethour, Clifford 332
Brewer, Theresa 331
Bridgewater, Carl **58–59**
Britain. *See* England
British child murders 59
Brooklyn, New York 57, **59–60**, 317–318, 333–335
Brooks, James 164
Brooks, Jamie 19
Brooks, Thomas L., Jr. 325
Brosso, Angela 60
Broussard, Felix 263
Brown, Ben 60
Brown, Carlene 316
Brown, Vivian 139

Buenos Aires Province, Argentina 224
Buffalo, New York 60–61
Bull, Gerald Victor 61–62
Bundy, Ted 290, 316, 333, 412, 414
Burdine, Toni-Anne 389
Burghard, Paul 281
Burk, William 62–63
Burke, Richard 63, 63–64
Burleson, Noelani 399
Burroughs, Krystal 276
Burton, Sheila 352
Burton, William 263
"Butcher of Mons" 64–65
Byers, Christopher 390
Byers, John 393

C

Cabo, Ronald 279
Cadieux, Cynthia 27
Cain, Jessica 176
Calvi, Roberto 67–68
Cambi, Susanna 250
Campbell, Amanda 35
Campbell, Howard 225
Capiola, Debra 389
Carfano, Anthony 69
Carlszen, Signe 90
Carpender, Henry 155
Carpenter, David 266
Carrier, Gary, Jr. 395
Carroll, Anna 128
Carter, Gloria 388
Carter, Leroy 70
Carter, Lucille 369
Cartwright, Una 394
castration murders 70–71
Castro, Fidel 198, 199, 201, 249
Castro, Gidget 353
"chain murders" 71–74
Chan, Karmein 262
Chaney, Trina 353
Chapman, Annie 183
Charach, Ted 204–205
Charlton, Judge 74–75
Chase, Richard and Russell 75
Chase, Valentine, and Pope, Henry 75–76
Chiang, Joyce 76
Chicago, Illinois 43–44, 97, 326–329
    child murders 76–77
    holdup murders (1971–72) 77
    holdup murders (1992) 77–78
"Chicago Ripper" 265
Child Abductions 78
China 148
Christiansen, Kenneth P. 93
Christopher, Joseph 61
Ciudad Juárez, Mexico 78–81, 265
Civil War
    Ayer, Dr. Benjamin 26
    Barmore, Seymour 31
    Brown, Ben 60
    Charlton, Judge 74
    Chase, Valentine and Pope, Henry 75
    Clayton, John Middleton 83
    Colgrove, O. R. 89
    Deason, Mat 103
    Diggs, Frank 110
    Haynes, A. J. 160
    Hindman, Thomas Carmichael, Jr. 163
    Hinds, James M. 164
    Jeffers, Perry 191

Leech, Alexander 216
Lowther, Henry 225
Martin, James 233
Mason, Simpson 235
Outlaw, Wyatt 293
Claremont Murders 81–83
Clark, James 327
Clark, Sophie 52
Clayton, John Middleton 83
Clayton, Powell 160, 164, 174, 195
Clery, Alexandra 17
Cleveland, Ohio 83–86
Cleveland Torso Murders 272
Clifford, Rochelle 270–271
Cloer, Betty 17
Clothier, Candace 358
Cochran, Frances Marie 86–87
Cohn, Lenora 188
Colby, Barbara 87–88
Cole, Colin 60
Cole, Jessica 389
Coleman, Eloise 123
Coleman, Guilford 88
Coleman, Linda 278
Coleman, Patricia 352
Coles, Frances 88–89
Colgrove, O. R. 89–90
Collier, Clarence 161
Collier, Myrtle 353
Collins, Diane 24
Collins, Kevin Andrew 90
Colombia 375
Colorado 90, 311–316
Columbus, Ohio 91
Connell, Julie 5
Conniff, Helen 105
Cook, Gale 142
Cook, Justin 173
Cook, Kelly 161
Cooke, Linda 400
"Cooper, D. B." 91–94
Corbin, Evelyn 52
Costa Rica 308
Cota, Celia 331
Côte d'Ivoire 211
County Kildare, Ireland 341
Courtemanche, Bernice 373
Cox, Scotty William 368
Craine, Louis 353
Crane, Bob 94–95
Crater, Joseph Force 95–96
Craven, Francis Leslie 305
Critchley, Elizabeth 374
Crockett, Brenda 130
Cromvoirt, Geoffrey von 170
Cross, Irene 335
Crossland, M.P. 96–97
Croy, Lily 364
Cruz, James 368
Cruz, Janelle Lisa 293
Culianu, Ioan Petru 97
Cummingsville, Ohio 98
Custer, Linda 178
Cutler, Julie 81
Cwik, Sandra 332

D

Dalquist, Erika Marie 241–243
Daniels, Jonathan Myrick 99–102, 100
Darlington, Pamela 161
"Dartman" 102

Dashiell, James 263
Davis, Caroline 290
Davis, Cindy 124
Davis, Emile 388
Davis, Raymond. See Avila, Robert, and Davis, Raymond
Davis, Robert Earl, Jr. 160
Days Inn murders 102
Deacon, Beryl 400
Deane-Tanner, Denis Cunningham 360
Deason, Mat 103
"Death Angels" 103–104
DeLay, "B. H." 2
DeLeon, Gloria 280
DeMello, Deborah 269
Deneveu, Leslie 288
Dennis, Patricia 352
Dennis, William 104–105
DeSalvo, Albert Henry 52
Dexter, Thurston 220
Diamond, John, Jr. ("Legs") 107, 107–109, 108, 322, 343
DiBenedetto, Linda 278
Dickerson, Elinor 307
Dickinson, John Q. 109–110
Diggs, Frank 110
Docker, Patricia 41
Dodson, Gary 307
Dogan, Richard 306
Dollar, William 110–111
Domingo, Cheri 139
"Doodler, The" 111
Dowd, Carol 129
Dowler, Amanda Jane 111–112
Downs, Janine 292
Dragna, Jack 344
Dubbs, Sandra 175
Duff, Edmund Creighton 352
Duff, Susan 161
Duggard, Jaycce Lee 36
"Dunes case" 265
Dunham, Anne 374
Dunmore, Denise 105
Dupree, Jack 112–113
Durkin, Jeanne 128

E

Eboli, Thomas 115
Echols, Damien 391
Edalji, George 172
Eddowes, Catherine 184
Edwards, Parker 60
Elam, Roberta 389
Ellison, Collette 17
Ellroy, Geneva 116–117
Ellroy, James 116–117
Ellwood, Russell 277–278
England
    Balchin, Olive 30
    Bingham family murders 42–43
    Bridgewater, Carl 58–59
    British child murders 59
    Dowler, Amanda Jane 111–112
    London. See London, England
    Queripel, Stacey 309
    South Croydon murders 352
    Wallace, Julia 382–383
    Wiltshire 400
Etchecolatz, Miguel Osvaldo 224
Ethier, Michel 252
Eustick, Robert 110

Evangelista murders **117**
Evans, Karry 32
Ewart, Angela 124
Ewell, Shari Dee Sampson 408
"Executioner, The" 265
Eyerly, Sherry 329
Eyton, Charles 360

F

Faelz, Tina 5
Fager, Kelli and Sherri 119
Fager, Phillip **119**
Fantazier, Joanne 274
Farr, Gary 112
Farrokhzad, Fereydoun **119–120**
"Fat Pat" 160
Fautenberry, John Joseph 368
Fechtel, Cathy 17
Federal Bureau of Investigation (FBI)
    aircraft crashes 3
    Anastasia, Albert 10
    anthrax murders 11–13
    Kennedy, John Fitzgerald 197,
        199–201
    Kennedy, Robert Francis 202
    King, Martin Luther, Jr. 205–206,
        208–209
    Monroe, Marilyn 246–250
    train derailments 365
    Wall Street bombing 383
    X, Malcolm 403–404
Fenton, Theresa 373
Ferguson, Mary 389
Ferrie, David 200
Feusi, Nancy 290
Ficklin, Gail 353
Field, Fred 372
Figg, Elizabeth 190
Finland 212
Finlayson, John **120**, *120*
Finn, Shirley **120–121**
Fitzsimmons, Frank 167, *167*
flat-tire murders **121**
Fleishman, Samuel **121–123**
Fleming, Mary 190
Florence, Italy 250–252
Floyd, Charles 266
Foggi, Giovanni 250
Forbes, Dennis 281
Ford, Eric 37
Ford, Wayne Adam 368
Fort Lauderdale, Florida **123**
Fort Wayne, Indiana **123**
Fort Worth, Texas **123–124**
Fossey, Dian **124–127**, *125*
Fountain, Albert Jennings **127–128**
France 29, 296, 365
"Frankford Slasher" **128–130**, *129*
Frazier, Etta 106
"Freeway Phantom" **130–131**
French, Jeanne Thomas **131–132**
Fried, Ellen 374
Fugate, Christy 178
Fuldauer, Robin 177
Fusco, Theresa 223

G

Gabriel, Karl 165
Gabriel, Viktoria 164
Gaida, William 224
Galante, Carmine **133–134**, *134*

Gallo, Joseph **134–135**
Gambino, Carlo 115
Garang De Mabior, John 4
Garcia, Cheryl 181
Garnett, Kevin 172
Gartner, Ramona 394
Garza, Ermilinda 143
Gaston, April 193
Gedalicia, Sara 331
Gency, Mary 389
Gentilcore, Pasquale 250
Gentile, Donna 331
Gera, Irena 261
Germany 157–160, 282–283
Gibson, Jane 155
Gibson, Margaret 361
Gidley, Nancy 290
Gilbert, Jeanne 102
Gill, Marty 102
Gilmore Lane Covalescent Hospital **136**
Glasscock, Mary Ann 177
Glennon, Ciara 81, 299
Glico-Morinaga Case **136–137**
Goble, Sean 368
Godart, Nathalie 64
Godfrey, Sir Edmund Berry **137–138**
Goetz, Fred 328–329
Goleta Murders **138–139**
Gonzalez, Pedro 280
Good, Danielle 329
Goodall, Leanne 272
Gooderham, Terry. *See* Arnold, Maxine, and
    Gooderham, Terry
Good Samaritan Hospital **139**
Gorlin, Ronnie 121
Gorman, Ken **139–140**
Gosch, John David **140–142**
Goudreau, Marie 161
Goulet, Dianne 402
Graff, Joann 52
Graham, Larry 36
Grant, Lucy 394
Great Basin **143–144**
Great Britain. *See* England
Greece 268
Green, Howard, and Marron, Carol **144**
Greenbaum, Gus **144–145**, *145*
Green Bicycle Case **145–147**
Greene County, Alabama 63–64, 88,
    233–234
Greenson, Ralph 247
Gricar, Ray Frank **147**
Grieve, Emily 412
Griffin, Canoscha 353
Griffin, Lisa 124
Griffin, Richard 362
Groden, Robert 200
Gross, Christy 316
Gruber, Andreas 164
Gruber, Cäzilia 164
"Guangzhou Ripper" **148**
Guida, Sheryl 280
Guihard, Paul **148–149**
Guimond, Josh 242–243
Gunness, Belle *149*, **149–151**
Guntersville, Alabama 305
Gusenberg, Frank and Pete 327–328
Gushrowski, Carol 332
Gustafsson, Nils Wilhelm 212–213
Gustavson, Cathy 352
Guy, William James 387

H

Ha, Oanh 161
Habyarimana, Juvénal 4
Hackney, Mary 98
Hagerman, Amber Renee **153**
Hakari, Judith 17
Haley, Lesa 175
Hall, Edward, and Mills, Eleanor **153–156**
Halstead, Dennis 224
Hammarskjöld, Dag 3
Hampton, Jerome 357
"Hampton Rapist" 261
Hancock, Sue 336
Hanes, Arthur, Sr. 207
Hanson, Ole 8
Hardwick, Thomas 8
Harper, Olga 394
Harriman, Tot Tran 177
Harrington, Frank 256
Harrington, Keith and Patrice 292
Harris, Ivory 357
Harris, King 263
Harry, Tonja 302
Haryono, Martadinata **156–157**
Hauptmann, Bruno Richard 220, 220–222
Hauser, Kaspar **157–160**
Hawkins, John Edward **160**
Hawkins, Patrick Lamont **160**
Hayes, Ben 241
Hayes, Clifford 154–156
Haynes, A. J. **160–161**
Haywood, William 385
Heller, Cindy 124
Helsel, Chandra 178
Henderson, Margaret 320
Herrera, Omar Torrijos 3
Hickey, Michael and Vincent 58
Hickie, Jim 272
Hickie, Robin 272
"Highway Killer(s)" (Canada) **161–162**
Highway Murders **162**
Hilburn, Carol 17
Hill, Dana 388
Hill, Timothy 19
Hill, Veronica 24
Hilliard, Derrick 234
Hindman, Thomas Carmichael, Jr. **162–164**
Hinds, James M. **164**, *164*
Hinterkaifeck Murders **164–165**
Hodges, Thomas 77
Hoey, Evelyn **165–166**
Hoffa, James Riddle *166*, **166–168**, 201, 202,
    249
Hollis, Jimmy 361
Holloway, Natalee Ann **168–171**, *169*
Holster, Ira 320
Holtz, David 241–242
"Honolulu Strangler" **171–172**
Hoover, Herbert 218, 328
Hoover, J. Edgar
    Anastasia, Albert 10
    Kennedy, John Fitzgerald 197, 201
    Kennedy, Robert Francis 202
    King, Martin Luther, Jr. 205, 209
    Lee, George Washington 214
    MacDonald, Jeffrey 228
    Meyer, Mary Pinchot 240
    Monroe, Marilyn 246, 250
    Wall Street bombing 384
    Wanderwell, Walter 386
    X, Malcolm 404

Hope, Edward 330
Horn, Jack 37
horse mutilations **172**
Hospital for Sick Children **172–173**
Housman, Angie 325
Houston, Texas decapitation murders **173**
Huffman, Jean 173
Hughes, Denise 171
Hughes, Paul 111
Huisentruit, Jodi Sue **174**
Hulbert, Sara 368
Hume, Margaret 32
Humphries, Ban **174**

I

I-35 murders (Texas) **175–176**
I-45 murders (Texas) **176–177**
I-70/I-35 murders **177–178**
"Independence Avenue Killer" **178**
India 356, 365, 366
Indianapolis, Indiana **178–179**
Interpol 211
Inturrisi, Louis 180
Iran 71–74
Irga, Ida 52
"Ironman" **179**
Isabella Stewart Gardner Museum **179–180**
Italy **180**
Ivers, Peter Scott **180**
Iverster, Karen 277
Ivins, Bruce 13

J

Jackson, Aaron 19
Jackson, Essie 302
Jackson, Mississippi **181**
Jackson, Wharlest **181–183**, *182*, 240, 260
"Jack the Ripper" Atlanta 183, 264, 274
"Jack the Ripper" London 88–89, **183–188**, 264, 336, 414
"Jack the Ripper" New York City **188–190**
"Jack the Stripper" **190–191**
Jacobs, Cecilia 105
Jamieson, Marie 161
Japan 365
Jascalevich, Mario 320, *320*
Jeffers, Perry **191–192**
Jenkins, Christopher 242–243
Jerome, Helene Adele **192–193**
Jesperson, Keith Hunter 368
Jessup, Georgia **193**
Johannesburg, South Africa **193–195**
John, JoAnne Betty Wyman 408
Johnly, Karen Louise 407
Johns, David 75
Johns, Jerry Lee 316
Johnson, A. M. **195**
Johnson, Cassandra 106
Johnson, Darlenia Denise 130
Johnson, Janelle 143
Johnson, Lois 105
Johnson, Lyndon 197, 202, 205
Johnson, Milton 265
Joliet, Illinois murders 265
Jolkowski, Jason **196**
Jones, Anton 281
Jones, Brian Maurice 332
Jones, Cori Louise 388
Jones, Ernest 60
Jones, Loretta 353
Jonz, Don 3

Jorgensen, Martin 267
Juan B. Castegnino Museum of Fine Art **196**
Jursa, Lori 289

K

Kalpoe, Deepak and Satish 168
Kamahele, Jeannette 290
Karamini, Mohammad 402
Karr, John Mark 37, 315
Kashka, Sara 124
Kelly, Mary 184
Kennedy, John Fitzgerald **197–202**, *198*
    Hoffa, James Riddle 167
    Kennedy, Robert Francis 202
    King, Martin Luther, Jr. 208
    Meyer, Mary Pinchot 240–241
    Monroe, Marilyn 246–247
    Moore, William L. 257, 259
    X, Malcolm 403
    Zwillman, Abner 418
Kennedy, Robert Francis **202–205**, *203*
    Hoffa, James Riddle 167
    Kennedy, John Fitzgerald 199
    King, Martin Luther, Jr. 208
    Monroe, Marilyn 247–248, 250
    Wales, Thomas Crane 379
    X, Malcolm 404
    Zwillman, Abner 418
Kennedy, Stetson 256
Kennedy, Steven 357
Key, Frank 175
Kgamedi, Nompumelelo 194
Khan, Karim Aga 341
Kimmell, Lisa Marie 143
King, Martin Luther, Jr. 200, 202, **205–209**, *206*, *207*, 214
King, Timothy 28
Kingman, William 275
Kinsey, Charlotte 291
Kiss, Bela **209–210**
Kitzmiller, Nancy 177
Klinsky, Mary 274
Kogut, John 223
Kotevski, Gordana 272
Kramer, Lillian 394
Krane, Debbie 358
Kraveichvili, Jean-Michel 251
Ku Klux Klan
    Adkins, Joseph 2
    Allen, Louis 6
    Ashburn, George W. 16
    Atlanta, Georgia, "child murders" 22
    Atlanta, Georgia, serial murders of women 24
    Ayer, Dr. Benjamin 26
    Barmore, Seymour 31
    Boyd, Alexander 54
    Brown, Ben 60
    Burk, William 63
    Burke, Richard 63
    Charlton, Judge 74
    Chase, Valentine and Pope, Henry 75
    Clayton, John Middleton 83
    Coleman, Guilford 88
    Colgrove, O. R. 89
    Crossland, M.P. 96
    Daniels, Jonathan Myrick 99–101
    Deason, Mat 103
    Dennis, William 104–105
    Dickinson, John Q. 109
    Diggs, Frank 110

Dollar, William 110
Finlayson, John 120
Fleishman, Samuel 121–122
Guihard, Paul 148
Hall, Edward, and Mills, Eleanor 156
Haynes, A. J. 160–161
Hindman, Thomas Carmichael, Jr. 164
Hinds, James M. 164
Humphries, Ban 174
Jackson, Wharlest 182
Jeffers, Perry 191
Johnson, A. M. 195
Kennedy, John Fitzgerald 199, 201–202
King, Martin Luther, Jr. 205, 207, 209
Lee, George Washington 214
Leech, Alexander 216–217
Lowther, Henry 225–226
Malcolm, Roger and Dorothy 231
Mallard, Robert 233
Martin, James 233
Mason, Simpson 235
Meadows, William R. 239
Metcalfe, George 240
Mincey, S. S. 244–245
Moore, Harry Tyson 253–256
Moore, O'Neal 256–257
Moore, William L. 257–258
Morris, Frank 260
Norman, Frank 283–284
Outlaw, Wyatt 293
Wetterling, Jacob Erwin 397
X, Malcolm 403
Kwan, Albert 380

L

Labokro **211**
"Lady of the Dunes" **211–212**
Laferte, Annie 267
Lake Bodom murders **212–213**
Lamplugh, Susannah **213–214**
Landcraft, Elizabeth 353
Lange, Willem de 194
Larey, Mary 361
Lass, Donna 17
Laumann, Sarah 275
Lawford, Peter 246, 248
Lawrence, Lillian 24
Lebese, Mpho 194
Leclercq, Jacqueline 64
Lee, George Washington **214–216**, *215*
Leech, Alexander **216–217**
Lenair, Angel 19
Leshefsky, Leah 394
Levy, Chandra **217–218**
Lewis, Cheryl 277
Light, Ronald Vivian 146
Limachi Sihuayro, Clemente 218
Lindbergh, Charles 218–222, *219*
Lindbergh, Charles, Jr. 218–222
Lindbergh kidnapping **218–222**, 313
"Lisbon Ripper" **222–223**, 307
List, John Emil 93
Listman, Jack 225
Livingston, Sherri 178
Lloyd, Anna 98
Locci, Barbara 250
Lockwood, Irene 190
Loganbill, Patricia 329
Lollar, Vernell 77
Lombardi, Anna 189

London, England
    Abdullah, Ahmet 1
    Adkins, Francis Roy 1–2
    Al Sane, Adnan Abdul Hameed 7
    Armstrong, Emily 15
    Arne, Peter 15
    Arnold, Maxine, and Gooderham, Terry 16
    Atherston, Thomas Weldon 18
    Austin, Annie 25
    Bailes, Marie 29–30
    Barham, Harry 31
    Coles, Frances 88–89
    "Jack the Ripper" **183–188**
    "Jack the Stripper" 190–191
    Lamplugh, Susannah 213–214
    "Operation Enigma" 292
    "Spring-Heeled Jack" 353–355
    Upchurch, Norma 371–372
Long, Bobby Joe 412
Long, Royal Russell 292
Long Island, New York 223–224
López, Jorge Juilo 224
Lordi, Cheresa 178
Los Angeles, California
    Avila, Robert, and Davis, Raymond 25–26
    Barcomb, Jill and Robinson, Kathleen 30–31
    Bauerdorf, Georgette Elise 32–34
    "Black Dahlia" Murder 44–48
    Bresciano, Adolfo 58
    Ellroy, Geneva 116–117
    Ellroy, James 16–117
    French, Jeanne Thomas 131–132
    holdup murders **224–225**
    Jerome, Helene Adele 192–193
    Mondragon, Rosenda 246
    Monroe, Marilyn 246–250
    racist drive-by murders 225
    random shootings 225
    "Southside Slayer" 352–353
    Taylor, William Desmond 359–361
    Trelstad, Laura 366
    Wallace, Christopher George Latore 380–382
    "West Side Rapist" 394–395
    Windham, Evelyn May 400
"Los Angeles Slasher" 265
Lovett, LaBrian 24
Lowe, Anna 275
Lowther, Henry **225–226**
Lozano, Pete 330
Lubin, Wilton 252
Lucas, Henry Lee 161, 175, 333
Lynch, Dennis 37

M

MacDiarmid, Sarah **227**
MacDonald, Jeffrey **227–230**
MacDonald, Mima 41
Machel, Samora Moisés 3
Machin, Edward 31
Mack, Dolores 277, 279
MacLean, Faith Cole 361
MacLeod, Frank and Willie 267
MacNiven, Donald 279
MacRae, Renee and Andrew **230**
Madden, Wendy 402
Madeiros, Debra 269, 270
Magers, Patricia 177

Maggio, Joseph 274
Mainardi, Paolo 250
Mäki, Anja Tuulikki 212
Malcolm, Pamela 234–235
Malcolm, Roger and Dorothy **231–232**
Malcolm X. See X, Malcolm
Mallard, Robert 232, **232–233**
Mallon, Kevin 341
Manhattan axe murders 233
Manning, Debra 138
Manson, Charles 228, 297, 414
Maphanga, Fezeka 195
Marco, Jennifer San 138
Marron, Carol. See Green, Howard, and Marron, Carol
Martarella, Jacqueline 223
Martin, Effie 394
Martin, James **233–234**
Martin, Michelle 130
Martin, Paul 362
Maryland gay murders **234**
Maryland unsolved murders **234–235**
Mason, Simpson 235
Massey, Rodney 175
Matthews, Charlie 254
Maurice, Malay 336
Mauriot, Nadine 251
Maxwell, Joseph 225
May, Catherine 363
May, John 327
McCann, Kate and Gerald 235–237
McCann, Madeleine Beth **235–237**, 236
McConnell, Deborah 270
McCown, Marilyn Renee **237–238**
McCown, Michael 177
McCoy, Richard Floyd, Jr. 93
McDonald, Mary 98
McElrath, Nesia 353
McElroy, Kenneth Rex **238–239**
McElveen, Ernest Ray 256–257
McGowan, Margaret 190
McGuire, Jimmy 234
McKenzie, Dorothy 274
McKeown, Elizabeth 394
McLaughlin, Susan 17
McLean, Barbara 161
McMillan, Colleen 161
McQueen, Arlette 106
McSpadden, Earl 362
McVey, Cynthia 332
Meador, Michael 225
Meadows, Okey, Jr. 395
Meadows, William R. **239**
Medeiros, Louise 171
Medes, Dawn 269–270
Medintsevaya, Kseniya 261
Mendenhall, Bruce 368
Mentzer, William 347
Merchant, Brenda 290
Metcalfe, George **240**
Metivier, Sebastien 252
Metzger, Vickie Sue 317
Mexico 78–81, 265, 290–291, 411
Meyer, Adam 327
Meyer, Cord 240–241
Meyer, Horst 251
Meyer, Mary Pinchot **240–241**
Meyers, Debra 316
Michigan 11, 32, 105–106, 142–143, **241**
"Midtown Slasher" 265
Midwest missing students **241–243**

Migliorini, Antonella 250
Mihelich, Kristine 27
Millbank, Thomas 355
Miller, Allana 173
Miller, Christine 402
Miller, Dorothy 234
Millican, Cathy 373
Mills, Charlotte 155
Mills, Eleanor. See Hall, Edward, and Mills, Eleanor
Mincey, S. S. **244–245**
Minter, Mary Miles 361
Misskelley, Jessie 393–394
Modafferi, Kristen **245–246**
Moffitt, Diana 331
Molloy, Patrick 58
Mondragon, Rosenda 246
Monk, Graham 272
Monroe, Marilyn **246–250**, 248
Monroe, Terry 329
"Monster of Florence" **250–252**
Monteiro, Christine 270
Monteiro, Linda 106
Montes de Oca, Rafael 281
Monti, Marina 292
Montreal, Québec, child murders **252**
Montreal, Québec, gay murders **253**
Montreal Museum of Fine Art robbery 252
Monzo, Lisa 5
Moore, Harry Tyson 253, **253–256**, 254, 255
Moore, James Michael 390
Moore, Lynda 374
Moore, Martha 307
Moore, O'Neal **256–257**
Moore, Polly Ann 362
Moore, Victoria 142
Moore, William L. **257–259**, 258
Moorman-Field, Sally 331
Moran, George "Bugs" 328
Morebeto, Mary 307
Moretti, Willie **259–260**
Morgan, Corinne 276
Morris, Frank 182, 240, **260**
Morrissey, Kelly 223
Morse, Eva 374
Morton, Janice 235
Morton, Samuel 390
Moscow decapitation murders 265
Moscow Murders **260–261**
Mosie, Maureen 161
Mosley, Priscilla 388
Mozynski, Joe 363
"Mr. Cruel" **261–262**
Mudd, Daniel 400
Mueller, Louise 98
Muentener, Mary 320
Muir, Ruth 331
mulatto axe murders **263–264**
Mumfre, Joseph 275
Murphy, Gary 173
Murphy, Paddy 390
Murray, Charles 188–189
Mvinjana, Nombovumo 195
Myojo 56 fire 264
mythical unsolved murders **264–266**

N

NAACP (National Association for the Advancement of Colored People)
    Allen, Louis 5
    Jackson, Wharlest 181–182

Lee, George Washington 214–216
Metcalfe, George 240
Moore, Harry Tyson 253–255
Morris, Frank 260
Wetterling, Jacob Erwin 397
Nahanni Valley, Canada 267
Napp, Elyse 121
Narciso, Filipina 11
Nastasia, Sherry 373
National Association for the Advancement of
Colored People. *See* NAACP
"National Reorganization Process" 224
Needham, Ben *268*, **268–269**, *269*
Neely, Richard 11
Neidig, Louisa 189
Nelles, Susan 173
New Bedford, Massachusetts 222–223,
269–272, 277
Newcastle, Australia 272
New Castle, Pennsylvania 86, **272–273**
New Haven, Connecticut **273–274**
New Jersey 274, 307
Newman, Lianne 112
New Orleans, Louisiana, "Axeman" murders
274–276
New Orleans, Louisiana, unsolved murders
(1987-88) **276**
New Orleans, Louisiana, unsolved murders
(1991-96) **276–279**
Newton, Vivian **279**
New York City. *See also* Brooklyn, New
York
anarchist bombings 8–9
Anastasia, Albert 9–10
Carfano, Anthony 69
Crater, Joseph Force 95–96
Diamond, John, Jr. 107–109
Eboli, Thomas 115
Galante, Carmine 133–134
Gallo, Joseph 134–135
gay murders 279–280
Hispanic gay murders 280
infant murders 280
"Jack the Ripper" **188–190**
strangulation murders 280
taxi murders 280–281
"trash bag murders" **281–282**
New Zealand 365
Ngubeni, Bongani 194
Nhlonetse, Bukeka 193
Nichols, Donna 235
Nichols, Mary 183
Nichols, Nina 52
Nihon Shintaku Ginko robbery **282**
Nikishina, Tatyana 261
Nilsson, Carl 311
Nitribitt, Rosalie Marie Auguste **282–283**
Nix, Tanya 319
Nixon, Charles 178
Nixon, Richard 167, *167*, 250, 342
Nixon, Rita 280
Noll, Michael 242
Nongiza, Zanele 193–194
Norman, Frank **283–284**
Normand, Mabel 360
Nuccio, Carmela De 250
Numfre, Joseph 265

O

Oakes, Sir Harry **285–288**
Oakland, California **288**

O'Bannion, Charles Dion **288–289**, 326, 389,
408
Obler, Martin 347
O'Brien, Charles 168
"occult murders" **289–290**
Ochoa y Plácido, Digna **290–291**
O'Dell, Laura 290
Offerman, Robert 138
O'Hara, Bridget 190
O'Hara, Ellen 139
Ohlig, Linda 17
Oklahoma City dismemberment murders **291**
Oklahoma City state fair murders **291–292**
Oldfield, Matthew 236
Olzef, Susan 128
"Operation Enigma" **292**
Original Night Stalker 139, **292–293**
Oswald, Henry 210
Oswald, Lee Harvey 197, 199
Otbert, Lesa 142
Outlaw, Wyatt **293–294**, *294*
Owens, Robert 309–310

P

Paiva, Nancy 269–270
Pallett, Cinda 291
Pankey, Jamie 178
Pascual, William 370
Patent, Helen 128
Patterson, John 267
Patton, Jeanie 395
Peart, Ruth 276
Peavey, Henry 360
Peiper, Joachim **295–296**
Pepitone, Mike 275–276
Perez, Leonora 11
Perkins, Vikki 143
Perm, Russia **296**
Perrett, Ruth 400
Perry, Arlis **296–198**
Perry, Cora 394
Perth, Australia **299**
Peru 218
Pesce, Linda 171
Peterson, Stacy **299–301**, *300*
Pettini, Stefania 250
Philadelphia, Pennsylvania 55–57, 128–130,
376–377
Philips, Eula 336
Phoenix, Arizona 60, 75, 145
Piirainen, Holly Kristen **301**
Player, Michael 265
Plotzman, Elizabeth. *See* Sisman, Ronald, and
Plotzman, Elizabeth
Pohlmann, Heinz 283
Poland 385
Polillo, Florence 84
"Pomona Strangler" **301**
Ponte, Kenneth 271
Poole, Bryan 330
Pope, Henry. *See* Chase, Valentine, and Pope,
Henry
Poppleton, Kelly Jean 5
Porter, Lola 278
Porter, Ronald Elliott 331
Portland, Oregon **302**
Portugal 222, 236, 307
Post, Edith 320
Potdevin, Ruth 233
Powers, Phil 267
Preparedness Day bombing *302*, **302–305**

Prevedini, Roberto Eduardo Viola 224
Priest Murders **305–306**
Prince Georges Hospital **306–307**
Princeton, New Jersey 307
Privot, Loletha 352
"Prostitute Hunter" **307–308**
Provenzano, Tony 167
"Psicópata" **308**
Purdy, Vicky 171
Purpura, Carma 369
Puttock, Helen 42

Q

Queripel, Gilliane 309
Queripel, Stacy 309
Quilintang, Yvonne 290
Quinn, Zebb Wayne **309–310**

R

railroad murders **311**
Ramey, Mary 335–336
Ramsey, Charles 218
Ramsey, JonBenét **311–316**
Randall, Norbert 263
Rawlins, Wyoming 316
Ray, James Earl 206–209, *207*
Real, Patricia 105
Reddick, Wanda Faye 319
Reddish, Olympia 193
Reddish, Tiffany 193
"Redhead Murders" **316–317**
Reed, Lorna 353
Rees, Gwynneth 190
Reles, Abraham **317–318**
Restivo, John 224
Rhoades, Robert Ben 368
Rhoads, Dyke and Karen **318–319**
Rhodes, Robin 270
Riberio, Alípio 237
Richards, Caty 373
Richardson, Diane 234
Richland, Georgia **319**
Rifendifer, Wayne 70
Rimmer, Jane 299
Rimmer, Jane Louise 81
Ring, Elizabeth 363
Ritter, Brenda 389
Ritter, Rosemarie 331
Riverdell Hospital murders **320**
Riviera, Reynaldo 306
Roberts, Clarence **320–321**
Roberts, Leona 17
Roberts, Marilyn 270
Roberts, Nelson 279
Robilant, Count Alvise di 180
Robinson, Amanda 272
Robinson, Jill 27
Robinson, Jim 59
Robinson, Kathleen. *See* Barcomb, Jill, and
Robinson, Kathleen
Robinson, Sharon 277
Rochester, New York 7, **321–322**
Rogers, Creed 256
Roherek, Melissa 161
Rohrbeck, Carl 320
Romano, Joseph 275
Rosansky, Patricia 32
Rosetti, Mary 275
Rothstein, Arnold *322*, **322–323**
Rouselle, Gayle 353
Roux-Bergevin, Denis 252

Rowlands, Walter 30
Ruby, Jack 197, 199–202
Rush, Susan 389

S

St. Louis, Missouri **325–326**
St. Valentine's Day Massacre 289, 326, **326–329**, *327*, 390
Sakamoto, Regina 171
Salazar, Luis 330
Salazar, Rita 175
Salem, Oregon **329–330**
Salim, Muhammad 281
Salsedo, Andrea 9
Salzburg, Austria **330**
Samans, Beverly 52
San Antonio, Texas, taxi cab murders **330**
Sanchez, Gregory 139
Sanders, Don and Terry 22
Sanders, Richard Allen 332
San Diego, California, gay murders **330**
San Diego, California, unsolved murders (1931–36) **330–331**
San Diego, California, unsolved murders (1985–88) **331–332**
Sandlin, Ronald 274
Sandoval, Melissa 331
Sands, Edward 360
San Francisco, California
    Carter, Leroy 70
    Collins, Kevin Andrew 90
    "Doodler, The" 111
    Modafferi, Kristen 245–246
    mythical unsolved murders 266
    Preparedness Day bombing 302–305
    train derailments 365
San Mateo, California **332–333**
Santa Monica, California
    Bacon, David 28–29
    Manhattan axe murders 233
    Monroe, Marilyn 246–250
    mythical unsolved murders 266
    Rothstein, Arnold 322–323
    Siegel, Benjamin 343–344
    "Soda Pop Slasher" 347–348
    Taylor, William Desmond 359–361
    "3X" murders 363–364
    Wall Street bombing 383
    Yale, Frankie 408–409
Santos, Mary 270
Savard, Ernest 267
Savino, Nancy 320
Savoy, Frederick 161
Scales, Lucy 355
Schacke, Linda 316
Schaefer, Gary 373
Scheiber, Isadore 307
Schiambra, Tony 274
Schilling, Sharon 175
Schneider, Ed 275
Schreiber, Barbara 121
Schuster, Arnold **333–335**
Schwimmer, Reinhard 327–328
Scialese, Mary 394
Sciortino, Theresa 128
Scotland 41
Scott, Janet 233
Scott, Lawanda 387
Scott, Lieutenant 77
Scretchings, Tammy 353
Sears, Charles 265

Seaside, California 398
Sedam, Crystal 367
Sellers, Marie 319
Sendejas, Jo Ann 177
Sennett, Mack 360
Sense, Uwe Rusch 251
Senter, Cassidy 325
Serra, Donna 27
"Servant Girl Annihilator" **335–336**
Shaffer, Brian **336–337**
Shakur, Tupac Amaru **337–339**, *338*
Shane, Michael 17
Sharp, Glenna Sue **339–340**
Sharp, Lena **183**
Sharp, Tina 339
Shaw, Eileen 320
Shaw, Jacqueline 273
Shaw, Sebastian Alexander 36
Shawcross, Arthur 321
Shea, Patricia 280
Shelby, Charlotte 361
Shelley, Eliza 335
Shergar 341
Sherman, Mary Stults **341–342**
Shook, Marty 70
Short, Elizabeth Anne 44, 246
Shrock, Sheila 27
"Sidney Sniper" **342–343**
Siebert, Daniel 353
Siegel, Benjamin (Bugsy) 48, 69, 144, *343*, **343–344**, 418
Silkwood, Karen Gay **344–346**
Silver Dollar Group 182, 240, 260
Simpara, Bakary 281
Sinatra, Frank 259
Sino, David 330
Sirhan, Sirhan Bishara 203
Sisman, Ronald, and Plotzman, Elizabeth **346–347**
Sithole, Moses 25
"Skid Row Slasher" 265, 266
Slessers, Anna 52
Sloot, Joran Van der 168, 170
Smartt, Marin 340
Smit, David 365
Smith, Emma 183
Smith, Garelle 357
Smith, Lyman and Charlene 292
Smith, Mollie 335
Smith, Patricia 177
Smith, Samuel 178
Smith, Tammy 178
Smith, William 330
Snyder, Sheila 276
"Soda Pop Slasher" **347–348**
Sodder children **348–350**
Sokoloff, Ethel 394
Solis, Jesus 224
"Somerton Man" **350–352**
"Son of Sam." *See* Berkowitz, David
Sousa, Olegário de 236
South Africa 25, 179
South Croydon murders **352**
"Southside Slayer" **352–353**
Sowley, Noel 363
Spangenberger, Robert 173
Sparks, Carole Denise 130
Spiers, Sarah 81, 299
"Spring-Heeled Jack" **353–355**, *354*
Starks, Virgil 362
Stean, Richard 77

Stebbins, Mark 27
Steidl, Gordon 318
Steinigewig, Alma 98
Stephens, Barbara 121
Stevens, Alan Michael 332
Stevens, Mary 353
Stevens, Robert 11
Stevens, William 154, 155
Stone, Theresa 272
"Stoneman" 356
Stout, James 37
Stoval, Lillian 352
Stride, Elizabeth 184
Strong, Maureen 289
Suarez, Fernando 282
Sullenberger, Mary Ellen 388
Sullivan, Jane 52
Sullivan, Mary 52
"Sunday Morning Slasher" 266
Sutton, Beatrice 372
Sutton, William Francis 333, *334*
Swartz, Amber 34
Sweden 24–25, 311
Swinney, Youell 362
Sydney, Vera 352
Sydney, Violet 352

T

Tabram, Martha 183
Tailford, Hannah 190
Tallant, Robert 275, 276
Tallman, Daisey May 407
Tapp, James, Jr. **357**
Taylor, Barbara Ann Hackman **357–359**
Taylor, Blake Raymond 332
Taylor, William Desmond *359*, **359–361**
Teske, Tonya 144
Teuber, Louise 331
Texarkana **361–362**
Texas **362–363**
    Fort Worth murders 123–124
    Hagerman, Amber Renee 153
    Hawkins, John Edward 160
    Hawkins, Patrick Lamont 160
    Houston decapitation murders 173
    I-35 murders 175–176
    I-45 murders 176–177
    Kennedy, John Fitzgerald 197–202
    mulatto axe murders 263–264
    mythical unsolved murders 256
    San Antonio taxi cab murders 330
    "Servant Girl Annihilator" 335–336
"Texas Strangler" 266
Thayer, Talmadge 404
Tholmer, Brandon 394
Thomas, Angela 290
Thomas, John Floyd 394
Thomas, William 77
Thompson, Susan 291
"3X" murders **363–364**
Tinsley, Marie 123
Tokyo, Japan 136–137, 264, 282
Tolokonnikova, Elena 261
"Toledo Clubber" **364–365**
Toole, Ottis 161, 175
Town Hospital murders **365**
Tracy, N. H. 235
"Trailside Killer" 266
train derailments **365–366**
Trans-Canada Highway 161
Trauernicht, Delia 317

Trayner, Phyllis 173
Trelstad, Laura **366**
"Truck Stop Killer" **366–369**
Trusty, Sarah 177
Tshabalala, Mshengu 194
Tulja, Smailj 65
"Tulsa bludgeonings" 266
Turkey 369, 371
Turner, Darryl Donnell 388
Tütengil, Cavit Orhan **369**
Twitty, Beth and George 168, 170
"Tylenol murders" **369–370**

U

Üçok, Bahriye 371
Upchurch, Norma **371–372**

V

"Valley Killer" **373–375**, *374*
"Vampire" murders 375
Vance, Gracie 335
Vance, Lee 181
Varela, Anna 331
Vasquez, Jacqueline **375–376**
Vasquez, Rosa 290
Vaughn, Marge 128
Vaughn, Sheryl 291
Vess, Amy 177
Vidocq Society **376–377**
Viens, Maurice 252
Villanueva, Julio 330
Vogal, Sylvia 394
Von Bülow, Claus 377, *378*
Von Bülow, Sunny **377–378**

W

Wales, Thomas Crane **379–380**
Wallace, Christopher George Latore **380–382**
Wallace, George 258–259
Wallace, Julia **382–383**
Wallace-Byas, Connie 178
Walls, Juanita 234

Wall Street bombing *383*, **383–385**, *384*
Walsh, Theresa 290
Wanderwell, Walter **385–387**
Warren Commission 198–200
Warsaw, Poland 387
Washington, D.C. 76, 130–131, 217–218
Washington, D.C., gay murders **387**
Washington, D.C., unsolved murders (1988)
    387–388
Washington, D.C., unsolved murders (1989)
    388
Washington, D.C., unsolved murders (1996–97)
    388–389
Washington, Pennsylvania 389
Watts, Coral Eugene 266
Webb, Patsy 352
Webb, Peter 372
Weber, Duane L. 93
Weber, Yvonne 289
Weinshank, Al 327
Weiss, Earl ("Hymie") 280, 326, **389–390**
Wellstone, Paul 4
Westbury, Cynthia 234
"West Memphis Three" **390–394**
"West Side Rapist" **394–395**
West Virginia Sniper *395*, **395–396**
Wetterling, Jacob Erwin **396–398**, *397*
Weys, Gale 161
Whitaker, Elliot 281
White, Fleet 313
White, Tera 161
White Plains, New York 266
Whitlock, Herb 318
Whittington, John 234
Wickliffe, George 400
Wilkerson, Angela 234
Williams, Christina Marie **398–399**
Williams, Connie 178
Williams, Diane 131
Williams, James 234, 387
Williams, Terry 273
Williams, Verna 353

Williams, Vickie 302
Williams, Wayne 20, 24
Willis, Delores 106
Wilson, Alvin 368
Wilson, Laurel and Erika 330
Wilson, Lee 77
Wilson, Sheily 352
Wiltshire, England 400
Windham, Evelyn May **400**
Wingate, Dana 339
Winn, Margie Lee **400–402**
Winters, Joan 402
Witthuhn, Manuela 293
Wood, Wilma 412
Woods, Doc 335
Woods, Jeanette 106
Woodstock, Laura 172
Woodward, Brenda Denise 130
Woonsocket, Rhode Island **402**
Worley, Phyllis 193
Wright, Bella 145
Wyche, Aaron 19

X

X, Malcolm **403–405**, *404, 405*

Y

Yakima, Washington **407–408**
Yale, Frankie 69, 289, *408*, **408–409**
Yerby, Faye 20

Z

Zapata Miranda, Laura Guadalupe **411**
Zephyrhills, Florida **411–412**
Zeterower, Belinda 121
Zia-ul-Haq, Muhammad 4
"Zodiac" 17, 190, 266, 290, **412–418**, *413*
Zolis, Amanda 272
Zwillman, Abner ("Longy") 69, 259, *418*,
    418–419
Zywicki, Tammy 367, 369